MASTERPIECES

IN

ENGLISH LITERATURE,

AND

LESSONS IN THE ENGLISH LANGUAGE,

WITH

A BRIEF STATEMENT OF THE GENEALOGY OF THE ENGLISH LANGUAGE, BIOGRAPHICAL SKETCHES, EXPLANATORY NOTES, SUGGESTIONS FOR EXPRESSIVE READING, METHODS OF ANALYSIS, ETC.

DESIGNED FOR USE IN

COLLEGES AND SCHOOLS.

BY

HOMER B. SPRAGUE,

Principal of the Adelphi Academy, Brooklyn, N. Y., and late Professor of Rhetoric in Cornell University.

IN FOUR BOOKS.

VOL. I.

NEW YORK:

J. W. Schermerhorn & Co.,

14 Bond Street.

1874.

LANGE, LITTLE & CO.,
PRINTERS, ELECTROTYPERS AND STEREOTYPERS,
108 TO 114 WOOSTER STREET, N. Y.

Being at some pause, looking back into that I have passed through, this writing seemeth to me, *si nunquam fallit imago*, as far as a man can judge of his own work, not much better than the noise or sound which musicians make while they are tuning their instruments; which is nothing pleasant to hear, but yet is a cause why the music is sweeter afterwards. So have I been content to tune the instruments of the muses, that they may play that have better hands.

FRANCIS BACON.

PREFACE.

WHAT shall we read? is becoming a serious question. A man can hardly find time for the daily newspapers, much less for even a glance over the pages of all the new books. But when he surveys the accumulation of literary treasures in a large library, he shrinks in despair from an effort to make them his own. The only resource is to select, and it is a good rule to always "get the best."

The productions that have stood the test of time and of multiplied criticisms, and are recognized as masterpieces, are comparatively few. Whatever else may be omitted, no intelligent man can afford to be unacquainted with these. But in the text-books of English Literature, one of two imperfections is almost always present. The first arises from an attempt to give, by mere description, correct and vivid ideas of literary creations; as if one should seek to impart a clear knowledge and awaken a just appreciation of the particular works in an art-gallery by merely talking about them to one who had never seen them. The second and more common mistake, is the endeavor to bring all the prominent authors at once within the scope of the student's observation. Under this process the book becomes little more than a "dictionary of poetical quotations" and a collection of smart or eloquent sayings in prose. To use our former comparison, it is an art-gallery which exhibits nothing but fragments; a foot of the *Venus de Medici*, a devil from Michael Angelo's *Last Judgment*, a marble chip from the *Parthenon*,—in fine, a multitude of specimens in all degrees of mutilation.

To obviate these faults we must, in the first place, give none but acknowledged MASTERPIECES, admitting very sparingly, if at all, the works of living authors. Secondly, we must give, whenever practicable, productions that are complete in themselves. Thirdly, in order to keep the book within dimensions that shall be convenient for class use, the number of selections must be somewhat limited, and additional series must be published in separate volumes.

In the following work, constituting the first series, and, indeed, in each of the subsequent volumes, the object is primarily and chiefly to present for study the masterpieces in English literature; but incidentally the attempt is made to show, in the first two volumes, something of the philosophy and development of the English language, and to awaken an interest in its critical study. In the third volume it is proposed to deduce the principles of rhetoric from the passages examined, and arrange them in a system. In the fourth volume the authors will be classified, and the whole field of English Literature surveyed, and a system of logic outlined.

In the present series, a brief biography is given of each author from whose works a selection is taken; for it is often quite important that we know the man in order to appreciate his book. In each volume much matter is suggested for original compositions.

As no test of a pupil's appreciation of a passage is better than to require him to read it aloud with due attention to delivery, such a compilation is one of the best books for drill in oral expression. All the wealth and beauty of the author should find utterance in the voice. This practice can hardly be too strongly urged. To facilitate this drill, a brief treatise is contained in the first series, showing the elements and principles of vocal expression, with striking examples to illustrate their application.

In a work involving such a multiplicity of details, the author cannot hope to have avoided errors and imperfections. With great diffidence, therefore, yet with confidence in the soundness of its method, and with the hope that scholars will look upon it indulgently as an earnest effort in the right direction, the author submits this work to his fellow teachers. He will be grateful for any criticisms made in a friendly spirit.

H. B. S.

ADELPHI ACADEMY,
BROOKLYN, N. Y., *June* 1, 1874.

CONTENTS OF VOL. I.

LANGUAGE.

CLASSIFICATION OF LANGUAGES.*

The languages of the world are classified as follows:

I. THE *Chinese stock*, spoken principally in China (see p. 13). Of this stock we remark that,

(1.) Every written character is an entire word.

(2.) Every written character is the symbol of an *idea*, rather than the representative of a *sound*.†

(3.) The languages are monosyllabic.

II. The *Shemitic stock*, consisting principally of,

(1.) The Arabic,‡ including the Ethiopic,

(2.) The Aramean, including the Syriac and the Chaldaic,

(3.) The Hebrew, connected with which are the Canaanitish and the Phœnician.

Of the Shemitic stock it is remarked, that, as a rule,

(1.) Each root is dissyllabic and contains three consonants.

(2.) All the Shemitic languages, except the Ethiopic, are written from right to left.

III. The *Indo-European stock.*

IV. The *African stock*, not including the Ethiopic. The Coptic, spoken by the descendants of the ancient Egyptians, has much in common with the Shemitic.

V. The *American stock*, comprising the tongues of the aboriginal inhabitants.

VI. The *Oceanic* or *Polynesian stock.*

THE INDO-EUROPEAN STOCK.

This is sometimes called the *Japhetic*, as the languages of Africa are called *Hamitic*, and those of Southwestern Asia, *Shemitic;* but the name *Indo-European* is more generally adopted. The Indo-European stock comprises the following divisions:

---

* Let the student consult his atlas as he studies this subject.

† Like an algebraic sign.

‡ The Koran is in this language.

1. *Sanskrit*, the language of the ancient Hindoos, and the parent of the languages now spoken in Hindostan; viz., the Hindostanee, the Bengalee, the Pali-Mahratta, etc. The most ancient type of Sanskrit is found in the hymns of the Vedas. The word Sanskrit means perfect, polished, or classical.
2. *Persian* or *Iranian*, the language of ancient *Persia* or *Iran*. It was the sacred idiom of the *Magi*. In it Zoroaster, the founder of the sect of fire-worshipers called Ghebers, wrote the Zend-Avesta? The Old Persian, or language of the Achæmenian cuneiform (wedge-shaped) inscriptions, was a dialect of this language. It is the mother of the languages now spoken in Persia.
3. *Latin*, the language of the ancient Romans. It is supposed to be more ancient than the Greek, and is the parent of the Italian, French, Provençal, Spanish, Portuguese, and Wallachian.
4. *Greek*, the language of ancient Greece, and the parent of the Romaic, or modern Greek.
5. *Celtic*, the language of the ancient Celts, who overspread the whole of western Europe. From the ancient Celtic are derived two modern families. One is called *Medo-Celtic* or *Gaelic;* comprising the Gaelic proper, or Highland Scotch; the Erse, or Irish; and the Manx, or dialect spoken by the inhabitants of the Isle of Man. The Manx is fast becoming extinct. The second family is called *Perso-Celtic*, *Cambrian*, or *Cymric*, including the Welsh and the Armoric (spoken in Brittany). The Cornish, or language of Cornwall, belonged to this family, but it became extinct about a hundred years ago.
6. *Gothic*, the language of the ancient Goths, who, later than the Celts, migrated to Western Europe. They occupied especially the island of Gothland and the southern shores of the Baltic; but early in the Christian era a large number of them quit the north of Europe, and established themselves on the coasts of the Black Sea. A portion of these were permitted by the Roman emperor Valens, in the fourth century, to settle in Mœsia, a very extensive country stretching four or five hundred miles west from the shores of the Black Sea, and bounded north by the river Danube. Those near the Black Sea were called Ostrogoths (East Goths); those further west were called Visigoths (West Goths). The Goths of Scandinavia are sometimes called Suio-Goths.

   Of the Gothic division there are two important branches:

   (1.) The Scandinavian; including the Icelandic or Old Norse, the Danish, the Swedish, the Norwegian, and the language of the Faroe islands.

   (2.) The Teutonic, comprising three families; the Mœso-Gothic (which is the oldest preserved type of the Gothic), the High German, and the Low German.

7. *Slavonic*, the language of the Russians, Bulgarians, Servians, Croats, Poles, and Bohemians. It closely resembles its mother tongue, the ancient Sanskrit.
8. *Lithuanian*, the language of the peasantry in Lithuania. Of all the European languages it approximates nearest to the Sanskrit.

THE LOW GERMAN OR SAXON FAMILY.

This family includes the following dialects:

(1.) The Frisian or Friesic; formerly prevailing in Friesland, north-east of the Zuyder Zee, but now on the eve of extinction.

(2.) The Dutch; spoken in Holland, and remarkable for the facility with which it forms compound words. The oldest literary specimen is from about the year 1280.

(3.) The Platt Deutsch (i. e., Low German); spoken in northern Germany by the common people, the descendants of the Old Saxons. The oldest specimen is *Heliand* (i. e., *Saviour*), a poem written in the eighth or ninth century.

(4.) The Anglo-Saxon; a dialect mixed of the idiom of the Angles and that of the Saxons. The oldest poetical specimen extant is probably the beginning of the Scripture paraphrase, by Cædmon, of the seventh century.

The Anglo-Saxon is the mother of the English, and, as such, is deserving of further attention from us.

GENEALOGY.

From what has been stated, the genealogy of the English language will be traced as follows: It is the daughter of the Anglo-Saxon dialect, of the Low Germanic family, of the Teutonic branch, of the Gothic division, of the Indo-European stock. The following diagram exhibits this relationship:

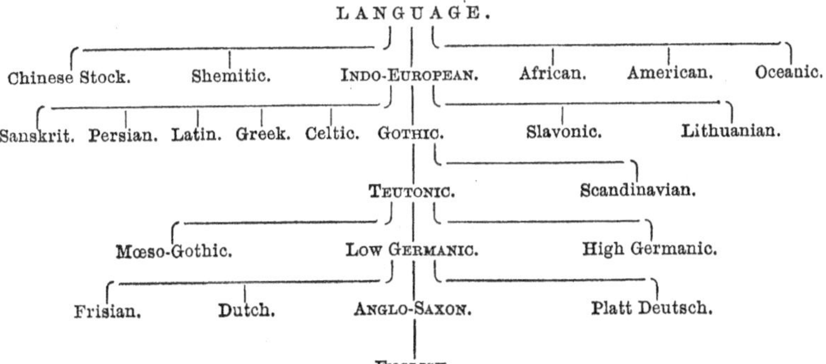

THE INTRODUCTION OF DIFFERENT ELEMENTS.

England had been for nearly four hundred years in the possession of the Romans, who, under Julius Cæsar, had partially wrested it from the Celts; but, about the middle of the fifth century of our era, the critical condition of affairs in Italy made it necessary to withdraw the Roman armies from Britain. Thereupon the Picts and Scots, fierce barbarians from the north part of the island, poured down upon the helpless people of the south, enfeebled and unwarlike from long subjection to their military masters. In their distress the sufferers invoked the aid of the Teutonic pirates of the lower Elbe.

"Then, sad relief, from the bleak coast that hears
The German ocean roar, deep-blooming, strong,
And yellow-haired, the blue-eyed Saxon came."

These auxiliaries, who first arrived A. D. 451, finally turned their arms against the feeble Celts whom they came to protect. Multitudes of the Britons fled for refuge to the mountains of Wales: others crossed the English Channel to the north-west corner of France, called *Brittany* or *Bretagne.*

The home of these *Saxons* (so called from *seax*, a short crooked sword carried under their loose garments) was a wide-spread territory south and south-west of Denmark. In the year 491 of the Christian era they established themselves in Sussex (i. e., South-Saxons), England; in 519, in Hampshire (formerly called *Wessex;* i. e., West-Saxons); and in 527, in Essex (i. e., East-Saxons).

The home of the *Angles* (from *angle*, a hook, or *angulus*, a corner) was probably Anglen, in Sleswick. In 527 they established themselves in Norfolk (i. e., North-folks); in 559, in Yorkshire and Northumberland.

The constant influx of Angles and Saxons filled England (i. e., Angle-land), and their blended language became established, to the exclusion of the old Celtic. To this statement one important exception should be made: a multitude of Celtic geographical names were retained in England, precisely as the old Indian names of rivers, lakes, districts, and mountains, have been preserved in America.

About the year 787, the Northmen, including Danes, Norwegians, and Swedes, began their aggressions upon England. Their inroads continued at intervals for nearly three centuries, and finally, in the year 1014, the Danish king, Sweyn, got complete possession of the country. In 1041 the Danish dynasty ceased, and the Anglo-Saxon rule was restored in the person of Edward the Confessor.

In 1066, William the Norman came to England at the head of sixty thousand men. The great battle of Hastings seated him upon the English throne. For two or three hundred years persistent efforts were made by the Norman French to substitute their language, a mixture of the Latin, the Celtic, and the Scandinavian, for the Anglo-Saxon. To only a limited extent was the attempt successful, about four-fifths of the words in actual use in England at this day being of Anglo-Saxon origin. Perhaps one-tenth of the words in common use are from the Norman French.

The different stages of the language of England may be thus designated by chronological periods:

(1.) Celtic, to the conquest of England by the Angles and Saxons in the sixth and seventh centuries; then,
(2.) Anglo-Saxon, five or six hundred years, to about the year 1150.
(3.) Semi-Saxon, one hundred years, from 1150 to 1250.
(4.) Old English, one hundred years, from 1250 to 1350.
(5.) Middle English, two hundred years, from 1350 to 1550.
(6.) Modern English, from 1550 to the present time.

In every hundred words, counting those which are repeated, but omitting proper names, Chaucer and Shakespeare employ, of Anglo-Saxon words, about ninety; Tennyson and Longfellow, about eighty-seven; Spenser, Milton, Addison, and Pope, about eighty-five; Macaulay, Everett, and Webster, about seventy-five.

NOTE 1.—For an admirable statement of the development of the English language, see Professor Hadley's *Brief History of the English Language,* prefixed to Webster's Unabridged Dictionary. Probably there is nothing of the kind superior to it. See Marsh's *Lectures on the English Language,* Max Müller's Lectures on the *Science of Language,* Whitney on *Language and the Study of Language, English Lessons for English People,* by Abbott and Seeley; *Teutonic Etymology,* by Prof. J. W. Gibbs, Gibbs's *Philological Studies,* Trench's *English, Past and Present,* Trench's *The Study of Words; Studies in English,* by Prof. M. Schele de Vere. See also the treatises of Blair, Quackenbos, Day, Campbell, Hart, and others, on *Rhetoric;* those of Craik, Arnold, Taine, and others, on *English Literature;* Fowler's *English Grammar* (Revised edition), Goold Brown's *Grammar of Grammars,* etc.

NOTE 2.—Besides the six great stocks of languages named on page 9, many philologists recognize a seventh, which they variously term Altaic, Ural-Altaic, Turanian, Mongolian, Tartaric, and Scythian. The last name is most favored. According to these authorities, the *Scythian stock* covers the whole of the northern portion of the eastern continent, and the greater part of central Asia. It includes the languages of the Laplanders, the Finns, the Magyars of Hungary, the Samoyed tribes, the Turks, the Mongols, and the Manchus. Some scholars would add to this list the tribes that inhabit the Dekhan, and the Japanese. The distinguishing characteristic of these languages is that they are *agglutinative;* that is, they "attach their formative elements somewhat loosely to a root which is not liable to variation." See Whitney on *Language and the Study of Language.*

Let the student write an essay on each of these *stocks;* on the Latin *division,* the Greek, the Celtic, the Gothic; on the Teutonic *branch;* on the Low Germanic *family;* on the Anglo-Saxon *dialect;* on *England* under the Romans, under the Saxons, under the Danes, under the Normans. Let him write an essay confirming or disproving any of the statements made in this chapter.

ABBREVIATIONS.

acc........................accent.
adj........................adjective.
Ad........................Addison.
A.D........................Anno Domini.
Ar........................Arabic.
Areop........................Areopagitica.
Arm........................Armoric.
A. S........................Anglo-Saxon.
Bac........................Bacon.
B. C........................before Christ.
Bun........................Bunyan.
Cf........................compare.
Class. Dic........................Classical Dictionary.
Com........................Comus.
D........................Dutch.
dat........................dative.
Dan........................Danish.
dissyl........................dissyllable.
Dry........................Dryden.
e. g........................for example.
E........................English.
Eng........................English.
es........................essay.
Eu........................European.
fr........................from.
Fr........................French.
Fries........................Friesic.
Gael........................Gaelic.
Ger........................German.
Goth........................Gothic.
Gr........................Greek.
Heb........................Hebrew.
i........................intransitive.
Ice........................Icelandic.
ind........................indicative.
Ind. Eu........................Indo-European.
inf........................infinitive.
Ir........................Irish.
It........................Italian.
L........................Low.
Lat........................Latin.
Mac........................Macbeth.
Mer. Ven........................Merchant of Venice.
Milt........................Milton.
Morn. Nat........................Hymn on The Morning of Christ's Nativity.
n........................noun.
Nor. Fr........................Norman French.
Norw........................Norwegian.
O........................old.
obs........................obsolete.
onomat........................onomatopoetic.
orig........................originally.
p........................page.
Par. L........................Paradise Lost.
Pers........................Persian.
Pil. Pr........................Pilgrim's Progress.
plu........................plural.
pos........................possessive.
pres........................present.
q. v........................quod vide = which see.
Sans........................Sanskrit.
Sax........................Saxon.
sc........................scene.
Scot........................Scotch.
Shak........................Shakespeare.
sing........................singular number.
Span........................Spanish.
Spen........................Spenser.
st........................stanza.
S. W........................South-west.
Sw........................Swedish.
syl........................syllable.
tris........................trisyllable.
v........................vide = see.
W........................Welsh.

GEOFFREY CHAUCER.

(From a Manuscript Copy, in vellum, of the "Canterbury Tales," adorned with Marginal Paintings, in the possession of the Marquis of Stafford.)

GEOFFREY CHAUCER.

1328–1400.

Dan Chaucer, well of English undefyled,
On Fame's eternal bead-roll worthy to be fyled.—SPENSER.

A perpetual fountain of good sense.—DRYDEN.

—That noble Chaucer, in those former times
Who first enriched our English with his rhymes,
And was the first of ours that ever broke
Into the Muses' treasures, and first spoke
In mighty numbers, delving in the mine
Of perfect knowledge.—WORDSWORTH.

—The morning star of song, who made
His music heard below ;

Dan Chaucer, the first warbler, whose sweet breath
Preluded those melodious bursts that fill
The spacious times of great Elizabeth
With sounds that echo still.—TENNYSON.

One of those rare authors, whom, if we had met him under a porch in a shower, we should have preferred to the rain!—LOWELL.

In the dim twilight of five hundred years ago, the "morning star of song" began to shine. Born about the year 1328, as we infer from an inscription on his tomb, Goeffrey Chaucer, the "father of English poetry," received a thorough education, at either Oxford or Cambridge, or both. It is pretty clear that he understood well the French and Latin tongues. Whether he was versed in Italian, may be doubted, though he spent some time in Italy, and was all his life a student.

In the autumn of 1359 Chaucer served in the army of Edward III. invading France, where he was captured at the siege of Retters. In the year 1367 we find him one of the king's *valets de chambre*, and receiving a yearly pension of twenty marks. About this time he married Philippa Roet, sister of the lady who afterwards became the wife of John of Gaunt, duke of Lancaster. In 1370 he was abroad in the king's service. In November, 1372, he was sent on a mission to Genoa, to treat of the choice of a port in England where the Genoese might form a commercial establishment. Having remained about a year in Genoa and Florence, we find him again in England in the latter part of 1373. The great Dante had died fifty years before, but Petrarch and Boccaccio, already famous, were still alive. He puts into the mouth of his "Clerk" or student, who is supposed to represent Chaucer himself, the following words in regard to the origin of the story of Patient Griselda:

"I will you tell a tale which that I
Learned at Padowe of a worthy clerk,
As proved by his wordes and his work;
He is now dead and nailed in his chest,

I pray to God to give his soule rest;
Francis Petrarch, the laureate poete,
Highte this clerk, whose rhetoric sweet
Enlumined all Itaille of poetry."

He repeatedly quotes Dante, but it is uncertain whether he was familiar with the writings of Boccaccio.

We find a curious record on the 23d of April, 1374, of a grant of a pitcher of wine daily by the king, soon afterwards commuted for another pension of twenty marks. On the 8th of the following June he was appointed controller of the customs and subsidies of wools, skins, and tanned hides, in London. Other tokens of the royal favor followed, and in the last year of Edward's long reign (1327–1377) we find him an ambassador, first to Flanders, and afterwards to France.

Soon after the accession of Richard II. Chaucer was sent to France to negotiate a treaty for a marriage between the boy king and a daughter of the French monarch. Returning soon to England, he was sent in May, 1378, to Lombardy, to treat of military matters. It was on this occasion that he nominated his brother poet, John Gower, whom he afterwards calls "Moral Gower," his attorney and legal representative during his absence. Gower, in his poem entitled *Confessio Amantis*, makes Venus say,

"And greet well Chaucer when ye meet,
As my disciple and my poete."

In 1386 he was elected knight of the shire, or county representative in parliament, for Kent. The session was very brief, and its proceedings were largely directed against Chaucer's particular friend and patron, John of Gaunt, Duke of Lancaster. Strongly enlisted on the side of the duke, Chaucer appears to have shared his fortunes, and to have lost the office of controller. Many years before, one Geoffrey Chaucer, probably our poet, had been fined two shillings for whipping a Franciscan friar in Fleet street; and now he became implicated in a London riot, and was obliged to flee to the Continent with his wife and children. After eighteen months he returned to England, to look after his property, but was seized and flung into the Tower. Yet he seems to have continued to receive, or at least to have been entitled to receive, his two pensions, until he sold them in 1388, being in great destitution. In May, 1389, he was again in favor at court, and in July of that year he was appointed "Clerk of the King's Works," with a pension of £36, and afterwards an annual pipe of wine.

Cloud and sunshine alternately filled his sky. In September, 1391, he was dismissed from office, but soon afterward was restored to public favor. Sixty-three years old, weary of public life, but not soured nor despondent, he retired to his house, given him at Woodstock by the noble duke, and sat down to write. There, and at Donington Castle, where an old tree long bore the name of *Chaucer's oak*, he composed his greatest work, *The Canterbury Tales.* One of the vellum manuscripts of these tales, in the possession of the Marquis of Stafford, has a striking picture of the poet; a portly figure, in a thoughtful attitude, his head inclining forward, his chin almost resting on his breast; a buttoned bonnet on his head, its folds hanging gracefully behind his shoulders; a loose frock of camlet reaching below the knee, its wide sleeves gathered and fastened at the waist; his shoes horned, and his hose supposed to be red. Silver locks peep out from beneath his bonnet. His beard is of moderate length and neatly trimmed. The expression of his face singularly unites cheerfulness and thoughtfulness. You can fancy a mirthful twinkle in the eye, and almost expect the grave face to relax into an arch smile as some funny thought flashes through his brain. This man has evidently a just sense of the vanity of all things earthly; but he has also a kind heart and a merry wit.

The accession of his patron's son, Henry IV., brought more sunshine; for within four days the new king granted him (Oct. 3, 1399) a yearly pension of forty marks. On the following Christmas he took the lease of a house at Westminster, near the spot where the magnificent chapel of Henry VII. now stands. Here he died, October 25, 1400, leaving two sons, one of whom became Speaker of the House of Commons.

On his death-bed Chaucer is said to have been filled with remorse at the thought that some of his writings had an immoral tendency. "Wo is me, that I cannot recall and annul these things! But, alas, they are continued from man to man, and I cannot do what I desire!" His last composition is said to have closed with the following stanza, in which the wisdom of threescore and ten years speaks with the voice of the dying man:

> That thee is sent, receive in buxomness; *
> The wrestling of this world asketh a fall.
> Here is no home! Here is but wilderness!
> Forth, pilgrim, forth! O beast, out of thy stall!
> Look up on high and thank thy God of all!
> Weyve thy lusts, and let thy ghost thee lead,
> And Truth shall thee deliver; it is no drede!

The chief characteristics of his writings are common sense, a keen observation, a sportive and even comic fancy, a genial and overflowing humor, deep tenderness, and an exquisite sensibility to the beauties of nature; in a word, all the wisdom, shrewdness, *naïveté*, mirthfulness, pathos, and delicacy, that could well be combined in a polished old gentleman.

Besides *Troilus and Creseide* (8,246 lines), *The Assembly of Fowls* (686 lines), *House of Fame* (2,190 lines), *Legend of Good Women* (2,722 lines), *The Book of the Duchess* (1,334 lines), and several minor pieces, he wrote the

CANTERBURY TALES (17,368 lines).

On the 29th of December, 1170, the famous archbishop Thomas à Becket was murdered before the altar in the Cathedral at Canterbury (58 miles E. S. E. of London). Canonized within three years after his death and placed high on the roll of saints, it became an act of exceedingly meritorious piety to make a pilgrimage to his shrine. We will let Chaucer speak for himself on this subject:

> When that Aprille, with his showers swoote,†
> The drought of March hath pierced to the roote,
> And bathed every vein in swich licour,
> Of which virtue engendered is the flower,—
> When Zephirus eke with his swete breath
> Enspired hath in every holt and heath
> The tender croppes; and the younge sun
> Hath in the Ram his halfe course yrun,
> And smalle fowles maken melodie,
> That sleepen all the night with open eye—
> So pricketh hem nature in their courages;—
> Then longen folks to go on pilgrimages,
> *   *   *   *   *   *
> And specially from every shires end
> Of Engeland to Canterbury they wend,
> The holy blissful martyr for to seek,
> That them hath holpen when that they were sick.

---

* **Buxomness,** *meekness.*—**Weyve,** *waive, put away.*—**It is no drede,** *there is no reason to fear.*—**Aprille.** Trisyl.—†**Swoote,** *sweet.* Dissyl.—**Swich,** *such.*—**Licour,** *liquor.* Acc. 2d syl.—**Eke,** *also.* Dissyl.—**Swete,** *sweet.* Dissyl.—**Croppes,** *crops.* Dissyl.—**Younge.** Dissyl.—**Ram.** The constellation *Aries,* into which the sun enters about March 21.—**Halfe.** Dissyl.—**Yrun,** *run.*—**Smalle.** Dissyl.—**Fowles.** Dissyl.—**Courages,** *heart, spirit.* Acc. 2d syl.

Befell that, in that season on a day,
In Southwark at the Tabard* as I lay,
Ready to wenden on my pilgrimage
To Canterbury, with full devout courage,
At night was come into that hostelry
Well nine and twenty in a company
Of sundry folk, by aventure yfall
In fellowship, and pilgrims were they all,
That toward Canterbury woulden ride.
The chambers and the stables weren wide,
And well we weren eased at the best.

These pilgrims agree to journey together; and, to beguile the way, each is to tell a tale both in going and in returning. Whoever shall relate the best is to have a supper at the others' expense, the fat, jolly landlord of the Tabard Inn, Harry Bailey, to be the judge. This plan would have required sixty stories, but only twenty-four are recorded.

The description of the different pilgrims, who represent almost all ranks in life, except the highest and the lowest, forms a matchless picture-gallery. Most of the tales are deeply interesting.

One of the best is *The Clerk's* (or Student's) *Tale*, which we have given entire. The substance of it existed before the time of Chaucer, in Latin and in Italian. It was dramatized and acted on the stage in France and Germany. It is found also, substantially, in Roberts' edition of *Old English and Scotch Ballads.* It was played on the English stage in the reign of Henry VIII. (1509–1547), and another dramatized version of it was made and acted in the London theatres in the time of Shakespeare.

Except in the last six stanzas, I have taken the liberty to modernize the spelling wherever it would not change the pronunciation of the word, outlandish orthography being no more essential to old English poetry than to modern wit.

It will materially assist, in reading Chaucer's verses, to observe the following general rules:

1. Pronounce, as a separate syllable, final *e* before a consonant; the final *es* in the plural; final *es* in the possessive singular; and *ed* in the past tense and participle.
2. Accent as in the original French the words that come from the Latin through that language.

The verse is called English Heroic, consisting of ten syllables, making five feet, every second syllable being accented. It had been used before in Italian and in French poetry, but perhaps not in English.

Each foot is regularly an *iambus;* that is, it consists of a short or unaccented syllable followed by a long or accented one. But two short syllables are often used instead of one, making the foot an *anapest.*

For some account of the life and works of Chaucer, the reader is referred to Thomas Wright's edition of the *Canterbury Tales;* Godwin's *Life of Chaucer;* Charles Cowden Clarke's *Life of Chaucer;* Tyrwhitt's *Chaucer's Works;* Taine's *History of English Literature;* Craik's *English Literature and Language;* Corson's edition of the *Legend of Good Women;* March's *Study of the English Language;* and Lowell's admirable essay on

---

* **Tabard,** the *Tabard Inn.* It is said to have been opposite the spot where Spurgeon's Tabernacle now stands.—**Wenden,** *wend.*—**Aventure,** *adventure, chance.*—**Yfall,** *fallen, happening.*—**Eased,** *made at ease, accommodated.* Dissyl.—**At the best,** or, as some manuscripts read, *atte best,* i. e., *in the best manner.*

Chaucer in *My Study Windows*. See also Arnold's, Collier's, Shaw's, Cleveland's, Spalding's, Chambers', Angus's works on *English Literature;* Allibone's *Dictionary of Authors; The Encyclopedia Britannica*, and *New American Cyclopedia; Home Pictures of English Poets*, etc. Let the student cull from these and other sources additional facts in regard to Chaucer.

THE CLERK'S TALE.

1. There is, right at the west side of Itaille,*
Down at the root of Vesulus the cold,
A lusty plain abundant of vitaille;
There many a town and tower thou mayest behold,
That founded were in time of fathers old,
And many another delitable sight;
And Saluces this noble country hight.
2. A marquis whilom lord was of that land,
As were his worthy elders him before;
And obeisant aye ready to his hand
Were all his lieges, bothe less and more.
Thus in delight he liveth and hath done yore,
Beloved and drad, through favor of fortune,
Both of his lordes and of his commune.
3. Therewith he was, to speaken of lineage,
The gentilest yborn of Lombardy,

---

* **Itaille** (O. Fr. from Lat. *Italia*), Italy. Accent the word on 2d syl.—**Vesulus**, now *Monte Viso*, about 13,000 feet high, one of the Alps on the boundary between Italy and France, and forty miles S. W. of Turin.—**Lusty** (A. S. *lust, lyst*, vigor; Dan. and Ice. *lyst*, fr. Ice. *liosta*, to strike), *fruitful*.—**Vitaille** (O. Fr. for *victuaille*, fr. Lat. *victualia*, fr. *victus*, nourishment, fr. *vivere, victum*, to live), *food*.—**There**, *where*. A. S. *thær*. This demonstrative came to be used as a relative, just as the word *that* is still used.—**Delitable** (Lat. *delectabilis*, fr. *delectare*, to delight), *delightful*.—**Saluces**, *Saluzzo*, formerly the name of a region, now a city in Piedmont. Trisyl.—**Hight** (A. S. *hâtan*, to call, name; be called; Ger. *heiszen*), *is called*. So Byron, "Childe Harold was he hight."—**Whilom** (A. S. *hwîlom*, old dat. plu. of *hwîl*, time; Ger. *weile*), *formerly*.—**Obeisant** (Fr. *obeissant*, fr. *obéir*, to obey; Lat. *obedire*, fr. *ob*, to, and *audire*, to give ear, perhaps akin to Lat. *auris* and Eng. *ear*), *obedient*. **Lieges** (either fr. Lat. *ligare*, to bind, denoting one bound by a feudal tenure, as a vassal to his lord; or fr. Ger. *ledig*, free, i. e., denoting one free fr. all obligation to *others*, being bound to one alone), *liegemen, vassals*.– **Bothe** (A. S. *bâ*, both, *tvâ*, two; akin to Lat. *ambo*, Gr. ἄμφω ?). Dissyl.—**Yore** (A. S. *geára*, formerly, *geár, gêr*, a year; or fr. A. S. *geo*, of old, and *ær*, before), *for a long time*.—**Drad** (A. S. *drædan*, to fear), *dreaded, revered*.—**Lordes** (Semi-Sax. plu. fr. A. S. *hlaford*, a bread-keeper, fr. *hlaf*, bread, and *weardian*, to ward or guard), *lords, nobles*. Dissyl.—**Commune** (Lat. *communis*, common, ordinary; perhaps allied to Ger. *gemein*), *common people*.—**Speaken** (O. En. infin., like *hearken*).—**Gentilest** (Lat. *gentilis*, fr. *gens*, a clan or race), *most noble in rank*. See *gentilesse* and note thereon, stanza 6. —**Yborn** (A. S. *ge-*, akin to Lat. *co-*, Ger. *ge-*, a particle often prefixed to A. S. verbs, and becoming, in O. Eng., *y-*). The student should test the accuracy of all these notes. Let him make free use of lexicons, cyclopedias, histories, classical dictionaries, etc. The sooner the habit of thorough and original investigation is formed, the better.

There is . . . . the west side. Th, when sonant as in *there*, has a *demonstrative* force; e. g., *that, then, this, there; the*. Give other examples of this.

A fair person* and strong and young of age
And full of honor and of courtesy;
Discreet enough his country for to gie,
Save in some thinges that he was to blame:
And Walter was this younge lordes name.

4. I blame him thus, that he considered nought
In time coming what might him betide,
But on his lust present was all his thought,
And for to hawk and hunt on every side:
Well nigh all other cures let he slide;
And eke he n'old (that was the worst of all)
Wedden no wife, for nothing that might befall.

5. Only that point his people bare so sore,
That flockmel on a day to him they went,
And one of them, that wisest was of lore,
(Or elles that the lord would best assent
That he should tell him what his people meant,
Or elles could he show well such matier,)
He to the marquis said as ye shall hear.

6. "O noble Marquis, your humanity
Assureth us and giveth us hardinesse,
As oft as time is of necessity,
That we to you may tell our heaviness.
Accepteth, Lord, now of your gentilesse,
That we with piteous heart unto you plain,
And let your eares not my voice disdain.

---

* **Person** (Fr. *personne*, fr. Lat. *persona*, a mask, fr. *personare*, to sound through). Acc. 2d syl.—**Gie**, *guide*.—**Thinges** (O. Semi-Sax. plu.). Dissyl.—**Younge** (A. S. *gêong; Ger. jung;* allied to Lat. *juvenis*). Dissyl.—**Lordes.** Dissyl. The A. S. pos. termination of many nouns in the sing. was *-es, -is*, or *-ys*. The *e, i*, or *y*, of this ending, was afterwards omitted by syncope, and the apostrophe took its place. Hence the mode of forming the possessive case in Eng.—**Time.** Dissyl.—**Lust** (A. S. *lystan*, to desire), *pleasure, wish*.—**Present.** Acc. 2d syl.—**Hawk,** to attempt to catch birds with hawks trained for the purpose, a favorite amusement of the O. Eng. nobility.—**Cures** (Lat. *cura*, care, fr. *quæro*, I seek, inquire), *cares*. Dissyl.—**Eke** (A. S. *eacan*, to add to; *eac*, also; Mœso-Goth. *auk*, allied to Lat. *ac*, and, or to *augere*, to increase), *also*.—**N'old** (A. S. *nillan*, to be unwilling; Lat. *nolle*), *was unwilling to*.—**Wedden** (Semi-Sax. and O. E. infin.), *wed*.—**No wife.** Observe the use of a double negative for emphasis.—**Flockmel,** *in flocks*.—**Lore** (A. S. *lâr*, fr. *læran;* Ger. *lehren*, to teach).—**Elles** (A. S. *elles;* pos. or genitive of the root of Gr. ἄλλος, Lat. *alius*, other), *else*. Dissyl.—**Matier** (O. Fr. fr. Lat. *materia*), *matter*.—**Giveth.** Monosyl.—**Hardiness,** *boldness*.—**Accepteth** (the imperative plu. in A. S. is written with the ending *dh;* in Early Eng., *th*), *accept*. The plu. is politely used for the sing.—**Gentilesse** (Lat. *gentilis*, fr. *gens*, race, stock, family, with a sense of noble or respectable, as we say a man of birth or family; whence *genteel*), *complaisance, gentleness*.—**Piteous,** sorrowful.—**Plain,** *complain*. Obs., except in poetry.—**Eares** (A. S. *eare;* Lat. *auris;* Gr. οὖς; Ger. *ohr*, ear), *ears*. Dissyl.—**Voice** (Gr. ὄψ; Lat. *vox*, voice; O. Fr. *vois;* Fr. *voix*).—**Disdain** (Lat. *dis*, asunder, apart, not; *dignari*, to deem worthy; O. Fr. *desdaigner*, to deem unworthy; Fr. *dédaigner*, to disdain).

Well nigh all other cures let he slide. *Sl*, as in *slide, slip, slime, sly, sleight, slink, slow*, (like *gl*,) denotes *smoothness* or *silent motion*. Other examples?

7. " And have I nought to don * in this matiere
More than another man hath in this place;
Yet, forasmuch as ye, my Lord so dear,
Have always showed me favor and grace,
I dare the better ask of you a space
Of audience, to showen our request,
And ye, my Lord, to don right as you lest.

8. " For certes, Lord, so well us liketh you
And all your work, and ever hath done, that we
Ne couthen not ourselves devisen how
We mighten live in more felicity;
Save one thing, Lord, if that your wille be,
That for to be a wedded man you lest;
Then were your people in sovereign hertes rest.

9. " Boweth your neck under that blissful yoke
Of sovereignety and not service,
Which that men clepen spousail or wedlock;
And thinketh, Lord, among your thoughtes wise,
How that our dayes pass in sundry wise;
For though we sleep, or wake, or roam, or ride,
Aye fleeth the time; it will no man abide.

10. " And though your greene youthe flower as yet,
In creepeth age alway as still as stone:
And death menaceth every age, and smit
In each estate, for there escapeth none.
And also certain as we know each one

---

* **Don** (A. S. *dôn*), *do.*—**Ye** (A. S. *ge*), *you.*—**Showed.** Dissyl.—**Favor.** Acc. 2d syl.—**Showen** (Semi-Sax. and Early Eng.), *show.*—**Lest** (A. S. *lystan*, *lustan*, incline, desire), *list, please.*—**Certes** (Lat. *certus*, sure; Fr. *certes*), *certainly.*—**Us** (dative, i. e. case of indirect object, after *liketh*).—**Liketh** (plu.; *you* and *work* being the subject nominative), *please. Us liketh* = are pleasing to us.—**Ne . . . . . not.** The double negative for emphasis.—**Couthen** (O. plu. past tense of A. S. *cunnan*, to know, *ic can*, I know; Ger. *können*, to know; akin to Lat. *gnoscere*, *noscere*, Gr. γιγνώσκω, to know), *knew, were able to.*—**Lest,** *incline, please.* See st. 7.—**Hertes** (Lat. *cor, cordis;* Gr. καρδία, κῆρ; Ger. *herz*), *heart's.*—**Boweth,** *bow.* Imperative.—**Which that,** *which.*—**Clepen** (A. S. *clepan*), *call.*—**Thinketh.** Imperative.—**Wise.** A. S. *wîs;* Ger. *weise;* akin to *wit;* A. S. *witan*, to know; Ger. *wissen;* Sans. *wid*, to know; Lat. *vid-ere*, to separate by the eye, Gr. ο-ἶδ-α).—**Sundry wise** (A. S. *synderig*, separate, fr. *sunder*, to separate. Hence *sundry=several*).—**Wise** (A. S. *wisian*, to direct; Ger. *weise*, mode, manner), *ways.*—**Aye** (A. S. *a, awa;* Lat. *ævum*, an age; Gr. ἀεί, ever), *ever.*—**Still as stone**='stone still.'—**Menaceth.** Acc. 2d syl.—**Smit** (A. S. *smitan;* Ger. *schmeiszen*, to smite. Hence *smith*, one "that smootheth with the hammer"), *smiteth.*—**None.** A. S. *nân*, fr. *ne*, not; *ân* one. Compare with this the Latin *nemo*, no one, fr. *ne*, not, *homo*, man.

And though your greene youthe flower as yet. *Fl* and *bl*, as in Lat. *flo, flare, flos, floreo*, Gr. φλόος, Ger. *blühen, blüthe, blume, blähen, blasen;* Eng. *flower, flourish, bloom, blossom, blow, blaze, blast, blister*, denotes a *blowing* or *blooming;* also *fl* denotes a *flowing*, as in Gr. φλέω, φλίω, φλύω; Lat. *fluo;* Ger. *fliessen, fluth*, Eng. *flow, flood*, Lat. *flere.* Let the student exercise his ingenuity in collecting other examples to illustrate these phonetic principles. Let him also carefully verify or disprove the statements in the foot-notes.

That we shall die, as uncertain * we all
Ben of that day when death shall on us fall.

11. "Accepteth then of us the true intent,
That never yet refused your behest,
And we will, Lord, if that you will assent,
Choose you a wife in short time at the mest,
Born of the gentilest and of the best
Of all this land, so that it ought to seem
Honor to God and you, as we can deem.

12. "Deliver us out of all this busy dread,
And take a wife, for highe Goddes sake!
For if it so befell, as God forbid,
That through your death your lineage should slake,
And that a strange successor should take
Your heritage, oh, wo were us on live!
Wherefore we pray you hastily to wive."

13. Hir meeke prayer and hir piteous cheer
Made the marquis for to have pity.
"Ye wold," quoth he, "mine owen people dear,
To that I never ere thought, constrainen me;
I me rejoiced of my liberty,
That selden time is found in marriage;
There I was free, I must ben in servage.

14. "But natheless I see your true intent,
And trust upon your wit, and have done aye.
Wherefore, of my free will, I will assent
To wedden me as soon as ever I may.
But thereas ye have proffered me to-day
To choosen me a wife, I you release
That choice, and pray you of your proffer cease.

---

* **Uncertain.** Acc. 1st and 3d syl.—**Ben** (O. Eng.), *be, are.*—**Mest** (A. S. *mæst*), *most.*—**Busy** (A. S. *bysig*, D. *bezig*, busy; Ice. *bisa*, to toil), *causing business* or *care.*—**Slake** (A. S. *slacian*, to slacken; *sleacian*, or *slacian*, to render less intense, mitigate), *fail.*—**Strange** (Lat. *extraneus*, foreign; *extra*, beyond). Dissyl. To make *strange* fr. *extraneus*, the prefix is dropped. So to form *uncle* fr. *avuncŭlus*, and *sample* fr. *exemplum.*—**Successor.** Acc. 1st and 3d syl.—**On live,** *in life.* Emphatic.—**Hir** (early Eng. pos.), *their.*—**Cheer,** *countenance.* See Index.—**Made.** Dissyl.—**Pity** (Fr. *pité*; Lat. *pietas*, filial affection, kindness). Acc. 2d syl.—**Wold** (A. S. *willan*; Ger. *wollen*; Lat. *velle*, *volo*; Fr. *vouloir*, *voudra*; Eng. *would*; Gr. *βούλομαι*), *would.* Auxil.—**Ere,** *before.*—**Selden** (A. S. *seldon* or *seldan*, rare), *seldom.*—**There,** *where.*—**Servage,** *servitude.*—**Natheless** (A. S. *na*; Lat. *ne*, no, not; *the*; *less*), *nevertheless.* In Milton we have *nathless.* Trisyl.—**Thereas,** *whereas.*—**Owen** (st. 13) is past participle of A. S. *âgan*, to possess.

Ben of that day when death shall on us fall. The sound of *a* in *fall*, as it requires the mouth to be opened wide to enounce it properly, and is rather large in volume, seems appropriate for *large* things, and for *serious* or *important* subjects. E. g., *all, lord, broad, law.* Other examples?

Deliver us out of all the busy dread. *Busy* has, perhaps, an *onomatopoetic* force. We speak of the *hum* of business. *Buzz* is clearly imitative of sound. *Z* final often denotes buzzing sounds, as in *whiz, buzz, buzfuz.* Give other examples.

15. "For God it wot,* that children often been
Unlike hir worthy elders them before.
Bountee cometh all of God, not of the streen
Of which they been engendered and ybore.
I trust in Goddes bounty, and therefore
My marriage and mine estate and rest
I him betake; he may do as him lest.

16. "Let me alone in choosing of my wife;
That charge upon my back I will endure!
But I you pray, and charge upon your life,
That, what wife that I take, ye me assure
To worship her, while that her life shall dure,
In word and work, both here and everywhere,
As she an emperores daughter were.

17. "And furthermore thus shall ye swear, That ye
Against my choice shall never grudge nor strive;
For since I shall forego my liberty
At your request, as ever mote I thrive,
There as mine heart is set, there will I wive;
And, but ye will assent in such mannere,
I pray you speak no more of this matiere."

18. With hertly will they sworen and assenten

---

* **Wot** (A. S. *witan*, to know), *knows.*—**Been,** *are.*—**Bountee** (Nor. Fr. *bountee;* Lat. *bonitas*, goodness; *bonus*, good; Fr. *bonte*), *goodness.*—**Streen** (A. S. *strynd*, stock, breed; *streon*, power), *race, stock, breed, descent.* In Shakespeare we have *strain* in this sense.—**Ybore,** *born.* The A. S. past tense, and often the past participle, took the prefix *ge*, at first with an *intensive* force. This *ge* became *y.*—**Marriage,** Tris.—**I him betake** (A. S. dative case is *him* or *hym* = to him), *I refer to him*, or *I entrust to him.*—**Him lest,** *it pleases him.* —**Dure** (Lat. *durare*, to harden, to last; *durus*, hard; Fr. *durer*, to last), *endure.*—**Emperores** (Lat. *imperator*, commander-in-chief; Fr. *empereur; emperores* being old pos.; the *e* of the old pos. being now dropped, and the apostrophe taking its place to form the pos.)—**Mote** (A. S. *mot;* O. Sax. *motan*), *must.* 1st sing. present.—**There as,** *there where, just where.*—**But ye** (A. S. *butan*, without, except; *be*, by, with; *utan*, out, abroad. *Be* is not here the imperative), *unless ye.*—**Hertly** (Ger. *herzlich. Herz* is akin to Lat. *cor*, *cord-is*, Eng. *heart;* Gr. *καρδία*), *hearty.* This word illustrates Grimm's famous law of consonant changes. This law embraces remarkable correspondences among the English, the German, and the classical languages; in fact, it extends to the whole Indo-European stock, though with many exceptions in particular words. The Sanskrit, Greek, Latin, Lithuanian, and Slavonic, are one class; the High German dialects, another; the Mœso-Gothic and Low German, a third. The mutes are divided into:

	Tenues. Smooth.	*Mediæ.* Middle.	*Aspiratæ.* Rough.
Labials (lip mutes)	P	B (V)	Ph (F).
Palatals (palatal mutes)	K (C)	G	Ch (H).
Linguals (tongue mutes)	T	D	Th (Z).

PRACTICAL APPLICATIONS OF GRIMM'S LAW.

To change Latin or Greek to English (or to A. S.), change smooth to rough, rough to middle, and middle to smooth. To change German to English, change rough to smooth, middle to rough, and smooth to middle. To change English to Latin or Greek, or to German, reverse these operations respectively. Thus Lat. *cor*, *cord-is*, Gr. *καρδία*, becomes Eng. *heart;* Lat. *corn-u* becomes Eng. *horn;* Lat. *tres* becomes Eng. *three;* Lat. *frater*, Eng. *brother;* Lat. *pater*, Eng. *father;* Lat. *frang-o*, *freg-i*, Eng. *break.* For further illustrations, see Index, Grimm's Law.—**Sworen.** O. plu.—The student should be taught to *scan* every line; that is, to distinguish and name the metrical feet of which each verse is composed.

Against my choice shall never grudge nor strive. *Str*, as in *strive*, seems to denote exertion; e. g., *strain, strenuous, stress, strike, stroke, streak, strip, strap, stripe, strife, string, strong, strength, strict, stretch, straight, struggle.* The fact is, it requires a considerable exertion to *articulate* properly this combination of consonants. Hence its fitness to express *effort.* Other examples?

To all this thing. There saide * no wight, "Nay;"
Beseeching him of grace, ere that they wenten,
That he would granten them a certain day
Of his spousail, as soon as ever he may.
For yet alway the peoplė somewhat dread
Lest that the marquis would no wife wed.

19. He granted them a day, such as him lest,
On which he would be wedded securely;
And said he did all this at their request;
And they with humble heart, full buxomly,
Kneeling upon their knees full reverently,
Him thanken all; and thus they have an end
Of their intent, and home again they wend.

20. And hereupon he to his officers
Commandeth for the feste to purvey;
And, to his privy knightes and squieres,
Such charge he gave as him list on them lay.
And they to his commandement obey,
And each of them doth all his diligence
To do unto the feast all reverence.

PARS SECUNDA.

21. Not far from thilke palace honorable,

---

* **Saide.** Dissyl.—**Wight** (A. S. *wiht*, a creature; *wagian*, to move; whence *wight* and *whit*), *person*.—**Spousail,** *marriage*. Acc. 2d syl.—**Him lest,** *pleased him*.—**Securely.** Acc. 1st syl.—**Buxomly** (A. S. *bugan*, to bow, bend, yield; A. S. *sum*, Gr. ὁμός, Lat. *similis*, Goth. *sama*, like, same; Ger. *biegsam*, O. Eng. *bocsom*, A. S. *bocsum*, pliable; A. S. *lic*, like), *obediently*. —**Feste** (Lat. *festum*, plu. *festa;* O. Fr. *feste;* Fr. *fete*, festival, holiday), *feast*. *Feste* is dissyl. —**Privy** (Lat. *privare*, to separate; *privus*, single; Fr. *prive*), *private*.—**Knightes** (A. S. *cniht*, a boy, attendant, military follower). Dissyl. A knight was a man admitted in feudal times to a certain military rank, and entitled to be addressed as *Sir*. "When the order of knighthood was conferred by the sovereign in the leisure of a court, imposing preliminary ceremonies were required of the candidate. He prepared himself by prayer and fasting, watched his arms at night in a chapel, and was then admitted with the performance of religious rites. Knighthood was conferred by the *accolade*, which, from the derivation of the name, should appear to have been originally an embrace; but afterwards consisted, as it still does, in a blow of the flat of a sword on the back of the kneeling candidate." *Brande*.—**Squieres** (Fr. *ecuyer*, shield-bearer; from *escu*, shield; Lat. *scutum*), *shield-bearers*, or *armor-bearers attendant* on a knight. Dissyl. Acc. 2d syl.—**As him list,** etc., as it pleased him to lay on them. *List* is A. S. *lystan*, *lustan*, to incline, to desire. Hence *lust*.—**Commandement.** Quadrisyllable.—**Thilke** (A. S. *thylc*, *thus lic*, thus-like; as A. Ward would say, "*Thusly*." The demonstrative element *th*, found in *this*, *that*, *the*, *there*, *they*, etc., is perhaps connected radically with the element of the second person singular, *th*, in *thou*), *this same*.—**Honorable.** Acc. 1st and 3d syllables. "The tendency of English accentuation has been to get as far back in words as it is possible for it to go."—*Corson*.

Not far from thilke palace honorable. *N*, as in *not*, denotes *negation;* e. g., Gr. ν in νήπιος; Lat. *ne*, *non;* Ger. *nicht*, *nein;* Welsh *na*, *ni*, not; Russian *ne;* It. *na*, *ni;* Sans. *na;* Pers. *neh;* Eng. *no*, *nor*, *nay*. The explanation of this fact I do not find; but I conceive it to be the *rejection*, by the *nose*, of disagreeable odors; whence *all* rejection, *all* refusal, comes to be expressed in the same way. The *n* is naturally prominent in the name of the nose, and in some operations in which that organ is used; as, *sneeze*, *sneer*, *snort*, *snuff*, *sniff*. Other examples?

Where as* this marquis schope his marriage,
There stood a thorp of sighte delitable,
In which that poore folk of that village
Hadden their beastes and their herbergage,
And of their labor took their sustenance,
After the earthe gave them abundance.

22. Among this poore folk there dwelt a man
Which that was holden poorest of them all;
But highe God sometime senden can
His grace unto a little oxe stall.
Janicula, men of that thorp him call.
A daughter had he, fair enough to sight,
And Griseldes this younge maiden hight.

23. But for to speak of virtuous beauty,
Then was she one the fairest under sun;
Full poorely yfostered up was she,
No licorous lust was in her heart yrun;
Well ofter of the well than of the tun
She drank, and, for she woulde virtue please,
She knew well labor, but none idle ease.

24. But though this maiden tender were of age,
Yet, in the breast of her virginity,
There was enclosed ripe and sad courage;
And in great reverence and charity
Her olde poore father fostered she;
A few sheep, spinning, on the field she kept;
She woulde not been idle till she slept.

25. And, when she homeward came, she woulde bring
Wortes and other herbes times oft,
The which she shred and seethe for hir living;

---

* **Where as,** *just where.*—**Schope** (A. S. *scapan;* Ger. *schaffen*), *shaped.*—**Marriage.** Trisyl. —**Thorp** (Dan. *thorp;* A. S. *thorp;* Lat. *turba?* Gr. *τύρβη?*), *hamlet.*—**Delitable.** The same as in the first stanza.—**Herbergage,** *pasture.*—**In which that poore,** *in which poor.*—**Sometime.** *E* final is often a syllable in Chaucer, as here.—**Oxe.** Dissyl.—**Younge.** Dissyl.—**Hight.** See 1st stanza.—**Poorely.** Trisyl.—**Yfostered.** The prefix *y*, so common in the old writers, as already remarked, grew out of the fuller form *ge*, the usual prefix of the past participle. A. S. *ge;* O. Sax. *gi;* Mœso-Gothic, *ga.* *G* in the A. S. is often changed to *y* in Eng.—**Licorous** (A. S. *liccian;* Ger. *lecken;* Fr. *lecher;* Lat. *lingere;* Gr. *λέιχειν*, to lick), *lickerish, greedy, lecherous.*—**Yrun,** *run.*—**Tun** (A. S. *tunne;* Ger. *tonne;* Fr. *tonne, tonneau*), cask (of liquor).—**For she woulde,** *because she would,* etc. *Woulde* is a dissyl.—**Sad** (A. S. *sad,* sated, weary, sick; Ger. *satt,* sated; Lat. *sat, satis,* enough), *steady, grave.*—**Been,** *be.*—**Wortes** (A. S. *wyrt, wirt,* herb, root, as in *liverwort, motherwort*), *worts, plants.* Dissyl.—**Times.** Dissyl.—**Shred** (A. S. *screadian,* Ger. *schroten,* to tear or cut), *to cut into small pieces* or *strips, to shred.*—**Seethe** (A. S. *seodhan*), *boiled, seethed.* —**Hir,** *their.* The pos. sing. masc. and neut. of *he* was in A. S. *his;* the pos. fem. was *hire* or *hyre;* the pos. plu. of all genders was *hira, heora,* often shortened to *hir, her.*

She woulde not been idle till she slept. *T,* as in *till, points out,* or demonstrates, and so is akin to *th.* E. g., Sans. *tat,* it; Gr. *τό,* the, *τοῦτο,* that; Lat. *tot,* so many, *talis,* such, *tantus,* so great, *tendere,* to stretch; Eng. *to, tend, tell.* Other instances?

And made her bed full hard and nothing soft;
And aye she kept her father's life on loft*
With every obeisance and diligence
That child may do to father's reverence.

26. Upon Griseldes, this poor creature,
Full often sithe this marquis set his eye,
As he on hunting rode peraventure;
And when it fell that he might her espy,
He, not with wanton looking of folly,
His eyen cast on her, but, in sad wise,
Upon her cheer he would him oft avise.

27. Commending in his heart her womanhead
And eke her virtue, passing any wight
Of so young age, as well in cheer as deed;
For though the people have no great insight
In virtue, he considered aright
Her bountee, and disposed that he would
Wed her only, if ever he wedden should.

28. The day of wedding came, but no wight can
Tellen what woman that it shoulde be;
For which mervaille wondered many a man,
And saiden, when they were in privity,
"Will not our lord yet leave his vanity?
Will he not wed? Alas, alas, the while!
Why will he thus himself and us beguile?

---

* **On loft** (A. S. *an*, on; *lyft*, the air), *aloft*.—**Obeisance.** Acc. 1st and 3d syl.—**Creature.** Acc. 1st and 3d syl.—**Sithe** (A. S. *sidh*, path, time, occasion), *times*.—**Peraventure,** *by chance*. Acc. 2d and 4th syl.—**Fell,** *fell out, happened*.—**Eyen** (A. S. *eage;* Ger. *auge;* Lat. *oculus;* D. *oog*, the eye; Gr. ὄσσε, two eyes), *eyes*. In A. S. the plu. very often ended in *n*, as *oxan*, oxen.—**Cheer** (Gr. κάρα, head; It. *ciera*, mien, face; Sp. *cara*, face; Gr. χαρά? joy; Fr. *chere*, entertainment, fare), *countenance, mien*.—**Avise** (Lat. *ad*, to, *videre*, to see), *to see to, observe, reflect*.—**Him oft avise,** *often take counsel with himself* (a *reflexive* use of avise).—**Womanhead** (A. S. *wif;* Ger. *weib*, woman; Sans. *ma*, to measure; *man*, to think, *mann*, the thinker, man; A. S. *wifman, wimman;* A. S. *had*, state; *hadian*, to ordain; Ger. *heit?* state, habit, condition), *womanhood, womanly character*.—**Wight,** person.—**Bountee.** See Index.—**Disposed,** arranged, *determined*.—**Mervaille** (Fr. fr. Lat. *mirabilis*, wonderful), *marvel*.—**The while** (A. S. *hwil*, Ger. *weile*, time), *the time*.—**Beguile** (*be* is orig. same as *by;* A. S., Ger., Sw., Dan., D., *be*, near, by, at; Goth., O. S., O. Ger., *bi*, Ger. *bei*. Sometimes this prefix gives emphasis, as in *bespatter, bedeck*. *Guile* is A. S. *wile*, Ice. *viel*, Eng. *wile*, fraud, deceit), *cheat, deceive*.

Upon Griseldes, this poor creature. The sound of *oo* in *poore* is soft and smooth. Hence it sometimes denotes softness and smoothness; as *soothe, smooth, cool, poor*. Other examples?

Will he not wed? Alas, alas, the while. The second *a* in *alas* has a sound naturally expressive of pain or grief. Its enunciation requires little besides the ordinary position of the organs of speech in a child, with the simple opening of the mouth and breathing. It is an unpleasant sound to the ear, perhaps from its association with the cries of infants and of sheep and calves. So the sound of *a* in *ah;* e. g. Heb. *ahh;* Gr. ἆ; Lat., Sans., Pers., Eng., Ger., *ah;* Ger. *ach;* Welsh *a;* Ir. *a*. As it is little more than a forcible *breathing*, it enters into some words denoting to *breathe, breath, air;* as Gr. ἄω, ἄημι; Lat. *halare*, to breathe; *aer*, air; Eng. *air*. Give other examples in illustration of these principles.

29. But natheless * this marquis hath done make
Of gemmes, set in gold and in azure,
Brooches and ringes for Griseldes sake;
And of her clothing took he the measure
Of a maiden like unto her in stature;
And eke, of other ornamentes, all
That unto such a wedding shoulde fall.

30. The time of undern of the same day
Approacheth that this wedding shoulde be,
And all the palace put was in array,
Both hall and chambers, each in his degree;
Houses of office stuffed with plenty.
There mayest thou see of dainteous vitaille
That may be found as fer as lasteth Itaille.

31. This real marquis, really arrayed,
Lordes and ladies in his company,
The which unto the feste weren prayed,
And of his retinue the bachelerie,
With many a sound of sundry melody,
Unto the village of the which I told,
In this array the righte way they hold.

32. Griseld of this, God wot, full innocent
That for her shapen was all this array,
To fetchen water at a well is went,
And cometh home as soon as ever she may;

---

* **Natheless.** See Index.—**Done make,** *caused to make, got made. Make* is here properly an infinitive.—**Gemmes** (Lat. *gemma*, gem, jewel). Dissyl.—**Azure** (Per. *lajuward*, azure; Ar. *azraq*, azure; Ger. *lasur*, azure-color; Sp. *azul*, the *lapis lazuli*, Ger. *lasurstein*, the stone of blue color). *Azure* or *blue*, the color of the sky, is the color of truth. So in Hudibras, "Presbyterian *true blue*." See Spenser's Epithalamium, 3d stanza.—**Brooches** (Lat. *brochus*, a projecting tooth; W. *proc*, a stab; Fr. *broche*, a spit, pin; Eng. *brooch*, a clasp, so called from the pin which fastens it), *clasps*.—**Ringes.** Dissyl.—**Undern** (A. S.), the third hour of the day, or nine in the morning.—**Same.** Dissyl.—**His degree,** *its degree.* The form *its*, as possessive, is quite modern, being very rarely found as early as in Shakespeare's time. In King James's version of the Bible, *his* is used instead of *its*.—**Stuffed.** Dissyl.—**Fer** (A. S.), *far*.—**Lasteth.** Monosyl.—**Real** (O. Fr. *real*; Lat. *regalis*, kingly, *rex*, king; Fr. *royal*), *royal*.—**Bachelerie** (W. *bach*, little, young; W. *baches*, a pretty little woman; O. Fr. *bacheler*, a young man; L. Lat. *baccalarius*, a soldier not old or rich enough to lead his retainers into battle with a banner), *knights of the lowest order*, or *young knights*.—**Righte.** Dissyl.—**Shapen** (see *schope*, st. 21), *made*.—**Went** (A. S. *wendan*, to turn, go; imperf. *went*), *gone*.—**Home.** A. S. *hâm*; O. Sax., O. Friesic, Sw., *hem*; Dan. *hiem*; Ice. *heimr*; Ger., D., *heim*; Goth. *haims*; Gr. *κῶμη*? village; Lith. *kaimas*?

To fetchen water at a well is went. The sound of *w*, in *water, well, went*, being a weak and flowing sound, is adapted to express *gentle motion, gentleness, weakness.* E. g. Lat. *vado* (for *v* in Latin often corresponds to *w*, the latter not being found in that language), Eng. *wade*; Lat. *vert-ĕre*, Eng. *-wards*, Ger. *-wärts*; Lat. *veho*, Eng. *way, wagon, wain*; Ger. *wallen*, to spring up, Eng. *well*; Ger. *wandern*, Eng. *wander*; Ger. *wehen*, to blow, Eng. *wind*, Lat. *vent-us*; Ger. *wenden*, to turn, Eng. *wend, went*; Ger. *winden*, Eng. *wīnd*; Eng. *wave, welter, wallow, warble, waddle, waft, wax, wane.* **Give other illustrations.**

For well she had heard say that thilke * day
The marquis shoulde wed, and, if she might,
She woulde fain have seen some of that sight.

33. She thought, "I will with other maidens stand
That be my fellows, in our door and see
The marquisesse, and therefore will I fond
To done at home, as soon as it may be,
The labor which that longeth unto me;
And then I may at leisure her behold,
If she this way unto the castle hold."

34. And as she would over the threshold gon,
The marquis came and gan her for to call.
And she set down her water-pot anon
Beside the threshold of this oxe stall,
And down upon her knees she gan to fall,
And with sad countenance she kneeleth still,
Till she had heard what was the lordes will.

35. This thoughtful marquis spake unto this maid
Full soberly, and said in this mannere,
"Where is your father, Griseldes?" he said,
And she with reverence and humble cheer
Answered, "Lord, he is all ready here."
And in she goeth, withouten longer let,
And to the marquis she her father fet.

36. He by the hand then taketh this old man,
And saide thus, when he him had aside:
"Janicula, I neither may nor can
Longer the pleasance of mine herte hide.
If that thou vouchesafe what so betide,

---

* **Thilke,** *this same.* See st. 21.—**Fellows** (A. S. *felaw,* fr. *fyligan, fylian,* to follow), *companions.*—**Fond** (Ice. *fana,* to act sillily; Scot. *fone,* to fondle; *fon,* to play the fool; O. Eng. *fond,* to dote on, fondle, caress), *be eager.*—**Which that,** *which.*—**Longeth,** *belongeth.*—**Leisure** (Lat. *licere,* to be at liberty; Fr. *loisir,* permission).—**Threshold** (A. S. *threscan,* to thresh; *wald, weald,* wood; A. S. *threscwald*).—**Gan,** *began.* A. S. *ginnan, gynnan,* begin. "The original sense of *ginnan* is to cut, split." *Webster.*—**Oxe,** dissyl. In Italy and some other countries the peasantry sometimes live under the same roof with their cattle.—**Sad.** See st. 24.—**Withouten** (A. S. *widh,* with; *utan,* out), *without.*—**Let** (A. S. *lettan,* to retard, make late; *lăt,* late), *hindrance, delay.*—**Fet** (A. S. *fetian,* to bring), *fetched.*—**Pleasaunce** (Lat. *placere,* to please; Fr. *plaisir,* to please; *plaisance*), *pleasure.*—**Vouchesafe** (*vouch* fr. Lat. *vocare,* the *c* changed to *ch* by Grimm's law; *vocare,* to call; O. Fr. *vocher;* Lat. *salvus,* Fr. *sauf,* safe; *vouchesafe,* vouch for safety, permit to be done safely), *permit.* Trisyl.—**What so betide,** *what* [I pray] *may happen so. Betide,* A. S. *tidan,* to happen. In the note on *beguile,* st. 28, it was shown that the prefix *be-* sometimes gives emphasis. Here observe another effect of the prefix; viz., it renders intransitive verbs transitive. E. g., *belie, befall.* Let the student look up other examples to illustrate both these points.

And down upon her knees she gan to fall. The sound of *kn,* in *knee* (and of *gn,* in the Lat. *genu,* knee, Gr. *γόνυ,* knee), was originally a broken sound, and so expressed a *breaking off suddenly.* E. g., *knot, knock, knell, knap, knit, knag, knead, knuckle, knurly.* So *gnarl.* Other examples?

Thy daughter will I take, ere that I wend,
As for my wife unto her lifes end.

37. "Thou lovest me, that wot I well certain,
And art my faithful liegeman* ybore,
And all that liketh me, I dare well sayn,
It liketh thee, and, specially, therefore,
Tell me that point that I have said before,
If that thou wilt unto this purpose draw,
To taken me as for thy son-in-law."

38. The sudden case the man astonied so
That red he wax, abashed, and all quaking
He stood, unnethes said he wordes mo;
But only this, "Lord," quoth he, "my willing
Is as ye will; against your liking
I will no thing, ye be my lord so dear,
Right as you list, governeth this matier."

39. "Then will I," quoth this marquis softely,
"That, in thy chamber, I and thou and she
Have a collation, and wost thou why?
For I will ask her if it her will be
To be my wife and rule her after me;
And all this shall be done in thy presence:
I will not speak out of thine audience."

40. And in the chamber while they were about
The treaty, which as ye shall after hear,
The people came unto the house without,
And wondered them in how honest mannere

---

* **Liegeman.** See *lieges*, st. 2.—**Liketh** (A. S. *lician*, to be pleased, to please), *pleaseth.*—**Sayn,** *say.*—**Astonied** (A. S. *stunian*, to stun; Ger. *staunen*, to be astonished; Lat. *attonare*, to thunder at; fr. *ad*, to, and *tonare*, to thunder; Fr. *étonner*; O. Eng. *astone*), *astonished.* So in the Bible; e. g., Dan. iv. 19.—**Wax** (A. S. *weaxen*; Ger. *wachsen*, to grow), *waxed, grew.*—**Unnethes** (A. S. *un*; Lat. *in*, not; A. S. *eadh*, ready, easy; Goth. *azets*, easy; Fr. *aisé*), *not easily, with difficulty.*—**Mo** (A. S. *mâ*; Scot. *mae*, more; A. S. *mâra*; Ger. *mehr*; Lat. *magis*, more), *more.*—**Against.** To make out the metre, pronounce *against* as a trisyl.—**Governeth.** Impera. plu. See *governance*, st. 134.—**Matier.** Acc. 2d syl.—**Collation** (Lat. *co-*, *con-*, *cum*, together, *latum*, to bring; *collatio*, a bringing together), *a conference, an interview.*—**Wost** (2d sing. fr. *wis*, pres. tense of A. S. *witan*, to know; *wiste*, knew; Lat. *vid-ere*, to separate with the eye, to see, becoming Eng. *wit* by Grimm's law, and the latter meaning to separate with the mind, to know, Gr. ὀϝίδα, I know), *knowest.* See *void*, in Index.—**Rule her,** *rule herself.*—**Audience,** *hearing.*—**Treaty** (Fr. *traité*; Lat. *tractatus*, a drawing out, agreement drawn up; Fr. *traho*, I draw), *agreement.*—**Which as** = which.—**Wondered them** (a reflexive combination, like 'bethought them'), *wondered.*—**Honest** (Lat. *honestus*, honorable), *respectable.* Acc. 2d syl.

Thou lovest me, that wot I well certain. The smooth sound of *l* is adapted to express what is *soft or soothing*; as in *lull, like, love, lave, lute*; Lat. *levis*, smooth; Gr. λεῖος; Lat. *libet* and *lubet*, it pleases. By analogy, especially at the end of words, it denotes slight or little things; as *satchel*, a little sack; Lat. *scutulum*, a little shield. Naturally it is employed to name actions in which the tongue, the organ that is chiefly used in enunciating the sound, is the main instrument; as Gr. λαλέω, to prate; Lat. *lallo*; Ger. *lallen*; Eng *loll*; Welsh. *llolian*; Gr. λάπτω; Eng. *lap*; Lat. *lambo*; Gr. λείχω; Lat. *lingo*, Eng. *lick*, Ger. *lecken*, Ir. *lighim*. Other examples?

And tenderly she kept her father dear.
But utterly Griseldes wonder might,
For never erst* ne saw she such a sight.

41. No wonder is, though that she be astoned
To see so great a guest come in that place.
She never was to none such guestes woned;
For which she looked with full pale face.
But shortly forth this matter for to chase,
These arn the wordes that the marquis said
To this benign, veray, and faithful maid.

42. "Griseld," he said, "ye shall well understand,
It liketh to your father and to me
That I you wed; and eke it may so stand,
As I suppose ye will that it so be.
But these demandes ask I first," quoth he,
"That since it shall be done in hasty wise,
Will ye assent, or elles you avise?

43. "I say this, 'Be ye ready with good heart
To all my lust, and that I freely may,
As me best thinketh, do you laugh or smart,
And never ye to grutchen night ne day,
And eke when I say yea, ye say not nay,
Neither by word ne frowning countenance?'
Swear this, and here I swear our alliance."

44. Wondering upon this thing, quaking for dread,
She saide, "Lord, undigne and unworthy
Am I to thilk honor that ye me bid;
But as ye will yourself, right so will I;
And here I swear that never willingly
In work, ne thought, I n'ill you disobey,

---

* **Erst** (superlative of *ere*, before; fr. A. S. *ær*, before; *ærest*, most before; Ger. *eher*, before; *erst*, first), *before*.—**Never . . . ne**. The double negative increases the negative force.—**Astoned.** Same as *astonied*, st. 38.—**Never . . . none**. Strengthened negation.—**Woned** (A. S. *wunian*, to dwell; O. Eng. *won*; Ger. *wohnen*), *wonted, accustomed*.—**Chase** (O. Fr. *chacier*; Fr. *chasser*; Lat. *captare*, to strive to seize, fr. *capere*, to take. See Grimm's law), *pursue*.—**Arn** (O. Eng. plu.), *are*.—**Veray** (Lat. *verus*, true), *true, very*.—**Avise**, *give counsel, advise*. See st. 26.—**Me best thinketh**, *seems best to me*.—**My lust**, *my wish* or *will*.—**Grutchen** (O. Fr. *groucher*, to murmur; Ger. *grunzen*, Eng. *grunt*. The *u* in these and many other words expresses low and obscure sounds), *grudge*.—**Ne**, *nor*. See *n'as*, st. 54.—**Alliance.** Acc. 1st and 3d. syl.—**Saide.** Dissyl.—**Undigne** (Lat. *in*, not, *dignus*, worthy), *undeserving*.—**Unworthy.** Acc. 1st and 3d syl.—**Thilk**, *this*. See st. 21.—**Honor.** Acc. 2d syl. **N'ill**, *will not*.—The reader will notice the large infusion of the French element in Chaucer's language. Contemporaries complained that he "imported a wagon-load of foreign words." Why may Chaucer have been predisposed to do this?

That I you wed, and eke it may so stand. To sound the *st*, as in *stand*, tends to bare and set the front teeth, and gives the face a look that denotes *firmness, stability*. Thus, Gr. ἵστημι, Lat. *stare*, Eng. *stand, staff, stake, stalk, stall, stay, steady, stem, stick, stiff, stock, stout, stub, stubborn, stump, sturdy*; Ger. *stein*, Eng. *stone*. Other illustrations of this?

For to be dead, though* me were loth to die."
45. "This is enough, Griselde mine," quoth he,
And forth he goeth, with a full sober cheer,
Out at the door, and after that came she ;
And to the people he said in this mannere :
"This is my wife," quoth he, "that standeth here.
Honoreth her and loveth her, I pray,
Whoso me loveth. There is no more to say."
46. And for that nothing of her olde gear
She shoulde bring into his house, he had
That women should despoilen her right there;
Of which these ladies weren nothing glad
To handle her clothes, wherein she was clad.
But natheless this maiden bright of hue,
From foot to head they clothed have all new.
47. Her haires have they kempt, that lay untressed
Full rudely, and with their fingers smale
A coroune on her head they have ydressed,
And set her full of nouches great and smale.
Of her array what should I make a tale ?
Unneth the people her knew for her fairness,
When she translated was in such richesse.
48. This marquis hath her spoused with a ring
Brought for the same cause, and then her set
Upon a horse snow-white and well ambling,
And to his palace, ere he longer let,

---

* **Though . . . die,** *though to die were grievous to me.*—**Honoreth.** Impera. plu. Acc. 2d syl.—**For that,** *because.*—**Gear** (A. S. *geara, gearwa,* provision, furniture ; *gearwian,* to prepare; Ger. *gärben,* to prepare leather, to tan), *clothing.*—**Clothes.** Dissyl.—**Haires.** Dissyl.—**Kempt** (A. S. *cemban ;* O. Eng. *kemben ;* Ger, *kämmen ;* to comb), *combed.*—**Rudely.** Trisyl.—**Coroune** (Lat. *corona*), *crown.*—**Ydressed**, *adjusted.*—**Nouches** (allied to *notch,* or from 'Late Latin' *nusca,* or *nosca, noschia,* a clasp), *clasps, buckles, jewels.*—**What,** *why.*—**Unneth,** *scarcely.* See *unnethes,* st. 38.—**Translated,** *transformed.*—**Richesse** (Fr. and O. Eng.), *riches.* A. S. *ric,* Ger. *reich,* rich. The word was originally in the singular number.—**Same.** Dissyl. —**Let** (A. S. *lat, late ; letian, lettan,* to make late, hinder), *delayed. Let* in the sense of *permit,* is from A. S. *lætan,* O. Sax. *latan,* Ger. *lassen.* The student should accustom himself to scrutinize closely the root-meanings of words. The teacher will find it a very profitable exercise, for pupils to look out and memorize with great care the roots, primitive meanings, and kindred forms, of a number of words regularly assigned for the purpose as a part of the daily lesson.

To handle her clothes, wherein she was clad. The sound of *cl,* as in *cloth* and *clad,* often denotes cleaving to, or *adhering.* E. g., *cleave, clay, cling, clinch, clutch, climb, clamber, clot, clod, clasp ;* Ger. *kleid,* garment. Shakespeare's lines illustrate this origin of the word *clothes :*

"New honors, come upon him,
Like our strange garments, cleave not to their mould,
But with the aid of use.—MACBETH, Act I., Scene 3.

This marquis hath her spoused with a ring. The sound of *r,* as in *ring,* denotes *interrupted* or *distorted* motion; as Lat. *rota,* wheel; Eng. *ring, round, cramp, crook, crown, gripe, grasp, reel, roll.* It also denotes broken or rattling noises, as Gr. κρίζω, κροτέω, κρώζω ; Eng. *croak, crack, cry, crash, creak, rattle.* Other examples ?

With joyful people that her led and met,
Conveyed her; and thus the day they spend
In revel, till the sunne gan* descend.

49. And shortly forth this tale for to chase,
I say that, to this newe marquisesse,
God hath such favor sent her of his grace
That it ne seemed not, by likeliness,
That she was born and fed in rudeness,
As in a cote, or in an oxe stall,
But nourished in an emperores hall.

50. To every wight she waxen is so dear
And worshipful, that folk there she was born,
And from her birthe knew her year by year,
Unnethes trowed they, but durst have sworn
That to Janicle, of which I spake biforn,
She daughter n'as; for, as by conjecture,
Hem thought she was another creature.

51. For though that ever virtuous was she,
She was increased in such excellence
Of thewes good yset in high bountee,
And so discreet and fair of eloquence,
So benign and so digne of reverence,
And couthe so the people's heart embrace,
That each her loveth that looketh in her face.

52. Not only of Saluces in the town
Públished was the bountee of her name,
But eke beside in many a regioun,
If one said well, another said the same.
So spreadeth of her high bountee the fame
That men and women, young as well as old,
Gon to Saluce, upon her to behold.

---

* **Gan,** *began.* See st. 34.—**Tale.** Dissyl.—**Rudeness.** Trisyl.—**Cote** (A. S. *cote, cyte,* a small house; Ice. *kot;* W. *cwt*), *cottage.*—**There,** *where.*—**Trowed** (A. S. *treowian;* Ger. *trauen,* to believe, trust), *thought.*—**Biforn,** *before.*—**N'as,** *was not.* "The *nasals, m* and *n,* are employed to express negation, being the natural sounds to express refusal." *Fowler.* Why?—**Hem thought** (them-thought, like *me-thought; him* being the A. S. dat. plu.; Semi-Sax. *heom;* O. Eng. *hem,* to them), *it seemed to them.*—**Creature.** Trisyl.—**Thewes** (A. S. *theaw, thau, thaw*), *manners, qualities.*—**Digne** (Lat. *dignus*), *worthy.*—**Couthe,** *knew how to, could.* See *couthen.* st. 8.—**Loveth.** This line reminds of Spenser's sweet encomium on Sir Philip Sidney :

"Was never eye did see that face,
Was never ear did hear that tongue,
Was never mind did mind his grace,
That ever thought the travel long ;
But eye and ear and every thought
Were with his sweet perfections caught."

Published. Acc. 2d syl.—**Gon** (A. S. *gangan;* Scot. *gang;* Ger. *gehen,* to go; O. Eng. plu, *gon,* for *goen*), *go.* *Went* comes from A. S. *wendan,* to turn, to go. Give the origin, root-meaning, allied forms, etc., of every word of the fifth line, fifty-second stanza.

53. Thus Walter lowly, nay, but really,*
Wedded with fortunate honestetee,
In Goddes peace liveth full easily
At home, and outward grace enough had he.
And for he saw that under low degree
Was ofte virtue hid, the people him held
A prudent man, and that is seen full seld.

54. Not only this Griseldes through her wit
Couth all the feat of wifely homeliness,
But eke when that the time required it,
The common profit coulde she redress.
There n'as discord, rancor, ne heaviness,
In all the land, that she ne could appease,
And wisely bring hem all in rest and ease.

55. Though that her husband absent were, anon,
If gentlemen, or other of that country,
Were wroth, she woulde bringen them at one;
So wise and ripe wordes hadde she,
And judgement of so great equity,
That she from heaven sent was, as men wend,
People to save and every wrong to amend.

56. Not longe time after that this Griseld
Was wedded, she a daughter hath ybore.
All had her lever han borne a knave child.
Glad was this marquis and the folk therefore;
For though a maiden child come all before,
She may unto a knave child attain
By likelihood, sith she n'is not barrein.

PARS TERTIA.

57. There fell, as falleth many times mo,

---

* **Really,** *royally.* See *real,* st. 31.—**Honestetee** (Lat. *honestas;* O. Fr. *honestetê;* Fr. *honnêtetê*), *virtue, good manners.*—**Couth,** *knew.* See st. 8.—**Feat** (Lat. *factum,* doing, deed; Fr. *fait;* Nor. Fr. *feat;* fr. *facere,* to act, do), *work, performance.*—**Homeliness** (A. S. *hâm,* home; Ger. *heim;* perhaps Gr. κώμη, by Grimm's law; *-li,* fr. A. S. *lic,* like; *-ness,* fr. A. S. *-ness, -niss;* O. Ger. *-nis, -nissa;* Ger. *-nisz;* denoting abstract quality, the termination *-ness* being found in about 1,300 Eng. words), *home management, domestic economy.* In some proper names *-ness* means *nose,* from A. S. *näse,* as Fifeness.—**Redress,** *set right again.*—**Ne,** *nor, not.*—**Anon** (O. Eng. for *in one*), *in one moment, quickly.*—**At one,** *to agreement.* Hence *atone*=to make one, to reconcile.—**Judgment.** Trisyl.—**Wend** (A. S. *wênan, wœnan;* Ger. *wähnen;* O. Eng. *ween;* to think), *weened, thought, fancied.*—**Ybore** (A. S. *beran;* Lat. *ferre;* Gr. φέρειν, to bear. See Grimm's law), *borne.*—**Lever** (A. S. *leof, leve,* dear; *lever* is the comparative degree), *more gladly, rather.*—**Knave** (A. S. *cnafa* or *cnapa,* offspring, boy; Ger. *knabe*), *a boy.*—**Sith** (A. S. *sith;* O. Eng. *sin, since;* Ger. *seit*), *since.*—**Mo,** *more.*

That she from heaven sent was, as men wend. *H*, as in *heaven*, is enounced with strong breathing. It therefore sometimes denotes *effort* and *aspiration;* as Lat. *halare*, to breathe, Eng. *haul*, *heave, hate, hurry, hent, hope, hark, high, holy.* Other examples?

When that this child had souked * but a throw,
This marquis in his herte longeth so
To tempt his wife, her sadness for to know,
That he ne might out of his herte throw
This marvellous desire his wife to assay:
Needless, God wot, he thought her to affray.

58. He had assayed her enough before,
And found her ever good. What needeth it
Her for to tempt, and alway more and more?
Though some men praise it for a subtle wit;
But as for me, I say that evil it sit
To assay a wife, when that it is no need,
And putten her in anguish and in dread.

59. For which this marquis wrought in this mannere;
He came alone anight, there as she lay,
With sterne face, and with full trouble cheer,
And saide thus: "Griseld," quoth he, "that day
That I you took out of your poor array
And put you in estate of high noblesse—
Ye have not that forgotten, as I guess.

60. "I say, Griseld, this present dignity,
In which that I have put you, as I trowe,
Maketh you not forgetful for to be
That I you took in poor estate full low,
For any weal you mote yourselve know,
Take heed of every word that I you say,
There is no wight that heareth it but we tway.

61. "Ye wot yourself how that ye comen here,
Into this house; it is not long ago;
And though to me that ye be lefe and dear,
Unto my gentils ye be nothing so.
They say, to them it is great shame and wo,

---

* **Souked** (A. S. *sûgan, sûcan;* Ger. *saugen;* Lat. *sugere*, to suck), *sucked.*—**Throw** (A. S. *thrag*, a period of time; or from A. S. *thrâwan*, to turn, twist, throw), *a little while.*—**Tempt** (Lat. *tentare*), *try, test.*—**Sadness,** *steadiness, constancy.*—**Assay** (Lat. *exigere*, to drive out, as dross; It. *assagiare;* Fr. *essayer*), *to try.*—**Needless,** *needlessly.*—**Thought,** *purposed.*—**Affray,** *frighten.* See *fray*, Index.—**Sit,** *becomes. Evil it sit = it ill becomes* or *suits.*—**Anight,** at night. —**There as,** *where.*—**Trouble** (Lat. *turbare*, to disturb; Fr. *troubler;* O. Fr. *tourbler*), *troubled.*—**Cheer,** *countenance, aspect.*—**Array,** *apparel.*—**Noblesse** (Fr.), *distinction, nobility.*—**Mote** (A. S. *môt*, ought; *mought;* Ger. *müssen*), *must.*—**Yourselve,** *yourself.*—**For any weal,** etc., *as to any goods that you possessed in your own right.*—**Tway** (Lat. *duo*, which, by Grimm's law, becomes *two;* Gr. δυω; A. S. *twegen, twâ;* Ger. *zwei*, by Grimm's law), *two.*—**Lefe** (A. S. *leof*, dear), *loved.* See *lever*, st. 56.—**Gentils** (Lat. *gentilis*), *persons of good birth, gentle-folk.* See *gentilesse*, Index.

When that this child had souked but a throw. Thr, as in *throw*, requiring much effort to articulate, indicates *violent motion;* as *thrush, throb, thrill, thrust, throng.* Other instances?

They say to them it is great shame and wo. The sound of *sh*, at the beginning of a word, being uttered with a forcible *expulsion* of the breath, and with the teeth set, sometimes expresses great *aversion;* as in *shame, pshaw.* Other illustrations?

For to ben subject and ben in servage *
To thee, that born art of a small linage.

62. "And, namely, sin thy daughter was ybore,
These wordes han they spoken, doubteless.
But I desire, as I have done before,
To live my life with them in rest and peace;
I may not in this case be reccheles;
I mote do with thy daughter for the best,
Not as I would, but as my people lest.

63. "And yet, God wot, this is full loth to me;
But, natheless, withouten your wityng
Will I not do; but this will I," quoth he,
"That ye to me assent as in this thing.
Show now your patience, in your working,
That ye me hight and swore in your village,
That day that maked was our marriage."

64. When she had heard all this, she, nought ameeved,
Neither in word, in cheer, or countenance,
(For as it seemed she was nought aggrieved,)
She saide, "Lord, all lieth in your pleasance,
My child and I, with hertly obeisance,
Ben youres all, and ye may save or spill
Your owen thing. Worketh after your will.

65. "There may no thing, so God my soule save!
Liken to you, that may displeasen me.
Ne I desire nothing for to have,
Ne dreade for to lese, save only ye.
This will is in mine heart, and aye shall be.
No length of time or death may this deface,
Ne change my courage to another place."

66. Glad was this marquis for her answering,
But yet he feigned as he were not so.
All dreary was his cheer and his looking,
When that he should out of the chamber go.

---

* **Servage,** *servitude.* The ending *-age* is said to be the Lat. *-atium.*—**Linage** (Lat. *linum,* flax; *linea,* linen thread, line; Fr. *ligne*), *family.* — **Sin,** *since.*—**Namely,** *particularly.*—**Reccheles** (A. S. *rêcan,* to care for; A. S. *leas,* Ger. *los,* destitute of; akin to Eng. *loose,* and *lose*), *without care, reckless.*—**Lest,** *please.*—**Loth,** *odious, disagreeable.*—**Witynge,** *knowledge.* See *wost,* Index.—**Patience.** Trisyl.—**Hight,** *promised.*—**Maked** (A. S. *macian,* to make), *made.* —**Marriage.** Trisyl.—**Ameeved** (Lat. *movere;* Fr. *mouvoir,* to move), *moved.* The *a* prefixed has a strengthening or intensive force. **Hertly,** *hearty.* See Index.—**Owen** (A. S. *agan,* to possess; Ger. *eigen;* O. Eng. *owen,* to possess), *possessed, own.*—**Courage** (Fr. *courage;* Lat. *cor,* the heart), *heart, inclination.*—**Marquis** (Fr. *marquis;* O. Fr. *markis;* fr. Ger. *mark,* a bound, border. Orig. the marquis was an officer appointed to guard the marches or frontiers).

Ben youres all, and ye may save or spill. The sound of *sp,* as in *spill,* at the beginning of a word, being made by a forcible puffing out of breath, naturally expresses *expulsion;* as *spit, spout, sputter, speak, spell, spew, spatter.* Give other examples.

Soon after this, a furlong way or two,
He privily hath told all his intent
Unto a man, and to his wife him sent.

67. A manner-sergeant * was this prive man,
The which he faithful often founden had
In thinges great, and eke such folk well can
Don execution in thinges bad.
The lord well knew that he him loved and drad.
And when this sergeant wist his lordes will,
Into the chamber he stalked him full still.

68. "Madam," he said, "ye mote forgive it me,
Though I do things to which I am constrained,
Ye ben so wise that full well knowen ye
That lordes hestes may not ben yfeigned.
They may well be bewailed and complained,
But men mote need unto her lust obey,
And so will I, there is no more to say.

69. "This child I am commanded for to take"—
And spake no more, but out the child he hent
Despitously, and gan a cheer to make
As though he would have slain it ere he went.
Griseld moot all suffer and all consent;
And as a lamb she sitteth meek and still,
And let this cruel sergeant do his will.

70. Suspicious was the defame of this man,
Suspect his face, suspect his word also,
Suspect the time in which he this began.
Alas her daughter, that she loved so!
She wend he would have slaien it right tho.
But natheless she neither wept ne siked,
Conforming her to that the marquis liked.

71. But at the last to speken she began,
And meekely she to the sergeant prayed,
So as he was a worthy gentilman,
That she might kiss her child, ere that it deyd.

---

* **Manner-sergeant,** *kind of sergeant. Of* is understood after *manner.* See *manner-governance,* Index.—**Prive,** *private, in private business* (Fr. *prive;* Lat. *privatus;* private; *privare,* to separate).—**Execution.** Five syl.—**Drad,** *dreaded.* See Index.—**Stalked** (A. S. *stælc, stealc,* high; *stælcan, stealcian,* to go slowly), *walked in a stealthy manner.*—**Hestes** (A. S. *hǣs;* fr. *hātan,* to call; Ger. *heiszen*), *commands.*—**Yfeigned** (Fr. *feindre;* Lat. *fingĕre,* to feign), *feigned, dissembled; concealed.*—**Her,** *their.*—**Lust,** *inclination.*—**Hent** (A. S. *hendan,* to seize; Ice. *henda;* Gr. χανδάνειν, to hold; Lat. *hend* in *prehendere,* to grasp; Eng. *hand*), *seized.*—**Despitously** (Lat. *despicĕre,* to despise; O. Eng. *despitous,* malicious), *spitefully, maliciously.*—**Cheer,** *appearance, face.*—**Moot,** *must.*—**Defame,** *ill repute.*—**Slaien** (A. S. *slahan, slagan,* to strike, slay; Ger. *schlagen;* Ice. *sla*), *slain.* Dissyl.—**Tho,** *then.*—**Siked** (A. S. *sican;* Ger. *seufzen,* to sigh), *sighed.*—**Speken,** *speak.*—**Meekely.** Trisyl.—**Sergeant** (Fr. *sergent,* fr. Lat. *serviens, servient-is,* pres. particip. of *servire,* to serve), a high officer, attending on the king; a *sergeant-at-arms.*—**Deyd** (O. Fries. and Ice. *deya,* to die), *died.*

And in her barm* this little child she leid
With full sad face, and gan the child to bless,
And lulled it, and after gan it kiss.

72. And thus she said in her benigne voice :
"Farewell, my child, I shall thee never see !
But sith I have thee marked with the crois,
Of thilke father blessed mote thou be,
That for us died upon a cross of tree :
Thy soule, little child, I him betake,
For this night shalt thou dien for my sake."

73. I trow that to a norice in this case
It had been hard this routhe for to see :
Well might a mother then have cried, "Alas !"
But natheless so sad steadfast was she
That she endured all adversity,
And to the sergeant meekely she said,
"Have here again your little younge maid.

74. "Goth now," quoth she, "and doth my lordes hest.
And one thing would I pray you of your grace,
But if my lord forbade you, at the lest,
Burieth this little body in some place,
That beastes ne no briddes it to-race."
But he no word will to the purpose say,
But took the child and went upon his way.

75. This sergeant came unto his lord again,
And of Griseldes wordes and her cheer
He told him point for point, in short and plain,
And him presented with his daughter dear.
Somewhat this lord had ruth in his mannere ;
But natheless his purpose held he still,
As lordes don, when they will have their will;

---

* **Barm** (A. S. *beorma*, bearm; Ger. *barme ;* fr. A. S. *beoran*, *beran*, to bear: fr. Lat. *ferre*, by Grimm's law; Gr. *φέρειν*), *bosom, lap.*—**Leid** (A. S. *lecgan ;* O. Eng. *leggen ;* Lat. *leg-ĕre*, to lay), *laid.*—**Lulled** (Lat. *lallare*, to sing *lalla*, or *lullaby ;* Ger. *lallen*), *soothed, quieted.*—**Crois** (O. Fr. *crois ;* Lat. *crux*, cross), *cross.*—**Mote,** *must.*—**Him betake,** *entrust to him.*—**Trow,** *believe.* See Index.—**Norice** (A. S., fr. Fr. *nourrice ;* Lat. *nutrix*, nurse, fr. *nutrire*, to nourish), *nurse.*—**Routhe** (A. S. *hreow*, grief), *ruth, grief.* See *ruth*, Index.—**Goth** (impera. plu. for sing.), *go.*—**Hest,** *command.* See *hestes*, Index.—**But if,** *unless.*—**Lest** (A. S. *lytel*, little ; *lassa*, less ; *last*, *lasest*, least), *least. At least, unless my lord forbade you.*—**Ne,** *nor.*—**Burieth.** Impera.—**Briddes** (A. S. *bird* or *brid*, fr. *bredan*, to nourish), *birds.*—**To-race** (Gr. *ῥάκος*, a rag ; *ῥήγνυμι*, to tear, to break ; Lat. *f-reg-i*, fr. *frango*, whence, by Grimm's law, *break*), *to rags, in pieces.*

And in her barm this little child she leid. The sound of *i*, in *little*, being very minute, is excellently adapted by nature to express diminutives. Hence the great majority of diminutives have this sound prominent. The effect is heightened in *little* by the sound of *l*, which, itself, often has a diminutive force. *Pill, little, nit, flit, whittle, giggle*, illustrate this principle, which is of very extensive application. See the word *diminutive*, in the Index.

Well might a mother then have cried, "Alas !" The sound of *m*, in *mother*, is very easily made by infants. Hence it is used to express the *mother* or *nurse*. E. g., Heb. *em*, mother ; Eng. *ma, mamma ;* Ger. *amme*, nurse. Other examples of this and the preceding ?

76. And bade the sergeant that he privily
Shoulde this childe softe wind and wrap
With alle circumstances tenderly,
And carry it in a coffer,* or in his lap;
But, upon peyne his head off for to swap,
That no man shoulde know of his intent,
Ne whence he came, ne whither that he went;

77. But at Boloygne, to his suster dear,
That thilke time of Panic was countess,
He should it take and show her this matiere,
Beseeching her to don her business
This child to foster in all gentleness;
And whose child that it was, he bade her hide
From every wight, for aught that might betide.

78. The sergeant goeth and hath fulfilled this thing;
But to the marquis now returne we;
For now goeth he full fast imagining,
If by his wifes cheer he mighte see,
Or by her wordes apperceive that she
Were changed; but he never could her find
But ever in one ylike sad and kind.

79. As glad, as humble, as busy in service,
And eke in love as she was wont to be,
Was she to him, in every manner wise;
Ne of her daughter not a word spake she;
Non accident for non adversity
Was seen in her, ne never her daughter name
Ne nempyned she in earnest ne in game.

80. In this estate there passed ben four year
Ere she with childe was; but, as God wold,
A knave child she bare by this Waltier,

---

* **Coffer** (Gr. *κόφινος*, a basket; Ger. and Dan. *koffer*), *a chest, trunk*.—**Peyne** (Gr. *ποινή*; Lat. *pœna*, penalty; A. S. *pin*; Ger. *pein*; O. Eng. *peyne, paine*), *penalty, pain*.—**Swap** (Ger. *schwappen*, to strike; whence 'swop,' to strike a bargain, to barter), *to strike*.—**Boloygne** (Lat. *Bononia*; Fr. *Bologne*; Ital. *Bologna*), a famous city of Italy, S.S.W. of Venice, N.N.W. of Rome, capital of the province of Bologna. Its population is about 90,000.—**Suster** (A. S. *sweoster, swyster, suster*; Ger. *schwester*; Lat. *soror*), *sister*.—**Don**, etc. (A. S. *don*, to do), to *make it* her business, *take pains*.—**Wifes** (A. S. *wif*; Ger. *weib*), *wife's*.—**Apperceive** (Fr. *appercevoir*; Lat. *ad, percipere*, fr. *per*, through, thoroughly, wholly, and *capĕre*, to take), *perceive*.—**Ever in one**, *continually*.—**Ylike** (A. S. *gelic*, fr. *ge-*, intensive, very, and *-lic*, like), *alike*.—**Non**, *no*.—**Every** *manner wise = every way*.—**Nempyned** (A. S. *nemnan, namian*, to name; Lat. *nominare*; Gr. *ὀνομάζω*; Ger. *nennen*; fr. root *no* or *gno*, by Grimm's law, Eng. *kno-w*; Sans. *naman*), *named*.—**Game** (A. S. *gamen*, game; fr. *gamian*, to play), *sport*.—**Year**, *years*.—**Wold**, *would, willed*. See *wolde*, Index.—**Knave**, *boy*.—**Daughter name**, in st. 79, must be considered equivalent to *daughter's name*. *Daughter* is A. S. *dohtor*; Ger. *tochter*; Gr. *θυγάτηρ*.

Shoulde this childe softe wind and wrap. The sound of *wr* in *wrap*, denotes *twisting* or *distorted motion*; as in *wrest, wring, wrong, wriggle, wrap, wreck, wrangle, wrench, wrist, wrestle, wreck, wrath, writhe, wry*. Give other illustrations of this.

Full gracious and fair for to behold;
And when that folk it to his father told,
Not only he, but all his country, merry
Was for this child, and God they thank and hery.*

81. When it was two year old, and from the breast
Departed from his norice, on a day
This marquis caughte yet another lest
To tempt his wife yet after, if he may.
Oh, needless was she tempted in assay!
But wedded men ne knowen no measure,
When that they find a patient creature.

82. "Wife," quoth this marquis, "ye have heard ere this,
My people sikely bearen our marriage;
And, namely, sin my son yboren is,
Now is it worse than ever in all our age;
The murmur sleth mine heart and my courage;
For to mine eares cometh the voice so smart
That it well nigh destroyed hath mine heart.

83. "Now say they thus: 'When Walter is agone,
Then shall the blood of Janicle succeed
And ben our lord, for other have we none.'
Such wordes saith my people, out of dread,
Well ought I of such murmur taken heed;
For certainly I dreade such sentence,
Though they not plainen in my audience.

84. "I wolde live in peace, if that I might;
Wherefore I am disposed utterly,
As I his sister served ere by night,
Right so think I to serve him privily.
This warn I you, that ye not suddenly,
Out of yourself for nothing should outraye.
Beth patient, and thereof I you pray."

***Hery** (A. S. *herian*, to praise; Goth. *hazjan*), *praise.*—**Norice,** *nurse.* See st. 73.—**After** (A. S. *æft*, *eft*, after, behind, again. "After seems to be the comparative degree of *af* or *aft.*" *Webster.* -R, or *-er*, the comparative ending, seems to be allied to Lat. *-ior*, and Gr. -ότερ-ος), *again.*—**Sikely** (A. S. *sican*, to sigh: O. Eng. *sike;* Ger. *seufzen*), *sorrowfully, with sighs.*—**Sin,** *since.*—**Sleth,** *slayeth.* See *slaien*, Index.—**Smart** (A. S. *smeortan;* Ger. *schmerzen;* perhaps akin to Lat. *mors*, death), *painful.*—**Audience,** *hearing.*—**Plainen** (Fr. *plaindre;* Lat. *plangere*, to beat the breast, to bewail), *complain.*—**Woulde.** Dissyl.—**Ere.** See *erst*, Index.—**Outraye** (Lat. *ultra*, beyond; Fr. *outrer*, to go beyond reason, to exaggerate; *outre*, extravagant), *be excessive, be outrageous.*—**Beth,** *be ye.* Impera. plu. The plu. of the impera. in Early Eng. ended in *-eth* or *-th;* but in Chaucer this ending is occasionally shortened to *e;* and frequently it is omitted altogether. The sing. of the impera. in O. Eng. is the same as the root of the verb.

The murmur sleth mine heart and my courage. The sound of *u* in *murmur*, being indistinct and produced low in the chest, expresses, when soft, *gentleness;* when loud, *harshness, discontent, muttering, smothered wrath.* E. g., Lat. *murmuro*, murmur; Ger. *murren;* Rus. *murtshu;* Gr. μύζω; Lat. *mutio, musso;* Eng. *mutter;* Eng. *grumble;* Dan. and Eng. *grum;* Welsh *grwm;* Gr. γρύζω, Lat. *grundio*, Ger. *grunzen*, Eng. *grunt.* Give other examples.

85. "I have," quoth* she, "said thus and ever shall,
I will nothing, ne nill no thing certain,
But as you list. Nought grieveth me at all,
Though that my daughter and my son be slain
At your commandement; that is to sayen,
I have not had no part of children twain,
But first sickness, and, after, wo and pain.

86. "Ye been our lord, doth with your owen thing
Right as you list, asketh no rede of me.
For as I left at home all my clothing
When I first came to you, right so," quoth she,
"Left I my will and all my liberty
And took your clothing. Wherefore I you pray
Doth your pleasaunce; I will your lust obey.

87. "And certes, if I hadde prescience
Your will to know, ere ye your lust me told,
I would it do withouten negligence.
But now I wot your lust, and what ye wold,
All your pleasaunce firm and stable I hold;
For wist I that my death would do you ease,
Right gladly would I dien, you to please.

88. "Death may not maken no comparison
Unto your love." And when this marquis say
The constance of his wife, he cast adown
His eyen two, and wondreth how she may
In patience suffer all this array.
And forth he goeth with dreary countenance,
But to his heart it was full great pleasaunce.

89. This ugly sergeant in the same wise
That he her daughter fette, right so he,
Or worse, if men can any worse devise,
Hath hent her son, that full was of beauty;
And ever in one so patient was she,

---

* **Quoth.** See Index.—**Nill** (A. S. *nillan* or *nyllan*, fr. *ne*, not, and *willan*, to will), *not will, refuse, reject.*—**Grieveth** (Lat. *gravare*, to burden; fr. *gravis*, heavy).—**Owen,** *own.*—**Rede** (A. S. *rædan*, to advise; *ræd*, counsel), *counsel.*—**Certes,** *surely.* See Index.—**Lust,** *pleasure.*—**Wot,** *know.*—**Wold,** *would, would have.*—**Wist,** *knew.*—**Dien** (O. Eng. infin. ending *-en*), *die.*—**Say** (A. S. *seon*, to see; Ger. *sehen;* A. S. *sehwan*, to see), *saw.*—**Cast** (Dan. *kaste;* Ice. and Sw. *kasta*), *cast.*—**Eyen,** *eyes.* See Index.—**Patience.** Trisyl.—**Fette,** *brought.* See Index.—**Hent,** *seized.* See Index.—**Ever in one,** *ever in one way, continually.* See st. 78.

Though that my daughter and my son be slain. The sound of *m* in *my*, being made with *closed lips*, is pre-eminently *internal* and personal to every one. It expresses the personal pronoun of the first person, on account of its subjective importance. E. g., Sans. *mam;* Gr. *μέ*; Lat. *me;* Eng. *me, my, mine.* Other examples? Other significance of this sound?

Hath hent her son, that full was of beauty. The sound of *fl*, as in *full* (corresponding by Grimm's law to πλ in Gr., *pl* in Lat., and *vl* in Ger.), is said to denote *fullness* or *extension*, from its swelling the cheeks, and filling the mouth. E. g. Gr. πλέος, πλήρης, πίμπλημι; Lat. *plere*, to fill; *plenus*, full; Ger. *füllen, voll;* Eng. *fill, full.* Other examples?

That she no cheere* made of heaviness,
But kissed her son, and after gan it bless.

90. Save this she prayed him, if that he might,
Her little son he would in earthe grave,
His tender limmes, delicate to sight,
From fowles and from beastes for to save.
But she none answer of him mighte have,
He went his way, as him nothing ne rought,
But to Boloygne he tenderly it brought.

91. This marquis wondreth ever lenger the mòre
Upon her patience, and if that he
Ne hadde soothly knowen therebefore
That parfitly her children loved she,
He would have weened that of some subtlety
And of malice, or of cruel courage,
That she had suffered this with sad visage.

92. But well he knew that, next himself, certain
She loved her children best in every wise.
But now of women would I aske fain
If these assayes mighten not suffice.
What could a sturdy husband more devise
To prove her wifehood and her steadfastness,
And he continuing ever in sturdiness?

93. But there ben folk of such condition
That, when they have a certain purpose take,
They cannot stint of their intention,
But, right as they were bounden to a stake,
They will not of their firste purpose slake.
Right so this marquis fully hath purposed
To tempt his wife, as he was first disposed.

94. He waiteth, if by word or countenance,
That she to him was changed of courage.
But never could he finden variance;
She was aye one in heart and in visage,

---

* **Cheere,** *appearance.*—**After,** *afterwards.* See Index.—**Grave** (A. S. *grafan,* to carve, dig; Gr. *γράφειν,* to scratch, write, grave; Ger. *graben;* Fr. *graver;* A. S. *graf,* a grave; Ger. *grab;* Russ. *grob*), *bury, entomb.*—**Limmes** (A. S. *lim;* O. Eng. *lyme*), *limbs.* Dissyl.—**Fowles** (A. S. *fleogan,* to fly; *fugel,* a bird; Ger. *vogel;* Ger. *fliegen,* to fly; *flog,* flew; O. E. *fowles,* flying animals), *birds.* **Rought** (A. S. *recan,* to reck, care for; Ger. *geruhen;* O. Dutch, *rochten*), *recked, cared.*—**Lenger** (A. S. *lang, long,* long; *lengdh,* length), *longer.*—**Soothly** (A. S. *sodh,* true; O. S. *soth,* truth; *lic,* like), *truly.*—**Therebefore,** *previously thereto.*—**Parfitly** (Lat. *perfectus,* perfect; fr. *perficĕre,* to complete; *per,* thoroughly; *facĕre,* to make or do; O. Fr. *parfit*), *perfectly.*—**Weened,** *thought.* See *wend,* Index.—**Courage,** *heart, spirit.* See Index.—**Fain** (A. S. *feaha,* gladness; *fagen,* glad; *gefeohan, fagnian,* to rejoice), *gladly.*—**Sturdy** (O. F. *estourdi,* stunned; Fr. *étourdi,* giddy, rash; Ice. *styrdir,* rigid), *foolishly obstinate, blunt, rude.*—**Wifehood,** *the state of wife.* See note on *womanhood,* st. 27.—**Condition.** Quadrisyl.—**Take,** *taken.*—**Stint** (A. S. *stintan,* to blunt; *stentan,* to be blunt, to be weary; Norw. *stinta,* to have enough), *restrain within bounds, weary of, desist from.*—**Slake,** *slacken, fail.* See Index.

And aye the further that she was in age,
The more true,* if that were possible,
She was to him, and more penible.

95. For which it seemed thus, that of them two
There was but oo will; for as Walter lest,
The same pleasaunce was her list also,
And, God be thanked! all fell for the best.
She shewed well, for no worldly unrest,
A wife, as of herself, nothing ne should
Will in effect, but as her husband would.

96. The sclander of Walter oft and wide spread,
That of a cruel heart he wickedly,
For he a poor woman wedded had,
Had murdered both his children privily.
Such murmur was among them commonly.
No wonder is; for, to the people's ear,
There came no word but that they murdered were.

97. For which, whereas his people therebefore
Had loved him well, the sclander of his defame
Made them that they him hateden therefor.
To ben a murderer is an hateful name.
But natheless, for earnest or for game,
He of his cruel purpose n'olde stent ;
To tempt his wife was set all his intent.

98. When that his daughter twelf year was of age,
He to the court of Rome, in subtil wise
Informed of his will, sent his message
Commanding hem such bulles to devise,
As to his cruel purpose may suffice ;
How that the pope, as for his people's rest,
Bade him to wed another, if him lest.

99. I say he bade, they shoulden counterfeit
The popes bulles, making mention

---

* **More true.** *More* a dissyl.—**Penible,** *painstaking, capable of pain.* See *peyne,* Index.—**Oo** (A. S. *an;* Fr. *un;* Lat. *un-us;* Gr. ἓν ; Ger. *ein;* Ir. and Gael. *aon, an,* one), *one.*—**Fell,** *happened.*—**Unrest,** *trouble, uneasiness, want of rest.*—**Would,** *would have it, would wish, wished.* See *wolde,* Index.—**Sclander** (Fr. *esclandre,* Lat. *scandalum,* Gr. σκάνδαλον, the stick or spring in a trap; a snare, offence, stumbling-block), *scandal.*—**Wide.** Dissyl.—**For he** = *because he.*—**Game,** *play, joke.* See Index.—**N'olde** = *ne would, would not.*—**Stent,** *to cease, desist.* See st. 93.—**Twelf,** *twelve* (Goth. *tva,* two ; *-lif,* ten).—**Message** (Fr. *messager,* to send word; Lat. *mittere,* to send), *messenger.*—**Hem,** *them.*—**Bulles** (Lat. *bulla,* anything rounded by art, a roll, a seal ; Fr. *bulle;* akin to *bill*), *bulls.*—**Counterfeit** (Lat. *contra,* against ; *facere,* to make ; Fr. *contrefaire, contrefait*).—**Popes,** etc. Scan this line. Name the root etc. of each word.

For which it seemed thus, that of them two. The sound of *tw* in *two* (corresponding by Grimm's law to δυ in Gr. and *du* in Lat.), in many words denotes *two.* No explanation is given.

The sclander of Walter oft and wide spread. The sound of *spr,* as in *spread,* denotes a *spreading out;* e. g., *sprawl, spray, sprinkle.* Other examples ?

That he had leave his firste wife to lete,*
As by the popes dispensation,
To stinten rancor and dissention
Betwixt his people and him. Thus said the bull;
The which they have published at the full.

100. The rude people, as no wonder is,
Wenden full well that it had been right so;
But when these tidings came to Griseldes,
I deeme that her heart was full of wo.
But she ylike sad forevermo
Disposed was, this humble creature,
The adversity of fortune all to endure.

101. Abiding ever his lust and his pleasance,
To whom that she was given, heart and all,
As to her very worldly suffisance.
But shortly if this story tell I shall,
This marquis written hath in special
A letter, in which he sheweth his intent,
And secretly he to Boloygne it sent.

102. To the earl of Panik, which that hadde tho
Wedded his sister, prayed he specially
To bringen home again his children two
In honorable estate all openly.
But one thing he him prayed utterly,
That he to no wight, though men would inquire,
Should not tellen whose children that they were;

103. But say the maiden should ywedded be
Unto the marquis of Saluce anon.
And as this earl was prayed, so did he,
For at day set, he on his way is gone
Toward Saluce, and lordes many on
In rich array, this maiden for to guide,
Her younge brother riding by her side.

104. Arrayed was toward her marriage,
This freshe maiden, full of gemmes clear;
Her brother, which that seven year was of age
Arrayed eke full fresh in his mannere.

---

* **Lete,** *leave.*—**Stinten,** *restrain, stop.*—**At the full** = *in full.*—**Wenden,** thought. See *wende*, Index.—**Ylike,** *alike.* See Index.—**Suffisance** (Fr. *suffisant*, sufficient; Lat. *sufficere*, to suffice), *sufficiency.*—**Tho** (A. S. *thonne*; O. Eng. *thanne*; Ger. *dann*), *then.*—**Utterly** (A. S. *ut*, out; *utter*, outer; *utemest*, outermost), *most particularly.*—**Many on,** *many a one.*—**Arrayed.** The *-ed* of preterites and past participles is regularly a separate syllable in Chaucer. So *-es* in the pos. and in the plu. The terminal "*e*" is usually a syllable in Chaucer.

That he to no wight, though men would inquire. The sound of *q* (= k) in *inquire*, is supposed to have a natural fitness to express *interrogation.* E. g., Sans. *kas*, Gr. -κος, whence comes κότερος; Lat. *quis*, who, Mœso-Goth. *hwas*, Lith. *kas*, Russ. *koi*, Gael. *co*, who? A. S. *hwa* (*h* for *k*, by Grimm's law); Eng. *who?* No explanation is found. Other examples?

And thus in great noblesse and with glad cheer,
Toward Saluces shaping her * journey,
From day to day they riden in hir way.

PARS QUINTA.

105. Among all this, after his wicked usage,
This marquis, yet his wife to tempten more
To the utterest proof of her courage,
Fully to have experience and lore,
If that she were as steadfast as before—
He on a day in open audience
Full boisterously hath said her this sentence:
106. "Certes, Griseld, I had enough pleasance
To have you to my wife, for your goodness
And for your truth and for your obeisance,
Not for your lineage, ne for your richesse;
But now know I, in very soothfastness,
That in great lordship, if I well avise,
There is great servitude in sundry wise.
107. "I may not do as every ploughman may:
My people me constraineth for to take
Another wife, and cryen day by day;
And eke the pope rancor for to slake
Consenteth it, that dare I undertake;
And trewely thus much I will you say,
My newe wife is coming by the way.
108. "Be strong of heart, and void anon her place,
And thilke dower that ye broughten me,

---

* **Shaping her . . . . . riden in hir.** *Her* and *hir* each = *their*. A. S. *hira*, *heora*, of them (genitive, or pos., plu.)—**Courage,** *disposition.*—**Lore,** *learning, knowledge.*—**Boisterously** (Ice. *bistr;* D. *byster*, stormy; O. Eng. *boistous*, furious; *boist*, swelling; akin to *boast;* W. *bwyst*, wild, savage; *bwystus;* Low Ger. *biester*, frowning, dark, ugly; Fr. *bis*, swarthy).—**Said her,** *said to her.*—**I had enough,** etc., I *was well enough* pleased to have you as my wife. —**For your goodness,** *on account of your goodness.*—**Soothfastness,** *truth.* See *soothly*, Index. For *-ness*, see *homeliness*, Index.—**Avise,** *observe, reflect.*—**Eke,** *also.* See Index.—**Pope** (A. S., Lat., It., Fr., Ger., D., Dan., Sp. *papa;* Gr. *πάππα, πάπα*, father; O. Eng. *pape*), *the bishop of Rome*, the chief dignitary of the Catholic Church. *Pope* is here dissyl.—**Rancor for to slake,** *to appease rancor.* **Rancor** (Lat. *rancor*, rancidity, an old grudge, rancor; Fr. *rancune*), *settled malignity.*—**Trewely** (A. S. *treowe, triwe*, faithful; Ger. *treu, getreu;* A. S. *treowian*, to believe, trust), *truly.* Trisyl.—**Will you say,** *will say to you.*—**Void** (Lat. *vid-uus*, separate, widowed; Fr. *vide*. *Vid*, the Lat., is the same as in *vid-ĕre*, to separate with the eye, to see. A. S. *weoduwe, widuwe;* Ger. *wittwe;* Lat. *vid-ua;* Eng. *wid-ow*), *make empty, quit.* See *wost*, Index.—**Thilke,** *that same.* Give root, root-meaning, etc., of each word in this line.

What power over foreign princes had the Pope in Chaucer's time? Was there then in England or on the Continent any form of Protestantism? What were Chaucer's religious sympathies? With what prominent English nobleman was he associated?

And thus in great noblesse and with glad cheer. The sound of *gl*, as in *glad*, denotes *smoothness* or *silent motion.* E. g., Ger. *glatt*, smooth, even; A. S. *glad;* Eng. *glide, glib.* This signification probably arises by analogy from the smooth sound. Other examples?

Take it again, I grant it of my grace.
Returneth * to your fatheres house," quoth he,
"No man may always have prosperity.
With even heart I rede you to endure
The stroke of fortune, or of adventure."

109. And she again answered in patience.
"My Lord," quoth she, "I wot and wist alway,
How that, betwixen your magnificence
And my poverty, no wight can ne may
Maken comparison, it is no nay.
I ne held me never digne in no mannere
To ben your wife, ne yet your chamberere.

110. "And in this house there ye me lady made,
(The highe God take I for my witness,
And all so wisly he my soule glad!)
I never held me lady ne mistress,
But humble servant to your worthiness,
And ever shall, while that my life may dure,
Aboven every worldly creature.

111. "That ye so long of your benignity
Han holden me in honor and nobley,
Whereas I was not worthy for to be,
That thank I God and you, to whom I pray
Foryeld it you; there is no more to say.
Unto my father gladly will I wend,
And with him dwell unto my life's end.

112. "There I was fostered as a child full small,
Till I be dead my life there will I lead,
A widow clean in body, heart, and all.

---

* **Returneth.** Impera. plu.—**Even heart,** *equanimity.*—**Rede,** *advise.* St. 86.—**Adventure** (Lat. *adventurus,* about to come; fr. *advenire,* to come on or to), *hap, chance.*—**Wist,** knew. See *wost,* Index.—**Betwixen** (A. S. *be,* and *twyg,* two; Lat. *duo.* See *tway,* st. 60), *between.*—**Poverty** (Lat. *paupertas,* poverty; *pauper,* poor; O. Fr. *poverte;* Fr. *pauvrete*). The 2d syl. is acc.; probably because it is so in the Lat.—**It is no nay.** It cannot be denied.—**Digne,** *worthy.*—**Chamberere** (Gr. καμάρα, Lat. *camera,* arched roof; Fr. *chambre,* chamber), *chambermaid.*—**There,** *where.*—**Wisly,** *certainly.*—**He my soule glad,** *may he gladden my soul!* **Soule,** dissyl.—**Han** (O. Eng. plu.), *have.*—**Nobley** (Lat. *no-scere,* to know; *nob-ilis,* well known, famous, noble; Fr. *noblesse,* nobility. See *nempyned,* st. 79), *distinction.*—**Foryeld** (A. S. *for,* forth, away, fr. *faran,* to go. *For,* as an inseparable preposition, denotes,—(1) simple *removal;* as in *forbid,* to bid away; *forsake,* to seek away, desert; (2) removal and *disappearance;* as, *forgive,* to give out of sight; *forget,* to let go out of mind; (3) removal and *going wrong;* as, *forswear;* (4) removal with added notion of *completeness;* as, *forlorn,* utterly lost; (5) the same as simple *for;* as, *forsooth,* for truth, in truth; (6) *fore;* as, *forward.* *Yield* is A. S. *gildan, geldan,* to pay, yield), *repay.*—**Wend,** *go, wend.* See *went,* Index.—**There,** *where.*

Unto my father gladly will I wend. The sound of *f* in *father* (corresponding by Grimm's Law to *p* or *ph* in Lat., and π or φ in Gr.), from the ease with which it is enounced, is employed to denote one of the first objects that interest the child. E. g., Sans. *pitar,* Zendish *paiter,* Pers. *padar,* Gr. πάτηρ, Lat. *pater,* Russ. *batia,* Ger. *vater,* Eng. *father,* and *papa,* Turk. *peder.*

For sith* I gave to you my maydenhede
And am your trewe wife, it is no drede,
God schilde such a lordes wife to take
Another man to husband or to make!

113. "And of your newe wife, God of his grace
So grante you weal and prosperity;
For I will gladly yelden her my place,
In which that I was blissful wont to be.
For sith it liketh you, my Lord," quoth she,
"That whilom weren all my heartes rest,
That I shall gon, I will go when you lest.

114. "But thereas ye me proffer such dowaire
As I first brought, it is well in my mind,
It were my wretched clothes, nothing faire,
The which to me were hard now for to find.
Oh, goode God! How gentle and how kind
Ye seemed by your speech and your visage,
That day that maked was our marriage!

115. "But soth is said, algate I find it true,
For in effect it proved is on me,
Love is not old, as when that it is new.
But certes, Lord, for none adversity
To dien in this case, it shall not be
That ever, in word or work, I shall repent
That I you gave mine heart in whole intent.

116. "My Lord, ye wot that in my father's place
Ye did me strip out of my poore weed,
And richely me cladden of your grace;
To you brought I nought elles out of drede
But faith and nakedness and maydenhede.

---

* **Sith,** *since.*—**Maydenhede** (A. S. *mag,* a boy; *magedh, magden,* a girl), *maidenhood* See *womanhood,* st. 27.—**Trewe,** *true.* Dissyl. See *trewely,* st. 107.—**It is no drede,** *there i no (occasion to) fear.* See *drad,* st. 2.—**Schilde** (A. S. *scild;* Ger. and Dan. *schild,* shield fr. Ice. and Sw. *skyla,* to cover, defend), *shield, forbid.*—**Make** (A. S. *macian;* Ger. *machen;* Dan *mage,* to make, frame, fashion; A. S. *maca, gemaca, gemacca,* mate, husband, companion; Ice *maki,* an equal, husband; Dan. *mage,* equal, mate, match, spouse; O. Eng. *macche*), *a companion a mate.*—**Yelden,** *yield.* See *foryelde,* st. 111.—**Gon,** *go.*—**Thereas,** *whereas.*—**Dowaire** (Fr *douer,* to endow; *douaire;* Lat. *dotare,* to endow, portion; fr. *dos,* a dowry, gift; fr. *do, dare,* t give, Gr. δίδωμι), *dowry.*—**Soth,** *sooth, true, truly.* See *soothly,* Index.—**Algate** (A. S. *álgeats,* fr *eall, al,* all, and *geat,* passage, door, way; Ger. *gasse,* path; Ice. and D. *gat,* opening), *always.*—**For none adversity,** etc., *for no adversity* (i. e., notwithstanding any adversity, even to th extent) *of dying in this case, shall it be that,* etc. The student's attention is called to the touching pathos of the last three lines of the preceding stanza. The whole speech is remarkable.—**Weed** (A. S. *wæd,* a garment; O. Fries. *wede;* fr. Goth. *vid-an,* to bind), *clothing.*

O goode God! How gentle and how kind. The sound of *o* in *God,* being a short sound, is more appropriate to express littleness than greatness. There is a sense of congruity in the enunciation of the word *jot;* but of incongruity in uttering the word *God.* Such an exception proves the rule. This sound sometimes denotes surprise or harshness. Examples?

And here again your clothing I restore,
And eke your wedding ring forevermore.

117. "The remnant of your jewels ready be
Within your chamber, dare I safely sayn.
Naked out of my father's house," quoth she,
"I came, and naked mote I turn again.
All your pleasaunce would I fulfill fain;
But yet I hope it be not your intent
That I smokles * out of your palace went."

120. "The smok," quoth he, "that thou hast on thy back,
Let it be still, and bear it forth with thee."
But well unnethes thilke word he spake,
But went his way for ruth and for pity.
Before the folk hirselven strippeth she,
And in her smok, with foot and head all bare,
Toward her father's house forth is she fare.

121. The folk her folwen weeping in hir way,
And fortune aye they cursen as they gone;
But she from weeping kept her eyen drey,
Ne in this time word ne spake she none.
Her father, that this tiding heard anon,
Curseth the day and time, that nature
Shope him to be a lives creature.

122. For, out of doubt, this olde poore man
Was ever in suspect of her marriage.
For ever he deemed, sith that it began,
That when the lord fulfilled had his courage,
Him woulde think that it were disparage
To his estate, so lowe for to light,
And voiden her as soon as ever he might.

123. Agains his daughter hastily goeth he;
For he by noise of folk knew her coming;

---

* **Smokles** (A. S. *smocc;* Ice. *smokkr,* chemise. As to *-les,* see *reccheles,* Index), *without under-garment.*—**Unnethes,** *with difficulty.* See Index.—**Ruth** (A. S. *hreowan,* to rue; Ger. *reuen*), *sorrow, compassion.*—**Fare** (A. S. and Goth. *faran,* to go; Ger. *fahren;* Ice. and Sw. *fara;* Dan. *fare*), *gone.*—**Folwen** (A. S. *folgian;* Ger. *folgen,* to follow), *follow.*—**Drey** (A. S. *dryg, dryge, drege,* dry; D. *droog;* Ger. *trocken*), *dry.*—**Time.** Dissyl.—**Shope,** *shaped.* See *schope,* Index.—**Lives** (A. S. *libban,* to live; *libbe,* surviving; *lif,* life; Ger. *leben,* to live), *live, living.*—**Courage,** *inclination.*—**Disparage** (Lat. *dispar,* unequal; *dis,* asunder; *par,* equal), *a disparagement.* Acc. 1st and 3d syl.—**Voiden,** *make empty, remove, cause to quit.* See *void,* Index.—**Agains** (A. S. *agen, ongegn;* Ger. *entgegen,* against; O. Eng. *agens;* A. S. *to-geanes, to genes,* toward, against; Fries. *aien, agen;* D. *tegens. Agains* is here probably the genitive case of an old noun), *towards, to meet.* To illustrate this origin of *agains,* or *against,* we may remark, that *since, amongst, betwixt, amidst,* and *whilst* are also old genitives. See Gibbs' *Teutonic Etymology.*

The smok, quoth he, that thou hast on thy back. The sound of *a* in *hast* and *back,* as well as that of *a* in *half,* being one of the very earliest and easiest, stands at the head of the Indo-European and some other languages, and often seems to be used where no *reason* exists for any *other* special vowel.

And with her olde coat,* as it might be,
He covereth her, full sorrowfully weeping.
But on her body might he it not bring,
For rude was the cloth, and more of age
By dayes fele than at her marriage.

124. Thus with her father for a certain space
Dwelleth this flower of wifely patience,
That neither by her wordes ne by her face,
Beforn the folk, nor eke in her absence,
Ne shewed she that her was done offence;
Ne of her high estate no remembrance
Ne hadde she, as by her countenance.

125. No wonder is, for in her great estate
Her ghost was ever in plain humility;
Ne tender mouth, no hearte delicate,
Ne pompe, ne semblant of realty;
But full of patient benignity,
Discreet and prideless, aye honorable,
And to her husband ever meek and stable.

126. Men speak of Job, and most of his humblesse,
As clerkes, when hem list, can well indite;
Namely, of men; but as in soothfastness,
Though clerkes praisen women but a lite,
There can no man in humblesse him acquite
As women can, ne can be half so true
As women ben, but it befall of new.

---

* **Coat,** *frock, gown.*—**Fele** (A. S. *fela, fele;* Ger. *viel,* many), *many.*—**Beforn** (A. S. *be-;* Goth. *bi-;* O. Ger. *pi-;* Ger., Sw., Dan., D., *be-*, originally the same as *by*, and denoting nearness of *place;* sometimes giving emphasis, as *bedeck, bedaub.* See note on *betide,* st. 4; and see *Teutonic Etymology,* by Prof. Gibbs. Often, as here, the original meaning of the prefix is lost. *Fore* is A. S. *for, fore;* Ger. *für, vor;* Lat. *pro;* Gr. πρό, in front; A. S. *beforan;* O. Eng. *beforn;* Ger. *bevor*), *in front, before.*—**Her was done,** *to her was done.*—**Ghost** (A. S. *gast,* breath; O. Eng. *gast;* Ice. *geysa,* to be impelled; whence *geyser,* a spouting spring of boiling water), *spirit.*—**Pompe.** Dissyl.—**Realty** (O. Fr. *roial, real.* The ending *-ty* is fr. Lat. *-itas,* which is much used in Lat. to form abstract substantives), *royalty.* See *real,* st. 31.—**Aye** (Gr. ἀεί, ever; αἰών, an age; Lat. *ævum;* Goth. *aivs;* Ice. *æfi;* A. S. *awa, aa, a,* always), *always.*—**Humblesse** (Lat. *humilitas,* humility; *humus,* the ground; Gr. χαμαί, on the ground; χαμαλός), *humility.*—**Clerkes** (Lat. *clerĭcus,* a clergyman; Gr. κληρικός, a priest; κλῆρος, a lot, the clergy, to whom lands were *allotted* for their support; A. S. *clerc, cleric, cleroc,* priest, clerk; afterwards any educated person, for the ministers of religion were almost the only literary men), *scholars.*—**Lite** (A. S. *lyt, lytel*), *little.*—**Him acquite,** *acquit himself, conduct himself.*—**But it befall of new,** *unless it happen recently.* The word *ben,* in this line, illustrates the O. Eng. plural in *-en.* So we have, four lines before, *praisen,* and, in st. 121, *folwen* and *cursen.* The loss of this ending and the dropping of inflections generally, accompany the transition from A. S. to Eng.

Ne of her high estate no remembrance. The sound of *m* in *remembrance,* being highly internal, made with closed lips, is exceedingly suggestive of subjectivity, belongs to one's own consciousness, and is indicative of important mental operations. E. g., Sans. *man,* to think; Gr. *μηνίω;* Lat. *moneo,* I remind; *memini,* I remember; Ger. *mahnen, meinen,* Eng. *mean,* to intend, imply; Lat. *mens,* Eng. *mind.* Hence, perhaps, the word *man,* A. S. *mann, mon,* means the *thinker.* Other examples?

PARS SEXTA.

127. From Boloygne is the Earl of Panik come,
Of which the fame up sprang to more and less;*
And to the peoples eares, all and some,
Was couth eke that a newe marquisess
He with him brought, in such pomp and richess,
That never was there seen with mannes eye
So noble array in all West Lombardy.

128. The marquis which that shope and knew all this,
Ere that this earl was come, sent his message
For thilke poore sely Griseldes.
And she with humble heart and glad visage,
Not with no swollen heart in her courage,
Came at his hest, and on her knees her sette,
And reverently and wisely she him grette.

129. "Griseld," quoth he, "my will is utterly,
This maiden, that shall wedded be to me,
Received be to-morrow as really
As it possible is in mine hous to be;
And eke that every wight in his degree
Have his estate in sitting and service,
In high pleasaunce, as I can best devise.

130. "I have no woman suffisant certain
The chambers for to array in ordinance
After my lust, and therefore would I fain,
That thine were all such manner governance.
Thou knowest eke of old all my pleasance.

---

* **More and less,** *great and small.*—**All and some,** *'all and singular,' each and all.*—**Couth,** *known.* See *couthen*, Index.—**Richess,** *riches.* See Index.—**Sely** (A. S. *sel*, good; *sælig*, *gesælig*, happy; Ger. *selig;* O. Eng. *seely*, lucky, inoffensive), *good.* This is the original of our word silly, the notion of *innocence* easily passing, in the minds of our naughty ancestors, into that of *folly.*—**Grette** (A. S. *gretan*, to address; Ger. *gruszen*, to greet), *greeted.*—**Really,** *royally.* See *really*, Index.—**Mine.** Monosyl.—**Sitting** (A. S. *sittan* for *sitian;* Ger. *sitzen*, to sit; Lat. *sedĕre.* See Grimm's law, by which *sed-* in *sedĕre* becomes *set* or *sit;* Gr. ἕζομαι. The suffix *-ing* has several uses: (1) to form a present active participle, it being then akin to Sans. *-ant;* Gr. -οντ; Lat. *-ent*, or *-ant;* A. S. *-ende*, *-and*, and *-ande;* Ger. *-end;* O. Eng. *-and*, as *glitterand* in Spenser; (2) to form an adjective, it being then the same in origin as the participle; (3) to form an abstract verbal noun, it being then the same as the Gothic *-eins;* Ice. *-ung;* D. *-ing;* Ger. and A. S. *-ung;* (4) to form, in A. S., patronymic nouns, as *Elising*, the son of Elisha; (5) to indicate, in the Saxon tongue, offspring, as *Browning*, brown offspring; (6) to denote meadow or field in O. Eng., as Rudd*ing*ton, town of the red *meadow*), *situation.*—**Suffisant** (Fr., fr. Lat. *sufficiens*), *sufficient.* See *suffisance*, Index.—**Ordinance,** *order, good order.*—**Lust,** *inclination, pleasure.*—**Manner governance,** *manner of direction.* See *manner sergeant*, st. 67. *Governance* is fr. Gr. κυβερνᾶν, to act as pilot; Lat. *gubernare;* Fr. *gouverner*, to govern; *gouvernance*, government.—**Knowest.** Give the derivation, root-meaning, etc., of each word in this line.

Not with no swollen heart in her courage. The sound of *sw* in *swollen* is said to denote *gentle motion*, this notion arising from the soft sound of *w* (which is the same nearly as *oo* in *fool* or *smooth*). E. g., *sway*, *swagger*, *sweep*, *swell*, *swerve*, *swing.* Other examples?

Though thine array be bad and evil byseye,*
Do thou thy devoir at the leste way."

131. "Not only, lord, that I am glad," quoth she,
"To don your lust, but I desire also
You for to serve and please in my degree,
Withoute fainting, and shall evermo.
Ne never for no weal, ne for no wo,
Ne shall the ghost within mine hearte stent
To love you best with all my true intent."

132. And with that word she gan the house to dight
And tables for to set and beddes make,
And pained her to don all that she might,
Praying the chambereres for Goddes sake
To hasten 'em and faste sweep and shake,
And she, the most serviceable of all,
Hath every chamber arrayed, and his hall.

133. Abouten undern gan this earl alight,
That with him brought these noble children twey;
For which the people ran to see the sight
Of her array, so richely byseye.
And then at erst amonges em they say
That Walter was no fool, though that him lest
To change his wife; for it was at the best.

134. For she is fairer, as they deemen all,
Than is Griseld, and more tender of age;
And fairer fruyt between them shoulde fall,
And more pleasant for her high lineage.
Her brother eke so fair was of visage

---

* **Byseye** (A. S. *beseon,* to view; fr. *be* and *see*), *beseen, adapted, adjusted.* **Evil byseye,** *ill to be seen.*—**Devoir** (Fr. fr. Lat. *debere,* to owe, fr. *de,* from, and *habere,* to have; *to have* something *from* another, and so *to owe*), *duty.*—**Leste** (A. S. *lytel,* little; A. S. *lassa, lasse,* less; *lasest, last,* least), *least.* **At the leste way,** at least.—**Stent,** *cease, be weary.* See *stint,* Index. —**Dight** (A. S. *dightan,* to dictate, arrange; fr. Lat. *dictare,* to dictate; fr. *dic-ere,* to speak; Ger. *dichten,* to write poetry), *set in order.*—**Pained,** *took pains.* Dissyl.—**Chamberes,** *chambermaid.* See Index.—**Undern,** *nine in the morning.* See st. 30.—**Twey,** *two.* See Index.—**Byseye,** *adjusted.* See above.—**Amonges** (A. S. *amang, onmang,* among, fr. *gemang,* mixture; Ger. and D. *mengen,* to mix; Dan. *mänge,* to mix: *-st* or *-est,* is usually the superlative ending; but here is probably an old genitive ending *-es;* O. Eng. *amonges,* in the crowd), *among.*—**Deemen** (A. S. *deman,* to think), *deem.* O. Eng. plu.—**Fruyt** (Lat. *fructus,* fruit; *frui,* to enjoy; Fr. *fruit*), *fruit, offspring.*

Ne never for no weal, ne for no wo. The sound of the first *e* in *never,* is really nothing more than the shortened sound of *a* in *hate.* The sound of *e* in the French word *feve* is akin to the sound of *a* in *care.* The sound of *e* in *her,* is the same as that of *u* in *fur.* *E* is a very frequent substitute for other vowels, as well as for the leading vowel. It is also often silent. These facts explain the frequent recurrence of the letter, without reference to the possible natural signification of the sound. When a *little* sound, however, it is not inappropriate to express *little* things and *little* actions. Thus *lancet, trumpet, pocket, streamlet, cockerel, pickerel, satchel, crackle* (once pronounced *crack-le* = *crack-ly*), diminutives from *lance, trump, pock, stream, cock, pike, sack, crack.* Give other illustrations.

That hem to seen the people hath caught pleasance,
Commending now the marquis' governance.*

135. O stormy people, unsad and ever untrue!
And undiscreet and changing as a fane,
Delighting ever in rumble that is new;
For, like the moone, waxen ye and wane.
Aye full of clapping, dear enough a jane,
Your doom is false, your constance evil previth
A full great fool is he that on you lieveth!

136. Thus saiden sade folk in that city,
When that the people gazed up and down;
For they were glad right for the novelty,
To have a newe lady of their town.
No more of this now make I mentioun,
But to Griseld again I will me dress,
And tell her constance and her business.

137. Full busy was Griseld in everything,
That to the feste was appertinent.
Right naught was she abashed of her clothing,
Though it were rude and some del eke to-rent;
But with glad cheere to the gate is went
With other folk, to greet the marquisesse,
And after that doth forth her business.

138. With so glad cheer his guestes she receiveth,
And cunningly everich in his degree,
That no defaute no man apperceiveth,
But aye they wondren what she mighte be,

---

* **Governance,** *management.* See *governance,* Index.—**Unsad,** *unsteady.* See *sad,* Index. —**Fane** (A. S. *fana,* a banner; Ger. *fahne,* D. *vaan;* O. Eng. *fane;* Goth. *fana,* a cloth), *vane, weathercock.*—**Rumble** (Fr. *romeler;* Ger. *rummeln.* This is one of the *onomatopoetic* class of words; i. e., those words whose sound, in pronouncing them, is like the sound they indicate, as *hiss, buzz*), *rumor.*—**Jane** (Lat. *Genua;* Low Lat. *janua;* O. Eng. *Jean; Genoa*), *a small coin of Genoa.*—**A Jane,** *at a farthing.*—**Preveth** (O. Fr. *prover;* Fr. *prouver,* to prove; Lat. *probare,* to try, approve, fr. *probus,* good; A. S. *profian;* Ger. *prufen, proben*), *proveth.*—**Lieveth** (A. S. *lefan,* to allow; *gelefan,* to believe; *leafa,* belief; Ger. *glauben,* to believe), *believeth.*—**Sade,** *thoughtful.* See *sad,* Index. Dissyl.—**Dress** (Lat. *dirigere,* to direct; *dis,* apart, *regĕre,* to straighten; Fr. *dresser,* to make straight), *direct.*—**Del** (A. S. *del,* part; *dælan,* to divide, deal out; Ger. *theilen,* to divide; *theil,* a portion), *part.*—**Somedel,** *somewhat.*—**To-rent** (A. S. *to;* Ger. *zu;* A. S. *rendan,* to rend; W. *rhanu,* to divide), *torn.*—**Went,** *gone.* See *went,* Index.—**Business** (A. S. *bysig, biseg,* busy; Ice. *bisa,* to work hard. For the suffix *-ness,* see *homeliness,* Index), *business.* Trisyl. —**Cunningly** (A. S. *cunnan,* to know, be able, can; O. Eng. *cun,* to know, *con,* to know, to study over; Goth. *kunnan;* D. *kunnen;* Ger. *konnen,* to know; O. Eng. *ken.* Is not this word allied to the root *gno-* in *i-gno-sco,* and γιγνώσκω?), *with skill.*—**Everich** (A. S. *æfer,* ever; Lat. *ævum,* an age; Gr. αἰών; A. S. *av,* eternity; *a,* always; *ylk,* same; *alc, elc,* each), *every one.*— **Defaute** (O. Fr. *defaulte;* Fr. *defaut,* deficiency; Lat. *de,* down; *fallere,* to deceive), *defect.*

O stormy people, unsad and ever untrue. The sound of *o* is produced by the muscles in a state of tension around the lips, accompanied by a forcible expiration (and sometimes inspiration). It is appropriate to express *pain, wonder, surprise.* Hence its universal use as an interjection. When prolonged, it may express *greatness.* Examples?

That in so poor array was for to see,
And couthe* such honour and reverence;
And worthily they praisen her prudence.

139. In all this mene while, she ne stent
This maid and eke her brother to commend,
With all her heart in full benigne intent,
So well that no man could her praise amend.
But at the last, when that these lordes wend
To sitten down to meat, he gan to call
Griseld, as she was busy in the hall.

140. "Griseld," quoth he, as it were in his play,
"How liketh thee my wife and her beauty!"
"Right well, my lord," quoth she, "for in good fay,
A fairer saw I never none than she.
I pray to God give her prosperity;
And so hope I that he will to you send
Pleasance enough unto your lives end.

141. "One thing beseech I you and warn also—
That ye ne pricke with no tormenting
This tender maiden, as ye have done mo.
For she is fostered in her nourishing
More tenderly, and, to my supposing,
She coulde not adversity endure
As could a poorly fostered creature."

142. And when this Walter saw her patience,
Her glade cheer and no malice at all,
And he so oft had done to her offense,
And she aye sad and constant as a wall,
Continuing ever her innocence over all,
This sturdy marquis gan his hearte dress
To rewe upon her wifely steadfastness.

143. "This is enough, Griselde mine," quoth he,
"Be now no more aghast, ne evil apaid,

---

* **Couthe,** knew. See *couthen*, Index.—**Mene** (Lat. *medius*, midst; Gr. *μέσος*; It. *mezzo*; Fr. *moyen*), *mean, middle.*—**Stent,** *stinted, withheld.* See *stint*, Index.—**Amend** (Lat. *emendo*, fr. *e*, out, and *menda*, spot, stain; whence *emendare*, to remove a spot or stain), *amend, correct, improve.*—**Wend,** *go.* See *went*, Index.—**Fay** (O. Fr. *fei*; Lat. *fides*; Fr. *foi*, faith; O. Eng. *feith, fayeth, fay*), *faith.*—**Pricke** (A. S. *priccian*; D. *prikken*, to prick; A. S. *prica*, a sharp point), *prick, sting.*—**Mo** (A. S. *me*; Goth. *mik*; Ger. *mich*; Lat. *me*; Gr. *μέ*; Sans. *mâ*, me), *me.* Is this a desperate attempt at rhyme?—**Creature.** Trisyl.—**Malice.** Acc. 2d syl.—**As a wall.** This reminds of the remark attributed to Gen. Lee, "There stands Jackson's brigade lik ea stone wall;" whence *Stonewall* Jackson.—**Dress,** *direct.* See st. 136.—**Rewe,** have compassion. See *ruth*, Index.—**Quoth** (Lat. *inquit*, said; A. S. *cwedhan*, to say; Mœso-Goth. *qitha, qath*; O. Ger. *quethan*; Dan. *qväde*; whence *-queath* in *bequeath*), *said.*—**Apaid,** *repaid.*

One thing beseech I you and warn also. The sound of *e* in beseech, requiring some tension of the muscles and closeness of the aperture made by the organs of speech, would seem to be appropriate to express *closeness, strain, pressure, effort*; as *squeeze, squeal, scream.* Care must be taken, however, in this case, as in all of these illustrations, not to press the analogy too far.

I have thy faith and thy benignity,
As well as ever woman was, assayed,
In great estate, and poorelich arrayed.
Now know I, deare wife, thy steadfastness."
And her in arms he took and gan her kiss.

144. And she for wonder took of it no keep :*
She hearde not what thing he to her said.
She ferde as she had start out of a sleep,
Till she out of her mazedness abraid.
"Griseld," quoth he, "by God that for us deyd,
Thou art my wife, none other I ne have,
Ne never had, as God my soule save !

145. "This is my daughter, which thou hast supposed
To be my wife. That other faithfully
Shall be mine heir, as I have aye purposed.
Thou bare them of thy body trewely.
At Boloygne have I kept them privily.
Take them again, for now mayst thou not say
That thou hast lorn none of thy children twey.

146. "And folk that otherwise have said of me—
I warn them well that I have done this deed
For no malice, ne for no cruelty,
But for to assay thee in thy womanhede,
And not to slay my children—God forbid!
But for to keep them privily and still,
Till I thy purpose knew and all thy will."

147. When she this heard, aswouned down she falleth
For piteous joy; and, after her swouning,
She both her younge children to her calleth,
And in her armes, piteously weeping,
Embraceth them, and tenderly kissing,
Full like a mother, with her salte tears,
She bathed both her visage and her hairs.

---

* **Keep** (A. S. *cepan ;* O. Eng. *kepen*, to retain), *heed.*—**Ferde** (A. S. *far*, a sudden coming upon, deceit, fear, danger ; Ger. *gefahr*. Akin to *ver-* in Lat. *vereor?*) *feared.*—**Start,** *started.*—**Mazedness** (A. S. *mase*, a whirlpool; Ice. *meis*, a winding, curve), *amazedness, confusion.*—**Abraid** (A. S. *abredian*, to draw out, move away), *awoke, aroused, recovered.* So in Spenser :

"For fear lest her unawares she should *abraid* " (i. e., awake).

Deyd (O. Fries. and Ice. *deya*, to die ; Goth. *divan*, to die), *died.* Spelled to rhyme with *abraid.*—**Lorn** (A. S. *leosan*, to lose ; *loren*, lost ; Ger. *ver-lieren*, to lose ; *verloren*, lost), *lost.*—**None.** The negative repeated for emphasis.—**Aswouned** (A. S. *swunan, āswunan*, to fail in intellect ; *swānian*, to faint ; *swimman*, to swim ; *svīma*, vertigo), *in a swoon, having swooned.*—**Piteous,** *sorrowful.*—**Swouning,** *swooning.*

And her in arms he took, and gan her kiss. The sound of *s* or *ss* as in *kiss*, is often *onomatopoetic*, or *imitative.* E. g. *his, siss, whisper, whistle.* As a rule, it is disagreeable ; though here we have a palpable exception ! *S* at the beginning of some words is supposed to have *a demonstrative force* ; as in *so, she, some.* Give other illustrations.

148. Oh, such a piteous thing it was, to see
Her swouning, and her humble voice to hear!
"*Grand mercy*,* Lord, God thank it you," quoth she,
"That ye have saved me my children dear.
Now reck I never to be dead right here;
Sith I stand in your love and in your grace,
No force of death, ne when my spirit pace.

149. "O tender, deare, younge children mine!
Your woful mother weened steadfastly
That cruel houndes or some foul vermine
Had eaten you. But God, of his mercy,
And your benigne father, tenderly
Hath done you keep!" And in that same stound
All suddenly she swapped down to ground.

150. And in her swough so sadly holdeth she
Her children two, when she gan them embrace,
That with great sleight and great difficulty
The children from her arm they gan arrace.
Oh, many a tear on many a piteous face
Down ran, of them that stooden her beside!
Unneth abouten her might they abide.

151. Walter her gladeth, and her sorrow slaketh.
She riseth up abashed from her trance,
And every wight her joy and feste maketh,
Till she had caught again her countenance.
Walter her doth so faithfully pleasance,
That it was dainty for to see the cheer
Betwix them two, now they be met in fere.

---

* **Grand mercy** (Lat. *grandis*, large; Lat. *misericors*, of pitying heart; fr. *miserēre*, to pity, and *cor*, the heart; or *mercy* is from Lat. *merces*, *mercedis*, pay, reward; Fr. *grand*, great, *merci*, thanks; *grand merci*, great thanks; usually *gramercy*), *great thanks*, expressing gratitude and surprise.—**God thank it you,** *may God recompense you for it.* *Thank* is A. S. *thanc*, *thonc*, thought, thanks; fr. *thencan*, to think, remember; Ger. *dank*.—**Reck** (A. S. *rêcan*, to care for; Ger. *geruhen*), *care.* **Reck I,** etc., *I am willing to die*, etc.—**Sith,** *since.* See Index.—**No force of,** *no matter for.*—**Pace** (Lat. *passus*, a step; Fr. *passer*, to pass), *passes*, *departs.* *Pace* follows, in construction, *no force of*..—**Houndes** (Ger. *hund*, dog; Gr. *κύων*, *κυνός*; Lat. *can-is*. By Grimm's law, Lat. *c*, or Gr. *κ* becomes Eng. *ch* or *h*), *hounds.* Dissyl.—**Done you keep,** *had you kept, caused you to be kept.*—**Stound** (A. S., Dan., Sw., Ice. *stund*; Ger. *stunde*, hour, period of time), *hour*, *time.*—**Swapped,** fell. See *swap*, Index. Perhaps the word *swap*, to fall, now obsolete, is allied to *swoop*.—**Swough,** *stupor.* See *aswouned*, Index.—**Sadly,** *steadily*, *firmly.* See *sad* st. 26. **Sleight** (Ice. *slägd*, cunning; Sw. *slögd*, workmanship; *slög*, skilled in art; Eng. *sly*; Ger. *schlau*), *skill.* Hence *sleight of hand*, legerdemain.—**Arrace** (Fr. *arracher*), *to pull away by force.*—**Slaketh,** *appeases.* See *slake*, Index.—**Fere** (A. S. *fera*, companion; *faran*, to go; Ger. *gefährte*, companion), *company.*

That cruel houndes or some foul vermine. The sound of *ou*, as in *houndes*, is rarely *onomatopoetic*; as *owl*, *howl*, *bow-wow*. *Ough*, as an interjection, expresses sudden pain.

She riseth up abashed from her trance. The sound of *sh* final, as in *abash*, is said to denote *silence*; also sounds and sights which end *suddenly*. E. g. *hush*, *clash*, *crash*, *flash*, *splash*, *dash*, *mash*. Clearly it is sometimes onomatopoetic. Other examples?

152. These ladies, when that they her time see,*
Have taken her, and into chamber gone,
And strippen her out of her rude array;
And in a cloth of gold, that bright shone,
With a coroune of many a riche stone
Upon her head, they into hall her brought,
And there she was honored as her ought.
153. Thus hath this piteous day a blissful end;
For every man and woman doth his might
This day in mirth and revel to dispend,
Till on the welkin shone the starres bright:
For more solempne in every mannes sight
This feste was, and greater of costage,
Than was the revel of her marriage.
154. Full many a year, in high prosperity,
Liven these two in concord and in rest;
And richely his daughter married he
Unto a lord, one of the worthiest
Of all Itaille; and then, in peace and rest,
His wife's father in the court he keepeth,
Till that the soul out of his body creepeth.
155. His son succeedeth in his heritage
In rest and peace, after his father's day;
And fortunate was eke in marriage,
Al put he not his wife in great assay.
This world is not so strong, it is no nay,
As it hath been in olde times yore;
And hearkneth what this author saith therefore.
156. This story is said, not for that wives should
Follow Griseld, as in humility;
For it were importable, though they would:
But for that every wight, in his degree,
Shoulde be constant in adversity
As was Griselde; therefore Petrarch writeth
This story, which with high style he inditeth.
157. For sith a woman was so patient

---

* **Her time,** *their proper time.* See *her* in '*shaping her*,' st. 104.—**As her ought,** *as was due to her.* See *owen*, Index. A. S. *ahte.*—**Solempne** (Oscan *sollus*, all; Lat. *annus*, year; Lat. *solemnis*, happening every year), *annually celebrated*, *solemn*, marked with religious pomp or ceremony.—**Costage,** *cost*, *expense.* *Cost* is Fr. *coût*, fr. Fr. *coûter*, fr. Lat. *constare*, to stand at, to cost: *-age* is Lat. *-atium.*—**Al put he,** *although he put.*—**It is no nay,** *it cannot be denied.*—**Hearkeneth,** *hear ye.* Impera.—**Importable** (Lat. *in*, not; *portare*, to bear), *intolerable.* Acc. 1st and 3d syl. The vowels were pronounced with a more open sound, probably, in Chaucer's time than now.

This world is not so strong, it is no nay. The hard sound of *g*, as in *strong* (though less marked in this word than in many others), seems to be appropriate to express hardness, strength, harshness; as in *tiger*, *eager*, *gripe*. Give other illustrations.

What is the significance of the phonetic element represented by *th?* by *n?* *str?* *wr?*

Unto a mortal man, well more we ought
Receiven all in gree,* that God us sent.
For great skill is he prove that he wrought;
But he ne tempteth no man that he bought,
As saith saint Jame, if ye his pistil read;
He proveth folk all day, it is no dread.

158. And suffereth us, as for our exercise,
With sharpe scourges of adversity,
Full often to be beat in sundry wise;
Not for to know our will; for, certes, he,
Ere we were born, knew all our freeletee;
And for our best is all his governance.
Let us then live in virtuous sufferance.

159. But one word, Lordes, hearkeneth ere I go.
It were full hard to finde, now-a-days,
In all a town, Griseldes three or two.
For if that they were put to such assays,
The gold of 'hem hath now so bad alays
With brass, that though the coin be fair at eye,
It woulde rather brest in two than plie.

160. For which here, for the Wifes love of Bath,—
Whose life and all her secte God maintain
In high maistrie, and elles were it scathe,—
I will, with lusty hearte fresh and green,
Say you a song to gladden you, I ween.
And let us stint of earnestful matiere.
Hearkeneth my song, that saith in this mannere:—

---

* **Gree** (Fr. *gré*, will, liking; Lat. *gratus*, pleased, grateful), *good will, good heart.*—**In gree,** *with content, thankfully.*—**For gret skill . . . . . wrought,** *for the sake of giving us skill, he proves his work.*—**Jame.** James i. 13, "God cannot be tempted with evil, neither tempteth he any man."—**Pistil** (Gr. ἐπιστολή, anything sent, fr. ἐπιστέλλειν, to send; Lat. *epistola*, a letter), *epistle.*—**It is no dread,** *there is no fear, have no apprehension.* The last two stanzas are a translation from Petrarch.—**For to know,** *in order to know.*—**Freeletee** (O. Fr. *frealté*; Lat. *fragilitas*, weakness, liability to break; fr. *frangĕre*, to break), *frailty.*—**Alays** (Fr. *aloyer*; Lat. *ad legem*, according to law; or A. S. *alecgan*, to lay down; Ger. *legen*, to put; or from Fr. *allier*, to mix; fr. Lat. *alligare*, to bind to; *ad*, to; *ligare*, to tie. The latter derivation is preferable, *alloy* and *allay* having been confounded in signification), *alloys.*—**Brest** (A. S. *berstan*; Ger. *berstan*, to burst), *burst.*—**Plie** (Fr. *plier*, to bend; Lat. *plicare*, to fold), *bend.*—**The Wifes.** *Wifes* is a dissyl. She was one of the Canterbury pilgrims.—**Secte** (Lat. *secare*, to cut; *sectum*, a cutting, a part cut off), *sex.*—**Maistrie** (O. Fr. *maistrie*, mastery; Lat. *magister*, master), *mastery, superiority.*—**Scathe** (A. S. *scathian*; Ger. *schaden*, to harm; A. S. *scedh*; Ger. *schade*), *harm, damage.*—**Stint,** *desist from.* See Index.—**Earnestful** (A. S. *eornost*; Ger. *ernst*), *serious.*

In high maistrie, for elles were it scathe. The sound of *sc* in *scathe* seems to denote *injurious motion.* Often, however, *sc* or *sk* apparently denotes merely *swift motion*; as in *scatter*, *scour*, *scud*, *scull*, *scamper*, *skew*, *skim*, *skip*, *skirmish*, *skate*, *skedaddle.* Give other examples.

Say you a song to gladden you, I ween. The sound of *ng*, as in *song*, is sometimes onomatopoetic, or imitative. E. g., *song*, *gong*, *ding-dong.* Sometimes it seems to express energetic motion; as in *fling*, *bring*, *swing*, *hang*, *slang*, *bang*, *mangle.* Other examples?

L'ENVOYE* DE CHAUCER.

161. Grisild is deed, and eek hir pacience,
And bothe at oones buried in Itayle:
For whiche I crye in open audience,
No weddid man so hardy be to assayle
His wyves pacience, in trust to fynde
Grisildes, for in certeyn he schal fayle.

162. O noble wyves, ful of heigh prudence,
Let noon humilité your tonges nayle:
Ne lat no clerk have cause or diligence
To write of yow a story of swiche mervayle
As of Grisildes pacient and kynde,
Lest Chichivache yow swolwe in hir entraile.

163. Folwith ecco, that holdith no silence,
But ever answereth at the countretayle:
Beth not bydaffed for your innocence,
But scharply tak on yow the governayle:
Empryntith wel this lessoun on your mynde,
For comun profyt, sith it may avayle.

164. Ye archewyves, stondeth at defens,
Syn ye ben strong, as is a greet chamayle;
Ne suffre not, that men don yow offens.
And sclendre wyves, felle as in batayle,
Beth egre as is a tyger yond in Inde;
Ay clappith as a mylle, I yow counsaile.

165. Ne drede hem not, do hem no reverence,
For though thin housbond armed be in mayle,
The arwes of thy crabbid eloquence

---

* **L'envoye** (Fr. *le*, the; *envoi*, sending; fr. Lat. *in*, in, and *via*, way), *the commendatory or explanatory postscript to a poem or other literary work.* Here follows a good specimen of Chaucer's characteristic humor. We give it in the antiquated orthography, following the text of Wright's edition.—**Oones,** *once.* Dissyl. *Ones* and *once* are the old genitive of *one.* —**Wyves.** Dissyl.—**Prudence.** Acc. 2d syl.—**Tonges** (Lat. *lingua*, tongue; A. S. and Dan. *tunge;* Ger. *zunge*), *tongues.* Dissyl.—**Mervayle,** *wonder.* See Index.—**Chichivache** (Fr. *chiche*, poor, sorry, stingy; Fr. *vache*, Lat. *vacca*), cow. *Chichevache* and *Bycorne* are two fabulous beasts in an old ballad. *Chichevache* is represented as feeding on patient wives; *Bycorne*, on obedient husbands. According to the story, Bycorne has plenty to eat and is fat; Chichevache is half-starved and lean!—**Folwith,** *follow ye.* Impera. See *accepteth*, st. 6, and *folwen*, st. 121.—**Countertayle** (Fr. *contre;* Lat. *contra*, against; Fr. *tailler*, to cut; whence *tally*, a notch cut), *counter-tally, a tally answering exactly to another.*—**Beth,** *be ye.* Impera.—**Bydaffed** (A. S. *daff*, a fool; Ice. *daufr*, stupid; A. S. *deaf*, deaf), *befooled.*—**Governayle,** *government.* See Index.—**Rede,** *advise.* See Index.—**Archewyves** (Gr. ἀρχ-, beginning, leading; whence *arch*, chief), *wives of a superior degree, or in the higher ranks; stout wives.*—**Syn,** *since.*—**Chamayle** (A. S. *camell;* Heb. *gâmal;* Ar. *gamal*, *jemel;* Gr. κάμηλος; Lat. *camēlus*), *camel.*—**Sclendre** (O. D. *slinder*, thin), *slender.*—**Batayle** (Fr. *bataille*, battle; fr. Lat. *battalia*, fighting and fencing; *batuĕre*, to strike, beat), *battle.*—**Clappeth** (A. S. *clappan;* Ger. *klopfen*, to knock), *strike ye.*—**Counsaile** (Fr. *conseiller*, to advise; Lat. *consiliari*, to receive or impart advice), *counsel.*—**Arwes** (Lat. *arma*, arms; A. S. *arewe;* Welsh *arv;* Arm. Fr., Gael., *arm*, weapon), *arrows.*—**Crabbid.** Akin to Ger. *herbe*, Lat. *acerbus*, W. *garv*, sour.

Schal perse his brest, and eek his adventayle: *
In gelousy I rede eek thou him bynde,
And thou schalt make him couche as doth a quayle.

166. If thou be faire, ther folk ben in presence
Schew thou thy visage, and thin apparaile:
If thou be foul, be free of thy despence,
To gete the frendes ay do thy travayle:
Be ay of chier as light as lef on lynde,
And let him care, and wepe, and wrynge and wayle! †

---

* **Adventayle** (Fr. *ventail*, the movable part of the front of a helmet; fr. Lat. *ventus*, wind), *the movable part of a helmet in front, the ventail.*—**Rede**, *advise.* See Index.—**Apparaile** (Fr. *appareil*, preparation, furniture; Fr. *pareil*, like, equal; Low Lat. *pariculus*, a little match; fr. *par*, an equal, a mate), *apparel.*—**Despence** (Lat. *dispendĕre*, fr. *dis*, apart, and *pendĕre*, to weigh out; *dispensare*, to distribute by weight, disburse), *expense.*—**Chier**, *countenance.* Give the origin, root-meaning, etc., of each word in this line.—**Lynde**, the *lime-tree.*

† We give on these last two pages the antiquated spelling, as in Wright's edition, for the comfort of those who attach great importance to the old orthography.

In gelousy I rede eek thou him bynde. The sound of *j* in *jealousy*, requiring or permitting considerable force to utter it properly, naturally expresses *energy;* and so we sometimes find it, as in *gyrate*, *gibe*, *gee* (to oxen), *gist.* Other examples?

Write a sketch of the life of Chaucer. Give some account of his different works. Write an essay on his life as a courtier and a politician. Write an essay on the revival of learning in Chaucer's age. Write an essay on his Canterbury Tales. Give in your own language the story of Patient Griselda. Name the peculiarities of his verse. Point out the beauties and the blemishes of this poem. Name other prominent authors of the fourteenth century, and the works they produced. Write an essay on the power of the Pope of Rome over foreign potentates in the time of Chaucer; one on the doctrines and career of Wickliffe; on Chaucer's religious tendencies; on the language of Chaucer; on Grimm's law of consonant changes. Let the teacher suggest other kindred topics for essays. The writing of brief compositions weekly, on subjects connected with the study of English Literature, will be found an invaluable exercise. The student should especially be encouraged to investigate for himself, and not take everything on the strength of the author's assertion.

SUMMARY OF ELEMENTARY SOUNDS AND THEIR PROPER SIGNIFICANCY.

The following list shows the *phonetic elements* in the English language, and, to some extent, their *proper significancy.** This interesting subject, however, has been only partially investigated. It still affords a field for further research. Let the student collect words and deduce principles.

	VOWEL SOUNDS.	SIGNIFICANCE.
1.	That of *e*, as in *we*.	Closeness, pressure, as some tension of the muscles is required to enunciate it properly ? See p. 52.
2.	" *i*, " *wit*.	This, perhaps the shortest and slightest sound in the language, is most appropriate to express *little* things and to form *diminutives*. See p. 37, and see note p. 61.
3.	" *a*, " *pale*.	
4.	" *e*, " *wet*.	A small sound, fit for unimportant things, or diminutives. See p. 50.
5.	" *a*, " *arm*.	Very easy for a child to utter, requiring only the opening of the mouth and breathing, it comes to express pain, grief, passion. Being so easily made, it is used where no reason exists for any special vowel. See p. 47.
5½.	" *a*, " *half*.	This is intermediate between the preceding and the following. See pp. 26, 47.
6.	" *a*, " *at*.	This is shortened from number five, and, like that, expresses *pain*. The sound is unpleasant, suggestive of crying infants and bleating sheep. It may express contempt, mockery, disgust. See pp. 26, 47.
7.	" *a*, " *all*.	Largeness, seriousness. There are many exceptions. See p. 22.
8.	" *o*, " *not*.	Surprise, harshness. Being short, it is less appropriate for large things.† See page 46.
9.	" *u*, " *fur*.	Produced low in the breast, it expresses, when soft, gentleness; when loud, harshness, discontent, smothered wrath, grumbling. See p. 39.
10.	" *u*, " *but*.	Obscure sound, akin to the preceding.

* In using the expression *proper significancy*, we must not be understood as holding that there is any *inherent* or *essential* significance in any sound; but simply that certain sounds have a natural fitness to express certain meanings. See Whitney on *Language and the Study of Language* (Lecture XI.); also Fowler's *Revised and Enlarged Grammar* (Chap. VII.).

† Hence the sense of incongruity in applying the short word and sound of the monosyllable in naming the Infinite Being. Young persons often try, unconsciously, to avoid the feeling of its unfitness, by prolonging the ŏ sound.

VOWEL SOUNDS.				SIGNIFICANCE.
11.	That of *o*, as in *so*.			Wonder, surprise; pain; calling. Prolonged, it may express greatness. See p. 51.
12.	" *o*, " *solo*.			[The second *o*.]
13.	" *oo*, " *boot*.			Soothing, smoothness. See p. 26.
14.	" *oo* or *w*, as in *foot*.			Weakness; wavy, gentle motion. See p. 27.

DIPHTHONGS.			SIGNIFICANCE.
15.	That of *i*, as in *five*,	5 + 2.*	
16.	" *u*, " *tune*,	2 + 14.*	The sound of *oo* here is made with the tip of the tongue in contact with the lower front teeth, and the lips in position as if to whistle. It approaches the French *u*.
17.	" *ou*, " *house*,	5 + 14.*	This is sometimes *onomatopoetic*, as in *bow-wow*. See p. 54.
18.	" *oi*, " *oil*,	7 + 2.*	

CONSONANT SOUNDS.			SIGNIFICANCE.
19.	That of *p*, as in *pat*.	Surd.†	This sound has in many languages been used to indicate *papa!* See p. 45. From the act of *puffing*, it has come to express contempt and aversion in some cases.
20.	" *b*, " *bat*.	Sonant.†	Akin to the preceding.
21.	" *f*, " *fan*.	Surd.	See p. 45.
22.	" *v*, " *van*.	Sonant.	Akin to the preceding.
23.	" *th*, " *think*.	Surd.	Akin to the following.
24.	" *th*, " *thine*.	Sonant.	Pointing out. See p. 19.
25.	" *t*, " *tin*.	Surd.	Pointing out strongly. Akin to the following. See p. 25.
26.	" *d*, " *din*.	Sonant.	Demonstrative; imparting.
27.	" *k*, " *kin*.	Surd.	Inquiry. Akin to *g* in *go*. See p. 43.
28.	" *g*, " *go*.	Sonant.	Harshness, hardness, strength. See p. 55.
29.	" *ch*,‡ " *chin*.	Surd.	Akin to the following.
30.	" *j*,‡ " *jest*.	Sonant.	Force. See p. 58.
31.	" *s*, " *sin*.	Surd.	Onomatopoetic; unpleasantly suggestive of snakes and geese! Sometimes it appears to be somewhat *demonstrative*. Akin to *z*. See p. 53.

* These numerals refer to the preceding list of vowel sounds, and they show which combine in the compound sound.

† *Surds* are mere whispering sounds. *Sonants* are pronounced with vocal tones. Instead of the words *surd* and *sonant*, the terms *sharp* and *flat*, or *aspirate* and *vocal*, or *atonic* and *subtonic* have been used. See Latham's *English Language*, Dr. Rush on *The Philosophy of the Human Voice*, Goold Brown's *Grammar of Grammars*, etc.

‡ These sounds are by many regarded as compound, equivalent to *tsh* and *dzh*, respectively.

CONSONANT SOUNDS.			SIGNIFICANCE.
32.	That of *z*, as in *zeal.*	Sonant.	Onomatopoetic, suggestive of bees, etc. See p. 22.
33.	" *sh*, " *shine.*	Surd.	When final, it denotes enjoined silence; when initial, aversion. See pp. 34, 54.
34.	" *z*, " *azure.*	Sonant.	Akin to the preceding.
35.	" *h*, " *hot.*	Aspirate.	Effort; aspiration. See p. 33.
36.	" *ng*, " *king.*	Nasal.	Sometimes is onomatopoetic; sometimes expresses energetic motion. See p. 56.
37.	" *m*, " *man.*	Labial nasal.	Infants easily utter this sound, and apply it to *mamma.* It has also a strong *subjective* force. See pp. 37, 40, 48.
38.	" *n*, " *no.*	Lingual nasal.	Negative; nose concerns. See p. 24.
39.	" *l*, " *lull.*	Smooth liquid.	Soft and soothing; littleness; tongue notions. See p. 29.
40.	" *r*, " *run.*	Rough liquid.	Rattling sounds; interrupted notions. See p. 31.

CONSONANT SOUNDS IN COMBINATION, AND THEIR APPROPRIATE SIGNIFICANCE.

41. *Bl*, *pl*, and *fl*, denote blowing, blooming, flowing. See pp. 21, 40.
42. *Kl* denotes cleaving or adhering. See p. 31.
43. *Br* and *kr*. The same substantially as *r*. See above.
44. *Gl* denotes smoothness, or silent motion. See p. 44.
45. *Gn*, *jn*, and *kn* denote a sudden breaking off. See p. 28.
46. *Gr*. Substantially like *r*. See above.
47. *Sc*. Swift motion. See p. 56.
48. *Shw* and *sw* denote gentle motion. See p. 49.
49. *Sl*. Like *gl*. See pp. 20, 44.
50. *Sn* denotes nose ideas. See *n* above, and p. 24.
51. *Spr* " a spreading out. See p. 42.
52. *St* " firmness or stability. See p. 30.
53. *Sp* " expulsion. See p. 35.
54. *Str* " exertion. See p. 23.
55. *Thr* " violent motion. See p. 34.
56. *Tw* " duality. See p. 42.
57. *Wr* " distorted motion. See p. 38.

NOTE.—The word QUIZ is said, in the unabridged dictionaries, to have had a singular origin. Whatever we may think of their explanation, the word is true to its phonetics. The first element denotes *inquiry;* the second, *smoothness* (its force not being very prominent in this word); the third, *littleness*, insignificance; the fourth, busy or *buzzing* action. Putting these together, we should, *a priori*, infer that the word would mean *buzzing inquiry*, *of a mild nature, on unimportant matters.* Let the student write an essay on this general subject of the natural fitness of articulate sounds to convey particular meanings, illustrating his views by numerous examples.

PHONETIC ANALYSIS.

The method of *phonetic analysis* is very simple.

EXAMPLE.

"There is, right at the west side of Itaille."

Here the first phonetic element is that represented by *th* in *thine* (No. 24, p. 60), a sonant. Its proper signification is demonstrative. [Give examples.] The next phonetic element is that represented by *a* in *at* (No. 6, p. 59), a vowel sound, shortened from the sound of *a* in *arm*. It is somewhat unpleasant to the ear, suggesting the cries of infants and some animals. [Give examples.] The next phonetic element is that represented by *r* in *run* (No. 40, p. 61). It is a rough liquid sound, naturally symbolical of rattling noise and interrupted notions. [Give examples.]

The next phonetic element is that represented by *i* in *wit* (No. 2, p. 59), a vowel sound. Being, perhaps, the shortest and slightest in the language, its use is very extensive to express littleness and to form diminutives. [Give examples.] The next phonetic element is that represented by *z* in *zeal* (No. 32, p. 61), a sonant. This sound is largely onomatopoetic, or imitative. [Give examples.]

N. B.—Let the student complete this analysis, and take further exercises, until he becomes perfectly familiar with the sounds and their primary significance, so far as ascertained.

NOTE.—The teacher will do well to direct the student's attention at this stage to the different theories of the origin of language, and particularly to the interjectional and the *onomatopoetic*. On this subject consult the lectures of Whitney, Max Müller, and G. P. Marsh, and the various treatises on Rhetoric. See *Excursus* in Prof. F. L. O. Roehrig's *Shortest Road to German*, pp. 217, 218, etc. Give examples of the power of sound to echo sense. Discriminate carefully between what is satisfactorily established, and what is merely fanciful. Assign themes to be investigated and written upon.

EDMUND SPENSER.

(From an original picture in the collection of the Right Honorable the Earl of Kinnoul.)

EDMUND SPENSER.

1553–1599.

——OUR sage and serious Spenser, whom I dare be known to think a better teacher than Scotus or Aquinas.—MILTON.

Nor shall my verse that elder bard forget,
The gentle Spenser, Fancy's pleasing son,
Who, like a copious river, poured his song
O'er all the mazes of enchanted ground.—THOMSON.

Of the childhood and youth of Chaucer, Spenser, and Shakespeare, the three great masters of English poetry previous to Milton, we know almost nothing. A few facts, however, in regard to Spenser's early life, have come down to us.

He was born in East Smithfield, hard by the Tower of London, about the year 1553. In his poems he repeatedly refers to his connection with the noble house of Spencer in Lancashire. Thus in his *Prothalamium:*

"At length they all to merry London came—
To merry London, my most kindly nurse,
That to me gave this life's first native source,
Though from another place I take my name,
An house of ancient fame."

His parents were probably poor, for, in May, 1569, we find him a sizar, or "poor student," in Pembroke Hall, Cambridge University. There he became intimate with Gabriel Harvey, a pedantic scholar, who afterwards introduced him to Sir Philip Sidney, and otherwise befriended him. Spenser received the degree of A. B. in 1573, and of A. M. in 1576.

Leaving the university, he went to the north of England, where he is supposed to have been employed as a teacher. There he fell in love. "Rosalind" did not reciprocate the attachment. Of course his sorrow found vent in poetry.

His first important production was *The Shepherd's Calendar*, published in 1579. The name suggests pastoral poetry; but a great part of the work is a discussion of ecclesiastical matters by shepherds, whom Campbell very appropriately calls "*parsons in disguise*," and who certainly ought to have confined their discourse to matters in which their four-footed sheep were more immediately interested. Passages of considerable beauty, however, abound in the poem. It is divided into twelve parts, or eclogues, each corresponding to some month and named after it. Five editions of the work, during his lifetime, attest its popularity.

Induced by Harvey, he had already come to London, and a warm friendship had sprung up between him and Sidney. Indeed, the *Shepherd's Calendar* is said to have been completed at Sidney's lordly mansion among the noble oaks of Penshurst, once the residence of the Saxon kings of Kent. The work was dedicated to Sidney, who introduced the young poet to his uncle, the powerful Earl of Leicester. The latter, in 1580, employed Spenser to write out the *Stemmata Dudleiana*, a statement, probably in poetry, of the earl's genealogy and ties of kindred.

In August, 1580, Spenser was secretary to Arthur Grey de Wilton, Lord Deputy to

Ireland. During two years of Grey's energetic administration of Irish affairs, Spenser was with him in that country. Fourteen years later, Spenser ably vindicated Lord Grey's course by his well-written treatise, the only prose work of the poet, entitled, *A View of the State of Ireland.*

For several years he now figured in the unenviable character of office-hunter and hanger-on at court, where he appears to have acquired that habit of gross flattery which is the greatest blemish in his writings. He made extraordinary efforts to secure the favor of Elizabeth's chief counsellor, Burleigh, who, with dogged obstinacy, sat on the lid of the treasury box whenever the queen was inclined to open it for the nice young man. It is related that she promised Spenser a hundred pounds, but that Burleigh pronounced the sum "beyond all reason." "Give him *reason*, then," replied the queen. Spenser, in a moment of boldness, sharply reminded the queen—

It pleased your grace, upon a time,
To grant me reason for my rhyme;
But from that time until this season,
I've heard of neither rhyme nor reason.

We pity the gentle poet for his ill success in obtaining position and pension; but doubtless it was best that the fulsome praise with which he larded the stingy treasurer and the conceited queen should meet with disappointment. Perhaps we owe *The Faerie Queene* and some of his other poems to the stimulus of poverty. At all events, it is a satisfaction to know that he became thoroughly disgusted with the business of office-seeking. In *Mother Hubbard's Tale*, a poem of about 1,400 lines, composed soon afterwards, and containing some satire on the court and the clergy, he speaks with warmth of this bitter experience:

Full little knowest thou, that hast not tried,
What hell it is, in suing long to bide;
To lose good days, that might be better spent;
To waste long nights in pensive discontent;
To speed to-day, to be put back to-morrow;
To feed on hope, to pine with fear and sorrow;
To have thy prince's grace, yet want her peer's;
To have thy asking, yet wait many years;
To fret thy soul with crosses and with cares;
To eat thy heart through comfortless despairs;
To fawn, to crouch, to wait, to ride, to run;
To spend, to give, to want, to be undone.
Unhappy wight, born to disastrous end,
That doth his life in so long tendance spend.

Through the influence of Grey, Leicester, and Sidney, he received in 1586, for his services as secretary, a grant of 3,028 acres in the county of Cork, it being a portion of the forfeited estate of the rebel earls of Desmond. As this grant was coupled with the condition that he should actually reside on the land and till it, there is reason to suspect that the shrewd lord-treasurer contrived, by this operation, to consign to honorable exile the protegé of his rival Leicester, in order that the poet might not become politically formidable with the pen.

Thenceforward Spenser lived, most of the time, on his estate in Ireland, making his home at Kilcolman Castle, two miles from Doneraile. It is still a beautiful and romantic spot; and when the country abounded with woodland, it may well have been a favorite residence for such a man. Looking southward from the ruined castle, one sees a lake like a mirror in a wide green frame of grassy land. On every side are distant mountains. The silver thread of the river Mulla winds through this region, which the poet's genius has made enchanted ground.

Hardly had it become his home, when a great sorrow befell him. His best friend and patron, the high-born Sidney, poet, scholar, warrior, prince of gentlemen,—"*my* Philip," as the queen loved to call him,—was mortally wounded in fighting the Spaniards near Zutphen. Three weeks he lingered, and then died. Spenser, who was almost of the same age, bewails his untimely death in several elegaic poems, written to console the mourning relatives. These pieces are characterized by childish conceits, but they contain passages of exquisite melody. We may say of them as he says of Sidney—

Did never love so sweetly breathe
In any mortal breast before;
Did never muse inspire beneath
A poet's brain with finer store!

Witness the following:

"When he descended from the mount,
His personage seemed most divine,
A thousand graces one might count
Upon his lovely cheerful eyne;
To hear him speak and sweetly smile,
You were in Paradise the while!

"A sweet attractive kind of grace—
A full assurance given by looks—
Continual comfort in a face—
The lineaments of gospel books.
I trow that countenance cannot lie,
Whose thoughts are legible in the eye!

"*Was never eye did see that face,*
Was never ear did hear that tongue,
Was never mind did mind his grace,
That ever thought the travel long;
But eyes and ears and every thought
Were with his sweet perfections caught."

The following lines tenderly express his faith in Sidney's immortality:

But that immortal spirit, which was decked
With all the dowries of celestial grace,
By sovereign choice from th' heavenly quires select,
And lineally deriv'd from angels' race,
O! what is now of it become aread?
Ah me, can so divine a thing be dead?

Ah! no: it is not dead, ne can it die,
But lives for aye, in blissful Paradise:
Where like a new-born babe it soft doth lie,
In bed of lilies wrapt in tender wise,
And compassed all about with roses sweet,
And dainty violets from head to feet.

There thousand birds, all of celestial brood,
To him do sweetly carol day and night;
And with strange notes, of him well understood,
Lull him asleep in angelic delight;
Whilst in sweet dream to him presented be
Immortal beauties, which no eye may see.

But he them sees, and takes exceeding pleasure
Of their divine aspects, appearing plain,
And kindling love in him above all measure;
Sweet love, still joyous, never feeling pain.
For what so goodly form he there doth see,
He may enjoy from jealous rancor free.

There liveth he in everlasting bliss,
  Sweet spirit, never fearing more to die :
Ne dreading harm from any foes of his,
  Ne fearing savage beasts' more cruelty;
Whilst we here, wretches, wail his private lack,
And with vain vows do often call him back.

But live thou there, still happy, happy spirit !
  And give us leave thee here thus to lament,
Not thee, that dost thy heaven's joy inherit,
  But our own selves, that here in dole are drent.
Thus do we weep and wail, and wear our eyes,
Mourning, in others, our own miseries.

Soon Sir Walter Raleigh, who had received twelve thousand acres of the same forfeited estate, visited Spenser, and, "under the green alders by the Mulla's shore," heard from his lips portions of the first three books of *The Faerie Queene.* Raleigh was charmed with the man and the poem, and seems to have thenceforward occupied the place which Sidney had filled, as the poet's most useful friend. He took Spenser to England to publish these three books. He also urged Spenser's claims upon Queen Elizabeth's bounty ; not in vain, for, in February, 1591, she rewarded him with a pension of £50. He is styled poet-laureate, but was not officially appointed.

In December, 1591, after his return to Ireland, he dedicates, "To the Right Worthy and Noble Knight, Sir Walter Raleigh, Captain of Her Majesty's Guard," a poem of about a thousand lines, entitled *Colin Clout's Come Home Again.* It is a pastoral, in which he sings of "the Shepherd of the Ocean," as he styles Raleigh ; of Queen Elizabeth, whom he calls "the Goddess Cynthia ;" of love, of beauty, and of the ocean.

Resuming his labor on his great poem, he completed the fourth, fifth, and sixth books of *The Faerie Queene*, the noblest allegorical poem in the English language. It was designed to consist of twelve books, each describing the adventures of a particular hero, who represents some one virtue. The first book relates the adventures of the Knight of the Red Cross, who typifies *holiness.* The second illustrates *temperance*, personified in Sir Guyon ; the third, *chastity*, represented by Britomartis, a lady knight ; the fourth, *friendship*, seen in Cambell and Triamond ; the fifth, *justice*, embodied in Artegal ; the sixth, *courtesy*, in Sir Calidore. It is doubtful whether Spenser developed the story beyond these six books. Perhaps it is well that the last half has not come down to us ; for there is a decided falling off in power after the first book ; and, although 'art is long,' as this poem in its present state abundantly testifies, yet life is short. In this busy age few have time to read more of Spenser than the 35,000 lines which it contains.

We may compare *The Faerie Queene* to the palace of the Vatican, with its thousands of apartments, its labyrinthian windings, its endless staircases and colonnades, its frescoes, statues, paintings, and beauties innumerable. The pure light of religion is over all.

I shall not exhibit a chip of marble from this vast structure, and call the fragment a specimen. But I may quote enough to give a faint glimpse of the spirit and genius of the poet. Take these two stanzas on the ministry of angels, as two strains from a grand symphony.

I.

And is there care in heaven ? And is there love
In heavenly spirits to these creatures base,
That may compassion of their evils move ?
There is :—else much more wretched were the case

Of men than beasts: But oh, th' exceeding grace
Of highest God, that loves his creatures so,
And all his works with mercy doth embrace,
That blessed angels he sends to and fro,
To serve to wicked man, to serve his wicked foe!

II.

How oft do they their silver bowers leave
To come to succor us that succor want!
How oft do they with golden pinions cleave
The flitting skies, like flying pursuivant,
Against foul fiends to aid us militant!
They for us fight, they watch and duly ward,
And their bright squadrons round about us plant;
And all for love, and nothing for reward:
Oh, why should heavenly God to men have such regard?

Take the following picture as a single figure from a great panorama:

A gentle knight was pricking on the plain,
Yclad in mighty arms and silver shield,
Wherein old dints of deep wounds did remain,
The cruel marks of many a bloody field;
Yet arms till that time did he never wield:
His angry steed did chide his foaming bit,
As much disdaining to the curb to yield:
Full jolly knight he seem'd, and fair did sit,
As one for knightly jousts and fierce encounters fit.

And on his breast a bloody cross he bore,
The dear remembrance of his dying Lord,
For whose sweet sake that glorious badge he wore,
And dead, as living ever, him ador'd.
Upon his shield the like was also scor'd,
For sovereign hope, which in his help he had.
Right faithful true he was in deed and word;
But of his cheer did seem too solemn sad;
Yet nothing did he dread, but ever was ydrad.*

Here is a personification of truth:

One day, nigh weary of the irksome way,
From her unhasty beast she did alight;
And on the grass her dainty limbs did lay
In secret shadow, far from all men's sight.
From her fair head her fillet she undight,
And laid her stole aside! Her angel's face,
As the great eye of heaven, shined bright,
And made a sunshine in the shady place!
Did never mortal eye behold such heavenly grace.

The stanza in which the *Faerie Queene* is written, was invented by Spenser, and is known as the *Spenserian*. It consists of eight lines of ten syllables each, and one of twelve. The latter line is called an *Alexandrine*, from a poem written in French on the life of Alexander and entitled the *Alexandriad*.

Despairing of doing anything like justice to Spenser by extracts from his *Faerie Queene*, I pass to some of his minor poems. Of these, one of the best is the *Epithalamium* or *Marriage Hymn*. It celebrates his nuptials with an Irish maiden, with whom he fell in love at the solid age of forty-one. He presents it to her "in lieu of many

* Dreaded.

ornaments." He calls her "the third Elizabeth," the first being his mother, and the second his queen. This passion had given birth to eighty-eight *Amoretti*, or love-sonnets, which are among the sweetest ever written. In one of these he says of her name:

Most happy letters! fram'd by skillful trade,
With which that happy name was first designed,
The which three times thrice happy hath me made,
With gifts of body, fortune, and of mind.
The first my being to me gave by kind,
From mother's womb deriv'd by due descent;
The second is my sovereign queen most kind,
That honour and large richesse to me lent;
The third, my love, my life's last ornament,
By whom my spirit out of dust was raised,
To speak her praise and glory excellent,
Of all alive most worthy to be praised.
  Ye three Elizabeths! for ever live,
  That three such graces did unto me give.

One day I wrote her name upon the strand;
But came the waves, and washed it away:
Again, I wrote it with a second hand;
But came the tide, and made my pains his prey.
Vain man, said she, that dost in vain assay
A mortal thing so to immortalize;
For I myself shall, like to this decay,
And eke my name be wiped out likewise!
Not so, quoth I; let baser things devise
To die in dust, but you shall live by fame:
My verse your virtues rare shall eternize,
And in the heavens write your glorious name;
  Where, when as death shall all the world subdue,
  Our love shall live, and later life renew.

The marriage hymn is conceded to be a masterpiece, the best of the kind in our language. The cool and judicious Hallam pronounces it "an intoxication of ecstasy, ardent, pure, and noble." Instead of a fragment from *The Faerie Queene*, I have preferred to give this *Epithalamium.*

Spenser was married in 1594. In 1596, he published, besides the fourth, fifth, and sixth books of *The Faerie Queene*, four noble hymns in honor of *love* and *beauty*. In 1597, he was appointed sheriff of Cork. We are not accustomed to think of the mild bard as an officer of justice, having to deal with stiff-necked and irascible "Corkonians"; but there is reason to believe he was faithful and efficient. We know from his prose work that he was in favor of "thorough" measures.

A happy future now seemed to stretch out before him. In the prime of life, honored by men like Raleigh, favored by the queen, happy in his marriage, blest with beautiful children, dwelling in a romantic and charming country, receiving a sufficient income, confessedly the first of living poets,—well might he thank God and take courage. But

"Let no man be called happy till his death!"

In October, 1598, the insurgent Irish gained the victory of Blackwater. By-and-by they pushed on to expel all Englishmen. They fell on the poet-sheriff like lightning. In a moment Kilcolman was shattered and desolate. In the terror and haste of flight, Spenser's infant child was left behind, and perished in the blazing pile. The exquisite sensibilities of the father were lacerated beyond endurance. In three months he died of a broken heart.

His last hours were embittered by poverty; but when it was known that the great poet was dead, a large concourse of the learned and noble gathered to honor his remains. A splendid funeral was arranged at the expense of the Earl of Essex. Brother poets bore his pall, each casting into the grave mourning verses and the pen that wrote them. In Westminster Abbey, near the spot where the body of Chaucer had been laid two hundred years before, the form of Spenser mouldered to dust. On his monument we read, "Here lyes (expecting the second comminge of our Saviour Jesus) the body of Edmond Spenser, the Prince of Poets in his tyme, whose divine spirit needs noe othir witnesse then the works which he left behinde him. He was borne in London, in the yeare 1553, and died in the yeare 1598."

"In person, Spenser was small and delicate, and in his dress precise, as became a man of taste. His face, well known from several portraits, has all the sweetness and delicacy that we require as accordant with the tone of his poetry. The mild, almond-shaped eye, brow slightly elevated, the mouth compressed just enough to suggest the idea that there was felt some need of patience, give an impression of dreamy repose not without pensiveness. The forehead is lofty, but less expanded than that of Shakespeare or Milton; and the whole countenance indicative more of an exalted tone than of great force of character."

Beauty, rather than sublimity, characterizes his writings. A mellow light plays over his pages, gilding or coloring all; but it never becomes lightning. The dreamy music, the sensuous sweetness that cloys, are indeed sometimes succeeded by stirring tones; but it is ever a flute and not a trumpet that is blown. The stream of his poetry goes on forever, but it is the Mulla, and not Niagara. Yet he will always be read, for his transparent style; the inexhaustible fertility of his fancy; the wondrous stores of learning transmuted into unbroken melody; and the purity, gentleness, and piety stamped upon every page.

Consult Hillard's edition of Spenser's Poems; Taine's *English Literature;* Hart's Essay on Spenser and the *Faerie Queene;* Warton on Spenser; Allibone's *Dictionary of Authors;* Campbell's *Specimens of British Poets;* Hallam's *Literature of Europe;* D'Israeli's *Amenities of Literature*, 2d vol.; the works on English Literature of Craik, Collier, Angus, Chambers, Cleveland, Shaw, Arnold, Spalding, Day, Gilman, and Hart. See also *Encyclopedia Britannica, New American Cyclopedia*, and Motley's *Rise of the Dutch Republic.* Collect other facts in regard to Spenser.

EPITHALAMIUM.*

1. Ye learned sisters, which have oftentimes
Been to me aiding, others to adorn
Whom ye thought worthy of your graceful rhymes,
That even the greatest did not greatly scorn
To hear their names sung in your simple lays,
But joyed in their praise;
And when ye list your own mishaps to mourn
Which death, or love, or fortune's wreck did raise,

---

* **Epithalamium** (Gr. ἐπί, upon; θάλαμος, bridal chamber, marriage), *marriage hymn.* The bride's name was Elizabeth.—**Sisters.** These were the nine Muses, Calliope, Clio, Erato, Euterpe, Melpomĕne, Polymnia, Terpsichore, Thalia, and Urania, daughters of Jupiter and Mnemosyne (memory). They were supposed to make Mount Helicon their home. They are "personifications of the inventive powers of the mind as displayed in the several arts." As deities they were believed to inspire poets. Hence the invocations with which Homer, Virgil, and others begin their poems. See the four stanzas prefixed to the first book of the *Faerie Queene;* also, the beginning of the *Paradise Lost.*—**Which have,** who have. *Which* was formerly used of persons. It is A. S. *hwylic*, fr. *hwa*, who, and *lic*, like. Note that "throughout the Indo-European languages, the interrogative or relative idea is expressed by *k*, or a modification of *k*." E. g., *qu*, in Lat. *qui*, who; *quot*, how many; *hu* or *h*, as *who, why, how;* κόσος, how much, etc. See p. 43.—**That even,** *so that even.* What kind of feet in these lines?

Your string could soon to sadder tenor* turn,
And teach the woods and waters to lament
Your doleful dreariment,—
Now lay those sorrowful complaints aside,
And, having all your heads with girlands crowned,
Help me mine own love's praises to resound;
Ne let the same of any be envied.
So Orpheus, for his bride;
So I, unto myself alone, will sing;
The woods shall to me answer, and my echo ring.

2. Early, before the world's light-giving lamp
His golden beam upon the hills doth spread,
Having dispersed the night's uncheerful damp,
Do ye awake; and, with fresh lustyhead,
Go to the bower of my beloved love,
My truest turtle dove;
Bid her awake; for Hymen is awake,
And long since ready forth his mask to move
With his bright tead that flames with many a flake,
And many a bachelor to wait on him
In their fresh garments trim.
Bid her awake, therefore, and soon her dight;
For, lo! the wished day is come at last,
That shall, for all the pains and sorrows past,
Pay to her usury of long delight:
And whilst she doth her dight,
Do ye to her of joy and solace sing,
That all the woods may answer, and your echo ring.

3. Bring with you all the nymphs that you can hear,
Both of the rivers and the forests green,
And of the sea that neighbors to her near;
All with gay garlands goodly well beseen.

---

* **Tenor**, *purport.* (Lat. *tenor*, a holding on in a continued course; fr. *tenēre*, to hold.)—**Dreariment**, *heaviness*, *sorrow*, *dreariness.* A. S. *dreorig*, bloody, sorrowful; Ger. *traurig*, sad. Note the alliteration in these lines and throughout the poem.—**Girlands** (It. *ghirlanda*, fr. root meaning to *twist;* O. Ger, *wieren*, to twist; Fr. *girande*, *girandole;* Gr. γῦρος, circle; Lat. *gyrare*, to turn round in a circle), *garlands*, *wreaths.*—**Orpheus**, a mythical Greek hero, noted for his miraculous skill in playing upon the lyre. He was the husband of Eurydice, who, bitten by a serpent, passed down to Hades. To recover her, Orpheus followed, and by his wonderful music entranced the inhabitants of that shadowy realm, and gained permission from Pluto to bring her back. See Class. Dictionary.—**Lustyhead** (*lusty*, strong; *head*, hood, state. See *womanhead*, Index), *lustiness*, *vigor.* See *lusty*, Index.—**Hymen** (Gr. Ὑμήν, god of marriage; Lat. *Hymen*), a supposed deity, said by some to have been the offspring of the heavenly muse Urania; by others, the son of Bacchus and Venus. He presided over marriages. The Latin poets picture him in a yellow robe, his temples wreathed with marjoram, his locks dropping with perfume, a nuptial torch in his hand.—**Tead** (Lat. *taeda*, torch; Gr. δαΐς, δᾷς), *a torch.*—**Bachelor.** See Index.—**Dight**, array, *adorn.* See Index.—**Usury**, *a large premium*, *abundant interest.*—**Nymphs** (Gr. νύμφη, a veiled one, a bride), *nymphs*, goddesses of mountains, woods, meadows, or waters (called, respectively, *oreădes*, *dryădes*, *limoniădes*, *naiădes*). The word is akin to Lat. *nubo*, *nubĕre*, to wear the bridal veil, to be a bride.—**Neighbors** (A. S. *neah*, nigh; *gebûr*, a dweller, boor; *boor* meaning originally a rustic), *dwells near*, *is a neighbor.*—**Beseen**, *adapted*, *adjusted.* See *byseye*, p. 50.

And let them also with them bring in hand
Another gay garland
For my fair love, of lilies and of roses,
Bound true-love-wise,* with a blue silk riband;
And let them make great store of bridal posies,
And let them eke bring store of other flowers
To deck the bridal bowers;
And let the ground whereas her foot shall tread,
For fear the stones her tender foot should wrong,
Be strewed with fragrant flowers all along,
And diapered like the discolored mead.
Which done, do at her chamber door await,
For she will waken straight.
The whiles do ye this song unto her sing,
The woods shall to you answer, and your echo ring.

4. Ye nymphs of Mulla, which with careful heed
The silver scaly trouts do tend full well,
And greedy pikes which use therein to feed—
Those trouts and pikes all others do excel—
And ye likewise which keep the rushy lake
Where none do fishes take;
Bind up the locks, the which hang scattered light,
And in his waters, which your mirror make,
Behold your faces as the crystal bright;
That, when you come whereas my love doth lie,
No blemish she may spy.
And eke, ye light-foot maids, which keep the deer
That on the hoary mountains use to tower;
And the wild wolves, which seek them to devour,
With your steel darts do chase from coming near;
Be also present here,
To help to deck her, and to help to sing,
That all the woods may answer, and your echo ring.

5. Wake now, my love, awake! for it is time.

---

* **True-love-wise,** *in the fashion of a true-love knot;* i. e., with many involutions, the emblem of intertwined affections.—**Blue silk.** Why blue? See *azure*, Index.—**Posies** (Gr. ποίησις, a making, composing; fr. ποιεῖν, to make; Lat. *poesis*, composition, poesy; whence *posy*, a verse made up for the occasion, *a motto sent with flowers*, or engraved on a ring), *nosegays* accompanied with mottoes, *bouquets.*—**Whereas,** *where.*—**Diapered** (Lat. *Jaspis*, a green-colored precious stone; Gr. ἴασπις; Fr. *diapré*, marbled, variegated), *diversified with colors.*—**Straight** (A. S. *streht*, past part. of A. S *streccan*, to stretch, extend), *directly, straightway.*—**Mulla,** a river running through the estate that Queen Elizabeth granted to Spenser, situated in the county of Cork, Ireland. The lake, mentioned five lines later, lay just south of Kilcolman Castle, Spenser's residence, and about two miles from Doneraile.—**Scattered light,** *scattered lightly*, or *loosely floating.*—**Come whereas,** *come where.*—**Use** (Lat. *uti*, to use; *usus*, use), *are wont.*—**Tower** (A. S. *torr;* Lat. *turris;* Gr. τύρσις; Fr. *tour;* Ger. *thurm;* a tower), soar, tower, *climb high.*—**Wolves** (Mœso-Goth. *wulfs;* A. S. *wulf;* D. *wolf;* Ger. *wolf;* Dan. *ulv;* Sw. *ulf;* Ice. *ulfr;* Lat. *vulpes.* The last word signifies *fox*). Is the change of *p* to *f*, in Lat. *vulpes* and Eng. *wolf*, in accordance with Grimm's Law?

The rosy morn long since left Tithon's* bed
All ready to her silver coach to climb;
And Phœbus 'gins to show his glorious head.
Hark how the cheerful birds do chant their lays,
And carol of Love's praise!
The merry lark her matins sings aloft,
The thrush replies, the mavis descant plays,
The ouzel shrills, the ruddock warbles soft;
So goodly all agree with sweet consent
To this day's merriment.
Ah, my dear love, why do ye sleep thus long,
When meeter were that ye should now awake
To await the coming of your joyous make,
And hearken to the birds' love-learned song
The dewy leaves among?
For they of joy and pleasaunce to you sing,
That all the woods them answer, and their echo ring.

6. My love is now awake out of her dream;
And her fair eyes, like stars that dimmed were
With darksome clouds, now show their goodly beams
More bright than Hesperus his head doth rear.
Come now, ye damsels, daughters of delight,
Help quickly her to dight.
But first come ye fair Hours, which were begot
In Jove's sweet paradise of day and night;
Which do the seasons of the world allot,
And all that ever in this world is fair,
Do make and still repair.
And ye three handmaids of the Cyprian queen,
The which do still adorn her beauty's pride,

---

* **Tithon,** *Tithonus*, husband of Aurora, the morn. She was a goddess; he, a man. In youth he was wondrously beautiful, and she, becoming enamored, obtained immortality for him from Jove, but forgot to ask perpetual youth. So he grew old and shrivelled, and finally became a *cicada*, or locust. Aurora is represented as a nymph crowned with flowers, with a star above her head, a torch in one hand, in the other roses, which she scatters as she stands in her chariot drawn by winged steeds. According to Prof. Max Müller, *Tithonus* (from θνήσκω, τέθνηκα, I die) signifies *the dying day*.—**Coach** (Gr. κόγχη, a muscle, a cockle; Lat. *concha*, a muscle-shell; Fr., Sp., *coche;* It. *cocca*, a vessel), *a chariot, coach*.—**Phœbus** (Gr. Φοῖβος, *the shining one*, Apollo), *the sun-god*.—**Mavis,** *the song thrush*.—**Ouzel,** the bird known as the water-ouzel, or dipper.—**Shrills,** utters a shrill note.—**Ruddock** (A. S. *rudduc;* W. *rhuddog*, having a redness, the redbreast; A. S. *rudu*, redness; *rud*, red; Gr. ἐρυθρός; Lat. *ruber;* Ger. *roth;* Fr. *rouge.* See Grimm's law), *redbreast*.—**Meeter,** *more meet, fitter*.—**Make,** *mate, consort.* See Index.—**Hesperus** (Gr. Ἕσπερος; Lat. *Vesper*), *the evening, evening star*.—**Hours** (Gr. Ὧραι; Lat. *Horae*), *the Hours, or Seasons.* They were three in number; though some name seven; others, ten; and later poets, twelve. Daughters of Jupiter and Themis (goddess of Justice and Law), they had charge of the gates of heaven, and presided over justice, peace, and order.—**Jove** (Gr. Ζεύς, Διός, root διϝ; Lat. *divus, diovis, Jovis;* Lith. *devas;* Lat. *deus;* Sans. *dyo, dyu*, the sky; akin to O. Eng. *Tuisco*), *Jupiter*, the supreme deity of the Romans, father of gods and men.—**Cyprian queen,** *Venus*, goddess of love and beauty, the *Aphrodite* of the Greeks. She sprang from the sea-foam near Cythera (now *Cerigo*). The soft west wind wafted her to Cyprus, where the gold-filleted Seasons received her, clothing her with immortal garments, and adorning her with a golden wreath, rings, and chains. She was worshipped chiefly at Cyprus and Cythera.—**Handmaids,** the three *Graces*, young and beautiful sisters, attendants of Venus. Their names were *Aglaia* (brightness), *Euphrosyne* (gladness), and *Thalia* (bloom). They may be regarded as "an æsthetic conception of all that is beautiful in the physical as well as in the social world"

Help to adorn my beautifulest bride;
And as ye her array, still throw between
Some graces to be seen;
And, as ye use to Venus, to her sing;
The whiles the woods shall answer, and your echo ring.

7. Now is my love all ready forth to come.
Let all the virgins therefore well await;
And ye fresh boys, that tend upon her groom,*
Prepare yourselves, for he is coming straight.
Set all your things in seemly good array
Fit for so joyful day,
The joyfulest day that ever sun did see.
Fair sun! show forth thy favorable ray,
And let thy lifeful heat not fervent be,
For fear of burning her sunshiny face,
Her beauty to disgrace.
O fairest Phœbus! father of the Muse!
If ever I did honor thee aright,
Or sing the thing that mote thy mind delight,
Do not thy servant's simple boon refuse.
But let this day, let this one day be mine:
Let all the rest be thine.
Then I thy sovereign praises loud will sing,
That all the woods shall answer, and their echo ring.

8. Hark! how the minstrels 'gin to shrill aloud
Their merry music, that resounds from far,
The pipe, the tabor, and the trembling crowd,
That well agree withouten breach or jar.
But most of all the damsels do delight,
When they their timbrels smite,
And thereunto do dance and carol sweet,
That all the senses they do ravish quite;
The whiles the boys run up and down the street,
Crying aloud with strong confused noise,
As if it were one voice.
"Hymen! Iö! Hymen! Hymen!" they do shout,
That even to the heavens their shouting shrill
Doth reach, and all the firmament doth fill;

---

* **Groom** (Lat. *homo*, man; *humanus*, of man; *humus*, ground; A. S. and Goth. *guma*, man; Scot. *grome*, man, lover), *bridegroom*.—**Lifeful,** *full of life, life-giving.* See *lives*, Index. *Full* is Gr. πλη in πίμπλημι, to fill; Lat. *ple-nus*, full; Ger. *voll;* A. S. and Sw. *full;* Goth. *fulls;* A. S. *fyllan*, to fill; Ger. *füllen.* See Grimm's Law.—**Shrill** (Sw. *skrälla;* Ger. *schrillen*), *to utter in a sharp, shrill tone.*—**Tabor,** *a small drum.* Fr. *tambour;* Ar. and Per. *tumbûr*, *tambûr*, a lute or guitar.—**Crowd** (Ir. and Gael. *cruit;* W. *crwth*), an ancient instrument of music with six strings, a kind of violin.—**Withouten** (O. Eng., fr. A. S. *widh*, with, and *ûtan*, out; *widhûtan*), *without.* See Index.—**The whiles,** *the intervening time, meanwhile, while.* See *the while*, Index.—**Hymen! Io! Hymen!** *Hymen! Huzza! Hymen!* Part of a Lat. song. See Index.

To which the people, standing all about,
As in approvance, do thereto applaud,
And loud advance her laud.*
And evermore they "Hymen! Hymen!" sing,
That all the woods them answer, and their echo ring.

9. Lo! where she comes along with portly pace,
Like Phœbe, from her chamber in the east,
Arising forth to run her mighty race,
Clad all in white, that seems a virgin best.
So well it her beseems that you would ween
Some angel she had been.
Her long loose yellow locks like golden wire,
Sprinkled with pearl, and pearling flowers atween,
Do like a golden mantle her attire;
And being crowned with a girland green,
Seem like some virgin queen.
Her modest eyes, abashed to behold
So many gazers as on her do stare,
Upon the lowly ground affixed are;
Ne dare lift up her countenance too bold,
But blush to hear her praises sung so loud,
So far from being proud.
Natheless do ye still loud her praises sing,
That all the woods may answer, and your echo ring.

10. Tell me, ye merchants' daughters, did ye see
So fair a creature in your town before?
So sweet, so lovely, and so mild as she,
Adorned with beauty's grace and virtue's store?
Her goodly eyes like sapphires shining bright,
Her forehead ivory white,
Her cheeks like apples which the sun hath rudded,
Her lips like cherries charming men to bite,
Her bosom like a bowl of cream uncrudded,
Her breasts like lilies budded,
Her snowy neck like to a marble tower,
And all her body like a palace fair,

---

* **Laud** (Lat. *laus, laudis*, praise; Fr. *louer*, to praise), *praise*.—**Portly** (Lat. *portare*; Fr. *porter*, to carry; *port*, carriage), *dignified, noble*.—**Phœbe** (fem. of *Phœbus*, for which see st. 5), *the moon goddess, Diana*.—**Seems,** *beseems, befits*.—**Long, loose,** etc. Note the alliteration, a subject well worthy of investigation. See the various treatises on Rhetoric. The comparison of a lady's auburn locks to golden wire is a favorite one with Spenser. Thus he says of Queen Elizabeth, in the *Faerie Queene*, Book II., canto iii., stanza 30: "Her yellow locks, crisped like golden wire." This simile seems to suggest Queen Elizabeth, who is mentioned four lines later.—**Girland.** See st. 1.—**Ne,** *nor, not*.—**Natheless,** *nevertheless*. (Index.)—**Ivory white.** So in *Faerie Queene*, Book II., canto iii., stanza 24: "*Her ivory forehead*."—**Rudded,** *made red*. See *ruddock*, st. 5.—**Uncrudded** (Scot. *crud*; Gael. *gruth*; Ir. *gruth, cruth*, curd; Ir. *cruthaim*, I milk), *uncurdled*. This description of his bride is strikingly like that contained in his Sonnets, LXIV., LXXXI.

Ascending up with many a stately stair,
To honor's seat and chastity's sweet bower.
Why stand ye still, ye virgins, in amaze,
Upon her so to gaze,
Whiles ye forget your former lay to sing,
To which the woods did answer, and your echo ring?

11. But if ye saw that which no eyes can see,
The inward beauty of her lovely spright,
Garnished with heavenly gifts of high degree,
Much more then would ye wonder at that sight,
And stand astonished, like to those which read *
Medusa's mazeful head.
There dwells sweet love, and constant chastity,
Unspotted faith, and comely womanhood,
Regard of honor, and mild modesty;
There virtue reigns as queen in royal throne,
And giveth laws alone,
The which the base affections do obey,
And yield their services unto her will;
Ne thought of things uncomely ever may
Thereto approach, to tempt her mind to ill.
Had ye once seen these her celestial treasures
And unrevealed pleasures,
Then would ye wonder, and her praises sing,
That all the woods should answer, and your echo ring.

12. Open the temple gates unto my love!
Open them wide that she may enter in;
And all the posts adorn as doth behove,
And all the pillars deck with girlands trim,
For to receive this saint with honor due
That cometh in to you.
With trembling steps and humble reverence
She cometh in, before the Almighty's view!
Of her, ye virgins, learn obedience,
When so ye come into those holy places,
To humble your proud faces.
Bring her to the high altar, that she may
The sacred ceremonies there partake,
The which do endless matrimony make;
And let the roaring organs loudly play

---

* **Which read,** *who perused; who attentively observed.*—**Medusa,** one of the three Gorgons. One legend makes her to have anciently been beautiful, and to have fascinated Neptune; but Minerva, angry because the lovers met in her temple, changed Medusa's locks into serpents, and made her head so horrible that whoever set eyes on it was instantly changed to stone. This head was cut off by the hero Perseus, and fixed upon the centre of Minerva's ægis or shield.—**The which,** *which.*—**Ne,** *no, nor, not.* **Holy places,** *temples.*

The praises of the Lord in lively notes;
The whiles with hollow throats,*
The choristers the joyous anthem sing,
That all the world may answer, and their echo ring.

13. Behold, whiles she before the altar stands,
Hearing the holy priest, that to her speaks,
And blesseth her with his two happy hands,
How the red roses flush up in her cheeks,
And the pure snow, with goodly vermeil, stain,
Like crimson dyed in grain!
That even the angels, which continually
About the sacred altar do remain,
Forget their service and about her fly,
Oft peeping in her face, that seems more fair
The more they on it stare.
But her sad eyes, still fastened on the ground,
Are governed with goodly modesty,
That suffers not one look to glance awry,
Which may let in a little thought unsound.
Why blush ye, love, to give to me your hand,
The pledge of all our band!
Sing, ye sweet angels! Alleluia sing!
That all the woods may answer, and your echo ring.

14. Now all is done, bring home the bride again.
Bring home the triumph of our victory:
Bring home with you the glory of her gain;
With joyance bring her and with jollity.
Never had man more joyful day than this,
Whom Heaven would heap with bliss:
Make feast, therefore, now all this live-long day:
This day to me forever holy is.
Pour out the wine without restraint or stay;
Pour not by cups, but by the bellyful;
Pour out to all that wull,
And sprinkle all the posts and walls with wine,
That they may sweat and drunken be withall.

---

* **Hollow throats,** *wide-open throats.*—**Happy hands.** This is, perhaps, the finest passage in the poem. The whole stanza is well conceived and exquisitely expressed. The very hands of the priest are conscious of joy!—**Vermeil** (Lat. *vermis,* a worm, fr. *vertĕre,* to turn, to wind; *vermiculus,* a little worm; Fr. *vermeil,* a little worm that furnishes the scarlet color), *vermilion,* a bright red.—**Grain** (Lat. *granum,* a grain, seed, kernel), a reddish dye made from the coccus insect, or kermes. **Dyed in grain,** dyed with the tint made from grain; dyed firmly; dyed in the wool or raw material.—**Alleluia** (Heb. *halelu,* praise; *yah,* Jehovah; *hallelujah,* praise ye Jehovah).—**Pour not by cups,** etc. The stupid custom, now happily obsolescent, of swilling down wine at weddings, is of great antiquity.—**Wull,** will. See *wolde,* Index.

Crown ye God Bacchus* with a coronal,
And Hymen also crown with wreaths of vine ;
And let the Graces dance unto the rest,
For they can do it best:
The whiles the maidens do their carol sing,
To which the woods shall answer, and their echo ring.

15. Ring ye the bells, ye young men of the town,
And leave your wonted labors for this day:
This day is holy: Do ye write it down,
That ye forever it remember may.
This day the sun is in its chiefest height
With Barnaby the bright,
From whence declining daily by degrees,
He somewhat loseth of his heat and light,
When once the crab behind his back he sees.
But for this time it ill ordained was,
To choose the longest day in all the year,
And shortest night, when longest fittest were.
Yet never day so long but it would pass.
Ring ye the bells, to make it wear away,
And bonefires make all day,
And dance about them, and about them sing,
That all the woods may answer, and your echo ring.

16. Ah! when will this long weary day have end
And lend me leave to come unto my love ?
How slowly do the hours their number spend!
How slowly does sad time his feathers move!
Haste thee, O fairest planet, to thy home
Within the western foam!
Thy tired steeds long since have need of rest.
Long though it be, at last I see it gloom,
And the bright evening star with golden creast
Appear out of the east.
Fair child of beauty! Glorious lamp of love!
That all the host of heaven in ranks dost lead,
And guidest lovers through the night's sad dread,

---

* **Bacchus,** the god of wine. He is said to have taught men how to cultivate the vine and spoil grapes by turning them into an intoxicating drink.—**Graces,** the three handmaids of the Cyprian queen, *Aglaia*, *Euphrosyne*, and *Thalia*. See *handmaids*, Index, Lat. *Gratiæ*.—**Chiefest height.** St. Barnabas' Day was June 22 (June 11, O. S.), 1594. This, then, was the marriage day of Spenser. About this time the sun reaches the solstice. Who is Barnaby? See Acts xiv., 12.—**Crab** (Gr. κάραβος; καρκίνος; D. *krab*, A. S. *crabba*, a crab), *Cancer*, one of the twelve signs of the zodiac, somewhat resembling a crab in form, and denoting the northern limit of the sun's course in summer. The sun enters it about the 21st or 22d of June, the longest day of the year.—**Bonefires** (W. *bàn*, high; *banffagl*, a lofty blaze; or fr. Fr. *bon*, Lat. *bonus*, good; or fr. Dan. *baun*, a beacon; Gr. πῦρ, fire; Lat. *pyra*, A. S. *fyr*; Ger. *feuer*; Fr. *feu*. See Grimm's Law), *bonfires*.—**Planet** (Gr. πλανάω, I wander; πλανήτης; Lat. *planēta*, a wandering body), *the sun*.—**Creast** (Lat. *crescĕre*, to grow; Lat. *crista*; A. S. *crĕsta*; Fr. *crête*), *crest*.

How cheerfully thou lookest from above
And seemst to laugh atween* thy twinkling light,
As joying in the sight
Of these glad many, which for joy do sing,
That all the woods them answer, and their echo ring!

17. Now cease, ye damsels, your delights forepast;
Enough it is that all the day was yours.
Now day is done and night is nighing fast;
Now bring the bride into the bridal bowers.
The night is come; now soon her disarray,
And in her bed her lay;
Lay her in lilies and in violets,
And silken curtains over her display,
And ordered sheets and arras coverlets.
Behold, how goodly fair my love does lie
In proud humility!
Like unto Maia, whenas Jove her took
In Tempe, lying on the flowery grass
'Twixt sleep and wake, after she weary was
With bathing in the Acidalian brook.
Now it is night, ye damsels may be gone
And leave my love alone,
And leave likewise your former lay to sing.
The woods no more shall answer, nor your echo ring.

19. Let no lamenting cries, nor doleful tears
Be heard all night within, nor yet without.
Ne let false whispers, breeding hidden fears,
Break gentle sleep with misconceived doubt.
Let no deluding dreams, nor dreadful sights
Make sudden sad affrights.
Ne let house fires, nor lightning's helpless harms,
Ne let the ponke nor other evil sprites
Ne let mischievous witches with their charms,
Ne let hob-goblins, names whose sense we see not,

---

* **Atween,** *between. A*, as a prefix, is explained subsequently. See *apace*, Index. *Tween* is A. S. *twegan*, *tweonan*, *twa;* Gr. δύω, Lat, *duo*, two ; Ger. *zwei.*—**Nighing,** *approaching.* See *neighbors*, Index.—**Arras** (so called because first made at *Arras* in France in the 14th century), *tapestry*, or hangings for rooms; woven stuffs decorated with a simple pattern.—**Maia,** one of the Pleiades, daughter of Atlas. She became the mother of Mercury.—**Tempe,** a most delightful vale in ancient Thessaly.—**Acidalian,** belonging to Acidalia, a fountain at Orchoměnus, in ancient Bœotia. This fountain was sacred to Venus, and in it the Graces were wont to bathe.—**Ponke** (an erroneous form of *pouke*, for *puck;* Scot. *puck;* Sw. *puke*, a nocturnal demon), *Puck*, Robin Goodfellow, a merry fiend in Shakespeare's *Midsummer Night's Dream;* called also *Pug*, Friar Rush, etc., in old ballads and legends.—**Sprites** (Lat. *spiritus*, breath, spirit; from *spiro*, to breathe), *spirits*, *ghosts*, *apparitions*.—**Hobgoblin** (*Hob*, abbreviated from Robin or Robin Goodfellow; *goblin* fr. Gr. κόβαλος; L. Lat. *gobelinus*, knave; Ger. *kobold*, knave, evil spirit; Eng. *cobalt*, the poisonous and troublesome metal), *phantom*, *hobgoblin.*—**Mischievous.** Acc. 2d syl. "This accentuation is still sometimes heard, though it is obsolescent." *Corson.*

Fray us * with things that be not.
Let not the screech-owl nor the stork be heard,
Nor the night raven, that still deadly yells;
Nor damned ghosts, called up with mighty spells,
Nor grisly vultures, make us once afeard.
Ne let the unpleasant choir of frogs still croaking
Make us to wish they're choking!
Let none of these their dreary accents sing;
Ne let the woods them answer, nor their echo ring.

20. But let still Silence true night-watches keep,
That sacred Peace may in assurance reign,
And timely Sleep, when it is time to sleep,
May pour his limbs forth on your pleasant plain;
The whiles an hundred little winged Loves,
Like divers-feathered doves,
Shall fly and flutter round about the bed,
And, in the secret dark that none reproves,
Their pretty stealths shall work, and snares shall spread
To filch away sweet snatches of delight,
Concealed through covert night.
Ye sons of Venus, play your sports at will;
For greedy Pleasure, careless of your toys,
Thinks more upon her paradise of joys
Than what ye do, albeit good or ill.
All night therefore, attend your merry play,
For it will soon be day.
Now none doth hinder you, that say or sing;
Ne will the woods now answer, nor your echo ring.

21. Who is the same, which at my window peeps?
Or whose is that fair face that shines so bright?
Is it not Cynthia, she that never sleeps,
But walks about high heaven all the night?
O fairest goddess, do not thou envy
My love with me to spy!
* * * * * * * * * *

22. And thou, great Juno, which with awful might
The laws of wedlock still dost patronize;
And the religion of the faith first plight
With sacred rites hast taught to solemnize,

* **Fray us** (*affray*, frighten; Fr. *effrayer*, to scare; Lat. *frigus*, cold, a cold shudder; Gr. ῥίγιον, colder, more awful, more chilling with fear), *frighten us*.—**Afeard** (A. S. *afæran*, *færan*, to frighten; *faran*, to impress fear), *afraid*.—**Choking!** Is it possible that Spenser ventures to be facetious?—**Sons of Venus.** Cupids. Simonides makes *Eros* or *Cupido* (Love) to have been the son of Venus and Mars.—**Albeit** (*all be it*, i. e., be it all, grant that it is all so), *although*, *whether it be*.—**Cynthia,** the same as *Phœbe*, st. 9.—**Juno,** wife of Jove.

And eke for comfort often called art *
Of women in their smart,
Eternally bind thou this lovely band,
And all thy blessings unto us impart.

* * * * * * * * * *

And thou, fair Hebe, and thou Hymen free,
Grant that it may so be.
Till which we cease your further praise to sing;
Ne any woods shall answer, nor your echo ring.

23. And ye high heavens, the temple of the gods,
In which a thousand torches flaming bright
Do burn, that to us wretched earthly clods
In dreadful darkness lend desired light;
And all ye powers which in the same remain,
More than we men can feign;
Pour out your blessing on us plenteously,
And happy influence upon us rain,
That we may raise a large posterity,
Which from the earth, which they may long possess
With lasting happiness,
Up to your haughty palaces may mount;
And for the guerdon of their glorious merit,
May heavenly tabernacles there inherit,
Of blessed saints for to increase the count.
So let us rest, sweet love, in hope of this,
And cease till then our timely joys to sing;
The woods no more us answer, nor our echo ring.

Song! made in lieu of many ornaments,
With which my love should duly have been deckt,
Which cutting off through hasty accidents,
Ye would not stay your due time to expect,
But promised both to recompense;
Be unto her a goodly ornament,
And for short time an endless monument!

---

* **Called art of,** *art called by.*—**Hebe** (Gr. Hβη, youth), *Hebe*, goddess of youth, daughter of Jupiter.—**Clods** (A. S. *clud*, rock, stone; Ger. *klosz*, clod, clump), lumps of earth or turf; dolts, gross or stupid fellows.—**Influence** (Lat. *influĕre*, to flow upon). This word carries us back to astrology. It was believed that the stars shed forth a mysterious and mighty power, which flowed down upon men and controlled their dispositions and destinies. One born under the *influence* of Jupiter (i. e., when this planet was high in heaven), would be *jovial;* born under that of Mercury, he would be *mercurial;* under Saturn, *saturnine*, etc.—**Haughty** (Lat. *altus*, high; *alĕre*, to nourish, feed; Fr. *haut*, high; formed fr. O. Fr. *hault*, *halt*), *high*, *lofty*.—**Guerdon** (O. Fr. *guerdon*, *guerredon;* Ger. *wider*, again, and Lat. *donum*, gift; or fr. O. Ger. *widarlôn*, recompense; A. S. *widherlean*), reward.—**Tabernacles** (Lat. *tabula*, a board, plank; Lat. *taberna*, a hut, a shed, a slightly built habitation), tents, temples, *mansions*.

Write a brief life of Spenser; an essay on his office-seeking; on his moral character; on his poetic genius; on the literary activity of the Elizabethan age; on the *Faerie Queene;* on this marriage hymn; on alliteration in poetry; on the changes in the English language between the times of Chaucer and Spenser; on the Spenserian stanza; on Spenser's connection with Sidney and Raleigh. Write some account of Robin Hood. (See Scott's *Ivanhoe;* Prof. F. J. Child's *Introduction to 5th vol. Eng. and Scot. Ballads;* Ritson's *Robin Hood, a Collection*, etc.). Write an essay on Astrology; one on the long-prevalent superstitions in regard to fairies, hobgoblins, etc.; one on the characters from heathen mythology named in this poem.

ORTHOGRAPHIC ANALYSIS.

For *orthographic analysis*, which treats of the *representatives* or *signs* of sounds, the student must understand and give the classifications of letters, the power or sound of each letter or combination of letters, and the equivalent letters (*i. e.*, those used to express the same sound). He should also apply the principles of syllabication.

These particulars are discussed with tolerable fulness in works on etymology, grammars, spelling-books, and the preliminary treatises in the large dictionaries. The teacher should see to it that the student forms the habit of original investigation by industriously consulting books of reference. The mode of orthographic analysis may be illustrated by the following.

EXAMPLE.

"Song made in lieu of many ornaments."

S is a surd sibilant consonant, representing a phonetic element (No. 31, p. 60). Its normal force is a hissing sound, as in *siss*. It has sometimes the sound of *z*, as in *reason;* of *sh*, as in *sure;* of *zh*, as in *pleasure;* and is sometimes silent, as in *island*. Its form, somewhat modified, is found in the Anglo-Saxon, Greek, and Latin. (But see Liddell & Scott's *Greek-English Lexicon*, revised edition.) It has, for an equivalent, *c*, before *e*, *i*, and *y*. *O* is a vowel, representing a phonetic element (No. 7, p. 59). Its normal force is the sound of *o* in *go*. It has also the sound of *o* in *not*, of *ŭ* in *won*, *oo* in *two*. Its form is found in the Anglo-Saxon, Greek, and Latin. It has for its equivalents, in the sound here represented, *au*, *aw*, *awe*, *al*, *o*, *oa*, *ou;* as in *Paul*, *law*, *awe*, *talk*, *or*, *broad*, *fought*. *N* is a nasal liquid consonant, representing, when alone, a phonetic element (No. 38, p. 61). It is silent when preceded in the same syllable by *m* or *l*. Its form is found in the Anglo-Saxon, Latin, and, as a capital letter, in the Greek. It has no equivalent. Here it is taken to form in combination with *g* a single sound. *G* is a palatal mute consonant, representing, when alone, and as its normal force, a sonant phonetic element (No. 28, p. 60). It often has, also, before *e*, *i*, or *y*, the sound of *j*, as in *gem*, and is silent before *m* or *n* in the same syllable. Its exact form is from the Latin, and is not found in the Anglo-Saxon nor the Greek. (See *G* and *C* in Webster's Unabridged Dictionary.) The combination, *ng*, is a compound sign, representing a single nasal-guttural consonant element (No. 36, p. 61). As such it has no equivalent.

Let the student go through the whole line in like manner.

Occasional exercises of this kind should be assigned by the teacher. See Blair's *Latin Pronunciation;* Max Müller's *Science of Language, Second Series;* Marsh's *Lectures on the English Language;* the Latin Grammars of Madvig, Zumpt, Allen and Greenough; Fowler's large English Grammar, etc. Write an essay on the original sounds and shapes of the vowels; one on those of the mute consonants; one on the other letters.

FRANCIS BACON.

FRANCIS BACON.

1561–1626.

—"Those two incomparable men, the Prince of Poets and the Prince of Philosophers, who made the Elizabethan age a more glorious and important era in the history of the human mind than the age of Pericles, of Augustus, or of Leo."—LORD MACAULAY.

To Sir Nicholas Bacon, Lord Keeper of the Great Seal of England, residing at York House in the Strand, Francis, the youngest of several sons, was born the twenty-second of January, 1561. The mother of Francis was Anne, a very learned and accomplished lady, daughter of Sir Anthony Cooke, tutor to Edward I. Sir Nicholas was a man of great business ability, and was noted for his fine personal appearance. Queen Elizabeth was wont to say of him, "My Lord Keeper's soul is well lodged." In childhood Francis exhibited remarkable precocity. On one occasion, when the queen inquired his age, he surprised her by replying, "I am two years younger than your Majesty's happy reign." Delighted with his wit and gravity, she used to call the boy "My young lord keeper."

At thirteen he entered Trinity College, Cambridge, where he remained three years. Like Milton, he conceived a strong distaste for the curriculum, and especially for the Aristotelian philosophy. We find him at sixteen in Paris, under the care of the English ambassador, Sir Amias Paulet, where he appears to have lived remarkably free from the vices for which that brilliant capital was then notorious. A passion for rich dress and equipage, and a love of art, beauty, and magnificence, seem to have been deeply imbibed at this time. From Paris he went to Poictiers, where he studied hard; investigating, among other subjects, that of *Echoes*, which had enlisted his attention in childhood, and *Cipher-writing*. He was already collecting materials for a literary work entitled, *Of the State of Europe.*

His father suddenly dying in February, 1579, young Bacon returned home. "I found it necessary," he says, "to think to live, instead of living to think." After in vain soliciting aid from his uncle, Lord Burleigh, who seems to have cherished a mean jealousy of Bacon's superior abilities, which were likely to make him a formidable rival to Burleigh's son, Francis became, in 1580, a student of law in Gray's Inn. In 1586 he became a "Bencher;" in 1588, "Lent Reader;" in 1589, "Counsel Learned Extraordinary to the Queen." In 1591 he endeavored to procure from his powerful uncle some lucrative appointment which should give him means and leisure for philosophical and scientific research. In his letter applying for such a position, he remarks, "Thirty-one years is a great deal of sand in the hour-glass." The Cecils rather stingily procured him the reversion of the Registership of the Star Chamber, worth, whenever it should fall into possession, some £1,600 a year. Unluckily, the prior occupant stubbornly refused to die, and Bacon had to wait twenty years for the commencement of the receipt of the income.

In February, 1592, he took his seat as member of Parliament for Middlesex, making his first speech on the twenty-fifth of that month. On the seventh of March he made another speech of great power, in favor of popular rights and economical reform. The queen was angered by his bold stand against the encroachments of royalty, and caused her displeasure to be communicated to him through several channels. After this,

Bacon was more cautious. As an orator he received the commendation of old Ben Jonson, who says, "There happened in my time one noble speaker, who was full of gravity in his speaking. His language, where he could spare or pass by a jest, was nobly censorious. No man ever spake more neatly, more pressly, more weightily, or suffered less emptiness, less idleness in what he uttered. No member of his speech but consisted of its own graces. His hearers could not cough or look aside from him without loss. He commanded when he spoke, and had his judges angry and pleased at his devotion. No man had their affections more in his power. The fear of every man that heard him was lest he should make an end."

Two great parties at court sought power and royal favor; one was headed by Bacon's uncle and cousin, the Cecils; the other, by the Earl of Essex, step-son of the Earl of Leicester. Bacon allied himself to Essex. The office of Solicitor-General becoming vacant in the spring of 1594, Bacon applied for it. He greatly needed the income, for he was always living beyond his means; in fact, this improvidence was the fountain of most of his subsequent difficulties and sorrows, and a knowledge of his pecuniary embarrassments is the key to the mysteries of his otherwise inexplicable misconduct. Essex exerted himself to the utmost for his friend, but in vain: the office was given to another.

Essex now made Bacon a present of an estate at Twickenham, worth £1,800. To the wayward queen, who had so unreasonably thwarted his wishes, Bacon obsequiously dedicated a treatise, written in 1596, but not published till after his death, on the elements and use of the common law. His object was to establish in this, as in every science, general principles that should diminish labor and be the foundation of discoveries.

In 1597 his first publication appeared. It was a small duodecimo volume, containing *Essays*, ten in number, *Religious Meditations*, and a *Table* of the *Colors* of *Good* and *Evil*. In 1598 appeared another edition; a third, with additions, in 1612; and a fourth in 1625. They were immediately translated into French, Italian, and Latin, and for two hundred and seventy years they have enjoyed an extraordinary degree of popularity.

In 1598 he made a strong effort to capture the affections of Lady Hatton, a widow of long purse and sharp tongue; but, fortunately, she was reserved to torment his great rival at the bar, Attorney-General Edward Coke. In the same year he wrote another law treatise, a luminous and profound work on the Statute of Uses.

In 1599 he exerted his best endeavors to dissuade Essex from the unfortunate expedition which ultimately proved the ruin of that warm-hearted but reckless and headstrong nobleman.

In 1600 it became his official duty to prosecute Essex for disobedience. A severe struggle ensued in Bacon's breast, but he decided to act against his former benefactor. The trial took place in June. Essex was convicted, suspended from office, and imprisoned during the pleasure of the queen. The fallen favorite soon engaged in his preposterous attempt to capture London and seize the queen. The plot utterly failing, Bacon again prosecuted him, this time for high treason. The trial began February 19, 1601. On the 25th of the same month, the prisoner was beheaded in the Tower. By the queen's command, Bacon wrote an "Account of the Treasonable Practices of Robert, Earl of Essex."

On the coronation of King James, May 23, 1603, some three hundred gentlemen were knighted, among whom was Bacon. It is said that his object in seeking this honor was to gratify the lady whom he married in 1606, Miss Alice, daughter of Alderman Barnham, a Cheapside merchant. In March, 1604, he took his seat as a member of Parliament for Ipswich. He spoke often, sat upon twenty-nine committees, and in six months was appointed "King's Counsel Learned in the Law," with two pensions, of forty and sixty pounds respectively.

In 1605 he published his work, *On the Proficiency and Advancement of Learning*, afterwards enlarged and published in Latin under the title, *De Augmentis Scientiarum*, which also is the first part of his gigantic work, *Instauratio Scientiarum*, the second part being the *Novum Organum*. Years before this, he had deliberately written of himself, "I have taken all knowledge to be my province!"

In 1607 he became Solicitor-General; in 1612, Judge of the Marshalsea Courts; in 1613, Attorney-General; in 1616, Member of the Privy Council; in 1617, Lord Keeper of the Great Seal; in January, 1618, Lord High Chancellor; in July, 1618, Baron Verulam; and in January, 1619, Viscount St. Albans. He had reached the summit of political distinction; but all such splendor grows pale in the light of his intellectual achievements. In 1620 was published in Latin his *Instauratio Magna*, of which the following synopsis may be given:

I. *De Augmentis Scientiarum*, giving a general summary of human knowledge, taking special notice of gaps and imperfections in science.

II. *Novum Organum*, explaining the inductive method of reasoning, on which his philosophy is founded. Of the nine sections into which he divides the subject, he fully treats of but one, the rest being only named.

III. *Sylva Sylvarum*, designed to give a complete View of Natural Philosophy and Natural History. He has discussed but four topics under this head, viz.: the History of Winds, of Life and Death, of Density and Rarity, of Sound and Hearing.

IV. *Scala Intellectus*, of which we have but a few pages, and those introductory.

V. *Prodromi*, of which but a few fragments were composed.

VI. *Philosophia Secunda*, never written.

This sketch is colossal. No one man of fewer years than Methuselah could hope to fill out the details of so vast a plan. To have conceived it and to have made so grand a beginning show the grasp of a mighty genius.

For thirty years he had been climbing, and now, on his sixtieth birthday, which he celebrated with great pomp, he seemed to have reached a higher summit of intellectual and political glory than had fallen to the lot of any other man. But in the twinkling of an eye all was changed. He

"Dropped from the zenith like a falling star."

Twenty-two distinct charges of bribery and corruption were made against him by the House of Commons in March, 1620. The case being investigated by the House of Lords, he substantially confessed in writing his guilt, and threw himself upon the mercy of his judges. The Lords appointed a committee to visit him and ask whether it was his own hand that was subscribed to the confession. He replied, "It is my act, my hand, my heart. I beseech your lordships, be merciful to a broken reed." He was fined £40,000, and sentenced to be imprisoned in the Tower during the king's pleasure, be forever incapable of holding office, and never come within the verge of the court. King James remitted the fine, and released him from the Tower after two days' imprisonment.

Sixty years old, he retired to his country home in Gorhambury. Here he spent the remainder of his life in reading, writing, and in scientific experiments. He composed, among other works, at this time, the *History of the Reign of King Henry VII.*, and the *Fable of the New Atlantis*, and also revised and enlarged his *Essays*. The last of his literary labors was his *Version of the Psalms*.

On the second of April, 1626, as he was riding near Highgate, while the ground was thinly covered with snow, the question occurred to him, whether meat might not be preserved in snow as well as in salt. Alighting, he scooped up a quantity in his hands, and having bought a hare and had it dressed, he himself stuffed and packed it with snow. Extremely chilled, he immediately fell sick, and, being unable to reach home, stopped at the house of the Earl of Arundel, where he was put into a damp bed. Violent fever ensued, and on the ninth of April he breathed his last. By his own request, his body was buried in the same grave with his mother's, in St. Michael's Church, near St. Albans. "For my name and memory," he says in his last will, "I leave it to men's charitable speeches, to foreign nations, and to the next ages."

See Montagu's *Life of Bacon*, prefixed to his edition of Bacon's Works; Macaulay's brilliant essay on Bacon; the compilations and treatises of English Literature cited in the case of Spenser, p. 69; the *Encyclopedias* and *Dictionary of Authors*, there named; the magazine articles referred to in *Poole's Index*, title *Bacon;* and the English Histories that treat of the reigns of Elizabeth and James I. Above all, in regard to *Bacon's Essays*, see Archbishop Whately's edition, containing that distinguished prelate's *Annotations*. Whately is one of the most stimulating and healthful of writers. Heard's *Student's Edition of Whately*, published by Lee & Sheppard, containing a Glossarial Index, should be in every reader's hands. Let not the student accept our statements in regard to Bacon without verifying them. Let him fill out with additional facts the meagre outline we have given.

PREFATORY EPISTLE.

TO. MR. ANTHONY BACON, HIS DEAR BROTHER.

Loving and beloved brother, I do now like some that have an orchard ill-neighbored, that gather their fruit before it is ripe, to prevent stealing. These fragments of my conceits were going to print: to labor the stay of them had been troublesome, and subject to interpretation; to let them pass had been to adventure the wrong they might receive by untrue copies, or by some garnishment, which it might please any that should set them forth to bestow upon them. Therefore I held it best discretion to publish them myself, as they passed long ago from my pen, without any further disgrace than the weakness of the author. And, as I did ever hold there might be as great a vanity in retiring and withdrawing men's conceits (except they be of some nature) from the world as in obtruding them; so in these particulars I have played myself the inquisitor, and find nothing to my understanding in them contrary or infectious to the state of religion or manners, but rather, as I suppose, medicinable. Only I dislike now to put them out, because they will be like the late new halfpence,* which though the silver were good, yet the pieces were small. But since they would not stay with their master, but would needs travel abroad, I have preferred them to you,† that are next myself; dedicating them, such as they are, to our love; in the depth whereof, I assure you, I sometimes wish your infirmities translated upon myself, that her majesty might have the service of so active and able a mind; and I might be with excuse confined to these contemplations and studies, for which I am fittest. So commend I you to the preservation of the Divine Majesty.

Your entire loving brother,

FRAN. BACON.

From my Chamber, at Gray's Inn,
this 30th of January, 1597.

---

* Coined in 1582-3, and in circulation till 1601.

† **I have preferred them to you.** I have *presented* or *dedicated* them to you. *Preferred* is Lat. *pre*, before, forward, akin to *pro* and *præ*, Gr. πρό; Lat. *fero*, I bring (whence, by Grimm's Law, Eng. *bear*); Gr. φέρω.

ESSAYS, CIVIL AND MORAL.

OF TRUTH (1625).

"What is truth?" * said jesting Pilate, and would not stay for an answer. Certainly there be that delight in giddiness, and count it a bondage to fix a belief; affecting free-will in thinking, as well as in acting. And though the sects of philosophers of that kind be gone, yet there remain certain discoursing wits which are of the same veins, though there be not so much blood in them as was in those of the ancients. But it is not only the difficulty and labor which men take in finding out of truth; nor again, that, when it is found, it imposeth upon men's thoughts, that doth bring lies in favor; but a natural, though corrupt love of the lie itself. One of the later schools of the Grecians examineth the matter, and is at a stand to think what should be in it, that men should love lies, where neither they make for pleasure, as with poets; nor for advantage, as with the merchant; but for the lie's sake. But I cannot tell: this same truth is a naked and open day-light, that doth not show the masques and mummeries, and triumphs of the world, half so stately and daintily as candle-lights. Truth may perhaps come to the price of a pearl, that showeth best by day; but it will not rise to the price of a diamond or carbuncle, that showeth best in varied lights. A mixture of a lie doth ever add pleasure. Doth any man doubt, that if there were taken out of men's minds vain opinions, flattering hopes, false valuations, imaginations as one would, and the like, but it would leave the

* **What is truth?** John xviii. 38.—**Jesting** (Lat. *gestum*, deed, fr. *gerĕre*, to accomplish; O. Fr. *geste*, exploit; O. Eng. *jest*. story of an exploit, good story, joke). Was Pilate jesting?—**Giddiness** (A. S. *gidig*, dizzy; *gyddian*, to be giddy), *instability*. See *homeliness*, p. 33.—**Fix a belief**, *settle upon a belief*.—**Affecting**, *aiming at*, *making a show of*.—**Discoursing** (Lat. *dis*, in different directions; *currĕre*, to run), *rambling*, *discursive*, *desultory*.—**Veins** (Lat. *vena*, vein; Fr. *veine*), *tempers*, *tendencies of disposition*.—**Blood.** Meaning?—**Ancients**, Democritus and other "laughing philosophers."—**Finding out of.** *Of* should be omitted (or the word *the* inserted before *finding*).—**What should be in it**, *the hidden cause*.—**Cannot tell.** What?—**Masques**, plays or festive entertainments in which the company wear masks; *masquerades*; masks.—**Mummeries** (Ger. *mummerei*; Fr. *momerie*, mummery), *farcical shows*, *maskings*, *buffooneries*.—**Triumphs** (Lat. *triumphus*, a magnificent procession with imposing ceremonies in honor of a victorious general at Rome), *stately shows*.—**Daintily**, *delicately*, *elegantly*. Either fr. Lat. *dignus*, worthy; or fr. W. *dain*, fine, delicate; or possibly fr. Lat. *dens*; W. *dant*; Ger. *zahn*; Gr. ὀ-δούς, ὀ-δόντ-ος, a tooth. See Grimm's Law.—**Carbuncle** (Lat. *carbo*, coal, carbon; *carbuncŭlus*, a little coal), *a beautiful red gem*, that in the sunlight looks like burning coal.—**Lie** (A. S. *lyge*; Ger. *lüge*, lug).—**But.** After *doubt that*, *but* should be omitted.—**Imaginations** (of things) **as one would** (like to have them).

Grammatical Equivalents.—Few exercises are more useful in giving a command of language, cultivating both fluency and elegance of speech, than the practice of finding equivalent grammatical expressions. He who would become an extemporaneous speaker, can hardly bestow too much time upon it. Even those who have no higher ambition in a rhetorical direction than to converse or write readily and correctly, should make it a daily exercise. The teacher will do well to give a few minutes' drill in it, if practicable, as an accompaniment to the recitations in Grammar, Composition, Rhetoric, Logic, and English Literature. We give a few illustrations, but *the instructor should take pains to supplement and continue the work by a multitude of similar exercises, and should always teach the pupil to choose wisely among the equivalents.* For convenience, the expressions which we select for the pupil to translate into other language, are placed at the bottom of the successive pages of the extracts from Bacon.

Affecting free-will in thinking = aiming at freedom of thought = desiring to attain intellectual freedom = endeavoring after intellectual liberty = striving to be free in thought = solicitous to be intellectually free, etc.

Discoursing wits = discursive wits = rambling wits = ingenious minds given to discourse = subtle intellects fond of light speculation, etc.

It imposeth upon men's thoughts = it lays restraint upon men's thoughts = it puts restrictions upon men's thoughts = it puts bounds to the license of speculation, etc.

Imaginations as one would = unrestrained imaginations = unbridled fancies. Other equivalents?

minds of a number of men poor shrunken things, full of melancholy and indisposition, and unpleasing to themselves? One of the fathers, in great severity, called poesy* "vinum dæmonum," because it filleth the imagination, and yet it is but with the shadow of a lie. But it is not the lie that passeth through the mind, but the lie that sinketh in and settleth in it, that doth the hurt, such as we spake of before. But howsoever these things are thus in men's depraved judgments and affections, yet truth, which only doth judge itself, teacheth that the inquiry of truth, which is the love-making or wooing of it; the knowledge of truth, which is the presence of it; and the belief of truth, which is the enjoying of it; is the sovereign good of human nature. The first creature of God, in the works of the days, was the light of the sense; the last was the light of reason; and his sabbath work, ever since, is the illumination of his Spirit. First, he breatheth light upon the face of the matter, or chaos; then he breatheth light into the face of man; and still he breatheth and inspireth light into the face of his chosen. The poet that beautified the sect that was otherwise inferior to the rest, saith yet excellently well, "It is a pleasure to stand upon the shore, and to see ships tossed upon the sea: a pleasure to stand in the window of a castle, and to see a battle, and the adventures thereof below: but no pleasure is comparable to the standing upon the vantage ground of truth (a hill not to be commanded, and where the air is always clear and serene), and to see the errors, and wanderings, and mists, and tempests, in the vale below:" so always that this prospect be with pity, and not with swelling or pride. Certainly it is heaven upon earth to have a man's mind move in charity, rest in providence, and turn upon the poles of truth.

To pass from theological and philosophical truth to the truth of civil business, it will be acknowledged, even by those that practice it not, that clear and round dealing is the honor of man's nature, and that mixture of

---

* **Poesy,** *poetry.* See *posies*, Index.—**Vinum dæmonum,** *wine of devils.* It was St. Augustine.—**Shadow of a lie.** Why so?—**Howsoever,** *however, although.* **Inquiry of,** *inquiry after, search for.*—**Belief.** Genuine belief issues in *action.* **Creature,** *creation.* —**Of the days.** See the account of the *Creation*, in Genesis. Note the beauty of this whole passage.—**Poet that beautified,** Lucretius, a profound Roman philosopher as well as poet. His great work, entitled *De Natura Rerum*, is considered by many scholars the greatest didactic poem in any language. He is said to have died by his own hand in 52 B. C. See *Lucretius*, in Class. Dict.—**The sect,** the *Epicureans. Epicurus*, the celebrated philosopher, was born in Samos in 341 B. C., and died in 270. He taught that ἐνδαιμόνεια, "supreme mental bliss," is the end and should be the purpose of life. St. Paul encountered the Epicureans at Athens. Lucretius was one of their greatest ornaments.—**Adventures** (Lat. *advenire*, to come to (pass), to happen), *hazards, bold exploits.*—**Vantage-ground** (Lat. *ab*, from, ante, *before;* Fr. *avant*, before; *avantage*, forward position), *advantageous position.*—**Commanded** (in a military sense), *held within control.*—**So always,** *on condition always, provided always.*—**Truth of civil business,** *truth exemplified in the business of society.*—**Round** (Fr. *rond;* Lat. *rotundus*, wheel-shaped, round; fr. *rota*, a wheel), *candid*, "*fair and square.*"

Unpleasing = distasteful. Other equivalents?

The sovereign good of human nature = man's highest welfare. Give six other equivalents.

The first creature of God = the first creation of God = the first of God's created works = the first object created by God = God's first creation = God's earliest creation = the earliest work of Jehovah = the earliest manifestation of the creative power of Deity = the very beginning of God's handiwork = the earliest production of the Omnipotent Hand = the "Offspring of Heaven first-born," etc.

Saith excellently well = saith very justly and fitly = saith very happily = makes the very appropriate and striking remarks. Give other grammatical equivalents.

See the adventures = witness the fortunes. Other equivalents?

So always that this prospect be = provided always that this prospect be accompanied. Other equivalents?

Clear and round dealing. Equivalents?

falsehood is like alloy in coin of gold and silver, which may make the metal work * the better, but it embaseth it. For these winding and crooked courses are the goings of the serpent, which goeth basely upon the belly, and not upon the feet. There is no vice that doth so cover a man with shame as to be found false and perfidious: and therefore Montaigne saith prettily, when he inquired the reason why the word of the lie should be such a disgrace, and such an odious charge, "If it be well weighed, to say that a man lieth, is as much as to say that he is brave towards God, and a coward towards men: for a lie faces God, and shrinks from man." Surely the wickedness of falsehood and breach of faith cannot possibly be so highly expressed as in that it shall be the last peal to call the judgments of God upon the generations of men, it being foretold that when "Christ cometh" he shall not "find faith upon earth."

OF DEATH (1612; enlarged 1625).

Men fear death as children fear to go into the dark; and as that natural fear of children is increased with tales, so is the other. Certainly, the contemplation of death, as the wages of sin and passage to another world, is holy and religious; but the fear of it, as a tribute due unto nature, is weak. Yet in religious meditations there is sometimes mixture of vanity and of superstition. You shall read in some of the friars' books of mortification, that a man should think with himself what the pain is, if he have but his finger's end pressed, or tortured, and thereby imagine what the pains of death are when the whole body is corrupted and dissolved. When, many times, death passeth with less pain than the torture of a limb; for the most vital parts are not the quickest of sense: and by him that spake only as a philosopher and natural man, it was well said, "Pompa mortis magis terret quam mors ipsa." Groans, and convulsions, and a discolored face, and friends weeping, and blacks and obsequies, and the like, show death terrible.

It is worthy the observing, that there is no passion in the mind of man so weak, but it mates and masters the fear of death; and, therefore, death is no such terrible enemy when a man hath so many attendants about him that can win the combat of him. Revenge triumphs over death; love

---

* **Work.** In what sense?—**Embaseth** (Fr. *em*, or *en;* Lat. *in;* Gr. βάσις, base; W. *bas*, shallow; Gr. βάσσων, deeper), *debaseth, lowers its value.*—**These.** This word is superfluous.—**Montaigne** (1533–1589), the earliest French essayist, distinguished for wit, subtlety, nice observation, and common sense. Montaigne quotes the saying in the text from Plutarch's Life of Lysander.—**As in that.** Supply the omitted words.—Divide this essay into paragraphs. Point out the best sentences. Rewrite the whole in your own language, amplifying if necessary.

Of death. This essay is partly taken from Seneca's Letters. Who was he? See p. 91.—**Fear to go,** etc. Would *fear darkness* be better? Why?—**Wages.** "The wages of sin is death."—**Friars' books.** What books? See Index.—**When many times,** *yet often.*—**Quickest of sense.** Meaning?—**Pompa,** etc. *The parade* (paraphernalia or array) *of death terrifies more than death itself.*—**Blacks,** *black dresses, mourning drapery,* etc. **Obsequies** (Lat. *obsequiæ*), *funeral rites.*—**Worthy the observing.** What form would be better?—**But it mates,** *but it matches, sets itself against as equal, vies with.*—**Win the combat of him.** Of whom? What defect in the English language in the matter of pronouns of the third person?

Embaseth it = vitiates it. Other equivalents?
Cannot be so highly expressed. Grammatical equivalents?
It mates = it subdues = it overcomes. Other equivalents?

slights it; honor aspireth to it; grief flieth to it; fear pre-occupateth it.* Nay, we read, after Otho the emperor had slain himself, pity, which is the tenderest of affections, provoked many to die out of mere compassion to their sovereign, and as the truest sort of followers. Nay, Seneca adds, niceness and satiety: "Cogita quamdiu eadem feceris; mori velle, non tantum fortis, aut miser, sed etiam fastidiosus potest." "A man would die, though he were neither valiant nor miserable, only upon a weariness to do the same thing so oft over and over." It is no less worthy to observe, how little alteration in good spirits the approaches of death make; for they appear to be the same men till the last instant. Augustus Cæsar died in a compliment: "Livia, conjugii nostri memor, vive et vale:" Tiberius, in dissimulation, as Tacitus saith of him, "Jam Tiberium vires et corpus, non dissimulatio, deserebant:" Vespasian, in a jest, ... "Ut puto Deus fio:" Galba with a sentence, "Feri, si ex re sit populi Romani," holding forth his neck: Septimus Severus in despatch, "Adeste, si quid mihi restat agendum;" and the like. Certainly the Stoics bestowed too much cost upon death, and by their great preparations made it appear more fearful. Better, saith he, "qui finem vitæ extre-

---

* **Fear pre-occupateth,** the fear of some greater evil lays hold of death as a refuge; *i. e.*, fear impels to suicide.—**We read** [that].—**Otho,** eighth Roman emperor, born A. D. 31 or 32; committed suicide, A. D. 68, after a reign of ninety-five days. Vitellius had revolted against him and been proclaimed emperor by the legions in Germany. After three victories, Otho was defeated. In his last moments he expressed an affectionate concern for his faithful followers, some of whom chose to die with him rather than live without him.—**Provoked** (Lat. *pro*, forth; *voco*, I call), *incited, induced.* This word is repeatedly used in the Bible in this sense.—**Niceness,** *fastidiousness.*—**Satiety,** *fulness beyond desire, ennui*, disgust arising from the appetite being cloyed.—**Cogita,** etc. *Think well how often you have done the same things over and over. One might wish to die, not only from bravery or misery, but even from ennui.*—**Worthy to,** *worth while to.*—**Good spirits.** By *spirits* does he mean souls, persons, men? Or does *good spirits* mean life, ardor, animation, courage, cheerfulness? If the latter, what is the antecedent of *they*, in *they appear to be the same men?*—**Augustus died,** A. D. 14, having reigned forty-four years. What can you say of him and his times? See Class. Dict.—**Livia,** etc. *Livia, remembering our wedlock, live and farewell.*—**Vive et vale,** *live and farewell*, or *Life and health to you!* the usual parting salutation among the Romans.—**Tiberius,** the successor of Augustus. Born B. C. 42; died A. D. 37, after a reign of twenty-three years. This great villain was remarkable for his dissimulation, though that was the least of his rascalities. Read his story in the classical dictionaries.—**Jam Tiberium.** *At length his powers and bodily strength, not dissimulation, were abandoning Tiberius.*—**Vespasian,** emperor of Rome A. D. 70, reigned nine years. It is a little remarkable, being a Roman emperor, that he died a natural death and was succeeded by his son.—**Ut puto.** "*As I suppose, I am turning into a god.*"—**Galba,** successor of Nero and predecessor of Otho, became emperor A. D. 68, and was slain at the end of seven months, being seventy-two years of age. To quell the mutiny which Otho had stirred up, Galba caused himself to be carried in a litter into the forum; but on the appearance of a band of Otho's armed adherents, Galba's followers dropped the litter and fled. As the assassins rushed upon him, he presented his neck, coolly addressing them in the words quoted above.—**Feri, si,** etc. *Strike, if it be for the advantage of the Roman people.*—**Septimus Severus.** After a reign of nearly eighteen years, this Roman emperor died at York, England, A. D. 211, at the age of sixty-five.—**In despatch,** *in business fashion.*—**Adeste.** *Attend, if anything remains for me to do.*—**Stoics,** so called from *Stoa*, a painted portico, the most famous in Athens. Here Zeno, who died B. C. 264, at the age of ninety-eight, taught his doctrines, and founded the sect of *Stoics.* They believed that a man should raise himself above pleasure, pain, fear, and all passion. They taught that virtue is the supreme good, and that death is no evil. On the latter point they laid so much stress, that Bacon affirms their eagerness to have had the contrary effect to what they had designed. See Index.—**Better saith he.** (*He* is emphatic.) Juvenal, the celebrated Roman satirist, is meant; born A. D. 40, or thereabouts; died when a little over eighty years of age. He is severe against the Stoics. In his Tenth Satire we find the line which Bacon quotes:

"*Qui spatium* [finem] *vitæ extremum inter munera ponat,*"

"who would count the last period of life among the boons" (of nature). The passage means, then, "Better than the dogmas of the Stoics is the sentiment of Juvenal, who would reckon death a boon." Boyd is mistaken in supposing that Bacon is careless in his style, and that here is an instance of it.

Fear pre-occupateth it = fear anticipates it. Other equivalents?

Pity provoked many = compassion excited many = tender sympathy induced a large number. Other equivalents?

mum inter munera, ponat naturæ." It is as natural to die as to be born; and to a little infant, perhaps, the one is as painful as the other. He that dies in an earnest pursuit is like one that is wounded in hot blood; who, for the time, scarce feels the hurt; and therefore a mind fixed and bent upon somewhat that is good, doth avert the dolors * of death. But, above all, believe it, the sweetest canticle is, "Nunc dimittis," when a man hath obtained worthy ends and expectations. Death hath this also, that it openeth the gate to good fame, and extinguisheth envy: "Extinctus amabitur idem." †

OF ADVERSITY (1625).

It was a high speech of Seneca after the manner of the Stoics, that the good things which belong to prosperity are to be wished, but the good things that belong to adversity are to be admired: "Bona rerum secundarum optabilia, adversarum mirabilia." Certainly, if miracles be the command over nature, they appear most in adversity. It is yet a higher speech of his than the other, much too high for a heathen, "It is true greatness to have in one the frailty of a man, and the security of a God:"—"Vere magnum habere fragilitatem hominis, securitatem Dei." This would have done better in poesy, where transcendencies are more allowed; and the poets, indeed, have been busy with it. For it is in effect the thing which is figured in that strange fiction of the ancient poets, which seemeth not to be without mystery; nay, and to have some approach to the state of a Christian; "that Hercules, when he went to unbind Prometheus, by whom human nature is represented, sailed the length of the great ocean in an earthen pot or pitcher, lively describing Christian resolution, that saileth in the frail bark of the flesh through the waves of the world." But, to speak in a mean, the virtue of prosperity is temperance, the virtue of adversity is fortitude, which in morals is the more heroical virtue. Prosperity is the blessing of

---

* **Dolors** (Lat. *dolor*, pain; *doleo*, to feel pain), *pangs.* — **Nunc dimittis.** *Now lettest thou.* This is the beginning of the Latin version of the aged Simeon's exclamation (Luke ii. 29) on beholding the infant Jesus. Here, as in all his quotations from the Scriptures in his essays, Bacon gives the language of the Latin Vulgate, or equivalent words.—**Extinctus,** etc. *When dead, the very one* (that had been envied) *will be loved.*

High speech, *a lofty, high-toned, remarkable, or excellent saying.*—**Seneca,** a celebrated Roman Stoic philosopher, born in Corduba (Cordova, Spain, whence the word *cordwainer* comes) about the beginning of the Christian era.—**Most in adversity.** Most what?—**Transcendencies** (Lat. *transcendere*, to climb over; from *trans*, beyond, and *scandere*, to climb), *soarings, hyperboles.*—**Poets,** Stesichorus, Apollodorus, and others.—**Nay, and,** *not only so, but also.*—**Hercules,** the most famous of Grecian heroes. See Class. Dict. for *Hercules* and *Prometheus.*—**Lively,** *with liveliness.*—**Frail bark.** So St. Paul, 2 Cor. iv. 7, "We have this treasure in earthen vessels."—**In a mean,** *in a moderate tone, with moderation.* —**Virtue of prosperity.** Meaning? Note the happy antitheses.

Avert the dolors of death = avert the pains of death = render unfelt the agonies of the last hour. Other equivalent expressions?

† Divide this essay into suitable paragraphs. Explain why Bacon quotes Latin so profusely. Turn the essay into your own language, being careful to express every thought fully and exactly.

A high speech = sublime declaration = a remark of great dignity and elevation. Give six other equivalent grammatical expressions.

Transcendencies are more allowed = lofty flights are more permissible = hyperbeles are more allowable. Other equivalent expressions?

To speak in a mean = to speak in a medium tone = to speak with moderation = to use unadorned language, avoiding flights of fancy and exaggerations. Other grammatical equivalents?

the Old Testament,* adversity is the blessing of the New, which carrieth the greater benediction, and the clearer revelation of God's favor. Yet even in the Old Testament, if you listen to David's harp, you shall hear as many hearselike airs as carols; and the pencil of the Holy Ghost hath labored more in describing the afflictions of Job than the felicities of Solomon. Prosperity is not without many fears and distastes; and adversity is not without comforts and hopes. We see in needleworks and embroideries, it is more pleasing to have a lively work upon a sad and solemn ground, than to have a dark and melancholy work upon a lightsome ground: judge, therefore, of the pleasure of the heart by the pleasure of the eye. Certainly virtue is like precious odors, most fragrant where they are incensed, or crushed: for prosperity doth best discover vice, but adversity doth best discover virtue.

OF STUDIES (1597).

Studies serve for delight, for ornament, and for ability. Their chief use for delight is in privateness and retiring; for ornament, is in discourse; and for ability, is in the judgment and disposition of business; for expert men can execute, and perhaps judge of particulars one by one: but the general counsels, and the plots and marshaling of affairs, come best from those that are learned. To spend too much time in studies is sloth; to use them too much for ornament is affectation; to make judgment wholly by their rules is the humor of a scholar: they perfect nature, and are perfected by experience. For natural abilities are like natural plants, that need pruning by study; and studies themselves do give forth directions too much at large, except they be bounded in by experience. Crafty men contemn studies, simple men admire them, and wise men use them; for they teach not their own use; but that is a wisdom without them, and above them, won by observation. Read not to contradict and confute, nor to believe and take for

---

* **The Old Testament** laid more stress on temporal rewards; the New, on spiritual. To lose all earthly blessing for Christ's sake, to be in *adversity* for him, was eventually the source of the highest blessing. See Rev. vii.—**Comforts and hopes.** So Paul "We glory in tribulations also." Rom. v.—**Lively,** *bright, in gay colors.*—**Lightsome,** *of light or joyous aspect.*—**Discover** (Fr. *découvrir*, to disclose; from Lat. *dis-*, denoting privation or negation; *co-* or *con-*, together, completely; and *operire*, to cover), *uncover, reveal, make manifest.* Divide this essay into paragraphs. See what improvement you can make in any sentences. Cull out the thoughts, and rewrite the essay in your own language, to see if you can improve upon the original. Specify in writing the twelve *labors* of Hercules. Write out the legend of Prometheus.

Privateness, *seclusion.* See *privy*, Index.—**Retiring** (Lat *re*, back, Fr. *tirer*, to draw), *freedom from business cares; withdrawal from society; modest leisure; unobtrusiveness.*—**General counsels,** *comprehensive counsels, plans embracing great and varied interests.*—**Judgments,** *plans, opinions.*—**Natural plants,** *plants that grow wild.*—**Crafty** (A. S. *cräft*, strength, art; Ger., Sw., and Dan. *kraft*, power; W. *cref*, strong) may here mean men of some craft, or skilled in some mechanical work; or it may be used in the sense of *cunning*. Which is preferable?—**Simple,** *unsophisticated.*

Lively work upon a sad and solemn ground = animated scenes and figures upon a dark and sober-looking ground. Other equivalents?

Most fragrant when they are incensed = most grateful to the sense of smell when they are burning. Other equivalents?

Their chief use for delight is in privateness = their principal use in giving pleasure is in privacy. Other equivalents?

To make judgment = to give judgment = to make decisions. Other equivalents?

The humor of a scholar = the predominant inclination of a learned man = the unreasoning fanciful inclination of a man of books. Other equivalents?

granted, nor to find talk and discourse, but to weigh and consider. Some books are to be tasted, others to be swallowed, and some few to be chewed and digested; that is, some books are to be read only in parts; others to be read, but not curiously; * and some few to be read wholly, and with diligence and attention. Some books also may be read by deputy, and extracts made of them by others; but that would be only in the less important arguments, and the meaner sort of books; else distilled books are, like common distilled waters, flashy things. Reading maketh a full man; conference, a ready man; and writing, an exact man: and, therefore, if a man write little, he had need have a great memory: if he confer little, he had need have a present wit; and if he read little, he had need have much cunning, to seem to know that he doth not. Histories make men wise; poets, witty; the mathematics, subtile; natural philosophy, deep; moral, grave; logic and rhetoric, able to contend. "Abeunt studia in mores:" nay, there is no stand or impediment in the wit, but may be wrought out by fit studies; like as diseases of the body may have appropriate exercises. Bowling is good for the stone and reins; shooting, for the lungs and breast; gentle walking, for the stomach; riding, for the head, and the like. So, if a man's wits be wandering, let him study the mathematics; for in demonstrations, if his wit be called away never so little, he must begin again. If his wit be not apt to distinguish or find differences, let him study the schoolmen; for they are "Cymini sectores." If he be not apt to beat over matters, and to call upon one thing to prove and illustrate another, let him study the lawyers' cases. So every defect of the mind may have a special receipt.†

OF MARRIAGE AND SINGLE LIFE (1612; slightly enlarged 1625).

He that hath wife and children hath given hostages to fortune; for they are impediments to great enterprises, either of virtue or mischief. Certainly the best works, and of greatest merit for the public, have proceeded from the unmarried or childless men; which, both in affection and means,

---

* **Curiously** (Lat. *cura*, care), *carefully, with eager attention.*—**Arguments,** *subjects, courses of thought.*—**Else** (genitive case of the root of Gr. ἄλλος: Lat. *alius*, other; A. S. *elles.* See p. 20), *in other cases in other circumstances.*—**Conference** (Lat. *con*, together; *fero*, Gr. φέρω, to bring; Lat. *conferentia*, a bringing together for comparison; Fr. *conférence*), *conversation.*—**Abeunt,** etc., *studies pass into habits, or manners.*—**Stand** (or **stond** in some editions), *disinclination to proceed.*—**Wit,** *intellect.*—**Wrought out,** *worked off, removed.*—**Schoolmen** (Gr. σχολή, leisure; Lat. *schola*, a school; Fr. *école;* Ger. *schule*). "The schoolmen were philosophers and divines of the Middle Ages who adopted the principles of Aristotle, and spent much time on points of nice and abstract speculation. They were so called because they taught in the schools of divinity established by Charlemagne."—**Cymini,** etc., *cumin-splitters, "hair-splitters."* Cumin is a plant, also the seed of the plant, like anise and caraway.—**Apt** (Lat. *aptus*, fit), *skillful, capable, able.*—**Beat over,** *scour, range over, drive over, go over with force and skill.*—**Receipt,** *recipe, formula prescribed for preparing medicine,* etc.—**Impediments** (Lat. *impedimentum*, hindrance; perhaps from *in*, against, and *pes, pedis*, the foot).

But not curiously = but not with eager attention. Other equivalents?
But that would be = but that should be done. Other equivalents?
Reading maketh a full man = what? *A ready man* = what? *An exact man* = what?
Seem to know that he doth not = seem to know that which he does not really know. Other equivalents?

---

† This admirable essay on studies has rarely or never been surpassed in concentration of thought. The student may profitably write out illustrations and expansions of the points made. Rewrite the thoughts in your own words, and then compare your work with Bacon's.

have married and endowed the public. Yet it were great reason that those that have children should have greatest care of future times, unto which they know they must transmit their dearest pledges. Some there are, who, though they lead a single life, yet their thoughts do end with themselves, and account future times impertinences. Nay, there are some other that account wife and children but as bills of charges. Nay, more, there are some foolish, rich, covetous men, that take a pride in having no children, because they may be thought so much the richer; for perhaps they have heard some talk, "Such an one is a great rich man," and another except to it, "Yea, but he hath a great charge of children;" as if it were an abatement to his riches. But the most ordinary cause of a single life is liberty; especially in certain self-pleasing and humorous minds, which are so sensible of every restraint, as they will go near to think * their girdles and garters to be bonds and shackles. Unmarried men are best friends, best masters, best servants, but not always best subjects; for they are light to run away; and almost all fugitives are of that condition. A single life doth well with churchmen; for charity will hardly water the ground where it must first fill a pool. It is indifferent for judges and magistrates; for, if they be facile and corrupt, you shall have a servant five times worse than a wife. For soldiers, I find the generals commonly, in their hortatives, put men in mind of their wives and children; and I think the despising of marriage among the Turks maketh the vulgar soldier more base. Certainly wife and children are a kind of discipline of humanity; and single men, though they be many times more charitable, because their means are less exhaust, yet, on the other side, they are more cruel and hard-hearted, good to make severe inquisitors, because their tenderness is not so oft called upon. Grave natures, led by custom, and therefore constant, are commonly loving husbands; as was said of Ulysses, "Vetulam suam prætulit immortalitati." Chaste women are often proud and froward, as presuming upon the merit of their chastity. It is one of the best bonds, both of chastity and obedience, in the wife, if she think her husband wise; which she will never do if she find him jealous. Wives are young men's mistresses, companions for middle age, and old men's

* **As they will go near to think,** *that they will almost think.*—**Light to run away,** *free from impediments to running away.* **Light,** *nimble.*—**Hortatives** (Lat. *hortari*, to excite). *exhortations.*—**Vulgar soldier,** *common soldier.*—**Vetulam suam,** etc. *He preferred his little old woman* [Penelope] *to immortality.* This refers to the Homeric narrative, which represents the nymph Calypso, daughter of Atlas, to have promised Ulysses immortality, if he would remain in the island of Ogygia. He chose to return to his aged wife, Penelope, after twenty years' absence.—**Presuming upon,** etc. This remark shows a keenness and depth of mental vision worthy of Shakespeare. Indeed, it has been argued, not without a degree of plausibility, that Bacon wrote Shakespeare's plays !

Account future times impertinences = account (regard, consider, reckon) future times (coming ages, the future) things wholly irrelevant (of no account, unimportant). Other equivalents ?

Bills of charges = bills of expense. Other equivalents ?

Humorous minds = fancy-ruled minds = minds under the dominion of some leading whim = minds subject to some predominant inclination. Other equivalents ? Whately suggests that humorous may here mean *self-conceited*.

As they will go near to think = that they will almost think. Other grammatical equivalents ?

Light to run away. Give half a dozen equivalents.

Their means are less exhaust = their pecuniary resources are more abundant. Other equivalents ?

nurses; so as a man may have a quarrel to marry* when he will. But yet he was reputed one of the wise men that made answer to the question when a man should marry, "A young man not yet, an elder man not at all." It is often seen, that bad husbands have very good wives; whether it be that it raiseth the price of their husbands' kindness when it comes, or that the wives take a pride in their patience. But this never fails if the bad husbands were of their own choosing, against their friends' consent, for then they will be sure to make good their own folly.

OF THE TRUE GREATNESS OF KINGDOMS AND ESTATES (1612; enlarged 1625).

The speech of Themistocles, the Athenian, which was haughty and arrogant in taking so much to himself, had been a grave and wise observation and censure, applied at large to others. Desired at a feast to touch a lute, he said, "he could not fiddle, but yet he could make a small town a great city." These words, holpen a little with a metaphor, may express two differing abilities in those that deal in business of estate. For, if a true survey be taken of counsellors and statesmen, there may be found, though rarely, those which can make a small state great, and yet cannot fiddle; as, on the other side, there will be found a great many that can fiddle very cunningly, but yet are so far from being able to make a small state great, as their gift lieth the other way; to bring a great and flourishing estate to ruin and decay. And, certainly, those degenerate arts and shifts, whereby many counsellors and governors gain both favor with their masters, and estimation with the vulgar, deserve no better name than fiddling; being things rather pleasing for the time, and graceful to themselves only, than tending to the weal and advancement of the state which they serve. There are also, no doubt, counsellors and governors which may be held sufficient, "negotiis pares," able to manage affairs, and to keep them from precipices and manifest inconveniences; which, nevertheless, are far from the ability to raise and amplify an estate in power, means, and fortune. But be the workmen what they may be, let us speak of the work; that is, the true greatness of kingdoms and estates, and the means thereof. An argument fit for great

---

* **Quarrel to marry** (Lat. *queror*, to complain; *querela*, complaint, cause of complaint; Fr. *querelle*), *cause to marry.* See Index. Whately suggests that it may be from the Lat. *quare*, wherefore.

Themistocles (B. C. 514–449), one of the most brilliant of Athenian statesmen. See Class. Dict. and Plutarch's Lives.—**Had been.** What mood? Common form?—**Applied.** What omission?—**Holpen** (passive participle of the A. S. *helpan*; Ger. *helfen*, to help: the *-en* in the A. S. is the ending of the past or perfect participle), *helped.* "*He hath holpen his servant Israel.*" Luke i. 54.—**Estate,** in the old English writers, means the same as *state.* (*St* denotes firmness, or stability; as in Gr. ἵστημι; Lat *stare*, to stand; Eng. *stick*; A. S. *standan*; Ger. *stehen.*)—**Those which,** *those who.*—**Cunningly** (A. S. *cunnan*, to know, to be able. Hence *cunningly* is *knowingly*, *ably.* See Index), *skillfully.*—**As their gift,** *that* (on the *contrary*) *their gift.*—**Estate,** as before.—**Governors which.** Modernize the expression. **Negotiis pares,** *equal to* (*i. e.*, able to transact) *business.*—**Which, nevertheless,** *who, nevertheless.*—**Argument,** *theme, subject.*

So as a man may have a quarrel to marry = so that a man may have a reason for marrying. Other equivalents?

Censure, applied, at large, to others = judgment, if stated as a general principle, applicable to others. Other grammatical equivalents?

Fiddle very cunningly = play a lute very skillfully. Other equivalents?

An argument fit for great and mighty princes to have in their hand = a subject appropriate for eminent and powerful monarchs to have in their intelligent consideration. Other equivalents?

These essays of Bacon, it is clear, are masterpieces of condensed *thought.* How say you of the verbal *expression?* Rewrite, in a more modern style, that on *Marriage and Single Life.*

and mighty princes to have in their hand; to the end, that neither by over-measuring their forces they lose themselves in vain enterprises; nor, on the other side, by undervaluing them, they descend to fearful* and pusillanimous counsels.

The greatness of an estate, in bulk and territory, doth fall under measure; and the greatness of finances and revenue doth fall under computation. The population may appear by musters; and the number and greatness of cities and towns, by cards and maps; but yet there is not anything, amongst civil affairs, more subject to error than the right valuation and true judgment concerning the power and forces of an estate. The kingdom of heaven is compared, not to any great kernel, or nut, but to a grain of mustard-seed; which is one of the least grains, but hath in it a property and spirit hastily to get up and spread. So are there states great in territory, and yet not apt to enlarge or command; and some that have but a small dimension of stem, and yet are apt to be the foundation of great monarchies.

Walled towns, stored arsenals and armories, goodly races of horse, chariots of war, elephants, ordnance, artillery, and the like,—all this is but a sheep in a lion's skin, except the breed and disposition of the people be stout and warlike. Nay, number itself in armies importeth not much, where the people are of weak courage; for, as Virgil saith, "it never troubles the wolf how many the sheep be." The army of the Persians, in the plains of Arbela, was such a vast sea of people as it did somewhat astonish the commanders in Alexander's army, who came to him, therefore, and wished him to set upon them by night. But he answered, "he would not pilfer the victory;" and the defeat was easy. When Tigranes, the Armenian, being encamped upon a hill with four hundred thousand men, discovered the army of the Romans, being not above fourteen thousand, marching towards him, he made himself merry with it, and said, "Yonder men are too many for an embassage, and too few for a fight:" but before

---

* **Fearful,** *full of fear, timid.*—**Doth fall under measure.** Modernize the expression. —**May appear,** *may be clearly shown.*—**Cards,** *charts* (Gr. χάρτης, a leaf of paper; Lat. *charta;* Fr. *carte*).

> All the quarters that they know
> I' the shipman's *card.*—*Macbeth.*

Compared. See the parable, Matthew xiii.—**Apt** (Lat. *aptus,* fit), *adapted, fit.*—**Stem . . . foundation.** Rhetorically incorrect. Why?—**All this is.** Would *all these are* be better?—**Except,** *unless.*—**Importeth not much.** Modernize.—**Virgil.** The great Roman poet, who lived B. C. 70–20. The allusion is said to be to the seventh Eclogue, where Virgil says,

> "We care as little for the cold as the wolf for the number (of the flock)."

Arbela, a city of Assyria near the small river Zabatus (*Zab*), which is a tributary of the Tigris. In the plain of Gangamela, near Arbela, a decisive battle was fought between Alexander the Great and Darius, B. C. 331.—**Alexander** (B. C. 356–323), son of Philip. In the battle of Arbela he commanded forty thousand infantry and seven thousand cavalry; to which Darius opposed one million infantry and forty thousand cavalry.—**Tigranes,** the self-styled King of Kings, was son-in-law of Mithridates. He was defeated by the Roman general Lucullus, B. C. 69, near Tigranocerta, the capital, which Lucullus captured, with eight thousand talents in ready money. The student will do well to write out in detail the history of the events referred to in this paragraph, and to illustrate the point by more recent examples.

Yet are apt to be = yet are qualified to be = are, notwithstanding, fitted to be = are, nevertheless, adapted to be. Other grammatical equivalents?

Importeth not much. Give six equivalent expressions.

Pilfer the victory = snatch the victory by stealth. Other equivalents?

the sun set, he found them enow* to give him the chase, with infinite slaughter. Many are the examples of the great odds between number and courage: so that a man may truly make a judgment, that the principal point of greatness in any state is to have a race of military men. Neither is money the sinews of war, as it is trivially said, where the sinews of men's arms in base and effeminate people are failing; for Solon said well to Crœsus, when in ostentation he showed him his gold, "Sir, if any other come that hath better iron than you, he will be master of all this gold." Therefore, let any prince, or state, think soberly of his forces, except his militia of natives be of good and valiant soldiers; and let princes on the other side, that have subjects of martial disposition, know their own strength, unless they be otherwise wanting unto themselves. As for mercenary forces, (which is the help in this case,) all examples show that, whatsoever estate, or prince, doth rest upon them, he may spread his feathers for a time, but he will mew them soon after.

The blessing of Judah and Issachar will never meet; that the same people, or nation, should be both the lion's whelp and the ass between burdens; neither will it be, that a people overlaid with taxes should ever become valiant and martial. It is true, that taxes, levied by consent of the estate, do abate men's courage less; as it hath been seen notably in the excises of the Low Countries, and, in some degree, in the subsidies of England. For, you must note, that we speak now of the heart, and not of the purse: so that, although the same tribute and tax, laid by consent or by imposing, be all one to the purse, yet it works diversely upon the courage. So that you may conclude, that no people overcharged with tribute is fit for empire.

Let states, that aim at greatness, take heed how their nobility and gentlemen do multiply too fast; for that maketh the common subject grow to be a peasant and base swain, driven out of heart, and, in effect, but a gentleman's laborer. Even as you may see in coppice woods; if you leave your staddles too thick, you shall never have clean underwood, but shrubs and

---

* **Enow** (A. S. *genōh*, Ger. *genug*, enough), *enough*. *Enow* was formerly supposed to be a plural, but was not always such.—**Make a judgment.** Equivalent to what?—**Trivially** (Lat. *tres*, three; and *via*, way, road; *trivium*, a place where three roads meet; hence *trivial*, belonging to the cross-roads or street corners, common, vulgar), *commonly*, *tritely*.—**Solon** (died about 559 B. C.), the celebrated lawgiver of the Athenians, and one of the seven wise men of Greece.—**Crœsus**, the rich king of Lydia, born about 591 B. C. His name is a synonym for *rich man*.—**Soberly**, *moderately*.—**He showed him** *his*. etc. Note again the defect in the English language. See p. 89.—**Prince or state think soberly of his.** Note the use of *his* with *state*. Is it correct?—**Unless**, etc., *if they would not in other respects be found wanting*.—**The help in this case.** In *what* case?—**Spread his feathers . . mew them.** Explain this metaphor by paraphrasing it.—**Mew** (Fr. *muer*, from Lat. *mutare*, to change), *to shed feathers*, *molt*, *cast*.—**Judah**, etc. See Genesis xlix. 8–12, 14, 15.—**Low Countries.** Why called *low?* Meaning of *Netherlands?*—**Excises** (*ex*, out, off; *cædere*, to cut). What, in particular, are *excises? subsidies?* Could the English monarch tax the people without the consent of parliament?—**By imposing.** Name English monarchs that levied taxes without authority of parliament, and state the consequences.—**Empire**, *exercising imperial power over others*, *acquiring dominion*.—**Maketh . . . . grow . . . . driven.** Modernize.—**Coppice woods** (Fr. *couper*, to cut), *woods of small growth*, or consisting of underwood or brushwood cut at certain times for fuel or other purposes. **Staddles** (the root is in Ἵστημι, and Lat. *stare*, A. S. *stadhol*, Eng. *steady*), *anything that supports*; a small tree in a forest. In America a tree is called a staddle after it is three or four years old, and until it is six or eight inches in diameter.

Think soberly = entertain moderate views = be modest in his estimate. Other equivalents?
Hath been seen notably = hath been seen in a remarkable manner. Other equivalents?
It works diversely = it works differently = it has a different aspect. Six other equivalents?

7

bushes. So in countries, if the gentlemen* be too many, the commons will be base; and you will bring it to that, that not the hundredth poll will be fit for a helmet; especially as to the infantry, which is the nerve of an army: and so there will be great population and little strength. This which I speak of hath been no where better seen than by comparing of England and France; whereof England, though far less in territory and population, hath been, nevertheless, an overmatch; in regard the middle people of England make good soldiers, which the peasants of France do not. And herein the device of King Henry the Seventh, whereof I have spoken largely in the history of his life, was profound and admirable; in making farms and houses of husbandry of a standard; that is, maintained with such a proportion of land unto them as may breed a subject to live in convenient plenty, and no servile condition; and to keep the plough in the hands of the owners, and not mere hirelings. And thus indeed ye shall attain to Virgil's character, which he gives to ancient Italy:

"Terra potens armis atque ubere glebæ."

Neither is that state, which, for any thing I know, is almost peculiar to England, and hardly to be found any where else, except it be perhaps in Poland, to be passed over. I mean the state of free servants and attendants upon noblemen and gentlemen, which are no ways inferior unto the yeomanry for arms. And, therefore, out of all question, the splendor and magnificence, and great retinues, the hospitality of noblemen and gentlemen received into custom, do much conduce unto martial greatness: whereas, contrariwise, the close and reserved living of noblemen and gentlemen causeth a penury of military forces.

By all means it is to be procured, that the trunk of Nebuchadnezzar's tree of monarchy be great enough to bear the branches and the boughs; that is, that the natural subjects of the crown or state bear a sufficient proportion to the strange subjects that they govern. Therefore, all states that are liberal of naturalization towards strangers are fit for empire: for to think that a handful of people can, with the greatest courage and policy in the

* **Gentlemen** (Eng. *genteel; gens*, a family of respectability), *men of good family having coats of arms.*—**Poll** (Low Ger. *polle*, the head; D. *bol*, a ball), *the head.* Hence *poll-tax*, a tax levied on each head or man.—**In regard,** *because.*—**Henry VII.** (1485–1509). Bacon wrote the history of this king, and began that of Henry VIII.—**Proportion of land** (Lat. *pro*, before; *portio*, share). The order was "that all houses of husbandry that were used with twenty acres of ground and upward, should be maintained and kept up for ever," etc. His object was to increase and perpetuate the great "middle class." Of this class were nearly all of Cromwell's best soldiers; but the independent yeomanry of England have now nearly disappeared.—**Virgil,** the celebrated Latin poet, author of the Æneid, Georgics, etc. See p. 96.—**Terra,** etc. *A land powerful by (reason of) arms and richness of soil.*—**State.** This word may here mean *class* or *order.*—**Great retinues** (Lat. *retinere;* Fr. *retenir*, to retain; hence *retinue*, a body of retainers, or men engaged to follow a prince or other distinguished person). It is said that Elizabeth would not permit any nobleman to retain more than a hundred followers; but her own retinue sometimes required twenty-four thousand horses for transportation. See Scott's *Kenilworth.*—**Received into custom,** *established as a custom.*—**Procured.** Modernize.—**Free of monarchy.** See Daniel iv.—**Strange subjects** (see *strange*, p. 62). Modernize.—**Fit for empire,** *fit for gaining and keeping dominion.*—**Policy** (πολιτεία, system of state management), *wisdom in state management.*

In regard = for the reason that = owing to the fact that = because. Other equivalents?

Neither is that state . . . . to be passed over = neither is that order (of men) . . . . to be omitted. Give ten equivalents, and select the best expression among them.

It is to be procured = it is to be contrived = it must be brought about = care must be taken. Other equivalents?

world, embrace* too large extent of dominion, it may hold for a time, but it will fail suddenly. The Spartans were a nice people in point of naturalization: whereby, while they kept their compass, they stood firm; but when they did spread, and their boughs were become too great for their stem, they became a windfall upon the sudden. Never any state was, in this point, so open to receive strangers into their body as were the Romans. Therefore it sorted with them accordingly, for they grew to the greatest monarchy. Their manner was to grant naturalization, which they called "jus civitatis," and to grant it in the highest degree; that is, not only "jus commercii, jus connubii, jus hæreditatis," but also "jus suffragii," and "jus honorum;" and this not to singular persons alone, but likewise to whole families; yea, to cities, and sometimes to nations. Add to this their custom of plantation of colonies, whereby the Roman plant was removed into the soil of other nations; and, putting both constitutions together, you will say, that it was not the Romans that spread upon the world, but it was the world that spread upon the Romans; and that was the sure way of greatness. I have marvelled sometimes at Spain, how they clasp and contain so large dominions with so few natural Spaniards. But sure the whole compass of Spain is a very great body of a tree, far above Rome and Sparta at the first. And, besides, though they have not had that usage to naturalize liberally, yet they have that which is next to it; that is, to employ, almost indifferently, all nations in their militia of ordinary soldiers; yea, and sometimes in their highest commands. Nay, it seemeth, at this instant, they are sensible of this want of natives; as by the pragmatical sanction, now published, appeareth.

It is certain, that sedentary and within-door arts, and delicate manufactures that require rather the finger than the arms, have in their nature a contrariety to a military disposition; and, generally, all warlike people are a little idle, and love danger better than travail. Neither must they be too much broken of it, if they shall be preserved in vigor. Therefore, it was great advantage in the ancient states of Sparta, Athens, Rome, and others, that they had the use of slaves, which commonly did rid those manufactures.

---

* **Embrace** (Fr. *en*, in; *bras*, arm; Lat. *brachium*, arm), *hold in their grasp.*—**It may hold, it** (*i. e.*, this opinion) *may prove true.*—**Nice,** *fastidious.*—**Compass** (Lat. *compassus*, a stepping together, circle; fr. *con-*, together; *passus*, a step), *circuit, moderate bounds.* Now obsolete in this sense.—**Windfall** (fruit blown down, or the tree itself blown down).—**Body** (politic).—**Sorted** (Lat. *sors*, a lot), *suited, succeeded, happened.*—**Jus civitatis,** *right of citizenship.*—**Jus commercii,** etc., *right of trading, right of marriage, right of inheritance, right of voting, right of honors* (*i. e.*, of holding office).—**Singular,** *single.* Obsolete?—**Constitutions,** *fundamental laws or usages, settled arrangements.*—**They clasp.** They?—**Contain,** *comprehend within their limits.*—**Natural Spaniards,** *native Spaniards.*—**That usage to.** Modernize.—**Pragmatical sanction,** a solemn ordinance established by the supreme power of a state upon weighty matters. Does Bacon refer to the most celebrated of these, the one issued by Charles VII. of France A. D. 1438, which was the foundation of the liberties of the Gallican Church, or to a more recent decree?—**Travail** (Fr. *travailler*, to labor; Sp. *trabar*, to check; Lat. *trabs*, a beam), *work, labor.*—**Broken of it.** Modernize.—**Which commonly,** etc., *who commonly cleared those manufactures out of the way* (of the fighting men).

The Spartans were a nice people = the Lacedæmonians were a fastidious people = the Spartans were hard to please. Other equivalents? Select the best expression to convey the sense.

Therefore it sorted with them accordingly = therefore it fared with them in a corresponding degree = therefore they succeeded proportionally. Other equivalents?

Not to singular persons = not to individuals. Other equivalents?

Love danger better than travail = love peril rather than toil. Other equivalents?

Which commonly did rid = who, as a general thing, dispatched. Other equivalents?

But that is abolished,* in greatest part, by the Christian law. That which cometh nearest to it is to leave those arts chiefly to strangers, which, for that purpose, are the more easily to be received, and to contain the principal bulk of the vulgar natives within those three kinds; tillers of the ground, free servants, and handicraftsmen of strong and manly arts, as smiths, masons, carpenters, etc., not reckoning professed soldiers.

But, above all, for empire and greatness, it importeth most, that a nation do profess arms as their principal honor, study, and occupation. For the things which we formerly have spoken of, are but habilitations towards arms; and what is habilitation without intention and act? Romulus, after his death, as they report or feign, sent a present to the Romans, that above all they should intend arms, and then they should prove the greatest empire of the world. The fabric of the state of Sparta was wholly, though not wisely, framed and composed to that scope and end. The Persians and Macedonians had it for a flash. The Gauls, Germans, Goths, Saxons, Normans, and others, had it for a time. The Turks have it at this day, though in great declination. Of Christian Europe, they that have it are, in effect, only the Spaniards. But it is so plain, that every man profiteth in that he most intendeth, that it needeth not to be stood upon. It is enough to point at it, that no nation, which doth not directly profess arms, may look to have greatness fall into their mouths. And, on the other side, it is a most certain oracle of time, that those states that continue long in that profession, as the Romans and Turks principally have done, do wonders; and those that have professed arms but for an age have, notwithstanding, commonly attained that greatness in that age which maintained them long after, when their profession and exercise of arms hath grown to decay.

Incident to this point is for a state to have those laws or customs which may reach forth unto them just occasions, as may be pretended, of war; for there is that justice imprinted in the nature of men, that they enter not upon wars, whereof so many calamities do ensue, but upon some, at the least,

---

* **That is abolished.** What?—**Which** (who) **for that purpose.** What purpose? —**Contain** (Lat. *con-*, together; *tenere*, to hold). *keep.*—**Vulgar** (Lat. *vulgus*, common people), *ordinary*, *common.*—**Importeth.** Modernize.—**Habilitations** (Lat. *habilis*, fit; fr. *habere*, to hold), *qualifications.*—**Intention** (Lat. *intendere*, to stretch on), *a stretching of the mind*, *earnest attention.*—**Present,** *a mandate*, *command.* The word is rarely found in this sense.—**Intend arms,** *bend their energies to war.* Military supremacy was the darling object of ambition to the Romans. See Æneid, VI., 848–855.—**For a flash,** *momentarily.*—**Profiteth,** *succeeds.*—**Intendeth,** *strives after.*—**Stood upon.** Modernize. —**Profess arms.** Equivalent to what?—**Fall into their mouths.** Equivalent?—**Oracle** (Lat. *orare*, to speak; fr. *os*, *oris*, the mouth), *divine utterance; wise and weighty decision.* What and where were the most famous oracles of antiquity?—**Grown to decay,** *fallen into decay.* Does the present condition of France, Turkey, or Spain, tend to confirm Bacon's argument? Does he not ignore the power of public opinion and the influence of Christianity?—**Incident to,** *appertaining to.*—**As may be pretended.** This doctrine is worthy of Machiavel or of Themistocles, not of Bacon. It would appear from this passage, and from much of his conduct, that he really believed the end to justify the means.

Habilitations towards arms = qualifications for a military life. Other equivalents? In all these cases where equivalent expressions are called for, the instructor will do well to insist on a judicious selection of the best.

Sent a present = sent a command. Other equivalents? "Know all men by these *presents*," is the law phraseology, the substance of which, in almost the same terms, is given by Shakespeare. The Latin is *literas presentes*, i. e., present letters.

Intend arms = pay attention to arms. Other grammatical equivalents?

As may be pretended = as may be put forward = as may be assigned for pretexts Other equivalents?

specious, grounds and quarrels.* The Turk hath at hand, for cause of war, the propagation of his law or sect, a quarrel that he may always command. The Romans—though they esteemed the extending the limits of their empire to be great honor to their generals when it was done, yet they never rested upon that alone to begin a war. First, therefore, let nations that pretend to greatness have this, that they be sensible of wrongs, either upon borderers, merchants, or politic ministers; and that they sit not too long upon a provocation. Secondly, let them be prest and ready to give aids and succors to their confederates, as it ever was with the Romans: insomuch as if the confederates had leagues defensive with divers other states, and, upon invasion offered, did implore their aids severally, yet the Romans would ever be the foremost, and leave it to none other to have the honor. As for the wars, which were anciently made on the behalf of a kind of party, or tacit conformity of state, I do not see how they may be well justified: as, when the Romans made a war for the liberty of Græcia; or, when the Lacedæmonians and Athenians made war to set up or pull down democracies or oligarchies; or, when wars were made by foreigners, under the pretence of justice or protection, to deliver the subjects of others from tyranny and oppression, and the like. Let it suffice, that no estate expect to be great, that is not awake upon any just occasion of arming.

No body can be healthful without exercise, neither natural body nor politic; and, certainly, to a kingdom, or estate, a just and honorable war is the true exercise. A civil war, indeed, is like the heat of a fever; but a foreign war is like the heat of exercise, and serveth to keep the body in health. For, in slothful peace, both courages will effeminate, and manners corrupt. But howsoever it be for happiness, without all question for greatness it maketh to be still for the most part in arms; and the strength of a veteran army (though it be a chargeable business), always on foot, is that which commonly giveth the law; or, at least, the reputation amongst all neighbor states, as may be well seen in Spain; which hath had, in one part or other, a veteran army almost continually, now by the space of six score years.

---

* **Quarrels,** *causes of dispute, grounds of hostility.* See the word *quarrel* in Bacon's Essa on Marriage and Single Life, p. 95. How far below Milton's is Bacon's conception of true greatness! "A state ought to be but as one huge Christian personage, one mighty growth and stature of an honest man, as big and compact in virtue as in body!" But Bacon's notions of morality and duty in some other respects never rose to the Christian standard.—**His law,** the doctrine of the Koran.—**Quarrel,** *cause of war.* See the Index.—**The extending** (of) **the limits.** "*The*" must be used before, and "*of*" after the participial noun, or both must be omitted. —**Have this.** This what?—**Politic,** *political. Politic ministers* are ambassadors, diplomatists, ministers of state.—**Sit not too long.** Meaning?—**Prest** (Fr. *prêt;* Lat. *præstus,* ready), *prompt.*—**As if the confederates,** *that if the confederates.*—**On the behalf,** etc., in favor of a political party, or for the sake of securing a *tacit* (*i. e.,* not openly avowed) correspondence in the form of the government.—**Græcia** (A. S. *Grec;* Lat. *Græcia*), *Greece.* So in Daniel viii. 21.—**Others,** *other governments.*—**Effeminate,** *grow womanish or weak.*—**Corrupt,** *become impure.*—**It maketh,** *it profits, makes for a nation's advantage.* See *make,* Index.—**Still** (A. S. *stille,* quietly), *continually.*—**Chargeable** (Lat. *carrus,* a cart; W. *cart;* A. S. *craet;* Fr. *charger,* to load; whence *cargo,*) *costly.*—**Reputation** (of being law-giver?)

A quarrel that he may always command. Equivalents?
Let them be prest = let them be prompt. Other equivalents?
Both courages will effeminate, and manners corrupt = what?
By the space of = what? See in Acts xx. 31, "By the space of three years I ceased," etc.

To be master of the sea is an abridgment of a monarchy. Cicero, writing to Atticus of Pompey's preparation against Cæsar, saith, "Consilium Pompeii plane Themistocleum est; putat enim, qui mari potitur, eum rerum potiri;" and, without doubt, Pompey had tired out Cæsar, if upon vain confidence he had not left that way. We see the great effects of battles by sea: the battle of Actium decided the empire of the world; the battle of Lepanto arrested the greatness of the Turk. There be many examples, where sea fights have been final to the war; but this is when princes, or states, have set up their rest upon the battles. But thus much is certain, that he that commands the sea is at great liberty, and may take as much and as little of the war as he will; whereas, those that be strongest by land are many times, nevertheless, in great straits. Surely, at this day, with us of Europe, the vantage of strength at sea, which is one of the principal dowries of this kingdom of Great Britain, is great; both because most of the kingdoms of Europe are not merely inland, but girt with the sea most part of their compass; and because the wealth of both Indies seems, in great part, but an accessory to the command of the seas.

The wars of later ages seem to be made in the dark, in respect of the glory and honor which reflected upon men from the wars in ancient time. There be now, for martial encouragement, some degress and orders of chivalry, which, nevertheless, are conferred promiscuously upon soldiers and no soldiers, and some remembrance perhaps upon the escutcheon, and some hospitals for maimed soldiers, and such like things. But, in ancient times, the trophies erected upon the place of the victory; the funeral laudatives and monuments for those that died in the wars; the crowns and garlands personal; the style of emperor, which the great kings of the world after borrowed; the triumphs of the generals upon their return; the great donatives and largesses upon the disbanding of the armies,—were things able to inflame all men's courages. But, above all, that of the *triumph* amongst the Romans was not pageants, or gaudery, but one of the wisest and noblest institutions that ever was. For it contained three things; honor to the general,

---

* **Abridgment** (Fr. *abréger*, to abbreviate; Lat. *brevis*), *compact form.* — **Cicero** (B. C. 107-43), the most celebrated of the Roman orators. — **Atticus,** friend and correspondent of Cicero. He committed suicide by starvation, B. C. 33.—**Pompey's** (B. C. 106-48). In some editions *Pompey's* is printed *Pompey his.* The old mode of indicating the possessive by adding *his*, appears to have originated in a blunder. The apostrophe with *s* comes from the old genitive (pos.) termination *es* (*is* or *ys*). The *e* being dropped the apostrophe takes its place, and the *s* is retained.—**Consilium,** etc. 'The plan of Pompey is clearly that of Themistocles; for he thinks that whoever is master of the sea is master of the world.'—**Actium,** a small promontory at the entrance of the Ambracian (modern *Arta*) gulf, famous for the decisive naval battle between Augustus and Mark Antony, B. C. 31.—**Lepanto,** a seaport town of Greece on the north coast of the Gulf of Lepanto. In this gulf the Turkish fleet was annihilated, A. D. 1571, by the combined fleets of the Christian states of the Mediterranean under Don John of Austria.—**That be strongest.** Note the frequent use of *be* for *are*, by the old writers.—**Final to the war.** Modernize.—**Set up their rest.** Meaning?—**Vantage,** *advantage.*—**Merely** (A. S. *mære*, pure, unmixed; Lat. *merus*), *completely.*—**Compass,** *circuit.* See Index.—**Degrees,** *titles of distinction.*—**Escutcheon** (Lat. *scutum*, a leather shield; Fr. *écu*), *coat of arms.*—**Laudatives,** *panegyrics.*—**Style,** *designation, title.*—**Triumphs,** *magnificent parades.* See Index. Describe a Roman 'triumph.'—**Donatives,** *gifts.*—**Pageants** (A. S. *pæcean*, to deceive by false appearances), *pompous display.*—**Gaudery** (Lat. *gaudium*, joy), *ostentatious finery, gauds.*

Are not merely inland = are not completely inland. Other equivalents?
Funeral laudatives = funeral eulogies = panegyrics. Other equivalents?

riches to the treasury out of the spoils, and donatives to the army. But that honor, perhaps, were not fit for monarchies, except it be* in the person of the monarch himself, or his sons; as it came to pass in the times of the Roman emperors, who did impropriate the actual triumphs to themselves and their sons, for such wars as they did achieve in person, and left only, for wars achieved by subjects, some triumphal garments and ensigns to the general.

To conclude: no man can, by care-taking, as the Scripture saith, "add a cubit to his stature," in this little model of a man's body. But in the great frame of kingdoms and commonwealths, it is in the power of princes, or estates, to add amplitude and greatness to their kingdoms. For, by introducing such ordinances, constitutions, and customs, as we have now touched, they may sow greatness to their posterity and succession. But these things are commonly not observed, but left to take their chance.

---

* **Except it be.** Equivalent?—**Impropriate,** *appropriate, assume* as one's own.—**Care-taking.** "Which of you with *taking thought,* can add to his stature one cubit?" Matt. vi., 27; Luke xii., 25.—**Touched** (upon), *treated of briefly.*

Who did impropriate = who appropriated. Other equivalents?
As we have now touched = as we have now slightly treated of. Other equivalents?

As with the preceding essays, the student will do well to write out the leading thoughts, and recast them in the form of one or more essays. Write an argument to confirm or refute any of the doctrines here advanced by Bacon. Make citations from *modern* history to illustrate or overthrow them. Compare the concentration of thought and language in Bacon with the diffusiveness of Spenser. Set forth in writing your views of true national greatness. Write an essay on Bacon's moral character, as far as it may be inferred from these essays that we have read. Write another on his intellectual power as evinced therein. Write separate sketches of his life at different periods, as in youth, in early manhood, in middle age, while chancellor, and after retirement from active business. Has Macaulay treated him fairly? What can you say of the Baconian philosophy?

WILLIAM SHAKESPEARE.

1564–1616.

NOTWITHSTANDING the investigations of scores of scholars and antiquarians, little is known of the early life of Shakespeare. No history records the successive steps by which he rose from the lowest depths of poverty and obscurity to the loftiest summits of intellect and fame.

His parents were illiterate, rarely, if ever, writing a word, but content to make their mark when called on for their signatures to any paper. His mother's name was Arden, a surname adopted by the Turchills, a family of some note that traced their lineage beyond the Norman conquest. Shakespeare is an old Warwickshire word. Lowell thinks that "one lobe of William's brain was Normanly refined, and the other Saxonly sagacious;" but other scholars will have it that he was purely Saxon. If we may confide in the accuracy of the painter of his bust, which had been colored to the life before Edmund Malone stultified himself by whitening it in imitation of marble, his eyes were of a light hazel color, his complexion fair, and his hair and beard auburn.

His mother had inherited some property. His father was a man of business; at various times, or perhaps all at once, farmer, wool-comber, butcher, and glover. In the little world of Stratford, he held successively the offices of "ale-taster," bailiff, justice of the peace, and chief alderman. At the age of thirteen, William found himself the oldest of thirteen living children, two sisters, born before him, having died in infancy.

In the Stratford free grammar-school, open to William at the age of seven, he probably acquired some knowledge of Latin and Greek, in addition to the common English branches. His extraordinary vocabulary, far surpassing in fullness and accuracy that of any other writer in any age, proves him to have been a most diligent student of language; while his learning in metaphysics, literature, logic, art, law, medicine, navigation, history, politics, mythology, shows him unequalled in keenness of observation, and in power of acquiring, classifying, and assimilating.

Doubtless the first twelve years of his life passed happily enough amid the comfort and respectability of home. But clouds now gathered. The little property which William's mother had brought her husband, was slowly dissipated. Unable to support his growing family, the father sank deeper and deeper in poverty. Though nominally an alderman, he for seven years dared not attend the meetings of the board, for fear of being arrested for debt. Skulking and hiding from constables, he was at length seized in 1587 and lodged in debtor's jail.

The distress of this once proud and respectable family must have been terrible. Mother and younger children naturally looked to the oldest boy, bright, strong, brave William, just entering manhood. Who knows but that the agonies of those nearest and dearest to him wrought in his sensitive spirit a determination to conquer all obstacles, and lift the family out of suffering and disgrace? The prodigious intellectual energies that he afterwards exhibited, must have had some great impelling force behind them, holding him to his work as with a giant's strength. Here may have been the source of his inspiration.

WILLIAM SHAKESPEARE.

Traditions, seemingly well-founded, show that William was withdrawn from school in consequence of his father's reverses, and apprenticed to a butcher. Old Aubrey says, "When he killed a calf, he would do it in high style and make a speech"! Very likely. No distress could check the buoyancy of so elastic a spirit. The torrent, dammed by temporary obstacles, becomes irresistible. I recognize in Shakespeare, as in most men of the highest genius, a singular force and intensity. More than any other writer, he loads words with meaning till they sink under the weight; vivifies nouns into verbs; injects his fiery emotion, incapable of cooling, through the rifts of granitic thought; vitalizes and incarnates the shadows of fiction, till no historic characters seem so real.

Yet one blunder, great and almost fatal, stands out in bold relief. At eighteen, having no visible means of supporting a family, he marries Anne Hathaway, a woman of twenty-six. Before he is twenty-one, three little Shakespeares are crying for bread!

To these embarrassments, which would have driven a small man to despair, a bad man to crime, a great man to sublime effort, there was added a yet deeper shadow. His marriage brought him little comfort. At twenty-one, or thereabouts, he quitted his wife, and for many years afterwards he rarely or never visited her. Do we have a casual negative hint of his home-misery in *Twelfth Night?*

> "Let still the woman take
> An elder than herself: so wears she to him;
> So sways she level in her husband's heart."

However this may be, in his last will and testament he omits all mention of his wife at first, and finally, on second thought, interlines this "item," "*I give unto my wife my second best bed.*" It is sad to lift the veil that hides this woe; but all mankind are probably the gainers. The love of this great soul, that might have blessed her alone, went to the drama instead.

> "You have a wife already whom you love,
> Your social theory,"

says Aurora Leigh. Shakespeare was married, not to a woman, but "to immortal verse."

We are told by tradition that young Shakespeare became a school-master, a statement not likely to have been a sheer fabrication. Unfavorable rumors of one's conduct are easily generated, usually exaggerated, willingly believed, and safely transmitted to posterity. Not so with the good which men do. Alas, we do not like to hear Aristides called "The Just!" We hug the aphorism, "No man is wholly good, or wholly bad," for it brings down the lofty, and perhaps lifts us. But how could a report that Shakespeare was a school-master originate and gain credence in Warwickshire, unless founded on fact? "He understood Latin pretty well, for he had been many years a school-master in the country," says Aubrey. Some confirmation may be found in the prominence which Shakespeare gives to school exercises, and in the marvellous fluency with which he uses those words and illustrations which are the stock-in-trade of Latin school-masters.

But the hum of pedagogy by day, or the monotony of hard study by night in a room where three babes exercise their musical prerogatives unquestioned, is dull experience for a youth conscious of gigantic powers and determined to scale the highest heaven of thought. The bow forever bent will either break, or lose its elasticity. As he had probably been inveigled into matrimony, he is supposed by White and other critics to have been drawn by some of his wild companions into the robbery of Sir Thomas Lucy's deer park, three miles from Stratford. Caught in the act, William and his young fellow-poachers show fight. The story runs that they were arrested for the trespass, and that William was obliged to leave town. The first scene in *Merry Wives of Windsor* is supposed to be partially founded on this incident.

We find him next in London; but for several years his history is a blank. Tradition fills it with vague reports of his joining the theatre, at first in a very humble capacity. It may have been.

After seven or eight years from the time of his arrival in the metropolis, he publishes what he styles "The first heir of my invention," the poem called *Venus and Adonis.* Brilliant and beautiful as much of it is, he should have burnt it; for "the trail of the serpent" is over it all. It ministers to the lowest appetite. A year later he publishes his second long poem, *The Rape of Lucrece,* dedicated to the same patron, Henry Wriothesly, Earl of Southampton, in language of remarkable significance: "What I have done is yours; what I have to do is yours; being part in all I have devoted yours." The tradition is that Southampton had presented him a thousand pounds.

About this time we find him joint owner in the new Globe Theatre, perhaps investing here the money that the earl had given or loaned him. In 1594, too, the greatest of then living poets, Edmund Spenser, names him with high commendation, and speaks of the heroic sound of his warrior name, the only recognition of him by any illustrious contemporary, if we except Ben Jonson's encomium written many years after Shakespeare's death. Spenser's lines are,

"And then, though last, not least is Ætion.
A gentler shepherd may nowhere be found;
Whose name, full of high thought's invention,
Doth like himself heroically sound."

This seems the place to mention his one hundred and fifty-four sonnets, though some of them were evidently written later in life. It is difficult, in reading them, to avoid the impression of a mysterious and profound sorrow, possessing his whole being. They contain few aspirations after anything noble; but there are vivid pictures of earthly love, strange flashes of ambition, a boundless exuberance of fancy, sublime premonitions of immortality; and revelations, too, it must be confessed, of conduct not creditable to any man's moral character. All of them are of love, and all of them could well have been omitted without damage to his fame.

He now (1587) entered upon his threefold career of dramatic author, actor, and manager. He wrote, or re-wrote (from 1587 to 1613), for it is not certain that he wholly originated any one of his plays, fourteen comedies, eleven tragedies, and ten histories.*

As to the seeds and sources of these plays, we find five comedies, *Taming of the Shrew*, *Merchant of Venice*, *All's Well that Ends Well*, *Much Ado About Nothing*, and *Measure for Measure*, Italian; two, *Comedy of Errors* and *Twelfth Night*, classical; two, *Midsummer Night's Dream*, and *As You Like It*, mediæval; one, *Two Gentlemen of Verona*, Spanish; one, *Merry Wives of Windsor*, English; one, *Love's Labor's Lost*, probably French; two, *Winter's Tale* and *Tempest*, unknown. We find, among the tragedies, four, *Timon of Athens*, *Coriolanus*, *Julius Cæsar*, and *Antony and Cleopatra*, classical; two, *Romeo and Juliet* and *Othello*, Italian; two, *Hamlet* and *Troilus and Cressida*, mediæval; three, *Cymbeline*, *Lear*, and *Macbeth*, from the legendary history of Britain. The ten histories are called by the names of the English kings, *Henry IV.* (Parts I. and II.), *Henry V.*, *Henry VI.* (Parts I., II., III.), *King John*, *Richard II.*, *Richard III.*, and *Henry VIII.*

His earliest plays were probably *Love's Labor's Lost*, *Comedy of Errors*, and *Two Gentlemen of Verona*. Between these youthful productions and the fruits of his maturer genius, an amazing progress is evident. *Hamlet*, written in or about the year 1600, may be taken as the dividing point between the first half and the last half of his dramas. Composed at the age at which Milton wrote his *Areopagitica*, it may be con-

* I omit *Pericles* and *Titus Andronicus.*

sidered, like the latter, as a peculiarly representative piece. *Midsummer Night's Dream* and *Merchant of Venice*, the two most popular of his comedies, came before *Hamlet; Macbeth* and *Lear*, the two sublimest of his tragedies, after it.

The struggles and distresses of his early years had taught him, most impressively, the value of money, and it is pretty clear that the lesson was not forgotten. Records exist of lawsuits brought by him to collect petty debts, even while he was growing rich. In 1602, he purchases one hundred and seven acres of land in Old Stratford. In 1605, he buys the moiety of a lease of all the tithes in Stratford, Old Stratford, Bishopton, and Welcombe, paying therefor £440.

Between 1610 and 1612, he resumed his residence at Stratford. Once or twice afterwards he visited London for a few days. On the twenty-fifth of March, 1616, he executed his will. On the twenty-third of the following April, probably the anniversary of his birth, he breathed his last. Of the cause of his death we have only a feeble tradition, recorded half a century after his death by John Ward, A. M., vicar of Stratford. Ward's language is, "Shakespeare, Drayton, and Ben Jonson had a merry-meeting, and, it seems, drank too hard; for Shakespeare died of a fever then contracted." We can hardly bring ourselves to believe that he fell a victim to intemperance, though such a catastrophe has befallen many a lesser genius.

By common consent his is one of the greatest names in literature. We recognize the following points in his intellectual supremacy:

1. His profound philosophical insight; his knowledge of human nature enabling him to seize unerringly upon the governing principle or master passion of a man or class of men.*

2. The creativeness of his imagination; exemplified in the multitude of striking characters, embodiments of the laws his intuition has detected. He names more than a thousand, each of whom expresses the thought or sentiment in fitting language and conduct.

3. The skillful grouping of characters, arrangement of scenes, construction and development of plots.

4. His style; that marvellous copiousness and felicity of speech, whereby is brought down to our midst the Shakespearian world, as perceived by an eye at once telescopic and microscopic, by an ear keenly sensitive to all harmonies and discords, by a mind at once the most piercing and the most comprehensive, by a heart tenderer than a mother's, yet stouter than that of Leonidas.

5. His wit and humor. Falstaff is the most comic character ever invented; yet he is but one of a multitude.

6. His power of portraying deep emotion. Others may have equalled him in single instances, but their successes in this particular are few to his.

Yet Shakespeare was but a half man, rarely looking beyond the uses of the theatre. Prince of dramatists, master of the revels to all mankind, chief caterer to human amusement—this is something: it is even noble. But it is not enough. Great intellectual, moral, and political movements are in progress in England and on the Continent during the whole of his career. Shall not the most consummate of artists play the man? Shall the foremost intellect of the race be insignificant in action and loose in conduct? see nothing but from the stand-point of his theatre? say nothing but as an actor on the stage? do nothing to lead the struggling millions to a higher life? But let us not judge hastily. We may be pardoned for the perhaps excessive charity of believing that, if his days had been prolonged, he would have atoned for the indifference or idleness of the past. Cut off suddenly at the age of fifty-two, what plans for human improvement may not have been buried with him! Given thirty years more,

* We must not, however, look to him for portraits that are in exact accordance with historical facts. His *Julius Cæsar*, for example, is a caricature.

he might have shown himself as sublime in action as in thought. We have here his own explicit declaration that the life of a trifler was distasteful to him:

"Alas! 'tis true I have gone here and there
And made myself a motley to the view,
Gored mine own thoughts, sold cheap what is most dear,
Made old offenses of affections new.
Most true it is that I have looked on truth
Askance and strangely . . . .

"Oh, for my sake do you with Fortune chide,
The guilty goddess of my harmful deeds,
That did not better for my life provide
Than public means which public manners breeds!
Thence comes it that my name receives a brand,
And almost thence my nature is subdued
To what it works in, like the dyer's hand!"

It is said that there have been published upwards of two thousand works treating of Shakespeare and his plays. Among them, consult White's *Shakespeare*, vol. 1; Drake's *Shakespeare and his Times;* Lowell's *Shakespeare Once More;* Hazlitt's *Characters of Shakespeare's Plays;* Whipple's *Lectures* and *Essays;* Johnson's *Preface to Shakespeare;* De Quincey's Essay on *Shakespeare* in the Encyclopedia Britannica; Campbell's *Essay on English Poetry;* Hudson's *Shakespeare;* Richardson's *Analysis of Shakespeare;* Stearns's *Shakespeare Treasury of Wit and Wisdom;* Mrs. Jameson's *Characteristics of Shakespeare's Women;* Schlegel's *Lectures on Dramatic Literature;* Pope's *Preface* to his edition of Shakespeare; Reed's *Lectures;* Price's *Wisdom and Genius of Shakespeare;* Emerson's *Shakespeare* in his *Representative Men.* See also the various works on English Literature cited at the close of our sketch of Spenser, p. 69. Let the student collect other facts in regard to Shakespeare.

MACBETH.

"Since *The Furies* of Æschylus nothing so grand and terrible has ever been composed. The Witches, it is true, are not divine Eumenides, and are not intended to be so; they are ignoble and vulgar instruments of hell. They discourse with one another like women of the very lowest class; for this was the class to which witches were supposed to belong. When, however, they address Macbeth, their tone assumes more elevation; their predictions have all the obscurity, the majestic solemnity, by which oracles have in all times contrived to inspire mortals with reverential awe. We here see that the witches are merely instruments; they are governed by an invisible spirit, or the operation of such great and dreadful events would be above their sphere. . . .

"Macbeth is an ambitious but noble hero, who yields to a deep-laid hellish temptation; and all the crimes to which he is impelled by necessity, to secure the fruits of his first crime, cannot altogether eradicate in him the stamp of native heroism. . . . . . In every feature we see a vigorous heroic age in the hardy North, which steels every nerve. The precise duration of the action cannot be ascertained; years, perhaps, according to the story; but we know that, to the imagination, the most crowded time appears to be the shortest. Here we can hardly conceive how so very much can be compressed into so narrow a space. Not merely external events, the very innermost recesses of the minds of the persons of the drama are laid open to us. It is as if the drags were taken from the wheels of time, and they rolled along without interruption in their descent. Nothing can equal the power of this picture in the excitation of horror. We need only allude to the circumstances attending the murder of Duncan, the dagger that hovers before the eyes of Macbeth, the vision of Banquo at the feast, the madness of Lady Macbeth;—what can we possibly say that will not weaken the impression? Such scenes stand alone, and are to be found only in this poet. Otherwise the tragic Muse might exchange her mask for the head of Medusa."—*Lectures on Dramatic Literature*, by A. W. Schlegel.

MACBETH.

PERSONS REPRESENTED.

DUNCAN, *King of* Scotland.
MALCOLM, DONALBAIN, } *his Sons.*
MACBETH, BANQUO, } *Generals of the King's Army.*
MACDUFF, LENOX, ROSSE, MONTEITH, ANGUS, CATHNESS, } *Noblemen of* Scotland.
FLEANCE, *Son to* Banquo.
SIWARD, *Earl of* Northumberland, *General of the English forces.*
YOUNG SIWARD, *his Son.*
SEYTON, *an Officer attending on* Macbeth.
Son to Macduff.
An English Doctor. A Scotch Doctor.
A Soldier. A Porter. An old Man.
LADY MACBETH.
LADY MACDUFF.
Gentlewoman *attending on* Lady Macbeth.
HECATE, *and* Witches.
Lords, Gentlemen, Officers, Soldiers, Murderers, Attendants, *and* Messengers.
The Ghost of Banquo, *and several other* Apparitions.

SCENE—*In the end of the Fourth Act, lies in* England; *through the rest of the play, in* Scotland, *and, chiefly, at* Macbeth's *Castle.*

ACT I.

SCENE I. *An open place.*

Thunder and lightning. Enter three Witches.

1st Witch. When shall we three meet again,
In thunder,* lightning, or in rain?
2d Witch. When the hurly-burly's done,
When the battle's lost and won.
3d Witch. That will be ere set of sun.
1st Witch. Where the place?
2d Witch. Upon the heath,
3d Witch. There to meet with Macbeth.
1st Witch. I come, Graymalkin!
All. Paddock calls:—Anon.
Fair is foul, and foul is fair:
Hover through the fog and filthy air. [Witches *vanish.*

* **Thunder** (A. S. *thunor;* D. *donder;* Ger. *donner;* Lat. *tonitru*, by Grimm's Law, Eng. *thunder;* Lat. *ton-are*, to thunder). The question appears to be not, "In *which* of the three, thunder, lightning, or rain, shall we meet?" but, "When shall we meet again in threatening or stormy weather?"—**Hurly-burly.** This word is formed by *onomatopœia*, which is thus defined by Peacham in 1577: "*Onomatopœia*, when we invent, devise, fayne, and make a name imitating the sound of that it signifieth; as *hurly-burly*, for an *uproar* or *tumultuous stir.*" Here it means the din of battle. See *Onomatopœia* in the treatises on Rhetoric.—**Heath** (A. S. *hädh*, Ger. and D. *heide*, heath, an evergreen shrub), a *place* overgrown with heath. Hence *heathen*, originally a dweller on the heath. Christianity having become established in *cities* sooner than in the *country*, the dwellers on the heath, or *heathen*, were still unbelievers; and so the word *heathen* came to have an opprobrious sense.—**Graymalkin** (or *Grimalkin*, fr. Fr. *gris*, gray), a common name for a *cat. Malkin* (pronounced *mawkin*) is from *Mary* and the diminutive ending *-kin*, which originally meant *child*, allied to Lat. *genus*, birth, race; as *manikin*, little man; *malkin*, little Mary. "Cats played an important part in witchcraft." *White.*—**Paddock** (A. S. *padde*, D. *pad*, a toad). One witch appears to have had some point of resemblance to a cat; perhaps in voice. For a like reason another is called "Paddock," or toad.—**Fair is foul,** etc. Fair weather is foul for witches, and *vice versa.*

SCENE II. *A Camp near* Forres.*

Alarum within. Enter King DUNCAN, MALCOLM, DONALBAIN, LENOX, *with* Attendants, *meeting a bleeding* Soldier.

Dun. What bloody man is that? He can report,
As seemeth by his plight, of the revolt
The newest state.
Mal. This is the sergeant,
Who, like a good and hardy soldier, fought
'Gainst my captivity. Hail, brave friend!
Say to the king thy knowledge of the broil,
As thou didst leave it.
Sold. Doubtful it stood;
As two spent swimmers, that do cling together,
And choke their art. The merciless Macdonwald
(Worthy to be a rebel, for to that
The multiplying villanies of nature
Do swarm upon him) from the Western Isles,
Of Kernes and Gallowglasses is supplied;
And Fortune, on his damned quarry smiling,
Show'd like a rebel's [——]. But all's too weak:
For brave Macbeth (well he deserves that name!)
Disdaining Fortune, with his brandished steel,
Which smoked with bloody execution,
Like Valor's minion,
Carved out his passage, till he faced the slave;
And ne'er shook hands, nor bade farewell to him,
Till he unseamed him from the nave to the chaps,
And fixed his head upon our battlements!
Dun. O, valiant cousin! worthy gentleman!

---

* **Forres,** or *Fores*, a Scotch parish, ten miles W. S. W. of Elgin. Near it is a remarkable obelisk called "Sweno's Pillar," probably erected in commemoration of a victory over the Danes. —**Sergeant** (Lat. *serviens*, serving; Fr. *sergent*), formerly an officer of importance, higher in rank than now.—**For to that,** *because*. Some critics interpret "for to that" as meaning "*for*, to that *end*."—**Western Isles,** *Hebrides*. Location? The population is Celtic; the language, Gaelic.—**Kernes,** light-armed Irish foot-soldiers. **Of Kernes,** *with* Kernes.—**Gallowglasses** (Ir. *giolla*, servant; *gleac*, to fight; *gallowglach*, a fighting servant), heavy-armed foot-soldiers from Ireland and the Western Isles. The gallowglass carried an axe; the kern, a sword and target. They are mentioned in Shakespeare's *King Henry VI.*, Part II., Act iv., Scene 9.—**Damned.** Dissyl.—**Quarry** (Lat. *quadratus*, square), *square*, *squadron*, *phalanx*. White and some other editors follow Dr. Johnson in reading *quarrel* instead of *quarry*. See *quarrel*, pages 95, 101.—**Showed like,** etc. Fortune smiled but to deceive.—**But all's too weak.** Mr. Hunter suggests that we should read *all-to*, i. e., *altogether*, *entirely*. See Judges ix. 53.—**Minion** (Lat. *min-us*, less; Eng. *minim*, something minute; Fr. *mignon*; O. High. Ger. *minni*, *minnia*, love, affection), *favorite*, *darling*. This word came afterwards to have an unfavorable sense, and to signify the *mean favorite* of a tyrant.

SUGGESTIONS FOR EXPRESSIVE READING.

(See *Summary of Results of Elocutionary Analysis*, post.)

What bloody man? *Surprise* and *excitement* blended are apt to be loud and quick. Read accordingly. Let the instructor unyieldingly insist upon correct vocal expression.

This is the sergeant. *Surprise*, *joy*, *gratitude*, and *admiration*, are mingled here. The utterance should be loud, quick, and high in "pitch" (or musical tone).

O, valiant cousin. *Excitement*, *surprise*, *joy*, *great admiration*. Loud, with full volume of voice, and rather high pitch, with "median stress" (i. e., the *middle* part of the accented vowel sound is enunciated forcibly).

Sold. As, whence* the sun 'gins his reflection,
Shipwrecking storms and direful thunders break;
So from that spring, whence comfort seemed to come,
Discomfort swells. Mark, King of Scotland, mark:
No sooner justice had, with valor armed,
Compelled these skipping Kernes to trust their heels;
But the Norweyan lord, surveying vantage,
With furbished arms and new supplies of men,
Began a fresh assault.
Dun. Dismayed not this
Our captains, Macbeth and Banquo?
Sold. Yes;
As sparrows, eagles; or the hare, the lion!
If I say sooth, I must report they were
As cannons overcharged with double cracks!
So they
Doubly redoubled strokes upon the foe.
Except they meant to bathe in reeking wounds,
Or memorize another Golgotha,
I cannot tell——
But I am faint, my gashes cry for help.
Dun. So well thy words become thee, as thy wounds!
They smack of honor both.—Go, get him surgeons. [*Exit* Soldier, *attended.*

Enter ROSSE.

Who comes here?
Mal. The worthy Thane of Rosse.
Len. What a haste looks through his eyes! So should he look,
That seems to speak things strange.
Rosse. God save the king!
Dun. Whence cam'st thou, worthy thane?
Rosse. From Fife, great king,
Where the Norweyan banners flout the sky,
And fan our people cold!
Norway himself, with terrible numbers,

---

* **As, whence,** etc. As shipwrecking storms and direful thunders break [from the east] whence the sun begins his reflection (*i. e.*, shining).—**Norweyan lord,** *Sweno.*—**Surveying vantage,** *seeing his advantage*, recognizing his opportunity. See *vantage*, p. 88.—**Sooth,** *truth.* See *soothly*, p. 41.—**Cracks,** *explosions*, *reports.* Gaelic and Irish *crac;* Fr. *craquer;* Ger. *krachen*, to burst into chinks. When was gunpowder invented? Any anachronism in this passage?—**Memorize,** *make memorable.*—**Golgotha.** See John xix. 17.—**Seems to speak,** seems about to speak.—**Thane,** a nobleman in A. S. and Dan. times; called a *baron* after the Norman Conquest. A. S. *thegan*, servant of the king.—**Fife,** a county of Scotland forming a peninsula, bounded by the Frith of Tay, Frith of Forth, and the North Sea, on the north, south, and east, respectively.—**Flout** (Goth. *flautan*, to boast; O. D. *fluyten*, to pipe, lie, flatter; A. S. *flitan*, to quarrel; Prov. Eng. *flite*, to scold), *mock.*—**Cold.** As if they brought the cold air of Norway.

As whence the sun. The sergeant is *blunt*, *brave*, *warm-hearted*, full of *admiration* for Macbeth, with a dash of *boastfulness.* He would speak *loud* even to his **king.** His voice **fails** him at the last. Read accordingly.
From Fife, great king. *Excitement*, *haste*, *joy*, *admiration.* Loud and quick.

Assisted by that most disloyal traitor,
The Thane of Cawdor,* began a dismal conflict;
Till that Bellona's bridegroom, lapped in proof,
Confronted him with self-comparisons,
Point against point rebellious, arm 'gainst arm,
Curbing his lavish spirit! And, to conclude,
The victory fell on us——

Dun. Great happiness!

Rosse. That now
The Norway's king craves composition;
Nor would we deign him burial of his men,
Till he disbursed, at Saint Colme's Inch,
Ten thousand dollars to our general use.

Dun. No more that thane of Cawdor shall deceive
Our bosom interest.—Go, pronounce his death,
And with his former title greet Macbeth.

Rosse. I'll see it done.

Dun. What he hath lost, noble Macbeth hath won. [*Exeunt.*

SCENE III. *A Heath.*

Thunder. Enter the three Witches.

1st *Witch.* Where hast thou been, sister?

2d *Witch.* Killing swine.

3d *Witch.* Sister, where thou?

1st *Witch.* A sailor's wife had chestnuts in her lap,
And mounched, and mounched, and mounched:—*Give me*, quoth I:
Aroint thee, witch! the rump-fed ronyŏn cries.
Her husband's to Aleppo gone, master o' the Tiger:
But in a sieve I'll thither sail,
And, like a rat without a tail,
I'll do, I'll do, and I'll do!

---

* **Cawdor,** or *Calder*, a parish of Scotland, in the counties of Nairn and Inverness. It is three and a half miles southwest of Nairn. Here is a castle, "an imposing feudal fortress, in which, it is said, Duncan was murdered by Macbeth."—**Till that,** *till.*—**Bellona's bridegroom.** Bellona, in mythology, is the goddess of war, sister (and wife, some say) of Mars. Here the bridegroom is Macbeth, as glorious in strength and beauty as Mars himself on his marriage day.—**Proof** (Lat. *probare*, to test), *proof*, *armor*, armor capable of resisting any impression.—**Self-comparisons,** *self matching self.* The expression is explained in the next line.—**Rebellious** (Lat. *re*, back; *bellum*, war), *warring back*, striking back. Originally *rebellion* meant bringing war back, making war again after having been vanquished.—**Composition** (Lat. *con-*, together; *ponĕre*, to place; *composition*, a putting together), *a peaceful agreement* or *settlement.*—**Saint Colme's inch** (*St. Columb;* Gael. *inis*, island; Lat. *insula;* the Celtic *inch*, island, being part of the name of many places on the coast of Ireland and Scotland), *Inchcolm*, or *Isle of Columba*, a small island in Edinburgh Frith, with an abbey upon it dedicated to St. Columb. *Colme's* is dissyl. St. Columb was a native of Ireland, said to have died A. D. 597. See New American Cyclopedia.—**Dollars** (Dan., D., Sw. *daler;* Ger. *thaler*, "a piece of money," says Wachter, "first coined about the year 1518, in Bohemia"). Any anachronism here?—**Mounched** (Lat. *masticare*, to masticate; *manducare*, to chew; Fr. *manger*, to eat), *munched*, *chewed with closed lips.*—**Aroint.** This word is also used in *King Lear*, Act iii., Scene 4. Perhaps from Fr. *arry avant*! away there! In the north of England milk-maids say '*rynt* thee,' to drive away a cow that has been milked. A. S. *ryman*, *rymde*, to make room.—**Rump-fed** (Sw. *rumpa*, a tail), *fed on offals.* Webster gives a different meaning to this word—crowded basement and empty attic.—**Ronyon,** "a vulgar term of reproach meaning 'scurvy drab.'" From Fr. *rogne*, itch; Lat. *ren*, *renes*, reins.—**Aleppo,** a great emporium of Asiatic Turkey in the north of Syria.—**Sieve.** In Shakespeare's time, writers on witchcraft affirmed that witches could sail in sieves.—**A tail.** The same writers asserted that witches could take the shape of any animal, but the tail would be wanting!—**I'll do,** etc. Gnaw a hole through the ship's hull?

2d Witch. I'll give thee a wind.
1st Witch. Thou art kind.*
3d Witch. And I another.
1st Witch. I myself have all the other,
And the very ports they blow,
All the quarters that they know
I' the shipman's card.
I will drain him dry as hay:
Sleep shall, neither night nor day,
Hang upon his pent-house lid:
He shall live a man forbid:
Weary sevennights, nine times nine,
Shall he dwindle, peak, and pine:
Though his bark cannot be lost,
Yet it shall be tempest-tossed.
Look what I have!
2d Witch. Show me, show me.
1st Witch. Here I have a pilot's thumb,
Wrecked, as homeward he did come. [*Drum within.*
3d Witch. A drum! a drum!
Macbeth doth come.
All. The weird sisters, hand in hand,
Posters of the sea and land,
Thus do go about, about;
Thrice to thine, and thrice to mine,
And thrice again to make up nine.
Peace!—the charm's wound up.

Enter MACBETH *and* BANQUO.

Macb. So foul and fair a day I have not seen.
Ban. How far is't called to Forres?—What are these,
So withered, and so wild in their attire,
That look not like the inhabitants o' the earth,
And yet are on't? Live you? or are you aught

---

* **Kind** (Gr. γένος, race, birth; Lat. *genus;* by Grimm's Law, Eng. *kin, kind;* A. S. *cyn, cynd,* race, offspring; Ger. *kind,* child), related by blood; consequently, *kind.* The word probably rhymed with wind.—**Ports** (Lat. *porta,* a gate; or *portus,* a harbor), the *gates* the winds blow *from,* or the *harbors* they blow *to?*—**Card** (Lat. *charta,* a leaf of papyrus, paper; Fr. *carte*), *chart.*—**Pent-house** (Lat. *pendĕre,* to hang; Fr. *pente,* slope), a shed standing aslope. Scott says, "Had there not lurked under the *pent-house* of his eye that sly epicurean twinkle."—**Forbid,** *interdicted, accursed, blasted.* See *foryeld,* p. 45.—**Peak,** *become sharp-featured.*—**Pine.** Marasmus was supposed to be produced by witchcraft. Holinshed thus describes the witchcraft used to destroy King Duff: "For as the waxen image [resembling the king's person] did waste afore the fire, so did the body of the king break forth in sweat; and as for the words of the enchantment, they served to keep him still waking from sleep."—**Weird** (A. S. *wyrd,* fate), *skilled in witchcraft, supernatural, wild.* Dissyl.—**Fair and foul,** *fair* because of *victory,* and *foul* because of the *weather.*

What are these, etc. *Wonder* with slight *awe,* 'Aspirated quality;' *i. e.,* with prominence given to the *consonants;* whispering; not loud, as not wishing to attract attention.

Live you, etc. *Boldness,* as of one having authority. *Loud,* with 'radical stress,' *i. e.,* with force on the first part of each accented vowel sound.

8

That man may question? You seem to understand me,
By each at once her choppy* finger laying
Upon her skinny lips.—You should be women,
And yet your beards forbid me to interpret
That you are so.

Macb. Speak, if you can.—What are you?

1st Witch. All hail, Macbeth! hail to thee, Thane of Glamis!

2d Witch. All hail, Macbeth! hail to thee, Thane of Cawdor!

3d Witch. All hail, Macbeth! that shalt be King hereafter.

Ban. Good sir, why do you start, and seem to fear
Things that do sound so fair?—I' the name of truth,
Are ye fantastical, or that indeed
Which outwardly ye show? My noble partner
You greet with present grace, and great prediction
Of noble having and of royal hope,
That he seems rapt withal: to me you speak not.
If you can look into the seeds of time,
And say which grain will grow, and which will not,
Speak then to me, who neither beg nor fear
Your favors nor your hate.

1st Witch. Hail!

2d Witch. Hail!

3d Witch. Hail!

1st Witch. Lesser than Macbeth, and greater.

2d Witch. Not so happy, yet much happier.

3d Witch. Thou shalt get kings, though thou be none:
So, all hail, Macbeth and Banquo!

1st Witch. Banquo and Macbeth, all hail!

Macb. Stay, you imperfect speakers; tell me more.
By Sinel's death, I know, I am Thane of Glamis;
But how of Cawdor? the Thane of Cawdor lives,
A prosperous gentleman; and to be king
Stands not within the prospect of belief,

---

* **Choppy,** *chapped.*—**Glamis,** Glammis, a Scotch parish, five and a half miles south-west of Forfar. It contains a venerable castle, the ancient residence of the Macbeths. The thaneship of Glamis was in the Macbeth family.—**Fantastical,** (creatures) *of fantasy.* Holinshed applies the same adjective to the witches. Macbeth's trance of thought is supposed by Hudson to indicate a wrong moral predisposition, and "a long course of secret inward preparation for the crimes that follow."—**Having,** *possession, fortune.* Here the allusion is to the thanedom of Cawdor, which is the 'present grace.'—**Royal hope,** hope of the crown.—**That he seems,** *so that he seems.*—**Rapt** (Lat. *rapĕre,* to snatch away; *raptus,* transported; Gr. ἁρπάζω, I seize), *transported, ravished.*—**Withal,** *with the rest, likewise, with it.*—**Sinel's death.** Sinel was Macbeth's father according to Boethius, whom Holinshed followed. The thaneship was inherited.—**Cawdor,** or Calder, p. 112. For all these geographical names, consult Lippincott's *Gazetteer* and a good atlas.

Good sir, why do you start, etc. A little of *wonder* at Macbeth's strange starting. For Macbeth had probably been thinking of becoming king, and he is struck by the astonishing coincidence of his thoughts with the witches' prediction! Spoken politely with rounded lips. Take great pains to read expressively.

I' the name of truth, etc. This address is *bold;* without a particle of fear, and in the last part with a tone of defiance. Loud and deliberate.

Stay, you imperfect speakers, etc. Earnest *appeal.* Spoken rapidly, but with occasional brief hesitation, as of one puzzled. Rather loud.

No more than to be Cawdor. Say from whence
You owe * this strange intelligence! or why
Upon this blasted heath you stop our way
With such prophetic greeting!—Speak, I charge you! [Witches *vanish.*
Ban. The earth hath bubbles, as the water has,
And these are of them.—Whither are they vanished?
Macb. Into the air; and what seemed corporal, melted
As breath into the wind.—'Would they had stayed!
Ban. Were such things here, as we do speak about?
Or have we eaten of the insane root,
That takes the reason prisoner?
Macb. Your children shall be kings.
Ban. You shall be king.
Macb. And Thane of Cawdor too: went it not so?
Ban. To the selfsame tune and words. Who's here?

Enter Rosse *and* Angus.

Rosse. The king hath happily receiv'd, Macbeth,
The news of thy success; and when he reads
Thy personal venture in the rebels' fight,
His wonders and his praises do contend,
Which should be, thine, or his. Silenced with that,
In viewing o'er the rest o' the selfsame day,
He finds thee in the stout Norweyan ranks,
Nothing afeard of what thyself didst make
Strange images of—death. As thick as tale,
Came post with post; and every one did bear
Thy praises in his kingdom's great defence,
And poured them down before him.
Ang. We are sent,
To give thee, from our royal master, thanks;
To herald thee into his sight, not pay thee.
Rosse. And, for an earnest of a greater honor,
He bade me, from him, call thee Thane of Cawdor:
In which addition, hail, most worthy Thane!
For it is thine.

---

* **Owe,** *possess.* See *owen*, p. 35.—**Insane root,** *henbane.* Batman says, "Henbane is called *insana*, mad . . . if it be eate or dronke it breedeth madness."—**Rebels' fight.** This was the first fight, before the Norwegians came.—**His wonders and his praises do contend** (with each other), **which should be** (*i. e.*, which should survive the other, wonder struggling with the *utterance* of praise, a struggle for existence), **thine** *or* **his** (*i. e.*, 'thine,' the praise; 'his,' the wonders.) This language is highly figurative. The next sentence throws light on it.—**Silenced with that.** The meaning is, *admiration* contends with ability to praise, overpowers his speech, and the result is silence.—**Afeard,** etc. Afraid of death, which thou didst make strange images of. Put a rhetorical pause before '*death.*'—**Tale** (A. S. *tale*, fr. *tellan*, to tell, to count; Ger. *zählen*, to number; *zahl*, number, counter), *count.* 'As thick as tale' means 'as fast as one could count.' *Tally* is fr. Fr. *tailler*, to cut.—**Earnest,** *pledge.* A. S. *eornost;* Goth. *arneis*, sure; or fr. O. Eng. *earles-penny*, part payment.—**Addition,** *title.*

The king hath happily, etc. *Bold, polite, joyful, declamatory, admiring.* Rather loud and rather fast. He has his speech all committed to memory.

Ban. What! can the Devil* speak true?
Macb. The Thane of Cawdor lives: Why do you dress me
In borrowed robes?
Ang. Who was the Thane, lives yet;
But under heavy judgment bears that life
Which he deserves to lose. Whether he was combined
With those of Norway, or did line the rebel
With hidden help and vantage; or that with both
He labored in his country's wreck, I know not;
But treasons capital, confessed and proved,
Have overthrown him.
Macb. [*Aside.*] Glamis, and Thane of Cawdor;
The greatest is behind.—Thanks for your pains.—
Do you not hope your children shall be kings,
When those that gave the Thane of Cawdor to me,
Promised no less to them?
Ban. That, trusted home,
Might yet enkindle you unto the crown,
Besides the Thane of Cawdor. But 'tis strange;—
And oftentimes, to win us to our harm,
The instruments of darkness tell us truths;
Win us with honest trifles, to betray us
In deepest consequence.—
Cousins, a word, I pray you.
Macb. Two truths are told,
As happy prologues to the swelling act
Of the imperial theme!—I thank you, gentlemen.—
This supernatural soliciting
Cannot be ill; cannot be good. If ill,
Why hath it given me earnest of success,
Commencing in a truth? I am Thane of Cawdor.
If good, why do I yield to that suggestion
Whose horrid image doth unfix my hair,
And make my seated heart knock at my ribs,
Against the use of nature? Present fears
Are less than horrible imaginings:

* **Devil,** the devil in the witches. Note that *devil* is shortened from Lat. *diabŏlus*, Gr. διάβολος, accuser; it being in accordance with the genius of the English language to make long words short, a process by which Voltaire said the English gain two hours a day!—**Line,** place alongside of for security, *strengthen.*—**Thanks.** Said to Rosse and Angus.—**Do you not.** Addressed to Banquo.—**Trusted home,** *trusted entirely.*—**Enkindle,** *fire, encourage.*—**Deepest consequence.** Elsewhere Shakespeare says, "It is a matter of small consequence."—**Prologues.** Before a dramatic performance, a brief discourse or poem was spoken to the audience. **Prologue** (Gr. πρό, before; λόγος, discourse), *preliminary speech.* **Happy prologues** are auspicious prologues.—**Swelling act,** a grand or imposing drama.—**Soliciting,** *incitement, temptation.*—**Earnest,** *assurance, pledge, token.* See p. 115.—**Suggestion,** the thought of the murder of Duncan. Shakespeare uses *suggest* in the sense of *tempt.*

Glamis, and Thane of Cawdor, etc. In the following soliloquies, of course, Macbeth speaks in an undertone. The interjected thanks to Rosse and Angus are in an ordinary tone of voice. The last part of the soliloquy is in a whisper.

My thought, whose murder yet is but fantastical,*
Shakes so my single state of man, that function
Is smothered in surmise; and nothing is,
But what is not!

Ban. Look, how our partner's rapt!

Macb. If chance will have me king, why, chance may crown me
Without my stir.

Ban. New honors, come upon him,
Like our strange garments, cleave not to their mould,
But with the aid of use.

Macb. Come what come may,
Time and the hour runs through the roughest day.

Ban. Worthy Macbeth, we stay upon your leisure.

Macb. Give me your favor:—my dull brain was wrought
With things forgotten. Kind gentlemen, your pains
Are registered where every day I turn
The leaf to read them.—Let us toward the king.—
Think upon what hath chanced: and, at more time,
The interim having weighed it, let us speak
Our free hearts each to other.

Ban. Very gladly.

Macb. Till then, enough.—Come, friends. [*Exeunt.*

SCENE IV. Forres. *A Room in the Palace.*

Flourish. Enter DUNCAN, MALCOLM, DONALBAIN, LENOX, *and* Attendants.

Dun. Is execution done on Cawdor? Are not
Those in commission yet returned?

Mal. My liege,
They are not yet come back; but I have spoke
With one that saw him die, who did report,
That very frankly he confessed his treasons;
Implored your highness' pardon; and set forth
A deep repentance. Nothing in his life
Became him like the leaving it: he died
As one that had been studied in his death,
To throw away the dearest thing he owed,
As 'twere a careless trifle.

---

* **Fantastical**, the creation of fancy.—**Single state**, "my inadequate, unsupported manhood," says White; "weak, feeble state," says Hudson. Webster defines single as "small, weak, silly;" Worcester, as "weak, silly."—**Function**, *action*, *performance*.—**Nothing is**, etc. The visible, tangible, and present, are as nothing; the invisible, intangible, and future, everything; fact is nothing; fancy, everything.—**Time and the hour.** Some suppose that Macbeth has in mind the hour-glass. The line appears to have been almost proverbial.—**Favor**, *countenance*, *good-will*.—**Wrought**, *exercised*.—**Pains**, *painstaking efforts*.—**The interim**, *in the meantime*.—**Free**, *free from guile, frank*.—**Studied**, *studiously prepared*.—**Owed**, *owned*, *possessed*. See *owen*, p. 35.—**Careless**, *uncared for*. It is supposed that in this description Shakespeare was thinking of the circumstances of the execution of the Earl of Essex. Was Shakespeare's friend Southampton connected with Essex?

My liege, they are not yet come back, etc. This is spoken in a business way, respectfully, of course, to the king; and it is commented upon with some earnestness and in a tone of surprise and disappointment.

Dun. There's no art,
To find* the mind's construction in the face:
He was a gentleman on whom I built
An absolute trust.—O worthiest cousin!

Enter MACBETH, BANQUO, ROSSE, *and* ANGUS.

The sin of my ingratitude even now
Was heavy on me. Thou art so far before,
That swiftest wing of recompense is slow
To overtake thee. Would thou hadst less deserved;
That the proportion both of thanks and payment
Might have been mine! Only I have left to say,
More is thy due than more than all can pay.
Macb. The service and the loyalty I owe,
In doing it, pays itself. Your Highness' part
Is to receive our duties: and our duties
Are, to your throne and state, children and servants;
Which do but what they should, by doing everything
Safe toward your love and honor.
Dun. Welcome hither:
I have begun to plant thee, and will labor
To make thee full of growing.—Noble Banquo,
That hast no less deserved, nor must be known
No less to have done so, let me enfold thee
And hold thee to my heart.
Ban. There if I grow,
The harvest is your own.
Dun. My plenteous joys,
Wanton in fulness, seek to hide themselves
In drops of sorrow!—Sons, kinsmen, thanes,
And you whose places are the nearest, know,
We will establish our estate upon
Our eldest, Malcolm; whom we name hereafter,
The Prince of Cumberland: which honor must
Not, unaccompanied, invest him only,

---

* **To find,** etc., to discern the *character* in the face.—**O worthiest.** To Macbeth. —**Ingratitude,** in not rewarding Macbeth sufficiently.—**Proportion,** etc., *that the proportioning of thanks and payment to your desert might have been mine*, i. e., in my power.—**The service,** etc. Virtue is its own reward.—**Duties,** etc. Our duties are as children and servants.—**Safe,** etc. This seems to have been taken from the customary saying in Lat., *salvo honore Dei*, the honor of God being safe; or the old Fr. phrase, *sauf votre honneur;* or, in Norman Fr., *saulf le foy que jeo doy a nostre seignor le roy*, a phrase of reservation in acknowledgments of allegiance or avowals of fealty.—**Nor . . . . no less.** The double negative here, as often in Shakespeare, strengthens the negation.—**Drops of sorrow,** *tears*.—**Cumberland** (A. S. *comb*, a valley, hollow), the land of hollows; *Cumberland*, the north-west county of England. Holinshed assigns this appointment of Malcolm as the cause of Macbeth's plot to murder Duncan and seize the throne. "Prince of Cumberland" was the title borne during the life of a king of Scotland by his appointed successor.

O worthiest cousin, etc. *Great joy, admiration, affection.* Loud, rather quick at first, with "median stress" (*i. e.*, with a *swell* of the voice on each long accented vowel). So in the following speeches of Duncan in this scene. The pitch is somewhat high.

But signs of nobleness, like stars, shall shine
On all deservers.—From hence to Inverness,*
And bind us further to you.
    Macb. The rest is labor, which is not used for you:
I'll be myself the harbinger, and make joyful
The hearing of my wife with your approach;
So, humbly take my leave.
    Dun.   My worthy Cawdor!
    Macb. The Prince of Cumberland!—That is a step   [*Aside.*
On which I must fall down, or else o'erleap,
For in my way it lies. Stars, hide your fires!
Let not light see my black and deep desires;
The eye wink at the hand; yet let that be,
Which the eye fears, when it is done, to see.   [*Exit.*
    Dun. True, worthy Banquo; he is full so valiant;
And in his commendations I am fed;
It is a banquet to me. Let us after him
Whose care is gone before to bid us welcome:
It is a peerless kinsman.   [*Flourish.* *Exeunt.*

SCENE V. Inverness. *A Room in* MACBETH'S *Castle.*

Enter Lady MACBETH, *reading a letter.*

Lady M. "*They met me in the day of success; and I have learned by the perfectest report, they have more in them than mortal knowledge. When I burned in desire to question them further, they made themselves—air, into which they vanished. Whiles I stood rapt in the wonder of it, came missives from the king, who all-hailed me,* Thane of Cawdor; *by which title, before, these weird sisters saluted me, and referred me to the coming on of time, with,* Hail, King that shalt be! *This have I thought good to deliver thee, my dearest partner of greatness, that thou mightest not lose the dues of rejoicing, by being ignorant of what greatness is promised thee. Lay it to thy heart, and farewell.*"
Glamis thou art, and Cawdor; and shalt be
What thou art promised!—Yet do I fear thy nature;
It is too full o' the milk of human kindness,
To catch the nearest way. Thou wouldst be great;
Art not without ambition; but without

* **Inverness.** See *Cawdor*, pp. 112, 114.—**Bind,** etc. Lay us under further obligations. —**Rest,** etc. *Rest*, if not taken for your sake, is *labor*.—**The Prince,** etc. Macbeth, passing out, soliloquizes. Meanwhile Duncan and Banquo converse unheard. When Macbeth is gone, Duncan exclaims aloud in reply to some remark of Banquo's, "True, worthy Banquo, he (*i. e.*, Macbeth) is full," etc.—**Banquet.** Is the word suggested by the name Banquo?—**Lady Macbeth.** Her name was *Gruach*. Wyntoun's Chronicle makes her to have been the wife of Duncan and, afterwards, of his murderer.—**Missives** (Lat. *mittĕre*, to send), *messengers*. The first part of this letter, or the whole of a previous one, is omitted.

The Prince of Cumberland, etc. Startled, angry, malicious, yet secret, so as not to be overheard or suspected. An undertone, or loud whisper.

They met me in the day of success, etc. Very *slow*, with pauses, to think out and take in the meaning of every word. So, *wherever the thought is greatly condensed*, or the words are very pregnant with meaning.

Glamis thou art, and Cawdor, etc. Decision; earnestness intense, yet under control; a hard, metallic voice; slow utterance. A tone of exultation running through the last part of the soliloquy.

The illness * should attend it. What thou wouldst highly,
That wouldst thou holily; wouldst not play false,
And yet wouldst wrongly win. Thou'dst have, great Glamis,
That which cries, "*Thus thou must do, if thou have it;*
And that which rather thou dost fear to do,
Than wishest should be undone." Hie thee hither,
That I may pour my spirits in thine ear;
And chastise with the valor of my tongue
All that impedes thee from the golden round,
Which fate and metaphysical aid doth seem
To have thee crowned withal.—What is your tidings?

Enter an Attendant.

Attend. The king comes here to-night.
Lady M. Thou'rt mad to say it.
Is not thy master with him? who, wer't so,
Would have informed for preparation.
Attend. So please you, it is true; our thane is coming:
One of my fellows had the speed of him;
Who, almost dead for breath, had scarcely more
Than would make up his message.
Lady M. Give him tending:
He brings great news. The raven himself is hoarse, [*Exit* Attendant.
That croaks the fatal entrance of Duncan
Under my battlements. Come, come, you spirits
That tend on mortal thoughts, unsex me here!
And fill me, from the crown to the toe, top-full
Of direst cruelty! make thick my blood,
Stop up the access and passage to remorse!
That no compunctious visitings of nature
Shake my fell purpose, nor keep peace between
The effect, and it! Come to my woman's breasts,

* **The illness,** *the evil nature, the wickedness.* **Thou'dst have,** etc. Thou wouldst have the crown, which (crown) cries, "Thus thou must do if thou have it (*i. e.*, the crown), and thou must do that (*i. e.*, the murder) which thou rather fearest to *do*, than wishest should be *undone*." **Metaphysical** (Gr. μετά, beyond; φύσις, nature), *beyond physical, supernatural.* **Seem to have,** *seem determined to have.*—**Master,** *Macbeth.*—**Fellows,** *companions.* See p. 28.—**Speed,** *start, advance.*—**Give him,** etc., give your breathless companion courteous attention.—**Entrance.** Good critics suppose this word to have the force of a trisyl. here; as if *enterance.*—**Raven . . . . hoarse . . . . croaks . . . . fatal . . . . battlements.** How the dark purpose of Lady Macbeth summons things of evil omen to suit her fierce and bloody mood! Contrast these images with those suggested by Duncan and Banquo in the commencement of the next scene, where all is hospitality and cheer. "If all this be accident," says Lowell, "it is at least one of those accidents of which only Shakespeare was ever capable."—**Spirits that tend on mortal thoughts,** spirits that incite to deadly crimes.—**Remorse,** *pity;* compassion; compunctions.—**Keep peace,** etc., *intervene between the fell purpose* and its *execution.*—**My woman's breasts,** the breasts of me, a woman.

What is your tidings, etc. Spoken sharply and quickly on the abrupt entrance of the attendant.
The raven himself is hourse, etc. A muttering, threatening tone. "Radical stress," the words being spitefully spit out through the set teeth. Fierce determination. The last part rather loud, violent, yet with small "volume" (or *size* of voice), it being a woman that speaks, and she not wishing to be overheard. "Aspirated quality," the consonant sounds being desperately hissed and blurted out. Take great pains in the reading.

And take my milk for gall, you murdering ministers, *
Wherever in your sightless substances
You wait on nature's mischief! Come, thick Night,
And pall thee in the dunnest smoke of hell!
That my keen knife see not the wound it makes;
Nor heaven peep through the blanket of the dark,
To cry, "*Hold, Hold!*"—Great Glamis! worthy Cawdor!

Enter MACBETH.

Greater than both, by the All-hail, hereafter!
Thy letters have transported me beyond
This ignorant present, and I feel now
The future in the instant.
Macb. My dearest love,
Duncan comes here to-night.
Lady M. And when goes hence?
Macb. To-morrow, as he purposes.
Lady M. O, never
Shall sun that morrow see!
Your face, my Thane, is as a book, where men
May read strange matters!—To beguile the time,
Look like the time; bear welcome in your eye,
Your hand, your tongue: look like the innocent flower,
But be the serpent under it! He that's coming
Must be provided for; and you shall put
This night's great business into my despatch,
Which shall to all our nights and days to come
Give solely sovereign sway and masterdom.
Macb. We will speak further.
Lady M. Only look up clear:
To alter favor ever is to fear.
Leave all the rest to me. [*Exeunt.*

SCENE VI. *The Same. Before the Castle.*

Hautboys. Servants *of* MACBETH *attending.* *Enter* DUNCAN, MALCOLM, DONALBAIN, BANQUO, LENOX, MACDUFF, ROSSE, ANGUS, *and* Attendants.

---

* **Take my milk for gall,** *exchange my milk for gall.*—**Pall** (Lat. *pallium;* A. S. *päll*, cloak, cover), *hide, cloak.*—**This ignorant present.** The present time, which is ignorant of the future.—**Instant,** *present.* Lat. *instare*, to stand on; to be urgent, to press.—**Favor,** *countenance*, the face. See Index.—**Scene VI.** After the intense excitement of Scene v, how calm and sweet is this repose! Note, however, the lack of anything like personal affection in Lady Macbeth's welcome, and that she overacts.

Great Glamis, etc. Rapturous admiration. Very loud; quick; very strong median stress; "pure quality" (*i. e.*, the vowel sounds being clear and full, and the consonant sounds not very prominent).

My dearest love, etc. *Love* for Lady Macbeth, blended with treacherous *malice* towards the king. Love is here soft in force, gently median in stress. Malice towards Duncan preponderates. It expresses itself by *decision* blended with *secrecy*. Radical stress.

Your face, my Thane, is as a book, etc. Sly exultation; malice mingled with affection. Suppressed force; quick utterance; small volume.

Dun. This castle hath a pleasant seat. The air
Nimbly and sweetly recommends itself
Unto our gentle senses.
Ban. This guest of summer,
The temple-haunting martlet,* does approve,
By his loved mansionry, that the heaven's breath
Smells wooingly here: no jutty, frieze,
Buttress, nor coigne of vantage, but this bird
Hath made his pendent bed and procreant cradle.
Where they most breed and haunt, I have observed,
The air is delicate.

Enter Lady MACBETH.

Dun. See, see! our honored hostess!
The love that follows us, sometime is our trouble;
Which still we thank as love. Herein I teach you,
How you shall bid God yield us for your pains,
And thank us for your trouble.
Lady M. All our service,
In every point twice done and then done double,
Were poor and single business to contend
Against those honors deep and broad, wherewith
Your Majesty loads our house. For those of old,
And the late dignities heaped up to them,
We rest your hermits.
Dun. Where's the Thane of Cawdor?
We coursed him at the heels, and had a purpose
To be his purveyor; but he rides well,
And his great love, sharp as his spur, hath holp him
To his home before us. Fair and noble hostess,
We are your guest to-night.

---

* **Martlet,** a kind of swallow, a *martin.*—**Approve,** give *proof.*—**Jutty,** *projection.*—**Frieze,** that part of the entablature of a column which is between the architrave and cornice. —**Coigne of vantage** (Lat. *cuneus*, wedge; Fr. *coin;* Gr. γωνία, angle), "a projecting angle in the masonry," advantageous corner.—**Delicate,** *soft, pure, and agreeable.*—**The love that,** etc., loving attentions to us are sometimes troublesome, yet we thank the giver for the spirit that prompts them.—**Herein,** by this illustration.—**Yield,** recompense. See *foryelde*, p. 45.—**Your pains,** the pains we compel you to take by coming so unceremoniously to your castle.—**Single business,** a slight matter. See *single state*, p. 117.—**Contend against,** *compare with.*—**Hermits** (Gr. ἐρῆμος, solitary; Lat. *eremita*, a hermit), *beadsmen*, persons bound to pray constantly for you, as hermits are wont.—**Coursed,** *pursued* as a hunter follows the game. —**Holp** (O. Eng.), *helped.* So *holpen* in Luke i. 54.

This castle hath a pleasant seat, etc. The first two speeches in this scene are full of *calmness and tranquillity.* The tone is pure (*i. e.*, free from *nasal, guttural, hissing*, and prominent *consonant* sounds); the force is soft; the pitch is medium (or average); the movement (or rate of utterance) is rather slow; the slides (*i. e.*, inflections, or changes of pitch on a single long sound) are moderate. All the delivery is gentle, yet glad.

See, see! our honored hostess, etc. Joy, benevolence, politeness. Rather loud and rather fast; radical and median stress.

All our service. Polite, ceremonious, yet with metallic hardness; not out-gushing, but measured. She "speaks a piece," which she has learned for the occasion; speaks it prettily, but with the lips merely, not the heart.

Where's the Thane of Cawdor, etc. A blunt, straightforward inquiry, in a good-natured, business way and tone.

Lady M. Your servants ever
Hath theirs, themselves, and what is theirs, in compt,*
To make their audit at your Highness' pleasure,
Still to return your own.

Dun. Give me your hand:
Conduct me to mine host. We love him highly
And shall continue our graces towards him.
By your leave, hostess. [*Exeunt.*

SCENE VII. *The same. A Room in the Castle.*

Hautboys and Torches. Enter, and pass over the Stage, a Sewer, *and divers* Servants *with Dishes and Service. Then enter* MACBETH.

Macb. If it were done, when 'tis done, then 'twere well
It were done quickly. If the assassination
Could trammel up the consequence, and catch,
With his surcease, success; that but this blow
Might be the be-all and the end-all here,
But here, upon this bank and shoal of time,—
We'd jump the life to come.—But, in these cases
We still have judgment here; that we but teach
Bloody instructions, which, being taught, return
To plague the inventor. This even-handed Justice
Commends the ingredients of our poisoned chalice
To our own lips.—He's here in double trust:
First, as I am his kinsman and his subject;
Strong both against the deed: then, as his host,
Who should against his murderer shut the door,
Not bear the knife myself. Besides, this Duncan
Hath borne his faculties so meek, hath been

* **In compt** (Lat. *computare*, to compute; *con-*, together, *putare*, to think, reckon; Fr. *compter*, to reckon; *compte*, computation), subject to *account* or computation.—**Audit,** examination (of accounts).—**Make their audit,** present their accounts for a hearing and settlement. Lat. *audit*, he hears.—**Return your own,** give back to you your own property.—**By your leave.** Perhaps taking her by the hand, or even kissing her.—**Sewer** (Fr. *asseoir*, to set, place; or O. E. *sew*, to follow; Lat. *sequi;* F. *suivre;* O. Fr. *sewer*, squire), an officer who had charge of the arrangement of table dishes and decorations in great houses. The French *essayeur* tasted each dish to show that there was no poison in the food.—**If it were done.** White puts a period after *well*, and no comma after *quickly*, and reads, "If it were *done* (*i. e.*, *ended*), when 'tis done (*i. e.*, *performed*), then it were (*i. e.*, *would be*) well. It were (*i. e.. would be*) done (*i. e.*, ended) quickly, if the assassination," etc. But the common interpretation is, perhaps, better: "If it were to be all over and ended as soon as the fatal blow is struck, then it would be well to strike it quickly."—**Trammel up,** *gather up and hold fast*, tie up.—**His surcease.** Surcease is cessation. His surcease may be the cessation of Duncan's life. So White understands it. Others construe *his* as *its*, which latter is rarely found in Shakespeare or Milton, and not at all in King James's version of the Bible. In this case, *surcease* means the completion of the bloody deed.—**Jump,** *risk*, *hazard. Jump the life to come*, run the risk of the life to come, disregard it. In *Coriolanus*, Act v., Scene 4. we have "Jump the after inquiry."—**Commends** (Lat. *con-*, completely; *manus*, hand; *do*, *dare*, to give; Lat. *commendare*, to give completely into the hands of), *commits*, delivers.—**Chalice** (Lat. *calix*, cup; by Grimm's Law). Is Macbeth thinking of the communion cup?

Your servants ever, etc. Another polished, ceremonious, heartless speech. A woman's voice, *soft*, but—*hard!*

If it were done, etc. *Secrecy;* slowness, because he is thinking out his plans, weighing consequences, and his language is weighty; his twisting thought requires long winding slides, *i. e.*, extensive changes of musical *pitch* on the accented vowels.

So clear* in his great office, that his virtues
Will plead like angels, trumpet-tongued, against
The deep damnation of his taking-off:
And Pity, like a naked new-born babe,
Striding the blast, or heaven's cherubin, horsed
Upon the sightless couriers of the air,
Shall blow the horrid deed in every eye,
That tears shall drown the wind!—I have no spur
To prick the sides of my intent; but only
Vaulting ambition, which o'erleaps itself,
And falls on the other——How now? what news?

Enter Lady MACBETH.

Lady M. He has almost supped. Why have you left the chamber?
Macb. Hath he asked for me?
Lady M. Know you not, he has?
Macb. We will proceed no further in this business.
He hath honored me of late; and I have bought
Golden opinions from all sorts of people,
Which would be worn now in their newest gloss,
Not cast aside so soon.
Lady M. Was the hope drunk,
Wherein you dressed yourself? hath it slept since?
And wakes it now, to look so green and pale
At what it did so freely? From this time,
Such I account thy love. Art thou afeard
To be the same in thine own act and valor
As thou art in desire? Wouldst thou have that
Which thou esteemest the ornament of life,
And live a coward in thine own esteem,

---

* **So clear**, so pure, so *upright*.—**Taking-off,** *murder*.—**Babe.** Suggested by the tenderness of pity?—**Striding,** *i. e., Pity, striding*, etc.—**Sightless couriers,** unseen swift messengers, *the winds*. Lat. *currĕre*, to run; Fr. *courir*, to run. "Who maketh the winds his messengers," Psalms civ. 4, usually translated, "Who maketh his angels spirits."—**Drown the wind!** A most extravagant metaphor. Sometimes during a shower the rain pours so copiously that it seems to cause a lull in the wind.—**Prick the sides of,** *stimulate*, as the spur does the horse.—**O'erleaps itself.** As we say "overreached himself," or "overshot himself." Possibly we should read "o'erleaps its sell," *sell* being an old word for saddle. Lat. *sella*, for *sedile*, fr. *sedes*, a "seat," by Grimm's law. Spenser says: "He left his lofty seat with yellow sell."—**Falls on the other,** *i. e., on the other side*. The sentence is unfinished, he being interrupted by the entrance of Lady Macbeth.—**Opinions.** In a previous scene *honors* are likened to garments.—**Would be worn,** *i. e., should* be worn. *Would* and *should*, as also *shall* and *will*, were not in Shakespeare's time fully differentiated.—**Hope . . . . dressed.** This is suggested by Macbeth's metaphor.—**Such I account.** Spoken with a disdainful gesture? Or does she mean to say she counts his love but a sickly affair?—**That which thou esteem'st,** *i. e., the crown*.—**And live,** *and* (yet) *live*.

Will plead like angels, etc. *Conscience* begins to be aroused; *horror* makes him shudder. By a kind of imitation, "trumpet-tongued" etc. should be uttered louder. Voice energetic but tremulous; aspirated (rough) quality.
I have no spur, etc. Impatience, abandonment of the plan.
How now? what news? The circumstances require whispers or undertone through this dialogue. Rapid utterance.
Was the hope drunk, etc. *Expostulation, ridicule, anger, contempt*. Rapid, 'jerky' utterance; radical (*i. e.*, initial) stress; as loud as the necessity of secrecy will permit; strongly aspirated quality, the words being blown out hissing.

Letting "I dare not"* wait upon "I would,"
Like the poor cat i' the adage?
  Macb. Pr'ythee, peace!
I dare do all that may become a man;
Who dares do more, is none.
  Lady M. What beast was 't, then,
That made you break this enterprise to me?
When you durst do it, then you were a man;
And, to be more than what you were, you would
Be so much more the man. Nor time nor place
Did then adhere, and yet you would make both.
They have made themselves, and that their fitness now
Does unmake you. I have given suck, and know
How tender 'tis to love the babe that milks me:
I would, while it was smiling in my face,
Have plucked my nipple from his boneless gums,
And dashed the brains out, had I so sworn, as you
Have done to this!
  Macb. If we should fail,——
  Lady M. We fail!
But screw your courage to the sticking place,
And we'll not fail. When Duncan is asleep,
(Whereto the rather shall his day's hard journey
Soundly invite him,) his two chamberlains
Will I with wine and wassail so convince
That memory, the warder of the brain,
Shall be a fume, and the receipt of reason
A limbeck only. When in swinish sleep

---

* **I dare not.** This is the grammatical object of *letting.*—**I would.** Grammat. object of *wait upon.*—**Cat.** In *Heywood's Proverbs*, published in 1566, we have the adage, "The catt wolde fish eat, but she wolde not wet her feet."—**Pr'ythee,** *I pray thee.*—**Become a man.** *Man* is emphatic.—**Beast.** *Beast* is to be emphasized. It was suggested by the mention of *man.*—**Adhere** (Lat. *ad*, to; *haerĕre*, to stick, cling to), *be consistent, favor.*—**Then adhere.** When?—**We fail.** Mrs. Siddons used to utter the *we* very slowly, and then, with an air of desperate determination, let the voice strike with downward slide and great emphasis on the word *fail.*—**Screw** (Fr. *écrou;* Ger. *schraube*). The strings of musical instruments are tightened by turning a peg on which one end of the string is wound. When the proper tension is reached, the peg is made to remain fast in its "sticking place."—**Whereto,** *to which.*—**Chamberlains.** The killing of the chamberlains appears to have been suggested to Shakespeare by the similar circumstance mentioned in Holinshed's account of the murder of King Duff.—**Wassail** (A. S. *wæs-hæl*, or *wes-hæl*, be in health, health to you, an ancient formula on drinking healths; A. S. *waes, wäs*, be, was; Ger. *wesen*, a being; A. S. *häl*, healthy; Gr. ὅλος, whole; Eng. *whole;* Ger. *heil;* Eng. *hale*), *quaffing, carousing*, intemperate indulgence in drink.—**Convince** (Lat. *con-*, completely; *vincĕre*, to conquer), *overcome.*—**Warder,** *guard, keeper.* The memory was supposed to be in the cerebellum, as a sort of a sentinel to warn the reason.—**Receipt,** *receptacle.* Here it is the cavity filled by the brain, the skull.—**Limbeck** (Ar. *al-ambiq;* Gr. ἄμβιξ, a cup, the cap of a still), the vessel in which the vapor of liquors is condensed in the process of distillation; an alembic. What did Shakespeare know about distilleries? Does alcohol accumulate in the cavity of the drunkard's cranium?

I have given suck, etc. Still more energy. Initial stress with expulsive force.
Dashed the brains, etc. Suppressed scream of wrathful energy, hurtling through the teeth and nostrils. Loud, quick, rough, convulsive voice, yet a constant effort to speak softly.
When Duncan is asleep, etc. Decision, precision, business-like, yet energetic; the last part with exultation, as if gloating over the successful accomplishment of the ingenious plan. Utterance rapid; radical stress; aspirated quality.

Their drenched* natures lie, as in a death,
What cannot you and I perform upon
The unguarded Duncan? what not put upon
His spongy officers, who shall bear the guilt
Of our great quell?

Macb. Bring forth men-children only!
For thy undaunted mettle should compose
Nothing but males. Will it not be received,
When we have marked with blood those sleepy two
Of his own chamber, and used their very daggers,
That they have done 't?

Lady M. Who dares receive it other,
As we shall make our griefs and clamor roar
Upon his death?

Macb. I am settled, and bend up
Each corporal agent to this terrible feat!
Away, and mock the time with fairest show:
False face must hide what the false heart doth know. [*Exeunt.*

ACT II.

SCENE I. *The Same. Court within the Castle.*

Enter BANQUO *and* FLEANCE, *and a* Servant *with a Torch before them.*

Ban. How goes the night, boy?

Fle. The moon is down: I have not heard the clock.

Ban. And she goes down at twelve.

Fle. I take 't, 'tis later, sir.

Ban. Hold, take my sword.—There 's husbandry in heaven:
Their candles are all out.—Take thee that too.—
A heavy summons lies like lead upon me,
And yet I would not sleep. Merciful Powers,
Restrain in me the cursed thoughts that nature
Gives way to in repose!—Give me my sword;—

Enter MACBETH, *and a* Servant *with a Torch.*

Who's there?

---

* **Drenched** (A. S. *drincan*, to drink; *drencan*, to give to drink; Ger. *tränken; Fr. trinquer*), *soaked in liquor.*—**Spongy**, absorbing liquor like a sponge.—**Quell** (O. E. *quellen*, kill; A. S. *cwelian;* Dan. *qväle*, to kill; Ger. *quälen*, to torment), *murderous act.*—**Received**, *accepted* as true.—**Other**, *otherwise.*

How goes, etc. Fleance understands the question as referring especially to *time.*—**Husbandry**, thrift, *frugality*, economy. Note the skill with which Shakespeare introduces the fact that it is a little past midnight, and that the sky is moonless and starless!—**Summons**, Nature's call to repose.—**Would not sleep**, because in my dreams comes the temptation to kill Duncan. Banquo's prayers against temptation strikingly contrast his heart with Macbeth's.

How goes the night, etc. The tone of ordinary conversation. Whenever there appears no special reason for something unusual in the utterance, the stress (*i. e.*, emphasis, or accent, or force, on the first part, middle part, or last part of an accented vowel), the time (*i. e.*, the rate or movement, whether fast or slow), the force (whether soft or loud), the pitch (*i. e.*, musical tone, whether high or low), the quality (*i. e.*, *musical* quality, whether pure or impure), the slides (*i. e.*, ascent or descent, musically speaking, of the voice on the long vowel sounds), and the volume (*i. e.*, the *bigness* or *size* of the voice, depending partly on the openness or closeness of the aperture of the vocal organs)—all these should be *moderate.*

Macb. A friend.
Ban. What, sir! not yet at rest? The king 's abed:
He hath been in unusual pleasure, and
Sent forth great largess* to your offices.
This diamond he greets your wife withal,
By the name of most kind hostess; and shut up
In measureless content.
Macb. Being unprepared,
Our will became the servant to defect,
Which else should free have wrought.
Ban. All 's well.
I dreamt last night of the three weird sisters:
To you they have showed some truth.
Macb. I think not of them;
Yet, when we can entreat an hour to serve,
Would spend it in some words upon that business,
If you would grant the time.
Ban. At your kind'st leisure.
Macb. If you shall cleave to my consent,—when 'tis,
It shall make honor for you.
Ban. So I lose none,
In seeking to augment it, but still keep
My bosom franchised and allegiance clear,
I shall be counselled.
Macb. Good repose the while!
Ban. Thanks, sir: the like to you! [*Exit* BANQUO.
Macb. Go, bid thy mistress, when my drink is ready,
She strike upon the bell. Get thee to bed.— [*Exit* Servant.
Is this a dagger which I see before me,
The handle toward my hand? Come, let me clutch thee:—
I have thee not, and yet I see thee still!
Art thou not, fatal vision, sensible

---

* **Largess** (Lat. *largitio*, a giving freely; bribery), bounty, *gifts.* —**Offices,** "rooms occupied by the officers of Macbeth's castle."—**Withal,** *with.*—**Shut up,** *concluded.*—**Will became,** etc. Our inclination to entertain the king sumptuously was subjected to the necessity imposed by defective means. Otherwise our will would have acted on a more liberal scale.—**All's well.** Your reception of the king is sufficiently hospitable.—**I dreamt,** etc. This refers to the "cursed thoughts" above mentioned?—**Consent** (Lat. *con-*, together; *sentire*, to feel), *accord*, *agreement;* or the company of those that are with me in sentiment, *my party.* White suspects here a misprint of *consort*, meaning company, and he quotes from *King Lear*, Act II., Scene i.: "Yes, Madam, he was of that consort;" also *The Two Gentlemen of Verona*, Act IV., Scene i.: "Wilt thou be of our consort?"—**When 'tis,** when the event, at which I hint, shall take place.—**None,** *no honor.*—**Franchised** (Fr. *franche*, free; Sp. *franqueza;* Ger. *frank;* Ice. *frî*, free), free from wrong.—**Clear,** clear of guilt.—**Counselled,** obedient to your counsel.—**Get thee to bed.** A careless dismissal for the night. *Thee* should not be emphasized.—**Clutch** (O. Eng. *clouch*, claw, grasp; O. Ger. *chluppe*, tongs, claw). Several times he tries to seize with his fingers the air-drawn dagger?

Get thee to bed, etc. Spoken carelessly in appearance.
Is this a dagger? etc. Alarm mingled with curiosity; a puzzled state of mind; full of horror and foreboding, yet overruled by desperate determination. Horror, when not passionate but akin to awe, speaks in a low pitch; fitful utterance, yet very slow, by reason of long *pauses*, guttural quality; slight force; large volume (not *loud*, however); falling slides, and tremulous (sometimes called "intermittent") stress.

To feeling, as to sight? Or art thou but
A dagger of the mind, a false creation,
Proceeding from the heat-oppressed brain?
I see thee yet, in form as palpable
As this which now I draw.
Thou marshall'st* me the way that I was going;
And such an instrument I was to use!
Mine eyes are made the fools o' the other senses,
Or else worth all the rest.—I see thee still;
And on thy blade and dudgeon gouts of blood,
Which was not so before!—There's no such thing:
It is the bloody business which informs
Thus to mine eyes.—Now o'er the one half world
Nature seems dead, and wicked dreams abuse
The curtained sleep: witchcraft celebrates
Pale Hecate's offerings; and withered Murder,
Alarumed by his sentinel, the wolf,
Whose howl 's his watch, thus with his stealthy pace,
With Tarquin's ravishing strides, towards his design
Moves like a ghost!—Thou sure and firm-set earth,
Hear not my steps, which way they walk, for fear
The very stones prate of my whereabout,
And take the present horror from the time,
Which now suits with it.—Whiles I threat, he lives:
Words to the heat of deeds, too cold breath gives.
I go, and it is done: the bell invites me. [*A bell rings.*
Hear it not, Duncan; for it is a knell
That summons thee to heaven, or to hell! [*Exit.*

SCENE II. *The Same.*

Enter Lady MACBETH.

Lady M. That which hath made them drunk, hath made me bold:

---

* **Marshall'st** (O. Ger. *marah*, horse; *scalc*, servant; A. S. *mear*, mare. See Webster's Dictionary), *leadest* as a harbinger; pointest out the path.—**Mine eyes**, etc. Either my eyes are deceived (made fools), or they are better than *touch* and the other senses (which are at fault, if my sight is trustworthy).—**Dudgeon,** *hilt, handle.* "Dudgeon is the root of box."—**Gouts** (Lat. *gutta*, Fr. *goutte*, a drop).—**Informs,** *takes form;* or gives *information.*—**Hecate.** "Hecate was a mystical Greek goddess, a divinity of the lower world, of whose individuality and functions the profoundest scholars and acutest investigators have found difficulty in obtaining an exact notion. Some of her attributes were those of the Greek Artemis and the Latin Diana. She was represented as having three heads; one of a horse, one of a dog, and one of a lion. A spectral being herself, she it was who sent at night demons and phantoms and disembodied souls upon the earth. Hence Shakespeare has been censured for mixing her up with vulgar Scotch witches, smelling of snuff and usquebaugh. But he sinned in this regard with many better scholars than himself; and had he not such companionship, his shoulders could bear the blame, as they also could that of pronouncing the name *Héc-at*, instead of *Hec-a-te.*" *White.*—**Tarquin's.** Sextus Tarquinius, guilty of the rape of Lucrece. Hence the words *ravishing strides*, long, cautious steps on tiptoe, such as one takes in a room where he does not wish to disturb sleepers. Shakespeare's nice observation is here apparent.—**The time.** What time was was it? See the beginning of Act II.

Thou sure and firm-set earth, hear not my steps, etc. Do not speak very loud in this utterance, as some actors do. I have heard good readers *shout* it so that not only the earth, but everybody in the neighborhood, could have heard it distinctly. It is midnight: Macbeth must not wake Duncan!

That which hath made, etc. Excitement, secrecy, boldness, determination. Undertone; rapid, convulsive utterance, yet with long pauses.

What hath quenched them hath given me fire!—Hark!—Peace!
It was the owl* that shrieked, the fatal bellman
Which gives the stern'st good night. He is about it!
The doors are open, and the surfeited grooms
Do mock their charge with snores. I have drugged their possets,
That death and nature do contend about them,
Whether they live or die.
Macb. [*Within*] Who's there?—what, ho!
Lady M. Alack! I am afraid, they have awak'd,
And 'tis not done!—the attempt and not the deed
Confounds us.—Hark!—I laid their daggers ready—
He could not miss them.—Had he not resembled
My father as he slept, I had done 't.—My husband!

Enter MACBETH.

Macb. I have done the deed!—Didst thou not hear a noise?
Lady M. I heard the owl scream, and the crickets cry.
Did not you speak?
Macb. When?
Lady M. Now.
Macb. As I descended?
Lady M. Ay.
Macb. Hark!—
Who lies i' the second chamber?
Lady M. Donalbain.
Macb. This is a sorry sight! [*Looking on his hands.*
Lady M. A foolish thought, to say a sorry sight.
Macb. There's one did laugh in his sleep, and one cried, "*Murder!*"
That they did wake each other; I stood and heard them.
But they did say their prayers, and addressed them
Again to sleep.
Lady M. There are two lodged together.
Macb. One cried, "*God bless us!*" and, "*Amen,*" the other,
As they had seen me, with these hangman's hands,

---

* **Owl** (Gr. ὀλολύζω, to howl; Lat. *ululare*, to howl; *ulŭla*, screech-owl; A. S. *ûle;* Ger. *eule*, owl; a word formed probably by onomatopœia). This mention of the owl heightens the borror.—**Bellman.** In Webster's *Duchess of Malfi*, we find the office of bellman thus described: "I am the common bellman that usually is sent to condemned persons the night before they suffer."—**Grooms.** See p. 73.—**Possets** (W. *posel*, curdled milk; fr. *pos*, gather), a kind of milk punch; a beverage of milk curdled with alcoholic liquor.—**The attempt . . . . deed,** *an unsuccessful attempt.*—**My father.** Here the woman's heart appears, more tender than she had herself imagined.—**As they had seen,** as *if* they had seen.

Who's there?—what, ho! Not very loud, but very quick.
Alack! I am afraid, etc. Same tone, etc., as before Macbeth speaks.
I have done the deed, etc. *Horror*, *consternation*, *remorse*, *secrecy*, all extreme. Lady Macbeth tries to speak calmly, in a *matter-of-fact* way, and she measurably succeeds; but Macbeth is a slave to *terror* and *remorse*. He speaks *convulsively*, *gaspingly*, with anguish. She gets out of patience with him, and finally scolds him quite sharply. His agony continues till they retreat at the sound of the knocking. In this scene, from the close of Macbeth's soliloquy to the entrance of the porter, there is intense excitement, but also a felt need of silence. Read rapidly in an undertone or whisper.

Listening their fear! I could not say "Amen,"
When they did say, "God bless us."
Lady M. Consider it not so deeply.
Macb. But wherefore could not I pronounce "Amen?"
I had most need of blessing, and "Amen"
Stuck in my throat.
Lady M. These deeds must not be thought
After these ways: so, it will make us mad.
Macb. Methought,* I heard a voice cry, "*Sleep no more!*
Macbeth does murder sleep—the innocent sleep—
Sleep, that knits up the ravelled sleave of care,
The death of each day's life, sore labor's bath,
Balm of hurt minds, great nature's second course,
Chief nourisher in life's feast"—
Lady M. What do you mean?
Macb. Still it cried, "*Sleep no more!*" to all the house:
"*Glamis hath murdered sleep, and therefore Cawdor*
Shall sleep no more: Macbeth shall sleep no more!"
Lady M. Who was it that thus cried?—Why, worthy Thane,
You do unbend your noble strength, to think
So brainsickly of things!—Go, get some water,
And wash this filthy witness from your hand.—
Why did you bring these daggers from the place?
They must lie there. Go, carry them, and smear
The sleepy grooms with blood.
Macb. I'll go no more.
I am afraid to think what I have done:
Look on 't again, I dare not.
Lady M. Infirm of purpose!
Give me the daggers! The sleeping and the dead
Are but as pictures: 'tis the eye of childhood,
That fears a painted devil! If he do bleed,
I'll gild the faces of the grooms withal,
For it must seem their guilt. [*Exit.—Knocking within.*
Macb. Whence is that knocking?
How is't with me, when every noise appals me?
What hands are here! Ha! they pluck out mine eyes!
Will all great Neptune's ocean wash this blood
Clean from my hand? No; this my hand will rather

---

* **Methought** (*me* is here the A. S. dative case), *it seemed to me.*—**Innocent.** An adjective belonging to sleep.—**Knits** (A. S. *cnyttan;* L. Ger. *knütten*, to form in knots; A. S. *cnot;* Lat. *nodus*, knot; Ger. *knoten*), *arranges* in good order (what care had discomposed).—**Sleave** (A. S. *slǽfan*, to put on, clothe; Ice. *slefa*, slender thread; Ger. *schleife*, a knot), a knot or snarl in thread, floss-silk. In Poole's *English Parnassus* (1657), hair is called "braided, dangling, sleavy, silken."—**The death,** etc. Warburton suggested *birth* in place of *death;* but a thousand poets, from the time of Job till now, have spoken gently of death as a rest for the weary.—**Glamis,** etc. This is probably the utterance of Macbeth's horror-stricken fancy.—**Gild . . . . guilt.** Punning is one of Shakespeare's besetting sins. But is it not here a desperate attempt of Lady Macbeth to bring her husband back to his senses?—**Neptune,** same as the Gr. Poseidon, god of the sea, son of Saturn, and brother of Jupiter and Pluto.

The multitudinous seas incarnadine,*
Making the green one red!

Re-enter Lady MACBETH.

Lady M. My hands are of your color, but I shame
To wear a heart so white! [*Knock.*] I hear a knocking
At the south entry—retire we to our chamber.
A little water clears us of this deed:
How easy is it, then! Your constancy
Hath left you unattended.—[*Knocking.*] Hark! more knocking!
Get on your nightgown, lest occasion call us,
And show us to be watchers.—Be not lost
So poorly in your thoughts.

Macb. To know my deed,—'twere best not know myself. [*Knock.*
Wake Duncan with thy knocking! I would thou couldst! [*Exeunt.*

SCENE III. *The Same.*

Enter a Porter. [*Knocking within.*]

Porter. Here's a knocking, indeed! If a man were porter of hell-gate, he should have old turning the key. [*Knocking.*] Knock, knock, knock! Who's there, i' the name of Beelzebub? Here's a farmer, that hanged himself on the expectation of plenty! Come in time; have napkins enough about you; here you'll sweat for't. [*Knocking.*] Knock, knock! Who's there, i' the other devil's name? 'Faith, here's an equivocator, that could swear in both the scales against either scale; who committed treason enough for God's sake, yet could not equivocate to heaven—O, come in, equivocator! [*Knocking.*] Knock, knock, knock! Who's there? 'Faith, here's an English tailor come hither, for stealing out of a French hose. Come in, tailor; here you may roast your goose. [*Knocking.*] Knock, knock! Never at quiet! What are you?—But this place is too cold for hell. I'll devil-porter it no further. I had thought to have let in some of all professions, that go the primrose way to the everlasting bonfire. [*Knocking.*] Anon, anon! I pray you, remember the porter. [*Opens the gate.*

---

* **Incarnadine** (Lat. *caro, carnis,* flesh), *make of flesh color.*—**Green,** etc., making the green waters one red mass. So Milton in *Comus,* "Make one blot of all the air."—**Constancy,** *firmness, resolution, courage.*—**Unattended,** without the courage that usually attended him. 'Constancy hath forsaken you.'—**Nightgown,** what we should call a *dressing-gown* or *robe de chambre,* rather than a modern nightgown. The latter was not used in Macbeth's time.—**Watchers** (Lat. *vigilare,* to watch; A. S. *weccan;* by Grimm's Law, Eng. *wake;* Ger. *wecken*), *persons not in* bed at night when most people are asleep.—**To know my deed,** etc. So long as I know of my deed, it were *best* to be lost in my thoughts.—**Scene III.** After the terrible scene just passed, the mind needs the change which the porter's nonsense brings. This is one view. In another light, this drunken levity adds to the horror. "Life, struck sharp on death, makes awful lightning." Taine, Voltaire, and all the French critics are shocked at what they call the inelegance, the savageness of Shakespeare. He was just as savage as nature and real life. **Old turning,** *frequent turning.* In *Merchant of Venice,* Act iv., Scene 2, we have the phrase 'old swearing'; in *Merry Wives of Windsor,* Act i., Scene 4, 'old abusing.'—**Hanged,** because plenty would bring down prices of farmer's produce.—**Napkins** (Lat. *mappa,* a napkin; Fr. *nappe,* a table-cloth; *kin,* fr. A. S. *cyn,* offspring, child. *Kin* is a diminutive ending. See *kind,* p. 113. *Napkin,* a little table-cloth), *handkerchiefs.*—**Equivocator.** This is said to mean a *Jesuit.* The members of this order were charged with having invented the doctrine of equivocation, or mental reservation. Lat. *æquus,* equal; *vox, vocis,* a word or voice; *æquivŏcus,* capable of double interpretation.—**Primrose** (Lat. *prima rosa,* first rose), *gay.* So "primrose path of dalliance," in *Hamlet.*—**Anon;** *i. e.,* I'll open the gate anon. See p. 33.

Enter MACDUFF *and* LENOX.

Macd. Was it so late, friend, ere you went to bed,
That you do lie so late?
Port. 'Faith, sir, we were carousing till the second cock. . . .
Macd. . . . .
Port. . . . .
Macd. I believe drink gave thee the lie last night.
Port. That it did, sir, i' the very throat o' me. But I requited him for his lie; and, I think, being too strong for him, though he took up my legs sometime, yet I made a shift to cast him.*
Macd. Is thy master stirring?—
Our knocking has awaked him; here he comes.

Enter MACBETH.

Len. Good-morrow, noble sir!
Macb. Good-morrow, both!
Macd. Is the king stirring, worthy Thane?
Macb. Not yet.
Macd. He did command me to call timely on him:
I have almost slipped the hour.
Macb. I'll bring you to him.
Macd. I know this is a joyful trouble to you;
But yet, 'tis one.
Macb. The labor we delight in physics pain.
This is the door.
Macd. I'll make so bold to call,
For 'tis my limited service. [*Exit* MACDUFF.
Len. Goes the king hence to-day?
Macb. He does—he did appoint so.
Len. The night has been unruly. Where we lay,
Our chimneys were blown down; and, as they say,
Lamentings heard i' the air; strange screams of death;
And prophesying, with accents terrible,
Of dire combustion, and confus'd events,
New hatched to the woful time. The obscure bird
Clamored the livelong night. Some say the earth
Was feverous and did shake.
Macb. 'Twas a rough night.
Len. My young remembrance cannot parallel
A fellow to it.

* **To cast him.** Vomit?—**Physics** (Gr. φυσική, science of nature; φύσις, nature; φύειν, to grow; hence, *physic*, the art of healing), *cures.*—**Limited,** *appointed.* Lat. *limes*, a prescribed boundary.—**He does—he did appoint so.** Truth momentarily struggles to his lips.—**Prophesying** (Gr. πρό, forth; φήμι, I speak), *utterance* (of strange, solemn, or important things).—**Parallel** (Gr. παρά, beside; ἀλλήλων, of one another; παράλληλος, alongside of one another), *bring alongside*, cite.

Faith, sir, etc. Spoken, like all of his gabble, in a rollicking way, with frequent hiccoughs?

Re-enter MACDUFF.

Macd. O horror! horror! horror! Tongue, nor heart,
Cannot conceive, nor name thee!
Macb., Len. What's the matter?
Macd. Confusion now hath made his masterpiece!
Most sacrilegious murder hath broke ope
The Lord's anointed* temple, and stole thence
The life o' the building!
Macb. What is't you say? the life?
Len. Mean you his majesty?
Macd. Approach the chamber, and destroy your sight
With a new Gorgon!—Do not bid me speak—
See, and then speak yourselves.—Awake! awake!—
[*Exeunt* MACBETH *and* LENOX.
Ring the alarum-bell! Murder! and treason!
Banquo! and Donalbain! Malcolm! awake!
Shake off this downy sleep, death's counterfeit,
And look on death itself!—up, up, and see
The great doom's image!—Malcolm! Banquo!
As from your graves rise up, and walk like sprights,
To countenance this horror! [*Bell rings.*

Enter Lady MACBETH.

Lady M. What's the business,
That such a hideous trumpet calls to parley
The sleepers of the house? speak, speak!——
Macd. O, gentle lady,
'Tis not for you to hear what I can speak!
The repetition, in a woman's ear,
Would murder as it fell——O Banquo! Banquo!

Enter BANQUO.

Our royal master's murdered!
Lady M. Wo, alas!
What, in our house?
Ban. Too cruel, anywhere!—

---

* **Anointed.** What can you say of the ceremony of anointing kings?—**Gorgon** (Gr. Γοργών). The Gorgons were three monstrous sisters of so terrific an aspect that the sight of them turned the beholder to stone. See *Medusa*, p. 75; also see Class. Dict.—**The great doom's image,** the image of the Judgment Day, when the dead are expected to rise.—**Sprights,** *spirits, ghosts.* See *spright*, Index.—**Parley** (Gr. παραβολή, a sentence, a parable; Lat. *parabŏla*, a comparison; O. F. *paroler;* Fr. *parler*, to speak), *conversation.*—**What, in our house?** No pity for Duncan, but a fear of being suspected!

O horror! horror! horror! etc. Here intense *horror* is followed by a *desire to* "*rouse* the neighborhood." The horror for an instant awes to silence, but it soon gives way to terror that shrieks "*Awake! awake!*" etc. We may suppose the language of Macduff, as far as "Awake! awake!" to be pronounced with shuddering *awe*, in a low pitch, median or final stress, aspirated quality, with rapid utterance.

Dear Duff, I pr'ythee, contradict thyself,
And say, it is not so.

Re-enter MACBETH *and* LENOX.

Macb. Had I but died an hour before this chance,
I had lived a blessed time; for, from this instant,
There's nothing serious in mortality;
All is but toys; renown and grace is dead;
The wine of life is drawn, and the mere lees
Is left this vault to brag of.

Enter MALCOLM *and* DONALBAIN.

Don. What is amiss?
Macb. You are, and do not know it:
The spring, the head, the fountain of your blood
Is stopped; the very source of it is stopped.
Macd. Your royal father's murdered.
Mal. O, by whom?
Len. Those of his chamber, as it seemed, had done 't:
Their hands and faces were all badged with blood;
So were their daggers, which, unwiped, we found
Upon their pillows:
They stared, and were distracted: no man's life
Was to be trusted with them.
Macb. O, yet I do repent* me of my fury,
That I did kill them.
Macd. Wherefore did you so?
Macb. Who can be wise, amazed, temperate and furious,
Loyal and neutral, in a moment? No man.
The expedition of my violent love
Outran the pauser reason.—Here lay Duncan,
His silver skin laced with his golden blood;
And his gashed stabs looked like a breach in nature,
For ruin's wasteful entrance! there, the murderers,
Steeped in the colors of their trade, their daggers
Unmannerly breeched with gore! Who could refrain,
That had a heart to love, and in that heart
Courage, to make his love known?
Lady M. Help me hence, ho!
Macd. Look to the lady.

---

* **Yet I do repent,** etc. Although they had killed Duncan, I nevertheless do repent of my killing them in my fury.—**Silver skin laced.** Observe these studied metaphors. They betray Macbeth, who, if innocent and really taken by surprise, would have used simpler language. Note, too, just before, the different styles in which Macduff and Macbeth respectively announce to Donalbain the murder of his father.—**Breeched,** *covered to the hilt,* or having the hilt covered thick with coagulated blood.

Had I but died, etc. *Assumed earnestness* and *pretended grief.* Loud; quick; median stress.
Who can be wise, amazed, etc. Assumed earnestness, loyalty, love, and anger. Sham excitement; loud; quick; median and radical stress, moderate pitch.

Mal. Why do we hold our tongues,
That most may claim this argument for ours?
Don. What should be spoken
Here, where our fate, hid in an auger-hole,
May rush, and seize us? Let's away; our tears
Are not yet brewed.*
Mal. Nor our strong sorrow
Upon the foot of motion.
} *Aside to each other.*

Ban. Look to the lady:— [Lady MACBETH *is carried out.*
And when we have our naked frailties hid,
That suffer in exposure, let us meet,
And question this most bloody piece of work,
To know it further. Fears and scruples shake us.
In the great hand of God I stand; and thence
Against the undivulged pretence I fight
Of treasonous malice!
Macb. And so do I.
All. So all.
Macb. Let's briefly put on manly readiness,
And meet i' the hall together.
All. Well contented.
[*Exeunt all but* MALCOLM *and* DONALBAIN.
Mal. What will you do? Let's not consort with them.
To show an unfelt sorrow is an office
Which the false man does easy. I'll to England.
Don. To Ireland, I: our separated fortune
Shall keep us both the safer. Where we are,
There's daggers in men's smiles. The near in blood,
The nearer bloody.
Mal. This murderous shaft that's shot,
Hath not yet lighted; and our safest way
Is to avoid the aim. Therefore, to horse.
And let us not be dainty of leave-taking,
But shift away. There's warrant in that theft
Which steals itself, when there's no mercy left. [*Exeunt.*

---

* **Brewed.** Macbeth has already brewed, or carefully premeditated, his tears; we have not.—**Foot of motion.** Our sorrow has not begun to step or move; Macbeth's has.—**Lady Macbeth is carried out.** Probably her fainting is genuine. She is unprepared for the other murders.—**Frailties**, etc. (Lat. *fragilitas*, brittleness; fr. *frangĕre*, to break). When we have clothed our bodies, now naked and suffering from cold. See *freeletee*, p. 56.—**Pretence** (Lat. *præ*, before; *tendĕre*, to stretch; *prætendĕre*, to hold out as an excuse or pretext), *design*, *intention*, pretext (which malice may allege).—**Nearer bloody.** Macbeth was own cousin to the princes.—**Murderous shaft . . . . lighted;** *i. e.*, Macbeth's fell purpose is not yet entirely accomplished.

And when we have our naked frailties hid, etc. *Decision*, *anger*, *solemnity*. At first, moderate time, pitch, and force, with radical stress; next, low pitch, soft force, slow time, and median stress; at last (*i. e.*, beginning with "*and thence against*"), moderate pitch, loud force, moderate time, and radical stress. The instructor should insist, all through this play, that every passage and every sentence shall be, in every particular, correctly read aloud. This will wonderfully bring out the merit of the play.

SCENE IV. *Without the Castle.*

Enter ROSSE *and an* Old Man.

Old M. Threescore and ten I can remember well:
Within the volume of which time, I have seen
Hours dreadful and things strange. But this sore night
Hath trifled former knowings.

Rosse. Ah, good father,
Thou seest, the heavens, as troubled with man's act,
Threaten his bloody stage. By the clock 'tis day;
And yet dark night strangles the travelling lamp.
Is it night's predominance, or the day's shame,
That darkness does the face of earth entomb,
When living light should kiss it?

Old M. 'Tis unnatural,
Even like the deed that's done. On Tuesday last,
A falcon, towering in her pride of place,
Was by a mousing owl hawked at and killed.

Rosse. And Duncan's horse, (a thing most strange and certain,)
Beauteous and swift, the minions of their race,
Turned wild in nature, broke their stalls, flung out,
Contending 'gainst obedience, as they would make
War with mankind.

Old M. 'Tis said, they ate each other.

Rosse. They did so; to the amazement of mine eyes,
That looked upon 't. Here comes the good Macduff——

Enter MACDUFF.

How goes the world, sir, now?

Macd. Why, see you not?

Rosse. Is 't known who did this more than bloody deed?

Macd. Those that Macbeth hath slain.

Rosse. Alas the day!
What good could they pretend?

Macd. They were suborned.
Malcolm and Donalbain, the king's two sons,
Are stolen away and fled; which puts on them
Suspicion of the deed.

Rosse. 'Gainst nature still!
Thriftless ambition, that will ravin up

---

* **Living light.** Holinshed tells us that, for six months after King Duff's murder, there appeared no sun, nor moon, but clouds, lightnings, and tempests.—**Pride of place** (a technical phrase in falconry), *highest soaring*, loftiness.—**Horse** (Sans. *hrêsh*, to neigh; A. S. *hors*, for *hros;* Ger. *ross*, horse), *horses*.—**Minions**, darlings. See p. 110.—**Ate each other.** So Holinshed, of Duff's horses.—**Pretend,** *design.* See *pretence*, p. 135.—**Ravin up** (Gr. ἁρπάζω, I snatch; Lat. *rapĕre*, to seize and carry away; Eng. *rapine*, forcible snatching and pillaging), *prey with rapacity upon*, devour ravenously. See "Benjamin shall *ravin* as a wolf," in Genesis xlix. 27. Spelled also, *raven*.

Threescore and ten, etc. *Awe.* Rather soft force, low pitch, slow time, and somewhat impure quality (*i. e.*, with slight prominence to consonant and hoarse pectoral sounds).

Thine own life's means!— Then, 'tis most like,
The sovereignty * will fall upon Macbeth.
Macd. He is already named, and gone to Scone
To be invested.
Rosse. Where is Duncan's body?
Macd. Carried to Colme-kill,
The sacred storehouse of his predecessors,
And guardian of their bones.
Rosse. Will you to Scone?
Macd. No, cousin: I 'll to Fife.
Rosse. Well, I will thither.
Macd. Well, may you see things well done there;—adieu!—
Lest our old robes sit easier than our new!
Rosse. Father, farewell.
Old M. God's benison go with you: and with those
That would make good of bad, and friends of foes! [*Exeunt.*

ACT III.

SCENE I. Forres. *A Room in the Palace.*

Enter BANQUO.

Ban. Thou hast it now, King, Cawdor, Glamis,—all,
As the weird women promised; and, I fear,
Thou playedst most foully for't. Yet it was said
It should not stand in thy posterity,
But that myself should be the root and father
Of many kings. If there come truth from them,
(As upon thee, Macbeth, their speeches shine,)
Why, by the verities on thee made good,
May they not be my oracles as well,
And set me up in hope? But, hush; no more.

---

* **Sovereignty.** After the sons of Duncan, the next heir was Macbeth.—**Scone.** At ancient Scone, in Scotland, County of Perth, the kings of that country used to be crowned sitting on a famous stone now preserved in Westminster Abbey. It is placed as the seat of a wooden chair, which is still used at coronations.—**Invested** (Lat. *vestire*, to clothe). *inaugurated.*—**Colme-kill,** *Icolmkill* (*Isle of Columb's Cell*), *Iona*, one of the Western Isles (Hebrides), the burial place, according to Holinshed, of the Scottish Kings. St. Columb, who flourished in the sixth century, was a native of Ireland. He is said to have founded an abbey here. *Cell*, Lat. *cella*, is chapel or church, the same as *kil* or *kill;* as in *Kilpatrick*, church of Patrick. For a long time Iona was the chief seat of learning in the north and the centre of missionary enterprise.—**Benison** (O. Fr. *beniçon*, blessing), *benediction.*

Speeches shine, predictions are sunshiny. "'Shine' means *prosper*," says Warburton: "Appear with all the lustre of conspicuous truth," is the stately paraphrase of Johnson.—**My oracles.** *My* is emphatic.

Thou hast it now, etc. This utterance I fancy to have been extremely slow, energetic, with long pauses. The *ou*, in *foully*, should be much prolonged, the diphthongal sound being struck on a moderate pitch, but the voice sliding down to a deep tremulous pectoral on the last part of the syllable.

Yet it was said, etc. This is uttered in a matter-of-fact way, as far as, "But, hush." "Circumflex slides" (the voice passing through what would be termed in music "higher, lower, and higher," or "lower, higher, and lower," making a *wave* in the pitch) prevail. This *wave* of the voice is on the long sounds of the accented syllables.

Sennet * *sounded. Enter* MACBETH, *as King;* Lady MACBETH, *as Queen;* LENOX, ROSSE, Lords, Ladies, *and* Attendants.

Macb. Here's our chief guest!
Lady M. If he had been forgotten,
It had been as a gap in our great feast,
And all things unbecoming.
Macb. To-night we hold a solemn supper, sir,
And I'll request your presence.
Ban. Let your Highness
Command upon me; to the which my duties
Are with a most indissoluble tie
Forever knit.
Macb. Ride you this afternoon?
Ban. Ay, my good lord.
Macb. We should have else desired your good advice
(Which still hath been both grave and prosperous)
In this day's council; but we'll take to-morrow.
Is't far you ride?
Ban. As far, my lord, as will fill up the time
'Twixt this and supper: go not my horse the better,
I must become a borrower of the night
For a dark hour, or twain.
Macb. Fail not our feast.
Ban. My lord, I will not.
Macb. We hear, our bloody cousins are bestowed
In England and in Ireland; not confessing
Their cruel parricide, filling their hearers
With strange invention. But of that to-morrow,
When, therewithal, we shall have cause of state
Craving us jointly. Hie you to horse. Adieu,
Till you return at night. Goes Fleance with you?
Ban. Ay, my good lord: our time does call upon us.
Macb. I wish your horses swift, and sure of foot;
And so I do commend you to their backs.
Farewell.— [*Exit* BANQUO.
Let every man be master of his time
Till seven at night. To make society
The sweeter welcome, we will keep ourself
Till supper-time alone. While then, God b' wi' you.
[*Exeunt* Lady MACBETH, Lords, Ladies, etc.

---

* **Sennet,** a particular time or mode of martial music.—**Solemn supper,** a banquet with form and ceremony. See *solempne*, Index.—**To the which,** *to which command;* or, *to whom* (*i. e.*, to your Highness).—**The better.** *Better* than to make night-travelling necessary.—**Cause of state,** *state affairs.*—**Commend.** See p. 123.—**While then,** *meanwhile, then;* or, perhaps, *till then.*—**God b' wi' you.** This expression is said to be the original of "*good-bye*," which would appear to be a mere contraction; but see the unabridged dictionaries.

Here's our chief guest, etc. The following dialogue requires only moderate force, time, etc., as far as, "Bring them before us."

Sirrah,* a word with you. Attend those men
Our pleasure ?
Atten. They are, my lord, without the palace gate.
Macb. Bring them before us.— [*Exit* Attendant.
To be thus is nothing;
But to be safely thus!—Our fears in Banquo
Stick deep; and in his royalty of nature
Reigns that which would be feared.—'Tis much he dares;
And, to that dauntless temper of his mind,
He hath a wisdom that doth guide his valor
To act in safety. There is none but he
Whose being I do fear; and, under him,
My genius is rebuked; as, it is said,
Mark Antony's was by Cæsar. He chid the sisters
When first they put the name of King upon me,
And bade them speak to him: then, prophet-like,
They hailed him father to a line of kings!
Upon my head they placed a fruitless crown,
And put a barren sceptre in my gripe,
Thence to be wrenched with an unlineal hand,
No son of mine succeeding. If it be so,
For Banquo's issue have I filed my mind;
For them the gracious Duncan have I murdered;
Put rancors in the vessel of my peace
Only for them; and mine eternal jewel
Given to the common enemy of man,
To make them kings!—the seed of Banquo kings!
Rather than so, come, Fate, into the list,
And champion me to the utterance!—Who 's there ?—

Re-enter Attendant, *with two* Murderers.

Now to the door, and stay there till we call. [*Exit* Attendant.
Was it not yesterday we spoke together ?
1st Mur. It was, so please your Highness.

---

* **Sirrah** (*Sir, ha!* O. Fr. *sire*, father; fr. Lat. *senior*, elder; *senex*, *senis*, old; Fr. *seigneur*, *sieur;* Ital. *signor;* Sp. *señor;* Eng. *sir;* or it may be fr. Ir. *sirreach*, poor, lean), *sir*. Now used rather contemptuously and rarely; but in Shakespeare's time used familiarly. It was usually addressed to males.—**Attend,** are in attendance on, *await.*—**Thus**, in the condition of a king.—**Would be feared.** *Would* and *should* were interchangeable in Shakespeare's time.—**And to that,** and *in addition* to that.—**None but he,** *none other than he. But* is primarily fr. *be*, be, and *utan*, outward, fr. *ût*, out. Is *but* a preposition when it has the sense of *except?* May it be followed by *him?*—**Mark Antony's was by Cæsar.** Octavius Cæsar is meant. See *Antony and Cleopatra*, Act ii., Scene 3, and *Plutarch's Lives.*—**Filed** (A. S. *fylan*, to pollute; akin to *filth* and *foul*), *defiled.*—**Enemy.** The word *Satan* means *adversary.*—**Utterance** (Fr. *à l'outrance*, to extremity, to the last drop of blood. See, also, A. S. *ût*, out; *uter*, exterior; *ûtōr*, outer), *utmost*, *extremity.*

To be thus is nothing, etc. Undertone, so as not to be heard far. Impatience and spite and, towards the last, remorse; ending with angry defiance. "Vanishing stress" on the most *impatient* utterances. The forcible utterance of the last part of an accented vowel, the voice being jerked out at the end of the syllable, is particularly appropriate in the expression of vexation, impatience, etc.

Macb. Well, then, now
Have you considered of my speeches? Know,
That it was he, in the times past, which held you
So under fortune; which, you thought, had been
Our innocent self. This I made good to you
In our last conference, passed in probation with you,*
How you were borne in hand; how crossed; the instruments;
Who wrought with them; and all things else, that might,
To half a soul, and to a notion crazed,
Say, "Thus did Banquo."
1st Mur. You made it known to us.
Macb. I did so; and went further, which is now
Our point of second meeting. Do you find
Your patience so predominant in your nature
That you can let this go? Are you so gospelled
To pray for that good man, and for his issue,
Whose heavy hand hath bowed you to the grave,
And beggared yours for ever?
1st Mur. We are men, my liege.
Macb. Ay, in the catalogue ye go for men;
As hounds, and greyhounds, mongrels, spaniels, curs,
Shoughs, water-rugs, and demi-wolves, are cleped
All by the name of dogs! The valued file
Distinguishes the swift, the slow, the subtle,
The house-keeper, the hunter,—every one
According to the gift which bounteous Nature
Hath in him closed; whereby he does receive
Particular addition, from the bill
That writes them all alike: and so of men.
Now, if you have a station in the file,
Not in the worst rank of manhood, say it;
And I will put that business in your bosoms,
Whose execution takes your enemy off;
Grapples you to the heart and love of us,
Who wear our health but sickly in his life,
Which in his death were perfect.

---

* **Probation with you,** *proving to you.*—**Borne in hand,** deluded by fair promises never fulfilled.—**Gospelled,** obedient to the Gospel, which bids us pray for those who wrong us.—**Spaniels** (Lat. *Hispania*, Spain; *Hispaniola*, little Spain, *i. e.*, Hayti, "where was the best breed of this dog").—**Shoughs** (A. S. *scacga*, a bush of hair, that which is shaggy; Sw. *skägg;* Dan. *skäg*, the beard; Eng. *shag*), *shock-dogs.* In Pope's *Rape of the Lock*, the dog is called *shock*, and the name is quite common.—**Cleped** (A. S. *clepan*, to call), *called.*—**Valued file,** descriptive *list* showing *values* and qualities.—**Particular addition,** particular *title.*

Are you so gospelled? etc. Here we have the circumflex slides again. This *wave* of the voice is especially adapted to irony, mockery, railing, etc. It usually expresses, indefinitely or conditionally, some idea contrasted with another to which the straight slide belongs.

Now, if you have a station, etc. This is uttered with decision and energy, so as to inspire confidence. It is bold; quite loud, but not so as to be overheard; with radical stress; rather quick time; rather aspirated quality; not much volume. This manner prevails to the end of the colloquy.

2d Mur. I am one, my liege,
Whom the vile blows and buffets of the world
Have so incensed that I am reckless what
I do to spite the world.

1st Mur. And I another,
So weary with disasters, tugged with fortune,
That I would set my life on any chance,
To mend it, or be rid on 't.

Macb. Both of you
Know Banquo was your enemy.

2d Mur. True, my lord.

Macb. So is he mine, and in such bloody distance*
That every minute of his being thrusts
Against my near'st of life; and though I could
With bare-faced power sweep him from my sight,
And bid my will avouch it, yet I must not,
For certain friends that are both his and mine;
Whose loves I may not drop, but wail his fall
Whom I myself struck down! and thence it is,
That I to your assistance do make love,
Masking the business from the common eye
For sundry weighty reasons.

2d Mur. We shall, my lord,
Perform what you command us.

1st Mur. Though our lives——

Macb. Your spirits shine through you. Within this hour, at most,
I will advise you where to plant yourselves,
Acquaint you, with a perfect spy, o' the time,
The moment on 't: for 't must be done to-night,
And something from the palace; always thought
That I require a clearness. And with him,
To leave no rubs nor botches in the work,
Fleance his son, that keeps him company,
Whose absence is no less material to me
Than is his father's, must embrace the fate
Of that dark hour. Resolve yourselves apart.
I'll come to you anon.

2d Mur. We are resolved, my lord.

---

* **Distance,** *enmity.* So Bacon uses it in his essay on *Seditions and Troubles.* Hudson interprets *distance* as here equivalent to *degree.* In fierce combat with swords, the less the distance, the bloodier the fight.—**With a perfect spy of,** etc. I will acquaint [inform] you, with [by means of] a perfect [thoroughly well-informed] spy, of [in regard to] the time, etc. Some prefer to read "*the* perfect spy," meaning "the sure means of spying or knowing;" but Mr. Collier's folio of 1632 has "*a* perfect spy."—**From** [at a distance from] **the palace.—Always thought,** it being always borne in mind that I must be unsuspected.—**Botches** (It. *bozza*, a swelling; Fr. *bosse*, bunch, swelling; Ger. *boll*, hard, bulbous), *bungling patches.*

So is he mine, etc. Secrecy, but such as befits a king: an undertone, therefore. Hate. Aspirated quality; low pitch; initial stress.

Macb. I'll call upon you straight: abide within.— [*Exeunt* Murderers.
It is concluded.—Banquo, thy soul's flight,
If it find heaven, must find it out to-night. [*Exit.*

SCENE II. *The Same. Another Room.*

Enter Lady MACBETH *and a* Servant.

Lady M. Is Banquo gone from court?
Serv. Ay, madam, but rĕturns again to-night.
Lady M. Say to the king, I would attend his leisure
For a few words.
Serv. Madam, I will. [*Exit.*
Lady M. Nought 's had, all 's spent,
Where our desire is got without content.
'Tis safer to be that which we destroy,
Than, by destruction, dwell in doubtful joy.

Enter MACBETH.

How now, my lord? why do you keep alone,
Of sorriest * fancies your companions making,
Using those thoughts which should indeed have died
With them they think on? Things without remedy,
Should be without regard: what's done, is done.
Macb. We have scotched the snake, not killed it!
She'll close, and be herself; whilst our poor malice
Remains in danger of her former tooth.
But let the frame of things disjoint,
Both the worlds suffer,
Ere we will eat our meal in fear, and sleep
In the affliction of these terrible dreams
That shake us nightly. Better be with the dead,
Whom we, to gain our place, have sent to peace,
Than on the torture of the mind to lie
In restless ecstasy. Duncan is in his grave;
After life's fitful fever, he sleeps well;
Treason has done his worst: nor steel, nor poison,
Malice domestic, foreign levy,—nothing,
Can touch him further!

---

* **Sorriest** (A. S. *sorg*, sorrow; O. E. *sorwe; sâr*, sore), *most unhappy.*—**Scotched** (Gael. *sgoch*, a slit, incision), chopped a bit of skin from, *scratched.*—**To gain our place.** Many read *peace* instead of *place.*—**Ecstasy** (Gr. ἐκ, out; στάσις, standing), that condition in which one is "beside himself," or, as the phrase is, "out of his head," out of his right mind, whether through pain or delight.—**Levy** (Fr. *lever*, to raise; Lat. *levare*, to raise; *levis*, light), raising of *troops*, preparation for war.

Nought 's had, etc. Spoken with sighs and weariness; high pitch.
How now, my lord? etc. Tenderness. Soft force, high pitch, median stress.
We have scotched the snake, etc. Decision; desperate resolve. Not loud, but forcible, with "expulsive stress" (the accented syllables being expelled with much breath); an earnest conversational tone.
Duncan is in his grave, etc. Sorrow and remorse. Vanishing stress; plaintive; half wailing distress; high pitch; aspirated.

Lady M. Come on, gentle my lord;*
Sleek o'er your rugged looks; be bright and jovial
Among your guests to-night.
Macb. So shall I, love;
And so, I pray, be you. Let your remembrance
Apply to Banquo: present him eminence, both
With eye and tongue: unsafe the while, that we
Must lave our honors in these flattering streams,
And make our faces vizards to our hearts,
Disguising what they are!
Lady M. You must leave this.
Macb. Oh, full of scorpions is my mind, dear wife!
Thou knowest that Banquo and his Fleance live.
Lady M. But in them nature's copy 's not eterne.
Macb. There's comfort yet; they are assailable.
Then be thou jocund. Ere the bat hath flown
His cloistered flight; ere, to black Hecate's summons,
The shard-borne beetle, with his drowsy hums,
Hath rung night's yawning peal, there shall be done
A deed of dreadful note.
Lady M. What 's to be done?
Macb. Be innocent of the knowledge, dearest chuck,
Till thou applaud the deed. Come, seeling night,
Scarf up the tender eye of pitiful day;
And, with thy bloody and invisible hand,
Cancel and tear to pieces that great bond
Which keeps me pale!—Light thickens, and the crow
Makes wing to the rooky wood;

* **Gentle my lord,** *my gentle lord.* This inversion is quite common in Shakespeare. —**Present,** etc. *Show him high honor.*—**Unsafe the while,** it being an unsafe state all the while. White makes "while" a substantive and interprets thus: "Unsafe is that time in which our royalty is obliged to stoop to flattery."—**Vizards** (Lat. *vidēre* to see, *visus, visum*, seen; Eng. *visor*, a part of a helmet perforated for the purpose of seeing through), *masks.*—**You must leave this;** *i. e.*, this way of thinking. Would it be in keeping with her humor to play upon the words *leave* and *lave?*—**Copy,** the copy of court rolls, being the evidence of a life-estate. Here Shakespeare's technical legal knowledge is supposed to be apparent. But is it necessary to regard *copy* as a legal term here?—**Shard-borne** (A. S *sceard*, a shearing, a part, share; A. S. *sceran*, to shear, cut; a fragment of earthenware or like brittle substance, a shell or scale; hence *pot-sherd*), *borne on scaly wings.*—**With his drowsy hums.** Gray evidently had this passage in mind in writing the second stanza of his "Elegy."—

"Save where the beetle wheels his droning flight,
And drowsy tinklings lull the distant folds."

Dearest chuck (A. S. *cicen*, chicken, whence *chuck;* or perhaps formed in imitation of the cluck of a hen), *chicken*, a pet name. So *chickens*, Act iv., Sc. 3.—**Seeling,** *blinding. Seeling* is said to be a term from *falconry;* to *seel* a hawk's eyes was to sew the eyelids together. Fr. *siller, ciller*, to wink, to seel, fr. *cil*, Lat. *cilium*, an eyelash.—**Bond,** Banquo's life. This word gives countenance to the explanation of *copy* as a technical law term. In *Cymbeline* we have "Cancel his bond of life, dear God, I pray."—**Thickens;** *i. e.*, it is growing dark.—**Rooky,** abounding in rooks. By such incidental allusions Shakespeare is shown to have been a close observer of nature.

Come on, gentle my lord, etc. Tender and soothing love. Soft; median; pure quality; high pitch.
So shall I, love, etc. Effort at hope; but weak from remorse and fear. Plaintive; high pitch; sighing, distressful; rising slides.
Oh, full of scorpions, etc. Distress. Vanishing stress; high; aspirated.
There's comfort yet, etc. He cheers himself. Decision. Initial stress.
Ere the bat hath flown, etc. Desperation, horror. Low pitch; slow; undertone.
Be innocent, etc. "Small volume," appropriate to *endearment*.
Come, seeling night, etc. Awe and horror. Low; slow; large volume; undertone; initial stress.

Good things of day begin to droop and drowse,
Whiles night's black agents to their preys do rouse.
Thou marvell'st at my words; but hold thee still:
Things, bad begun, make strong themselves by ill.
So, pr'ythee, go with me. [*Exeunt.*

SCENE III. *The Same.*

A Park or Lawn, with a Gate leading to the Palace.

Enter three Murderers.

1st Mur. But who did bid thee join with us?
3d Mur. Macbeth.
2d Mur. He needs not our mistrust; since he delivers *
Our offices, and what we have to do,
To the direction just.
1st Mur. Then stand with us.
The west yet glimmers with some streaks of day.
Now spurs the lated traveller apace,
To gain the timely inn; and near approaches
The subject of our watch.
3d Mur. Hark! I hear horses.
Ban. [*Within.*] Give us a light there, ho!
2d Mur. Then it is he; the rest
That are within the note of expectation,
Already are i' the court.
1st Mur. His horses go about.
3d Mur. Almost a mile; but he does usually,
So all men do, from hence to the palace gate
Make it their walk.

Enter BANQUO *and* FLEANCE, *a* Servant *with a Torch preceding them.*

2d Mur. A light, a light!
3d Mur. 'Tis he.
1st Mur. Stand to 't.
Ban. It will be rain to-night.
1st Mur. Let it come down! [*Assaults* BANQUO.
Ban. Oh, treachery! Fly, good Fleance, fly, fly, fly!
Thou may'st revenge.—O slave! [*Dies.* FLEANCE *and* Servant *escape.*
3d Mur. Who did strike out the light?

---

* **He delivers,** etc. He communicates Macbeth's directions accurately to us. This third murderer is supposed to be the "perfect spy" that was to acquaint the other two with the particulars of Banquo's approach, etc.—**Apace** (Lat. *passus*, a step), at a quick step, rapidly. See *apace*, Index.—**Note of expectation,** *list of expected guests.*—**It will be rain.** Then it was cloudy and, consequently, dark!—**Fleance and servant escape.** Fleance fled to Wales. He was an ancestor of James I., in compliment to whom, as is supposed, Shakespeare represents Banquo as innocent of Duncan's murder, though history shows him to have been equally guilty with Macbeth. Was Shakespeare justifiable in thus perverting history to flatter the thick-headed pedantic Scotchman?

Oh, treachery! etc. Surprise; shouting; scorn. Loud; quick; strongly aspirated; explosive.

1st Mur. Was 't not the way?
3d Mur. There's but one down: the son is fled!
2d Mur. We have lost best half of our affair.
1st Mur. Well, let's away, and say how much is done. [*Exeunt.*

SCENE IV. *A Room of State in the Palace. A Banquet prepared.*

Enter MACBETH, Lady MACBETH, ROSSE, LENOX, Lords, *and* Attendants.

Macb. You know your own degrees; sit down. At first
And last, the hearty welcome.
Lords. Thanks to your majesty.
Macb. Ourself will mingle with society,
And play the humble host.
Our hostess keeps her state;* but, in best time,
We will require her welcome.
Lady M. Pronounce it for me, sir, to all our friends;
For my heart speaks, they are welcome.

Enter first Murderer *to the door.*

Macb. See, they encounter thee with their heart's thanks:——
Both sides are even. Here I'll sit 'i the midst.
Be large in mirth; anon, we'll drink a measure
The table round.—There's blood upon thy face. [*Approaching the door.*
Mur. 'Tis Banquo's then.
Macb. 'Tis better thee without, than he within.
Is he dispatched?
Mur. My lord, his throat is cut; that I did for him.
Macb. Thou art the best o' the cut-throats! Yet he's good
That did the like for Fleance: if thou didst it,
Thou art the nonpareil.
Mur. Most royal sir,
Fleance is 'scaped.
Macb. Then comes my fit again! I had else been perfect,
Whole as the marble, founded as the rock,
As broad and general as the casing air;
But now I am cabined, cribbed, confined, bound in
To saucy doubts and fears. But Banquo's safe?

* **Her state.** State is chair, or royal seat. It was upon the canopied dais and at the head of the table. Macbeth descends.—**Encounter thee.** The guests encounter Lady Macbeth with their thanks.—**Thy face.** He steps aside to the door and whispers, "There's blood," etc.—**He within,** *within him.* So the editors generally. But possibly Macbeth means, for he has not yet been informed of Banquo's death, "'Tis better for thee to be without [outside] the palace, than that he [Banquo] should be within it," implying that the murderer has intruded, leaving Banquo's murder, or his body, unattended to.—**Non-pareil** (Fr. *non*, not; *pareil*, equal; fr. Lat. *par*, equal), the *peerless*, the unmatched.—**Cabined** (W., Ir., and Gael. *caban*, a hut or booth, cot), shut up as in a cabin.—**Cribbed** (A. S. *crybb*; Ger. *krippe*, a manger), caged, *cramped*, straitened.

You know your own degrees, etc. Polished courtesy, avoiding command. Soft; median; quick.
There's blood, etc. Secrecy. Whispering; initial stress.
Then comes my fit, etc. Great impatience. Vanishing stress; aspirated quality; undertone; quick; small volume.

Mur. Ay, my good lord: safe in a ditch he bides,
With twenty trenched* gashes on his head,
The least a death to nature.
Mach. Thanks for that!——
There the grown serpent lies. The worm, that's fled,
Hath nature that in time will venom breed,
No teeth for the present.—Get thee gone. To-morrow
We'll hear ourselves again. [*Exit* Murderer.
Lady M. My royal lord,
You do not give the cheer. The feast is sold,
That is not often vouched, while 'tis a making,
'Tis given with welcome. To feed were best at home;
From thence, the sauce to meat is ceremony;
Meeting were bare without it.
Mach. Sweet remembrancer!—
Now, good digestion wait on appetite,
And health on both!
Len. May it please your Highness sit?
[*The Ghost of* BANQUO *rises, and sits in* MACBETH'S *place.*
Mach. Here had we now our country's honor roofed,
Were the graced person of our Banquo present;
Whom may I rather challenge for unkindness,
Than pity for mischance!
Rosse. His absence, sir,
Lays blame upon his promise. Please it your Highness
To grace us with your royal company?
Mach. The table 's full.
Len. Here 's a place reserved, sir.
Mach. Where?
Len. Here, my good lord. What is 't that moves your Highness?
Mach. Which of you have done this?
Lords. What, my good lord?
Mach. Thou canst not say I did it. Never shake
Thy gory locks at me!
Rosse. Gentlemen, rise; his Highness is not well.
Lady M. Sit, worthy friends.—My lord is often thus,
And hath been from his youth. Pray you, keep seat;

---

* **Trenched** (Lat. *truncare*, to cut off; Fr. *trancher*, to cut; Eng. *trench*, a ditch cut in the earth), *deep cut*.—**To feed**, etc. J. Wilkes Booth quoted this in his diary, when, after the assassination of the President, he was clandestinely fed by a friend who dared not seat him openly at his table.—**Meeting.** Alas, the quibble! Lady Macbeth seems to have had a weakness for puns.—**Whom may I**, *whom may I*, a wish.—**Thou canst not say**, etc. One Dr. Forman in his Diary, preserved in the Ashmolean Museum, records his seeing the play of Macbeth at the Globe Theatre, April 20, 1610. He describes the consternation of Macbeth on turning and beholding the ghost, after "drinking a carouse to the noble Banquo, and wishing he were there." See note in White's Shakespeare. See also Hudson's note on this ghost scene. Evidently the ghost is a 'subjective' one, seen by Macbeth only.

My royal lord, etc. Rather loud, but polite; median; circumflex; slight volume; pure quality.
Thou canst not say I did it, etc. Terror. Very loud; tremulous; quick; explosive; rising slides.
Sit, worthy friends, etc. Courteous, but authoritative; polite, earnest appeal. High; quick; loud.

The fit is momentary: upon a thought*
He will again be well. If much you note him,
You shall offend him and extend his passion.
Feed, and regard him not.—Are you a man ?
Macb. Ay, and a bold one, that dare look on that
Which might appal the devil!
Lady M. O proper stuff! [*Aside to* MACBETH.
This is the very painting of your fear.
This is the air-drawn dagger, which, you said,
Led you to Duncan! Oh, these flaws and starts
(Impostors to true fear) would well become
A woman's story at a winter's fire,
Authorized by her grandam! Shame itself!
Why do you make such faces ? When all 's done,
You look but on a stool.
Macb. Pr'ythee, see there! behold! look! lo! how say you ?—
Why, what care I ? If thou canst nod, speak too.—
If charnel-houses and our graves must send
Those that we bury back, our monuments
Shall be the maws of kites! [Ghost *disappears.*
Lady M. What! quite unmanned in folly ?
Macb. If I stand here, I saw him.
Lady M. Fie! for shame!
Macb. Blood hath been shed, ere now, i' the olden time,
Ere human statute purged the gentle weal:
Ay, and since, too, murders have been performed
Too terrible for the ear. The times have been,
That, when the brains were out, the man would die,
And there an end; but now, they rise again,
With twenty mortal murders on their crowns,
And push us from our stools! This is more strange
Than such a murder is.
Lady M. My worthy lord,
Your noble friends do lack you.

---

* **Upon a thought,** as quick as thought.—**Extend his passion,** *prolong his suffering.*—**Flaws** (Norw. *flage, flaag,* a sudden gust of wind; Lat. *flare,* to blow; Eng. *blast,* by Grimm's Law?), *sharp gusts.*—**Impostors to,** impostors *in comparison with.*—**Become,** *befit;* like Lat. *convenire,* to come together, to be fitting.—**Authorized,** *vouched for.*—**Grandam** (Fr. *grand,* great; *dame,* lady; Lat. *grandis, domina*), *grandmother.*—**Pr'ythee.** To Lady Macbeth.—**Why, what care I?** To the ghost.—**If charnel-houses.** To Lady Macbeth, in an undertone or whisper.—**Maws.** Spenser says, "Be not entombed in the raven or the kite."—**Gentle weal,** etc. "Ere human statute made the commonwealth gentle by purging or cleansing it from the pollutions of barbarism." *Hudson.*—**My worthy lord.** This, of course, is spoken aloud.

Are you a man? O proper stuff, etc. Reproach, impatience, scorn. Radical; nasal; aspirated; "expulsive" stress; quick.
Pr'ythee! etc. Secrecy. Loud whisper to his wife; spasmodic utterance.
Why, what care I? etc. Loud defiance, which instantly melts into *terror.* "Intermittent stress" at the last.
Blood hath been shed, etc. Undertone to his wife; tremor; gasping.
My worthy lord, etc. Quite loud, cheerful, re-assuring.

Macb. I do forget.—
Do not muse* at me, my most worthy friends.
I have a strange infirmity, which is nothing
To those that know me. Come, love and health to all;
Then I'll sit down.—Give me some wine: fill full.
I drink to the general joy of the whole table,
Ghost *rises.*
And to our dear friend Banquo, whom we miss.
'Would he were here! to all, and him, we thirst,
And all to all.

Lords. Our duties, and the pledge.

Macb. Avaunt! and quit my sight! Let the earth hide thee!
Thy bones are marrowless, thy blood is cold!
Thou hast no speculation in those eyes
Which thou dost glare with!

Lady M. Think of this, good peers,
But as a thing of custom. 'Tis no other;
Only it spoils the pleasure of the time.

Macb. What man dare, I dare:
Approach thou like the rugged Russian bear,
The armed rhinoceros, or the Hyrcan tiger,
Take any shape but that, and my firm nerves
Shall never tremble! Or, be alive again,
And dare me to the desert with thy sword—
If trembling I inhabit then, protest me
The baby of a girl! Hence, horrible shadow!
Unreal mockery, hence!—Why, so;—being gone, [Ghost *disappears.*
I am a man again.—Pray you, sit still.

Lady M. You have displaced the mirth, broke the good meeting,
With most admired disorder.

Macb. Can such things be,
And overcome us like a summer's cloud,
Without our special wonder? You make me strange,

---

* **Muse,** *wonder*, be in an eager study. Fr. *muser*, to loiter, trifle; Ger. *musze*, leisure; Lat. *musa;* Gr. μοῦσα, a muse, a fabled goddess; fr. μάω, to seek out, invent.—**All to all.** Proverbial. May all good things be to you all; or, we all drink to the health of all.—**Speculation,** *seeing;* or *intelligence.*—**Hyrcan,** *Hyrcanian.* Hyrcania was a large country to the south-east of the Caspian. In Hamlet, Act ii., Scene 2, we have, "The rugged Pyrrhus, like the Hyrcanian beast."—**Trembling I inhabit,** *inhabit trembling;* as in Ps. xxii., 3, we read, "Thou that *inhabitest the praises* of Israel." Others interpret the passage thus: If, trembling, I remain in any habitation when thou dost dare me to the desert. Pope changed *inhabit* to *inhibit;* Steevens changed *then* to *thee;* Dyce adopts both alterations.—**Baby,** *doll.* So White.—**Admired** (Lat. *ad*, at; *miror*, I wonder), *wonderful.*—**Overcome,** come over, *pass over.*

I do forget, etc. Apologetic, courteous, confused; desperate attempt at cheerfulness. Fits and starts in the voice, with stammering; radical now; now median; rather high pitch.

Avaunt! etc. A scream of terror—defiance yielding instantly to consternation. Very loud; very quick; very high; guttural quality at last, with convulsive gasps.

Think of this, etc. Very decided and emphatic, but polite; assumed indifference.

What man dare, etc. Frantic terror, gradually giving way to frantic spasmodic courage; convulsive tremor; very loud; very quick; explosive radical stress on the last.

Can such things be, etc. Wonder. He slowly recovers from his terror.

Even to the disposition that I owe,*
When now I think you can behold such sights
And keep the natural ruby of your cheek,
When mine is blanched with fear.

Rosse. What sights, my lord?

Lady M. I pray you, speak not. He grows worse and worse:
Question enrages him. At once, good night:—
Stand not upon the order of your going,
But go at once.

Len. Good night, and better health
Attend his Majesty!

Lady M. A kind good night to all!

[*Exeunt* Lords *and* Attendants.

Macb. It will have blood! They say, blood will have blood!
Stones have been known to move, and trees to speak;
Augurs, and understood relations have,
By magot-pies, and choughs, and rooks, brought forth
The secret'st man of blood.—What is the night?

Lady M. Almost at odds with morning, which is which.

Macb. How say'st thou, that Macduff denies his person
At our great bidding?

Lady M. Did you send to him, sir?

Macb. I hear it by the way; but, I will send:
There 's not a man of them, but in his house
I keep a servant feed. I will to-morrow
(And betimes I will) to the weird sisters.
More shall they speak; for now I am bent to know,
By the worst means, the worst. For mine own good,
All causes shall give way. I am in blood
Stept in so far, that, should I wade no more,
Returning were as tedious as go o'er.
Strange things I have in head, that will to hand;
Which must be acted, ere they may be scanned.

Lady M. You lack the season of all natures, sleep.

Macb. Come, we 'll to sleep. My strange and self-abuse
Is the initiate fear, that wants hard use:—
We are yet but young in deed. [*Exeunt.*

---

* **Owe,** *possess.* Here we have the original meaning of *owe.* See *owen*, p. 35.—**Stand not,** etc. Do not stand waiting in order to pass out according to your rank.—**Augurs,** *auguries, divinations.* So Singer, who, however, spells the word *augures.* Why not *augurs*, in its proper signification?—**Understood relations,** proofs based on circumstantial evidence.—**Magot-pies** (Lat. *margarita*, a pearl; Gr. μαργαρίτης; O. Fr. *Margot*, diminutive of *Marguerite;* abbreviated to *Maggie* and *Mag;* Lat. *pica*, a bird of the magpie kind), *magpies.*—**Choughs** (probably onomatopoetic), *a kind of crow.*—**How say'st thou?** What say you to this circumstance?—**Feed,** *paid a fee*, under pay.—**Season,** that which gives a relish, *seasoning.*—**Initiate fear,** fear that attends the initiatory steps of guilt.

I pray you, speak not, etc. Anxious appeal; decision blended with entreaty. High; quick; median.
It will have blood, etc. Suppressed remorse, fear, and despair.
I hear it, etc. Decision; reckless resolve. Quick; radical.

SCENE V. *The Heath. Thunder.*

Enter HECATE, *meeting the three* Witches.

1st Witch. Why, how now, Hecate? * you look angerly.
Hec. Have I not reason, beldams, as you are,
Saucy and overbold? How did you dare
To trade and traffic with Macbeth
In riddles and affairs of death;
And I, the mistress of your charms,
The close contriver of all harms,
Was never called to bear my part,
Or show the glory of our art?
And, which is worse, all you have done
Hath been but for a wayward son,
Spiteful and wrathful; who, as others do,
Loves for his own ends, not for you.
But make amends now. Get you gone,
And at the pit of Acheron
Meet me i' the morning. Thither he
Will come to know his destiny.
Your vessels and your spells, provide,
Your charms, and every thing beside.
I am for the air: this night I 'll spend
Unto a dismal and a fatal end.
Great business must be wrought ere noon.
Upon the corner of the moon
There hangs a vaporous drop profound:
I'll catch it ere it come to ground:
And that, distilled by magic sleights,
Shall raise such artificial sprights,
As, by the strength of their illusion,
Shall draw him on to his confusion:
He shall spurn fate, scorn death, and bear
His hopes 'bove wisdom, grace, and fear:
And you all know, security
Is mortals' chiefest enemy.

---

* **Hecate.** See p. 128.—**Beldam.** "Beldam probably meant originally mother-in-law, and hence the opprobrium which it finally came to convey." *White.* Fr. *beau-père*, fine or handsome father; *belle-mère*, fine or handsome mother; Fr. *dame*, lady; *belle-dame*, mother-in-law.—**Acheron** (Gr. Ἀχέρων; ἄχος, ache, pain; ῥέω, I flow; ῥῶν, flowing), flowing with pain, *Acheron*, the river over which the souls of the dead were first conveyed. "Sad Acheron, of sorrow black and deep." *Milton.* Here, and often, the word is synonymous with *hell.*—**Corner of the moon.** Was Milton thinking of this when he wrote, among the concluding lines of *Comus*,

"And from thence can soar as soon
To the corners of the moon"?

—**Profound,** of deep or hidden power.—**Sleights** (Ice. *slägd*, cunning), subtle arts. See Index. Many critics suppose this whole scene to be an interpolation by some inferior pen. Certainly it is of a weak, milk-and-water quality.

Have I not reason, etc. Scolding. Aspirated; loud; radical; rather quick.

[Song,* *accompanied, within. "Come away, come away," etc.*]

Hark, I am called; my little spirit, see,
Sits in a foggy cloud and stays for me! [*Exit.*

1st Witch. Come, let 's make haste; she 'll soon be back again. [*Exeunt.*

SCENE VI. Forres. *A Room in the Palace.*

Enter LENOX *and another* Lord.

Len. My former speeches have but hit your thoughts,
Which can interpret further. Only, I say,
Things have been strangely borne. The gracious Duncan
Was pitied of Macbeth.—Marry, he was dead!—
And the right-valiant Banquo walked too late;
Whom you may say, if it please you, Fleance killed;
For Fleance fled. Men must not walk too late.
Who cannot want the thought, how monstrous
It was for Malcolm and for Donalbain
To kill their gracious father? damned fact!
How it did grieve Macbeth! did he not straight,
In pious rage, the two delinquents tear,
That were the slaves of drink and thralls of sleep?
Was not that nobly done? Ay, and wisely too;
For 'twould have angered any heart alive,
To hear the men deny it. So that, I say,
He has borne all things well: and I do think,
That, had he Duncan's sons under his key,
(As, an 't please heaven, he shall not,) they should find
What 'twere to kill a father; so should Fleance.
But, peace!—for from broad words, and 'cause he failed
His presence at the tyrant's feast, I hear,
Macduff lives in disgrace. Sir, can you tell
Where he bestows himself?

Lord. The son of Duncan,
From whom this tyrant holds the due of birth,
Lives in the English court; and is received

---

* **Song.** In Middleton's *Witch*, Act III., Scene 3, we find a song beginning thus:

" Come away, come away,
Hecate, Hecate, come away!
Hec. I come, I come, I come, I come,
With all the speed I may.
Where's Stadlin?
[*Voice above.*] Here," etc.

Marry, he was dead. *Marry* is a petty oath, meaning, *By Mary!*—**Who cannot want,** etc. Most critics are inclined to think Lenox, that is, Shakespeare, blunders, and that he means, "Who *can* want," etc. But perhaps *want* should be interpreted *wish for.* The meaning would then be, "Who cannot desire to cherish the thought, how monstrous it was," etc., the whole being ironical. Keightley would change "*who*" to "*we*," and put a period after father.

The gracious Duncan was pitied, etc. Irony. Circumflex. Whenever the thought is *winding, crooked, sarcastic*, etc., the *wave* (or *circumflex*) is likely to be appropriate.
The son of Duncan, etc. Matter of fact, business style.

Of the most pious Edward * with such grace
That the malevolence of fortune nothing
Takes from his high respect. Thither Macduff
Is gone to pray the holy king, upon his aid
To wake Northumberland and warlike Siward;
That, by the help of these, with Him above
To ratify the work, we may again
Give to our tables meat, sleep to our nights;
Free from our feasts and banquets bloody knives;
Do faithful homage, and receive free honors;—
All which we pine for now. And this report
Hath so exasperate the king, that he
Prepares for some attempt of war.

Len. Sent he to Macduff?

Lord. He did; and with an absolute, "*Sir, not I,*"
The cloudy messenger turns me his back,
And hums, as who should say, "*You 'll rue the time
That clogs me with this answer.*"

Len. And that well might
Advise him to a caution, to hold what distance
His wisdom can provide. Some holy angel
Fly to the court of England, and unfold
His message ere he come; that a swift blessing
May soon return to this our suffering country
Under a hand accursed!

Lord. I'll send my prayers with him! [*Exeunt.*

ACT IV.

SCENE I. *A dark Cave. In the middle, a Caldron boiling.*

Thunder. Enter the three Witches.

1st Witch. Thrice the brinded cat hath mewed.
2d Witch. Thrice; and once the hedge-pig whined.
3d Witch. Harpier cries.—'Tis time, 'tis time.
1st Witch. Round about the caldron go;
In the poisoned entrails throw.—

* **Edward.** *Edward the Confessor* (1042-1066).—**Northumberland** (north-Humber-land; *i. e.*, the land north of the Humber, an estuary of the east coast of England between Yorkshire and Lincolnshire), the most northerly county of England, having Scotland on the northwest.—**Free from our feasts,** *remove from our feasts.*—**Exasperate,** *exasperated.*—**Turns me.** Me is expletive, as is often the Lat. *mihi.*—**Hedge-pig.** The hedge-hog, owing to its ugliness, solitary habits, and supposed diabolic character, figured extensively in demonology.—**Harpier.** I would fain believe that Shakespeare meant this word to be equivalent to *Harpie*, or *Harpy*, a fabulous monster, winged, ravenous, and filthy, with long claws, the face of a woman, and the body of a vulture. See Virgil's *Æneid*, III., 212, 365, etc.—**Suffering country under,** i. e., *country suffering under.*

You'll rue the time. "Circumflex" on *rue* and *time.*
Some holy angel. Solemn, but fervent. Median; quick utterance, because instant and rapid action is sought.

Toad, that, under [the] cold stone,*
Days and nights hast thirty-one
Sweltered venom, sleeping got,
Boil thou first i' the charmed pot!

All. Double, double toil and trouble;
Fire, burn; and, caldron, bubble.

2d Witch. Fillet of a fenny snake,
In the caldron boil and bake:
Eye of newt and toe of frog,
Wool of bat and tongue of dog,
Adder's fork and blind-worm's sting,
Lizard's leg and owlet's wing,—
For a charm of powerful trouble,
Like a hell-broth boil and bubble.

All. Double, double toil and trouble;
Fire, burn; and, caldron, bubble.

3d Witch. Scale of dragon; tooth of wolf;
Witch's mummy; maw and gulf
Of the ravined salt-sea shark;
Root of hemlock, digged i' the dark;
Liver of blaspheming Jew;
Gall of goat, and slips of yew
Slivered in the moon's eclipse;
Nose of Turk, and Tartar's lips;
Finger of birth-strangled babe,
Ditch-delivered by a drab,—
Make the gruel thick and slab:
Add thereto a tiger's chaudron,
For the ingredients of our caldron.

All. Double, double toil and trouble;
Fire, burn; and, caldron, bubble.

2d Witch. Cool it with a baboon's blood:
Then the charm is firm and good.

Enter HECATE.

Hec. O, well done! I commend your pains;
And every one shall share i' the gains.
And now about the caldron sing,
Like elves and fairies in a ring,
Enchanting all that you put in.

---

* **Under [the] cold stone.** *The* was inserted by Pope to make out the metre. —**Sweltered,** *exuded.* A. S. *sweltan*, to hunger, fail, faint; be overcome with heat.—**Blind-worm,** *slow-worm.* Its eyes are almost invisible.—**Gulf** (Gr. κόλπος, bosom, bay; modern Gr. κόλφος, gulf; Ger. *golf*, by Grimm's Law ?), *throat.*—**Ravined,** *ravenous.* Such use of the participle is common in Shakespeare. See p. 136, *ravin.*—**Slivered,** *split into thin pieces*, splintered, cleft. A. S. *slifan*, to split.—**Slab** (Ice. *slapp*, mire; Ir. *slaib*, mud deposited by a river), *thick, glutinous, viscous.*—**Chaudron.** "This seems to have been the *omentum* or rim: it was certainly some part of the entrails." *White.*

[MUSIC AND A SONG.*

Black spirits and white,
Red spirits and gray;
Mingle, mingle, mingle,
You that mingle may.]

2d Witch. By the pricking of my thumbs,
Something wicked this way comes:
Open, locks, whoever knocks.

Enter MACBETH.

Macb. How now, you secret, black, and midnight hags!
What is 't you do?

All. A deed without a name.

Macb. I conjure you, by that which you profess,
(Howe'er you come to know it,) answer me.
Though you untie the winds, and let them fight
Against the churches; though the yesty waves
Confound and swallow navigation up;
Though bladed corn be lodged, and trees blown down;
Though castles topple on their warders' heads;
Though palaces and pyramids do slope
Their heads to their foundations; though the treasure
Of nature's germins tumble altogether,
Even till destruction sicken,—answer me
To what I ask you!

1st Witch. Speak.

2d Witch. Demand.

3d Witch. We 'll answer.

1st Witch. Say, if thou 'dst rather hear it from our mouths,
Or from our masters'—

Macb. Call 'em, let me see 'em.

1st Witch. Pour in sow's blood, that hath eaten
Her nine farrow; grease, that 's sweaten

---

* **Song.** In Middleton's *Witch*, Act v., Scene 2, this song also may be found, as follows:

"Black spirits and white, red spirits and gray,
Mingle, mingle, mingle, you that mingle may!
Titty, Tiffin, keep it stiff in:
Fire-drake, Puckey, make it lucky;
Lizard, Robin, you must bob in.
Round, around, around, about, about!
All ill come running in, all good keep out!"

By the pricking. The superstition still lives, which regards pricking sensations in the thumbs, burnings in the ear, etc., as omens.—**Yesty** (A. S. *gist*, yeast; Ger. *gäscht*, froth, ferment), *yeasty*, foamy. So in Byron's apostrophe to the ocean, in *Childe Harold*,—

"These are thy toys, and as the snowy flake
They melt into thy *yeast* of waves."

Lodged, *laid prostrate.*—**Germins,** *sprouting seeds*, all germs.—**Eaten her nine.** It is nothing uncommon for the swine mother to eat her new-born young!—**Farrow** (A. S. *fearh*, pig; A. S. *foor*, hog; Ger. *ferkel*, pig; Lat. *porcus*, hog, pork; by Grimm's Law), *litter of pigs.*

How now, you . . . . hags, etc. Bold, slow, scornful, defiant. Loud, large volume.
I conjure you, etc. Same. Radical stress, as is always the case in commands.

From the murderer's gibbet, throw
Into the flame.
All. Come, high or low;
Thyself and office deftly * show!

Thunder. An Apparition *of an armed Head rises.*

Macb. Tell me, thou unknown power,—
1st Witch. He knows thy thought:
Hear his speech, but say thou nought.
App. Macbeth! Macbeth! Macbeth! beware Macduff;
Beware the Thane of Fife.—Dismiss me.—Enough. [*Descends.*
Macb. Whate'er thou art, for thy good caution, thanks!
Thou hast harped my fear aright.—But one word more:—
1st Witch. He will not be commanded. Here 's another
More potent than the first.

Thunder. An Apparition *of a bloody Child rises.*

App. Macbeth! Macbeth! Macbeth!—
Macb. Had I three ears, I'd hear thee.
App. Be bloody, bold,
And resolute. Laugh to scorn the power of man,
For none of woman born shall harm Macbeth. [*Descends.*
Macb. Then live, Macduff! What need I fear of thee?
But yet I'll make assurance doubly sure,
And take a bond of Fate. Thou shalt not live;
That I may tell pale-hearted fear, it lies,
And sleep in spite of thunder.—What is this,

Thunder. An Apparition *of a Child crowned, with a Tree in his Hand, rises.*

That rises like the issue of a king,
And wears upon his baby brow the round
And top of sovereignty?
All. Listen, but speak not to 't.
App. Be lion-mettled, proud; and take no care
Who chafes, who frets, or where conspirers are;
Macbeth shall never vanquished be, until

---

* **Deftly** (Goth. *daban*, to be fit; A. S. *däft*, fit), *dexterously*.—**Nought.** Silence was necessary during the incantations. Hence, a little further on, "Listen, but speak not."—**Thane of Fife,** *Macduff*.—**Harped,** *sounded forth*, uttered.—**Bloody child.** This is supposed to represent Macduff, who was born by the Cæsarean operation. The "armed head" symbolizes Macbeth's own head, which was to be severed from his body. The "child crowned" is Malcolm, the tree representing Birnam wood. See Act v., Scene 5.—**Three ears,** as if responsive to the three utterances of the word "Macbeth."—**Of woman born.** Holinshed tells us that Macbeth would have put Macduff to death, but for the assertion of a certain witch that none of woman born should harm Macbeth. She also made the prediction in regard to Birnam wood.—**Round and top.** The "round" is the part encircling the head; the "top" is the crest or ornament above the "round." "The crown not only completes and rounds, as with the perfection of a circle, the claim to sovereignty; but it is figuratively the top, the summit, of ambitious hopes."—*White.* See White's comment on this passage.

Tell me, thou unknown power, etc. Awe. Low; slow.
Then live, Macduff, etc. Very determined, yet soliloquizing, and so not very loud. Radical.
What is this? etc. *Wonder*, without fear. Somewhat aspirated. Moderate force; slow.

Great Birnam wood to high Dunsinane* hill
Shall come against him. [*Descends.*
Macb. That will never be.
Who can impress the forest? bid the tree
Unfix his earth-bound root? Sweet bodements! good!
Rebellion's head, rise never till the wood
Of Birnam rise, and our high-placed Macbeth
Shall live the lease of nature, pay his breath
To time and mortal custom!—Yet my heart
Throbs to know one thing:—tell me, (if your art
Can tell so much,) shall Banquo's issue ever
Reign in this kingdom?
All. Seek to know no more.
Macb. I will be satisfied! Deny me this,
And an eternal curse fall on you! Let me know:—
Why sinks that caldron? and what noise is this? [*Hautboys.*
1st Witch. Show!
2d Witch. Show!
3d Witch. Show!
All. Show his eyes, and grieve his heart!
Come like shadows, so depart.

Eight Kings appear, and pass over the Stage in order; the last with a Glass in his Hand; BANQUO'S *Ghost following.*

Macb. Thou art too like the spirit of Banquo; down!
Thy crown does sear mine eyeballs!—And thy hair,
Thou other gold-bound brow, is like the first.—
A third is like the former.—Filthy hags!
Why do you show me this?—A fourth?—Start, eyes!
What! will the line stretch out to the crack of doom?
Another yet?—A seventh?—I'll see no more!—
And yet the eighth appears, who bears a glass,
Which shows me many more; and some I see,
That twofold balls and treble sceptres carry!

* **High Dunsinane.** *Dunsinane* in this line has the accent on the 2d syl.; elsewhere, on the 1st.—**Impress,** *press into service.*—**Rebellion's head.** So the folio of Mr. Collier, 1632. Others read, "rebellious head."—**Show his eyes,** etc. See 1 Samuel, ii., 33, "to consume thine eyes and to grieve thine heart." What other evidence can you give of Shakespeare's familiarity with the Bible?—**Bears a glass.** Just as fortune-tellers now, Druid-like, will show you in a glass the likeness of some sainted friend, whom you never saw, or your future husband or wife, whom you never will see. Magic mirrors were much used in the old enchantments. See the *Squire's Tale* in Chaucer; also *Fairy Queen*, III. 2; and *Measure for Measure*, II. 2.—**Twofold balls,** typifying the two islands of Great Britain and Ireland. Some would refer the expression to the two independent crowns of England and Scotland. White prefers the former.—**Treble sceptres.** The three kingdoms of England, Scotland, and Ireland, united under James I., in compliment to whom this is inserted by Shakespeare. See the beautiful compliment to Queen Elizabeth in *Midsummer Night's Dream*, Act II., sc. 2.

That will never be, etc. Elated. Loud; quick; radical.
Tell me, if your art, etc. Earnest appeal.
I will be satisfied, etc. Fiery and fierce anger. Aspirated; guttural; initial stress; quick.
Thou art too like, etc. Surprise, alarm, defiance, anger, fear, horror. Aspirated; loud; spasmodic; explosive; tremulous; deep guttural; shuddering.

Horrible sight!—Aye, now, I see, 'tis true;
For the blood-boltered * Banquo smiles upon me,
And points at them for his.—What! is this so?
1st Witch. Aye, sir: all this is so. But why
Stands Macbeth thus amazedly?—
Come, sisters, cheer we up his sprights,
And show the best of our delights.
I'll charm the air to give a sound,
While you perform your antic round;
That this great king may kindly say,
Our duties did his welcome pay. [*Music. The* Witches *dance, and vanish.*
Macb. Where are they? Gone?—Let this pernicious hour
Stand aye accursed in the calendar!
Come in, without there!

Enter LENOX.

Len. What 's your grace's will?
Macb. Saw you the weird sisters?
Len. No, my lord.
Macb. Came they not by you?
Len. No, indeed, my lord.
Macb. Infected be the air whereon they ride,
And damned all those that trust them!—I did hear
The galloping of horse. Who was 't came by?
Len. 'Tis two or three, my lord, that bring you word,
Macduff is fled to England.
Macb. Fled to England?
Len. Aye, my good lord.
Macb. Time, thou anticipat'st my dread exploits:
The flighty purpose never is o'ertook,
Unless the deed go with it. From this moment,
The very firstlings of my heart shall be
The firstlings of my hand. And even now,
To crown my thoughts with acts, be it thought and done:
The castle of Macduff I will surprise;
Seize upon Fife; give to the edge o' the sword
His wife, his babes, and all unfortunate souls
That trace him in his line. No boasting like a fool:
This deed I 'll do, before this purpose cool.
But no more sights!—Where are these gentlemen?
Come, bring me where they are. [*Exeunt.*

* **Blood-boltered,** *blood-besmeared, blood-clotted. Boltered* is a Warwickshire word, meaning "matted" or "clotted" [with the blood].—**Sprights,** spirits. See *sprites*, pp. 78, 133.—**Weird.** Dissyl. See p. 113.—**Purpose . . . . unless the deed,** etc. The execution of the purpose lags behind.—**Trace** (Lat. *trahere*, to draw), *follow in the steps of*, follow, succeed.

Infected be the air, etc. Anger; hate; desperation. Aspirated; loud; quick; expulsive radical. *Time, thou anticipat'st*, etc. Undertone; quick; rough; radical.

SCENE II. Fife. *A Room in* MACDUFF'S *Castle.*

Enter Lady MACDUFF, *her* Son *and* ROSSE.

L. Macd. What had he done to make him fly the land?
Rosse. You must have patience, madam.
L. Macd. He had none;
His flight was madness. When our actions do not,
Our fears do make us traitors.*
Rosse. You know not,
Whether it was his wisdom or his fear.
L. Macd. Wisdom! to leave his wife, to leave his babes,
His mansion, and his titles, in a place
From whence himself does fly? He loves us not:
He wants the natural touch; for the poor wren,
The most diminutive of birds, will fight,
Her young ones in her nest, against the owl.
All is the fear, and nothing is the love.
As little is the wisdom, where the flight
So runs against all reason.
Rosse. My dearest coz,
I pray you, school yourself. But, for your husband,
He is noble, wise, judicious, and best knows
The fits o' the season. I dare not speak much further:
But cruel are the times, when we are traitors,
And do not know ourselves; when we hold rumor
From what we fear, yet know not what we fear,
But float upon a wild and violent sea,
Each way and move.—I take my leave of you.
Shall not be long but I 'll be here again.
Things at the worst will cease, or else climb upward
To what they were before.—My pretty cousin,
Blessing upon you!
L. Macd. Fathered he is, and yet he 's fatherless.
Rosse. I am so much a fool, should I stay longer,
It would be my disgrace, and your discomfort.
I take my leave at once. [*Exit* ROSSE.
L. Macd. Sirrah, your father 's dead;
And what will you do now? How will you live?

---

* **Make us traitors,** *make us appear traitors, convict us of being traitors.*—**Natural touch,** *natural affection, natural feeling.* Shakespeare elsewhere speaks of the "inly touch of love," and the "touch of nature," that makes all the world our kindred.—**Young ones,** etc.; i. e., *if her young ones are in her nest.*—**Fits** (A. S. *feoht*, fight, attack), *passing humors, vicissitudes,* impulsive irregular actions, paroxysms, convulsions, fits.—**Hold rumor,** etc. *Our fears, though vague, engender rumors.*—**Each way and move,** *each way and each motion.* —**Shall not be long,** *it shall not be long.* The pronoun is not seldom omitted in Shakespeare. —**Cousin.** The boy.

He had none, etc. Impatience. High; quick; vanishing.
Wisdom, etc. Impatience; complaint. Vanishing stress; high.
I pray you, school yourself, etc. Matter of fact; kindness. Soft force; rather quick.

Son. As birds do, mother.

L. Macd. What, with worms and flies?

Son. With what I get, I mean; and so do they.

L. Macd. Poor bird! thou 'dst never fear the net, nor lime,
The pitfall, nor the gin.

Son. Why should I, mother? Poor birds they are not set for.
My father is not dead, for all your saying.

L. Macd. Yes, he is dead. How wilt thou do for a father?

Son. Nay, how will you do for a husband?

L. Macd. Why, I can buy me twenty at any market.

Son. Then you 'll buy 'em to sell again.

L. Macd. Thou speak'st with all thy wit; and yet i' faith,
With wit enough for thee.

Son. Was my father a traitor, mother?

L. Macd. Ay, that he was.

Son. What is a traitor?

L. Macd. Why, one that swears and lies.

Son. And be all traitors that do so?

L. Macd. Every one that does so is a traitor, and must be hanged.

Son. And must they all be hanged that swear and lie?

L. Macd. Every one.

Son. Who must hang them?

L. Macd. Why, the honest men.

Son. Then the liars and swearers are fools; for there are liars and swearers enough to beat the honest men and hang up them.

L. Macd. Now, God help thee, poor monkey! But how wilt thou do for a father?

Son. If he were dead, you 'd weep for him: if you would not, it were a good sign that I should quickly have a new father.

L. Macd. Poor prattler! how thou talk'st!

Enter a Messenger.

Mess. Bless you, fair dame! I am not to you known,
Though in your state of honor* I am perfect.
I doubt, some danger does approach you nearly.
If you will take a homely man's advice,
Be not found here: hence, with your little ones.
To fright you thus, methinks, I am too savage:
To do worse to you, were fell cruelty,
Which is too nigh your person. Heaven preserve you!
I dare abide no longer. [*Exit* Messenger.

L. Macd. Whither should I fly?

* **In your state of honor,** etc. *I am perfectly aware of your honorable rank.*

As birds do, mother. This small talk, and all light conversation or unimportant matter, should be spoken rapidly. A child's voice.
Bless you, fair dame, etc. Hurry, and earnest kindness. Very quick; loud; radical.

I have done no harm. But I remember now
I am in this earthly world; where, to do harm
Is often laudable; to do good sometime
Accounted dangerous folly. Why then, alas!
Do I put up that womanly defence,
To say, I have done no harm?—What are these faces?

Enter Murderers.

Mur. Where is your husband?
L. Macd. I hope, in no place so unsanctified,
Where such as thou may'st find him.
Mur. He 's a traitor.
Son. Thou liest, thou shag-haired * villain.
Mur. What, you egg! [*Stabbing him.*
Young fry of treachery!
Son. He has killed me, mother!
Run away, I pray you. [*Dies.*
[*Exit* Lady MACDUFF, *crying murder, and pursued by the* Murderers.

SCENE III. England. *A room in the King's Palace.*

Enter MALCOLM *and* MACDUFF.

Mal. Let us seek out some desolate shade, and there
Weep our sad bosoms empty.
Macd. Let us rather
Hold fast the mortal sword, and, like good men,
Bestride our down-fallen birthdom. Each new morn,
New widows howl; new orphans cry; new sorrows
Strike heaven on the face, that it resounds
As if it felt with Scotland, and yelled out
Like syllable of dolor.
Mal. What I believe, I 'll wail;
What know, believe; and, what I can redress,
As I shall find the time to friend, I will.
What you have spoke, it may be so, perchance.
This tyrant, whose sole name blisters our tongues,

---

* **Shag-haired** (A. S. *sccacga*, a bush of hair), *bushy-haired*, a term of abusive slang. —**Young fry** (O. Fr. *fraye*, M. Fr. *frai*, spawning, spawn of fishes), *small fry*.—**Scene III.** In this scene Shakespeare follows very closely the account in Holinshed's Chronicle. —**Bestride.** As a brave warrior stands over his fallen friend in battle, to defend him.— **Birthdom** (*-dom* is A. S. *dom*; Ger. *-thum*; Lat. *-tium*; Sans. *tvan*; and denotes *quality*, as *wisdom*; *act*, as *martyrdom*; *state*, as *thraldom*, *freedom*; *appurtenances* or *possessions*, as *dukedom*; by metonymy the *collective concrete*, as *Christendom*), *birth-place*, *native land*.— **Like syllable,** *similar utterance*.—**To friend,** *to befriend*.—**Whose sole name,** *whose mere name*.

I have done no harm, etc. Earnest; alarmed. Quick; rather loud.
What are these faces? etc. Fright. Loud; very quick.
I hope in no place, etc. Bold, defiant, scornful. Loud; radical; quick.
He has killed me, mother, etc. Do not read this tamely.
Let us seek out, etc. Weak, despondent. Slow; feeble; median.
Let us rather hold fast, etc. Bold; energetic. Loud; quick; radical.
What I believe, etc. Assumed weakness. Moderate; median; becoming cool and business-like.

Was once thought honest. You have loved him well.
He hath not touched you yet. I am young; but something
You may deserve* of him through me; and wisdom
To offer up a weak, poor, innocent lamb,
To appease an angry god!

Macd. I am not treacherous.

Mal. But Macbeth is.
A good and virtuous nature may recoil
In an imperial charge. But I shall crave your pardon.
That which you are, my thoughts cannot transpose;
Angels are bright still, though the brightest fell;
Though all things foul would wear the brows of grace,
Yet grace must still look so.

Macd. I have lost my hopes.

Mal. Perchance, even there where I did find my doubts.
Why in that rawness left you wife and child,
Those precious motives, those strong knots of love,
Without leave-taking?—I pray you,
Let not my jealousies be your dishonors,
But mine own safeties. You may be rightly just,
Whatever I shall think.

Macd. Bleed, bleed, poor country!
Great tyranny, lay thou thy basis sure,
For goodness dares not check thee!—Wear thou thy wrongs:
The title is affeered!—Fare thee well, lord:
I would not be the villain that thou think'st
For the whole space that 's in the tyrant's grasp,
And the rich East to boot.

Mal. Be not offended:
I speak not as in absolute fear of you.
I think our country sinks beneath the yoke;
It weeps, it bleeds; and each new day a gash
Is added to her wounds. I think, withal,
There would be hands uplifted in my right;

---

* **May deserve . . . . me,** *may earn some favor from him by destroying me.* This is said with some bitterness by the distrustful Malcolm.—**Imperial charge,** *the execution of a royal commission.* Shakespeare had not read English history to no purpose. Illustrate, by citation of instances, the truth of this assertion of Malcolm's.—**Look so,** *look like herself, look beautiful.*—**Rawness,** *hasty manner.* Malcolm here asks a very pertinent and incisive question.—**Wear thou.** To Malcolm. But some refer it to tyranny incarnated in Macbeth. —**Title.** This is usually explained as meaning Macbeth's title to the crown; but perhaps it means Malcolm's title to the wrongs he wears.—**Affeered** (Fr. *affier*, to reduce to a certainty. Webster gives a different etymology), *confirmed.*—**Rich East.** So Milton's expression, "The gorgeous East with richest hand."

But Macbeth is, etc. Moderation; assumed despondency.
Perchance, even there where I, etc. Circumflex; or it may be read in a *business* way.
Why in that rawness, etc. Pointed inquiry. Rather sharp, metallic voice; quick; radical.
I pray you, let not my jealousies, etc. Circumflex, as the thought winds.
Bleed, bleed, poor country, etc. Grief and despondency. Slow; median; high.
I would not be the villain, etc. Indignation. Rather loud; expulsive; rather quick; aspirated.
Be not offended, etc. Assumed coolness and hardness; putting on the mocking unsympathizing tone of a villain.

And here, from gracious England, have I offer
Of goodly thousands. But, for all this,
When I shall tread * upon the tyrant's head,
Or wear it on my sword, yet my poor country
Shall have more vices than it had before;
More suffer, and more sundry ways than ever,
By him that shall succeed.
Macd. What should he be?
Mal. It is myself I mean; in whom I know
All the particulars of vice so grafted,
That, when they shall be opened, black Macbeth
Will seem as pure as snow; and the poor state
Esteem him as a lamb, being compared
With my confineless harms.
Macd. Not in the legions
Of horrid hell can come a devil more damned
In evils, to top Macbeth!
Mal. I grant him bloody,
Luxurious, avaricious, false, deceitful,
Sudden, malicious, smacking of every sin
That has a name. But there 's no bottom, none,
In my voluptuousness! . . . .
. . . .
. . . . and my desire
All continent impediments would o'erbear,
That did oppose my will. Better Macbeth,
Than such a one to reign.
Macd. Boundless intemperance
In nature is a tyranny. It hath been
The untimely emptying of the happy throne,
And fall of many kings. But fear not yet
To take upon you what is yours: you may
Convey your pleasures in a spacious plenty,
And yet seem cold, the time you may so hoodwink.
. . . .
. . . .
Mal. With this, there grows,

---

* **When I shall tread**, etc. Malcolm here enters upon a most ingenious, a crucial test of Macduff's sincerity.—**Confineless harms.** *boundless vices.*—**Top Macbeth,** *surpass* or tower above Macbeth.—**Sudden,** *passionate.*—**Continent** (Lat. *continere*, to keep together, hold within bounds), *restraining.*—**Convey,** *take by stealth.* See *Lear*, Act I., Scene 2.

It is myself I mean, etc. Coolness and sneering.
Not in the legions, etc. Anger. Loud; quick; radical; aspirated.
I grant him bloody, etc. Circumflex; mocking; cold and heartless; dismissing his assumed diabolic thoughts as mere matter of course, not to be ashamed of, but rather as ground for malicious satisfaction! A guttural, sensual tone.
Boundless intemperance, etc. Apologetic; persuasive; argumentative.
With this there grows, etc. Assumed malicious hardened avarice. Avoid the median; rather low pitch; guttural and growling.

In my most ill-composed affection, such
A stanchless avarice, that, were I king,
I should cut off the nobles for their lands;
Desire his jewels, and this other's house;
And my more-having would be as a sauce
To make me hunger more; that I should forge
Quarrels unjust against the good and loyal,
Destroying them for wealth.
Macd. This avarice
Sticks deeper, grows with more pernicious root
Than summer-seeming* lust, and it hath been
The sword of our slain kings. Yet do not fear:
Scotland hath foisons to fill up your will,
Of your mere own. All these are portable,
With other graces weighed.
Mal. But I have none. The king-becoming graces,
As justice, verity, temperance, stableness,
Bounty, perseverance, mercy, lowliness,
Devotion, patience, courage, fortitude,—
I have no relish of them; but abound
In the division of each several crime,
Acting it many ways. Nay, had I power, I should
Pour the sweet milk of concord into hell,
Uproar the universal peace, confound
All unity on earth.
Macd. O Scotland! Scotland!
Mal. If such a one be fit to govern, speak.
I am as I have spoken.
Macd. Fit to govern!
No, not to live!—O nation miserable,
With an untitled tyrant bloody-sceptred,
When shalt thou see thy wholesome days again,
Since that the truest issue of thy throne
By his own interdiction stands accursed,
And does blaspheme his breed?—Thy royal father
Was a most sainted king; the queen, that bore thee,
Oftener upon her knees than on her feet,
Died every day she lived. Fare thee well!

---

* **Summer-seeming;** "seeming to last but a summer," says White; "hot as summer," says Steevens; "burns awhile like summer, and, like summer, passes away," says Hudson.—**Foisons** (Fr. *foison;* Lat. *fusio*, a pouring, fr. *fundĕre*, to pour), *plenty*.—**Portable**, *endurable*.—**Perseverance.** Acc. 2d syl.—**Died,** *i. e.*, died unto sin. Paul says, "I die daily."

This avarice, etc. Serious, and somewhat emphatic.
Yet do not fear, etc. Persuasive; moderate argument.
But I have none. Pretended swaggering and boastfulness of a villain proud of his villany. Coarse; guttural; loud; slow, cool, scornful; aspirated; radical.
O Scotland! Scotland! etc. Great grief. Loud; quick; high; vanishing.
Fit to govern! No, not to live! etc. Intense wrathful energy. Very loud; explosive radical.
O nation miserable, etc. Loud grief, ending in despair.

These evils thou repeat'st upon thyself
Have banished me from Scotland.—O, my breast!
Thy hope ends here!
Mal. Macduff, this noble passion,
Child of integrity, hath from my soul
Wiped the black scruples, reconciled my thoughts
To thy good truth and honor. Devilish Macbeth
By many of these trains hath sought to win me
Into his power; and modest wisdom plucks me
From over-credulous haste. But God above
Deal between thee and me; for even now
I put myself to thy direction, and
Unspeak mine own detraction; here abjure
The taints and blames I laid upon myself,
For strangers to my nature. I am yet
Unknown to woman; never was forsworn;
Scarcely have coveted what was mine own;
At no time broke my faith; would not betray
The devil to his fellow; and delight
No less in truth, than life: my first false speaking
Was this upon myself. What I am truly,
Is thine, and my poor country's, to command:
Whither, indeed, before thy here-approach,
Old Siward, with ten thousand warlike men,
Already at a point,* was setting forth.
Now we 'll together; and the chance of goodness
Be like our warranted quarrel!—Why are you silent?
Macd. Such welcome and unwelcome things at once,
'T is hard to reconcile.

Enter a Doctor.

Mal. Well; more anon.—Comes the king forth, I pray you?
Doct. Aye, sir: there are a crew of wretched souls,
That stay his cure. Their malady convinces
The great assay of art; but, at his touch,
Such sanctity hath heaven given his hand,
They presently amend.
Mal. I thank you, Doctor. [*Exit* Doctor.
Macd. What 's the disease he means?
Mal. 'Tis called the Evil:

---

* **Ready at a point,** *minutely, perfectly ready.* Thus in *Hamlet,* "armed to point."—**Warranted quarrel,** *just cause.* May the chance of goodness be as fair as our cause is just.—**Convinces,** *overcome.*—**His touch,** etc. King Edward, the Confessor, is said to have been the first, and Queen Anne the last, English sovereign, who "touched" to cure scrofula, or "the King's Evil." The latter tried the remedy without effect on Samuel Johnson in his infancy.

Macduff, this noble passion, etc. Malcolm's whole manner now changes. He becomes cheerful, noble, emphatic in his purity and truth; closing with exultation. Loud; radical and median; pure quality; large volume.

A most miraculous work in this good king,
Which often, since my here-remain in England,
I have seen him do. How he solicits Heaven,
Himself best knows: but strangely-visited people,
All swoln and ulcerous, pitiful to the eye,
The mere despair of surgery, he cures,
Hanging a golden stamp* about their necks,
Put on with holy prayers: and 'tis spoken,
To the succeeding royalty he leaves
The healing benediction. With this strange virtue,
He hath a heavenly gift of prophecy;
And sundry blessings hang about his throne,
That speak him full of grace.

Enter ROSSE.

Macd. See, who comes here?
Mal. My countryman; but yet I know him not.
Macd. My ever-gentle cousin, welcome hither.
Mal. I know him now. Good God, betimes remove
The means that make us strangers!
Rosse. Sir, amen.
Macd. Stands Scotland where it did?
Rosse. Alas, poor country!
Almost afraid to know itself! It cannot
Be called our mother, but our grave: where nothing,
But who knows nothing, is once seen to smile;
Where sighs, and groans, and shrieks that rend the air,
Are made, not marked; where violent sorrow seems
A modern ecstacy; the dead man's knell
Is there scarce asked, for who; and good men's lives
Expire before the flowers in their caps,
Dying or ere they sicken.
Macd. Oh, relation
Too nice, and yet too true!
Mal. What is the newest grief?
Rosse. That of an hour's age doth hiss the speaker.
Each minute teems a new one.
Macd. How does my wife?
Rosse. Why,—well.
Macd. And all my children?

---

* **Golden stamp,** a coin called an *angel.* See *Merchant of Venice,* II., 6.—**Modern,** *ommon, trite.*—**Ecstacy,** alienation of mind, unusual state of mind. *Modern ecstacy,* "a slight iervousness," says White. See ecstacy, p. 142.—**For who,** *for whom.* Shakespeare repeatedly ises *who* for *whom:* but perhaps we should read *whom* in this place. Lowell says that Shake-peare was "incapable of bad grammar."

---

1 *most miraculous work,* etc. Slight admiration. Rather loud; median and radical.
1las, poor country! etc. Distress. Loud; median and vanishing.
Vhy, well . . . . No; they were, etc. Long pauses; slow; slight force.

Rosse. Well too.
Macd. The tyrant has not battered at their peace?
Rosse. No;—they were well at peace when I did leave them.
Macd. Be not a niggard of your speech. How goes it?
Rosse. When I came hither to transport the tidings,
Which I have heavily borne, there ran a rumor
Of many worthy fellows that were out;
Which was to my belief witnessed the rather,
For that I saw the tyrant's power afoot.
Now is the time of help! Your eye in Scotland
Would create soldiers, make our women fight,
To doff* their dire distresses.
Mal. Be it their comfort,
We are coming thither. Gracious England hath
Lent us good Siward and ten thousand men:
An older and a better soldier, none
That Christendom gives out.
Rosse. Would I could answer
This comfort with the like! But I have words,
That would be howled out in the desert air,
Where hearing should not latch them.
Macd. What concern they?
The general cause? or is it a fee-grief,
Due to some single breast?
Rosse. No mind, that 's honest,
But in it shares some wo; though the main part
Pertains to you alone.
Macd. If it be mine,
Keep it not from me: quickly let me have it.
Rosse. Let not your ears despise my tongue for ever,
Which shall possess them with the heaviest sound
That ever yet they heard.
Macd. Humph! I guess at it.
Rosse. Your castle is surprised; your wife, and babes,
Savagely slaughtered: to relate the manner,
Were, on the quarry of these murdered deer,
To add the death of you.
Mal. Merciful Heaven!—
What, man! ne'er pull your hat upon your brows;
Give sorrow words: the grief that does not speak,
Whispers the o'erfraught heart, and bids it break.

---

* **Doff** (*do off*, as *don* is *do on*), *put off*.—**Latch,** *catch*, as a door-latch catches the door.—**Fee-grief,** grief that has but one owner, *private grief*. *Fee* is A. S. *feoh*, cattle; and, as cattle were used for money or a medium of payment, *fee* came to mean *money, property*. So the Lat. *pecunia*, money, is from *pecus*, small cattle, sheep.—**Quarry,** a heap of dead game.—**Grief that does not,** etc. See, in Tennyson's *Princess*, the exquisite song beginning, "Home they brought her warrior dead."—**O'erfraught** (Dan. *fragt;* Fr. *fret;* Ger. *fracht;* freight of a ship), *overloaded*, overburdened.

Macd. My children too ?
Rosse. Wife, children, servants,—all
That could be found.
Macd. And I must be from thence !—
My wife killed too ?
Rosse. I have said.
Mal. Be comforted.
Let 's make us medicines of our great revenge,
To cure this deadly grief.
Macd. He has no children.*—All my pretty ones ?
Did you say, all ?—O, hell-kite !—All ?
What! all my pretty chickens and their dam
At one fell swoop ?
Mal. Dispute it like a man.
Macd. I shall do so;
But I must also feel it as a man:
I cannot but remember such things were,
That were most precious to me.—Did heaven look on,
And would not take their part ? Sinful Macduff,
They were all struck for thee! Naught that I am,
Not for their own demerits, but for mine,
Fell slaughter on their souls. Heaven rest them now!
Mal. Be this the whetstone of your sword. Let grief
Convert to anger: blunt not the heart; enrage it.
Macd. Oh, I could play the woman with mine eyes,
And braggart with my tongue!—But, gentle Heaven,
Cut short all intermission; front to front,
Bring thou this fiend of Scotland and myself;
Within my sword's length set him; if he 'scape,
Heaven forgive him too!
Mal. This tune goes manly.
Come, go we to the king. Our power is ready:
Our lack is nothing but our leave. Macbeth
Is ripe for shaking, and the powers above
Put on their instruments. Receive what cheer you may;
The night is long that never finds the day. [*Exeunt.*

* **He has no children.** The thought of revenge perhaps suggests to Macduff that Macbeth has no children. But is it not more likely that Macduff refers to Malcolm's being childless and therefore unable to sympathize fully with Macduff?—**Dispute,** etc. Contend with this terrible blow like a man.—**Swoop** (A. S. *swâpan;* O. Fries. *swepa;* Goth. *sveipan;* Ice. and Swed. *sopa*, to sweep), a falling on and seizing.—**Intermission,** *intervening time, delay.*—**Forgive him too.** Note the intensive and pregnant force of *too.*—**Put on their instruments,** incite, encourage, or *urge forward us*, who are their instruments.

All my pretty ones? etc. An agony of grief. High; convulsive.
O, hell-kite! etc. Intensest wrath hissing.
But I must also feel it as a man, etc. Under this crushing blow, his voice falters, sobs, and wails
Sinful Macduff, etc. Self-reproach, with tears and sobs.
Be this the whetstone, etc. Loud, cheerful, decisive.
Front to front, etc. Frenzied anger and hate. Very much aspirated; explosive; very loud
This tune goes manly, etc. Cheerful. Loud; quick.

ACT V.

SCENE I.* Dunsinane. *A room in the Castle.*

Enter a Doctor *of Physic, and a waiting* Gentlewoman.

Doct. I have two nights watched with you, but can perceive no truth in your report. When was it she last walked?

Gent. Since his Majesty went into the field, I have seen her rise from her bed, throw her night-gown upon her, unlock her closet, take forth paper, fold it, write upon it, read it, afterwards seal it, and again return to bed; yet all this while in a most fast sleep.

Doct. A great perturbation in nature!—to receive at once the benefit of sleep, and do the effects of watching.—In this slumbery agitation, besides her walking and other actual performances, what, at any time, have you heard her say?

Gent. That, sir, which I will not report after her.

Doct. You may to me; and 'tis most meet you should.

Gent. Neither to you, nor any one, having no witness to confirm my speech.

Enter Lady MACBETH, *with a Taper.*

Lo you, here she comes! This is her very guise; and, upon my life, fast asleep! Observe her: stand close.

Doct. How came she by that light?

Gent. Why, it stood by her: she has light by her continually: 'tis her command.

Doct. You see her eyes are open.

Gent. Aye, but their sense is shut.

Doct. What is it she does now? Look, how she rubs her hands!

Gent. It is an accustomed action with her to seem thus washing her hands. I have known her continue in this a quarter of an hour.

Lady M. Yet here 's a spot!

Doct. Hark, she speaks! I will set down what comes from her, to satisfy my remembrance the more strongly.

Lady M. Out, damned spot! out, I say!—One: two. Why, then 't is time to do 't!—Hell is murky!—Fie, my lord, fie! a soldier, and afeared? What need we fear who knows it, when none can call our power to account?—Yet who would have thought the old man to have had so much blood in him?

Doct. Do you mark that?

---

* **Scene I.** This scene is especially worthy of study, as one of the most wonderful in dramatic literature.—**Hell is murky!** etc. We must suppose her to be scornfully repeating this language uttered by her husband.—**Fie** (Gr. φεῦ; Ger. *pfui;* Fr. *fi.* Origin of the word?).

I have two nights watched, etc. Undertone till Lady M. enters, and then whispering.
Lo, you, here she comes, etc. Whispering.
Yet here 's a spot, etc. A cry of anguish. High; aspirated with sighs.
Out, damned spot! etc. Radical; aspirated; high; slow.
One: two, etc. She counts the striking of the clock. Slow, and then quick, on the words, "Why, then 't is time," etc.
Hell is murky! etc. Scornful, sneering. Pause after it. Aspirated.
Yet who would have thought, etc. Horror. Low; slow; soft; shuddering; aspirated.

Lady M. The Thane of Fife had a wife! Where is she now?—What! will these hands ne'er be clean?—No more o' that, my lord, no more o' that! you mar all* with this starting.

Doct. Go to, go to: you have known what you should not.

Gent. She has spoke what she should not, I am sure of that! Heaven knows what she has known!

Lady M. Here 's the smell of the blood still! all the perfumes of Arabia will not sweeten this little hand. Oh! oh! oh!

Doct. What a sigh is there! The heart is sorely charged.

Gent. I would not have such a heart in my bosom for the dignity of the whole body.

Doct. Well, well, well!—

Gent. 'Pray God, it be, sir.

Doct. —this disease is beyond my practice. Yet I have known those which have walked in their sleep, who have died holily in their beds.

Lady M. Wash your hands, put on your night-gown; look not so pale.—I tell you yet again, Banquo 's buried: he cannot come out of his grave.

Doct. Even so?

Lady M. To bed, to bed: there 's knocking at the gate. Come, come, come, come, give me your hand. What 's done, cannot be undone. To bed, to bed, to bed. [*Exit* Lady MACBETH.

Doct. Will she go now to bed?

Gent. Directly.

Doct. Foul whisperings are abroad. Unnatural deeds
Do breed unnatural troubles. Infected minds
To their deaf pillows will discharge their secrets.
More needs she the divine, than the physician.—
God, God, forgive us all! Look after her;
Remove from her the means of all annoyance,
And still keep eyes upon her.—So, good night.
My mind she has mated, and amazed my sight.
I think, but dare not speak.

Gent. Good night, good doctor. [*Exeunt.*

---

* **You mar all.** Her mind wanders from the blood on her hands to the scene at the supper, where the ghost of Banquo terrified Macbeth.—**The smell of the blood.** There is a parallel passage in the *Agamemnon* of Æschylus, where Cassandra, in prophetic spell or trance, scents the odor of blood and the exhalations from the tomb. What evidence is there that Shakespeare had read Æschylus? See Lowell's Essay on Shakespeare.—The question has been asked why this terrible scene should have been written in prose. In answer it may be said, first, that there is a kind of rhythm running through much of it; secondly, that the irregular and fitful utterances of a somnambulist would hardly seem natural, if expressed in perfect metre; and, thirdly, that whispered questions and answers are not easily capable of rhythm, which requires distinct vowel sounds.—**Mated** (Fr. *mater*, to fatigue, enfeeble, checkmate; Ger. *matt*, faint, exhausted; O. Fr. *matté*, overcome, confounded, dismayed), *astounded, overcome.*

The Thane of Fife had a wife, etc. Wailing. High; slow; pure tone.
What! will these hands, etc. Impatient distress. Vanishing.
No more o' that, etc. Command; decision. Quick, firm voice, yet in undertone; radical.
Here 's the smell of the blood, etc. A cry of anguish. Very high; vanishing; slow.
Wash your hands, etc. Undertone; quick; impetuous; angry, aspirated.
To bed, to bed, etc. Very quick; much aspirated.
Foul whisperings, etc. Very solemn. Low; slow; soft.
Look after her, etc. Serious; business tone.

SCENE II. *The Country near* Dunsinane.*

Enter, with Drum and Colors, MENTETH, CATHNESS, ANGUS, LENOX, *and* Soldiers.

Ment. The English power is near, led on by Malcolm,
His uncle Siward, and the good Macduff.
Revenges burn in them; for their dear causes
Would, to the bleeding and the grim alarm,
Excite the mortified man.
Ang. Near Birnam wood
Shall we well meet them: that way are they coming.
Cath. Who knows if Donalbain be with his brother?
Len. For certain, sir, he is not. I have a file
Of all the gentry. There is Siward's son,
And many unrough youths, that even now
Protest their first of manhood.
Ment. What does the tyrant?
Cath. Great Dunsinane he strongly fortifies.
Some say, he 's mad; others, that lesser hate him,
Do call it valiant fury; but, for certain,
He cannot buckle his distempered cause
Within the belt of rule.
Ang. Now does he feel
His secret murders sticking on his hands;
Now minutely revolts upbraid his faith-breach;
Those he commands move only in command,
Nothing in love. Now does he feel his title
Hang loose about him, like a giant's robe
Upon a dwarfish thief.
Ment. Who, then, shall blame
His pestered senses to recoil and start,
When all that is within him does condemn
Itself for being there!
Cath. Well, march we on,
To give obedience where 'tis truly owed:
Meet we the medicine of the sickly weal;
And with him pour we, in our country's purge,
Each drop of us.
Len. Or so much as it needs,
To dew the sovereign flower, and drown the weeds.
Make we our march towards Birnam. [*Exeunt, marching.*

* **Dunsinane,** p. 156.—**Uncle Siward.** Duncan's wife, who was Malcolm's mother, was the sister (or, as some say, the daughter) of Siward, Earl of Northumberland.—**Mortified,** *ascetic, deadened by religious discipline.* "Mortify, therefore, your members which are upon the earth."—Col. iii. 5.—**Unrough,** *smooth-faced, beardless.*—**Minutely** (adjective), *happening every minute*; (or it may be adverbial,) *minute by minute.*—**Condemn itself,** etc. He is filled with self-loathing.—**March we.** Imperative 1st person plural.—**Medicine,** *the physician, i. e.* Malcolm.—**Weal.** State, commonwealth? A. S. *wela;* O. Eng. *wele*, welfare.

The English power is near, etc. Matter of fact. Moderation, therefore, in pitch, time, etc.

SCENE III. Dunsinane. *A Room in the Castle.*

Enter MACBETH, Doctor, *and* Attendants.

Macb. Bring me no more reports: let them fly all.
Till Birnam wood remove to Dunsinane,
I cannot taint with fear. What 's the boy Malcolm?
Was he not born of woman? The spirits that know
All mortal consequences, have pronounced me thus:
"*Fear not, Macbeth: no man that 's born of woman,*
Shall e'er have power on thee."—Then fly, false thanes,
And mingle with the English epicures.*
The mind I sway by, and the heart I bear,
Shall never sag with doubt, nor shake with fear.

Enter a Servant.

The devil damn thee black, thou cream-faced loon!
Where got'st thou that goose look?
Serv. There is ten thousand—
Macb. Geese, villain?
Serv. Soldiers, sir.
Macb. Go, prick thy face, and over-red thy fear,
Thou lily-livered boy! What soldiers, patch?
Death of thy soul! those linen cheeks of thine
Are counsellors to fear. What soldiers, whey-face?
Serv. The English force, so please you.
Macb. Take thy face hence.—Seyton!—I am sick at heart,
When I behold—Seyton, I say!—This push
Will chair me ever, or disseat me now.
I have lived long enough. My way of life
Is fallen into the sear, the yellow leaf;
And that which should accompany old age,
As honor, love, obedience, troops of friends,
I must not look to have; but, in their stead,
Curses, not loud, but deep; mouth-honor, breath;
Which the poor heart would fain deny, but dare not.
Seyton!—

---

* **Epicures,** followers of Epicurus (B. C. 341–270), *voluptuaries.* Scotch abstemiousness was proverbial. Holinshed notices the fact that the English introduced gormandizing and luxury into Scotland.—**Sag** (A. S. and O. Ger. *sîgan*, to fall, sink), *sink with its own weight.*—**Loon** (A. S. *lun*, poor, needy; Fr. *liun*, idle, lazy; Scotch *loun, lown, loon*, a stupid man), *a sorry, stupid fellow.* But perhaps Macbeth means the northern swimming bird called loon.—**Patch,** *wretch, fool.* The name owes its origin perhaps to the patched or motley coat worn by the professional fool. The word is akin to *botch*, p. 141.—**Cream-faced, goose-look, lily-livered, linen cheeks, whey-face,** etc. What a vocabulary!—**Chair me,** *seat me permanently.*—**Sear** (A. S. *searian*, to dry; Gr. ξηρός, dry), *dry, withered.*—**Fain deny,** *gladly refuse* or *reject.*

Bring me no more reports, etc. Excitement; anger; scorn; exultation. Loud; high on emphatic syllables; explosive radical; large volume; aspirated; quick.
The devil, etc. Great anger. Very loud; very rough; very quick; explosive; large volume.
Go, prick thy face, etc. Anger. Contempt at littleness and at boyish cowardice may make the volume moderate or even small.
I'm sick at heart, etc. Distressful; disgusted; impatient. Aspirated; expulsive, vanishing.
I have lived long enough, etc. Plaintive.
Curses, not loud but deep, etc. Aspirated; varying pitch, forcible; radical, vanishing.

Enter SEYTON.

Sey. What is your gracious pleasure?
Macb. What news more?
Sey. All is confirmed, my lord, which was reported.
Macb. I'll fight till from my bones my flesh be hacked!
Give me my armor.
Sey. 'Tis not needed yet.
Macb. I'll put it on.
Send out more horses, skirr* the country round.
Hang those that talk of fear.—Give me mine armor.—
How does your patient, Doctor?
Doct. Not so sick, my lord,
As she is troubled with thick-coming fancies,
That keep her from her rest.
Macb. Cure her of that.
Canst thou not minister to a mind diseased;
Pluck from the memory a rooted sorrow;
Raze out the written troubles of the brain;
And, with some sweet oblivious antidote,
Cleanse the stuffed bosom of that perilous stuff
Which weighs upon the heart?
Doct. Therein the patient
Must minister to himself.
Macb. Throw physic to the dogs! I'll none of it.—
Come, put mine armor on: give me my staff:—
Seyton, send out.—Doctor, the thanes fly from me.—
Come, sir, despatch.—If thou couldst, Doctor, cast
The water of my land, find her disease,
And purge it to a sound and pristine health,
I would applaud thee to the very echo,
That should applaud again.—Pull 't off, I say.—
What rhubarb, senna, or what purgative drug,
Would scour these English hence?—Hear'st thou of them?
Doct. Aye, my good lord; your royal preparation
Makes us hear something.
Macb. Bring it after me.—
I will not be afraid of death and bane,
Till Birnam forest come to Dunsinane. [*Exit.*

* **Skirr** (A. S. *scûr*, a scouring; Ger. *scheuern*, fr. Lat. *ex*, out, and *curare*, to take care of, to look to? Low Ger. *schüren*, to flee away; Fr. *écurer*, to scour, clean), *scour; scud over*. See note on the significance of the sound of *sc*, p. 56.—**Patient**, Lady Macbeth.—**Stuffed . . . . stuff.** Another play on words?—**Staff**, *lance, spear*.—**Cast the water**, inspect the water, as physicians do.—**Pull 't off.** He is talking of his dress or a part of his armor.—**Bring it after me.** He refers to some of his accoutrements.—**Birnam forest**, a forest covering and surrounding a high hill twelve miles N.W. of Perth, and about the same distance W.N.W. of Dunsinane.

I'll fight, etc. Savage energy. Very loud; quick; radical; impure; large volume.
Cure her of that, etc. Calmer, but yet in a beseeching tone.
Throw physic, etc. Anger; contempt; haste. Loud; quick; radical; aspirated; small volume.
If thou couldst, Doctor, cast, etc. Grim humor. Radical, business tone, with energy.

Doct. Were I from Dunsinane away and clear,
Profit again should hardly draw me here. [*Exit.*

SCENE IV. *Country near* Dunsinane. *A Wood in view.*

Enter, with Drum and Colors, MALCOLM, *old* SIWARD, *and his* Son, MACDUFF, MENTETH, CATHNESS, ANGUS, LENOX, ROSSE, *and* Soldiers, *marching.*

Mal. Cousins, I hope the days are near at hand
That chambers will be safe.*
Ment. We doubt it nothing.
Siw. What wood is this before us?
Ment. The wood of Birnam.
Mal. Let every soldier hew him down a bough,
And bear 't before him. Thereby shall we shadow
The numbers of our host, and make discovery
Err in report of us.
Sold. It shall be done.
Siw. We learn no other but the confident tyrant
Keeps still in Dunsinane, and will endure
Our setting down before 't.
Mal. 'Tis his main hope:
For where there is advantage to be given,
Both more and less have given him the revolt;
And none serve with him but constrained things,
Whose hearts are absent too.
Macd. Let our just censures
Attend the true event, and put we on
Industrious soldiership.
Siw. The time approaches
That will with due decision make us know
What we shall say we have, and what we owe.
Thoughts speculative their unsure hopes relate;
But certain issue, strokes must arbitrate:
Towards which, advance the war. [*Exeunt, marching.*

SCENE V. Dunsinane. *Within the Castle.*

Enter, with Drums and Colors, MACBETH, SEYTON, *and* Soldiers.

Macb. Hang out our banners on the outward walls.
The cry is still, "*They come!*" Our castle's strength
Will laugh a siege to scorn. Here let them lie

---

* **Chambers will be safe,** alluding to the murder of Duncan; or, perhaps, to the paid spies of Macbeth in their houses.—**For where . . . . advantage,** etc. Where Macbeth's subjects occupy advantageous positions in which they might assist him and injure us.—**More and less,** *high and low.*—**Censures . . . . event,** *judgments await the actual result.*—**What we shall say,** etc. The time draws near when we shall know what we can truly claim as ours, and what duties we owe to the government.—**Arbitrate,** *determine.* —**War,** *army.*

Cousins, I hope, etc. Matter of fact through this scene. All the vocal elements moderate.
Hang out our banners, etc. Command. Loud; bold; scornful.

Till famine and the ague eat them up.
Were they not forced* with those that should be ours,
We might have met them dareful, beard to beard,
And beat them backward home.—What is that noise?
[*A cry within, of women.*
Sey. It is the cry of women, my good lord. [*Exit.*
Macb. I have almost forgot the taste of fears.
The time has been, my senses would have cooled
To hear a night-shriek; and my fell of hair
Would at a dismal treatise rouse and stir
As life were in 't. I have supped full with horrors:
Direness, familiar to my slaughterous thoughts,
Cannot once start me.—Wherefore was that cry? [*Re-enter* SEYTON.
Sey. The queen, my lord, is dead.
Macb. She should have died hereafter;
There would have been a time for such a word.—
To-morrow, and to-morrow, and to-morrow,
Creeps in this petty pace from day to day,
To the last syllable of recorded time;
And all our yesterdays have lighted fools
The way to dusty death. Out, out, brief candle!
Life 's but a walking shadow; a poor player,
That struts and frets his hour upon the stage,
And then is heard no more: it is a tale
Told by an idiot, full of sound and fury,
Signifying nothing!—

Enter a Messenger.

Thou com'st to use thy tongue:—thy story—quickly!
Mess. Gracious my lord,
I shall report that which I say I saw,
But know not how to do it.
Macb. Well, say it, sir.
Mess. As I did stand my watch upon the hill,
I looked toward Birnam, and anon, methought,
The wood began to move.
Macb. Liar and slave! [*Striking him.*
Mess. Let me endure your wrath, if 't be not so.

---

* **Forced,** *reinforced.*—**Fell** (A. S. and Ger. *fell;* akin to Lat. *pellis,* skin. See Grimm's law), the skin of a beast, particularly of a sheep with the wool on it; *scalp,* or *head* of hair. See "lion-fell," in *Midsummer Night's Dream,* Act v., Scene 1.—**Treatise,** etc. Even a dismal tale in a book would make my hair stand on end, as if it were alive.—**Such a word,** *such a message, such tidings.*—**To-morrow,** etc. Note the deep pathos of the situation and the language.

Till famine, etc. Defiant. Loud; quick; radical.
I have almost forgot, etc. Serious. Low; slow; small volume.
She should have died, etc. Sorrow. Low; slow; soft; small volume.
To-morrow, and to-morrow, etc. Solemn; despairing. Low pitch, monotone; slow; slight force.
Thou comst to use, etc. Angry. Quick; loud.
Liar and slave! etc. Great anger. Very loud and quick.

Within this three mile may you see it coming:
I say, a moving grove.
Macb. If thou speak'st false,
Upon the next tree shalt thou hang alive
Till famine cling* thee: if thy speech be sooth,
I care not if thou dost for me as much.—
I pull in resolution; and begin
To doubt the equivocation of the fiend,
That lies like truth: "*Fear not, till Birnam wood*
Do come to Dunsinane;"—and now a wood
Comes toward Dunsinane.—Arm, arm, and out!—
If this, which he avouches, does appear,
There is nor flying hence, nor tarrying here.
I 'gin to be a-weary of the sun,
And wish the estate o' the world were now undone.—
Ring the alarum-bell!—Blow, wind! come, wrack!
At least we 'll die with harness on our back. [*Exeunt.*

SCENE VI. *The Same. A Plain before the Castle.*

Enter, with Drums and Colors, MALCOLM, *old* SIWARD, MACDUFF, etc., *and their Army with Boughs.*

Mal. Now near enough: your leavy screens throw down,
And show like those you are.—You, worthy uncle,
Shall, with my cousin, your right noble son,
Lead our first battle: worthy Macduff and we
Shall take upon us what else remains to do,
According to our order.
Siw. Fare you well.—
Do we but find the tyrant's power to-night,
Let us be beaten, if we cannot fight.
Macd. Make all our trumpets speak: give them all breath,
Those clamorous harbingers of blood and death.
[*Exeunt. Alarums continued.*

SCENE VII. *The Same. Another part of the Plain.*

Enter MACBETH.

Macb. They have tied me to a stake; I cannot fly,
But bear-like, I must fight the course.—What 's he
That was not born of woman? Such a one
Am I to fear, or none.

---

* **Cling** (A. S. *clingan*, to wither), *shrivel, wither, pinch.*—**Sooth,** *truth.* See *soothly*, p. 41.—**Harness** (W. *haiarn*, iron; O. Fr. *harnas*, iron armor; Fr. *harnais*), *armor.*—**First battle,** *advanced force.*—**Fight the course.** An expression taken from bear-baiting. The bear was tied to a stake, and the dogs were then let loose upon him.

To doubt the equivocation, etc. Puzzled; alarmed. Very rapid; small volume; aspirated.
Arm, arm, and out! etc. Excited command. Very loud; quick; large volume.
Blow, wind, etc.! Shouting defiance.

Enter young SIWARD.

Yo. Siw. What is thy name?
Macb. Thou'lt be afraid to hear it.
Yo. Siw. No; though thou call'st thyself a hotter name
Than any is in hell.
Macb. My name 's Macbeth.
Yo. Siw. The devil himself could not pronounce a title
More hateful to mine ear.
Macb. No, nor more fearful.
Yo. Siw. Thou liest, abhorred tyrant! with my sword
I'll prove the lie thou speak'st. [*They fight, and young* SIWARD *is slain.*
Macb. Thou wast born of woman:—
But swords I smile at, weapons laugh to scorn,
Brandished by man that 's of a woman born. [*Exit.*

Alarums. Enter MACDUFF.

Macd. That way the noise is.—Tyrant, show thy face!
If thou be'st slain, and with no stroke of mine,
My wife and children's ghosts will haunt me still.
I cannot strike at wretched kernes,* whose arms
Are hired to bear their staves: either thou, Macbeth,
Or else my sword, with an unbattered edge,
I sheathe again undeeded. There thou shouldst be;
By this great clatter, one of greatest note
Seems bruited. Let me find him, Fortune!
And more I beg not. [*Exit. Alarum.*

Enter MALCOLM *and old* SIWARD.

Siw. This way, my lord;—the castle 's gently rendered:
The tyrant's people on both sides do fight;
The noble thanes do bravely in the war;
The day almost itself professes yours,
And little is to do.
Mal. We have met with foes
That strike beside us.
Siw. Enter, sir, the castle. [*Exeunt. Alarum.*

Re-enter MACBETH.

Macb. Why should I play the Roman fool, and die
On mine own sword? Whiles I see lives, the gashes
Do better upon them.

---

* **Kernes.** "Here the word seems to mean the lowest order of mercenary soldiers." *White.* See note on *Kernes,* Act I., sc. 2.—**Bruited,** *noised abroad.* Fr. *bruire,* to roar; *bruit,* noise.—**Gently rendered,** *quietly surrendered.*—**Strike beside us,** *strike wide of the mark,* try not to hit us.—**Roman.** He is thinking of the suicide of Cato, Brutus, and others.

Tyrant, show thy face! etc. Loud defiance.
This way, my lord, etc. Joyful. Quick; loud; median; pure; large.
Why should I play the Roman fool, etc. Scorn. Radical; loud; aspirated with sneers.

Re-enter MACDUFF.

Macd. Turn, hell-hound, turn!
Macb. Of all men else I have avoided thee:
But get thee back: my soul is too much charged
With blood of thine already.
Macd. I have no words:
My voice* is in my sword, thou bloodier villain
Than terms can give thee out! [*They fight.*
Macb. Thou losest labour:
As easy mayest thou the intrenchant air
With thy keen sword impress, as make me bleed.
Let fall thy blade on vulnerable crests.
I bear a charmed life, which must not yield
To one of woman born.
Macd. Despair thy charm!
And let the angel whom thou still hast served
Tell thee, Macduff was from his mother's womb
Untimely ripped!
Macb. Accursed be that tongue that tells me so!
For it hath cowed my better part of man!
And be these juggling fiends no more believed,
That palter with us in a double sense;
That keep the word of promise to our ear,
And break it to our hope!—I'll not fight with thee.
Macd. Then yield thee, coward,
And live to be the show and gaze o' the time!
We'll have thee, as our rarer monsters are,
Painted upon a pole, and underwrit,
"*Here may you see the tyrant!*"
Macb. I 'll not yield,
To kiss the ground before young Malcolm's feet,
And to be baited with the rabble's curse.
Though Birnam wood be come to Dunsinane,
And thou opposed, being of no woman born,
Yet I will try the last! Before my body
I throw my warlike shield! lay on, Macduff;
And damned be he that first cries, "*Hold! enough!*" [*Exeunt, fighting.*

---

* **My voice**, etc. So Casca, in *Julius Cæsar*, says, "Speak, *hands*, for me!"—**Intrenchant**, that which cannot be trenched or cut. See *trenched*, p. 146.—**Charmed life**, a life protected by magic charms. In the age of chivalry, a champion in a tournament was obliged to swear that he used no charmed weapons.—**Palter**, act in an insincere or false manner; *shift*, dodge, trifle, haggle. Low Ger. *palte*, rag; Fries. *palt;* Sw. *palta;* Scot. *paltrie*, trash; Eng. *paltry*, mean, worthless.—**Baited** (A. S. *bate*, contention), *provoked*, harassed, worried, as a chained bear is annoyed by dogs.—**Hold! enough!** By the old codes of honor, the mode of separating combatants was to cry "*Hold!*"

Turn, hell-hound, etc. The first half of this dialogue is loud, bold, defiant.
Accursed be that tongue, etc. Imprecating; desponding; distrustful; feeble. Aspirated; small volume.
Then yield thee, coward, etc. Scorn; ridicule. Loud; radical; circumflex; small volume.
I 'll not yield, etc. He rouses himself grandly, and dies with a heroic bravery that partially wins back our respect.

Retreat. Flourish. Re-enter, with Drum and Colors, MALCOLM, *old* SIWARD, ROSSE, LENOX, ANGUS, CATHNESS, MENTETH, *and* Soldiers.

Mal. I would the friends we miss were safe arrived.
Siw. Some must go off;* and yet, by these I see,
So great a day as this is cheaply bought.
Mal. Macduff is missing, and your noble son.
Rosse. Your son, my lord, has paid a soldier's debt;
He only lived but till he was a man:
The which no sooner had his prowess confirmed
In the unshrinking station where he fought,
But like a man he died.
Siw. Then he is dead?
Rosse. Aye, and brought off the field. Your cause of sorrow
Must not be measured by his worth, for then
It hath no end.
Siw. Had he his hurts before?
Rosse. Aye, on the front.
Siw. Why then, God's soldier be he!
Had I as many sons as I have hairs,
I would not wish them to a fairer death.
And so his knell is knolled.
Mal. He 's worth more sorrow,
And that I 'll spend for him.
Siw. He 's worth no more.
They say, he parted well, and paid his score:
So, God be with him!—Here comes newer comfort.

Re-enter MACDUFF, *with* MACBETH'S *Head on a Pole.*

Macd. Hail, King! for so thou art. Behold, where stands
The usurper's cursed head: the time is free.
I see thee compassed with thy kingdom's pearl,
That speak my salutation in their minds;
Whose voices I desire aloud with mine.—
Hail, King of Scotland!
All. King of Scotland, hail! [*Flourish.*
Mal. We shall not spend a large expense of time,
Before we reckon with your several loves,
And make us even with you. My thanes and kinsmen,
Henceforth be Earls,—the first that ever Scotland

* **Some must go off,** some must be *slain.*—**Fairer death.** This incident is related in *Camden's Remaines.*—**Pearl.** A collective noun, meaning a *string of pearls.* Spoken of the heroes that encircled Malcolm.—**Henceforth be Earls.** Holinshed gives the same explanation of this change of name.

I would, the friends we miss, etc. This dialogue is quite rapid.
Then he is dead? etc. The old Spartan must have spoken this with deep sorrow; from which, however, he instantly recovers.
Hail, king, etc. Great joy. Very loud; quick; median.
We shall not spend, etc. Joy; gratitude; business. Rather loud; rather quick; median; rather large volume.

In such an honor named. What 's more to do,
Which would be planted newly with the time,—
As calling home our exiled friends abroad,
That fled the snares of watchful tyranny;
Producing forth the cruel ministers
Of this dead butcher, and his fiendlike queen;
Who, as 'tis thought, by self and violent hands
Took off her life;—this, and what needful else
That calls upon us, by the grace of Grace,
We will perform in measure, time, and place.
So thanks to all at once and to each one,
Whom we invite to see us crowned at Scone.* [*Flourish. Exeunt.*

* **Scone.** See note on *Scone*, Act II., sc. 2., p. 137.

What's more to do, etc. Business tone with something of joy. Radical; rather loud; moderate in time, pitch, and volume.

Write a sketch of the life of Shakespeare; an account of his writings. Write an essay upon his moral character; one upon his genius; one upon the theatre. Sketch the life of Macbeth as it appears in history; the character of Macbeth as it appears in this play; of Lady Macbeth; of Duncan; of each of the other prominent personages. Write your views of the propriety or impropriety for dramatic effect, of the sequence of scenes in this play. Relate the story as developed in each act. Write out the moral or lessons conveyed by this play, and give your reasons for your conclusions on that subject. Write an essay upon alliteration; one upon English heroic verse; one upon Shakespeare's vocabulary, and what is proved by its fullness and accuracy. Argue the rightfulness or wrongfulness of Shakespeare's course in ignoring the practical questions of his age. Explain the fact that the great men of Shakespeare's time did not appreciate him. Give your views of Shakespeare's sympathies, as regards Puritanism, democracy, progress. Is the world likely to see another Shakespeare? Why? The instructor should give out other themes, the investigation of which will throw light upon the literature of Shakespeare and of the Elizabethan age. No exercise will be found more profitable than brief compositions at regular intervals on topics suggested by the reading of the author. These should be read in the hearing of the class, and the teacher should comment upon them.

SUMMARY OF RESULTS OF ELOCUTIONARY ANALYSIS.*

Among the elements of vocal expression revealed by the simplest analysis, are the following:—

1. *Force;* the degree of loudness or softness.

2. *Time;* the movement, or rate of utterance, whether fast or slow.

3. *Pitch;* the key-note, or musical tone, whether low or high.

4. *Slides;* changes in pitch, during the utterance of a single vowel or syllable. The change may be very slight, passing through about a semi-tone, or it may sweep through a whole octave or more.

5. *Stress;* change in force, during the utterance of a single vowel or syllable.

6. *Quality;* purity or impurity in tone.

7. *Volume;* the size, so to speak, of the voice. Thus we hear of a "thin voice," and Shakespeare tells us of a "big, manly voice," which elocutionists call "orotund."

In the employment of these elements, as we have already to some extent seen,† there is a principle of imitation and of analogy. "The sound should seem an echo to the sense," says Pope. This principle has a multitude of applications.

1. A loud utterance naturally characterizes descriptions of loud sounds. Thus:

> The wakeful trump of doom must thunder through the deep
> With such a horrid clang as on Mount Sinai rang,
> When the red fire and smouldering clouds outbrake.—MILTON.

A soft voice belongs to descriptions of what is soft, gentle, or quiet. Thus:

> Oft in the stilly night, ere Slumber's chain has bound me,
> Fond Memory brings the light of other days around me;
> The smiles, the tears, of boyhood's years;
> The words of love then spoken;
> The eyes that shone, now dimmed and gone;
> The cheerful hearts now broken.—MOORE.

2. Slowness of motion should generally be expressed by slowness of speech.‡ Thus:

> Hear the tolling of the bells, iron bells!
> . . . .
> And who, tolling, tolling, tolling,
> In that muffled monotone, etc.—POE.

---

* See the foot-notes to MACBETH, *passim.*

† Thus, in reading the dialogue between Lady Macduff and her son, the voice may be modified in a slight degree to suit those characters.

‡ There are two mechanical methods of securing slowness in speech. One is by long pauses between sounds, syllables, words, and sentences. The other is by prolonging the phonetic elements. In the slowest passages, the two methods are combined.

Rapid motion is expressed by quick-utterance. Thus:

Hurrah! the foes are moving! Hark to the mingled din
Of fife and steed and trump and drum and roaring culverin!
The fiery duke is pricking fast across St. André's plain
With all the hireling chivalry of Guelders and Almayne.
Now, by the lips of those ye love, fair gentlemen of France,
Charge for the golden lilies! Upon them with the lance!—
A thousand spurs are striking deep, a thousand spears in rest,
A thousand knights are pressing fast behind the snow-white crest!
And in they burst, and on they rushed, while, like a guiding star,
Amidst the thickest carnage blazed the helmet of Navarre!—MACAULAY.

The impression of *distance* is given by prolonging the sound. For example, notice the effect of protracting the word *far* in the following line:*

So seemed, far off, the flying fiend.—MILTON.

3. In *pitch*, the voice naturally glides into the low (not necessarily soft) notes in speaking of deep, grave tones. Thus:

Oh, it is monstrous, monstrous!
Methought the billows spoke and told me of it;
The winds did sing it to me; and the thunder,
That deep and dreadful organ-pipe, pronounced
The name of Prosper: it did bass my trespass.—SHAKESPEARE.

But in describing the fine, high-pitched note of the musquito, we involuntarily change to a higher key, as, forgetting ourselves, we think of the penetrating musical sound. The voice of a child, as we saw in *Macbeth*, Act IV., Scene 2, is high (not necessarily loud) in pitch. Thus:

You must wake and call me early, call me early, mother dear;
To-morrow 'll be the happiest time of all the glad new year;
Of all the glad new year, mother, the maddest, merriest day!
For I 'm to be queen of the May, mother, I 'm to be queen of the May!—TENNYSON.

4. In respect to *quality*, we may observe that purity, sweetness, and smoothness in objects, require corresponding vocal qualities: *i. e.*, there is no prominence of consonant sounds, and there is an absence of husky, hoarse, nasal, or guttural tones. Thus:

"Sweet day, so cool, so calm, so bright,
Bridal of earth and sky,
The dew shall weep thy fall to-night;
For thou, alas, must die!

"Sweet rose, in air whose odors wave,
And color charms the eye,
Thy root is ever in its grave,
Thou too, alas, must die!

---

* Another case in which great slowness of speech is required, is where the thought is very much condensed, and the mind needs considerable time to appreciate the full meaning, as was remarked of the passage where Lady Macbeth enters reading the letter. Thus, "Now if the fall of them be the riches of the world, and the diminishing of them the riches of the Gentiles, how much more their fullness!"—Rom. xi. 12. On the contrary, where the writer does not plough deep, there the voice is nimble, and gets over the ground fast. Thus: "Certainly my conscience will serve me to run from the Jew, my master. The fiend is at mine elbow, and tempts me, saying to me, 'Gobbo, Launcelot Gobbo, good Launcelot, or good Gobbo, or good Launcelot Gobbo, use your legs, take the start, run away.' My conscience says, 'No, take heed, honest Launcelot; take heed, honest Gobbo; or, as aforesaid, honest Launcelot Gobbo, do not run; scorn running with thy heels, etc."—SHAKESPEARE.

"Sweet spring, of days and roses made,
Whose charms in beauty vie;
Thy days depart, thy roses fade;
Thou, too, alas, must die!

"Only a pure and holy soul
Hath charms that never fly!
While days depart and seasons roll,
This lives, and cannot die!"

What is impure, noisy, or rough, is best described with corresponding impurity or harshness of voice, the consonant sounds being given forcibly, and, sometimes, with a loud hissing, wheezing, snarling, whining, or growling, or as if the utterance were choked with emotion. For instance, Lear, in the howling of the storm, exclaims:

Blow, wind, and crack your cheeks! Rage! Blow!
You cataracts and hurricanoes, spout
Till you have drenched the steeples, drowned the cocks!
You sulphurous and thought-executing fires,
Vaunt-couriers to oak-cleaving thunderbolts,
Singe my white head! And thou all-shaking thunder,
Strike flat the thick rotundity of the world!
. . . .
Crack Nature's molds, all germens spill at once
That make ingrateful man!—SHAKESPEARE.

5. In *stress*, the voice sometimes swells and sinks in unison with the sound described. Thus in Webster:

"It was the last swelling peal of yonder organ, 'Their bodies rest in peace, but their name liveth evermore.' I catch the solemn sound; I echo that lofty strain of funeral triumph, 'Their name liveth evermore.'"

Here on each long sound the voice makes a sort of *crescendo* and *diminuendo*, styled by elocutionists *median* stress.

In Campbell we have,

But when the gun's tremendous flash is o'er.

Here an explosive tone marks the word *gun;* a burst of sound instantly waning. So on the word *flash.* This is termed *initial* or *radical* stress.

"And when the voice of the trumpet sounded long, and waxed louder and louder, Moses spake."

Here on the diphthong in the word *louder*, the last part of the sound may be the most forcible, constituting the *final* or *vanishing* stress.

6. As to *volume*, vast objects should have full volume; *i. e.*, large, not always *loud*, voice. Thus:

The Bunker Hill monument is completed. Here it stands. Fortunate in the natural eminence on which it is placed, higher, infinitely higher in its objects and purposes, it rises over the land and over the sea; and, visible, at their homes, to three hundred thousand citizens of Massachusetts, it stands, a memorial of the past, and a monitor to the present and all succeeding generations.—WEBSTER.

Contrast with this, Shakespeare's description of Queen Mab:

Oh, then I see Queen Mab hath been with you!
She is the fairies' midwife, and she comes
In shape no bigger than an agate stone,

On the forefinger of an alderman,
Drawn by a team of little atomies
Athwart men's noses as they lie asleep, etc.

Contrast Byron's,

Roll on, thou deep and dark blue ocean, roll!

with Burns's lines to a mouse,

Wee sleekit, timorous, cowerin beastie,
Oh what a panic 's in thy breastie! etc.

7. Again, in the matter of *slides*, there is, to say the least, a curious analogy between straightforward thoughts and straight slides; as also between crooked, indirect thoughts, and that winding which is called the "circumflex" slide. The voice in mockery, irony, sarcasm, often seems to wriggle through several notes up and down, or down and up. Thus:

The gracious Duncan
Was pĭtied of Macbeth . . . . .
And the right valiant Banquo walked too lâte!
Whom you may say, if 't please you, Flêance killed,
For Fleance fled. Men must not walk too lâte.
. . . .
How it did griêve Macbeth! Did he not straight
In pious rage the two delinquents tear?
. . . .
Was not that nôbly done?—SHAKESPEARE.

But besides this evident propriety in making voice correspond with sense, there is a deeper analogy, a more wonderful responsiveness; in short, a possibly perfect adaptation between sound and feeling. Cowper says, "There is in souls a sympathy with sounds." This truth underlies the whole art of vocal expression. It perhaps finds its highest illustration in the miracles wrought by Beethoven's genius; but it lies at the very threshold of elocution. Its philosophy need not now be discussed: but let him who would become a good reader or speaker, give his days and nights, first, to the scientific analysis which shall enable him to discern the precise mental act or state to be expressed, and the appropriate voice that may body it forth; and, secondly, to the reducing of his theory to practice, till correct vocal delivery becomes spontaneous.

With a view to putting the student on the right path for original investigation and independent practice, and not, by any means, with the idea of presenting a complete system, we suggest the following brief statement of such correspondences, and

SUGGESTIONS IN REGARD TO VOCAL EXPRESSION.

TRANQUILLITY is usually of medium force, or a little less; rather slow movement; middle pitch tending to low; pure quality; moderate or slight volume; gentle and median stress;* moderate slides (*i. e.*, slight transitions in the pitch of a single sound). Thus:

* *Stress* is "*compound*," where the initial and the final are combined; "*thorough*," *where* the *whole* sound is very loud; and "*intermittent*" where the voice *trembles*.

"I've seen the moon climb the mountain's brow;
I've watched the mist o'er the river stealing;
But ne'er did I feel in my breast, till now,
So pure, so calm, and so holy a feeling."

So the remarks of Duncan and Banquo on the pleasant situation and surroundings of the castle. (*Macbeth*, Act I., Scene 6.)

CHEERFULNESS is usually of medium force, or a little greater; quick movement; middle pitch, or a little higher; pure quality; moderate or slight volume; initial stress, sometimes median; moderate or longer slides, often rising. Thus:

Pleasant was the journey homeward:
All the birds sang loud and sweetly
Songs of happiness and heart's ease.
Sang the blue-bird, the Owaissa,
"Happy are you, Hiawatha,
Having such a wife to love you!"
Sang the robin, the Opechee,
"Happy are you, laughing water,
Having such a noble husband!"—LONGFELLOW.

MIRTH, if the degree of fun be considerable, and the person be demonstrative, is usually of rather loud force; quick movement; high pitch; pure quality, except in imitation of impure; moderate or small volume; initial stress; extensive, often circumflex, slides. Thus:

Falstaff. Harry, I do not only marvel where thou spendest thy time, but also how thou art accompanied; for though the camomile, the more it is trodden on, the faster it grows, yet youth, the more it is wasted, the sooner it wears. That thou art my son, I have partly thy mother's word, partly my own opinion; but chiefly, a villanous trick of thine eye, and a foolish hanging of thy nether lip, that doth warrant me. If then thou be son to me, here lies the point! why, being son to me, art thou so pointed at? Shall the blessed *sun of heaven* prove a micher, and eat blackberries? a question not to be asked. Shall the son of England prove a thief, and take purses? a question to be asked. There is a thing, Harry, which thou hast often heard of, and it is known to many in this land by the name of pitch. This pitch, as ancient writers do report, doth defile; so doth the company thou keepest. For Harry, now I do not speak to thee in drink, but in tears; not in pleasure, but in passion; not in words only, but in woes also! And yet there is a virtuous man, whom I have often noted in thy company, but I know not his name.

Prince Henry. What manner of man, an it like your majesty?

Falstaff. A good portly man, in faith, and a corpulent; of a cheerful look, a pleasing eye, and a most noble carriage! and, as I think, his age some fifty, or, by 'r-lady, inclining to three score. And now I remember me, his name is Falstaff! If that man should be lewdly given, he deceiveth me; for, Harry, I see virtue in his looks.—SHAKESPEARE.

In this passage, however, mirth may be *imitative*, and a tone of mock seriousness, and the coarse voice of Falstaff, might be adopted. The degree to which imitation should be carried, and the vocal expression varied to hit that which is burlesqued, parodied, or laughed at, will differ with different readers. Usually, attempts to personate are failures.

HUMOR is more quiet than mirth, and is more under control. It usually has moderate force; moderate or quick movement; moderate pitch; pure quality; slight volume; initial, but not explosive, stress; moderate slides. Thus:

I am not without suspicion that I have an undeveloped faculty of music within me. For, thrumming, in my wild way, on my friend A.'s piano, the other morning, while he was engaged in an adjoining parlor, on his return he was pleased to say, "he thought it could not be the maid!" On his first surprise at hearing the keys touched in somewhat an airy and masterful way, not dreaming of me, his suspicions had lighted on *Jenny*.—LAMB.

JOY is usually of loud force, brisk movement, high pitch, pure quality, full volume, median stress, long slides. Thus:

Joy! joy, forever! My task is done!
The gates are passed and heaven is won!
Oh, am I not happy? I am! I am!—MOORE.

(See Duncan's speech beginning, "My plenteous joys," in *Macbeth*, Act I., Scene 4.)

ADMIRATION, which always contains something of joy, is of rather loud force; rather high pitch; moderate time, sometimes quick; pure quality; median stress; moderate volume, sometimes large when the object is large; long slides.

The splendor falls on castle walls
  And snowy summits old in story;
The long light shakes across the lakes,
  And the wild cataract leaps in glory.—TENNYSON.

DELIGHT is between *joy* and *cheerfulness*. Its manifestation differs little from that of *cheerfulness*. The movement is rather fast; the slides are moderate; the quality is very pure. Thus:

Hear the mellow wedding bells, golden bells:
What a world of happiness their harmony foretells!
Through the balmy air of night
How they ring out their delight!
From the molten golden notes,
  And all in tune,
What a liquid ditty floats
To the turtle-dove that listens, while she gloats
  On the moon!
Oh, from out the sounding cells,
What a gush of euphony voluminously wells!
How it swells! How it dwells
On the future! How it tells
Of the rapture that impels
To the swinging and the ringing of the bells, bells, bells—
Of the bells, bells, bells, bells, bells, bells, bells,—
To the rhyming and the chiming of the bells.—POE.

LOVE, undisturbed by fear, is usually of moderate force; moderate movement, inclining to quick; rather high pitch; very pure quality; moderate or slight volume; soft median stress; moderate slides, often rising. Thus:

For the moon never beams, without bringing me dreams
Of the beautiful Annabel Lee;
And the stars never rise, but I feel the bright eyes
Of the beautiful Annabel Lee:
And so all the night-tide I lie down by the side
Of my darling, my darling, my life and my bride,
In that kingdom by the sea—
In that tomb by the deep-sounding sea.—POE.

TENDERNESS is usually of slight force; moderate or slow movement; rather high pitch; pure quality; slight volume; gentle median stress, sometimes tremulous; short or moderate slides, which are oftener rising than falling. Thus:

Take her up tenderly,
  Lift her with care,
Fashioned so slenderly,
  Young and so fair.—HOOD.

If the tenderness is playful, the slides may be long and circumflex.

SORROW is of various kinds. When allied to tenderness and pity it has usually slight force; slow movement; high pitch; pure quality, sometimes aspirated; slight volume; median stress, sometimes intermittent; moderate or long slides, often rising. Thus:

O sacred Head, now wounded,
  With grief and shame bowed down!
O sacred brow, surrounded
  With thorns, thine only crown!—GERHART.

PITY is usually of slight force; rather slow time; very high pitch; pure quality; small volume; median, or slight radical stress; moderate slides, often rising. Thus:

Do you hear the children weeping, O my brothers!
  Ere the sorrow comes with years?
They are leaning their young heads against their mothers,
  And that cannot stop their tears.
The young lambs are bleating in the meadows,
  The young birds are chirping in the nest,
The young fawns are playing with the shadows,
  The young flowers are blowing towards the west;—
But the young, young children, O my brothers,
    They are weeping bitterly!
They are weeping in the playtime of the others,
    In the country of the free!—MRS. BROWNING.

DISTRESS is of several kinds and degrees. It is usually of loud force (by paroxysms); very high pitch; quick time, with occasional long sounds of grief; aspirated quality; moderate volume; vanishing stress, rarely median; long slides. Thus:

O nation miserable,
With an untitled tyrant bloody-sceptered!
When shalt thou see thy wholesome days again?
Since that the truest issue of thy throne
By his own interdiction stands accursed,
And does blaspheme his breed! . . . .
. . . .
O my breast,
Thy hope ends here!—SHAKESPEARE.

IMPATIENCE is usually of loud force; very quick time; high pitch; harsh, impure quality; moderate or small volume; strong vanishing* stress; long, usually falling slides. Thus:

Shame! shame! that in such a proud moment of life,
  Worth ages of history, when, had you but hurled
One bolt at your bloody invader, that strife
  Between freemen and tyrants had spread through the world.

---

* As if, the longer the mind dwelt on the thought, the more intense the feeling became.

That then! O disgrace upon manhood! e'en then
  You should falter; should cling to your pitiful breath;
Cower down into beasts when you might have stood men;
  And prefer a slave's life to a glorious death!—MOORE.

CONTEMPT is usually of slight force, quick or moderate time, moderate pitch; expulsive initial stress, aspirated whispering quality, small volume, moderate slides. Thus:

Go, preach to the coward, thou death-telling seer!
Or, if gory Culloden so dreadful appear,
Draw, dotard, round thy old wavering sight,
This mantle, to cover the phantoms of fright!—CAMPBELL.

SCORN is similar to contempt; but louder, and of larger volume and longer slides.

MALICE, which is a settled state of the mind, is usually of moderate force, moderate or slow time, low pitch, initial stress, aspirated or guttural quality, small volume, short slides. Thus:

I 'll have my bond. Speak not against my bond.
I 've sworn an oath that I will have my bond.
Thou call'dst me dog, before thou hadst a cause;
But, since I am a dog, beware my fangs.—SHAKESPEARE.

SCOLDING is own sister to Impatience. It is usually of loud force; quick time; high pitch, but may growl in a low pitch; impure quality; small volume; marked radical stress; short slides, often circumflex. Thus:

Capulet. How now! how now, chop-logic! What is this?
"Proud"—and, "I thank you"—and, "I thank you not;"
And yet "not proud!" mistress minion, you,
Thank me no thankings, nor proud me no prouds;
But fettle your fine joints 'gainst Thursday next
To go with Paris to St. Peter's church;
Or I will drag thee on a hurdle thither!
You tallow face!

Lady Capulet. Fie! fie! what, are you mad?

Juliet. Good father, I beseech you on my knees,
Hear me with patience but to speak a word.

Capulet. Hang thee, young baggage! disobedient wretch!
I tell thee what,—get thee to church o' Thursday,
Or never after look me in the face!
Speak not; reply not; do not answer me!
My fingers itch!—SHAKESPEARE.

ANGER, when it has not settled into cool malice, is usually of loud force; quick time; moderate or high pitch; very impure in quality, the words being hissed or growled; small volume, the teeth being set; abrupt explosive initial stress, sometimes vanishing; long slides, sometimes circumflex. Thus:

Villains! you did not so when your vile daggers
Hacked one another in the sides of Cæsar!
You showed your teeth like apes, and fawned like hounds,
And bowed like bondmen, kissing Cæsar's feet,
Whilst damned Casca, like a cur, behind,
Struck Cæsar on the neck! SHAKESPEARE.

RAGE and FURY are usually of very loud force, very quick time, very high pitch,* very impure quality,* large volume,* very abrupt initial stress, long slides. Thus:

All the stored vengeance of heaven fall
On her ingrateful top! Strike her young bones,
You taking airs, with lameness! . . . .
You nimble lightnings, dart your blinding flames
Into her scornful eyes!—SHAKESPEARE.

DEFIANCE is usually of loud force, quick time, high pitch, large volume, very impure quality, abrupt initial stress, long slides. Thus:

Whence and what art thou, execrable shape?
That dar'st, though grim and terrible, advance
Thy miscreated front athwart my way
To yonder gates? Through them I mean to pass—
That be assured—without leave asked of thee.—MILTON.

COMMAND is usually of loud force; moderate or quick time; moderate or high pitch; large volume; pure quality, unless angry; marked radical stress; long falling† slides. Thus:

Uzziel! Half these draw off, and coast the south
With strictest watch. These other, wheel the north.—MILTON.

DECISION is usually of rather loud force; rather quick time; moderate pitch; medium or pure quality; moderate volume; marked, but not explosive radical stress; moderate falling slides. Thus:

I stand at Cæsar's judgment seat, where I ought to be judged. To the Jews have I done no wrong, as thou very well knowest.—ST. PAUL.

BUSINESS, or MATTER OF FACT, is usually of moderate force; moderate time; moderate pitch; medium quality; small volume; initial, but not marked stress; short slides, variable. Thus:

I have no more doubt, that, before the expiration of winter, this bill will pass, than I have that the annual tax bills will pass; and greater certainty than this, no man can have; for Franklin tells us, that there are but two things certain in this world—death and taxes.‡

SECRECY is usually of slight force, quick time; and is carried on in a whisper or undertone.

FEAR is usually of soft force, except when frantic; very quick time; low pitch, except in great fright; strongly aspirated quality; little volume; tremulous, or spasmodic initial stress; short slides. Thus:

Macbeth. I have done the deed! Didst thou not hear a noise?
Lady Macbeth. I heard the owl scream and the crickets cry.
Did you not speak?
Macbeth. When?
Lady M. Now.

---

* This element may be varied by frenzy.

† The falling slide indicates completed thought; the rising denotes expectant or tentative thought. The suspended voice (*i. e.*, neither rising nor falling) denotes incomplete thought. The voice takes the downward slide on that word which mainly conveys the thought, or which, when uttered, makes the sense to be apprehended.

‡ *Emphasis* usually makes the prominent word or words higher in musical pitch than the others; and the greater the emphasis, the higher the pitch. Increasing seriousness or solemnity, however, may cause the pitch in emphasis to fall lower. *Accent* does the same for the accented *syllable*, relatively to the other syllables, that emphasis does for the emphatic *word*, relatively to the other words.

Macbeth. As I descended?
Lady M. Aye.
Macbeth. Hark! Who lies in the second chamber?
Lady M. Donalbain.—SHAKESPEARE.

TERROR, when the victim is not paralyzed,* is usually of very loud force, shrieking; very quick time; very high pitch; very impure quality, but the high notes may be very pure; variable volume, usually large; spasmodic initial stress, may be thorough or trembling; long slides. Thus:

Avaunt! and quit my sight! Let the earth hide thee!
Thy bones are marrowless, thy blood is cold;
Thou hast no speculation in those eyes
Which thou doth glare with!
. . . .
Take any shape but that, and my firm nerves
Shall never tremble: or be alive again,
And dare me to the desert with thy sword;
If trembling I inhabit then, protest me
The baby of a girl. Hence, horrible shadow!
Unreal mockery, hence!—SHAKESPEARE.

AWE is usually of slight force; slow time; low pitch; median, sometimes initial stress; sometimes pure, often impure, quality, the voice being low down in the chest; large volume; short, mostly falling slides. Thus:

O eloquent, just, and mighty death! Whom none could advise, thou hast persuaded; what none hath dared, thou hast done; and whom all the world hath flattered, thou only hast cast out of the world and despised. Thou hast drawn together all the far-stretched greatness, all the pride, cruelty, and ambition of man, and covered it over with these two narrow words, *Hic jacet!*—SIR WALTER RALEIGH.

SOLEMNITY is usually of slight or moderate force, slow time, low pitch, median stress, pure quality, moderate or large volume, short slides. Thus:

In truth, there is no sadder spot on earth than that little cemetery. Death is there associated, not, as in Westminster Abbey and St. Paul's, with genius and virtue, with public veneration and imperishable renown; not, as in our humblest churches and churchyards, with everything that is most endearing in social and domestic charities; but with whatever is darkest in human nature and in human destiny; with the savage triumph of implacable enemies; with the inconstancy, the ingratitude, the cowardice of friends; with all the miseries of fallen greatness and of blighted fame. Thither have been carried, through successive ages, by the rude hands of gaolers, without one mourner following, the bleeding relics of men who had been the captains of armies, the leaders of parties, the oracles of senates, and the ornaments of courts. Thither was borne, before the window where Jane Grey was praying, the mangled corpse of Guilford Dudley. Edward Seymour, Duke of Somerset and Protector of the realm, reposes there by the brother whom he murdered. There has mouldered away the headless trunk of John Fisher, Bishop of Rochester and Cardinal of St. Vitalis, a man worthy to have lived in a better age and died in a better cause. There are laid John Dudley, Duke of Northumberland, Lord High Admiral; and Thomas Cromwell, Earl of Essex, Lord High Treasurer. There, too, is another Essex, on whom nature and fortune had lavished all their bounties in vain, and whom valor, grace, genius, royal favor, popular applause, conducted to an early and ignominious doom. Not far off sleep two chiefs of the great house of Howard, Thomas, fourth Duke of Norfolk, and Philip, eleventh Earl of Arundel. Here and there, among the thick graves of unquiet and aspiring statesmen, lie more delicate sufferers; Margaret of Salisbury, the last of the proud name of Plantagenet, and those two fair queens who perished by the jealous rage of Henry. Such was the dust with which the dust of Monmouth mingled.—MACAULAY.

---

* Terror affects different persons differently. It is here supposed to be extreme, so that the sufferer loses all self-control.

SERIOUSNESS is usually of moderate force, sometimes loud, sometimes soft; rather slow time; rather low pitch; slightly median stress, sometimes radical; pure quality; moderate volume; moderate slides. Thus:

Fourscore and seven years ago, our fathers brought forth upon this continent a new nation, conceived in liberty and dedicated to the proposition that all men are created equal. Now we are engaged in a great civil war, testing whether that nation, or any nation so conceived and so dedicated, can long endure. We are met on a great battle-field of that war. We are met to dedicate a portion of it as the final resting place of those who have given their lives that that nation might live.—LINCOLN.

REVERENCE differs little from solemnity in its expression. Love, however, usually blends with it, and so at times does joy, giving it a somewhat higher pitch. Thus:

Thou art, O God, the life and light
Of all this wondrous world we see!
Its glow by day, its smile by night,
Is but reflection caught from thee!—MOORE.

HORROR is deeper than awe. It does not drive frantic like terror. It chills and paralyzes. It is usually of soft force; very low pitch; very slow time; slight median stress; sometimes tremulous, impure, guttural quality; large volume; short slides, or none. This combination of elements gives rise to the *monotone*, in which supernatural visitants are sometimes represented in the theatres as conversing on awful subjects. Thus the ghost in *Hamlet:*

. . . . My hour is almost come,
When I to sulphurous and tormenting flames
Must render up myself! . . . . .
. . . . I am thy father's spirit;
Doomed for a certain term to walk the night,
And for the day confined to fast in fires,
Till the foul crimes done in my days of nature
Are burnt and purged away. But that I am forbid
To tell the secrets of my prison house,
I could a tale unfold whose lightest word
Would harrow up thy soul; freeze thy young blood;
Make thy two eyes like stars start from their spheres;
Thy knotted and combined locks to part,
And each particular hair to stand on end
Like quills upon the fretful porcupine.—SHAKESPEARE.

REMORSE, when great, is usually of loud, convulsive force, sometimes suppressed; quick time, with irregular intervals; high pitch, sometimes moderate or low, as horror comes in; impure quality, guttural, with sobbing or sighing; small volume, sometimes moderate; final stress, with tremor; moderate slides, mostly falling. Thus:

Macbeth. Methought I heard a voice cry, "Sleep no more!
Macbeth does murder sleep, the innocent sleep!
Sleep that knits up the ravelled sleave of care,
The death of each day's life, sore labor's bath,
Balm of hurt minds, great Nature's second course,
Chief nourisher in life's feast"—
Lady M. What do you mean?

Macbeth. Still it cried, "Sleep no more!" to all the house:
"Glamis hath murdered sleep; and therefore Cawdor
Shall sleep no more! Macbeth shall sleep no more!"—SHAKESPEARE.

DESPAIR is usually of slight force; slow time; low pitch; moderately pure quality, slightly aspirated; small volume; tremulous stress; short slides, mostly falling. Thus:

Man. I am now a man of despair, and am shut up in it, as in this iron cage. I cannot get out; Oh, *now* I cannot.

Christian. But how camest thou into this condition?

Man. I left off to watch and be sober; I laid the reins upon the neck of my lusts; I sinned against the light of the word, and the goodness of God; I have grieved the Spirit, and he is gone; I tempted the devil, and he is come to me; I have provoked God to anger, and he has left me; I have so hardened my heart that I cannot repent."

Then said Christian to the Interpreter, "But are there no hopes for such a man as this?"
"Ask him," said the Interpreter. Then said Christian:

Is there no hope, but you must be kept in the iron cage of despair?

Man. No, none at all.

Christian. Why, the Son of the Blessed is very pitiful.

Man. I have crucified him to myself afresh; I have despised his person; I have despised his righteousness; I have counted his blood an unholy thing; I have done despite to the spirit of grace: therefore I shut myself out of all the promises, and there now remains to me nothing but threatenings, dreadful threatenings, fearful threatenings, of certain judgment and fiery indignation, which shall devour me as an adversary.

Christian. For what did you bring yourself into this condition?

Man. For the lusts, pleasures, and profits of this world; in the enjoyment of which I did then promise myself much delight; but now every one of those things also bites me, and gnaws me like a burning worm.

Christian. But canst thou not now repent and turn?

Man. God hath denied me repentance. His word gives me no encouragement to believe; yea, himself hath shut me up in this iron cage, nor can all the men in the world let me out! O Eternity! Eternity! How shall I grapple with the misery that I must meet with in eternity!

Then said the Interpreter to Christian, "Let this man's misery be remembered by thee, and be an everlasting caution to thee."

"Well," said Christian, "this is fearful! God help me to watch and be sober, and to pray that I may shun the cause of this man's misery."—BUNYAN.

SURPRISE is usually of loud force; high pitch; quick and slow movement, alternately; aspirated quality; expulsive radical stress; small volume; long slides. Thus:

Attendant. The king comes here to-night.

Lady Macbeth. Thou 'rt mad to say it! Is not thy master with him? who, were 't so, would have informed for preparation.—SHAKESPEARE.

WONDER is usually of moderate force, sometimes loud; moderate pitch; irregular time, slow, and sometimes quick; aspirated quality, sometimes nearly pure; expulsive initial stress; small volume, sometimes moderate or large; long slides. Thus:

And thou hast walked about—how strange a story!
  In Thebes' streets, three thousand years ago!
When the Memnonium was in all its glory,
  And time had not begun to overthrow
Those temples, palaces, and piles stupendous,
Of which the very ruins are tremendous!

ADMIRATION, *blended with secrecy*, takes some of the characteristics of the latter, the union resulting in slight force; moderate pitch; moderate or quick time; aspirated whispering quality; expulsive initial stress; small volume; short or moderate slides. Thus:

> What is 't? a spirit?
> Lord, how it looks about! Believe me, Sir,
> It carries a brave form: but 'tis a spirit!
> . . . . I might call him
> A thing divine; for nothing natural
> I ever saw so noble.—SHAKESPEARE.

The preceding passage illustrates the *mingling of different emotions, sentiments*, and *passions*. Rarely is one found unmixed; but they are blended in infinite variety. Of course, that which predominates will most color the expression, and much skill may be requisite to rightly adjust the characteristics of vocal utterance so as to represent the ingredients which compose the passage.

From all that has been said, we deduce the following directions for elocutionary analysis:—

1. Ascertain the prevailing tone or spirit of the piece, and adhere to it, adapting the elements of vocal expression to it wherever you perceive no cause for deviation.

2. Ascertain the deviations from the general spirit of the piece, and adapt the elements of expression to the spirit of the individual sentences and words. Be careful, where mental states or acts are blended, to give each its due representation.

3. Make a phonetic analysis of the emphatic words, and practise especially the enunciation of the elements of such words, singly and combined.

We subjoin for illustration the following commencement of an analytical examination of the stanzas preliminary to Milton's *Hymn on the Morning of Christ's Nativity*, as a model of elecutionary analysis. The whole ode will be found on subsequent pages.

I.

> This is the month, and this the happy morn,
> Wherein the Son of Heaven's Eternal King,
> Of wedded Maid and Virgin Mother born,
> Our great redemption from above did bring;
> For so the holy sages once did sing,
> That he our deadly forfeit should release,
> And with his Father work us a perpetual peace.

II.

> That glorious form, that light unsufferable,
> And that far-beaming blaze of majesty,
> Wherewith he wont at Heaven's high council-table
> To sit the midst of Trinal Unity,
> He laid aside; and here with us to be,
> Forsook the courts of everlasting day,
> And chose with us a darksome house of mortal clay.

III.

> Say, heavenly Muse, shall not thy sacred vein
> Afford a present to the Infant God?—
> Hast thou no verse, no hymn, or solemn strain,

To welcome him to this his new abode,
Now, while the heaven, by the sun's team untrod,
  Hath took no print of the approaching light,
And all the spangled host keep watch in squadrons bright?

IV.

See, how, from far, upon the eastern road,
The star-led wizards haste with odors sweet!
O, run, prevent them with thy humble ode,
And lay it lowly at his blessed feet!
Have thou the honor first thy Lord to greet,
  And join thy voice unto the angel choir,
From out his secret altar touched with hallowed fire.

The prevailing tone of the hymn is *serious.* Hence it must, for the most part, be read with moderate force, somewhat slowly, in a rather low pitch, with slightly median stress, pure quality, moderate volume, and moderate slides.

The first stanza, beginning, "This is the month," has joy as well as seriousness. Joy predominates. Hence it should be read with rather loud force, rather brisk movement, rather high pitch, very pure quality, rather full volume, decided median stress, rather long slides.

Make a phonetic analysis * of "*this,*" "*morn,*" "*redemption,*" "*peace;*" and then read the stanza aloud.†

The next stanza, beginning, "That glorious form," has, in the first four lines, deep admiration blended equally with deep reverence and love. Hence those lines should be read with moderate force, moderate pitch, rather slow time, very pure quality, rather large volume, full median stress, moderate slides.

The next three lines, beginning, "He laid aside," have tenderness combined with reverence; tenderness preponderating in the first two, and reverence in the last. Hence to be read with slight force, slow movement; ‡ moderate pitch, median stress, very pure quality, moderate volume, short slides. Read it aloud. Proceed in this manner with every stanza.

* See method of phonetic analysis, p. 62; also list of phonetic elements, pp. 59, 60, 61.

† "How loud?" Loud enough, whatever the piece may be, to be distinctly heard by all the audience, without the slightest effort on their part; and, in addition, loud enough to sufficiently bring into *relief*, as it were, the strong features of the passage. The student will do well to consult the admirable *Treatise on Elocution* by Prof. Mark Bailey, of Yale College. It is prefixed to Hillard's Fifth and Sixth Readers.

‡ After the manner of many elocutionists, we have used the words "movement" and "time" as interchangeable.

JOHN MILTON.

1608–1674.

Nor second HE, that rode sublime
Upon the seraph wings of ecstasy,
The secrets of th' abyss to spy.
He passed the flaming bounds of place and time:
The living throne, the sapphire blaze,
Where angels tremble while they gaze,
He saw; but, blasted with excess of light,
Closed his eyes in endless night.—GRAY.

Thy soul was like a star, and dwelt apart:
Thou hadst a voice, whose sound was like the sea,
Pure as the naked heavens, majestic, free.
So didst thou travel on life's common way,
In cheerful godliness; and yet thy heart
The lowliest duties on herself did lay.—WORDSWORTH.

O mighty-mouthed inventor of harmonies!
O skilled to sing of time and eternity!
God-gifted organ voice of England!
Milton, a name to resound through ages.—TENNYSON.

JOHN MILTON was born in London, December 9, 1608. His father was a scrivener, or writer of law papers, who had been disinherited for a change in his religion, but by diligence and economy had accumulated a considerable property. A man of learning, and something of a poet and musician, he took extraordinary pains with the education of his son. John probably imbibed on his father's knee that taste for these elegant accomplishments, and that hatred of tyranny, which distinguished him in after life. At the age of eleven his father sent him to St. Paul's school, then under the charge of Alexander Gill, a name somewhat famous among pedagogues. Here the boy made wonderful progress in his studies. One fruit of his youthful genius is a beautiful version, written while at school, of the one hundred and thirty-sixth Psalm, beginning,—

Let us, with a gladsome mind,
Praise the Lord, for he is kind;
For his mercies shall endure
Ever faithful, ever sure!

At the age of sixteen his father sent him to Christ's College, Cambridge. He entered as a pensioner, or paying student. It was in the year 1625. In this college he remained four years, until his graduation as Bachelor of Arts; after which he continued at the University three years, pursuing more advanced studies, and finally taking the degree of Master of Arts in 1632.

As a college student it is pretty clear, notwithstanding all that has been said to the contrary, that his career was uncommonly successful. He appears not to have liked the curriculum, nor some of the tutors; but the college productions which Masson quotes and translates, to say nothing of the magnificent *Hymn on the Morning of Christ's Nativity*, show a depth of scholarship, and a grasp, a subtlety, a loftiness,

JOHN MILTON.

(From a miniature of the same size, by Faithorne, *anno* 1667, in possession of William Falconer, Esq.)

and an intensity of thought, such as the world has rarely seen in one so young. We have his own unquestioned testimony to the fact of his great industry. He tells us that, from the age of twelve to thirty, he seldom left his books before midnight.

His bodily appearance at leaving the University was of almost ideal perfection. He was a little below the medium stature; his hair was light brown, and, parted in the middle, it hung in rich curling locks down to his shoulders; his complexion a delicate pink and white, rose blending with lily; his eyes clear and of a dark gray; his voice cheery and musical; his form of wondrous symmetry; his movements manly, graceful, and bold. So beautiful and so refined had he been, that he was commonly called "the Lady of Christ's College;" yet his contemporary, Anthony Wood, tells us that, with all his elegance, "his gait was erect and manly, bespeaking courage and undauntedness."

His father had removed his residence from London to Horton, Buckinghamshire. Thither our handsome scholar, now about twenty-four years of age, went from Cambridge, and there he made his home for nearly six years. His father and mother would have been glad to see their brilliant son become a minister of the established church. But to his bold and independent spirit, the condition of the church seemed such that he who would take orders must write himself down a slave, and conscientious scruples arose. "I thought," says he, "to prefer a blameless silence before the sacred office of speaking, bought and begun with servitude and forswearing." He engaged at Horton in an almost ceaseless round of reading and study, occasionally dashing off a letter or a poem, or running down to London for books or a visit with friends. *Comus*, *Lycidas*, *L'Allegro*, and *Il Penseroso*, poems that "wear the stamp of immortality" as much as anything in the English language, are among the fruits of these six years of toil.

Upon his mother's death, about the beginning of the year 1638, he determined to go abroad. His father furnished him ample funds, and the young man set out, accompanied by a servant, and bearing letters from and to distinguished men. At Paris he saw the great Grotius; at Florence, the greater Galileo, "a prisoner to the Inquisition," says Milton, "for thinking in astronomy otherwise than the Franciscan and Dominican licensers thought." At Rome he attended parties given by the famous Cardinal Barberini. Here he saw and heard Leonora Baroni, a sweet singer, whose melody fascinated him, and to whom he wrote three Latin sonnets. He was preparing to cross over into Sicily, and then to Greece; but on learning that civil war was breaking forth in England, he hastened to return. "I thought it base," he says, "to be travelling for amusement abroad, while my fellow-citizens were fighting for liberty at home."

He arrived in 1639, after an absence of fifteen months. He was eager to join in the great struggle that had already begun, which was destined to shake off the heavy prelatical and political yoke that Laud and Wentworth had so long been fastening about the neck of the nation. In the great awakening of the English people, Milton thought he saw the way opening to a higher liberty, civil and religious, than England had yet seen, and he threw himself with all his might into the conflict. He was strongest with the pen, and he began those famous treatises on religious reformation, that are so much praised but so little read, of which Macaulay says, "They contain passages compared with which the finest declamations of Burke sink into insignificance. They are a perfect field of cloth of gold. The style is stiff with gorgeous embroidery."

But he must have an income. He opens a private school, takes a few pupils, and enters heartily into the work of their education. This subject commands his attention; he becomes sensible of its vast importance, and writes his famous letter to Samuel Hartlib, delineating with care the plan of "a complete and generous education, to fit a man to perform justly, skilfully, and magnanimously, all the offices, public and private, of peace and war." This treatise is remarkable for its recommendation of certain features which some of the best schools now exhibit, but which were practically unknown in his day; such as systematic gymnastic and military drill, original investigations in natural history, object-teaching, business studies, theoretical and practical agriculture, and making language the key to science.

In 1643, Milton strolled away from London to Forest Hill, Oxfordshire. It was his spring vacation.

"In the spring a young man's fancy lightly turns to thoughts of love."

His ostensible business was to collect a debt of £500, due to his father from Mr. Richard Powell, a justice of the peace. Whether he knew of the existence of Mr. Powell's daughter Mary, may be questioned; but it would appear that here was a genuine case of love at first sight. The handsome scholar probably encountered no opposition from the young lady, and still less from the father, who saw in the speedy marriage not only a desirable match for his daughter, but a quasi settlement, at least for a time, of the long-standing debt. After a month's absence, says Milton's nephew Phillips, he returned with a wife. Married in haste, he repented at leisure. A few weeks revealed the utter unfitness of the alliance. There was not only nothing in common between the two, but there was an utter contrariety of sympathies and of views on the most important subjects. She hated the studious habits of her schoolmaster husband, and longed for her old home. They do not appear to have parted in anger; but they saw no more of each other for two years, and it is certain that her desertion of him was voluntary.

In the early fall he wrote to her to return. It seems a little singular that he did not make the short journey in person to the spot where he had wooed and won her. Had he awakened to the fact that he had been entrapped by the artful debtor, who had palmed off an indifferent daughter upon him instead of paying the old claim in current funds? To his letter, twice repeated, he received no response. He then despatched a messenger to bring the lady, but she refused an interview.

Important consequences grew out of this quarrel, if so we may call it. He wrote four long treatises to prove that reason and Scripture justify a divorce from the bands of matrimony, whenever there exists "any cause, in nature unchangeable, hindering and ever likely to hinder the main benefits of conjugal society." An avalanche of argument and of obloquy descended upon the head of the bold advocate of divorce. There is no reason to suppose that he ever retracted his views; but his magnanimous conduct in forgiving and receiving back the erring wife, and taking beneath his hospitable roof her father's family, to shelter them from the storm that soon threatened all royalists, shows the goodness of his heart, whatever we may think of the soundness of his opinions.

The year 1644 was one of his busiest. In it, while his wife was absent, he wrote his *Areopagitica*, or *Speech for the Liberty of Unlicensed Printing*. In some respects this is the best of his prose works. We have given it entire. It will be found an excellent discipline and a valuable preparation for public life, for the student to master the argument in all its details. "Every statesman," says Macaulay, "should bind this treatise as a sign upon his hand and as frontlets between his eyes."

His nephew Phillips tells us there was, about the year 1647, some talk of making Milton Adjutant-General, and Masson gives us good reason to believe that Milton had carefully studied military tatics. We know from his own statement that he was an adroit fencer. Conceive of our poet in military uniform! He had doubtless admirable qualifications, courage, quickness, energy, enthusiasm combined with coolness; but there was one sufficient obstacle; his eyesight was failing. An inherited weakness of vision had been aggravated by intense study in many a midnight. He appears to have continued to teach until about the time of the execution of the king, January 30, 1649.

Immediately after this extraordinary and astonishing event, he published an able treatise entitled, "*The Tenure of Kings and Magistrates: Proving that it is Lawful and hath been so Held in all Ages, for any that have the Power, to Call to Account a Tyrant or Wicked King, and, after Conviction duly had, to Depose and Put him to Death, if the ordinary Magistrate have neglected or denied to do the same: And that they who, of late, so much blame Deposing, are the Men that did it Themselves.*" This is a remarkable document. In it he sets forth, with great clearness and energy, the very principles on which, a century and a quarter afterwards, our fathers of the American Revolution, the "Jeffersonian Democracy" of our nascent republic, based their resistance against British tyranny. Not even in our famous Declaration of American Independence, are presented more vividly and more eloquently than in this treatise, the principles of the natural equality and freedom of man, of the foundation of all the just authority of magistrates upon the consent of the governed, and of the right of the people to alter or abolish a form of government that proves destructive of their interests or dangerous to their rights.

Hardly had he given this to the world, when he was called to the position of Latin Secretary to the Council of State. The council requested him to answer Bishop Gauden's *Εἰκὼν Βασιλική* [*Icon Basilike*, The King's Image], *A Portraiture of His Sacred Majesty in His Solitudes and Sufferings*, purporting to have been written by the king himself in his last days. The book was having an unprecedented sale, and apparently turning the tide of popular sentiment in favor of monarchy. Milton's smashing answer was entitled *Εἰκονοκλάστης* [*Iconoclastes*, The Image Breaker], for which parliament voted him a thousand pounds.

Now came the world-renowned controversy with Salmasius. Claudius Salmasius [Claude Saumaise], professor in the University of Leyden, had been hired and flattered by Prince Charles, afterwards Charles II., into writing a treatise in defence of Charles I. and of monarchical principles. The treatise was producing a great effect not only in England, but on the continent. The Council of State voted "that Mr. Milton do prepare something in answer to the book of Salmasius." But Milton's eyesight was now so precarious that his physicians forbade him to engage in literary labor, on penalty of total blindness. "I did not long balance," says Milton, "whether my duty should be preferred to my eyes." Accordingly he wrote his *Defence of the People of England*, a work in the sledge-hammer style of argument and abounding with terrible invective. Salmasius was annihilated. The controversy was in Latin. It was disfigured by the personal abuse in which the best men of that period were too prone to indulge; but we must not judge them too harshly for their lack of familiarity with the amenities of a later age.

The service which Milton rendered to the cause of liberty by this treatise and his subsequent publications in the same controversy was felt to be very great, and his fame spread over Europe. But the effort cost him his eyes. There is nothing sublimer than the attitude of this giant champion of human rights, when darkness had settled upon him forever. Read this calm utterance of a heroic soul:

TO CYRIACK SKINNER.

Cyriack, this three years day, these eyes, though clear,
To outward view, of blemish or of spot,
Bereft of light, their seeing have forgot;
Nor to their idle orbs doth sight appear
Of sun, or moon, or star, throughout the year,
Or man or woman. Yet I argue not
Against Heaven's hand or will, nor bate a jot
Of heart or hope; but still bear up and steer
Right onward. What supports me, dost thou ask?
The conscience, friend, to have lost them overplied

In liberty's defence, my noble task,
Of which all Europe rings from side to side.
This thought might lead me through the world's vain mask,
Content, though blind, had I no better guide.

On the death of Cromwell, in 1658, Milton was filled with forebodings. Popular sentiment was becoming strong in favor of the restoration of monarchy. Milton issued pamphlet after pamphlet, urging the establishment of a republic, and setting forth, in striking language, the dangers and inconvenience of kingship. To the final moment he lifted up his voice like a trumpet, "the last words of expiring liberty," as he himself characterizes them. One favorite plan of his, which now, after two hundred years, seems really to be in process of gradual accomplishment, was to abolish monarchy and the House of Lords, and to concentrate power in the House of Commons.

His worst fears were more than realized. The shameful period of the Restoration is best described by Macaulay. "Then came those days, never to be mentioned without a blush; the days of servitude without loyalty, and sensuality without love; of dwarfish talents and gigantic vices; the paradise of cold hearts and narrow minds; the golden age of the coward, the bigot, and the slave. The king cringed to his rival, that he might trample on his people; sunk into a viceroy of France, and pocketed, with complacent infamy, her degrading insults and more degrading gold. The caresses of harlots and the jests of buffoons regulated the measures of a government which had just ability enough to deceive, and just religion enough to persecute."

Powerful friends appear to have saved Milton from the fate that befell good Sir Harry Vane and so many others in those dark days. And now, with singular calmness, when the cherished hopes of his manhood had all been blasted, and the great battle of twenty years had gone against him, he turned to the fulfillment of a dream of his youth. He knew his strength. In prose, he said he had but the use of his left hand. For six years he labored on his *Paradise Lost.*

This poem has been much criticised of late. One essayist finds fault with its Latinisms; another with its learned allusions; another, with its occasional imitations of the language of Homer or Virgil, instead of the language of the street; another, with its incorrect theology; another, with its representation of Adam and Eve as persons of learned and philosophic minds, instead of babes or semi-monkeys; another, with the language and arguments which Milton, after the manner of the Bible, attributes to the Deity; another with Milton's evident moral purpose, his desire to teach a lesson; another, with his conception of the angels as having material bodies, as if everybody knew that there is not a particle of matter in them; another, because, contrary to orthodox views, his Satan is not wholly bad; another, because he makes Sin and Death allegorical personages; another, because he introduces the devils and angels as joking and punning, contrary to their actual usage. The best way to answer these critics, as Hazlitt remarks, is to take down the book and read it. Read it in a loving, sympathetic spirit, from the author's stand-point, as a poem and not as a philosophical or theological treatise. Whoever fails to recognize its power and beauty, after careful study, may well ask himself whether he is not more likely to be mistaken in judgment than the great critics from Addison and Johnson to Coleridge, Channing, Emerson, and Macaulay.

Paradise Lost was published in 1667. For the first edition of this, the greatest epic poem in the language, he received only five pounds; and a like sum for the second edition! In 1671 he produced his *Paradise Regained*, pronounced by Macaulay the second best epic in English. In the same year he wrote *Samson Agonistes*, the best modern imitation of a classic Greek tragedy. He also compiled a Latin Grammar, a treatise on logic, and a Latin lexicon; wrote grand sonnets, some happy translations, a history of England, and several religious works. Among the last named, was an elaborate system of theology, written in Latin and built up wholly of scriptural arguments and citations. The manuscript of this work was lost for a hundred and fifty years; but in 1824 it was discovered in the State Paper Office at London. It has been translated. Whatever may be thought of its premises or its conclusions, it fully sustains his reputation as a scholar and a Christian.

On the eighth of November, 1674, this great man died. I cannot better express my opinion of him than by quoting the language of the learned Dr. Symmons, one of the editors of Milton's prose works. "We have now completed the history of John Milton, a man in whom were illustriously combined all the qualities that could adorn or could elevate the nature to which he belonged; a man who at once possessed beauty of countenance, symmetry of form, elegance of manners, benevolence of temper, magnanimity and loftiness of soul, the brightest illumination of intellect, knowledge the most various and extended, virtue that never loitered in her career nor deviated from her course; a man, who, if he had been delegated as the representative of his species to one of the superior worlds, would have suggested a grand idea of the human race, as of beings affluent in moral and intellectual treasure, raised and distinguished in the universe as the favorites and heirs of heaven."

Consult lives of Milton by Phillips, Ellwood, Toland, Todd, Fenton, Newton, Warton, Symmons, Johnson, Mitford, Griswold, E. P. Hood, Keightly, Brydges; and, especially, Masson, two volumes of whose *Life and Times of John Milton* have been published. See also essays on Milton by Macaulay, Channing, Coleridge, Hazlitt, Ralph Waldo Emerson, and others. Allibone's *Dictionary of Authors* should not be omitted, nor the works on English Literature by Taine, Collier, Craik, Chambers, Angus, Arnold, Cleveland, Minto, Hart, etc. See also Whipple's *Essays* and Reed's *Lectures*, and the article on Milton in the *Encyclopedia Britannica.*

AREOPAGITICA:*

A SPEECH FOR THE LIBERTY OF UNLICENSED PRINTING.

TO THE PARLIAMENT OF ENGLAND.

EVERY statesman should bind this treatise as a sign upon his hand, and as frontlets between his eyes.—MACAULAY.

Every word leaps with intellectual life.—E. P. WHIPPLE.

Τοὐλεύθερον δ' ἐκεῖνο, εἴ τις θέλει πόλει
Χρηστόν τι βούλευμ' εἰς μέσον φέρειν, ἔχων.
Καὶ ταῦθ' ὁ χρῄζων, λαμπρὸς ἔσθ', ὁ μὴ θέλων,
Σιγᾷ· τί τούτων ἐστιν ἰσαίτερον πόλει;—EURIPID. HICETID.

This is true liberty, when freeborn men,
Having to advise the public, may speak free.
Which he who can, and will, deserves high praise;
Who neither can, nor will, may hold his peace.
What can be juster in a state than this?—EURIPID. HICETID.

They, who to states and governors of the commonwealth direct their

---

* **Areopagitica** (Ἄρης, the god of war among the Greeks, Mars; πάγος, a district. Hence, *Areopagus*, Mars' Hill. So called because Mars was said to have been the first person tried there for murder, the murder of Halirrhothius, a son of Neptune), *pertaining to the Areopagus or Mars' Hill at Athens.* The Council of the Areopagus, having supreme judicial authority at Athens in cases of murder, and the general superintendence of religion, morals, education, and the public treasury, was the most august tribunal of heathen antiquity. It used to hold its sessions in the night, on the twenty-seventh, twenty-eighth, and twenty-ninth days of every month. Before this court, St. Paul is supposed to have been arraigned, (see Acts xvii. 19,) and there he pronounced his brief but masterly speech, telling them that Jehovah was "the unknown god" whom they ignorantly worshipped. The British parliament in 1644 occupied a position in some respects similar to that of the Areopagus. But probably the controlling consideration which induced Milton to style this speech *Areopagitica*, was the similarity between his circumstances and those of the Athenian Isocrates, who, in one of his best discourses, which he styles *Areopagiticus*, counsels the Athenians to change their democracy by re-establishing the constitution of Solon in a modified form.

speech, High Court* of Parliament, or, wanting such access in a private condition, write that which they foresee may advance the public good,—I suppose them, as at the beginning of no mean endeavor, not a little altered and moved inwardly in their minds; some with doubt of what will be the success, others with fear of what will be the censure; some with hope, others with confidence of what they have to speak. And me, perhaps each of these dispositions, as the subject was whereon I entered, may have at other times variously affected, and likely might in these foremost expressions now also disclose which of them swayed most; but that the very attempt of this address thus made, and the thought of whom it hath recourse to, hath got the power within me to a passion, far more welcome than incidental to

---

* **High Court.** Parliament had, and, in the last resort, still has, judicial powers. So it was with the colonial legislatures of this country, before the adoption of their constitutions vested the legislative, judicial, and executive powers in separate branches of the government. Accordingly the legislature was often called *the general court* (as, "The General Court of Massachusetts").—**Parliament** (Fr. *parler*, to speak; Lat. *-mentum*, which is a suffix denoting a means for the performance of the action of the verb, so that *parliament* is strictly, in the language of Thomas Carlyle, "the *talking apparatus*" of a nation).—**I suppose them.** The sentence begins, *They, who,* etc.; and *they* has no predicate verb. The sense is, They . . . . I suppose, as at the beginning . . . . are not a little, etc. What is *anacoluthon?* Is this an instance of it? Reconstruct the sentence in several ways.—**As the subject was,** according as the subject was; according to the nature of the subject.—**Likely,** it is likely that each of these dispositions (doubt, fear, hope, confidence) might in these introductory expressions disclose, etc.—**Attempt . . . . thought.** These two things are so blended that Milton treats them as forming a nominative singular, the subject of *hath got* (*i. e.*, hath aroused).

SYNONYMES.—"All languages tend to clear themselves of synonymes as intellectual culture advances, the superfluous words being taken up and appropriated by new shades and combinations of thought evolved in the progress of society."—*De Quincey.*

Beginning, commencement, entry upon. Distinguish among the meanings and uses of these words. Incorporate each in a sentence or in sentences, that shall illustrate its peculiar significance. Thus:—

"*Begin*, in German *beginnen*, is compounded of *be* and *ginnen*, probably a frequentative of *gehen*, signifying 'to *go* first to' a thing. [Noah Webster gives a different etymology, making A. S. *ginnan* mean to *cut*, to split; so that *begin* would mean *cut in!*] *Commence*, in Fr. *commencer*, is not improbably derived from the Lat. *commendo*, signifying 'I betake myself to' a thing. *Enter*, in Lat. *intro*, within, signifies, with the preposition *upon*, to go into a thing.

"Begin and commence are so strictly allied in signification that it is not easy to discover the difference in their application; although a minute difference does exist. To *begin* respects the order of time. 'When *beginning* to act your part, what can be of greater moment than to regulate your plan of conduct with the most serious attention?'—*Blair.* To *commence* implies the exertion of setting about a thing. 'By the destination of his Creator, and the necessities of his nature, man commences at once an active, not merely a contemplative being.'—*Blair.* Whoever *begins* a dispute is termed the aggressor; no one should *commence* a dispute, unless he can calculate the consequences, and, as this is impracticable, it is better never to *commence* disputes, particularly such as are to be decided by law. *Begin* is opposed to *end; commence*, to *complete:* a person *begins* a thing with a view of ending it; he *commences* a thing with a view of completing it.

"To *begin* is either transitive or intransitive; to *commence* is mostly transitive. A speaker *begins* by apologizing; he *commences* his speech with an apology. Happiness frequently *ends* where prosperity *begins;* whoever *commences* any undertaking, without estimating his own power, must not expect to succeed.

"To *begin* is used either for things or persons; to *commence*, for persons only. All things have their *beginning;* in order to effect anything, we must make a *commencement.* A line *begins* with a particular word; a person *commences* his career. Lastly, *begin* is more colloquial than *commence.* Thus we say, to *begin* the work; to *commence* the operation; to *begin* one's play; to *commence* the pursuit; to *begin* to write; to *commence* the letter.

"To *commence* and *enter upon* are as closely allied in sense as the former words; they differ principally in application. To *commence* seems rather to denote the making [of] an experiment; to *enter upon*, that of first doing what has not been tried before. We *commence* an undertaking; we *enter upon* an employment. Speculating people are very ready to *commence* schemes; considerate people are always averse to *entering upon* any office, until they feel themselves fully adequate to discharge its duties."—*Crabb's English Synonymes*, 10th edition (1858), p. 292.

In like manner let the student write out concisely the respective meanings and uses of the following synonymes, with appropriate sentences to fully illustrate each:

Attempt, endeavor, effort, exertion, trial, struggle. See Crabb's *Synonymes*, Worcester's *Unabridged Dictionary*, Webster's *Unabridged Dictionary*, Roget's *Thesaurus*, Graham's *English Synonymes*, etc.

a preface. Which though I stay not to confess * ere any ask, I shall be blameless, if it be no other than the joy and gratulation which it brings to all who wish and promote their country's liberty; whereof this whole discourse proposed will be a certain testimony, if not a trophy.

For this is not the liberty which we can hope, that no grievance ever should arise in the commonwealth. That let no man in this world expect. But when complaints are freely heard, deeply considered, and speedily reformed, then is the utmost bound of civil liberty attained that wise men look for. To which if I now manifest, by the very sound of this which I shall utter, that we are already in good part arrived, and yet from such a steep disadvantage of tyranny and superstition grounded into our principles as was beyond the manhood of a Roman recovery, it will be attributed, first, as is most due, to the strong assistance of God, our deliverer; next, to your faithful guidance and undaunted wisdom, Lords and Commons of England!

Neither is it, in God's esteem, the diminution of his glory, when honorable things are spoken of good men and worthy magistrates. Which if I now first should begin to do, after so fair a progress of your laudable deeds and such a long obligement upon the whole realm to your indefatigable virtues, I might be justly reckoned among the tardiest and the unwillingest of them that praise ye. Nevertheless, there being three principal things, without which all praising is but courtship and flattery; first, when that only is praised which is solidly worth praise; next, when greatest likelihoods are brought, that such things are truly and really in those persons to whom they are ascribed; the other, when he who praises, by showing that such his actual persuasion is of whom he writes, can demonstrate that he flatters not; the former two of these I have *heretofore* endeavored, rescuing the employment from him who went about to impair your merits with a trivial and malignant encomium. The latter, as belonging chiefly to *mine own* acquittal, that whom I so extolled I did not flatter, hath been reserved opportunely to this occasion.

For he who freely magnifies what hath been nobly done and fears not to declare as freely what might be done better, gives ye the best covenant of his fidelity, and that his loyalest affection and his hope waits on your pro-

* **Which though I stay** (delay or hesitate) **not to confess.** A Latin construction, equivalent to, *And though I delay not to confess this passion.*—**If it be no other,** *if this passion be no other.* —**Whereof,** *of which liberty.*—**Trophy.** He claims that this very discourse may be considered a testimonial (almost a trophy) of liberty, for its boldness proves that England is free.—**When complaints,** etc. How comprehensive and how admirable is this statement!—**Roman.** Even the old Romans, with all their manhood (*virtus*, manliness, from *vir*, a man), could not have regained their liberty under such disadvantages. It is a steep ascent from a very low level. —**Roman.** Why Roman?—**Which if I now first,** etc., and if I now, for the first time, should begin to do this (*i. e.*, to speak honorable things of parliament).—**Obligement,** etc., *obligation* (resting) *upon the whole realm* (*i. e.*, after the whole realm has been so long indebted to your indefatigable virtues).—**Praise ye.** This use of *ye* (A. S. *ge*) as an object after a transitive verb is mostly poetic.—**Nevertheless,** etc., notwithstanding my previous commendation of you, it remains for me to complete it, and to show my own sincerity.—**Heretofore endeavored.** This probably refers to his panegyric in the *Apology for Smectymnuus.*—**Him who went,** etc. Bishop Hall, whose encomium appeared insipid and insincere, "damning with faint praise."—**Affection . . . . hope.** The two emotions unite in producing one state of mind, and hence the use of a singular verb, *waits*, where we should use the plural.

Distinguish the respective meanings of *flattery*, *adulation*, *compliment*, *obsequiousness*. Illustrate by sentences.

ceedings. His highest praising is not flattery, and his plainest advice is a kind of praising. For though I should affirm and hold by argument, that it would fare better with truth, with learning, and the commonwealth, if one of your published orders which I should name, were called in; yet at the same time it could not but much redound to the lustre of your mild and equal government, whenas* private persons are hereby animated to think ye better pleased with public advice, than other statists have been delighted heretofore with public flattery. And men will then see what difference there is between the magnanimity of a triennial parliament, and that jealous haughtiness of prelates and cabin counsellors that usurped of late; whenas they shall observe ye in the midst of your victories and successes more gently brooking written exceptions against a voted order, than other courts, which had produced nothing worth memory but the weak ostentation of wealth, would have endured the least signified dislike at any sudden proclamation.

If I should thus far presume upon the meek demeanor of your civil and gentle greatness, Lords and Commons, as what your published order hath directly said, that to gainsay, I might defend myself with ease, if any should accuse me of being new or insolent, did they but know how much better I find ye esteem it to imitate the old and elegant humanity of Greece, than the barbaric pride of a Hunnish and Norwegian stateliness. And out of those ages, to whose polite wisdom and letters we owe that we are not yet Goths and Jutlanders, I could name him who from his private house wrote that discourse to the parliament of Athens, that persuades them to change

* **Whenas,** *while, when* (like the Lat. *cum* with the subjunctive).—**Statists,** *statesmen, politicians.*—**Triennial,** *continuing three years.* Sometimes the word means *happening once in three years* (Lat. *tres*, three; *annus*, a year). The Long Parliament commenced its session in November, 1640.—**Haughtiness.** Baxter, in his *Dying Thoughts*, also complains of them as follows: "They too easily believe that either their grandeur, reverence, names, or numbers, must give them the reputation of being orthodox and in the right, and will warrant them to account and defame him as erroneous, heretical, schismatical, singular, factious, or proud, that presumeth to contradict them and to know more than they."—**Prelates** (Lat. *prælātus*, preferred), a clergyman in authority over the lower orders, as an archbishop, bishop, etc.—**Cabin,** *cabinet, confidential, private.* (See *cabined*, p. 145.) He refers to Wentworth and Laud and the Star-chamber.—**Victories.** The battles of Edgehill, Grantham, Newberry, and Winceby had been fought, and the great victory of Marston Moor had just been won by the parliamentary army.—**Sudden proclamation.** Note the antithetic words in this vigorous sentence, as he contrasts the rule of Charles I. with that of the Long Parliament: "magnanimity," and "haughtiness;" "triennial parliament," and "prelates and cabin counsellors that usurped;" "victories and successes," and "weak ostentation;" "written exception," and "least signified (*i. e.* intimated) dislike;" "voted order," and "sudden proclamation."—**Humanity,** mental cultivation and refinement of manners. *Greek authors* were diligently studied in those times by all who aimed at distinction in politics or literature. The spirit of the Greek classics is eminently favorable to freedom.—**Hunnish.** About the middle of the fifth century (A. D. 447) of the Christian era, Attila, at the head of an immense army of the Huns, advanced to the very gates of Constantinople. Theodosius II. bought him off; and a year or two later Attila led his barbarian army westward, invading Gaul and Italy with fire and sword.—**Norwegian.** "In the twelfth century the Norwegians had carried the terror of their arms to distant lands, and swayed the sceptre, not over Norway merely, but over many parts of the coasts of Britain and the adjacent islands, more especially the Orkneys and the Hebrides."—**Stateliness,** loftiness, haughtiness.—**Those ages,** the ages when Greek literature and art flourished.—**Not yet Goths,** not still (continuing to be) Goths.—**Goths.** A people of Asiatic origin. In the third century they lived in the countries adjacent to the Black Sea and the Danube. Some of them made their way to Scandinavia. Towards the end of the fourth century the Goths, under their king, Alaric, captured and plundered Rome. The word *Goth* became a synonym for *barbarian.* Chesterfield uses it as equivalent to a rude, ignorant person.—**Jutlanders.** Jutes, inhabitants of Jutland, a low, flat peninsula of Denmark. Milton has in mind the fierce and warlike pirates who anciently inhabited Denmark.—**Him.** Isocrates (B. C. 436–338), a distinguished Athenian writer of orations and teacher of rhetoric. See the first note (on *Areopagitica*). Milton, in one of his sonnets, that to Lady Margaret Leigh, styles Isocrates, "that old man eloquent."

the form of democraty which was then established. Such honor was done in those days to men who professed the study of wisdom and eloquence, not only in their own country, but in other lands, that cities and signiories* heard them gladly and with great respect, if they had aught in public to admonish the state. Thus did Dion Prusæus, a stranger and a private orator, counsel the Rhodians against a former edict; and I abound with other like examples, which to set here would be superfluous. But if, from the industry of a life wholly dedicated to studious labors, and those natural endowments haply not the worst for two and fifty degrees of northern latitude, so much must be derogated as to count me not equal to any of those who had this privilege, I would obtain to be thought not so inferior as yourselves are superior to the most of them who received their counsel. And how far you excel them, be assured, Lords and Commons, there can no greater testimony appear, than when your prudent spirit acknowledges and obeys the voice of reason, from what quarter soever it be heard speaking, and renders ye as willing to repeal any act of your own setting forth as any set forth by your predecessors.

If ye be thus resolved, as it were injury to think ye were not, I know not what should withhold me from presenting ye with a fit instance wherein to show, both that love of truth which ye eminently profess, and that uprightness of your judgment which is not wont to be partial to yourselves, by judging over again that order which ye have ordained "to regulate print-

* **Signiories** (Lat. *senior*, older; Ital. *signor*, Mr.; *signoria*, the country under the dominion of a lord), *seigniories*, lordly domains.—**Heard them.** This means the *sophists* in particular, who travelled from city to city delivering lectures on politics.—**Dion Prusæus.** *Dion*, a native of *Prusa*, a city of Bithynia. He lived in the first century of the Christian era and in the beginning of the second, and was a stoic and a sophist. On account of the beauty of his style he was surnamed *Chrysostom, the golden-mouthed.* When Vespasian had first been proclaimed emperor, he consulted Dion as to his proper course, and Dion had the candor to advise him to restore the republic.—**Rhodians.** The island of Rhodes is off the south-west coast of Asia Minor. The chief city, also called Rhodes, famous for its colossus, was in the north-eastern part of the island.—**Not so inferior**, etc. A very handsome compliment, both to himself and to the Long Parliament. "Old Montaigne would have been satisfied with this self confidence." *J. A. St. John.*—**From what quarter.** Milton here seems to allude to a pleasant remark of Socrates in the *Phædrus* of Plato: "The ministers of the Dodonæan Jupiter inform us, my friend, that the first oracles were delivered from an oak; and the people of those days, not being so wise as we are now become, cared not, so that what they heard were true, whether it proceeded from a rock or a tree."—**Presenting ye.** *Ye* (A. S. *ge*) was often used as the objective form by the old English writers. See p. 201.—**Judging over again,** *reconsidering.*—**That order.** This order was made June 14, 1643. It is more minute in its details than the part which Milton quotes. See extract below.[1] See Rushworth's *Hist. Col.* v., 335.

(1) "It is therefore Ordered by the Lords and Commons in *Parliament*, That no Order or Declaration of both, or either House of *Parliament* shall be printed by any, but by order of one or both the said Houses: Nor other Book, Pamphlet, paper, nor part of any such Book, Pamphlet, or paper, shall from henceforth be printed, bound, stitched or put to sale by any person or persons whatsoever, unlesse the same be first approved of and licensed under the hands of such person or persons as both, or either of the said Houses shall appoint for the licensing of the same, and entered in the Register Book of the Company of *Stationers*, according to Ancient custom, and the Printer thereof to put his name thereto. And that no person or persons shall hereafter print, or cause to be reprinted any Book or Books, or part of Book, or Books heretofore allowed of and granted to the said Company of *Stationers* for their relief and maintenance of their poore, without the licence or consent of the Master, Wardens and Assistants of the said Company; Nor any Book or Books lawfully licenced and entred in the Register of the said Company for any particular member thereof, without the licence and consent of the owner or owners thereof. Nor yet import any such Book or Books, or part of Book or Books formerly Printed here, from beyond the Seas, upon paine of forfeiting the same to the Owner, or Owners of the Copies of the said Books, and such further punishment as shall be thought fit.

"And the Master and Wardens of the said Company, the Gentleman Usher of the House of *Peers*, the Sergeant of the Commons House and their deputies, together with the persons formerly appointed by the Committee of the House of Commons for Examinations, are hereby authorized and required, from time to time, to make diligent search in all places, where they

ing; that no book, pamphlet, or paper shall be henceforth printed, unless the same be first approved and licensed by such, or at least one of such, as shall be thereto appointed." For that part which preserves justly every man's copy* to himself, or provides for the poor, I touch not; only wish they be not made pretences to abuse and persecute honest and painful men who offend not in either of these particulars. But that other clause of licensing books, which we thought had died with his brother *quadragesimal* and *matrimonial* when the prelates expired, I shall now attend with such a homily, as shall lay before ye, first, the inventors of it to be those whom ye will be loth to own; next, what is to be thought in general of reading, whatever sort the books be, and that this order avails nothing to the suppressing of scandalous, seditious, and libellous books, which were mainly intended to be suppressed; last, that it will be primely to the discouragement of all learning and the stop of truth, not only by disexercising and blunting our abilities in what we know already, but by hindering and cropping the discovery that might be yet further made both in religious and civil wisdom.

I deny not, but that it is of greatest concernment in the church and

---

* **Every man's copy.** Lord Mansfield laid great stress upon this passage as an authority in favor of copyright. He says, "The single opinion of such a man as Milton, speaking after much consideration on the very point, is stronger than any inferences from gathering acorns and seizing a vacant piece of ground." (Haliday's *Life of Lord Mansfield*, p. 232.)—**Painful men,** *painstaking, laborious men.* Fuller, Jeremy Taylor, and Dryden, use the word *painful* in this now obsolete sense.—**Quadragesimal** (Lat. *quadragesimus*, fortieth; *quadragesima*, the forty days of fast preceding Easter), *pertaining to Lent, lenten.* This word *quadragesimal* is found in Cartwright's comedy entitled *The Ordinary*,

"But Quadragesimal wits, and fancies lean
As Ember weeks."

A *quadragesimal license* must have been a permission granted to eat certain meats in Lent. "Queen Elizabeth used to say that she would never eat flesh in Lent without obtaining license from her 'little black husband,' as she called Archbishop Whitgift." The *matrimonial license* was no longer necessary, as, during this interval or interregnum, marriages were, by act of Parliament, authorized to be solemnized before a civil magistrate.—**Prelates expired,** i. e., the *power* of the prelates expired.—**Homily** (ὁμιλία, communion, assembly, sermon), *sermon*, or *serious discourse.* Milton now marks out very clearly and concisely the plan of this treatise.—**Disexercising**, *depriving of exercise, leaving untrained.*—**I deny not,** etc. This magnificent passage extending as far as, "But lest I should be condemned," has been universally admired.

Learning. Synonymes, *erudition, lore, learning, scholarship, science, knowledge, wisdom, letters, literature.* Give sentences to illustrate.

---

shall think meete, for all unlicensed Printing Presses, and all Presses any way imployed in the printing of scandalous or unlicensed Papers, Pamphlets, Books, or any Copies of Books belonging to the said Company, or any member thereof, without their approbation and consents, and to seize and carry away such Printing Presses Letters, together with the Nut, Spindle, and other materialls of every such irregular Printer, which they find so misimployed, unto the Common Hall of the said Company, there to be defaced and made unserviceable according to Ancient Custom; And likewise to make diligent search in all suspected Printing-houses, Ware-houses, Shops and other places for such scandalous and unlicensed Books, papers, Pamphlets, and all other Books, not entred, nor signed with the Printers name as aforesaid, being printed, or reprinted by such as have no lawfull interest in them, or any way contrary to this Order, and the same to seize and carry away to the said common hall, there to remain till both or either House of *Parliament* shall dispose thereof, And likewise to apprehend all Authors, Printers, and other persons whatsoever imployed in compiling, printing, stitching, binding, publishing and dispersing of the said scandalous, unlicensed, and unwarrantable papers, books and pamphlets as aforesaid, and all those who shall resist the said Parties in searching after them, and to bring them afore either of the Houses or the Committee of Examinations, that so they may receive such further punishments, as their Offences shall demerit, and not to be released untill they have given satisfaction to the Parties imployed in their apprehension for their paines and charges, and given sufficient caution not to offend in like sort for the future. And all Justices of the Peace, Captaines, Constables and other officers, are hereby ordered and required to be aiding, and assisting to the aforesaid persons in the due execution of all, and singular the premisses and in the apprehension of all Offenders against the same. And in case of opposition to break open Doores and Locks.

"And it is further ordered, that this Order be forthwith Printed and Published, to the end that notice may be taken thereof, and all Contemners of it left inexcusable."

commonwealth, to have a vigilant eye how books demean themselves, as well as men; and thereafter to confine, imprison, and do sharpest justice on them as malefactors. For books are not absolutely dead things,* but do contain a potency of life in them to be as active as that soul was whose progeny they are: nay, they do preserve as in a phial the purest efficacy and extraction of that living intellect that bred them. I know they are as lively and as vigorously productive as those fabulous dragon's teeth, and, being sown up and down, may chance to spring up armed men. And yet, on the other hand, unless wariness be used, as good, almost, kill a man as kill a good book. *Who kills a man, kills a reasonable creature, God's image; but he who destroys a good book, kills reason itself, kills the image of God, as it were in the eye. Many a man lives a burden to the earth; but a good book is the precious life blood of a master spirit, embalmed and treasured up on purpose to a life beyond life!*

It is true no age can restore a life, whereof perhaps there is no great loss; and revolutions of ages do not oft recover the loss of a rejected truth, for the want of which whole nations fare the worse. We should be wary, therefore, what persecution we raise against the living labors of public men, how we spill that seasoned life of man, preserved and stored up in books: since we see a kind of homicide may be thus committed, sometimes a martyrdom, and if it extend to the whole impression, a kind of massacre; whereof the execution ends not in the slaying of an elemental life, but strikes at the ethereal and fifth essence, the breath of reason itself, *slays an immortality rather than a life!*

But lest I should be condemned of introducing license while I oppose licensing, I refuse not the pains to be so much historical as will serve to show what hath been done by ancient and famous commonwealths against this disorder, till the very time that this project of licensing crept out of the Inquisition, was catched up by our prelates, and hath caught some of our presbyters.

In Athens, where books and wits were ever busier than in any other part of Greece, I find but only two sorts of writings which the magistrate cared to take notice of; those either blasphemous and atheistical, or libellous.

---

* **Dead things.** Milton's, at least, are not. "Every word" of this Areopagitica, says Whipple, "leaps with intellectual life."—**Dragon's teeth.** There are two leading myths in reference to the sowing of serpent's or *dragon's* teeth, which sprang up armed men. One of these represents Cadmus as sowing them in Bœotia, at that place where Thebes afterwards stood. The other describes Jason as yoking two flame-breathing, brazen-hoofed bulls, ploughing with them a piece of ground, and then sowing the serpent's teeth. In each case, the teeth sprang up armed men, whom the hero had the art to set a-fighting among themselves, and then he slew them.—**Fifth essence,** *quintessence* (Lat. *quinta*, fifth; *essentia*, essence; the fifth, or last and highest, essence in alchemy), *the pure essence.*—**Condemned of,** *condemned for*. (A Latinism.)—**Inquisition.** The Spanish Inquisition was established at Seville by a papal bull in 1480. The first *auto de fé* was held January 6, 1481, when six heretics were burned alive.—**Catched,** *caught*. Butler in *Hudibras* uses this (now nearly obsolete) word,

"As if divinity had catched
The itch, on purpose to be scratched."

—**Presbyters.** Milton concludes one of his sonnets with the line,

"New Presbyter is but old priest, writ large!"

which, at that time, was at least *etymologically* true. (A. S. *prêost*; Lat. *presbyter*; Gr. πρεσβύτερος, an *elder*.)

Atheistical. Differences in meaning of *atheist*, *unbeliever*, and *infidel*?

Thus the books of Protagoras* were, by the judges of Areopagus, commanded to be burnt, and himself banished the territory for a discourse begun with his cónfessing not to know "whether there were gods, or whether not." And against defaming, it was agreed that none should be traduced by name, as was the manner of Vetus Comœdia; whereby we may guess how they censured libelling. And this course was quick enough, as Cicero writes, to quell both the desperate wits of other atheists, and the open way of defaming; as the event showed. Of other sects and opinions, though tending to voluptuousness and the denying of divine providence, they took no heed. Therefore we do not read that either Epicurus, or that libertine school of Cyrene, or what the Cynic impudence uttered, was ever questioned by the laws. Neither is it recorded, that the writings of those old comedians were suppressed, though the acting of them were forbid. And that Plato commended the reading of Aristophanes, the loosest of them all, to his royal scholar Dionysius, is commonly known; and may be excused, if holy Chrysostom, as is reported, nightly studied so much the same author, and had the art to cleanse a scurrilous vehemence into the style of a rousing sermon!

That other leading city of Greece, Lacedæmon—considering that Lycurgus, their lawgiver, was so addicted to elegant learning as to have been the first that brought out of Ionia the scattered works of Homer, and sent the poet Thales from Crete to prepare and mollify the Spartan surliness with his smooth songs and odes, the better to plant among them law and civility—it is to be wondered how museless and unbookish they were, minding nought but the feats of war. There needed no licensing of books among them; for they disliked all but their own Laconic apothegms, and took a slight occasion to chase Archilochus out of their city; perhaps for composing in a higher strain than their own soldiery ballads and roundels could reach

---

* **Protagoras,** a Grecian philosopher (B. C. 480–411) who wrote many treatises, not now extant, on logic, metaphysics, ethics, and politics.—**Vetus Comœdia,** *the old comedy.* The most ancient theatrical plays in Greece (the "Old Comedy") were exceedingly rude, libellous, and indecent; often singling out individuals by name and holding them up to ridicule.—**Cicero,** B. C. 107–43.—**Epicurus,** B. C. 341–270.—**Cyrene,** a famous city on the northern coast of Africa, south from Greece. Here Aristippus (about 392 B. C.) founded the "Cyrenaic sect" or "libertine school," above-named. He taught that "good is pleasure, and pain is evil."—**Cynic.** The word *Cynic* is derived by some from κύων, a dog, and, is, in that view, most appropriate to describe the *snarling* and impudent conduct of Diogenes and other Cynics. The sect was founded by Antisthenes (born about 420 B. C.).—**Plato,** B. C. 429–348.—**Aristophanes,** B. C. 456–380. The most celebrated comic dramatist of antiquity.—**Dionysius,** the younger, tyrant of Syracuse B. C. 367–343. The father, Dionysius the Elder, employed Plato to instruct the son.—**Chrysostom** (A. D. 347–407), a celebrated Christian patriarch of Constantinople. His father's name was Secundus. The son, St. John, like Dion of Prusa, already mentioned in this treatise, was surnamed Chrysostom (Gr. Χρυσόστομος, golden-mouthed) on account of his eloquence. He is said to have habitually slept with the comedies of Aristophanes under his pillow.—**Lacedæmon,** also called *Sparta*, a celebrated city of Greece, the capital of Laconia.—**Lycurgus,** about 820 B. C., probably.—**Ionia,** a district on the western coast of Asia Minor. Here Homer probably lived, if he lived at all. The Arundelian marbles fix his date at 907 B. C., but no dependence can be placed upon this.—**Thales,** B. C. 636–546. Here is certainly an error, perhaps of the printer. The poet meant by Milton was probably *Thaletas;* but he, too, flourished ages after Lycurgus, about 620 B. C. Milton follows the common account, which is sufficient for the purposes of his argument.—**Crete,** *Candia.*—**Laconic,** from *Laconia*, the southeast country of the Morea. Its chief city was Lacedæmon or Sparta.—**Archilochus** flourished in the first part of the seventh century.—**Roundel** (Fr. *rondeau*, something that goes round; *i. e.*, returns upon itself; a species of lyric poetry that has a *refrain* recurring according to fixed law. Fr. *rond;* Lat. *rotundus*, round), *a roundelay*, a sort of ancient poem of thirteen verses, divided into couplets and containing equivocal or punning repetitions.

Defame. Distinguish, and illustrate by sentences, *defame*, *asperse*, *disparage*, *detract from*, *vilify*, *slander*, *libel*, *calumniate.*

to; or, if it were for his broad verses, they were not therein so cautious, but they were as dissolute in their promiscuous conversing; whence Euripides * affirms in *Andromache* that their women were all unchaste. Thus much may give us light after what sort of books were prohibited among the Greeks.

The Romans, also, for many ages trained up only to a military roughness resembling most the Lacedæmonian guise, knew of learning little but what their twelve tables and the pontific college, with their augurs and flamens, taught them in religion and law; so unacquainted with other learning, that when Carneades and Critolaus, with the stoic Diogenes, coming ambassadors to Rome, took thereby occasion to give the city a taste of their philosophy, they were suspected for seducers by no less a man than Cato the censor; who moved it in the senate to dismiss them speedily, and to banish all such Attic babblers out of Italy. But Scipio and others of the noblest senators withstood him and his old Sabine austerity, honored and admired the men, and the censor himself at last, in his old age, fell to the study of that whereof before he was so scrupulous. And yet at the same time, Nævius and Plautus, the first Latin comedians, had filled the city with all the borrowed scenes of Menander and Philemon. Then began to be considered there also what was to be done to libellous books and authors; for Nævius was quickly cast into prison for his unbridled pen, and released by the tribunes upon his recantation. We read also that libels were burnt, and the makers punished, by Augustus. The like severity no doubt was used, if aught were impiously written against their esteemed gods. Except in these two points, how the world went in books, the magistrate kept no reckoning. And therefore Lucretius,

* **Euripides** (B. C. 480–406), a celebrated Athenian tragic poet.—**Andromache,** wife of the bravest Trojan hero, Hector. Here the word is the title of a drama. See the passage beginning with verse 595 in the *Andromache.*—**Unchaste.** Aristotle (*Politics*, L. II., c.7) says the same thing in substance.—**Twelve Tables.** A celebrated body of Roman laws framed by decemvirs appointed four hundred and fifty years before Christ, on the return of commissioners who had been sent to Greece to examine into foreign laws and institutions. They consisted partly of selected foreign laws, partly of new provisions; but mainly, perhaps, of laws and usages under the ancient Roman kings.—**Pontific college,** *the body of Roman priests*, their hierarchy.—**Flamen,** a Roman priest devoted to the service of a particular god.—**Carneades,** of Cyrene in Africa, was the founder of a sect called the Third or New Academy. **Critolaus,** of Phaselis in Lycia, went to Athens to study philosophy. He became the head of the Peripatetics (so called from περί, about, and πατεῖν, to walk; because Aristotle, the founder of the sect, gave instruction while walking in the Lyceum at Athens).—**Diogenes,** the Stoic; not Diogenes the Cynic. Cicero calls Carneades an orator of surpassing keenness and copiousness. These philosophers were sent by the Athenians to Rome, B. C. 155 —**Cato,** the stern old Roman censor, who used to close his speeches on all subjects with the words, *Præterea censeo Carthaginem esse delendam,* "*I am, moreover, of the opinion that Carthage ought to be blotted out.*" He lived B. C. 234-149.—**Attic,** of *Attica* (that part of Greece of which Athens was the capital). It is a triangular peninsula, some eighty miles long, by forty, more or less, wide.—**Scipio,** Publius Cornelius Scipio Africanus (B. C. 241–184), the conqueror of Hannibal and the Carthaginians.—**Sabine.** The early youth of Cato was spent among the brave and austere Sabines, who inhabited a district in the interior of Italy to the north-east of Rome.—**Nævius,** a dramatic (chiefly comic) poet of Rome. He died, according to Cicero, about 204 B. C.—**Plautus.** A celebrated Roman comic (dramatic) poet, B. C. 254–184. On the Roman comic writers, see preliminary treatise of Heinsius, prefixed to the Elzevir edition of Terence.—**Menander,** a celebrated comic poet of Athens, B. C. 342–292.—**Philemon,** a Greek comic poet, contemporary and rival of Menander.—**Augustus Cæsar,** who "found Rome brick, and left it marble," was born B. C. 62, and died A. D. 14. He was emperor from 31 B. C. till his death.—**Lucretius** (B. C. 95-51), one of the most illustrious of Roman epic poets. At the request of his patron, Memmius, he wrote his great work, *De Rerum Natura*, a truly magnificent poem, setting forth the philosophy of Epicurus. "Lucretius is, perhaps, the only poet inspired by materialism." See note on *poet that beautified*, p. 88.

Dissolute. Differentiate *dissolute, licentious, lax, loose, unrestrained, debauched.*

without impeachment, versifies his Epicurism* to Memmius, and had the honor to be set forth the second time by Cicero, so great a father of the commonwealth; although himself disputes against that opinion in his own writings. Nor was the satirical sharpness or naked plainness of Lucilius, or Catullus, or Flaccus, by any order prohibited. And for matters of state, the story of Titus Livius, though it extolled that part which Pompey held, was not therefore suppressed by Octavius Cæsar of the other faction. But that Naso was by him banished in his old age for the wanton poems of his youth, was but a mere covert of state over some secret cause; and besides, the books were neither banished nor called in. From hence we shall meet with little else but tyranny in the Roman empire, that we may not marvel, if not so often bad as good books were silenced. I shall therefore deem to have been large enough, in producing what among the ancients was punishable to write; save only which, all other arguments were free to treat on.

By this time the emperors were become Christians; whose discipline in this point I do not find to have been more severe than what was formerly in practice. The books of those whom they took to be grand heretics were examined, refuted, and condemned in the general councils, and not till then were prohibited, or burned, by authority of the emperor. As for the writings of heathen authors, unless they were plain invectives against Christianity, as those of Porphyrius and Proclus, they met with no interdict that can be cited, till about the year four hundred, in a Carthaginian council; wherein bishops themselves were forbid to read the books of gentiles, but heresies they might read: while others long before them, on the contrary, scrupled more the books of heretics, than of gentiles. And that the primitive councils and bishops were wont only to declare what books were not commendable, passing no further, but leaving it to each one's conscience to read or to lay by, till after the year eight hundred, is observed already by Padre Paolo, the great unmasker of the Trentine council.

---

* **Epicurism** (from Epicurus, the philosopher, born in Samos, B. C. 341, and dying B. C. 270), *the supposed doctrines of Epicurus;* particularly, that the gods have no concern in human affairs, and that pleasure-seeking is true wisdom.—**To be set forth,** *to be edited.* There is a tradition that Cicero revised and published the great work of Lucretius.—**Father.** For his distinguished services, particularly in suppressing the conspiracy of Catiline, Cicero was hailed by the Romans as the father of his country.—**Lucilius,** a famous satirical writer, B. C. 148–103.—**Catullus,** a noted Latin poet, B. C. 87–40.—**Flaccus.** I think he means *Horace* (Horatius Flaccus, B. C. 65–8), rather than *Valerius*, who died as late as A. D. 88. Horace ridicules unsparingly the vague theories of the philosophers, especially of the Stoics. But there is no venom in his wit.—**Livius.** Livy, the famous historian, B. C. 59 to A. D. 17.—**Pompey,** *the Great*, B. C. 106 to B. C. 48.—**Octavius,** the same as *Augustus*, above-mentioned.—**Naso,** *Publius Ovidius Naso*, the famous poet *Ovid*, B. C. 43 to A. D. 18.—**Covert of state,** *political pretext.* The reason for his banishment is still matter of conjecture.—**That we may,** *so that we may.*—**Deem,** etc., *deem* myself to have been copious enough.—**Save only which,** *except which alone* (*i. e.*, and omitting this).—**Porphyrius** (A. D. 233–305), a native of Tyre. He was an elegant writer, but an inveterate enemy to the Christian faith.—**Proclus,** a very learned philosopher, a native of Constantinople (A. D. 412–485).—**Paolo Sarpi** (1552–1623), a celebrated Italian monk, historian, and philosopher. His history of the Council of Trent is a work of great brilliancy and power.—**Trentine council,** one of the great Œcumenical councils of the Catholic Church. It held twenty-five sessions at Trent in the Tyrol, from 1545 to 1563.

Refuted. Distinguish, and illustrate by sentences, the differences among *refute*, *confute*, *rebut*, *oppugn*, *overthrow*, *disprove*.

After which time* the popes of Rome, engrossing what they pleased of political rule into their own hands, extended their dominion over men's eyes, as they had before over their judgments, burning and prohibiting to be read what they fancied not; yet sparing in their censures, and the books not many which they so dealt with, till Martin the Fifth, by his bull, not only prohibited, but was the first that excommunicated the reading of heretical books. For, about that time, Wickliffe and Huss, growing terrible, were they who first drove the papal court to a stricter policy of prohibiting. Which course Leo the Tenth and his successors followed, until the council of Trent and the Spanish Inquisition, engendering together, brought forth or perfected those catalogues and expurging indexes that rake through the entrails of many an old good author, with a violation worse than any could be offered to his tomb. Nor did they stay in matters heretical; but any subject that was not to their palate, they either condemned in a prohibition, or had it straight into the new purgatory of an index. To fill up the measure of encroachment, their last invention was to ordain that no book, pamphlet, or paper, should be printed, (as if St. Peter had bequeathed them the keys of the press also, as well as of paradise!) unless it were approved and licensed under the hands of two or three gluttonous friars. For example:—

Let the chancellor Cini be pleased to see if in this present work be contained aught that may withstand the printing.

Vincent Rabbata, Vicar of Florence.

I have seen this present work, and find nothing athwart the Catholic faith and good manners. In witness whereof I have given, etc.

Nicolo Cini, Chancellor of Florence.

Attending the precedent relation, it is allowed that this present work of Davanzati may be printed.

Vincent Rabbata, etc.

It may be printed, July 15.

Friar Simon Mompei d' Amelia,
Chancellor of the Holy Office in Florence.

Surely they have a conceit, if he of the bottomless pit had not long

---

* **After which time**; *i. e.*, after the year 800, or thereabouts.—**Martin the Fifth** (1417-1431). There have been about two hundred and forty popes, reckoning from St. Peter, who is claimed to have been the first bishop of Rome.—**Wickliffe.** John Wickliffe (1324-1384), a native of Yorkshire, England, was a man of very great learning, power, and boldness. He has been styled "the Morning Star of the Reformation." He is famous for having given to the English the first translation of the Bible in their native tongue.—**Huss.** John Huss, a Bohemian religious reformer, was born in 1373, and was burned at the stake at Constance in 1415.—**Leo the Tenth,** one of the most celebrated of the popes. He held the papal office from 1513 to Dec.,1521.—**The Spanish Inquisition,** as already stated, was established at Seville by a papal bull in 1480.—**Purgatory** (Lat. *purgare*, to purify), a state, believed to exist after death, in which offences that do not deserve eternal punishment are expiated.—**Keys.** See Matt. xvi. 19.—**Friars** (Fr. *frère;* Lat. *frater*, brother), brother members of a religious order, especially of one of the four mendicant orders; viz., Gray Friars, or Franciscans; Black Friars, or Dominicans; White Friars, or Carmelites; and Augustines, also called White Friars.—**Attending the precedent relation,** *paying due heed to the preceding reference;* in virtue of the preceding reference and finding, it is allowed, etc.—**Davanzati** (1529-1606), a Florentine author, whose work Milton probably had before his eyes when he wrote this treatise.

Ordain. Distinguish and exemplify, as before, *appoint*, *order*, *prescribe*, *ordain*, *direct*.
Withstand. Exemplify *withstand*, *oppose*, *resist*, *combat*, *contest*, *fight*, *thwart*.

since broke prison, that this quadruple exorcism would bar him down! . .

. . . .

. . . . Vouchsafe to see another of their forms, the Roman stamp:—

Imprimatur,* If it seem good to the reverend Master of the Holy Palace,

Belcastro, Vicegerent.

Imprimatur.

Friar Nicolo Rodolphi, Master of the Holy Palace.

Sometimes five *imprimaturs* are seen together dialogue-wise in the piazza of one title-page, complimenting and ducking each to other with their shaven reverences, whether the author, who stands by in perplexity at the foot of his epistle, shall to the press or to the spunge!

These are the pretty responsories, these are the dear antiphonies, that so bewitched of late our prelates and their chaplains with the goodly echo they made, and besotted us to the gay imitation of a lordly *imprimatur*, one from Lambeth house, another from the west end of Paul's; so apishly Romanizing that the word of command still was set down in Latin! As if the learned grammatical pen that wrote it, would cast no ink without Latin! or perhaps, as they thought, because no vulgar tongue was worthy to express the pure conceit of an *imprimatur!* but rather, as I hope, for that our English, the language of men ever famous and foremost in the achievements of liberty, will not easily find servile letters enow to spell such a dictatory presumption Englished!

And thus ye have the inventors and the original of book-licensing, ripped up and drawn as lineally as any pedigree. We have it not, that can be heard of, from any ancient state, or polity, or church; nor by any statute left us by our ancestors elder or later; nor from the modern custom of any reformed city or church abroad: but from the most antichristian council, and the most tyrannous inquisition that ever inquired. Till then, books were ever as freely admitted into the world as any other birth. The issue of the brain was no more stifled than the issue of the womb. No envious Juno sat crosslegged over the nativity of any man's intellectual offspring. But if it proved a monster, who denies but that it was justly burnt, or sunk

---

* **Imprimatur**, (Lat.), *it may be printed.*—**Shaven reverences**, "priests all shaven and shorn."—**Responsories**, the *alternate responses* of the people to the priest in the church service.—**Antiphonies**, anthems or psalms of which the alternate verses were sung or chanted by a choir or congregation divided into two parts. The word *antiphony* (A. S. *antefen*, fr. Gr. *ἀντίφωνα*, returning a sound, fr. *αντί*, against, *φωνή*, sound; or fr. *ἀντί*, and *ὕμνος*, song) is the original of *anthem.*—**Lambeth house**, *Lambeth palace*, on the Thames, nearly opposite the new houses of parliament in London. It has been the town residence of the archbishop of Canterbury since 1197.—**Paul's**, *St. Paul's Cathedral.* The original building was destroyed in the great fire of 1666. The present splendid structure was designed by Sir Christopher Wren, who lived to see its completion in 1710. It is not far from the centre of London.—**Enow.** See Index.—**Ripped up and drawn.** This metaphor looks like an allusion to the old mode of executing criminals by disemboweling them, "hanging, *drawing*, and quartering." But do the words, *as lineally as any pedigree*, favor the supposition?—**Pedigree** (Fr. *par*, by; *degrés*, degrees, *i. e.*, of consanguinity.) Some derive *pedigree* from Fr. *pied-de-grue*, crane's foot, on account of the shape of the heraldic genealogical tree. Others make it fr. *père*, father, and *degré*, a stair; others still, fr. *pied*, foot, *de*, of, *grès* (Lat. *gradus*, a step), *pied-de-grés*, "a stem of lineage."—**Juno**, whom Milton places in so picturesque an attitude, was greatly exercised at the birth ("nativity") of the numerous illegitimate children of Jupiter, her brother and husband.

into the sea? But that a book, in worse condition than a peccant* soul, should be to stand before a jury ere it be born to the world, and undergo yet in darkness the judgment of Rhadamanth and his colleagues, ere it can pass the ferry backward into light, was never heard before, till that mysterious Iniquity, provoked and troubled at the first entrance of reformation, sought out new limbos and new hells wherein they might include our books also within the number of their damned! And this was the rare morsel so officiously snatched up, and so ill-favoredly imitated by our inquisiturient bishops and the attendant minorites, their chaplains. That ye like not now these most certain authors of this licensing order, and that all sinister intention was far distant from your thoughts when ye were importuned the passing it, all men who know the integrity of your actions, and how ye honor truth, will clear ye readily.

But some will say, "What though the inventors were bad? The thing, for all that, may be good." It may so. Yet, if that thing be no such deep invention, but obvious and easy for any man to light on, and yet best and wisest commonwealths through all ages and occasions have forborne to use it, and falsest seducers and oppressors of men were the first who took it up, and to no other purpose but to obstruct and hinder the first approach of reformation; I am of those who believe it will be a harder alchymy than Lullius ever knew, to sublimate any good use out of such an invention. Yet this only is what I request to gain from this reason; that it may be held a dangerous and suspicious fruit, as certainly it deserves for the tree that bore it, until I can dissect one by one the properties it has. But I have, first, to finish, as was propounded, what is to be thought in general of reading books, whatever sort they be; and whether be more, the benefit or the harm that thence proceeds.

Not to insist upon the examples of Moses, Daniel, and Paul, who were skilful in all the learning of the Egyptians, Chaldeans, and Greeks, which could not probably be without reading their books of all sorts,—in Paul especially, who thought it no defilement to insert into Holy Scripture the

---

* **Peccant** (Lat. *peccare*, to sin), *sinful*.—**Should be to stand,** *should be necessitated* or *forced* to stand.—**Rhadamanth.** *Rhadamanthus*, in Roman mythology, was one of the three judges of the dead in the lower world. Minos and Æacus were his associate judges.—**Ferry backward.** This was the ferry over the river Acheron in the infernal regions. The spirits of the departed were ferried across by Charon for from three to ten cents apiece.—**Limbos** (Lat. *limbus*, a border. *Limbus patrum*, the limbo of the fathers, was a region *bordering* on hell. In it the souls of good men were believed to await the coming of our Saviour. There were, besides, a *limbus infantum* for unbaptized infants, and a *limbus fatuorum*, or fool's paradise, regarded as a receptacle for all vanity and nonsense), places of confinement or restraint. In regard to the formation of the plural, it may be observed, that nouns ending in *o* preceded by a vowel form their plurals regularly; *i. e.*, by simply adding *s*: if the *o* is preceded by a consonant, *es* is usually added; but *canto*, *grotto*, *junto*, *portico*, *rotundo*, *salvo*, *solo*, *tyro*, *duodecimo*, *octavo*, *quarto*, and *limbo*, have simply *s*.—**Inquisiturient,** too inquisitive; *hankering after the Inquisition*. Obsolete. The ending *-urio*, in Latin, appended to the roots of simple verbs, forms *desideratives*.—**To light on,** to come upon by chance, to find without effort.—**Alchymy** (Ar. *al*, the; *kîmîâ*; Gr. χημεία, for χυμεία, fr. χυμός, juice, liquid), *alchemy*, an ancient science which aimed to transmute metals into gold, to find a panacea, etc.—**Lullius** (A. D. 1235–1315), *Raymond Lully*, a famous Spanish philosopher, born at Palma, the capital of the island of Majorca. He is said to have written more books than a man could transcribe in the course of an ordinary life!—**Sublimate** (Lat. *sublimare*, to raise; fr. *sublimis*, high; fr. *sub*, from beneath, and *levare*, to raise), to bring a solid by heat into a state of vapor, and then, by cooling, condense the vapor again into a solid; *to sublime*. It is a refining process.—**For the tree,** *on account of the tree*.

Invention. Exemplify the special meanings of *invent*, *discover*, *reveal*, *find out*, *uncover*.

sentences of three Greek poets,* and one of them a tragedian,—the question was, notwithstanding, sometimes controverted among the primitive doctors, but with great odds on that side which affirmed it both lawful and profitable: as was then evidently perceived, when Julian the Apostate, and subtlest enemy to our faith, made a decree forbidding Christians the study of heathen learning. "For," said he, "they wound us with our own weapons, and with our own arts and sciences they overcome us." And, indeed, the Christians were put to their shifts by this crafty means, and so much in danger to decline into all ignorance, that the two Apollinarii were fain, as a man may say, to coin all the seven liberal sciences out of the Bible, reducing it into divers forms of orations, poems, dialogues, even to the calculating of a new Christian grammar! But, saith the historian Socrates, the providence of God provided better than the industry of Apollinarius and his son, by taking away that illiterate law with the life of him who devised it. So great an injury they then held it to be deprived of Hellenic learning; and thought it a persecution more undermining and secretly decaying the church, than the open cruelty of Decius or Diocletian.

And perhaps it was with the same politic drift that the devil whipped St. Jerome in a lenten dream, for reading Cicero! or else it was a phantasm, bred by the fever which had then seized him. For had an angel been his discipliner, unless it were for dwelling too much on Ciceronianisms, and had chastised the reading, not the vanity, it had been plainly partial; first, to correct him for grave Cicero, and not for scurrile Plautus, whom he confesses to have been reading not long before; next, to correct him only, and let so many more ancient fathers wax old in those pleasant and florid studies without the lash of such a tutoring apparition! Insomuch that Basil teaches how some good use may be made of *Margites*, a sportful poem, not

---

* **Three Greek poets.** *Aratus*, in Acts xvii. 28; *Euripides* (or Menander). 1 Cor. xv. 33; *Epimenides*, Tit. i. 12. But there is some doubt on these points.—**Julian the Apostate** (331-363), a celebrated Roman emperor, who had been bred a Christian, but who, on assuming imperial power at Constantinople, A. D. 361, openly professed the old pagan religion of Rome, and sacrificed as high-priest to the gods.—**Forbidding.** Gibbon says of this matter: "The edict itself, which is still extant among the epistles of Julian, may be compared with the loose invectives of Gregory. . . . The Christians were *directly* forbid to teach, they were *indirectly* forbid to learn; since they would not frequent the schools of the pagans. . . . Julian contemptuously observes that the men who exalt the merit of implicit faith are unfit to claim or to enjoy the advantages of science; and he vainly contends that, if they refuse to adore the gods of Homer and Demosthenes, they ought to content themselves with expounding Luke and Matthew in the churches of the Galileans," etc. *Decline and Fall of the Roman Empire*, iv., 111, 112, *and note.*—**Apollinarii,** the *Apollinarii*, or *Apolinarii*, father and son. They were Phrygians, citizens of Laodicea. See an interesting and striking account of them in Mrs. Browning's *Essays on the Greek Christian Poets*, pp. 30-34. They repelled the attacks of Julian, who affected to despise his Christian antagonists.—**Seven liberal sciences,** *Grammar*, *Logic*, and *Rhetoric*, constituting the *trivium*, or triple road to eloquence; *Arithmetic*, *Music*, *Geometry*, and *Astronomy*, constituting the *quadrivium*, or fourfold way to eloquence.—**Socrates.** A native of Constantinople. Wrote an ecclesiastical history in the middle of the fifth century.—**Illiterate,** *hostile to literature.*—**Hellenic** (fr. *Hellen*, the fabled progenitor of the Greeks), *Grecian.*—**Decaying,** *causing to decay*, *impairing*, *enfeebling.*—**Decius,** a cruel persecutor of the Christians. He was Roman emperor from 249 to 251.—**Diocletian.** Roman emperor from 284 to 305. He, too, persecuted the Christians.—**Was with the same politic drift,** *was with the same politic* (*i. e.*, sagacious) *drift* (*i. e.*, aim); viz., to undermine and enfeeble the church.—**Jerome** (A. D. 342-420), a saint and doctor of the Catholic Church, famous for his religious treatises, and his Latin version (the *Vulgate*) of the Scriptures.—**Lenten,** pertaining to Lent; happening in Lent; caused by the abstinence of Lent.—**Dream.** Jerome himself insists that it was not a dream: "*Nec vero sopor ille fuerat, aut vana somnia, quibus sæpe deludimur*, nor in truth was that a sleep, or empty dream, such as we are often deluded by."—**Basil** *the Great* (*Saint*, A. D. 328-379), an illustrious theologian and orator, archbishop of Cæsarea.—**Margites.** This was a satire on some blockhead. Aristotle attributes it to Homer.

now extant, writ by Homer. And why not then of *Morganté*, an Italian romance much to the same purpose? But if it be agreed we shall be tried by visions, there is a vision recorded by Eusebius,* far ancienter than this tale of Jerome to the nun Eustochium, and, besides, has nothing of a fever in it.

Dionysius Alexandrinus was, about the year two hundred forty, a person of great name in the church for piety and learning, who had wont to avail himself much against heretics by being conversant in their books, until a certain presbyter laid it scrupulously to his conscience, how he durst venture himself among those defiling volumes. The worthy man, loth to give offense, fell into a new debate with himself, what was to be thought; when suddenly a vision sent from God, (it is his own epistle that so avers it,) confirmed him in these words, "Read any books whatever come to thy hands; for thou art sufficient both to judge aright and to examine each matter." To this revelation he assented the sooner, as he confesses, because it was answerable to that of the apostle to the Thessalonians, "Prove all things, hold fast that which is good." And he might have added another remarkable saying of the same author, "To the pure, all things are pure;" not only meats and drinks, but all kind of knowledge, whether of good or evil. The knowledge cannot defile, nor consequently the books, if the will and conscience be not defiled. For books are as meats and viands are; some of good, some of evil substance; and yet God, in that unapocryphal vision, said without exception, "Rise, Peter, kill and eat;" leaving the choice to each man's discretion. Wholesome meats to a vitiated stomach differ little or nothing from unwholesome; and best books to a naughty mind are not unapplicable to occasions of evil. Bad meats will scarce breed good nourishment in the healthiest concoction. But herein the difference is of bad books, that they, to a discreet and judicious reader, serve in many respects to discover, to confute, to forewarn, and to illustrate. Whereof what better witness can ye expect I should produce, than one of your own now sitting in parliament, the chief of learned men reputed in this land, Mr. Selden? whose volume of natural and national laws proves, not only by great authorities brought together, but by exquisite reasons and theorems almost mathematically demonstrative, that all opinions, yea, errors, known, read, and collated, are of main service and assistance toward the speedy attainment of what is truest.

I conceive therefore, that when God did enlarge the universal diet of man's body, saving ever the rules of temperance, he then also, as before, left arbitrary the dieting and repasting of our minds, as wherein every mature man might have to exercise his own leading capacity.

How great a virtue is temperance! how much of moment through the

---

* **Eusebius** (264-340), a very learned historian and Christian teacher.—1 **Thessalonians** v. 21.—**Unapocryphal**, canonical; not apocryphal; not spurious; *genuine*.—**Concoction**, *digestion*.—**To discover**, etc. The point here made is one of great importance.—**Selden** (John Selden, 1584-1654), a celebrated English lawyer and author, and true friend of liberty.—**Arbitrary**, dependent on mere will, *discretionary*.

Romance. Illustrate the peculiar meaning of *fable*, *romance*, *novel*, *fiction*, *legend*, *myth*, *tale*, *apologue*, *parable*, *allegory*.

whole life of man! Yet God commits the managing so great a trust, without particular law or prescription, wholly to the demeanor of every grown man. And therefore, when he himself tabled * the Jews from heaven, that omer, which was every man's daily portion of manna, is computed to have been more than might have well sufficed the heartiest feeder thrice as many meals. For those actions which enter into a man, rather than issue out of him, and therefore defile not, God uses not to captivate under a perpetual childhood of prescription, but trusts him with the gift of reason to be his own chooser. There were but little work left for preaching, if law and compulsion should grow so fast upon those things which heretofore were governed only by exhortation. Solomon informs us, that much reading is a weariness to the flesh; but neither he, nor other inspired author tells us that such or such reading is unlawful. Yet certainly, had God thought good to limit us herein, it had been much more expedient to have told us what was unlawful, than what was wearisome.

As for the burning of those Ephesian books by St. Paul's converts, it is replied, the books were magic. The Syriac so renders them. It was a private act, a voluntary act, and leaves us to a voluntary imitation. The men in remorse burnt those books which were their own. The magistrate by this example is not appointed. *These* men practised the books; *another* might perhaps have read them in some sort usefully.

Good and evil we know in the field of this world grow up together almost inseparably; and the knowledge of good is so involved and interwoven with the knowledge of evil, and in so many cunning resemblances hardly to be discerned, that those confused seeds which were imposed upon Psyche as an incessant labor to cull out and sort asunder, were not more intermixed. It was from out the rind of one apple tasted, that the knowledge of good and evil, as two twins cleaving together, leaped forth into the world! And perhaps this is that doom which Adam fell into of knowing good and evil; that is to say, of knowing good by evil.

As, therefore, the state of man now is, what wisdom can there be to choose, what continence to forbear, without the knowledge of evil? *He that can apprehend and consider vice with all her baits and seeming pleasures, and yet abstain, and yet distinguish, and yet prefer that which is truly better, he is the true warfaring Christian!* I cannot praise a fugitive and cloistered virtue,

---

* **Tabled,** *supplied with food.* Obsolete in this sense.—**Omer,** a Hebrew measure, the tenth of an ephah. Ex. xvi., 36. According to Josephus, it would appear to have been nearly four quarts (.867 of a gallon); according to the rabbinists, about half as much. Cruden and Dr. A. Clark make it about three quarts.—**God uses not,** *God is not wont.*—**Captivate,** *lead captive, enslave.*—**Solomon** (reigned B. C. 1015-975).—**More expedient,** etc. Note the adroitness of this reasoning.—**Ephesian books.** Acts xix. 19. Ephesus was the headquarters of magic, or "the black art." Plutarch mentions the "*Ephesian letters,*" which were regarded as a charm, and, when written down, were carried about as amulets.—**Syriac** (version of the New Testament). —**Inseparably.** See Matt. xiii. 24-31.—**Psyche.** Venus, being angry with Psyche, assigned her, as a day's work, to separate into parcels by themselves, so that each parcel should contain but one kind, all the grains of wheat, barley, millet, vetches, beans, and lentils, that were confusedly mixed in a vast heap in the temple. Cupid, in his compassion for his wife (Psyche), stirred up an innumerable multitude of ants, which took the seeds, grain by grain, sorting each kind to its proper parcel.—**Adam.** See Genesis ii. 17; iii. 5.—**I cannot praise,** etc. The reader will mark the suggestiveness of this paragraph. Milton practised what he preached, devoting the whole of his vast powers to the service of humanity.

Wearisome. "Differentiate" *irksome, tiresome, tedious, fatiguing, annoying, wearisome, vexatious.*

unexercised and unbreathed, that never sallies out and sees her adversary, but slinks out of the race where that immortal garland is to be run for, not without dust and heat! *

Assuredly, we bring not innocence into the world: we bring impurity much rather. That which purifies us is trial, and trial is by what is contrary. That virtue, therefore, which is but a youngling in the contemplation of evil, and knows not the utmost that vice promises to her followers, and rejects it, is but a blank virtue, not a pure: her whiteness is but an excremental whiteness. Which was the reason why our sage and serious poet Spenser, whom I dare be known to think a better teacher than Scotus or Aquinas, describing true temperance under the person of Guion, brings him in with his Palmer through the cave of Mammon and the bower of earthly bliss, that he might see and know, and yet abstain.

Since, therefore, the knowledge and survey of vice is in this world so necessary to the constituting of human virtue, and the scanning of error to the confirmation of truth, how can we more safely, and with less danger, scout into the regions of sin and falsity, than by reading all manner of tractates, and hearing all manner of reason? And this is the benefit which may be had of books promiscuously read.

But of the harm that may result hence, three kinds are usually reckoned.

First, is feared the infection that may spread. But then all human learning and controversy in religious points, must remove out of the world; yea, the Bible itself: for that ofttimes relates blasphemy not nicely; it describes the carnal sense of wicked men not unelegantly; it brings in holiest men passionately murmuring against Providence through all the arguments of Epicurus. In other great disputes, it answers dubiously and darkly to the common reader. And ask a Talmudist what ails the modesty of his marginal *keri*, that Moses and all the prophets cannot persuade him to pronounce the textual *chetiv*. For these causes, we all know the Bible itself put by the papist into the first rank of prohibited books.

The ancientest fathers must be next removed, as Clement of Alexandria, and that Eusebian book of Evangelic Preparation, transmitting our ears

---

* **Dust and heat.** He seems to have in mind the famous lines with which Horace begins his first ode, "*Sunt quos curriculo pulverem Olympicum,*" etc. "There are those who delight in having gathered Olympic dust," etc.—**Not a pure.** "He here, perhaps, contemplated Plato's beau ideal of a judge; an old man, who, in advancing through his long career, has, by observing the conduct of others, obtained a thorough knowledge of vice and injustice, without ever suffering the slightest taint of either to appear on his own soul." *J. A. St. John.*—**Spenser.** Milton was a great admirer of Spenser. In *Fairy Queen*, Book II., Cantos vii. and xii., we have these experiences of Sir Guion, who personates temperance.—**Scotus,** Duns Scotus, a very learned and subtle teacher of philosophy and theology at Oxford University, lived 1274–1308. His followers were proud to call themselves *Dunses;* whence our word *dunce!*—Saint Thomas **Aquinas** (1224–1274), a great scholar and theologian, who taught at Cologne, Paris, Rome, Bologna, Pisa, etc.—**Mammon** (Gr. μαμμῶνας, riches; Heb. *matmon*, subterranean treasury.)—**Holiest men.** See, for example, the murmurings of Job.—**Arguments of Epicurus.** See the book of Ecclesiastes.—**Talmudist**, one versed in the *Talmud;* which is a book containing the body of Hebrew laws, traditions, and explanations.—**Keri . . . . chetiv** (Heb. *keri-chetib*, what is read, what is written. Whenever the name *Jehovah* occurred in the Hebrew Scriptures, the pious Jews would scrupulously decline to pronounce it, and would read instead of it the word *Adonai*, written in the margin).—**Clement** flourished between A. D. 192 and 217. He attempted to blend heathen tenets with Christian doctrines. Alexandria, where he taught, was founded by Alexander the Great, B. C. 332. It contained the most famous library of antiquity.—**Eusebian.** *Eusebius* was mentioned on page 213. *Præparatio Evangelica* is the name of his work.

through a hoard of heathenish obscenities to receive the gospel. Who finds not that Irenæus,* Epiphanius, Jerome, and others, discover more heresies than they well confute, and that oft for heresy which is the truer opinion?

Nor boots it to say for these and all the heathen writers of greatest infection, if it must be thought so, with whom is bound up the life of human learning, that they writ in an unknown tongue; so long as we are sure those languages are known as well to the worst of men, who are both most able and most diligent to instil the poison they suck, first, into the courts of princes, acquainting them with the choicest delights and criticisms of sin. As perhaps did that Petronius, whom Nero called his *arbiter*, the master of his revels; and that notorious ribald of Arezzo, dreaded, and yet dear to the Italian courtiers. I name not him, for posterity's sake, whom Henry the Eighth named in merriment his "vicar of hell!" By which compendious way, all the contagion that foreign books can infuse, will find a passage to the people far easier and shorter than an Indian voyage, though it could be sailed either by the north of Cataio eastward, or of Canada westward, while our Spanish licensing gags the English press never so severely.

But on the other side, that infection which is from books of controversy in religion, is more doubtful and dangerous to the learned than to the ignorant; and yet those books must be permitted untouched by the licenser. It will be hard to instance where any ignorant man hath been ever seduced by any papistical book in English, unless it were commended and expounded to him by some of that clergy. And indeed all such tractates, whether false or true, are as the prophecy of Isaiah was to the eunuch, not to be "understood without a guide." But of our priests and doctors, how many have been corrupted by studying the comments of Jesuits and Sorbonists, and how fast they could transfuse that corruption into the people, our experience is both

---

* **Irenæus** (born about A. D. 108, may have suffered martyrdom in 202), a disciple of Polycarp, and bishop of Lyons, in France.—**Epiphanius** (320–403), a Christian bishop of Salamis in Cyprus.—**Jerome.** See note several pages *ante*.—**Discover,** *reveal, bring to light.*—**Boots it** (A. S. *bôt*, compensation; *bet*, better; *betan*, to improve; Goth. *bôtan*, to profit, help).—**Infection**, tainting, corrupting, *poisoning influence*, contagion.—**If it must be thought** *to be infection.*—**Petronius.** "Being in favor at court, and cherished as the companion of the Emperor Nero (A. D. 37–68) in all his select parties, he was allowed to be the *arbiter* of taste and elegance."—**Ribald.** I suppose that Milton refers to *Pietro Aretino* (1492–1557), who was honored with an extraordinary number of presents and distinctions from popes, dukes, lords, and emperors; but was called, on account of his keen satires, "the scourge of princes." Says J. A. St. John, "Time has now so effectually buried his profligate writings in oblivion, that few but bibliographers appear to know of their existence. In fact, mankind are generally so just, and endued with so fine a feeling for whatever is excellent, that scarcely any but good works survive; contempt and neglect at length overwhelm all others."—**Arezzo** (Lat. *Arretium*). A city thirty-eight miles southeast of Florence. The city is famous for having given birth to many eminent men.—**Henry** VIII. reigned 1509–1547.—**Compendious** (Lat. *con*, together; *pendere*, to weigh. *Compendium*, that which is weighed, saved, shortened. Eng. *compend*, a brief compilation of the principal heads or general principles of a larger work; an abridgment, epitome), *abridged, short.*—**Cataio** (Cathay, China).—**Isaiah** (B. C. 758–698), Acts viii. 31.—**Jesuits** (Jesus). A religious order founded by Ignatius Loyola, and approved in 1540 under the title of *The Society of Jesus.* It consists of two classes: *Scholars*, who take vows simply of poverty, chastity, and obedience, and who can leave the society or be dismissed; and *Priests*, who take the same vows, but whose connection cannot be so severed. The society was first established in the United States in 1807. See *New Am. Cyclopedia.*—**Sorbonists.** The Sorbonne, a college of the University of Paris, was founded by Robert de *Sorbonne* in 1252. Some of the most eminent theologians in the fourteenth, fifteenth, sixteenth, and seventeenth centuries were educated there. It was suppressed in 1789.

Compendious. Exemplify the peculiar meaning of this word, and of *short, summary, abridged, succinct, brief, laconic, concise.*

late and sad. It is not forgot, since the acute and distinct Arminius * was perverted merely by the perusing of a nameless discourse written at Delft, which at first he took in hand to confute.

Seeing therefore that those books, and those in great abundance which are likeliest to taint both life and doctrine, cannot be suppressed without the fall of learning and of all ability in disputation; and that these books of either sort are most and soonest catching to the learned, from whom to the common people whatever is heretical or dissolute may quickly be conveyed; and that evil manners are as perfectly learned without books a thousand other ways which cannot be stopped; and evil doctrine not with books can propagate, except a teacher guide, which he might also do without writing, and so beyond prohibiting;—I am not able to unfold, how this cautelous enterprise of licensing can be exempted from the number of vain and impossible attempts. And he who were pleasantly disposed, could not well avoid to liken it to the exploit of that gallant man, who thought to pound up the crows by shutting his park gate.

Besides, another inconvenience. If learned men be the first receivers out of books, and dispreaders both of vice and error, how shall the licensers themselves be confided in, unless we can confer upon them, or they assume to themselves above all others in the land, the grace of infallibility and uncorruptedness? And again, if it be true that a wise man, like a good refiner, can gather gold out of the drossiest volume, and that a fool will be a fool with the best book, yea, or without book; there is no reason that we should deprive a wise man of any advantage to his wisdom, while we seek to restrain from a fool, that which, being restrained, will be no hinderance to his folly. For if there should be so much exactness always used to keep that from him which is unfit for his reading, we should, in the judgment of Aristotle not only, but of Solomon, and of our Saviour, not vouchsafe him good precept, and by consequence not willingly admit him to good books; as being certain that a wise man will make better use of an idle pamphlet, than a fool will do of sacred Scripture.

It is next alleged, we must not expose ourselves to temptations without necessity; and, next to that, not employ our time in vain things.

To both these objections one answer will serve out of the grounds already laid; that to all men such books are not temptations, nor vanities, but useful drugs and materials wherewith to temper and compose effective and strong medicines, which man's life cannot want. The rest, as children and childish men who have not the art to qualify and prepare these working minerals, well may be exhorted to forbear; but hindered forcibly they

* **Arminius,** the great Dutch theologian (1560-1609). He undertook to defend the doctrine of absolute predestination, but, before the completion of his argument, he embraced the opposite views.—**Delft,** a city of Holland, nine miles northwest of Rotterdam. Here are the tombs of William I. of Orange, Hugo Grotius, Admiral Van Tromp, and other famous men. —**Not with books can,** *cannot with books.*—**Cautelous,** *cautious to excess, cunning, insidious.* So in Shakespeare's *Julius Cæsar*, Act II., Scene 1.—**Aristotle** (B. C. 384-322), the greatest, in some respects, of all the philosophers of antiquity.—**Solomon.** Prov. xxvi., 4.—**Cannot want,** *cannot dispense with, cannot do without, must have.*

Advantage. Exemplify this and *benefit, utility, service, profit, avail, use, gain.*

cannot be, by all the licensing that sainted Inquisition could ever yet contrive. Which is what I promised to deliver next; that this order of licensing conduces nothing to the end for which it was framed, and hath almost prevented me * by being clear already while thus much hath been explaining. See the ingenuity of Truth, who, when she gets a free and willing hand, opens herself faster than the pace of method and discourse can overtake her!

It was the task which I began with, to show that no nation, or well-instituted state, if they valued books at all, did ever use this way of licensing; and it might be answered, that this is a piece of prudence lately discovered. To which I return, that, as it was a thing slight and obvious to think on, so, if it had been difficult to find out, there wanted not among them long since who suggested such a course. Which they not following, leave us a pattern of their judgment, that it was not the not knowing, but the not approving, which was the cause of their not using it.

Plato, a man of high authority, indeed, but least of all for his Commonwealth, in the book of his laws which no city ever yet received, fed his fancy with making many edicts to his airy burgomasters; which they who otherwise admire him, wish had been rather buried and excused in the genial cups of an academic night-sitting. By which laws he seems to tolerate no kind of learning, but by unalterable decree, consisting most of practical traditions, to the attainment whereof a library of smaller bulk than his own dialogues would be abundant; and there also enacts, that no poet should so much as read to any private man what he had written, until the judges and law keepers had seen it and allowed it. But that Plato meant this law peculiarly to that commonwealth which he had imagined, and to no other, is evident. Why was he not else a lawgiver to himself, but a transgressor, and to be expelled by his own magistrates, both for the wanton epigrams and dialogues which he made, and his perpetual reading of Sophron, Mimus, and Aristophanes, books of grossest infamy? and also for commending the latter of them, though he were the malicious libeller of his chief friends, to be read by the tyrant Dionysius, who had little need of such trash to spend his time on? but that he knew this licensing of poems had reference and dependence to many other provisos there set down in his fancied republic, which in this world could have no place? And so neither he himself, nor any magistrate or city ever imitated that course, which, taken apart from those other collateral injunctions, must needs be vain and fruitless. For if

---

* **Prevented me,** *anticipated* my efforts.—**I return,** I reply.—**Plato** (429-348), the great Athenian philosopher. He founded the famous "*Academy*" at Athens. His *Commonwealth* or *Republic* (Πολιτεία), is a poetic dream or vision of a perfect political state, in which one leading idea is that every man should be put exactly where he belongs. He proposed, among other strange regulations, a community of property and even of wives!—**Sophron,** a native of Syracuse and a contemporary of Plato.—**Mimus.** The text is perhaps faulty. Should it be **Sophron's Mimes?** If we retain *Sophron Mimus*, we may interpret *Mimus*, the *comedian* or *writer of Mimes*. A *Mime* was a kind of farce in which real characters were depicted.—**Aristophanes** has already been mentioned. So *Dionysius*. See, in Anthon's Classical Dictionary, an interesting statement of intercourse between Plato and Dionysius.

Fruitless. Exemplify by sentences the meanings of *fruitless*, *barren*, *useless*, *unprofitable*, *idle*, *abortive*, *ineffectual*, *profitless*, *futile*, *vain*.

they fell upon one kind of strictness, unless their care were equal to regulate all other things of like aptness to corrupt the mind, that single endeavor, they knew, would be but a fond labor; * to shut and fortify one gate against corruption, and be necessitated to leave others round about wide open.

If we think to regulate printing, thereby to rectify manners, we must regulate all recreations and pastimes, all that is delightful to man. No music must be heard, no song be set or sung, but what is grave and Doric. There must be licensing dancers, that no gesture, motion, or deportment be taught our youth, but what, by their allowance, shall be thought honest. For such Plato was provided of. It will ask more than the work of twenty licensers to examine all the lutes, the violins, and the guitars in every house. They must not be suffered to prattle as they do, but must be licensed what they may say. And who shall silence all the airs and madrigals that whisper softness in chambers? The windows also, and the balconies must be thought on. These are shrewd books, with dangerous frontispieces, set to sale. Who shall prohibit them? Shall twenty licensers? The villages also must have their visitors to inquire what lectures the bagpipe and the rebec reads, even to the ballatry and gamut of every municipal fiddler. For these are the countryman's Arcadias and his Monte Mayors.

Next, what more national corruption, for which England hears ill abroad, than household gluttony? Who shall be the rectors of our daily rioting? And what shall be done to inhibit the multitudes that frequent those houses where drunkenness is sold and harbored? Our garments also should be referred to the licensing of some more sober work-masters, to see them cut into a less wanton garb. Who shall regulate all the mixed conversation of our youth, male and female together, as in the fashion of this country? Who shall still appoint what shall be discoursed, what presumed, and no further? Lastly, who shall forbid and separate all idle resort, all evil company? These things will be, and must be: but how they shall be least hurtful, how least enticing, herein consists the grave and governing wisdom of a state.

To sequester out of the world into Atlantic and Eutopian politics, which never can be drawn into use, will not mend our condition; but to ordain

---

* **Fond labor,** *foolish labor.*—**Doric,** pertaining to Dorians, a people of ancient Greece. In music, *Doric* means severe, austere, grave; the *Lydian* was soft, sweet, pathetic; *Phrygian*, sprightly, animated; *Ionic*, airy, fanciful.—**Madrigal,** a brief pastoral poem, usually a love-song.—**Rebec** (Fr. *rebec*, from the Arabic), a stringed instrument like a violin or guitar. (It was the original of our violin, and probably a Moorish invention.) **Ballatry** (balladry. This word is now obsolete), a *song*, a *jig*.—**Arcadias.** The *Arcadia* of Sir Philip Sidney is a pastoral romance, published in 1590; "the only original production of the kind worthy of notice," says Hallam, "which our older literature can boast."—**Monte Mayor** is a town in Spain. Here it is the title of a book.—**Hears ill,** *is blamed. Hear* was used in the sense of *to be called, to hear one's self called.* With *ill* it meant *to be in bad repute.* Thus Holland says of Fabius, "He *heard ill* for his temporizing and slow proceedings." The Latin *audio* was used in the same way; also the Greek ἀκούω. So, "Hear'st thou rather pure, ethereal stream?" *i. e.*, "Dost thou rather hear thyself called pure ethereal stream?" *Paradise Lost*, III., 7.—**Inhibit,** *check.*—**Sequester,** *retire.*—**Atlantic,** pertaining to the *New Atlantis*, an imaginary paradise of utilitarian philosophers, described by Lord Bacon in his unfinished work entitled *New Atlantis.* The *old* Atlantis was described by Plato as a vast and beautiful island which was sunk beneath the Atlantic Ocean nine thousand years before his day!—**Utopia** is an imaginary island described by Sir Thomas More in his celebrated work bearing that title. He represents society and government there as absolutely perfect.

Aptness. Distinguish among the synonymes, *aptness*, *fitness*, *meetness*, *suitableness*, *appropriateness.*

wisely, as in this world of evil, in the midst whereof God hath placed us unavoidably. Nor is it Plato's licensing of books will do this, which necessarily pulls along with it so many other kinds of licensing as will make us all both ridiculous and weary, and yet frustrate: but those unwritten, or at least unconstraining laws of virtuous education, religious and civil nurture, which Plato there mentions as the bonds and ligaments of the commonwealth, the pillars and the sustainers of every written statute,—these they be which will bear chief sway in such matters as these, when all licensing will be easily eluded.

Impunity and remissness for certain are the bane of a commonwealth. But here the great art lies, to discern in what the law is to bid restraint and punishment, and in what things persuasion only is to work.

If every action which is good or evil in man at ripe years, were to be under pittance, and prescription, and compulsion, what were virtue but a name? What praise could be then due to well-doing? What gramercy * to be sober, just or continent?

Many there be that complain of Divine Providence for suffering Adam to transgress. Foolish tongues! When God gave him reason, he gave him freedom to choose; for reason is but choosing. He had been else a mere artificial Adam, such an Adam as he is in the motions. We ourselves esteem not of that obedience, or love, or gift, which is of force. God therefore left him free, set before him a provoking object, ever almost in his eyes. Herein consisted his merit, herein the right of his reward, the praise of his abstinence. Wherefore did he create passions within us, pleasures round about us, but that these rightly tempered are the very ingredients of virtue?

They are not skilful considerers of human things, who imagine to remove sin by removing the matter of sin. For, besides that it is a huge heap increasing under the very act of diminishing, though some part of it may for a time be withdrawn from some persons, it cannot from all in such a universal thing as books are; and when this is done, yet the sin remains entire. Though ye take from a covetous man all his treasure, he has yet one jewel left; ye cannot bereave him of his covetousness. Banish all objects of lust, shut up all youth into the severest discipline that can be exercised in any hermitage,—ye cannot make them chaste, that came not thither so. Such great care and wisdom is required to the right managing of this point.

Suppose we could expel sin by this means. Look, how much we thus expel of sin, so much we expel of virtue; for the matter of them both is the same. Remove that, and ye remove them both alike. This justifies the high providence of God, who, though he commands us temperance, justice, continence, yet pours out before us, even to a profuseness, all desirable things, and gives us minds that can wander beyond all limit and satiety.

---

* **Gramercy** (Fr. *grand merci*, great thanks), *thanks*. See *grand-mercy*, p. 54.—**In the motions,** *in the puppet shows. Motions* in this sense is now obsolete.—**Esteem not of,** *esteem not, admire not.* This splendid argument in justification of divine Providence for leaving man free in the midst of temptations, is well worth attention.

Covetous. Give examples of the respective meanings of *covetous*, *avaricious*, *parsimonious*, *penurious*, *miserly*, *niggardly*, *stingy*.

Why should we, then, affect a rigor contrary to the manner of God and of nature, by abridging or scanting those means, which books freely permitted are, both to the trial of virtue and the exercise of truth ?

It would be better done to learn that the law must needs be frivolous which goes to restrain things uncertainly and yet equally working to good and to evil. And were I a chooser, a dram of well-doing should be preferred before many times as much the forcible hinderance of evil-doing. *For God sure esteems the growth and completing of one virtuous person, more than the restraint of ten vicious!*

And albeit, whatever thing we hear or see, sitting, walking, travelling, or conversing, may be fitly called our book, and is of the same effect that writings are; yet grant the thing to be prohibited were only books, it appears that this order hitherto is far insufficient to the end which it intends. Do we not see, not once or oftener, but weekly, that continued court libel* against the parliament and city ? printed, as the wet sheets can witness, and dispersed among us, for all that licensing can do. Yet this is the prime service, a man would think, wherein this order should give proof of itself. "If it were executed," you will say. But certain, if execution be remiss or blindfold now, and in this particular, what will it be hereafter, and in other books ?

If then the order shall not be vain and frustrate, behold a new labor, Lords and Commons. Ye must repeal and proscribe all scandalous and unlicensed books already printed and divulged, after ye have drawn them up into a list, that all may know which are condemned, and which not; and ordain that no foreign books be delivered out of custody, till they have been read over. This office will require the whole time of not a few overseers, and those no vulgar men. There be also books which are partly useful and excellent, partly culpable and pernicious. This work will ask as many more officials, to make expurgations and expunctions, that the commonwealth of learning be not damnified. In fine, when the multitude of books increase upon their hands, ye must be fain to catalogue all those printers who are found frequently offending, and forbid the importation of their whole suspected typography. In a word, that this your order may be exact, and not deficient, ye must reform it perfectly, according to the model of Trent and Seville; which I know ye abhor to do. Yet though ye should condescend to this, (which God forbid!) the order still would be fruitless and defective to that end whereto ye meant it. If to prevent sects and schisms, who is so unread or uncatechised in story, that hath not heard of many sects refusing books as a hinderance, and preserving their doctrine unmixed, for many ages,

---

Court libel. A weekly paper entitled *Mercurius Aulicus*, put forth by Sir John Birkenhead to extol the king and royalists, and ridicule the parliament party. It appeared regularly from 1642 to 1645, and occasionally afterwards. It was usually in one sheet, sometimes more, in quarto.—**For all that licensing can do,** *in spite of all that licensing can do.*—**No vulgar men,** *no common men.*—**Expunctions,** *expungings, erasures.* Lat. *expungĕre*, to prick out, blot out by puncturing or by smoothing with the stylus. The word is not akin to *sponge.*—**Trent,** a city of Austria, in the Tyrol. Here the celebrated Council of Trent held its sittings, 1545–1563.—**Seville,** a famous city of Spain, containing about one hundred and fifty thousand inhabitants. Here the Spanish Inquisition held its first regular session in 1480.

Expunctions. Synonymes, *expunge, efface, erase, obliterate, cancel, blot out, wipe out, destroy?*

only by unwritten traditions? The Christian faith (for that was once a schism!) is not unknown to have spread all over Asia, ere any gospel or epistle was seen in writing. If the amendment of manners be aimed at, look into Italy and Spain, whether those places be one scruple the better, the honester, the wiser, the chaster, since all the inquisitorial rigor that hath been executed upon books!

Another reason whereby to make it plain that this order will miss the end it seeks, consider by the quality which ought to be in every licenser. It cannot be denied but that he who is made judge to sit upon the birth or death of books, whether they may be wafted into this world or not, had need to be a man above the common measure, both studious, learned, and judicious.* There may be else no mean mistakes in the censure of what is passable or not; which is also no mean injury. If he be of such worth as behoves him, there cannot be a more tedious and unpleasing journey-work, a greater loss of time levied upon his head, than to be made the perpetual reader of unchosen books and pamphlets, ofttimes huge volumes. There is no book that is acceptable, unless at certain seasons. But to be enjoined the reading of that at all times, and in a hand scarce legible, whereof three pages would not down at any time in the fairest print, is an imposition which I cannot believe how he that values time and his own studies, or is but of a sensible nostril, should be able to endure. In this one thing I crave leave of the present licensers to be pardoned for so thinking, who doubtless took this office up, looking on it through their obedience to the parliament, whose command perhaps made all things seem easy and unlaborious to them. But that this short trial hath wearied them out already, their own expressions and excuses to them who make so many journeys to solicit their license, are testimony enough. Seeing, therefore, those who now possess the employment, by all evident signs wish themselves well rid of it, and that no man of worth, none that is not a plain unthrift of his own hours, is ever likely to succeed them, except he mean to put himself to the salary of a press corrector; we may easily foresee what kind of licensers we are to expect hereafter; either ignorant, imperious, and remiss, or basely pecuniary.

This is what I had to show, wherein this order cannot conduce to that end whereof it bears the intention.

I lastly proceed from the no good it can do, to the manifest hurt it causes, in being, first, the greatest discouragement and affront that can be offered to learning and to learned men.

It was the complaint and lamentation of prelates, upon every least breath of a motion to remove pluralities and distribute more equally church reve-

---

* **Both studious, learned, and judicious.** *Both*, as a conjunction, properly precedes the first of *two* co-ordinate words or phrases; not properly the first of three.—**Would not down,** *would not be taken down; i. e.*, would not be willingly read.—**Sensible nostril,** *sensitive nostril; i. e., delicate taste.*—**Pluralities.** The possession, by a clergyman, of more church livings or benefices than one, is a plurality. Each benefice so held is called a plurality. The revenue of such additional endowed church is also sometimes termed a plurality.

Perpetual. Give sentences to illustrate *constant, continual, perpetual, eternal, unceasing, everlasting, perennial, continuous, endless, ceaseless, interminable.*

nues, that then all learning would be for ever dashed and discouraged. But as for that opinion, I never found cause to think that the tenth part of learning stood or fell with the clergy: nor could I ever but hold it for a sordid and unworthy speech of any churchman who had acompetency left him.* If, therefore, ye be loath to dishearten utterly and discontent, not the mercenary crew of false pretenders to learning, but the free and ingenuous sort of such as evidently were born to study and love learning for itself, not for lucre or any other end but the service of God and of truth, and perhaps that lasting fame and perpetuity of praise which God and good men have consented shall be the reward of those whose published labors advance the good of mankind; then know, that so far to distrust the judgment and the honesty of one who hath but a common repute in learning and never yet offended, as to not count him fit to print his mind without a tutor and examiner, lest he should drop a schism or something of corruption, is the greatest displeasure and indignity to a free and knowing spirit that can be put upon him.

What advantage is it to be a man over it is to be a boy at school, if we have only escaped the ferular to come under the fescue of an *imprimatur?* if serious and elaborate writings, as if they were no more than the theme of a grammar lad under his pedagogue, must not be uttered without the cursory eyes of a temporizing and extemporizing licenser? He who is not trusted with his own actions, his drift not being known to be evil, and standing to the hazard of law and penalty, has no great argument to think himself reputed, in the commonwealth wherein he was born, for other than a fool or a foreigner!

When a man writes to the world, he summons up all his reason and deliberation to assist him. He searches, meditates, is industrious, and likely consults and confers with his judicious friends. After all which done, he takes himself to be informed in what he writes, as well as any that writ before him. If in this, the most consummate act of his fidelity and ripeness, no years, no industry, no former proof of his abilities, can bring him to that state of maturity as not to be still mistrusted and suspected, unless he carry all his considerate diligence, all his midnight watchings and expense of Palladian oil, to the hasty view of an unleisured licenser; perhaps much his younger, perhaps far his inferior in judgment, perhaps one who

* **Competency left him.** Milton, in his *Animadversions on the Remonstrant's Defence*, had vehemently inveighed against the supposition that the riches of the church were of importance in the support of learning.—**Ferular** (Lat. *ferula*, fr. *ferire*, to strike), *ferule*, a flat, straight, thin piece of wood, used formerly at school in drawing straight lines, and, for want of the predestined *birch*, in whipping unruly children.—**Fescue** (Lat. *festuca*), a straw, little stick, or wire, used to point out letters for children learning to read.—**Imprimatur** (Lat.), it may be printed; *a license to print.*—**Drift**, *tendency.*—**When a man writes.** Here is an admirable statement of the best method of preparation for composition. First, the writer should carefully, comprehensively, and thoroughly, examine the subject by the light of his own reason. Next, he should as carefully search out the best thoughts of the best authors, if any there are, that have treated of the subject; and then he should confer with judicious friends.—**That state of maturity as,** *such a state of maturity as.*—**Palladian oil.** *Pallas Athene* (Greek name of the Lat. *Minerva*) was the goddess of wisdom and skill among the ancient Greeks. "Palladian oil" is that which burns in the student's midnight lamp.

Peculiar meaning of *pedagogue? schoolmaster? tutor? teacher? pedant? instructor?* Show these meanings by appropriate sentences.

never knew the labor of book-writing; and if he be not repulsed, or slighted, must appear in print like a puny* with his guardian, and his censor's hand on the back of his title to be his bail and surety, and that he is no idiot or seducer: it cannot be but a dishonor and derogation to the author, to the book, to the privilege and dignity of learning. And what if the author shall be one so copious of fancy as to have many things well worth the adding come into his mind after licensing, while the book is yet under the press; which not seldom happens to the best and diligentest writers, and that perhaps a dozen times in one book? The printer dares not go beyond his licensed copy. So often then must the author drudge to his leave-giver, that those his new insertions may be viewed; and many a jaunt will be made, ere that licenser, for it must be the same man, can either be found, or found at leisure. Meanwhile, either the press must stand still, which is no small damage, or the author lose his accuratest thoughts, and send the book forth worse than he had made it; which to a diligent writer is the greatest melancholy and vexation that can befall.

And how can a man teach with authority, which is the life of teaching; how can he be a doctor in his book, (as he ought to be, or else had better be silent,) whenas all he teaches, all he delivers, is but under the tuition, under the correction of his patriarchal licenser, to blot or alter what precisely accords not with the hide-bound humor which he calls his judgment? when every acute reader, upon the first sight of a pedantic license, will be ready with these like words to ding the book a quoit's distance from him! "I hate a pupil teacher: I endure not an instructor that comes to me under the wardship of an overseeing fist. I know nothing of the licenser, but that I have his own hand here for his arrogance. Who shall warrant me his judgment?" "The state, sir," replies the stationer; but has quick return, "The state shall be my governors, but not my critics; they may be mistaken in the choice of a licenser, as easily as this licenser may be mistaken in an author. This is some common stuff." And he might add from Sir Francis Bacon, that "such authorized books are but the language of the times." For though a licenser should happen to be judicious more than ordinary, which will be a great jeopardy of the next succession, yet his very office and his commission enjoins him to let pass nothing but what is vulgarly received already.

Nay, which is more lamentable, if the work of any deceased author, though never so famous in his lifetime and even to this day, comes to their hands for license to be printed or reprinted; if there be found in his book one sentence of a venturous edge, uttered in the height of zeal, (and who knows whether it might not be the dictate of a divine spirit?) yet not suiting with every low decrepit humor of their own; though it

---

* **Puny** (Fr. *puîné*, *puisné*, younger; Lat. *post*, afterwards; *natus*, born), a young person, a *minor*.—**Doctor** (Lat. *doctor*, teacher; *docere*, to teach), *teacher*.—**Whenas all,** *when all*.—**Ding**, *hurl*.—**Quoit's** (D. *koot;* Welsh *coitan*, a quoit), a circular ring or piece of iron, stone, or other material, pitched in play at a fixed object, or thrown to a distance, as a trial of skill or strength.—**Bacon.** See ante, p. 83.—**Vulgarly received,** *commonly approved*.

Arrogance. Syn., *haughtiness*, *disdain*, *conceit*, *pride*, *vanity*, *presumption*.

were Knox* himself, the reformer of a kingdom, that spake it; they will not pardon him their dash. The sense of that great man shall to all posterity be lost, for the fearfulness or the presumptuous rashness of a perfunctory licenser. And to what an author this violence hath been lately done, and in what book of greatest consequence to be faithfully published, I could now instance, but shall forbear till a more convenient season. Yet if these things be not resented seriously and timely by them who have the remedy in their power, but that such iron-moulds as these shall have authority to gnaw out the choicest periods of exquisitest books, and to commit such a treacherous fraud against the orphan remainders of worthiest men after death; the more sorrow will belong to that hapless race of men, whose misfortune it is to have understanding. Henceforth let no man care to learn, or care to be more than worldly wise; for certainly in higher matters to be ignorant and slothful, to be a common steadfast dunce, will be the only pleasant life, and only in request.

And as it is a particular disesteem of every knowing person alive, and most injurious to the written labors and monuments of the dead, so to me it seems an undervaluing and vilifying of the whole nation. I cannot set so light by all the invention, the art, the wit, the grave and solid judgment which is in England, as that it can be comprehended in any twenty capacities, how good soever; much less that it should not pass except their superintendence be over it, except it be sifted and strained with their strainers, that it should be uncurrent without their manual stamp. Truth and understanding are not such wares as to be monopolized and traded in by tickets, and statutes, and standards. We must not think to make a staple commodity of all the knowledge in the land, to mark and license it like our broadcloth and our woolpacks. What is it but a servitude like that imposed by the Philistines, not to be allowed the sharpening of our own axes and coulters, but we must repair from all quarters to twenty licensing forges?

Had any one written and divulged erroneous things and scandalous to honest life, misusing and forfeiting the esteem had of his reason among men; if, after conviction, this only censure were adjudged him, that he should never henceforth write, but what were first examined by an appointed officer, whose hand should be annexed to pass his credit for him, that now he might be safely read; it could not be apprehended less than a disgraceful punishment. Whence to include the whole nation, and those that never

---

* John **Knox**, the leader of the Protestant reformation in Scotland (about 1505–1572). —**Dash,** *sudden check, frustration, abashment;* e. g. "His hopes received a dash." But perhaps we should interpret *dash* in this instance to mean *the obliterating stroke of a pen.*—**Perfunctory,** *acting mechanically, acting without interest, acting with indifference.* —**To what an author . . . . in what book.** This is supposed by Holt White to refer to the posthumous portion of *Coke's Institutes*, first printed in 1641.—**Orphan remainders;** *i. e.*, the books which were as dear as children.—**Judgment which is in England.** In his *Reason of Church Government*, Milton speaks with patriotic pride of the English people, as "a right pious, right honest, and right hardy nation."—**Twenty.** By a decree of the Star Chamber, published in Charles's reign, twenty master-printers are named to have the use of printing presses, etc.—**Philistines.** See 1 Samuel, xiii. 19–22.

Fearfulness. Peculiar signification of this word? of *timidity? cowardice? pusillanimity? timorousness? fear?* Illustrate.

yet thus offended, under such a diffident and suspectful prohibition, may plainly be understood what a disparagement it is. So much the more, whenas debtors and delinquents may walk abroad without a keeper, but unoffensive books must not stir forth without a visible jailer in their title!

Nor is it to the common people less than a reproach. For if we be so jealous over them as that we dare not trust them with an English pamphlet, what do we but censure them for a giddy, vicious, and ungrounded people, in such a sick and weak estate of faith and discretion as to be able to take nothing down but through the pipe of a licenser? That this is care or love of them, we cannot pretend; whenas, in those popish places where the laity are most hated and despised, the same strictness is used over them. Wisdom we cannot call it, because it stops but one breach of license; nor that neither: whenas, those corruptions which it seeks to prevent, break in faster at other doors which cannot be shut.

And, in conclusion, it reflects to the disrepute of our ministers also, of whose labors we should hope better, and of the proficiency which their flock reaps by them, than that, after all this light of the gospel which is and is to be, and all this continual preaching, they should be still frequented with such an unprincipled, unedified, and laic * rabble, as that the whiff of every new pamphlet should stagger them out of their catechism and Christian walking! This may have much reason to discourage the ministers, when such a low conceit is had of all their exhortations, and the benefiting of their hearers, as that they are not thought fit to be turned loose to three sheets of paper without a licenser! that all the sermons, all the lectures preached, printed, vended in such numbers and such volumes as have now well nigh made all other books unsaleable, should not be armor enough against one single Enchiridion, without the Castle of St. Angelo of an *imprimatur!*

And lest some should persuade ye, Lords and Commons, that these arguments of learned men's discouragement at this your order are mere flourishes and not real, I could recount what I have seen and heard in other countries, where this kind of inquisition tyrannizes; when I have sat among their learned men, for that honor I had, and been counted happy to be born in such a place of philosophic freedom as they supposed England was: while themselves did nothing but bemoan the servile condition into which learning amongst them was brought; that this was it which had damped the glory of Italian wits; that nothing had been there written now these many years but flattery and fustian. There it was that I found and visited the famous Galileo, grown old, a prisoner to the Inquisition for

* **Laic** (Gr. λαός, the people), belonging to the laity or people, as distinguished from the clergy; hence, *ignorant.*—**Enchiridion** (Gr. ἐν, in; χείρ, the hand), a *hand-book* or *manual.* —**Castle of St. Angelo.** The citadel of Rome, on the right bank of the Tiber. It serves for a state prison.—**Happy to be born,** *happy to have been born.*—**Galileo** (1564–1642), the famous Italian mathematician and philosopher, who invented the telescope, discovered the satellites of Jupiter, and taught the Copernican theory of astronomy. It would appear from this passage that he was still a prisoner when Milton saw him in 1638 or 1639.

Prohibition, interdict, inhibition, disallowance. Wherein do these words differ in meaning? Illustrate.

thinking in astronomy otherwise than the Franciscan* and Dominican licensers thought! And though I knew that England then was groaning loudest under the prelatical yoke, nevertheless I took it as a pledge of future happiness, that other nations were so persuaded of her liberty.

Yet was it beyond my hope, that those worthies were then breathing in her air, who should be her leaders to such a deliverance as shall never be forgotten by any revolution of time that this world hath to finish. When that was once begun, it was as little in my fear that what words of complaint I heard among learned men of other parts uttered against the Inquisition, the same I should hear by as learned men at home uttered in time of parliament against an order of licensing! and that so generally, that when I had disclosed myself a companion of their discontent, I might say, if without envy, that he whom an honest quæstorship had endeared to the Sicilians was not more by them importuned against Verres, than the favorable opinion which I had among many who honor ye, and are known and respected by ye, loaded me with entreaties and persuasions, that I would not despair to lay together that which just reason should bring into my mind, toward the removal of an undeserved thraldom upon learning.

That this is not therefore the disburdening of a particular fancy, but the common grievance of all those who had prepared their minds and studies above the vulgar pitch to advance truth in others, and from others to entertain it, thus much may satisfy. And in their name I shall for neither friend nor foe conceal what the general murmur is; that, if it come to inquisitioning again, and licensing, and that we are so timorous of ourselves and suspicious of all men, as to fear each book, and the shaking of every leaf, before we know what the contents are; if some who, but of late, were little better than silenced from preaching, shall come now to silence us from reading, except what they please: it cannot be guessed what is intended by some but a second tyranny over learning, and will soon put it out of controversy that bishops and presbyters are the same to us, both name and thing.

That those evils of prelaty, which, before, from five or six and twenty sees were distributively charged upon the whole people, will now light wholly upon learning, is not obscure to us; whenas now the pastor of a small unlearned parish on the sudden shall be exalted archbishop over a large diocese

---

* **Franciscan.** The Franciscans were monks of the order of St. Francis, founded in 1209. —**Dominican.** The Dominicans were the order of St. Dominic, established in 1215. They were called *black* friars, while the Franciscans were styled *gray* friars, and the Augustines and Carmelites, *white*. See p. 209.—**Verres,** a Roman prætor, notorious for his oppression of Sicily. He was a contemporary of Cicero, the *honest* quæstor. The quæstor had, among other duties, the collection of the revenues.—**Bishops and presbyters** (Gr. Ἐπίσκοποι, overseers; fr. ἐπί, over; σκοπέω, I look. Gr. Πρεσβυτέροι, elders; fr. πρέσβυς, old). This reminds us of Milton's irregular sonnet, to which allusion has already been made, printed about the time of his *Areopagitica*, and closing with the words already quoted, "New *Presbyter* is but old *Priest* writ large." Note that, as a rule, French words, coming into English, and Latin words coming through the French, drop a part of their original form. Consult Webster's Dict., for illustration, in regard to *palsy*, *doubt*, *marvel*, *moiety*, *treason*, *miscreant*, *peril*, *poor*, *priest*, *surname*, *muster*, *measure*, *grant*, *chance*, *blame*, *count*, *cost*, *daunt*, *due*, *gourd*, *preach*, *rill*, *seal*, *sure*.—**Sees** (Lat. *sedes*, seat; Gr. ἕδος, seat; O. Eng. *se*, *see;* Fr. *siége*), *seats*, *thrones*. The office, or jurisdiction, of a pope or bishop was called a *see*.

Thraldom, *servitude*, *slavery*, *bondage*, *vassalage*, *serfdom*. Difference? Illustrate.

of books, and yet not remove, but keep his other cure* too, a mystical pluralist! He, who, but of late, cried down the sole ordination of every novice bachelor of art, and denied sole jurisdiction over the simplest parishioner, shall now at home in his private chair assume both these over worthiest and excellentest books and ablest authors that write them.

This is not the covenants and protestations that we have made! This is not to put down prelaty! This is but to chop an episcopacy! This is but to translate the palace metropolitan from one kind of dominion into another! This is but an old canonical slight of commuting our penance! To startle thus betimes at a mere unlicensed pamphlet, will, after a while, be afraid of every conventicle, and a while after will make a conventicle of every Christian meeting. But I am certain that a state governed by the rules of justice and fortitude, or a church built and founded upon the rock of faith and true knowledge, cannot be so pusillanimous.

While things are yet not constituted in religion, that freedom of writing should be restrained by a discipline imitated from the prelates, and learned by them from the Inquisition to shut us up all again into the breast of a licenser, must needs give cause of doubt and discouragement to all learned and religious men. Who cannot but discern the fineness of this politic drift, and who are the contrivers? that while bishops were to be baited down, then all presses might be open; it was the people's birthright and privilege in time of parliament; it was the breaking forth of light? But now, the bishops abrogated and voided out of the church, as if our reformation sought no more but to make room for others into their seats under another name, the episcopal arts begin to bud again! the cruise of truth must run no more oil! liberty of printing must be enthralled again under a prelatical commission of twenty! the privilege of the people nullified! and, which is worse, the freedom of learning must groan again, and to her old fetters! All this, the parliament yet sitting! Although their own late arguments and defences against the prelates, might remember them that this obstructing violence meets for the most part with an event utterly opposite to the end which it drives at: instead of suppressing sects and schisms, it raises them and invests them with a reputation!

"The punishing of wits enhances their authority," saith the viscount St. Albans; "and a forbidden writing is thought to be a certain spark of truth that flies up in the faces of them who seek to tread it out." This order

---

* **Cure** (Lat. *cura*, care), the office of curate.—**Mystical** (Gr. μύστης, one initiated in mysteries; fr. μύειν, to shut the eyes), *involving mysticism, allegorical, emblematical.*—**Pluralist.** A clergyman who holds more ecclesiastical benefices than one, with cure of souls, is *a pluralist.* See p. 222.—**Chop,** exchange, barter.—**Sleight,** *trick, artifice.* See p. 54.—**Discern the fineness** (*fineness* is Fr. *finesse*, fr. Lat. *finitus*, finished; *finis*, end), discern the *subtlety.*—**Baited down.** See *baited*, Index. Milton conceives a bishop to have been attacked by the presses, as a bear is harassed by dogs.—**Cruise** (Lat. *crucibulum*, a hanging lamp or earthen pot for melting metals, a crucible. Perhaps fr. Lat. *crux*, cross; as crucibles were marked with the sign of the cross to prevent the devil from interfering to spoil the chemical operation! So *curse* is said to be from *crux*, and to have meant, originally, to imprecate evil in the name of the cross. Fr. *cruche*, pitcher; Low Ger. *kroos, kruus*, a mug, jar), *a small cup or bottle.* See 1 Kings xvii. 9-17.—**Remember them,** *put them in mind, remind them.*—**Viscount** (Lat. *vice*, in place of; *comes*, a companion of the king, a count, or earl), formerly an officer who took the place of a count or earl; a sheriff; a nobleman next in rank below an earl; the title of such a nobleman. Sir Francis Bacon is the man quoted from. See p. 83.

therefore may prove a nursing mother to sects, but I shall easily show how it will be a step-dame to truth; and, first, by disenabling us to the maintenance of what is known already.

Well knows he who uses to consider, that our faith and knowledge thrive by exercise, as well as our limbs and complexion. Truth is compared in Scripture to a streaming fountain; if her waters flow not in a perpetual progression, they sicken into a muddy pool of conformity and tradition.

*A man may be a heretic in the truth; and if he believe things only because his pastor says so, or the assembly so determines, without knowing other reason, though his belief be true, yet the very truth he holds, becomes his heresy.**

There is not any burden that some would gladlier post off to another, than the charge and care of their religion. There be (who knows not that there be?) of Protestants and professors who live and die in as arrant an implicit faith, as any lay papist of Loretto.

A wealthy man, addicted to his pleasure and to his profits, finds religion to be a traffic so entangled, and of so many piddling accounts, that of all mysteries he cannot skill to keep a stock going upon that trade. What should he do? Fain he would have the name to be religious: fain he would bear up with his neighbors in that. What does he therefore, but resolves to give over toiling, and to find himself out some factor, to whose care and credit he may commit the whole managing of his religious affairs? Some divine of note and estimation, that must be. To him he adheres, resigns the whole warehouse of his religion, with all the locks and keys, into his custody; and indeed makes the very person of that man his religion; esteems his associating with him a sufficient evidence and commendatory of his own piety. So that a man may say his religion is now no more within himself, but is become a dividual movable, and goes and comes near him, according as that good man frequents the house. He entertains him, gives him gifts, feasts him, lodges him. His religion comes home at night, prays, is liberally supped, and sumptuously laid to sleep! rises, is saluted, and after the malmsey,

* **The very truth . . . . becomes his heresy,** etc. Milton here states a principle not yet generally appreciated. What multitudes of religionists mistake credulity for faith! *Heresy* is Gr. ἅιρεσις, a taking, a choosing; an *unreasonable* or *wilful* choice; a sect; a denial of some essential doctrine of Christianity. Locke (*Essay on the Human Understanding*, IV., ch. 19) observes: "There are few lovers of truth *for truth's sake*, even amongst those who persuade themselves they are so. How a man may know whether he be so in earnest, is worth inquiry; and I think there is one unerring mark of it; viz., the not entertaining any proposition with greater assurance than the proofs it is built upon will warrant. Whoever goes beyond this measure of assent, it is plain, receives not truth in the love of it; loves not truth for truth's sake, but for some other by-end."—**Arrant** (Lat. *errare*, to wander; O. Eng. *errant*, wandering, vagabond, vile), *in right earnest*, *unmistakable; notorious.*—**Loretto.** A city in Central Italy, in the Marches, three miles from the Adriatic, famous for a shrine of the Virgin and for the trade in relics and rosaries.—**Piddling** (another form, perhaps, of *peddle*, from *paddle*, diminutive of A. S. *pad*, a path, *pad*, to go), *dealing in trifles, trivial. Diminutive nouns* end in *-kin*, as *manikin*, little man; *lambkin*, little lamb; *Peterkin*, little Peter;—in *-ock*, as *hillock*, little hill; *bullock*;—in *-ie*, as *wifie*, little wife; *Johnnie*, little John;—in *-et*, as *streamlet, lancet, trumpet*;—in *-el*, as *cockerel, pickerel*;—in *-ling*, as *darling*, little dear; *lordling*, little lord. Some are formed by a change of vowel, as *kitten*, little *cat; chick*, little *cock; tip*, little top. The short sound of *i*, being one of the smallest sounds in language, is especially adapted to express *little* things. The student will be surprised to find how multitudinous are the words that illustrate the natural significance of this little sound.—**Mysteries** (Lat. *magisterium*, mastery, magistracy; O. Eng. *maisterie*, a trade), *callings* or *occupations* requiring peculiar skill, or some knowledge which is a secret to others; the word being probably associated unconsciously with *mystery* in its usual sense.—**Cannot skill,** *cannot have skill* or *be skilful.*

Heresy, schism, heterodoxy. Difference in these? Example of each in a sentence.

or some well spiced brewage, and better breakfasted than he whose morning appetite would have gladly fed on green figs between Bethany * and Jerusalem, his religion walks abroad at eight, and leaves his kind entertainer in the shop trading all day without his religion!

Another sort there be, who, when they hear that all things shall be ordered, all things regulated and settled, nothing written but what passes through the custom-house of certain publicans that have the tonnaging and poundaging of all free-spoken truth, will straight give themselves up into your hands, make them and cut them out what religion ye please. There be delights, there be recreations and jolly pastimes that will fetch the day about from sun to sun, and rock the tedious year as in a delightful dream. What need they torture their heads with that which others have taken so strictly and so unalterably into their own purveying? These are the fruits which a dull ease and cessation of our knowledge will bring forth among the people. How goodly, and how to be wished were such an obedient unanimity as this! What a fine conformity would it starch us all into! Doubtless a staunch and solid piece of frame work as any January could freeze together!

Nor much better will be the consequence even among the clergy themselves. It is no new thing never heard of before, for a parochial minister who has his reward, and is at his Hercules' Pillars in a warm benefice, to be easily inclinable, if he have nothing else that may rouse up his studies, to finish his circuit in an English Concordance and a topic folio; the gatherings and savings of a sober graduateship; a Harmony and a Catena; treading the constant round of certain common doctrinal heads, attended with their uses, motives, marks, and means. Out of which, as out of an alphabet or *sol fa*, by forming and transforming, joining and disjoining variously, a little bookcraft and two hours' meditation might furnish him unspeakably to the performance of more than a weekly charge of sermoning; not to reckon up the infinite helps of interlinearies, breviaries, synopses, and other loitering gear! But as for the multitude of sermons ready printed and piled up, on every text that is not difficult—our London trading St. Thomas in his vestry, and add to boot St. Martin and St. Hugh, have not within their hallowed limits more vendible ware of all sorts ready made. So that penury he never need fear of pulpit provision, having where so plenteously to refresh his

---

* **Bethany,** a village of Palestine, on the east slope of the Mount of Olives and two miles east of Jerusalem. Matt. xxi. 18, 19.—**Tonnaging and poundaging.** Goods exported or imported were taxed by the *ton* or *pound*. Ships paid duties according to their tonnage. Tonnage and poundage correspond to custom-house duties and internal revenue taxes.—**Parochial** (Gr. παρά, beside, near; οἶκος, house; πάροικος, dwelling near; Lat. *parochia*, parish), *relating to a parish*.—**Hercules' Pillars.** Gibraltar on the north, and Apes' Hill (Mount Abyla) on the south of the entrance to the Mediterranean, were called by the ancients the *Pillars of Hercules*, and were regarded by those who dwelt on the coasts of the Mediterranean as the western boundary of the world. "Hercules was fabled to have placed them there as monuments of his travels westward, and as bounds beyond which no mortal could pass." He is said to have placed on them the inscription, *Ne plus ultra*. "They long remained deeply fixed in the Greek mind as a terminus of human adventure and aspiration."—**Topic folio,** a book containing a collection of topics.—**Harmony,** a work showing parallel passages in the Gospels.—**Catena** (Lat., *a chain*), a series of passages illustrating a subject.—**Sol fa**, *the gamut* or musical scale (*do, re, mi, fa, sol, la, si, do*).—**To boot** (see *boots it*, p. 216), *in addition, over and above, besides*.

Recreation, amusement, entertainment, diversion, sport, pastime. Differences? Illustrate.

magazine. But if his rear and flanks be not impaled,* if his back-door be not secured by the rigid licenser, but that a bold book may now and then issue forth, and give the assault to some of his old collections in their trenches; it will concern him then to keep waking, to stand in watch, to set good guards and sentinels about his received opinions, to walk the round and counter-round with his fellow inspectors, fearing lest any of his flock be seduced, who also then would be better instructed, better exercised and disciplined. And God send that the fear of this diligence which must then be used, do not make us affect the laziness of a licensing church!

For if we be sure we are in the right, and do not hold the truth guiltily, which becomes not; if we ourselves condemn not our own weak and frivolous teaching, and the people for an untaught and irreligious gadding rout; what can be more fair, than when a man, judicious, learned, and of a conscience, for aught we know, as good as theirs that taught us what we know, shall, not privily from house to house, which is more dangerous, but openly by writing, publish to the world what his opinion is, what his reasons, and wherefore that which is now thought, cannot be sound? Christ urged it, as wherewith to justify himself, that he preached in public. Yet writing is more public than preaching, and more easy to refutation, if need be, there being so many whose business and profession merely it is to be the champions of truth; which if they neglect, what can be imputed but their sloth or inability?

Thus much we are hindered and disinured, by this course of licensing, toward the true knowledge of what we seem to know. For how much it hurts and hinders the licensers themselves in the calling of their ministry, more than any secular employment, if they will discharge that office as they ought, so that of necessity they must neglect either the one duty or the other, I insist not, because it is a particular; but leave it to their own conscience, how they will decide it there.

There is yet behind of what I purposed to lay open, the incredible loss and detriment that this plot of licensing puts us to, more than if some enemy at sea should stop up all our havens and ports and creeks. It hinders and retards the importation of our richest merchandise, truth. Nay, it was first established and put in practice by antichristian malice and mystery, on set purpose to extinguish, if it were possible, the light of reformation, and to settle falsehood; little differing from that policy wherewith the Turk upholds his Alcoran, by the prohibiting of printing. It is not denied, but gladly confessed, we are to send our thanks and vows to heaven, louder than most of nations, for the great measure of truth which we enjoy; especially in those main points between us and the pope, with his appurtenances, the prelates. But he who thinks we are to pitch our tent here, and have attained the utmost prospect of reformation that the mortal glass, wherein

---

* **Impaled** (Lat. *in*, in; *palus*, a stake), fenced with stakes; *fortified*.—**Gadding rout**, *gadding rabble*. For *rout*, see Index.—**Christ urged.** See John xviii. 20.—**Disinured** (Lat. *dis*, asunder, without, not; *in*, in; Scot. *ure*, practice, use; O. Eng. *ure*, to exercise; Nor. Fr. *ure*, use; *enuer*, to inaugurate; Fr. *inaugurer*; Lat. *inaugurare*; Lat. *augurium*, prophecy), *rendered unfamiliar*.—**Alcoran** (Ar. *al*, the, and *koran*, book), *the Koran*.

we contemplate, can show us till we come to beatific vision,—that man by this very opinion declares that he is yet far short of truth.

Truth indeed came oncé into the world with her divine master, and was a perfect shape most glorious to look on. But when he ascended, and his apostles after him were laid asleep, then straight arose a wicked race of deceivers; who, as that story goes of the Egyptian Typhon with his conspirators, how they dealt with the good Osiris,* took the virgin Truth, hewed her lovely form into a thousand pieces, and scattered them to the four winds. From that time ever since, the sad friends of Truth, such as durst appear, imitating the careful search that Isis made for the mangled body of Osiris, went up and down, gathering up limb by limb still as they could find them. We have not yet found them all, Lords and Commons, nor ever shall do, till her master's second coming. He shall bring together every joint and member, and shall mould them into an immortal feature of loveliness and perfection! Suffer not these licensing prohibitions to stand at every place of opportunity, forbidding and disturbing them that continue seeking, that continue to do our obsequies to the torn body of our martyred saint.

We boast our light. But if we look not wisely on the sun itself, it smites us into darkness. Who can discern those planets that are oft combust, and those stars of brightest magnitude that rise and set with the sun, until the opposite motion of their orbs bring them to such a place in the firmament, where they may be seen evening or morning? The light which we have gained, was given us, not to be ever staring on, but by it to discover onward things more remote from our knowledge. It is not the unfrocking of a priest, the unmitring of a bishop, and the removing him from off the Presbyterian shoulders, that will make us a happy nation. No, if other things as great in the church and in the rule of life, both economical and political, be not looked into and reformed, we have looked so long upon the blaze that Zwinglius and Calvin have beaconed up to us, that we are stark blind.

There be who perpetually complain of schisms and sects, and make it such a calamity, that any man dissents from their maxims! It is their own pride and ignorance which causes the disturbing, who neither will hear with meekness, nor can convince; yet all must be suppressed which is not found in their Syntagma. They are the troublers, they are the dividers of unity, who neglect and permit not others to unite those dissevered pieces which are yet wanting to the body of truth. To be still searching what we know not by what we know, *still closing up truth to truth as we find it*, (for all her

---

* **Osiris**, one of the principal Egyptian deities, brother and husband of *Isis*. He reigned in Egypt. His brother **Typhon** (from τύφω, to *smoke*, and so a personification of volcanic eruptions) murdered him, and cut up his body into twenty-six parts, which were divided among the conspirators who had aided in the murder. (See *Typhon*, Index.) *Isis* made search for these pieces, and found them all but one. This she replaced with an imitation of sycamore wood. See Plutarch's treatise, *Of Isis and Osiris*.—**Combust**, *burned; eclipsed;* so near the sun as to be obscured by his light.—**Zwinglius**, *Ulric Zwingle* (1484–1531), a Swiss patriot and reformer, greatly distinguished for his learning, religious zeal, and heroic courage.—**Calvin**, *John* (1509–1564), "the theologian and organizing genius of the Reformed churches."—**Syntagma** (Greek), *connected system.*

Conspirators. Define *conspiracy*, *plot*, *cabal*, *combination*. Illustrate.

body is homogeneal and proportional,) *this is the golden rule in theology as well as in arithmetic*, and makes up the best harmony in a church; not the forced and outward union of cold and neutral and inwardly divided minds!

Lords and Commons of England! Consider what nation it is, whereof ye are, and whereof ye are the governors; a nation not slow and dull, but of a quick, ingenious, and piercing spirit; acute to invent, subtle and sinewy to discourse, not beneath the reach of any point the highest that human capacity can soar to. Therefore the studies of learning in her deepest sciences have been so ancient and so eminent among us, that writers of good antiquity and able judgment have been persuaded that even the school of Pythagoras * and the Persian wisdom took beginning from the old philosophy of this island. And that wise and civil Roman, Julius Agricola, who governed once here for Cæsar, preferred the natural wits of Britain before the labored studies of the French.

Nor is it for nothing that the grave and frugal Transylvanian sends out yearly, from as far as the mountainous borders of Russia and beyond the Hercynian wilderness, not their youth, but their staid men, to learn our language and our theologic arts. Yet that which is above all this, the favor and the love of heaven, we have great argument to think in a peculiar manner propitious and propending towards us. Why else was this nation chosen before any other, that out of her, as out of Sion, should be proclaimed and sounded forth the first tidings and trumpet of reformation to all Europe? And had it not been the obstinate perverseness of our prelates against the divine and admirable spirit of Wickliffe, to suppress him as a schismatic and innovator, perhaps neither the Bohemian Huss and Jerome, no, nor the name of Luther, or of Calvin, had been ever known: the glory of reforming all our neighbors had been completely ours!

But now, as our obdurate clergy have with violence demeaned the matter, we are become hitherto the latest and the backwardest scholars of whom God offered to have made us the teachers. Now once again, by all concurrence of signs and by the general instinct of holy and devout men, as they daily and solemnly express their thoughts, God is decreeing to begin some new and great period in his church, even to the reforming of reformation itself. What does he, then, but reveal himself to his servants, and, as his

* **Pythagoras** (B. C. 580–504?), a Greek philosopher, founder of a religious, philosophical, and political association in southern Italy. He was a native of Samos, and a man of wonderful wisdom.—**Persian wisdom.** This suggests the *Magi*, "the wise men from the east."—**This island.** The Druids knew geometry, medicine, natural philosophy, and something of astronomy.—**Agricola** (A.D. 40–93), a celebrated Roman commander in England in the reign of Domitian. See Tacitus, *Agric.* XXI.—**Transylvanian.** Transylvania lay mostly in the basin of the Danube, east of Hungary.—**Hercynian wilderness,** a very extensive forest of Germany, including, among others, what is known as the Black Forest, the Hartz Forest, etc.—**Propending** (Lat. *pro*, forward; *pendēre*, to hang or be suspended), *leaning*, *inclining*.—**Sion.** The largest of the hills on which Jerusalem was built. It was the strongest part of the city, and became the royal residence of David and his successors. Hence, Jerusalem itself.—**Wickliffe. . . . Huss,** Already mentioned on page 209. Wickliffe was a much more splendid character than is commonly supposed. See p. 209.—**Jerome** (1378–1416), Jerome of Prague. Suffered martyrdom by decree of the Council of Constance.—**Luther** (1483–1546).—**Calvin** (1509–1564).

Subtle, *cunning*, *crafty*, *sly*, *wily*, *acute*, *refined*, *shrewd*, *discerning*. Discriminate among these. Illustrate.

manner is, first to his Englishmen? I say, as his manner is, first to us, though we mark not the method of his counsels, and are unworthy.

Behold now this vast city! a city of refuge, the mansion-house of liberty, encompassed and surrounded with his protection! The shop of war hath not there more anvils and hammers waking, to fashion out the plates and instruments of armed justice in defence of beleaguered truth, than there be pens and heads there, sitting by their studious lamps, musing, searching, revolving new notions and ideas wherewith to present, as with their homage and their fealty, the approaching reformation! others as fast reading, trying all things, assenting to the force of reason and convincement!

What could a man require more from a nation so pliant and so prone to seek after knowledge? What wants there to such a towardly and pregnant soil but wise and faithful laborers, to make a knowing people, a nation of prophets, of sages, and of worthies? We reckon more than five months yet to harvest. There need not be five weeks, had we but eyes to lift up. The fields are white already.

Where there is much desire to learn, there of necessity will be much arguing, much writing, many opinions. For opinion in good men is but knowledge in the making. Under these fantastic terrors of sect and schism, we wrong the earnest and zealous thirst after knowledge and understanding, which God hath stirred up in this city. What some lament of, we rather should rejoice at; should rather praise this pious forwardness among men to reassume the ill deputed care of their religion into their own hands again. A little generous prudence, a little forbearance of one another, and some grain of charity, might win all these diligences to join, and unite into one general and brotherly search after truth, could we but forego this prelatical tradition of crowding free consciences and Christian liberties into canons and precepts of men.

I doubt not, if some great and worthy stranger should come among us, wise to discern the mould and temper of a people, and how to govern it; observing the high hopes and aims, the diligent alacrity of our extended thoughts and reasonings in the pursuance of truth and freedom; but that he would cry out as Pyrrhus did, admiring the Roman docility and courage, "If such were my Epirots, I would not despair the greatest design that could be attempted to make a church or kingdom happy."

Yet these are the men cried out against for schismatics and sectaries! As if, while the temple of the Lord was building, some cutting, some squaring the marble, others hewing the cedars, there should be a sort of irrational men, who could not consider there must be many schisms and many dissections made in the quarry and in the timber, ere the house of God can be built. And when every stone is laid artfully together, it cannot be united

---

* **Towardly,** turned to do or learn; *apt*, docile, compliant with duty.—**Pyrrhus** (B. C. 318–272), king of Epirus (a country of Greece lying along the Adriatic), invaded Italy B. C. 280. —**Laid artfully together,** *laid skillfully together with the rest.* This paragraph is one of extraordinary beauty. The argument is especially felicitous.

Religion, theology, morality, piety, sanctity, holiness, devotion. Discriminate and illustrate.

into a continuity: it can but be contiguous in this world. Neither can every piece of the building be of one form. Nay, rather, the perfection consists in this, that out of many moderate varieties and brotherly dissimilitudes that are not vastly disproportional, arises the goodly and the graceful symmetry that commends the whole pile and structure.

Let us therefore be more considerate builders, more wise in spiritual architecture, when great reformation is expected. For now the time seems come, wherein Moses,* the great prophet, may sit in heaven rejoicing to see that memorable and glorious wish of his fulfilled, when not only our seventy elders, but all the Lord's people are become prophets. No marvel then though some men, and some good men too perhaps, but young in goodness, as Joshua then was, envy them. They fret, and, out of their own weakness, are in agony, lest these divisions and subdivisions will undo us. The adversary again applauds, and waits the hour. "When they have branched themselves out," saith he, "small enough, into parties and partitions, then will be our time." Fool! He sees not the firm root, out of which we all grow, though into branches; nor will beware until he see our small divided maniples cutting through at every angle of his ill-united and unwieldly brigade. And that we are to hope better of all these supposed sects and schisms, and that we shall not need that solicitude, honest perhaps, though over-timorous, of them that vex in this behalf; but shall laugh in the end at those malicious applauders of our differences, I have these reasons to persuade me:—

First, when a city shall be, as it were, besieged and blocked about, her navigable river infested, inroads and incursions round, defiance and battle oft rumored to be marching up even to her walls and suburb trenches; that then the people, or the greater part, more than at other times, wholly taken up with the study of highest and most important matters to be reformed, should be disputing, reasoning, reading, inventing, discoursing, even to a rarity and admiration, things not before discoursed or written of; argues, first, a singular good will, contentedness, and confidence in your prudent foresight and safe government, Lords and Commons, and from thence derives itself to a gallant bravery and well grounded contempt of their enemies. As if there were no small number of as great spirits among us as his was, who, when Rome was nigh besieged by Hannibal, being in the city, bought that piece of ground at no cheap rate, whereon Hannibal himself encamped his own regiment.

Next, it is a lively and cheerful presage of our happy success and victory. For, as, in a body when the blood is fresh, the spirits pure and vigorous, not only to vital but to rational faculties, and those in the acutest and the

* **Moses** (B. C. 1500). See Numbers xi. 29.—**When a city,** etc. It must be remembered that the nation was at this time in the midst of the civil war which overthrew the monarchy and established the commonwealth.—**Hannibal** (B. C. 247–183), one of the greatest of warriors, and the most formidable enemy of Rome. He led a powerful army of Carthaginians across the Alps into Italy. When the incident related in the text took place (B. C. 211), Hannibal is said to have retorted by putting up for sale at auction the shops in the vicinity of the Roman Forum.

Contiguous. Synonymes, *adjoining*, *adjacent*, *neighboring*. Meanings?

pertest operations of wit and subtlety, it argues in what good plight and constitution the body is; so, when the cheerfulness of the people is so sprightly up as that it has not only wherewith to guard well its own freedom and safety, but to spare, and to bestow upon the solidest and sublimest points of controversy and new invention; it betokens us not degenerated, nor drooping to a fatal decay, but casting off the old and wrinkled skin of corruption to outlive these pangs, and wax young again, entering the glorious ways of truth and prosperous virtue, destined to become great and honorable in these latter ages. Methinks I see in my mind a noble and puissant nation, rousing herself like a strong man after sleep, and shaking her invincible locks! Methinks I see * her as an eagle, mewing her mighty youth, and kindling her undazzled eyes at the full mid-day beam, purging and unscaling her long abused sight at the fountain itself of heavenly radiance! while the whole noise of timorous and flocking birds, with those also that love the twilight, flutter about, amazed at what she means, and in their envious gabble would prognosticate a year of sects and schism!

What should ye do then? Should ye suppress all this flowery crop of knowledge and new light sprung up and yet springing daily in this city? Should ye set an oligarchy of twenty engrossers over it, to bring a famine upon our minds again, when we shall know nothing but what is measured to us by their bushel? Believe it, Lords and Commons, they who counsel ye to such a suppressing, do as good as bid ye suppress yourselves! And I will soon show how. If it be desired to know the immediate cause of all this free writing and free speaking, there cannot be assigned a truer than your own mild and free and humane government. It is the liberty, Lords and Commons, which your own valorous and happy counsels have purchased us; liberty, which is the nurse of all great wits! This is that which hath rarefied and enlightened our spirits like the influence of heaven! This is that which hath enfranchised, enlarged, and lifted up our apprehensions degrees above themselves! Ye cannot make us now less capable, less know-

---

* **Methinks I see**, etc. These are truly Miltonic images.[1]—**Mewing** (Lat. *mutare*, to change; Fr. *muer*), molting, casting the feathers, *renewing*. See *mew*, Index.—**Twenty engrossers.** The twenty master-printers, named in the fifteenth section of the Star Chamber decree promulgated in the thirteenth year of King Charles I. An engrosser was one who purchased the whole (*gross*, Fr. *gros*, *grosse*) of the articles for sale in a market, so as to be able to demand what price he pleased. Having a perfect monopoly, he could "bring a famine" in respect to those wares.

[1] It will be found that a rhythmical movement pervades the finest prose pieces. This passage has been thus divided:—

"Methinks I see in my mind a noble and puissant nation
Rousing herself like a strong man after sleep,
And shaking her invincible locks! Methinks
I see her as an eagle muing her mighty youth,
And kindling her undazzled eyes at the full mid-day beam;
Purging and unscaling her long-abused sight
At the fountain itself of heavenly radiance!
While the whole noise of timorous and flocking birds,
With those also that love the twilight,
Flutter about; amazed at what she means,
And in their envious gabble would prognosticate
A year of sects and schisms." (See the sketch of Bunyan's life.)

Puissant, *potent*, *powerful*, *mighty*, *strong*, *vigorous*, *forcible*. Give and exemplify the true meaning of each of these.

ing, less eagerly pursuing of the truth, unless ye first make yourselves, that made us so, less the lovers, less the founders of our true liberty. We can grow ignorant again, brutish, formal, and slavish, as ye found us. But you then must first become that which ye cannot be; oppressive, arbitrary, and tyrannous, as they were from whom ye have freed us. That our hearts are now more capacious, our thoughts more erected to the search and expectation of greatest and exactest things, is the issue of your own virtue propagated in us. Ye cannot suppress that, unless ye reinforce an abrogated and merciless law, that fathers may despatch at will their own children! And who shall then stick closest to ye and excite others? Not he who takes up arms for coat and conduct,* and his four nobles of Danegelt. Although I dispraise not the defense of just immunities, yet love my peace better, if that were all. *Give me the liberty to know, to utter, and to argue freely according to conscience, above all liberties!*

What would be best advised then, if it be found so hurtful and so unequal to suppress opinions for the newness, or the unsuitableness to a customary acceptance, will not be my task to say. I shall only repeat what I have learned from one of your own honorable number, a right noble and pious lord, who, had he not sacrificed his life and fortunes to the church and commonwealth, we had not now missed and bewailed a worthy and undoubted patron of this argument. Ye know him, I am sure; yet I, for honor's sake, (and may it be eternal to him!) shall name him, the lord Brooke. He, writing of episcopacy, and by the way treating of sects and schisms, left ye his vote, or rather now the last words of his dying charge, which I know will ever be of dear and honored regard with ye, so full of meekness and breathing charity, that, next to His last testament who bequeathed love and peace to his disciples, I cannot call to mind where I have read or heard words more mild and peaceful. He there exhorts us to hear with patience and humility those, however they may be miscalled, that desire to live purely, in such a use of God's ordinances as the best guidance of their conscience gives them, and to tolerate them, though in some disconformity to

---

* **Coat and conduct.** [In some editions, as in the *English Reprints* of Alex. Murray and Sons, *coat* is printed *cote.* "*Cote*" means *cottage, cot.* Does *cote and conduct*, then, mean "firesides, and freedom of travel or commerce?" Or does *coat* mean *coat-of-arms, hereditary rank, armorial bearings?* Does *conduct* mean *convoy?* Was the expression *coat and conduct* (or *cote and conduct*) proverbial?]—**Noble.** A *noble*, "half a mark," was a gold coin equivalent to about $1.61. So called because gold was regarded as a *noble* metal.—**Danegelt** (Low Lat. *Dacini*, fr. *Dacia*, the original home of the Danes? A. S. *gild;* Dan. *gield;* A. S., Ger., D., *geld*, money), *Dane-money*, an annual tax imposed, Webster says, by the Danes on the English people. Better, an assessment, at first one shilling, afterwards two, on every "hide" of land, either to maintain troops to oppose the Danes, or to buy peace. It was a tax on real-estate, first levied in the reign of Ethelred in the year 991, and discontinued in the reign of Henry II., in the year 1173. (Spelled also *Danegeld.*)—**If that** (*i. e.*, exemption, or immunity) **were all.**—**Brooke,** *Robert Greville, Lord Brooke* (1607–1642). Not to be confounded with the poet *Fulke* Greville, Lord Brooke, who died in 1628. Robert Greville's book on the nature of English Episcopacy was printed in 1641. The manner of his death recalls (it perhaps suggested) Milton's famous sentence, "He who destroys a good book kills reason itself, kills the image of God, as it were, *in the eye.*" Lord Brooke commanded the parliamentary forces attacking the Church-close at Litchfield, March 2, 1642. "Though harnessed with plate-armor *cap-à-pie,* he was shot from the church in the eye by one Diot, a clergyman's son (who could neither hear nor speak), as he stood in a door (whither he came to see the occasion of a sudden shout made by the soldiers), of which he instantly died."—*A. à-Wood, Athenæ Oxonienses*, II., 433, Bliss's edition, 1815. (Let the student correct this quotation from Wood.)

Immunities, privileges, prerogatives, exemptions, rights. Distinguish, and give appropriate sentences in illustration.

ourselves. The book itself will tell us more at large, being published to the world, and dedicated to the parliament by him, who, both for his life and for his death, deserves that what advice he left, be not laid by without perusal.

And now the time in special is, by privilege to write and speak what may help to the further discussing of matters in agitation. The temple of Janus,* with his two controversial faces, might now not unsignificantly be set open. *And though all the winds of doctrine were let loose to play upon the earth, so Truth be in the field, we do injuriously by licensing and prohibiting to misdoubt her strength. Let her and Falsehood grapple! Who ever knew Truth put to the worse, in a free and open encounter?* Her confuting is the best and surest suppressing. He who hears what praying there is for light and clear knowledge to be sent down among us, would think of other matters to be constituted, beyond the discipline of Geneva framed and fabricked already to our hands.

Yet when the new light which we beg for, shines in upon us, there be who envy and oppose, if it come not first in at their casements. What a collusion is this, whenas we are exhorted by the wise man to use diligence, "to seek for wisdom as for hidden treasures," early and late, that another order shall enjoin us to know nothing but by statute?

When a man hath been laboring the hardest labor in the deep mines of knowledge, hath furnished out his findings in all their equipage, drawn forth his reasons as it were a battle ranged, scattered and defeated all objections in his way, calls out his adversary into the plain, offers him the advantage of wind and sun, if he please, only that he may try the matter by dint of argument; for his opponents then to skulk, to lay ambushments, to keep a narrow bridge of licensing where the challenger should pass, though it be valor enough in soldiership, is but weakness and cowardice in the wars of Truth. *For who knows not that Truth is strong, next to the Almighty? She needs no policies, nor stratagems, nor licensings, to make her victorious!* Those are the shifts and the defences that Error uses against her power. Give her but room, and do not bind her when she sleeps; for then she speaks not true, as the old Proteus did, who spake oracles only when he was caught and bound: but then rather she turns herself into all shapes, except her own, and perhaps tunes her voice according to the time, as Micaiah did before Ahab, until she be adjured into her own likeness. Yet is it not impossible that she may have more shapes than one? What else is all that rank of things indifferent, wherein Truth may be on this side, or on the other, without being unlike herself? What but a vain shadow else is the abolition of "those ordinances, that hand-writing nailed to the cross"?

* **Janus,** an old Italian deity, the sun-god. He was represented with a face on the front, and another on the back of his head. The gates of the principal temple of Janus at Rome were always open in time of war, and shut in time of peace.—**Proteus,** in Greek mythology, a sea-god, the shepherd of Neptune's flocks. He had the gift of prophecy, but whoever would avail himself of it was obliged to seize and bind him. Whereupon Proteus would turn himself into many strange shapes; but, if held fast, he would finally resume his proper form and utter truthful predictions.—**Micaiah.** See 1 Kings, xxii., especially the 15th, 16th, and 17th verses.—**Vain shadow.** See Colossians ii. 14.

Stratagem, artifice, trick, fraud, cunning, duplicity, deceit, finesse, chicanery. Meanings?

What great purchase is this Christian liberty which Paul so often boasts of? His doctrine* is, that he who eats or eats not, regards a day or regards it not, may do either to the Lord. How many other things might be tolerated in peace, and left to conscience, had we but charity, and were it not the chief strong hold of our hypocrisy to be ever judging one another!

I fear yet this iron yoke of outward conformity hath left a slavish print upon our necks. The ghost of a linen decency yet haunts us. We stumble and are impatient at the least dividing of one visible congregation from another, though it be not in fundamentals; and through our forwardness to suppress, and our backwardness to recover any enthralled piece of truth out of the gripe of custom, we care not to keep truth separated from truth; which is the fiercest rent and disunion of all. We do not see that while we still affect by all means a rigid external formality, we may as soon fall again into a gross conforming stupidity, a stark and dead congealment of "wood and hay and stubble" forced and frozen together, which is more to the sudden degenerating of a church than many subdichotomies of petty schisms. Not that I can think well of every light separation; or that all in a church is to be expected "gold and silver and precious stones." It is not possible for man to sever the wheat from the tares, the good fish from the other fry. That must be the angels' ministry at the end of mortal things.

Yet if all cannot be of one mind, as who looks they should be? this doubtless is more wholesome, more prudent, and more Christian, that many be tolerated, rather than all compelled. I mean not tolerated popery, and open superstition, which, as it extirpates all religious and civil supremacies, so itself should be extirpate; provided first that all charitable and compassionate means be used to win and regain the weak and the misled. That also which is impious or evil absolutely, either against faith or manners, no law can possibly permit, that intends not to unlaw itself. But those neighboring differences, or rather indifferences, are what I speak of, whether in some point of doctrine or of discipline; which, though they may be many, yet need not interrupt the unity of spirit, if we could but find among us the bond of peace.

In the mean while, if any one would write, and bring his helpful hand to the slow moving reformation which we labor under; if Truth hath spoken to him before others, or but seemed at least to speak; who hath so bejesuited us that we should trouble that man with asking license to do so worthy a deed? and not consider this, that if it come to prohibiting, there is not aught more likely to be prohibited than truth itself? whose first appearance to our eyes, bleared and dimmed with prejudice and custom, is more unsightly and unplausible than many errors, even as the person is of many a great man, slight and contemptible to see to.

---

* **Doctrine** (Lat. *doctrina*, teaching; *docere*, to teach). See Romans xiv. 6.—**Wood, hay,** etc. See 1 Corinthians iii. 12.—**Wheat,** Matthew xiii. 24-30; 47. 48.—**Tolerated popery,** etc. So Milton excepts popery, as he calls it, and bases his exception on civil grounds. It must be remembered that the popes in those ages aimed at political supremacy, and pretended to absolve all their adherents from obedience to the civil Protestant power.—**Impious or evil absolutely.** Like the pamphlet entitled, *Killing no Murder*.—**Contemptible to see to,** *contemptible to the outward vision.*

And what do they tell us vainly of new opinions, when this very opinion of theirs, that none must be heard but whom they like, is the worst and newest opinion of all others, and is the chief cause why sects and schisms do so much abound, and true knowledge is kept at a distance from us? Besides yet a greater danger which is in it.

For when God shakes a kingdom, with strong and healthful commotions, to a general reforming, it is not untrue that many sectaries and false teachers are then busiest in seducing. But yet more true it is, that God then raises to his own work men of rare abilities and more than common industry, not only to look back and revise what hath been taught heretofore, but to gain further, and to go on some new enlightened steps in the discovery of truth. For such is the order of God's enlightening his church, to dispense and deal out by degrees his beam, so as our earthly eyes may best sustain it.

Neither is God appointed and confined, where and out of what place these his chosen shall be first heard to speak. For he sees not as man sees, chooses not as man chooses; lest we should devote ourselves again to set places, and assemblies, and outward callings of men, planting our faith one while in the old Convocation * house, and another while in the chapel at Westminster; when all the faith and religion that shall be there canonized, is not sufficient, without plain convincement and the charity of patient in-

* **Convocation,** the assembly of the representatives of the English Church at the opening of every new parliament. Among other powers, it had authority to examine and censure heretical and schismatical books and persons. "The convocation was prorogued in 1717, and has never sat again for any business." *Hallam.*—**Chapel.** There are nine chapels in a semicircle around the east end of Westminster Abbey. The most interesting are that of Edward the Confessor, and the famous chapel of King Henry VII. The latter is here referred to. *Chapel* is said to be from Low Lat. *capella*, a *hood* or *cowl*. "The kings of France in war carried St. Martin's hat, *capella*, into the field. As a precious relic it was kept in a tent which was also thence called *capella*, Fr. *chapelle*. The name was afterwards given to inferior places of worship. The priest who had the custody of the tent and the hat, was called *capellanus*, now *chaplain*." The word is akin to Lat. *caput*, head; A. S. *heáfod*, head; Ger. *haupt;* Gr. κεφαλή; Fr. *chapeau*.[1]—**Westminster.** The city of Westminster is the west part of the metropolis of London. Its population is about two hundred and seventy-five thousand.

Abilities, gifts, endowments, talents, capacities, faculties. Define and illustrate each.

[1] NOTE.—*Grimm's Law* (p. 23) is here exemplified. To refresh the student's memory, we repeat certain points. To change Latin or Greek to English, *change smooth mutes to rough; rough to middle; middle to smooth.* To change Latin or Greek to German, *change smooth to middle; middle to rough; rough to smooth.* With some exceptions, the following words illustrate these principles:

		Lat.	Eng.	Ger.
Lat. *c* (for *k*) becomes *h* (for *kh*) in Eng. and Ger.	Thus,	*centum,*	*hundred,*	*hundert.*
	"	*cannabis,*	*hemp,*	*hanf.*
" *h* (for *kh*) " *g* " "	"	*hostis,*	*guest,*	*gast.*
	"	*hædus,*	*goat,*	*geiss.*
" *g* " *k* or *c* " "	"	*granum,*	*corn, kernel,*	*corn, kern.*
	"	*gena,*	*chin,*	*kinn.*
" *t* " *th* in Eng., and *d* in Ger.	"	*tonitru,*	*thunder,*	*donner.*
	"	*tres,*	*three,*	*drei.*
" *th* (Gr. *th*) " *d* " " *t* "	" Gr.	*thugater,*	*daughter,*	*tochter.*
	" "	*ther,*	*deer,*	*thier.*
" *d* " *t* " " *z* "	" Lat.	*decem,*	*ten.*	*zehn.*
	" "	*dens,*	*tooth,*	*zahn.*
" *p* *f* " *f* or *v* "	" "	*pater,*	*father,*	*vater.*
	" Gr.	*pente,*	*five,*	*fünf.*
" *f* " *b* " "	" Lat.	*fagus,*	*beech,*	*buche.*
" *b* " *p* " *f* "	" "	*cannabis,*	*hemp,*	*hanf.*

See Fowler's English Grammar, p. 176 (unabridged, edition of 1868).

struction, to supple the least bruise of conscience, to edify the meanest Christian who desires to walk in the spirit and not in the letter of human trust, for all the number of voices that can be there made. No! though Harry the Seventh* himself there, with all his liege tombs about him, should lend them voices from the dead to swell their number.

And if the men be erroneous who appear to be the leading schismatics, what withholds us but our sloth, our self-will, and distrust in the right cause, that we do not give them gentle meetings and gentle dismissions? that we debate not and examine the matter thoroughly with liberal and frequent audience, if not for their sakes, yet for our own? seeing no man who hath tasted learning, but will confess the many ways of profiting by those, who, not contented with stale receipts, are able to manage and set forth new positions to the world. And were they but as the dust and cinders of our feet, so long as in that notion they may yet serve to polish and brighten the armory of truth, even for that respect they were not utterly to be cast away. But if they be of those whom God hath fitted for the special use of these times with eminent and ample gifts, and those perhaps neither among the priests nor among the Pharisees, and we in the haste of a precipitant zeal shall make no distinction, but resolve to stop their mouths, because we fear they come with new and dangerous opinions, as we commonly fore-judge them ere we understand them; no less than woe to us, while, thinking thus to defend the gospel, we are found the persecutors!

There have been not a few since the beginning of this parliament, both of the presbytery and others, who, by their unlicensed books to the contempt of an *imprimatur*, first broke that triple ice clung about our hearts, and taught the people to see day. I hope that none of those were the persuaders to renew upon us this bondage which they themselves have wrought so much good by contemning. But if neither the check that Moses gave to young Joshua, nor the countermand which our Saviour gave to young John, who was so ready to prohibit those whom he thought unlicensed, be [not] enough to admonish our elders how unacceptable to God their testy mood of prohibiting is; if neither their own remembrance what evil hath abounded in the church by this let of licensing, and what good they themselves have begun by transgressing it, be [not] enough, but that they will persuade and execute the most Dominican part of the Inquisition over us, and are already with one foot in the stirrup, so active at suppressing; it would be no unequal distribution in the first place to suppress the suppressors themselves, whom the change of their condition hath puffed up, more than their late experience of harder times hath made wise.

And as for regulating the press, let no man think to have the honor of advising ye better than yourselves have done in that order published next

---

* **Henry the Seventh** (1456-1509) built the beautiful chapel called by his name, at the east end of Westminster Abbey.—**Beginning of this parliament.** The famous *Long Parliament*, which met for the first time in November, 1640. It was violently dissolved by Cromwell in April, 1653.—**Check that Moses,** etc. See Numbers xi. 24-30.—**Young John.** See Luke ix. 49, 50.—**Let,** hinderance, *impediment.* See p. 28.—**Dominican.** See this word, p. 227.—**That order.** The order made by the House of Commons, January 29, 1641-2.

before this, "That no book be printed, unless the printer's and the author's name, or at least the printer's, be registered." Those which otherwise come forth, if they be found mischievous and libellous, the fire and the executioner will be the timeliest and the most effectual remedy that man's prevention can use. For this authentic Spanish policy of licensing books, if I have said aught, will prove the most unlicensed book itself within a short while, and was the immediate image of a star-chamber * decree to that purpose, made in those very times when that court did the rest of those her pious works, for which she is now fallen from the stars with Lucifer. Whereby ye may guess what kind of state prudence, what love of the people, what care of religion, or good manners, there was at the contriving; although with singular hypocrisy it pretended to bind books to their good behavior. And how it got the upper hand of your precedent order so well constituted before, if we may believe those men whose profession gives them cause to inquire most, it may be doubted there was in it the fraud of some old patentees and monopolizers in the trade of bookselling; who, under pretence of the poor in their company not to be defrauded, and the just retaining of each man his several copy, which God forbid should be gainsaid! brought divers glozing colors to the house. Which were indeed but colors, and serving to no end except it be to exercise a superiority over their neighbors; men who do not therefore labor in an honest profession, to which learning is indebted, that they should be made other men's vassals.

Another end is thought was aimed at by some of them, in procuring by petition this order; that having power in their hands, malignant books might the easier escape abroad, as the event shows. But of these sophisms and *elenchs* of merchandise, I skill not. This I know, that errors, in a good government and in a bad, are equally almost incident. For what magistrate may not be misinformed, and much the sooner, if liberty of printing be reduced into the power of a few? But to redress willingly and speedily what hath been erred, and in highest authority to esteem a plain advertisement more than others have done a sumptuous bribe, is a virtue, honored Lords and Commons, answerable to your highest actions, and whereof none can participate but greatest and wisest men!

---

* **Star-chamber,** so called from the gilded stars on the ceiling of the council-chamber in the palace of Westminster. (Webster, however, suggests that it was "so called either from A. S.) *steoran, styran,* to steer, to govern; or from being held in a room at the exchequer, where the chests containing certain Jewish contracts and obligations called *starrs,* from the Hebrew *shetar* pronounced *shtar* were kept.") This court is mentioned as early as the time of Edward III. (1327–1377). It sat in cases not capital, and without the intervention of a jury. In 1641 it was abolished by act of parliament.—**Decree.** This decree was made in July, 1637.—**Lucifer** (Lat. *lux, lucis,* light; *fero.* I bear; the English words following Grimm's Law, it will be observed), *the bringer of light; the planet* which is the morning star. See Isaiah xiv. 12, where the prophet, by a bold metaphor, applies the name to the King of Babylon. The mention of the *star*-chamber seems to suggest its Lucifer-like fall. The name Lucifer is often used to designate Satan.—**The just retaining,** etc. We should say, *the just retaining* (or *retention*) *by each man of his,* etc.—**Elenchs** (Lat. *elenchus,* from the Gr. ἔλεγχος, confutation), *tricky arguments,* fallacies adapted to deceive.—**Skill not,** *have no skill.* See *cannot skill,* p. 229.—**This I know,** etc. Reconstruct this sentence so as to make it more euphonious and clear.—**Advertisement** (Lat. *ad,* to; *vertĕre,* to turn; Eng. *advert.* to turn the mind or attention to; *advertise,* to give notice to, or give notice of), *notification,* act of giving information.

Remedy, cure, medicine, physic, relief, counteraction, antidote, reparation, aid, help, assistance. Explain each, and embody in sentences.

Write out a synopsis of Milton's reasoning in this celebrated treatise. Select those arguments that seem to you the most conclusive, and write an essay setting forth and illustrating each. Suggest other arguments, not named by Milton, in favor of freedom of the press. What limitations or checks, if any, has experience shown to be needful? Trace the successive steps by which the press has become free in America. What degree of freedom of the press prevails in other countries? Was Milton consistent in denying entire toleration to what he terms "popery?" Who, besides Milton, have been great literary champions of freedom? What could be learned of Milton, if we possessed only this treatise? What effect, if any, was produced in the time of the Commonwealth by this treatise? To what extent was the press unrestricted under Cromwell? Write an essay covering the ground of each of these questions.

ODE ON THE MORNING OF CHRIST'S NATIVITY.

"The *Ode on the Nativity* is perhaps the finest in the English language."—*Hallam.*

The *Ode on the Morning of Christ's Nativity* is thus referred to by Milton himself, in an elegy written in Latin, a few days after Christmas, 1629, to his friend Charles Diodati :—

"We are engaged in singing the heavenly birth of the King of Peace, and the happy age promised by the holy books, and the infant cries and cradling, in a manger, under a poor roof, of that God who rules, with his Father, the Kingdom of Heaven ; and the sky with the new-sprung star in it, and the ethereal choirs of hymning angels, and the gods of heathen eld suddenly fleeing to their endangered fanes. This is the gift which we have presented to Christ's natal day. On that very morning, at daybreak, it was first conceived. The verses, which are composed in the vernacular, await your criticism : you shall be the judge to whom I shall recite them."

This little poem unites, in an extraordinary degree, thought, feeling, imagery, and personification ; a fusion which has been admired by some critics as an excellence peculiar to Shakespeare. There are in some stanzas an exquisite airiness and delicacy, while in others the tone rises and swells into thunderous melody. In its lyric fire Milton is equalled by few among the English poets. He is particularly happy in the choice of his subject, whose tender sweetness and royal glory captivated his young heart. Dryden's *Ode on St. Cecilia's Day* seems comparatively on a small theme and by a small man.

ON THE MORNING OF CHRIST'S NATIVITY.

THIS is the month, and this the happy morn,
  Wherein the Son of Heaven's Eternal King,
Of wedded maid and virgin mother born,
  Our great redemption from above did bring; *(Joyous yet serious.*)*
  For so the holy sages† once did sing,
That He our deadly forfeit should release,
And with His Father work us a perpetual peace.

That glorious form, that light unsufferable,
  And that far-beaming blaze of majesty,
Wherewith He wont at Heaven's high council-table *(Reverence and admiration with love.)*
  To sit the midst of trinal Unity,
  He laid aside, and here with us to be,
Forsook the courts of everlasting day,
And chose with us a darksome house of mortal clay.

---

* This marginal analysis is designed to aid in reading. The student should make it more minute. See p. 193.

† **Sages** (Lat. *sapĕre*, to be wise; Fr. *sage*, wise), the Hebrew prophets.—**Forfeit** (Lat. *foris*, out of doors; *facere*, to do; *forisfactum*, an out-of-the-way act, a crime ; hence, *penalty.*)—**Wont,** was accustomed. See *woned*, p. 30.

Say, heavenly Muse,* shall not thy sacred vein
  Afford a present to the Infant God?
Hast thou no verse, no hymn, or solemn strain,
  To welcome Him to this His new abode,
  Now while the heaven, by the sun's team untrod,
Hath took no print of the approaching light,
And all the spangled host keep watch in squadrons bright?

Animation and seriousness.

See, how, from far, upon the eastern road,
  The star-led wizards haste with odors sweet!
Oh! run, prevent them with thy humble ode,
  And lay it lowly at His blessed feet:
  Have thou the honor first thy Lord to greet,
And join thy voice unto the angel choir,
From out His secret altar touched with hallowed fire.†

Animation.

---

1. It was the winter wild—
While the heaven-born Child
  All meanly wrapt in the rude manger lies!
Nature, in awe to Him,
Had doffed her gaudy trim,
  With her great Master so to sympathize:
It was no season then for her
To wanton with the sun, her lusty paramour.

Awe.

2. Only with speeches fair,
She woos the gentle air
  To hide her guilty front with innocent snow;
And on her naked shame,
Pollute with sinful blame,
  The saintly veil of maiden white to throw;
Confounded, that her Maker's eyes
Should look so near upon her foul deformities.

Awe and tenderness.

---

* **Muse.** The "heavenly Muse" with Milton is the Holy Spirit. So in the beginning of the seventh book of *Paradise Lost.*—**Vein,** *disposition* or *cast of genius; course of thought.*—**Wizards.** *Magi.* See Matthew ii. *Wizard* is fr. *wise*, and the suffix *-ard*, of Teutonic origin. This suffix is A. S. *heard*, strong; akin to the Ger. *hart*, Fr. *-arde;* Eng. and D. *hard.* It denotes some characteristic trait; as *Reinhart*, strong in counsel; *Godard* or *Goddard*, strong in God; *Bernhart* or *Bernard*, strong like a bear; *Gebhart*, strong in giving, bountiful; or it enlarges the meaning and denotes some *excess*, as *drunkard*, a hard drinker; so *dullard*, *laggard*, *haggard*, *niggard*, *sluggard*, *wizard*, *braggart*, *dotard*, *bastard*, *coward*, *buzzard.* See, however, the termination *-ard* in Worcester's Dict. In some words the enlarged meaning is less obvious, or has faded entirely out; as in *billiard*, *bombard*, *hazard*, *mustard*, *poniard*, *standard*, *tankard.* —**Touched** *with fire.* See Isaiah vi. 6, 7.—**Doffed** (*do* and *off*, the opposite of *don*, *do* and *on*).—**Gaudy trim.** Her green garments embroidered with flowers.

† It will be observed that these four preliminary stanzas correspond precisely in poetical form with those of the extract from Chaucer. In the hymn proper, the first, second, fourth, and fifth lines of the stanza contain, each, three iambic feet; the third and sixth lines are English heroic, containing the usual five iambic feet; the seventh line has four iambic; the eighth, which is an Alexandrine, contains six. The combination is agreeable, though highly artificial.

Distinguish and illustrate the meanings of *wizards*, *magi*, *seers*, *soothsayers*, *necromancers*, *diviners*, *conjurers*, *fortune-tellers*, *clairvoyants*, *sorcerers.* Other synonymes?

Tranquillity passing into calm joy.

3. But He, her fears to cease,
Sent down the meek-eyèd Peace.
She, crowned with olive* green, came softly sliding
Down through the turning sphere,
His ready harbinger,
With turtle wing the amorous clouds dividing;
And, waving wide her myrtle wand,
She strikes a universal peace through sea and land.

Tranquillity and awe.

4. No war, or battle's sound,
Was heard the world around:
The idle spear and shield were high up hung;
The hooked chariot stood
Unstained with hostile blood;
The trumpet spake not to the armed throng;
And kings sat still with awful eye,
As if they surely knew their sovereign Lord was by!

Tranquillity.

5. But peaceful was the night,
Wherein the Prince of Light
His reign of peace upon the earth began;
The winds, with wonder whist,
Smoothly the waters kissed,
Whispering new joys to the mild Ocean,
Who now hath quite forgot to rave,
While birds of calm sit brooding on the charmed wave.

Tranquillity.

6. The stars, with deep amaze,
Stand fixed in steadfast gaze,
Bending one way their precious influence;
And will not take their flight,
For all the morning light,
Or Lucifer that often warned them thence;
But in their glimmering orbs did glow,
Until the Lord himself bespake, and bid them go.

7. And though the shady gloom
Had given day her room,

---

* **Olive.** The olive branch was an emblem of peace. So the turtle-dove.—**Turning sphere.** The whole heavens were supposed to move around the earth.—**Amorous**, the very clouds are personified and share in the feeling of love.—**Myrtle.** The myrtle, sacred to Venus, came to typify *love.*—**No war.** "In a longitudinal line of four thousand miles, and within a circuit of ten thousand, the energies of Roman genius had hushed all wars."—**Hooked.** The war chariots of antiquity sometimes had long crooked steel blades or scythes, fastened to the axles, or to the fellies of the wheels. *Hooked* is dissyl.—**Ocean.** Trisyllable. Lat. *oceanus.*—**Birds of calm**, the *halcyŏnes.* According to the Greek legend, the sea preserved a perfect calmness during the fourteen days in which this bird was supposed to be making its floating nest and laying its eggs. Hence the words "halcyon days." These were said to be the seven days preceding, and the seven following the winter solstice.—**Charmed.** Even the water is entranced!

Influence, *authority*, *ascendency*, *sway*. Distinguish, and embody in sentences.

Tranquillity and admiration.

The sun himself withheld * his wonted speed,
And hid his head for shame,
As his inferior flame
The new-enlightened world no more should need:
He saw a greater sun appear
Than his bright throne, or burning axletree, could bear.

Tranquillity with small volume.

8. The shepherds on the lawn,
Or e'er the point of dawn,
Sat simply chatting in a rustic row:
Full little thought they then,
That the mighty Pan
Was kindly come to live with them below:
Perhaps their loves, or else their sheep,
Was all that did their silly thoughts so busy keep.

Tranquillity with calm, admiring joy.

9. When such music sweet
Their hearts and ears did greet,
As never was by mortal finger strook;
Divinely-warbled voice
Answering the stringed noise,
As all their souls in blissful rapture took:
The air, such pleasure loth to lose,
With thousand echoes still prolongs each heavenly close.

Tranquillity and calm admiring joy.

10. Nature, that heard such sound
Beneath the hollow round
Of Cynthia's seat, the airy region thrilling,
Now was almost won
To think her part was done,
And that her reign had here its last fulfilling:
She knew such harmony alone
Could hold all heaven and earth in happier union.

Wonder and joy.

11. At last surrounds their sight
A globe of circular light,
That with long beams the shamefaced night arrayed;
The helmed cherubim,
And sworded seraphim,
Are seen in glittering ranks with wings displayed,

---

* **Withheld.** The nights just preceding Christmas are the longest of the year.—**Shepherds.** See Luke ii. 8-15.—**Or e'er** (*or* is A. S. *ær*, ere, before), before ever, *sooner than.* —**Pan,** the god of shepherds.—**Strook,** *struck.*—**Close,** *cadence,* the end of a strain in music (Lat. *clausus,* a shutting: *claudĕre,* to shut).—**Hollow round.** the vault of heaven (beneath the moon).—**Cynthia's** (from *Cynthus, Monte Cintio,* a mountain in Delos, where Apollo and Diana Cynthius and Cynthia, were born), the same as Diana, the moon-goddess. She was the goddess of chastity, and she presided over the birth of children. She was called *Selene* in the sky, *Artemis* or *Diana* on the earth, and *Hecate* or *Proserpina* in hell.—**Union.** Trisyl.

Union, unity, junction, combination, oneness, association. Illustrate by sentences.

Harping, in loud and solemn choir,
With unexpressive* notes, to Heaven's new-born heir.

12. Such music as, 'tis said,
Before was never made,
But when of old the sons of morning sung;
While the Creator great
His constellations set,
And the well-balanced world on hinges hung,
And cast the dark foundations deep,
And bid the weltering waves their oozy channel keep.

Wonder, admiration, joy, solemnity.

13. Ring out, ye crystal spheres!
Once bless our human ears,
If ye have power to touch our senses so;
And let your silver chime
Move in melodious time;
And let the bass of heaven's deep organ blow;
And, with your ninefold harmony,
Make up full concert to the angelic symphony!

Joy and admiration.

14. For, if such holy song
Enwrap our fancy long,
Time will run back and fetch the age of gold;
And speckled vanity
Will sicken soon and die;
And leprous sin will melt from earthly mould;
And hell itself will pass away,
And leave her dolorous mansions to the peering day.

Tranquil joy.

15. Yea, Truth and Justice then
Will down return to men,
Orbed in a rainbow; and, like glories wearing,
Mercy will sit between,
Throned in celestial sheen,
With radiant feet the tissued clouds down steering;

Solemn joy and gladness.

---

* **Unexpressive,** *inexpressible.* **Sons of morning.** See Job xxxviii. 7.—**Crystal spheres.** "Pythagoras taught that each planet is fixed in a crystal sphere, or transparent shell, and that the celestial spheres in which the planets move, striking upon the ether through which they pass, produce sounds." He thought that the sphere of Saturn gives the deepest tone, the moon the highest or shrillest, and that the other heavenly spheres complete the musical octave.—**Ninefold.** "This music of the spheres, proceeding from the rapid motion of the heavens, is so loud, various, and sweet, as to exceed all aptitude or proportion of the human ear, and therefore is not heard by men. Moreover, this spherical music consists of eight unisonous melodies; the ninth is a concentration of all the rest, or a diapason of all those eight melodies." *T. Warton.*—**Age of gold.** The fabulous age of primeval simplicity, purity, and happiness. The poets of many nations have delighted to sing of the imaginary Eden.—**Orbed in a rainbow.** Nothing can surpass the beauty of this picture of Truth, Mercy, and Justice.

Melodious, harmonious, musical, symphonious. Distinguish and exemplify.

And heaven, as at some festival,
Will open wide the gates of her high palace hall!

16\. But wisest Fate says no,
This must not yet be so;
  The babe yet lies in smiling infancy,
That on the bitter cross
Must redeem our loss;
  So both himself and us to glorify:
Yet first, to those ychained* in sleep,
The wakeful trump of doom must thunder through the deep

Pity, loud alarm.

17\. With such a horrid clang
As on Mount Sinai rang,
  While the red fire and smouldering clouds outbrake!
The aged earth, aghast
With terror of that blast,
  Shall from the surface to the centre shake;
When, at the world's last session,
The dreadful Judge in middle air shall spread His throne!

Alarm, awe and terror; deep solemnity.

18\. And then at last our bliss
Full and perfect is;
  But now begins; for, from this happy day,
The old Dragon, under ground
In straiter limits bound,
  Not half so far casts his usurped sway;
And, wroth to see his kingdom fail,
Swinges the scaly horror of his folded tail.

Tranquil, joyous; horror.

19\. The oracles are dumb:
No voice or hideous hum
  Runs through the arched roof in words deceiving.
Apollo from his shrine
Can no more divine,
  With hollow shriek the steep of Delphos leaving.
No nightly trance, or breathed spell,
Inspires the pale-eyed priest from the prophetic cell.

Solemn fear.

---

* **Ychained,** *chained.* See *yborn*, p. 19.—**Trump.** 1 Thessalonians iv. 16. This line is greatly admired for its swell and roll. No poet ever surpassed Milton in the sonorous melody and ring of his verse. Hence the term *Miltonic*, which suggests this wondrous combination of sweetness and majesty in the "God-gifted, organ voice of England."—**Sinai.** Ex. xix. 16, and the following verses.—**Session.** Trisyl.—**Dragon.** Rev. xx. 2.—**Straiter** (Lat. *strictus*, drawn tight, from *stringĕre*, to draw tight), narrower.—**Swinges** (A. S. *swingan*, to swing, whip), *to move as a lash.* Obs.—**Dumb.** Milton's conception of the heathen gods as amazed and confounded by this great event, and as fleeing in terror, is original and sublime. Here, too, as more fully in *Paradise Lost*, he groups all the false gods of antiquity and thrusts them down to hell! Eusebius first propounded the opinion that "the oracles became silent ever after the birth of Christ."—**Apollo,** the god of prophecy. His oracle at Delphi, on the southern slope of Mount Parnassus, was the most famous of antiquity. The shrine was said to have been built over a cave, from which issued an intoxicating or inspiring vapor, which the priestess inhaled. See Class. Dictionary, article *Delphi.*

20. The lonely mountains o'er,
And the resounding shore,
  A voice of weeping heard and loud lament;
From haunted spring and dale,
Edged with poplar pale,
  The parting genius* is with sighing sent;
With flower-inwoven tresses torn,
The nymphs in twilight shade of tangled thickets mourn.

Solemn fear.

21. In consecrated earth,
And on the holy hearth,
  The Lars and Lemures moan with midnight plaint;
In urns, and altars round,
A drear and dying sound
  Affrights the Flamens at their service quaint;
And the chill marble seems to sweat,
While each peculiar power foregoes his wonted seat.

Solemn fear.

22. Peor and Baälim
Forsake their temples dim,
  With that twice-battered god of Palestine;
And mooned Ashtaroth,
Heaven's queen and mother both,
  Now sits not girt with tapers' holy shine;
The Lybic Hammon shrinks his horn;
In vain the Tyrian maids their wounded Thammuz mourn.

Awe and silent exultation.

23. And sullen Moloch, fled,
Hath left in shadows dread

---

* **Genius,** the guardian deity of a man, of a place, or a thing.—**Nymphs,** goddesses of mountains, woods, waters, etc.—**Lars and Lemures.** The *Lemures* were the spirits of the departed. They were also called *Manes.* Solemn rites, called *Lemuria*, were celebrated at midnight for three alternate days beginning on the ninth of May. If these spirits were beneficent, they were called *Lares*, and were considered as the guardian spirits of houses and families. If malevolent, they were called *Larvæ.*—**Flamens,** priests devoted to the service of some particular god.—**Peor.** The same as Baal-Peor, Numbers xxv., 3, 18; Deut. iv., 3.—**Baalim** is the plural of Baal, who was the supreme male divinity of the Phœnician and Canaanitish nations, as *Ashtoreth* (Ashtaroth) was their supreme female divinity. 1 Kings xi., 5, 33. Baal is the sun; Ashtoreth, the moon. Ashtoreth appears also to have been identified with the goddess Venus and the planet of that name. See *Paradise Lost*, Book I., 422, 438.—**Twice-battered.** Poor Dagon, the national god of the Philistines, was represented with the face and hands of a man, and the tail of a fish. His sufferings are described in 1 Samuel v.—**Mooned,** in the form of the crescent moon, or adorned with the crescent.—**Lybic** (*Lybia*, Africa), *Lybian, African.*—**Hammon.** *Jupiter Ammon.* This god had a famous oracle at the Oasis of *Seewah* or *Siwah*, 310 miles W.S.W. of Cairo. His statue had the head and *horns* of a ram.—**Horn,** a symbol of strength or exaltation. (Deut. xxxiii., 17; Hab. iii., 4; Zech. i., 18, etc.) Among the Druses of Mount Lebanon the married women wear silver horns on their heads.—**Thammuz.** Ezekiel viii., 14. Jerome attempts to identify Thammuz with Adonis, and Milton poetically accepts this theory. Adonis, beloved of Venus, was killed by a wild boar. On every anniversary of his death, he was mourned, especially by the women. See *Paradise Lost*, Book I., 446-454.—**Moloch** (Heb. *molech, king*), the national god of the Ammonites. He was the god of fire, and appears to have been worshipped with human sacrifices. According to Jewish tradition the image of Moloch was of brass, hollow within, having the face of a calf, and its arms stretched forth as if to receive something. It was heated red hot, and the child that was offered to Moloch was placed in its burning arms. See *Paradise Lost*, I., 304. The Hebrews fell into this idolatry (see 1 Kings xi., 7; 2 Kings xvii., 16, 17), and practised it chiefly in the valley of Tophet, east of Jerusalem.

His burning idol all of blackest hue;
In vain, with cymbals'* ring,
They call the grisly king,
In dismal dance about the furnace blue;
The brutish gods of Nile as fast,
Isis and Orus and the dog Anubis haste.

Awe and silent exultation.

24. Nor is Osiris seen
In Memphian grove or green,
Trampling the unshowered grass with lowings loud;
Nor can he be at rest
Within his sacred chest;
Nought but profoundest hell can be his shroud:
In vain, with timbrelled anthems dark,
The sable-stoled sorcerers bear his worshipped ark.

Awe and silent exultation.

25. He feels from Juda's land
The dreaded infant's hand;
The rays of Bethlehem blind his dusky eyn;
Nor all the gods beside
Longer dare abide;
Not Typhon huge ending in snaky twine:
Our babe, to show his Godhead true,
Can in his swaddling bands control the damned crew.

Solemn joy.

26. So, when the sun in bed,
Curtained with cloudy red,
Pillows his chin upon an orient wave,
The flocking shadows pale
Troop to the infernal jail;
Each fettered ghost slips to his several grave;

Admiration.

* **Cymbals**, among the ancients, probably resembled our kettle-drums. These, it is said, were beaten to drown the cries of the children sacrificed.—**Brutish.** Animal worship was the strangest feature in the religion of the Egyptians. Splendid temples, adorned with superb vestibules and lofty porticoes, were build for the beasts. "If you enter the penetralia," says Clemens, "and inquire for the image of the god, one of the priests approaches with a solemn and mysterious aspect, and, putting aside the curtain, suffers you to peep in and obtain a glimpse of the divinity. There you behold a snake, a crocodile, or a cat, or some other beast, a fitter inhabitant of a cavern or a bog than a temple!"—**Isis** (p. 232), one of the principal deities of the Egyptians, the goddess of fecundity. She was often represented as a woman with the horns of a cow. She was said to be sister and wife of **Osiris** (p. 232), who was worshipped under the form of a bull. **Orus** was their son. **Anubis**, the son of Osiris and Nephthys, had the head of a dog.—**Chest** (Gr. κίστη, Lat. *cista;* A. S. *cest;* Ger. *kiste*). By fraud Osiris was shut up in a chest, which was flung into the Nile.—**Ark** (Lat. *arcere*, to inclose; *arca*, a chest; A. S. *ark*). Pictures on the walls of Egyptian temples show this ark as borne by the priests in religious processions. It may have represented the chest in which Osiris was confined.—**Typhon** (p. 232) here is the same as the snake-giant Apophis, the enemy of gods and men.

Brutish. Discriminate the meanings of *brutish, beastly, brutal, bestial, ferocious.*
Control, curb, restrain, govern, manage, check. Differentiate the meanings.

And the yellow-skirted fays
Fly after the night-steeds,* leaving their moon-loved maze.

27. But see, the Virgin blest
Hath laid her Babe to rest!
Time is, our tedious song should here have ending:
Heaven's youngest teemed star
Hath fixed her polished car,
Her sleeping Lord with handmaid lamp attending;
And all about the courtly stable
Bright harnessed angels sit in order serviceable.

Hushed admiration and reverential joy.

* **Night-steeds,** the steeds that draw the chariot of night. See *Comus*, 553.—**Maze.** See *Paradise Lost*, Book I., 781-787. The superstitious belief, expressed in this stanza, is akin to that stated in Shakespeare as follows:

"I have heard,
The cock, that is the trumpet to the morn,
Doth, with his lofty and shrill-sounding throat,
Awake the god of day; and, at his warning,
Whether in sea or fire, in earth or air,
The extravagant and erring spirit hies
To his confine."—*Hamlet*, Act I., sc. 1.

So the ghost retreats as morning approaches, and, at parting, says to Hamlet:

"Fare thee well at once.
The glow-worm shows the water to be near,
And 'gins to pale his uneffectual fire."—*Hamlet*, Act I., sc. 5.

Harnessed, *clad in armor.* So *Macbeth*, Act V., sc. 5, says,

"At least we 'll die with *harness* on our back."—

Serviceable. Acc. 1st and 3d syl. "The tendency of English accentuation has been to get as far back in words as it is possible for it to go." *Corson.* Thus *character* was once accented on the 2d syl. A multitude of illustrations of this tendency may be found in comparing the language of the old English writers with that of the modern.

Write an essay on this ode, showing its origin, its beauties, its peculiarities. Supposing its author entirely sincere, what kind of man, mentally and morally, does this ode show him to have been? Write an essay on Milton's college life; on lyric poetry. (See Masson's Milton.)

COMUS: A MASK.

The loftiest poem in praise of female purity in any language.—*Emerson.*

THE PERSONS.

The ATTENDANT SPIRIT afterwards in the habit of THYRSIS, personated by Henry Lawes.
COMUS, with his crew.
THE LADY, personated by Lady Alice Egerton.
FIRST BROTHER, " Lord Brackley.
SECOND BROTHER, " Mr. Thos. Egerton.
SABRINA, the Nymph.

The first Scene discovers a wild wood. The attendant Spirit descends or enters.

1. Before the starry threshold of Jove's court
My mansion is; where those immortal shapes
Of bright aerial spirits live insphered*
In regions mild of calm and serene air,

* **Insphered,** in the sphere whither departed spirits pass from earth. The opposite of *unsphered* in *Il Penseroso.*

Calm, serene, placid, tranquil, still, quiet, undisturbed, unruffled, peaceful, composed. Explain and illustrate each.

Above the smoke and stir of this dim spot
Which men call earth; and, with low-thoughted care,
Confined and pestered* in this pinfold here,
Strive to keep up a frail and feverish being,
Unmindful of the crown that virtue gives,
After this mortal change, to her true servants,
Amongst the enthroned gods on sainted seats.
Yet some there be that, by due steps, aspire
To lay their just hands on that golden key,
That opes the palace of eternity.
To such my errand is; and, but for such,
I would not soil these pure ambrosial weeds
With the rank vapors of this sin-worn mold.
But to my task. Neptune, besides the sway
Of every salt flood and each ebbing stream,
Took in by lot, 'twixt high and nether Jove,
Imperial rule of all the sea-girt isles,
That, like to rich and various gems, inlay
The unadorned bosom of the deep;
Which he, to grace his tributary gods,
By course commits to several government,
And gives them leave to wear their sapphire crowns,
And wield their little tridents. But this isle,
The greatest and the best of all the main,
He quarters to his blue-haired deities;
And all this tract that fronts the falling sun,
A noble peer, of mickle trust and power,
Has in his charge, with tempered awe to guide
An old and haughty nation, proud in arms:
Where his fair offspring, nursed in princely lore,
Are coming to attend their father's state
And new-intrusted sceptre. But their way
Lies through the perplexed paths of this drear wood,
The nodding horror of whose shady brows
Threats the forlorn and wandering passenger;
And here their tender age might suffer peril,
But that, by quick command from sovereign Jove,
I was dispatched for their defence and guard:
And listen why; for I will tell you now
What never yet was heard in tale or song,

---

* **Pestered,** *crowded, encumbered.*—**Pinfold** (*pen*, inclosure; *fold*. a sheep-pen) *a pound.* —**Golden key,** virtue.—**High and nether Jove.** *High Jove* is Jupiter; *nether Jove* is Pluto.—**By course,** *by methodical procedure.*—**Tridents,** three-pronged sceptres. (*Tres*, three, *dentes*, teeth.)—**Isle,** England, Scotland, and Wales.—**Quarters,** *allots.*—**Blue-haired,** *blue* because the ocean is blue.—**Mickle** (obs., except in Scotch). *much, great.* Akin to Lat. *magnus*, Gr. *μέγας*, Eng. *much*. See Grimm's Law, pp. 23, 197.—**Nation,** the Welsh.—**Father's.** This father, the peer of mickle trust and might, is the Earl of Bridgewater, the governor of the Welsh.—**State,** *inauguration*, or entry with pomp upon the duties of his high office.

From old or modern bard, in hall* or bower.
  Bacchus, that first from out the purple grape
Crushed the sweet poison of misused wine,
After the Tuscan mariners transformed,
Coasting the Tyrrhene shore, as the winds listed,
On Circe's island fell. (Who knows not Circe,
The daughter of the Sun, whose charmed cup
Whoever tasted, lost his upright shape,
And downward fell into a grovelling swine?)
This nymph, that gazed upon his clustering locks
With ivy berries wreathed, and his blithe youth,
Had by him, ere he parted thence, a son
Much like his father, but his mother more.
Whom, therefore, she brought up, and Comus named:
Who, ripe and frolic of his full-grown age,
Roving the Celtic and Iberian fields,
At last betakes him to this ominous wood,
And, in thick shelter of black shades imbowered,
Excels his mother at her mighty art,
Offering, to every weary traveller,
His orient liquor in a crystal glass,
To quench the drought of Phœbus; which as they taste,
(For most do taste, through fond intemperate thirst,)
Soon as the potion works, their human countenance,
The express resemblance of the gods, is changed
Into some brutish form, of wolf, or bear,
Or ounce, or tiger, hog, or bearded goat,
All other parts remaining as they were;
And they, so perfect is their misery,
Not once perceive their foul disfigurement,
But boast themselves more comely than before,
And all their friends and native home forget,
To roll with pleasure in a sensual sty.
Therefore, when any, favored of high Jove,
Chances to pass through this adventurous glade,

* **In hall.** "The allusion is to the ancient mode of entertaining a splendid assembly, by singing or reciting tales." *T. Warton.*—**Bacchus,** the god of wine and revelry. See p. 77. —**Tuscan mariners transformed.** A Latinism (*post nautas Tyrrhenos mutatos*), after the transformation of the Tuscan mariners, the Tyrrhene pirates, who are represented as having been transformed into dolphins by Bacchus.—**Tyrrhene,** the same as Tuscan.—**Circe** personifies the brutalizing power of the intoxicating cup. She occupies a large space in ancient myths and legends.—**Ivy** was a favorite plant with Bacchus. In *L'Allegro* we have *ivy-crowned Bacchus.*—**Blithe** (A. S. *blidhe*, gay, merry), joyous, sprightly.—**Comus** (Gr. κῶμος, a revel, fr. κώμη, a village, whence comedy?), in the latter age of Rome a god of festive mirth and joy. But Milton has forever stamped his character as that of a reveller and vile enchanter. —**Celtic and Iberian,** *French and Spanish.*—**Orient** (Lat. *oriens*, the rising of the sun, the east), *radiant*, bright.—**Phœbus** (Gr. φάω, to shine; *Phœbus*, the shining one, the sun-god, Apollo), *the sun.*—**Drought** (A. S. *drugâdh*, from *dryge*, Eng. *dry*), *aridity*, *dryness.*—**Is changed.** In the tenth book of Homer's *Odyssey*, the companions of Ulysses are changed by Circe to swine by a stroke of her wand, after they have drunk of her wine.—**Ounce** (Lat. *uncia felis*), an animal resembling the leopard.

Liquor, liquid, juice, humor, fluid. Explain, etc.

Swift as the sparkle* of a glancing star
I shoot from heaven, to give him safe convoy;
As now I do. But first I must put off
These my sky-robes, spun out of Iris' woof,
And take the weeds and likeness of a swain
That to the service of this house belongs,
Who, with his soft pipe, and smooth-dittied song,
Well knows to still the wild winds when they roar,
And hush the waving woods; nor of less faith,
And in this office of his mountain watch,
Likeliest, and nearest to the present aid
Of this occasion. But I hear the tread
Of hateful steps: I must be viewless now.

COMUS *enters with a charming-rod in one hand, his glass in the other; with him a rout of monsters, headed like sundry sorts of wild beasts, but otherwise like men and women, their apparel glistering. They come in, making a riotous and unruly noise, with torches in their hands.*

Comus. The star that bids the shepherd fold,
Now the top of heaven doth hold;
And the gilded car of day
His glowing axle doth allay
In the steep Atlantic stream;
And the slope sun his upward beam
Shoots against the dusky pole,
Pacing toward the other goal
Of his chamber in the east.
Meanwhile, welcome joy and feast,
Midnight shout and revelry,
Tipsy dance and jollity.
Braid your locks with rosy twine,
Dropping odors, dropping wine.
Rigor now is gone to bed;

---

* **Sparkle.** A beautiful simile.—**Iris,** the goddess of the rainbow.—**Woof** (A. S. *wefan*, to weave), the threads across the warp; *cloth.* So, in the *Hymn on the Nativity*, Milton represents Truth, Justice, and Mercy, as wearing rainbow colors.—**Swain** (A. S. *swân*), a young rustic. The name of the person who acted the part of the Attendant Spirit and of the swain Thyrsis, has come down to us. It was Thomas Lawes, a musician and poet, immortalized in Milton's Eighth Sonnet.—**Less faith** (than skill in magical music).—**Top of heaven,** *the zenith.*—**Glowing axle.** In *Hymn on the Nativity*, we have "burning axle-tree."—**Allay,** etc., abate the intense heat of the sun-god's chariot-axle, cool the "burning axle-tree."—**Atlantic stream.** Around the earth, which was supposed to be flat and circular, the ocean-stream was said to flow. On the western coast of Europe it flowed from south to north; then, passing east along the Arctic lands, it afterwards flowed south along the eastern coast of Asia. Those who lived in the far west were said to sometimes hear the hiss of the burning wheels, as they dipped at sunset in the ocean-stream. Some would have it that a winged boat conveyed the sun-god from the western horizon round by the northern part of the earth, and back to his place of rising.—**Steep,** sloping at a great angle with the plane of the horizon; hence, *very swift.*—**Slope sun,** sun travelling on an inclined plane, or in an oblique direction.

Sparkle, flash, gleam, glitter, glow, scintillation, glimmer, glisten, glare. Distinguish, etc.
Odors, smell, scent, perfume, fragrance. Differentiate, etc.

And Advice, with scrupulous head,
Strict Age, and sour Severity,
With their grave saws,* in slumber lie.
We, that are of purer fire,
Imitate the starry quire,
Who, in their nightly watchful spheres,
Lead in swift round the months and years.
The sounds and seas, with all their finny drove,
Now to the moon in wavering morrice move;
And, on the tawny sands and shelves,
Trip the pert fairies and the dapper elves.
By dimpled brook and fountain-brim,
The wood-nymphs, decked with daisies trim,
Their merry wakes and pastimes keep:
What hath night to do with sleep?
Night hath better sweets to prove:
Venus now wakes, and wakens Love.
Come, let us our rites begin:
'Tis only daylight that makes sin;
Which these dun shades will ne'er report.
Hail, goddess of nocturnal sport,
Dark-veiled Cotytto! to whom the secret flame
Of midnight torches burns; mysterious dame,
That ne'er art called but when the dragon womb
Of Stygian darkness spits her thickest gloom,
And makes one blot of all the air;
Stay thy cloudy ebon chair,
Wherein thou ridest with Hecate, and befriend
Us, thy vowed priests, till utmost end
Of all thy dues be done, and none left out;
Ere the blabbing eastern scout,
The nice Morn, on the Indian steep,
From her cabined loop-hole peep,
And to the tell-tale sun descry,
Our concealed solemnity.

---

* **Saws.** *Sayings, maxims.* So Shakespeare in *As You Like It*, "full of wise *saws*."—**Purer fire.** The deities were supposed to have bodies made of a fiery essence, an "empyreal substance." See *Paradise Lost*, I., 117, II., 215. **Morrice** (Sp. *morisco*, Fr. *moresque*, from *Moro*, a Moor), *morris*, a Moorish dance, first brought into England on the return of John of Gaunt from Spain in the time of Chaucer.—**Dapper** (Ger. *tapfer*, valiant), little and active; spruce, smart.—**Wakes,** vigils; night-revels; sitting up late for solemn or festive purposes. A. S. *wacan;* Ger. *wachen*, to wake; Lat. *vigilāre*, to watch. See Grimm's Law, p. 240.—**'Tis only daylight that makes sin.** "A sentiment worthy of Comus."—**Cotytto,** the goddess of licentiousness, worshipped with rites of the grossest indecency in private at Athens.—**Stygian,** "of, or pertaining to, Styx, fabled by the ancients to be a river of hell; hence, hellish." *Webster.*—**Makes one blot.** So Shakespeare's "*making the green one red*," in *Macbeth*, II., 1, p. 131.—**Hecate.** As Diana personifies the moonlight splendor, so Hecate represents night's darkness and terrors. See *Cynthia*, pp. 79, 246, and *Phœbe*, p. 74.—**Blabbing,** *talkative, tale-telling.* Shakespeare (*Henry* VI., Part 2, Act IV., Scene 1, first line) speaks of "the gaudy, blabbing, and remorseful day."—**Nice,** *fastidious.*—**Loop-hole.** The scout, on the top of one of the steep mountains of India, looks from the loop-hole of a fortification which is no larger than a cabin or tent. But see *cabined*, p. 145.

Come, knit hands, and beat the ground
In a light fantastic round.

The Measure.

Break off, break off! I feel the different pace
Of some chaste footing near about this ground.
Run to your shrouds * within these brakes and trees:
Our number may affright!—Some virgin sure,
(For so I can distinguish by mine art,)
Benighted in these woods. Now to my charms
And to my wily trains. I shall, ere long,
Be well stocked with as fair a herd as grazed
About my mother Circe. Thus I hurl
My dazzling spells into the spongy air,
Of power to cheat the eye with blear illusion,
And give it false presentments, lest the place
And my quaint habits breed astonishment,
And put the damsel to suspicious flight;
Which must not be, for that's against my course.
I, under fair pretence of friendly ends,
And well-placed words of glozing courtesy,
Baited with reasons not unplausible,
Wind me into the easy-hearted man,
And hug him into snares. When once her eye
Hath met the virtue of this magic dust,
I shall appear some harmless villager,
Whom thrift keeps up about his country gear.
But here she comes. I fairly step aside,
And hearken, if I may, her business here.

The Lady *enters.*

Lady. This way the noise was, if mine ear be true,
My best guide now. Methought it was the sound
Of riot and ill-managed merriment;
Such as the jocund flute and gamesome pipe
Stirs up among the loose unfettered hinds,
When, for their teeming flocks, the granges full,
In wanton dance they praise the bounteous Pan,
And thank the gods amiss. I should be loath

---

* **Shrouds** (A. S. *scrûd*, a garment), *covered places, retreats.*—**Trains** (Lat. *traho*, to draw), things which draw, *enticements, artifices.*—**Fair a herd.** Circe had about her not only swine, the victims of her transforming power, but lions, tigers, wolves, etc., tamed by her magic arts.—**Spongy** (Gr. σπογγία, σπόγγος; Lat. *spongia;* A. S. *sponge*), having the quality of imbibing like a sponge.—**Gear,** *business matters, affairs.* See p. 31.—**Fairly,** *softly, gently.* (Obs. in this sense).—**Hinds,** peasants, *boors.*—**Granges,** Fr. *grange*, a barn; Lat. *granum*, a grain; (Eng. *corn* by Grimm's Law), *barns, granaries.*

Fantastic, visionary, fanciful, chimerical, whimsical, wild, capricious, ideal, imaginary. Explain, etc.

To meet the rudeness and swilled* insolence
Of such late wassailers: yet, oh! where else
Shall I inform my unacquainted feet
In the blind mazes of this tangled wood?
My brothers, when they saw me wearied out
With this long way, resolving here to lodge
Under the spreading favor of these pines,
Stepped, as they said, to the next thicket-side,
To bring me berries, or such cooling fruit
As the kind hospitable woods provide.
They left me then, when the gray-hooded Even,
Like a sad votarist in palmer's weed,
Rose from the hindmost wheels of Phœbus' wain.
But where they are, and why they came not back,
Is now the labor of my thoughts. 'Tis likeliest,
They had engaged their wandering steps too far;
And envious darkness, ere they could return,
Had stole them from me. Else, O thievish Night,
Why shouldst thou, but for some felonious end,
In thy dark lantern thus close up the stars
That nature hung in heaven, and filled their lamps
With everlasting oil, to give due light
To the misled and lonely traveller?
This is the place, as well as I may guess,
Whence even now the tumult of loud mirth
Was rife, and perfect in my listening ear.
Yet nought but single darkness do I find.
What might this be? A thousand fantasies
Begin to throng into my memory,
Of calling shapes, and beckoning shadows dire,
And aëry tongues, that syllable men's names
On sands and shores and desert wildernesses.
These thoughts may startle well, but not astound
The virtuous mind that ever walks attended
By a strong-siding champion, Conscience.
O, welcome, pure-eyed Faith, white-handed Hope,
Thou hovering angel, girt with golden wings!

---

* **Swilled** (A. S. *swilgan*, to swallow) *drunken. Swilled insolence.* insolence caused by greedy drinking of alcoholic liquors. See *Paradise Lost*, I., 502.—**Wassailers**, those who drink *wassail* (A. S. *wes-hæl*, be in health), *revellers*. See note on *wassail*, *Macbeth*, Act I., sc. 7, p. 125.—**Votarist**, *votary*, one devoted to worship.—**Palmer**, a religious pilgrim who had visited the Holy Land, and, in token thereof, used to carry a branch of palm. He was designedly a homeless vagrant.—**Phœbus' wain** (*wain* from A. S. *wæn*, wagon; Lat. *vehĕre*, to carry. See Grimm's Law, pp. 23, 240), the sun-god's car. See *glowing axle*, p. 254.—**Engaged**, *involved*, rendered liable.—**Lamps**. In *Macbeth*, in the beginning of Act II., sc. 1, p. 126, the stars are called *candles*. So in *Romeo and Juliet*, Act III., sc. 5.—**Perfect**, perfectly distinct, complete.—**Single**, unmixed.—**Aery tongues**. In *Romeo and Juliet* (which Milton would seem to have just been reading when he wrote Comus), we find the "*airy tongues*" of echo mentioned, Act II., sc. 2.—**Syllable**, pronounce.—**Hovering**. "This word is applied with peculiar propriety to the angel Hope, in sight, on the wing." *T. Warton.*

And thou unblemished form of Chastity!
I see ye visibly, and now believe
That He, the Supreme Good, to whom all things ill
Are but as slavish officers of vengeance,
Would send a glistering * guardian, if need were,
To keep my life and honor unassailed.
Was I deceived, or did a sable cloud
Turn forth her silver lining on the night?
I did not err: there does a sable cloud
Turn forth her silver lining on the night,
And casts a gleam over this tufted grove.
I cannot halloo to my brothers, but
Such noise as I can make to be heard farthest,
I'll venture; for my new enlivened spirits
Prompt me; and they, perhaps, are not far off.

SONG.

Sweet Echo, sweetest nymph, that liv'st unseen
Within thy airy shell,
By slow Meander's margent green,
And in the violet-embroidered vale,
Where the love-lorn nightingale
Nightly to thee her sad song mourneth well;
Canst thou not tell me of a gentle pair
That likest thy Narcissus are?
O, if thou have
Hid them in some flowery cave,
Tell me but where,
Sweet queen of parley, daughter of the sphere!
So mayest thou be translated to the skies,
And give resounding grace to all heaven's harmonies.

Enter COMUS.

Comus. Can any mortal mixture of earth's mold

---

* **Glistering** (A. S. *glisian*, to shine. From the same root come *glow*, *gleam*, *glare*, *glory*, *glimmer*, etc.), *shining*, *sparkling*.—**Guardian.** "Are they not all ministering spirits?" *Paul.* See the fine lines on the ministry of angels, quoted in the biographical sketch of Spenser.—**Silver lining.** Even in the night, the dark cloud often has a silver lining. —**Echo,** daughter of Air (Jupiter) and Earth (Tellus). See Class. Dict.—**Airy shell.** "Hurd and Warburton observe that *shell* means the horizon, the hollow circumference of the heavens." *Cleveland.* This explanation, which makes the *horizon* a *shell* and a *circumference*, and that circumference the circumference of the heavens, and hollow besides, is, to say the least, not very accurate. In ancient astronomy the *spheres* were imagined to be concentric, transparent shells encompassing the earth. Within the nearest of these lives Echo. See *crystal spheres*, p. 247. —**Meander** (now the *Mender* or *Minder*), a river in the southwest of Asia Minor, flowing into the Grecian Archipelago.—**Margent,** *margin*.—**Love-lorn,** "bereft of her loved one."—**Likest,** most like in beauty.—**Narcissus,** beloved of Echo, became enamored of his own image mirrored in a fountain; and he pined away with longing for it, until he was changed into the flower that bears his name.—**Daughter of the sphere.** "Milton supposes her to owe her first existence to the reverberation of the spheres." *Warburton.*—**So mayest.** On condition that thou shalt tell me, I wish that thou mayest be transferred to the skies, and echo the divine melody of heaven.

Margent, *margin*, *border*, *edge*, *rim*, *brim*, *brink*, *verge*. Distinguish, etc.

Breathe such divine enchanting ravishment?
Sure something holy* lodges in that breast,
And with these raptures moves the vocal air
To testify his hidden residence.
How sweetly did they float upon the wings
Of silence, through the empty-vaulted night,
At every fall smoothing the raven-down
Of darkness, till it smiled! I have oft heard
My mother Circe, with the Sirens three,
Amidst the flowery-kirtled Naiades,
Culling their potent herbs and baleful drugs,
Who, as they sung, would take the prisoned soul,
And lap it in Elysium: Scylla wept,
And chid her barking waves into attention,
And fell Charybdis murmured soft applause:
Yet they in pleasing slumber lulled the sense,
And in sweet madness robbed it of itself;
But such a sacred and home-felt delight,
Such sober certainty of waking bliss,
I never heard till now. I'll speak to her,
And she shall be my queen. Hail, foreign wonder!
Whom certain these rough shades did never breed,
Unless the goddess that in rural shrine
Dwell'st here with Pan, or Sylvan, by blest song
Forbidding every bleak unkindly fog
To touch the prosperous growth of this tall wood.
Lady. Nay, gentle shepherd, ill is lost that praise
That is addressed to unattending ears:
Not any boast of skill, but extreme shift
How to regain my severed company,
Compelled me to awake the courteous Echo
To give me answer from her mossy couch.
Comus. What chance, good lady, hath bereft you thus?
Lady. Dim darkness and this leafy labyrinth.
Comus. Could that divide you from near-ushering guides?

* **Something holy.** Here is a striking tribute to the power of music. Even Comus is fascinated and for the moment ennobled.—**Fall,** *cadence*.—**Sirens** (Lat. *Siren*, Gr. Σειρήν), maidens, celebrated in fable, who occupied an island, near Caprera in the Mediterranean, on the shores of which they used to sit and sing to mariners passing by. Their voices were so melodious that the listeners forgot home and friends and were lured on to destruction.—**Flowery-kirtled.** A *kirtle* is a gown.—**Naiades** (Ναιάς, from νάειν, to flow, Lat. *naias*, *naïs*), *Naiads*, inferior deities in the form of young and beautiful virgins, who presided over rivers, brooks, and fountains. Pronounced *Nā-ya-dēs.* Acc. 1st syl.—**Elysium** (Lat. *Elysium*) the abode of the spirits of the blessed. Homer locates it in the far west of earth; Virgil, under the earth; Hesiod and Pindar, in the Isles of the Blessed, or Fortunate Islands, in the Atlantic Ocean.—**Scylla,** once a beautiful maiden, changed by Circe into a monster having six heads and surrounded by serpents and barking dogs.—**Charybdis,** a dangerous whirlpool. Charybdis and Scylla were fabled to be on opposite sides of the straits of Messina.—**Sylvan** (Lat. Sylvanus or Silvanus), a deity among the Romans. He had the care of fields, herds, woods, etc. (From *sylva* or *silva*, a forest.)

Ravishment, rapture, ecstasy, transport, bliss, exultation. Distinguish, etc.

Lady. They left me, weary, on a grassy turf.
Comus. By falsehood, or discourtesy, or why?
Lady. To seek, i' the valley, some cool friendly spring.
Comus. And left your fair side all unguarded, lady?
Lady. They were but twain, and purposed quick return.
Comus. Perhaps forestalling night prevented them.
Lady. How easy my misfortune is to hit!
Comus. Imports there loss, beside the present need?
Lady. No less than if I should my brothers lose.
Comus. Were they of manly prime, or youthful bloom?
Lady. As smooth as Hebe's,* their unrazored lips.
Comus. Two such I saw, what time the labored ox
In his loose traces from the furrow came,
And the swinked hedger at his supper sat;
I saw them under a green mantling vine,
That crawls along the side of yon small hill,
Plucking ripe clusters from the tender shoots;
Their port was more than human, as they stood:
I took it for a faery vision
Of some gay creatures of the element,
That in the colors of the rainbow live,
And play i' the plighted clouds. I was awe-struck,
And, as I passed, I worshipped; if those you seek,
It were a journey like the path to heaven,
To help you find them.
Lady. Gentle villager,
What readiest way would bring me to that place?
Comus. Due west it rises from this shrubby point.
Lady. To find out that, good shepherd, I suppose,
In such a scant allowance of star-light,
Would overtask the best land-pilot's art,
Without the sure guess of well-practised feet.
Comus. I know each lane, and every alley green,
Dingle, or bushy dell, of this wild wood,
And every bosky bourn from side to side,
My daily walks and ancient neighborhood;
And if your stray attendants be yet lodged,
Or shroud within these limits, I shall know
Ere morrow wake, of the low-roosted lark

---

* **Hebe,** daughter of Juno and goddess of youth. She was cup-bearer to the gods.—**Swinked,** *over-labored, tired.*—**Hedger,** one who works at making or repairing hedges.—**Port** (A. S. *port;* Lat. *portus*), *carriage, bearing.* **Faery** (Lat. *fata*), fairy.—**Vision** (trisyl., like *union*, p. 246, and *session*, p. 248).—**Element,** *the air, atmosphere.*—**Plighted.** "We are to understand the braided or embroidered clouds, in which certain airy elemental beings are most poetically supposed to sport, thus producing a variety of transient and dazzling colors." *T. Warton.*—**Without the sure guess.** *Unless he had the sure guess.*—**Dingle,** a small, secluded and embowered valley.—**Dell,** *a ravine.*—**Bosky,** *woody*, or *bushy.*—**Bourn,** *a rivulet, a brook.* (Hence the meaning of a *bound*, or *limit*, a stream being a natural boundary.)—**Shroud,** *take shelter.* See *shrouds*, p. 256.

From her thatched pallet* rouse; if otherwise,
I can conduct you, lady, to a low
But loyal cottage, where you may be safe
Till further quest.
Lady. Shepherd, I take thy word,
And trust thy honest-offered courtesy,
Which oft is sooner found in lowly sheds,
With smoky rafters, than in tapestry halls,
And courts of princes, where it first was named,
And yet is most pretended: in a place
Less warranted than this, or less secure,
I cannot be, that I should fear to change it.
Eye me, blessed Providence, and square my trial
To my proportioned strength. Shepherd, lead on. [*Exeunt.*

Enter the TWO BROTHERS.

First Br. Unmuffle, ye faint stars; and thou, fair moon,
That wont'st to love the traveller's benison,
Stoop thy pale visage through an amber cloud,
And disinherit Chaos, that reigns here
In double night of darkness and of shades:
Or, if your influence be quite dammed up
With black usurping mists, some gentle taper,
Though a rush-candle, from the wicker hole
Of some clay habitation, visit us
With thy long-levelled rule of streaming light,
And thou shalt be our star of Arcady,
Or Tyrian cynosure.
Sec. Br. Or, if our eyes
Be barred that happiness, might we but hear
The folded flocks penned in their wattled cotes,
Or sound of pastoral reed with oaten stops,

---

* **Pallet** (Lat. *palea*, chaff; Fr. *paille*, straw), a small poor bed.—**Quest** (Lat. *quærĕre*, to ask, seek), search *inquiry*.—**Warranted**, *made secure, assured of safety, guaranteed.* (*Guaranty* and *warranty* are the same word.) *G* at the beginning of a word, especially when sounded like *h*, as in German, easily disappears. Hence Fr. *guerre* becomes *war; guise, wise; guile, wile*, etc.—**That I should fear,** *so as to make me fear.*—**Square**, *adjust, accommodate.*—**Wont'st** (A. S. *wunian*, to dwell; *wuna*, custom; Ger. *gewohnt*, accustomed), *art accustomed.*—**Benison,** *blessing*, benediction.—**Amber,** yellowish and translucent. Milton is fond of this word, or of the color designated.—**Chaos,** the unorganized condition of matter, when "the earth was without form and void"; the oldest of the Greek gods.—**Rush-candle,** a small taper made by dipping a rush in tallow.—**Wicker hole,** the window covered with osiers or willow twigs.—**Long-levelled.** Whoever has noted a beam of light streaming through dusty or foggy air, especially at night, will recognize the beauty of this epithet.—**Arcady.** Jupiter changed Callisto, daughter of Lycaon, King of Arcadia, into the constellation *Ursa Major*, and changed her son Arcas into *Ursa Minor*, called also *Cynosura* (the Dog's tail). The *Cynosura* as containing the polar star, has the eyes of all mariners directed to itself. The Tyrians (Phœnicians) were the most celebrated seamen of antiquity, and from them the smaller Bear was sometimes called *Phœnice.*—**Wattled,** formed of platted or interwoven twigs.—**Cotes,** *sheep folds.*—**Reed,** a musical instrument made of the hollow joint of some plant.—**Oaten stops,** apertures closed by the finger in a pipe of oat straw.

Courtesy, politeness, refinement, urbanity, good-breeding, civility, complaisance, gentility, courtliness, elegance. Distinguish, etc.
Conduct, escort, suite, guide, lead. Distinguish, etc.

Or whistle from the lodge,* or village cock
Count the night watches, to his feathery dames,
'Twould be some solace yet, some little cheering,
In this close dungeon of innumerous boughs.
But, oh, that hapless virgin, our lost sister!
Where may she wander now, whither betake her
From the chill dew, among rude burs and thistles?
Perhaps some cold bank is her bolster now,
Or 'gainst the rugged bark of some broad elm
Leans her unpillowed head, fraught with sad fear.
What, if in wild amazement and affright,
Or, while we speak, within the direful grasp
Of savage hunger, or of savage heat?
First Br. Peace, brother be not over exquisite
To cast the fashion of uncertain evils:
For, grant they be so, while they rest unknown,
What need a man forestall his date of grief,
And run to meet what he would most avoid?
Or if they be but false alarms of fear,
How bitter is such self-delusion!
I do not think my sister so to seek,
Or so unprincipled in virtue's book,
And the sweet peace that goodness bosoms ever,
As that the single want of light and noise
(Not being in danger, as I trust she is not)
Could stir the constant mood of her calm thoughts,
And put them into misbecoming plight.
Virtue could see to do what virtue would,
By her own radiant light, though sun and moon
Were in the flat sea sunk. And wisdom's self
Oft seeks to sweet retired solitude,
Where, with her best nurse, Contemplation,
She plumes her feathers and lets grow her wings,
That, in the various bustle of resort,
Were all-to ruffled, and sometimes impaired.
He that has light within his own clear breast
May sit i' the centre, and enjoy bright day:
But he that hides a dark soul and foul thoughts,
Benighted walks under the mid-day sun;
Himself is his own dungeon.

---

* **Lodge,** a small house in a forest.—**Innumerous,** *countless.* This word is now obsolete.—**Cast,** *compute, predict,* to reckon on the future.—**Delusion,** four syllables.—**So to seek,** so needing to seek, so at a loss, *so without resources.*—**Bosoms,** incloses in the bosom, *cherishes.*—**Seeks to** (Lat. *sequi,* to follow), *resorts to, courts.* See Isaiah xi., 10.—**Contemplation.** -*Tion* is here a dissyllable.—**All-to,** *altogether.* Webster prefers to join the *to* in such a phrase, to the following word. This would then read all to-ruffled. See Worcester's and Webster's Unabr. Dict. under *all.*

Amazement, astonishment, surprise, wonder. Discriminate, etc.

Sec. Br. 'Tis most true,
That musing meditation most affects
The pensive secrecy of desert cell,
Far from the cheerful haunt of men and herds,
And sits as safe as in a senate-house;
For who would rob a hermit of his weeds,
His few books, or his beads, or maple dish,
Or do his gray hairs any violence?
But beauty, like the fair Hesperian* tree,
Laden with blooming gold, had need the guard
Of dragon-watch, with unenchanted eye,
To save her blossoms, and defend her fruit,
From the rash hand of bold incontinence.
You may as well spread out the unsunned heaps
Of miser's treasure by an outlaw's den,
And tell me it is safe, as bid me hope
Danger will wink on opportunity,
And let a single helpless maiden pass
Uninjured in this wild surrounding waste.
Of night, or loneliness, it recks me not;
I fear the dread events that dog them both,
Lest some ill-greeting touch attempt the person
Of our unowned sister.
First Br. I do not, brother,
Infer, as if I thought my sister's state
Secure, without all doubt or controversy;
Yet, where an equal poise of hope and fear
Does arbitrate the event, my nature is
That I incline to hope, rather than fear,
And gladly banish squint suspicion.
My sister is not so defenceless left
As you imagine; she has a hidden strength,
Which you remember not.
Sec. Br. What hidden strength,
Unless the strength of Heaven, if you mean that?
First Br. I mean that, too, but yet a hidden strength,
Which, if Heaven give it, may be termed her own;
'Tis chastity, my brother; chastity:
She that has that is clad in complete steel;

* **Hesperian.** At the wedding of Jupiter and Juno, the bride received, as a present from the goddess of earth, a tree with golden apples growing on its branches. This tree was intrusted to the keeping of the Hesperides, or "Western Maidens," assisted by a hundred-headed dragon. See Class. Dict.—**Unsunned,** *not exposed to the sun*, carefully concealed.—**Dog,** *follow closely.*—**Unowned,** *unclaimed*, unattended.—**Squint,** *looking obliquely*, suspiciously, or by side glances.—**Complete steel.** So in *Hamlet*, the ghost is in "complete steel." Act I., sc. 4.

Suspicion, doubt, mistrust, scruple, indecision, hesitation, distrust, jealousy, envy. **Discriminate, etc.**

And, like a quivered nymph,* with arrows keen,
May trace huge forests, and unharbored heaths,
Infamous hills, and sandy perilous wilds,
Where, through the sacred rays of chastity,
No savage fierce, bandit, or mountaineer,
Will dare to soil her virgin purity.
Yea, there, where very desolation dwells,
By grots and caverns shagged with horrid shades,
She may pass on with unblenched majesty,
Be it not done in pride, or in presumption.
Some say, no evil thing that walks by night,
In fog or fire, by lake or moorish fen,
Blue meagre hag, or stubborn unlaid ghost
That breaks his magic chains at curfew time,
No goblin, or swart fairy of the mine,
Hath hurtful power o'er true virginity.
Do ye believe me yet, or shall I call
Antiquity from the old schools of Greece,
To testify the arms of chastity?
Hence had the huntress Dian her dread bow,
Fair silver-shafted queen, for ever chaste,
Wherewith she tamed the brinded lioness
And spotted mountain-pard, but set at nought
The frivolous bolt of Cupid: gods and men
Feared her stern frown, and she was queen of the woods.
What was that snaky-headed Gorgon shield
That wise Minerva wore, unconquered virgin,
Wherewith she freezed her foes to congealed stone,
But rigid looks of chaste austerity,
And noble grace, that dashed brute violence
With sudden adoration and blank awe?

---

* **Quivered nymph.** He is thinking of Diana, goddess of chastity, whose favorite occupation it was to hunt with bow and full quiver.—**Trace** (Lat. *trahere*, to draw), to track, walk over, pass through.—**Unharbored,** *affording no shelter.*—**Unblenched,** not baffled, *not blinded.* (*Blench* from *blanch*, to grow white. Fr. *blanc*, white.)—**Unlaid,** *not pacified, not caused to disappear.* "An unlaid ghost," says T. Warton, "was among the most vexatious plagues of the world of spirits. The metaphorical expression of *breaking his magic chains* for being suffered to wander abroad is "beautiful." The seven lines beginning, "Some say, no evil thing," suggest a kindred seven lines beginning, "Some say that ever 'gainst that season comes," near the end of the first scene in *Hamlet.*—**Curfew** (Fr. *couvre-feu; couvrir*, to cover; *feu*, fire. By command of William the Conqueror, 1066–1087, a bell was rung at nightfall as a signal to the inhabitants to cover fires, extinguish lights, and retire to rest). As to the habits of spirits that "walk the night," see the passage just cited in *Hamlet.* See also stanza 26 of *Ode on the Morning of Christ's Nativity.*—**Fairy**. "In the Gothic system of pneumatology, mines were supposed to be inhabited by various sorts of spirits." *T. Warton.*—**Dian,** *Diana.* goddess of the chase, and always chaste. See *Hecate*, pp. 128, 255. —**Cupid's bolt,** the arrow of Cupid, son of Venus, and god of love.—**Gorgon.** The Gorgons were three frightful sisters who turned into stone all who looked on them. The hero Perseus slew Medusa, one of the Gorgons, and, cutting off her head, gave it to the goddess of wisdom, Minerva, who fastened it in the centre of her ægis or shield. *Paradise Lost*, II., 611.—**Freezed** (obsolete) *froze.* This passage, explaining the myth of the Gorgon's head and ascribing the power of Diana and Minerva to their chastity, is original and beautiful. The delicacy and purity of the language well correspond with the thought. See Class. Dict.

Bandit, outlaw, brigand, robber, buccaneer, pirate, highwayman, thief, freebooter, pilferer. **Distinguish,** etc.

So dear to Heaven is saintly chastity,
That, when a soul is found sincerely so,
A thousand liveried angels lackey her,
Driving far off each thing of sin and guilt;
And, in clear dream and solemn vision,
Tell her of things that no gross ear can hear;
Till oft converse with heavenly habitants
Begin to cast a beam on the outward shape,
The unpolluted temple of the mind,
And turns it, by degrees, to the soul's essence,*
Till all be made immortal. But when lust,
By unchaste looks, loose gestures, and foul talk,
But most by lewd and lavish act of sin,
Lets in defilement to the inward parts,
The soul grows clotted by contagion,
Imbodies, and imbrutes, till she quite lose
The divine property of her first being.
Such are those thick and gloomy shadows damp,
Oft seen in charnel vaults and sepulchres,
Lingering and sitting by a new-made grave,
As loth to leave the body that it loved,
And linked itself, by carnal sensuality,
To a degenerate and degraded state.
Sec. Br. How charming is divine philosophy!
Not harsh and crabbed, as dull fools suppose,
But musical as is Apollo's lute,
And a perpetual feast of nectared sweets,
Where no crude surfeit reigns.
First Br. List! list! I hear
Some far-off halloo break the silent air.
Sec. Br. Methought so, too; what should it be?
First Br. For certain,
Either some one, like us, night-foundered here,
Or else some neighbor woodman; or, at worst,
Some roving robber calling to his fellows.
Sec. Br. Heaven keep my sister. Again, again, and near!
Best draw, and stand upon our guard.
First Br. I'll halloo:
If he be friendly, he comes well; if not,
Defense is a good cause, and Heaven be for us.

---

* **Soul's essence,** etc. This seems to have been a favorite thought with Milton. See *Paradise Lost*, v., 468–505. See, too, the beginning of Milton's treatise on *Reformation in England*.—**Loth to leave.** Note the alliteration. The thought here and throughout the whole of this speech of the elder brother, well deserves the compliment the younger brother immediately pays it.—**Apollo,** god of music, played upon the lyre invented by Mercury.—**Nectared.** Nectar was the drink of the gods, as ambrosia was their food.—**Night-foundered** (*founder*, from Lat. *fundus*, bottom; Old French *fondre*, to sink), foundered, or sunk, in night, or in darkness. *Paradise Lost*, I., 204.—**Draw,** *i. e.*, draw the sword.

Enter the attendant Spirit, habited like a Shepherd.

That halloo I should know; what are you ? speak.
Come not too near: you fall on iron stakes else.
Spir. What voice is that ? my young lord ? speak again.
Sec. Br. O brother, 'tis my father's shepherd, sure.
First Br. Thyrsis ?* whose artful strains have oft delayed
The huddling brook to hear his madrigal,
And sweetened every musk-rose of the dale ?
How camest thou here, good swain ? Hath any ram
Slipped from the fold, or young kid lost his dam ?
Or straggling wether the pent flock forsook ?
How couldst thou find this dark sequestered nook ?
Spir. O, my loved master's heir, and his next joy,
I came not here on such a trivial toy
As a strayed ewe, or to pursue the stealth
Of pilfering wolf: not all the fleecy wealth
That doth enrich these downs is worth a thought
To this my errand, and the care it brought.
But, oh, my virgin lady! where is she ?
How chance she is not in your company ?
First Br. To tell thee sadly, shepherd, without blame
Or our neglect, we lost her as we came.
Spir. Ah me unhappy! then my fears are true.
First Br. What fears, good Thyrsis ? Pr'ythee, briefly show.
Spir. I'll tell ye. 'Tis not vain or fabulous,
Though so esteemed by shallow ignorance,
What the sage poets, taught by the heavenly muse,
Storied of old, in high immortal verse,
Of dire chimeras, and enchanted isles,
And rifted rocks whose entrance leads to hell;
For such there be, but unbelief is blind.
Within the navel of this hideous wood,
Immured in cypress shades, a sorcerer dwells,
Of Bacchus and of Circe born, great Comus,
Deep skilled in all his mother's witcheries;
And here, to every thirsty wanderer,
By sly enticement gives his baneful cup,

---

* **Thyrsis**, the name of a herdsman in Theocritus and of a shepherd in Virgil, is used in the pastoral poets as a generic name for shepherd.—**Artful strains**, cunning notes, *skilful tones*.—**Huddling**, crowding confusedly forward.—**Madrigal** (Lat. *Mandra*, a stall, a herd of cattle; It. and O. Span. *mandra*, a flock), a brief pastoral poem, usually a love-story or song. See p. 219.—**Sweetened.** How exquisite the music that could add perfume to the rose!—**Forsook** (obs. as participle), *forsaken*.—**Dire chimeras.** The *chimera* was a fire-vomiting monster, having the head of a lion, the body of a goat, and the tail of a dragon. *Paradise Lost*, II., 628.—**Rifted,** *rent asunder*, split. Near Tænarus (Cape Matapan) was a cave, which the poets fabled to be the entrance to hell, and through which Hercules was said to have dragged up the three-headed dog Cerberus.—**Navel.** So Delphi was called by the Greeks the navel of earth.—**Sorcerer** (Lat. *sors*, a lot).

Immortal, deathless, imperishable, incorruptible. Other synonymes ?

With many murmurs* mixed, whose pleasing poison
The visage quite transforms of him that drinks,
And the inglorious likeness of a beast
Fixes instead, unmolding reason's mintage
Charactered in the face. This have I learned,
Tending my flocks hard by i' the hilly crofts
That brow this bottom-glade; whence, night by night,
He and his monstrous rout are heard to howl
Like stabled wolves or tigers at their prey,
Doing abhorred rites to Hecate,
In their obscured haunts of inmost bowers.
Yet have they many baits and guileful spells,
To inveigle and invite the unwary sense
Of them that pass unweeting by the way.
This evening late, by then the chewing flocks
Had ta'en their supper on the savory herb
Of knot-grass dew-besprent, and were in fold,
I sat me down to watch upon a bank
With ivy canopied, and interwove
With flaunting honeysuckle, and began,
Rapt in a pleasing fit of melancholy,
To meditate my rural minstrelsy,
Till fancy had her fill: but, ere a close,
The wonted roar was up amidst the woods,
And filled the air with barbarous dissonance;
At which I ceased, and listened them awhile,
Till an unusual stop of sudden silence
Gave respite to the drowsy-flighted steeds
That draw the litter of close-curtained sleep.
At last, a soft and solemn-breathing sound
Rose like a steam of rich distilled perfumes
And stole upon the air, that even Silence
Was took ere she was ware, and wished she might

---

* **Murmurs,** muttered magic words or verses. In preparing this enchanted cup, the iarm of many barbarous, unintelligible words was intermixed to quicken and strengthen its peration.—**Mintage** (A. S. *mynet*, money, co n, Lat. *monēta*, the adviser; from *monēre*, to warn. *onēta* was a surname of Juno, in whose temple money was co ned), that which has been inted, or stamped at a mint. *Reason's mintage* is the form or look as expressing reason.—**haractered.** Here we have the old cus omary accent on the second sy lable. See note on *rviceable*, p. 251.—**Crofts** (Gr. κρύπτη, fr. κρύπτειν, to conceal; Lat. *crypta;* A. S. *croft*, by rimm's Law), small inclosed fields.—**Brow,** form a brow to, *overlook*.—**Rout** (Old French *ute*, troop; Lat. *rupta*, from *rumpere, to break*), concourse, *rabble* that commits a breach of the ace.—**Hecate** (Trisyl.). See pp. 128, 150, 2 5.—**Unweeting** (*un*, not; O. Eng. *weet*, to know), norant, *unknowing*. Obs.—**By then,** at the time when.—**Knot-grass,** a weed-like p ant, iot-weed.—**Besprent** (*sprent*, A. S. *sprengan*, or *sprencan*, to sprinkle), besprinkled.—**Sat** **e down** (*sat* is reflexive here), seated myself.—**Flaunting,** *ostentatious*.—**Rapt** (Lat. *raptus*, raptured, from *rapere*, to seize and carry off), *transported*, ravished.—**Meditate** (Lat. *editari*), *practice*.—**Close,** the end of a strain of music; cadence. See p. 246.—**Steeds,** night-steeds," as they are called in the *Hymn on the Nativity*. So Campbell has the line, Chased on his night-steed by the star of day."—**Took,** taken prisoner, captivated.

Transform, metamorphose, alter, change, vary, diversify, shift, turn to or *into, transmute.* istinguish, etc.

Deny her nature and be never more,
Still to be so displaced. I was all ear,
And took in strains that might create a soul
Under the ribs* of death! But, oh, ere long,
Too well I did perceive it was the voice
Of my most honored lady, your dear sister.
Amazed I stood, harrowed with grief and fear:
And, O poor hapless nightingale! thought I,
How sweet thou sing'st, how near the deadly snare!
Then down the lawns I ran with headlong haste,
Through paths and turnings often trod by day,
Till, guided by mine ear, I found the place
Where that damned wizard, hid in sly disguise,
(For so by certain signs I knew,) had met
Already, ere my best speed could prevent,
The aidless innocent lady, his wished prey,
Who gently asked if he had seen such two,
Supposing him some neighbor villager.
Longer I durst not stay, but soon I guessed
Ye were the two she meant: with that I sprung
Into swift flight, till I had found you here;
But further know I not.

Sec. Br. O Night, and Shades!
How are ye joined with hell in triple knot
Against the unarmed weakness of one virgin,
Alone and helpless! Is this the confidence
You gave me, brother?

First Br. Yes, and keep it still:
Lean on it safely: not a period
Shall be unsaid for me. Against the threats
Of malice, or of sorcery, or that power
Which erring men call chance, this I hold firm:
Virtue may be assailed, but never hurt;
Surprised by unjust force, but not inthralled:
Yea, even that, which mischief meant most harm,
Shall in the happy trial prove most glory:
But evil on itself shall back recoil,
And mix no more with goodness; when, at last,
Gathered like scum, and settled to itself,
It shall be in eternal restless change

---

* **Ribs**, etc. In Herman Hugo's *Pia Desideria* is an emblem representing a soul in the figure of an infant inside the ribs of a skeleton, with the motto, "O wretched man that I am. Who shall deliver me from the body of this death?" So Francis Quarles, Book v., for his eighth emblem, in like manner represents a youth within the ribs of a human skeleton. See Rom. vii., 24. These speeches, though very fine, delay the action too much. Shakespeare would have hastened on to the denouement.

Signs, mark, symptom, indication, note, token, signal. Distinguish, etc.

Self-fed * and self-consumed: if this fail,
The pillared firmament is rottenness,
And earth's base built on stubble. But come, let's on.
Against the opposing will and arm of Heaven
May never this just sword be lifted up;
But for that damned magician, let him be girt
With all the grisly legions that troop
Under the sooty flag of Acheron,
Harpies and hydras, or all the monstrous forms
'Twixt Africa and Ind,—I'll find him out,
And force him to return his purchase back,
Or drag him by the curls to a foul death,
Cursed as his life.
Spir. Alas! good venturous youth,
I love thy courage yet, and bold emprise;
But here thy sword can do thee little stead.
Far other arms and other weapons must
Be those that quell the might of hellish charms:
He with his bare wand can unthread thy joints,
And crumble all thy sinews.
First Br. Why, pr'ythee, shepherd,
How dost thou then thyself approach so near,
As to make this relation?
Spir. Care, and utmost shifts,
How to secure the lady from surprisal,
Brought to my mind a certain shepherd lad,
Of small regard to see to, yet well-skilled
In every virtuous plant and healing herb
That spreads her verdant leaf to the morning ray.
He loved me well, and oft would beg me sing,
Which, when I did, he on the tender grass
Would sit, and hearken even to ecstasy;
And, in requital, ope his leathern scrip,
And show me simples of a thousand names,
Telling their strange and vigorous faculties.

---

* **Self-fed**, etc. Warburton says: "This image is wonderfully fine. It is taken from the conjectures of astronomers concerning the dark spots which, from time to time, appear on the surface of the sun's body, and, after a while, disappear again; which they suppose to be the scum of that fiery matter which first breeds it, and then breaks through and consumes it."—**Pillared**. Homer represents Atlas as keeping "the tall pillars which hold heaven and earth asunder." This line has a Miltonic energy.—**Legions** (trisyl.)—**Acheron,** here as in Virgil, designates the lower world, hell.—**Harpies** (ἅρπυιαι, from ἁρπάζω, I snatch), monsters having the faces of women, and the bodies, wings, and claws of birds. They are personified storm-winds, or demons of the tempest. See Virgil's *Æneid*, III., 210. etc.—**Hydras** (ὕδρα, from ὕδωρ, water, Lat. *hydra*, a water-snake). The Lernæan hydra, destroyed by Hercules, had a huge body with nine heads, eight mortal and one immortal.—**Ind**, *India*.—**Emprise**, enterprising spirit; enterprise.—**Stead,** advantage.—**Relation,** statement.—**Regard,** *aspect.*—**To see to,** *to look at.*—**Scrip** (Icel. *skreppa*), *a wallet, small bag.*—**Simples** (*semel*, once; or *sine*, without; *plica*, fold), medicinal plants; each plant being supposed to possess its simple or particular virtue, and to be a simple remedy.

Vigorous, energetic, forcible, powerful, lively. Other synonymes?

Amongst the rest, a small unsightly root,
But of divine effect, he culled me out.
The leaf was darkish, and had prickles on it,
But in another country, as he said,
Bore a bright golden flower, but not in this soil:
Unknown, and like esteemed,* and the dull swain
Treads on it daily with his clouted shoon:
And yet more medicinal is it than that moly,
That Hermes once to wise Ulysses gave.
He called it hæmony, and gave it me,
And bade me keep it as of sovereign use
'Gainst all enchantments, mildew, blast, or damp,
Or ghastly furies' apparition.
I pursed it up, but little reckoning made,
Till new that this extremity compelled:
But now I find it true; for by this means
I knew the foul enchanter, though disguised,
Entered the very lime-twigs of his spells,
And yet came off. If you have this about you,
(As I will give you when we go,) you may
Boldly assault the necromancer's hall;
Where if he be, with dauntless hardihood,
And brandished blade, rush on him; break his glass,
And shed the luscious liquor on the ground,
But seize his wand. Though he and his cursed crew
Fierce sign of battle make, and menace high,
Or, like the sons of Vulcan, vomit smoke,
Yet will they soon retire, if he but shrink.
First Br. Thyrsis, lead on apace, I'll follow thee;
And some good angel bear a shield before us.

---

* **Like esteemed**, etc., not known and not esteemed.—**Clouted**, patched. See Josh. ix., 5.—**Shoon**, the old plural form of shoe. The old plural ending, common in Semi-Sax., is still retained in *oxen*. In Shakespeare and Byron we have *sandal shoon*.—**Moly**, a fabulous herb, said to have been given by Mercury to Ulysses, as a counter-charm against the spells of Circe. Homer (*Odyssey* x., 304. 305) says it was "black in the root, and its flower was like unto milk; and the gods call it Molu. It is difficult for mortal men to dig it up; but the gods can do everything"—**Hermes**, *Mercury*, the god of eloquence, and messenger of Jupiter. He wore a winged cap and winged sandals.—**Ulysses** (Odysseus), the most cunning and the wisest of all the Greek chieftains at the siege of Troy. His wanderings after the capture of that city are related in Homer's *Odyssey*.—**Hæmony.** *Hæmonia* was a poetical name of Thessaly. This country was more famous than almost any other for incantations, witchcraft, magic drugs, etc. See *Odes of Horace*. Book I., 27.—**Apparition** (five syllables).—**Pursed**, put in a purse or wallet. —**Lime-twigs**, twigs smeared with lime, which was a viscous substance for catching small birds.—**Necromancer** (νεκρός, dead; μαντέια, divination), one who professes to foretell events by communication with departed spirits; a conjurer.—**Vulcan**, god of fire, blacksmith and worker in metals generally, who had his forges under Ætna, seems to have been a personification of volcanic (*vulcanic*) force. The sons of Vulcan are probably the Cyclopes, and these again but symbolize volcanic forces. See Class. Dict. —**Apace**, with quick pace; rapidity. See *apace*, Index.

Apparition, vision, phantom, spectre, ghost. Distinguish, etc.
Extremity, exigency, emergency, crisis. Distinguish, etc.

The scene changes to a stately palace, set out with all manner of deliciousness: soft music, tables spread with all dainties. COMUS *appears with his rabble, and the* LADY, *set in an enchanted chair, to whom he offers his glass, which she puts by, and goes about to rise.*

Comus. Nay, lady, sit; if I but wave this wand,
Your nerves are all chained up in alabaster,
And you a statue; or, as Daphne* was,
Root-bound, that fled Apollo.
Lady. Fool, do not boast;
Thou canst not touch the freedom of my mind
With all thy charms, although this corporal rind
Thou hast immanacled, while Heaven sees good.
Comus. Why are you vexed, lady? Why do you frown?
Here dwell no frowns, nor anger; from these gates
Sorrow flies far. See, here be all the pleasures
That fancy can beget on youthful thoughts,
When the fresh blood grows lively and returns
Brisk as the April buds in primrose season.
And first behold this cordial julep here,
That flames and dances in his crystal bounds,
With spirits of balm and fragrant syrups mixed.
Not that Nepenthes, which the wife of Thone,
In Egypt, gave to Jove-born Helena,
Is of such power to stir up joy as this,
To life so friendly, or so cool to thirst.
Why should you be so cruel to yourself,
And to those dainty limbs, which nature lent
For gentle usage and soft delicacy?
But you invert the covenants of her trust,
And harshly deal, like an ill borrower,
With that which you received on other terms;
Scorning the unexempt condition
By which all mortal frailty must subsist,
Refreshment after toil, ease after pain,
That have been tired all day without repast,
And timely rest have wanted. But, fair virgin,
This will restore all soon.
Lady. 'Twill not, false traitor!
'Twill not restore the truth and honesty

---

* **Daphne.** Phœbus Apollo, love-smitten, pursued the fair nymph Daphne, who, as he was on the point of overtaking her, was changed into a bay-tree. Ever afterwards this tree (*laurus*) was a favorite with Apollo.—**Immanacled** (*in*. *upon*; *manus*, the hand), handcuffed, *manacled*.—**Julep** (Pers. *gul*, rose, *âb*, water).—**Nepenthes** (νη-, not; πένθος, grief), a drug used by the ancients to remove pain and produce exhilaration.—**Wife of Thone.** *Polydamna*, wife of Thone, gave to Helena, daughter of Jove and fairest of all women, *nepenthes*, among other "cunning and excellent drugs." See *Odyssey*, IV., 219–233.

Immanacled, *manacled*, *chained*, *fettered*, *shackled*, *bound*. Distinguish, etc.

That thou hast banished from thy tongue with lies.
Was this the cottage and the safe abode
Thou told'st me of? What grim aspects * are these,
These ugly-headed monsters? Mercy guard me!
Hence with thy brewed enchantments, foul deceiver!
Hast thou betrayed my credulous innocence
With visored falsehood and base forgery?
And wouldst thou seek again to trap me here
With liquorish baits, fit to ensnare a brute?
Were it a draught for Juno when she banquets,
I would not taste thy treasonous offer. None,
But such as are good men, can give good things;
And that which is not good is not delicious
To a well-governed and wise appetite.
Comus. O foolishness of men! that lend their ears
To those budge doctors of the Stoic fur,
And fetch their precepts from the Cynic tub,
Praising the lean and sallow abstinence!
Wherefore did nature pour her bounties forth
With such a full and unwithdrawing hand,
Covering the earth with odors, fruits, and flocks,
Thronging the seas with spawn innumerable,
But all to please and sate the curious taste?
And set to work millions of spinning worms,
That in their green shops weave the smooth-haired silk,
To deck her sons; and, that no corner might
Be vacant of her plenty, in her own loins
She hutched the all-worshipped ore and precious gems,
To store her children with. If all the world
Should, in a pet of temperance, feed on pulse,
Drink the clear stream, and nothing wear but frieze,
The All-giver would be unthanked, would be unpraised,
Not half his riches known, and yet despised;

---

* **Aspects.** As in Shakespeare, this word is accented on the last syllable in Milton. See note on *serviceable*, p. 251.—**Brewed.** See the description of the "poisoned caldron" in *Macbeth*.—**Visored,** wearing a visor (the part of a helmet perforated, to see through), *masked*.—**Liquorish** (A. S. *liccian*, to lick; Fr. *lécher*. to lick; A. S. *liccera*, a glutton), tempting the appetite. *dainty*.—**Wise appetite,** an appetite controlled by wisdom.—**Budge** (Irish *bolc. bolg, balg*, a bag, sack. Budge was lamb-skin fur, formerly much used as an ornamental edging of the gowns of scholars; hence), *scholastic, austere*.—**Stoic** (στόα, a roofed colonnade, a porch in Athens, where Zeno and his successors taught that men should be free from passion, unmoved by joy or grief), *pertaining to the Stoics*. See *Stoics*, p. 90.—**Fur** (Icel. *fôdr*, lining. Strips of fur were used on garments for lining or ornament), *robe*.—**Cynic,** pertaining to the school of philosophers founded by Antisthenes (who flourished about 375, B. C.). Of this school, Diogenes, who lived in a *tub*, was the most famous disciple. Antisthenes inculcated a rigid discipline, which he meant as a protest against luxury and effeminacy. See p. 206.—**Hutched** (A. S. *hwecca*. a chest), laid up as in a chest, hoarded.—**Pet** (*pout*, to protrude the lips), a slight fit of peevishness.—**Pulse,** the fruit or seed of leguminous plants, as beans, peas, etc.—**Frieze** (Fr. *frise*; W. *ffris*), a woollen cloth from Friesland, coarse, with a nap on one side.

Innocence, guiltlessness, harmlessness. Other synonymes? Differentiate, etc.
Temperance, modesty, moderation, continence, sobriety. Distinguish, etc.

And we should serve Him as a grudging master,
As a penurious niggard* of his wealth;
And live like Nature's bastards, not her sons;
Who would be quite surcharged with her own weight,
And strangled with her waste fertility;
The earth cumbered, and the winged air darked with plumes,
The herds would over-multitude their lords,
The sea, o'erfraught, would swell, and the unsought diamonds
Would so imblaze the forehead of the deep,
And so bestud with stars that they below
Would grow inured to light, and come at last
To gaze upon the sun with shameless brows.
List, lady; be not coy, and be not cozened
With that same vaunted name, virginity.
Beauty is Nature's coin, must not be hoarded,
But must be current; and the good thereof
Consists in mutual and partaken bliss,
Unsavory in the enjoyment of itself:
If you let slip time, like a neglected rose,
It withers on the stalk with languished head.
Beauty is Nature's brag, and must be shown
In courts, at feasts, and high solemnities,
Where most may wonder at the workmanship.
It is for homely features to keep home:
They had their name thence. Coarse complexions
And cheeks of sorry grain will serve to ply
The sampler, and to tease the housewife's wool.
What need a vermeil-tinctured lip for that,
Love-darting eyes, or tresses like the morn?
There was another meaning in these gifts:
Think what, and be advised: you are but young yet.

Lady. I had not thought to have unlocked my lips
In this unhallowed air, but that this juggler
Would think to charm my judgment, as mine eyes,
Obtruding false rules pranked in reason's garb.
I hate when vice can bolt her arguments,
And virtue has no tongue to check her pride.

---

* **Niggard** (Ice. *hnöggr*, sparing; Dan. *gnier*, a niggard), a *miser*, a *stingy wretch*.—**Over-multitude,** outnumber the multitude of.—**Coy** (Lat. *quies*, rest, *quietus*, quiet), *shy*.—**Cozened** (*cousin*, to pretend relationship; or it may be from Ger. *kosen*, Fr. *causer*, to talk, chat, wheedle), *deceived*.—**Grain.** (See note on "*dyed in grain*," in the 13th stanza of Spenser's Epithalamium, p. 76), *dye, color*.—**Ply,** to work busily at.—**Sampler,** a pattern of work, a collection of needle-work patterns.—**Tease** (A. S. *tæsan*, to pluck), *comb* or *card*.—**Vermeil-tinctured** (Lat. *vermiculus*, the little worm that furnishes the scarlet color), tinged with vermilion.—**Like the morn.** All the poets tell of the "golden hair" of the sun, or that of Aurora, "floating on the eastern clouds."—**Pranked** (Ger. *prangen*, *prunken*, to shine, make a show; Icel. *pranga*, Dan. *prange*, *prunke*, allied to *prink*), ostentatiously dressed.—**Bolt.** Webster defines this word in this connection, "to throw precipitately, blurt out, utter or throw out." (From A. S. *bolt*. Akin to Gr. βάλλειν, to throw.)

Niggard, miser. Other synonymes? Differentiate, etc.

Impostor! do not charge most innocent Nature,
As if she would her children should be riotous
With her abundance. She, good cateress,
Means her provision only to the good,
That live according to her sober laws,
And holy dictate of spare temperance.
If every* just man, that now pines with want,
Had but a moderate and beseeming share
Of that which lewdly-pampered luxury
Now heaps upon some few with vast excess,
Nature's full blessings would be well dispensed
In unsuperfluous even proportion,
And she no whit encumbered with her store:
And then the Giver would be better thanked,
His praise due paid; for swinish gluttony
Ne'er looks to heaven amidst his gorgeous feast,
But, with besotted base ingratitude,
Crams, and blasphemes his Feeder. Shall I go on?
Or have I said enough? To him that dares
Arm his profane tongue with contemptuous words
Against the sun-clad power of chastity,
Fain would I something say;—yet to what end?
Thou hast nor ear, nor soul, to apprehend
The sublime notion, and high mystery,
That must be uttered to unfold the sage
And serious doctrine of virginity;
And thou art worthy that thou shouldst not know
More happiness than this thy present lot.
Enjoy your dear wit, and gay Rhetoric,
That hath so well been taught her dazzling fence:
Thou art not fit to hear thyself convinced.
Yet, should I try, the uncontrolled worth
Of this pure cause would kindle my rapt spirits
To such a flame of sacred vehemence
That dumb things would be moved to sympathize,
And the brute earth would lend her nerves, and shake,
Till all thy magic structures, reared so high,
Were shattered into heaps o'er thy false head.
Comus. She fables not; I feel that. I do fear

---

* **If every,** etc. She answers specifically the argument of Comus. See the speech of Comus just preceding.—**Lewdly-pampered** (*lewd* is from A. S. *læwd*, laical; fr. Gr. λαός, the people), *wantonly pampered. Pampered* (Lat. *pampinus*, a vine-leaf. Old Fr. *pamprer*, to cover with vine-leaves, to nurse into luxuriant growth. Akin to O. Ger. *pampen*, to cram).—**Dazzling fence,** dazzling sword-play, as it were, of argument or repartee.—**I feel that** she fables not. Sympson suggested this punctuation instead of, *I feel that I do fear*, etc.

Dictate, command, injunction, order, direction, admonition, suggestion. Discriminate, etc.
Pines, flags, droops, languishes, dwindles, withers, decays. Give the peculiar meanings, etc.

Her words set off by some superior power;
And though not* mortal, yet a cold shuddering dew
Dips me all o'er, as when the wrath of Jove
Speaks thunder and the chains of Erebus
To some of Saturn's crew. I must dissemble,
And try her yet more strongly. Come, no more.
This is mere moral babble, and direct
Against the canon-laws of our foundation:
I must not suffer this: 'tis but the lees
And settlings of a melancholy blood;
But this will cure all straight. One sip of this
Will bathe the drooping spirits in delight
Beyond the bliss of dreams. Be wise, and taste.

The BROTHERS *rush in with swords drawn, wrest his glass out of his hand, and break it against the ground: his rout make sign of resistance, but are all driven in. The* ATTENDANT SPIRIT *comes in.*

Spir. What, have you let the false enchanter 'scape?
Oh ye mistook: you should have snatched his wand,
And bound him fast. Without his rod reversed,
And backward mutters of dissevering power,
We cannot free the lady that sits here
In stony fetters fixed and motionless.
Yet stay, be not disturbed: now I bethink me,
Some other means I have, which may be used,
Which once of Melibœus old I learnt,
The soothest shepherd that e'er piped on plains.
There is a gentle nymph, not far from hence,
That with moist curb sways the smooth Severn stream:
Sabrina is her name, a virgin pure.
Whilom she was the daughter of Locrine,

* **Though not,** though I am not. T. Warton says: "Here is the noblest panegyric on the power of virtue, adorned with the sublimest imagery. It is extorted from the mouth of a magician and a preternatural being, who, although actually possessed of his prey, feels all the terrors of human nature at the bold rebuke of innocence, and shudders with a sudden cold sweat, like a guilty man."—**Chains,** the object of *speaks* in the sense of *threatens.*—**Erebus** (see *Merchant of Venice*, Act v., Scene 1, and Class. Dict.), a dark region in the lower world; hell.—**Crew** (*Terra*, Earth, bore to *Cœlus* or *Uranus*, Heaven, the Titans, six males and six females, Saturn being the youngest male), the Titans, or the Giants.—**Canon-laws,** the church laws of Rome; established moral laws. (Lat. *canon*, a measuring line; Gr. *κανών*).—**Lees,** *dregs.* Hurd says, "I like the manuscript reading best: '*This is mere moral stuff, the very lees,*'" etc.—**Blood.** The quality of the blood was supposed to determine the disposition.—**Backward mutters,** the words of the charm pronounced in the reverse order.—**Bethink me,** make myself think, call to mind.—**Melibœus,** a shepherd in Virgil's First Eclogue. The prose tale of Melibœus is one of the Canterbury Tales.—**Soothest** (A. S. *sôdh*, truth), *truest;* most pleasing.—**Severn** (Lat. *Sabrina*) rises, in Wales, in a small lake on the east side of Plinlimmon. It is 210 miles long.—**Sabrina.** It being the principal river in this part of England and not far from Ludlow Castle, there was a special propriety in summoning the goddess of this stream. The story of Sabrina is in Sackville's "*Mirror for Magistrates,*" Drayton's "*Polyolbion,*" and in the Second Book of "*Fairy Queen.*" See also Fletcher's "*Faithful Shepherdess,*" which Milton evidently had before him in writing this part of Comus.—**Locrine.** Anchises, of Trojan fame, was the father of Æneas; Æneas, of Ascanius; Ascanius, of Silvius; Silvius of Brutus; Brutus, of Locrine. See Milton's Translation from *Geoffrey of Monmouth;* also Milton's *History of England*, Book I.

Dissemble, conceal, disguise, cloak, cover, pretend. Distinguish, etc.

That had the sceptre from his father Brute.
She, guiltless damsel, flying the mad pursuit
Of her enraged* stepdame, Guendolen,
Commended her fair innocence to the flood,
That stayed her flight with his cross-flowing course.
The water-nymphs, that in the bottom played,
Held up their pearled wrists and took her in,
Bearing her straight to aged Nereus' hall;
Who, piteous of her woes, reared her lank head,
And gave her to his daughters to imbathe
In nectared lavers, strewed with asphodel;
And through the porch and inlet of each sense
Dropt in ambrosial oils, till she revived
And underwent a quick immortal change,
Made goddess of the river. Still she retains
Her maiden gentleness, and oft at eve
Visits the herds along the twilight meadows,
Helping all urchin blasts and ill-luck signs
That the shrewd meddling elf delights to make;
Which she with precious vialled liquors heals.
For which the shepherds, at their festivals,
Carol her goodness loud in rustic lays,
And throw sweet garland wreaths into her stream,
Of pansies, pinks, and gaudy daffodils;
And, as the old swain said, she can unlock
The clasping charm, and thaw the numbing spell,
If she be right invoked in warbled song:
For maidenhood she loves, and will be swift
To aid a virgin, such as was herself,
In hard-besetting need. This will I try,
And add the power of some adjuring verse.

SONG.

Sabrina fair,
Listen where thou art sitting

* **Enraged.** Trisyl.—**Guendolen,** a divorced wife of Locrine.—**Nereus,** a sea deity, son of Pontus and Terra. In Homer he is styled ἅλιος γέρων, "old man of the sea." Hesiod represents him as distinguished for wisdom, truth, peace, and justice. He married the ocean nymph Doris, and the Nereids are their daughters.—**Lavers,** large basins for washing.—**Asphodel,** a perennial plant with beautiful flowers.—**Helping,** curing.—**Urchin** (Lat. *ericius. erinaceus;* Fr. *herisson*). T. Warton remarks: "The urchin or hedgehog, from its solitariness, the ugliness of its appearance, and from a popular opinion that it sucked or poisoned the udders of cows, was adopted into the demonologic system; and its shape was sometimes supposed to be assumed by mischievous elves."—**Blasts,** *blights* (caused by mischievous spirits in the form of hedgehogs). Webster, in his dictionary, makes the singular blunder of defining the word *urchin* in this passage as meaning *rough, pricking, piercing.*—**Shrewd,** *troublesome.* See *be-* in the Index.—**Elf** (A. S. *elf;* Celtic *Alp*, a mountain? Is *Elf* originally a *mountain* spirit?), a diminutive spirit, delighting in mischievous tricks.—**Vialled** (*vial* is from Gr. φιάλη, Lat. *phiala*, a broad, flat, shallow cup), *in a vial.*—**Daffodils** (Lat. and Gr. *asphodelus*, Fr. *fleur d'asphodèle*).—**Thaw,** *dissolve.*—**Right** (A. S. *riht;* Ger. *recht;* Lat. *rectus*, straight, *regere*, to straighten), *rightly.*

Meddling, interfering. Other synonymes? Differentiate, etc.

Under the glassy, cool, translucent wave,
In twisted braids of lilies knitting*
The loose train of thy amber-dropping hair.
Listen, for dear honor's sake,
Goddess of the silver lake;
Listen and save.
Listen, and appear to us,
In name of great Oceanus!
By the earth-shaking Neptune's mace,
And Tethys' grave majestic pace;
By hoary Nereus' wrinkled look,
And the Carpathian wizard's hook;
By scaly Triton's winding shell,
And old soothsaying Glaucus' spell;
By Leucothea's lovely hands,
And her son that rules the strands;
By Thetis' tinsel-slippered feet,
And the songs of Sirens sweet;
By dead Parthenope's dear tomb,
And fair Ligea's golden comb,
Wherewith she sits on diamond rocks,
Sleeking her soft alluring locks;
By all the nymphs that nightly dance
Upon thy streams with wily glance;—
Rise, rise, and heave thy rosy head
From thy coral-paven bed,

---

* **Knitting.** Sea nymphs, mermaids, and the like, are often represented as braiding and combing their locks. See, some eighteen or twenty lines below, *Ligea.*—**Amber.** "Amber, when applied to water, means a luminous clearness." *T. Warton.* See *amber*, line 333.—**Oceanus,** the god of the ocean-stream, offspring of *Cœlus* (Heaven) and *Terra* (Earth).—**Earth-shaking.** Homer constantly gives this epithet to *Poseidon* (Neptune).—**Mace,** a staff, borne by a magistrate or before him as an emblem of authority; a *sceptre.*—**Tethys,** wife of Oceanus. These two were the happy parents of the *Oceanides* or ocean-nymphs, three thousand in number!—**Nereus.** See note on line 835.—**Carpathian wizard, Proteus,** a sea-deity, son of Oceanus and Tethys, or as some say, of Neptune and Phœnice. He is called a wizard because he used to turn himself into many shapes. See note on his name in the *Areopagitica*, p. 238. He is called *Carpathian* from the island of *Carpathus*, between Rhodes and Crete, with the Carpathian sea in its vicinity. His *hook* is his "shepherd's crook;" for he tended the flocks of Neptune. See Virgil's *Georgics*, IV., 387, and following.—**Triton,** a sea-god, trumpeter of Neptune, son of Neptune and Amphitrite.—**Winding,** sounding with notes prolonged and mutually involved.—**Shell** (A. S. *scell, scealu, scalu;* Dan. *skal.* a shell), a shell used as a musical instrument. See p. 2:8.—**Glaucus,** a sea-deity, much given to prophecy and soothsaying. Some make him the same as Neptune: others, Neptune's son.—**Leucothea** (λευκός, white; θεά, goddess, the white goddess), the name borne by Ino, wife of Athamas, after she had leaped into the sea with her infant son, to escape from her insane husband, and had become a sea goddess. The child, whose name had been Melicerta, became a sea god with the name Palæmon. He and his mother were reputed kind to mariners, and were often invoked by them.—**Thetis,** one of the Nereids, wife of Peleus and mother of Achilles.—**Parthenope,** one of the sirens. She was cast upon the shore at Naples, which was anciently called Parthenope.—The siren **Ligea** (Gr. Λιγεία, clear-voiced) is mentioned as a *wood-nymph* in Virgil (*Georgics* IV., 336). Poe's lines will readily be recalled:—

"Ligea! Ligea!
My beautiful one,
Whose harshest idea
Will to melody run."

Translucent, transparent, pellucid. Other synonymes? Distinguish, etc.
Moist, humid, damp, wet. Other synonymes? Distinguish, etc.

And bridle * in thy headlong wave,
Till thou our summons answered have.
Listen and save!

SABRINA *rises, attended by water-nymphs, and sings.*

By the rushy-fringed bank,
Where grow the willow and the osier dank,
My sliding chariot stays,
Thick set with agate and the azure sheen
Of Turkis blue, and emerald green,
That in the channel strays;
Whilst from off the waters fleet,
Thus I set my printless feet
O'er the cowslip's velvet head,
That bends not as I tread.
Gentle swain, at thy request,
I am here.
Spir. Goddess dear,
We implore thy powerful hand
To undo the charmed band
Of true virgin, here distressed
Through the force and through the wile
Of unblessed enchanter vile.
Sabr. Shepherd, 'tis my office best
To help ensnared chastity.
Brightest lady, look on me.
Thus I sprinkle on thy breast
Drops, that, from my fountain pure,
I have kept, of precious cure;
Thrice upon thy finger's tip,
Thrice upon thy rubied lip:
Next, this marble venomed seat,
Smeared with gums of glutinous heat,
I touch with chaste palms, moist and cold.
Now the spell hath lost its hold,
And I must haste, ere morning hour,
To wait in Amphitrite's bower.

SABRINA *descends, and the Lady rises out of her seat.*

Spir. Virgin, daughter of Locrine,
Sprung of old Anchises' line,
May thy brimmed waves, for this,

---

* **Bridle.** See line 825.—**Sheen,** *brightness* So in line 1003, and in the *Hymn on the Nativity*, stanza 15.—**Turkis,** *turquois*, a Persian mineral of a bluish-green color and esteemed precious. Its color was supposed to change with the health of the wearer.—**Look on me.** See Acts iii., 4.—**Amphitrite,** daughter of Nereus and Doris. She was wife of Neptune.—**Daughter,** etc. See notes on lines 825, 826.

Their full tribute never miss
From a thousand petty rills,
That tumble down the snowy hills:
Summer drought, or singed air,
Never scorch thy tresses fair;
Nor wet October's torrent* flood
Thy molten crystal fill with mud.
May thy billows roll ashore
The beryl and the golden ore;
May thy lofty head be crowned
With many a tower and terrace round,
And here and there, thy banks upon,
With groves of myrrh and cinnamon!
Come, lady, while Heaven lends us grace,
Let us fly this cursed place,
Lest the sorcerer us entice
With some other new device.
Not a waste or needless sound,
Till we come to holier ground.
I shall be your faithful guide
Through this gloomy covert wide;
And not many furlongs thence
Is your father's residence,
Where this night are met in state
Many a friend to gratulate
His wished presence; and, beside,
All the swains, that there abide,
With jigs and rural dance resort.
We shall catch them at their sport,
And our sudden coming there
Will double all their mirth and cheer.
Come, let us haste: the stars grow high,
But night sits monarch yet in the mid sky.

The scene changes, presenting Ludlow town and the President's castle; then come in, country dancers; after them, the attendant SPIRIT, *with the* TWO BROTHERS *and the* LADY.

SONG.

Spir. Back, shepherds, back. Enough your play
Till next sun-shine holiday.

* **Torrent** (A. S. *teran*, *tær*, *toren*, tear, tore, torn; Mæso-Goth. *tairan;* Ger. *zerren;* W. *torri*, to break), *tearing*, rapidly rolling or rushing.[1]—**Be crowned.** Milton perhaps has in mind the "turreted Cybele" of the classics.—**Jigs**, light, brisk, musical movements; also frolicsome dances to such music. From Fr. *gigue*, a dance, tune, romp; Ger. *geigen*, to fiddle).

Petty, *trifling*, *trivial*, *frivolous*, *futile*, *little*. Other synonymes? Distinguish, etc.

[1] I venture to dissent from the common etymology, which derives this word from *torrēre*, to parch or scorch. See, however, the unabridged dictionaries.

Here be,* without duck or nod,
Other trippings to be trod
Of lighter toes, and such court guise
As Mercury did first devise
With the mincing Dryades,
On the lawns and on the leas.

This second Song presents them to their Father and Mother.

Noble lord, and lady bright,
I have brought ye new delight.
Here behold so goodly grown
Three fair branches of your own.
Heaven hath timely tried their youth,
Their faith, their patience, and their truth;
And sent them here, through hard assays,
With a crown of deathless praise,
To triumph in victorious dance,
O'er sensual folly and intemperance.

The dances being ended, the SPIRIT *epilogises.*

Spir. To the ocean now I fly,
And those happy climes that lie
Where day never shuts his eye
Up in the broad fields of the sky!
There I suck the liquid air,
All amidst the gardens fair
Of Hesperus, and his daughters three
That sing about the golden tree.
Along the crisped shades and bowers
  Revels the spruce and jocund Spring,
The Graces and the rosy-bosomed Hours
  Thither all their bounties bring:
There eternal Summer dwells,
And west winds, with musky wing,
About the cedarn alleys fling
Nard and cassia's balmy smells:
Iris there, with humid bow,
Waters the odorous banks, that blow

---

* **Here be,** etc., here *are*. Often in Shakespeare and the Bible we have *be* for *are*. See Abbott's *Shakespearian Grammar*, 300.—**Duck or nod.** These words allude to the awkwardness of the rustics in dancing.—**Mercury.** See note on *Hermes*, line 637.—**Mincing,** stepping short pretty steps. See Dict.—**Dryades** (Δρῦς, a tree), nymphs of the trees and woods.—**Hesperus.** See note on line 393. There are several versions of the story of Hesperus. Milton follows partly the account of Diodorus. See the Classical Dictionaries.—**Crisped,** curled, twisted, wreathed, interwoven.—**Graces.** See Spenser's *Epithalamium*, sixth stanza. "They were an æsthetic conception of all that is beautiful and attractive in the physical as well as in the social world."—**Hours.** See notes on *Hours* and *handmaids*, p. 72.—**Iris.** See p. 254.—**Blow,** cause to blossom.

Jocund, *lively*, *sprightly*, *vivacious*, *sportive*, *merry*, *jolly*, *lively*. Other synonymes? Discriminate, etc.

Flowers of more mingled hue
Than her purfled* scarf can shew;
And drenches with Elysian dew
(List, mortals, if your ears be true)
Beds of hyacinths and roses,
Where young Adonis oft reposes,
Waxing well of his deep wound
In slumber soft; and on the ground
Sadly sits the Assyrian queen:
But far above, in spangled sheen,
Celestial Cupid, her famed son, advanced,
Holds his dear Psyche sweet entranced,
After her wandering labors long,
Till free consent the gods among
Make her his eternal bride;
And from her fair unspotted side
Two blissful twins are to be born,
Youth and Joy: so Jove hath sworn.
But now my task is smoothly done,
I can fly, or I can run,
Quickly to the green earth's end,
Where the bowed welkin slow doth bend,
And from thence can soar as soon
To the corners of the moon.
Mortals, that would follow me,
Love virtue: she alone is free.
She can teach ye how to climb
Higher than the sphery chime;
Or, if virtue feeble were,
Heaven itself would stoop to her.

---

* **Purfled** (Old Fr. *pourfiler; pour*, for; *fil*, Lat. *filum*, thread; Ital. *profilare*, to embroider), with flowered border; *embroidered*.—**Scarf**, the rainbow.—**Elysian.** See note on line 257.—**Adonis**, etc. See *Thammuz*, p. 249. See *Fairy Queen*, Book III.; Canto vi., 46. Adonis was famed for his beauty. He was greatly beloved by Venus, who used to entreat him not to expose himself to the dangers of the chase. At last he lost his life by the tusk of a wild boar.—**Assyrian queen,** *Venus.* "There is no other of the Olympians of whom the foreign origin is so probable as this goddess, and she is generally regarded as being the same with the Astarte (Ishtar) of the Phœnicians."—**Psyche.** See *Fairy Queen*, Book III.; Canto vi., st. 50, 51. The legend or allegory of Cupid and Psyche is one of the most beautiful of ancient mythology. The story is charmingly told in Bulfinch's *Age of Fable.* "The Greek name for a *butterfly* is Psyche, and the same word means the *soul.* Perhaps there is no illustration of the immortality of the soul more striking and beautiful than that furnished by the butterfly, bursting on brilliant wings from the tomb in which it has lain, after a dull, grovelling, caterpillar existence, to flutter in the blaze of day and feed on the most fragrant and delicate productions of the spring. Psyche, then, is the human soul, which is purified by sufferings and misfortunes, and is thus prepared for the enjoyment of true and pure happiness."—**Welkin** (A. S. *wolcen*, cloud, sky), the vault of heaven, the sky. *Bowed welkin*, "a curve which bends, or descends *slowly* from its great sweep." *Cleveland.*—**Sphery chime,** the music of the spheres. See note on *crystal spheres* in *Hymn on the Nativity*, p. 247.—**Stoop,** etc. The moral of this elegant poem is summed up with exquisite felicity in these concluding lines. Well does Emerson pronounce *Comus* "the loftiest poem in praise of female purity in any language."

Virtue, chastity, purity. Other synonyms? Distinguish, etc.

Write out the story of *Comus*. To what extent was Milton indebted to Fletcher and other poets for the plan or leading thoughts? What can you say of the species of composition called *Masques?* Point out the beauties or blemishes in this poem. Write out a statemant of the origin and the exhibition of this Masque. It is the fashion with modern critics, Taine, Froude, White, and others, to disparage and even censure the appearance of any didactic purpose in a poem; to count it a blemish; and to regard as a great merit the fact that a poet is careless of the moral lesson his work conveys. Try *Comus* by this standard, and write your views of such a criterion. Is it matter of commendation in Shakespeare that he "carries his persons indifferently through right and wrong?" Write an essay on Milton's boyhood and youth; one on him as a politician; as a reformer; as a poet; one on his blindness; on his marriages; on his place in English literature; on Milton as a schoolmaster; on *Paradise Lost;* on his imitators. Compare Shakespeare's originality as an author with that of Milton. What sacrifices of taste and inclination did Milton make in joining the Puritans? What intimations does he give in youth or early manhood, of his intention to write a great poem? (These themes for essays are intended as suggestions to teachers, who should be fertile in devising and ingenious in selecting others. The student should be encouraged especially to rely on his own investigations and not to accept facts or principles at second-hand.)

HISTORICAL ANALYSIS OF WORDS.

An historical analysis should give a history of each word. It should state, if practicable, the root form, the primary meaning, and the successive changes these have undergone. The prefixes and suffixes should be treated in the same way. If the period in which the term or element was introduced into the English language can be determined, it will be well to specify it. Something of comparative philology may be added.

We have already, in the explanatory foot-notes, dipped, in a desultory way, into this interesting subject; but it will be well to be henceforth more systematic. If convenient, the student should consult, among other books, *Trench on the Study of Words*, *English Past and Present*, *Diversions of Purley*, Swinton's *Word Analysis*, Max Müller's and Marsh's *Lectures*, Goold Brown's *Grammar of Grammars*, Abbot's *Shakespearian Grammar*, and especially Wedgewood's *Dictionary of English Etymology*. If no other book can be had, Webster's or Worcester's *Unabridged Dictionary* will tolerably answer the purpose. The practice of examining reference-books of all kinds ought to become a confirmed habit. Let the teacher insist on this. Something should be done daily, for a year or more, in historical analysis. The following may serve as an

EXAMPLE.

"Whom we invite to see us crowned at Scone."—SHAKESPEARE.

Whom is from A. S. *hwá*, who; dative, *hwám*, to whom; masc. accusative (*i. e.*, objective) *hwone*, *whäne*, whom; Mæso-Goth. *hwas*, who; *hwana*, whom; Ger. *wer*, who; *wen*, whom. The first two letters, *hw*, appear to have an interrogative (and often a relative) force. They are akin to Lat. *qu* in *qui*, who; *quot*, how many; and to Sans. *k* in *kas*, who; Gr. *κόσος*, how much. By a peculiar and unexplained caprice in orthography, they in the eleventh or twelfth century became permanently transposed to *wh*. The termination *m* or *n* is the common sign of the accusative singular, masc. and fem., in the Indo-European languages.

We. A. S. *we;* Ger. *wir;* Dan. *vi.* *W* is from *u*, an element of the first pers. plu. in our pronoun of the first person; as in *we*, *our*, *ours*, *us*.

Invite. Lat. *invitare*, to invite. *In* is Sans. *antu*, *ontu*, *on;* Gr. *ἐν*, in; Lat., Goth., Ger., Ital., Dutch, *in;* Gr. *εἰν*; Ice., Sw., Dan. *i;* Fr. *en;* —meaning *within*, *into*, *to*. Or it may be Gr. *ἀν*, *ἀ*, Sans. *an*, *a*, akin to *ἄνευ*, without; Ger. *ohne;* Lat. *in-*, not; Ger. *un-;* Eng. *in-* and *un-* not.

Vite is from what? connected with Lat. *vitare*, to shun? or with Lat. *vita*, life?

To is A. S. *tô;* Goth. *du;* Ger. *zu;* perhaps fr. Lat. *ad* by transposition; indicating primarily approach and arrival. In A. S., *to* was used with the dative of the infinitive, and this usage became general with the infinitives in all situations. It perhaps originally had a demonstrative force. See the element *t*, p. 60.

See. A. S. *seon*, for *sehwan ;* Goth. *saihwan*, *saiwan ;* Ger. *sehen ;* Dan. *see ;* Ice. and O. Fries. *sía ;* all meaning *to see.* Perhaps fr. Gr. θεάομαι, to see.

Us. A. S. *ús*, *úsih*, *usic*, accusative plu. of *Ic*, *I ;* Goth. and Ger. *uns ;* Lat. *nos ;* O. Sax., O. Fries., Low Ger. *us.* See *We* above.

Crowned. Lat. *coronare ;* Fr. *couronner ;* Ger. *krönen ;* Dutch *kroonen*, to crown ; fr. Lat. *corona ;* O. Eng. *corone*, *coroun ;* Fr. *couronne ; a crown.* The *-ed* is probably abridged from an ancient auxiliary verb signifying *to do.* The most ancient English verbs express the past tense by an internal inflection or change of vowel, as *sing*, *sang*, *sung.* Those which add *-d* or *-ed* are more recent accessions to the language.

At. A. S. *æt ;* Goth., O. Sax., Ice., and Dan. *at ;* Lat. *ad.* It is supposed to be another form of *to*, and to mean, primarily, *near*, *present*, or *towards.* See *to* on p. 283.

Scone. Old Scotch *Scoon.* See p. 137.

JOHN BUNYAN, 1682.

JOHN BUNYAN.

1628–1688.

" Ingenious dreamer, in whose well-told tale
Sweet fiction and sweet truth alike prevail;
Whose humorous vein, strong sense, and simple style
May teach the gayest, make the gravest smile;
Witty, and well employed, and, like thy Lord,
Speaking in parables his slighted word;
I name thee not, lest so despised a name
Should move a sneer at thy deserved fame;
Yet e'en in transitory life's late day,
That mingles all my brown with sober gray,
Revere the man, whose pilgrim marks the road,
And guides the progress of the soul to God."—COWPER.

JOHN BUNYAN, the author of the most popular allegory in any language, was born in 1628 at Elstow, about two miles from Bedford, the county-seat of Bedfordshire, England. He got a little instruction in reading and writing at the village school, but lost it nearly all before he came of age. He represents himself as having been in youth exceedingly depraved; but this self-depreciation was probably the utterance of religious enthusiasm, or of a conscience morbidly acute. He was at least perfectly chaste, and does not appear to have ever been drunk. "The four chief sins of which he was guilty," says Macaulay, "were dancing, ringing the bells of the parish church, playing at 'tipcat,' and reading the *History of Sir Bevis of Southampton.*" To these I think we may add sabbath-breaking, ale-tippling, and profane swearing; but on being reproved for the last-named vice by a "loose and ungodly" woman, who protested that even she was shocked at his blasphemy, he at once and forever abandoned it.

During a great part of his youth and early manhood he was on the verge of insanity. His self-inquisitorial habit amounted to a disease. His vivid imagination was ever summoning up the most frightful images of hell and devils, and himself in the midst of them. In the commonest events he was sure he recognized the miraculous interposition of a supernatural hand, often terrible, sometimes merciful. "God [illegible]d not utterly leave me. Once I fell into a creek of the sea, and hardly escaped drowning. Another time I fell out of a boat into Bedford River; but mercy yet preserved me; besides, another time, being in the field with my companions, it chanced that an adder passed over the highway; so I, having a stick, struck her over the back, and having stunned her, I forced open her mouth with my stick and plucked her sting out with my fingers; by which act, had not God been merciful to me, I might by my desperateness have brought myself to my end. This also I have taken notice of with thanksgiving; when I was a soldier, I with others were [was] drawn out to go to such a place to besiege it; but when I was just ready to go, one of the company desired to go in my room; to which, when I had consented, he took my place, and, coming to the siege, as he stood sentinel, he was shot in the head with a musket bullet, and died. Here, as I said, were judgments and mercy." *

---

* *Grace Abounding to the Chief of Sinners:* by John Bunyan.

These were but transient gleams. "Often, after I had spent this and the other day in sin, I have been greatly afflicted, while asleep, with the apprehension of devils and wicked spirits, who, as I then thought, labored to draw me away with them. . . . . These things, I say, when I was but a child but nine or ten years old, did so distress my soul. . . . . I was also then so overcome with despair of life and heaven, that I should often wish either that there had been no hell, or that I had been a devil, supposing that they were only tormentors! that, if it needs must be that I went thither, I might be rather a tormentor than be tormented myself!" *

He feared he had committed "the unpardonable sin," and an aged godly man, whom in his distress he consulted on the subject, concurred with him in this apprehension. Day and night he felt himself driven by devils to sell Christ. "Sell him, sell him, sell him!" rang in his ears, and was whispered to him by a thousand fiendish tongues. "Never! never! not for thousands of worlds," he replied, hour after hour; till at last, amid unspeakable agony, he exclaimed, "Let him go, if he will!" No words can paint the horrible visions and despair that succeeded. "I lifted up my head, but methought I saw as if the sun that shineth in the heavens did grudge to give me light; and as if the very stones in the streets, and tiles upon the houses, did bend themselves against me. Oh, how happy now was every creature over I was! For they stood fast and kept their station, but I was gone and lost." †

Other fantasies came to torment him. "At one time he took it into his head that all persons of Israelite blood would be saved, and tried to make out that he partook of that blood; but his hopes were speedily destroyed by his father, who seems to have had no ambition to be regarded as a Jew.

"At another time Bunyan was disturbed by a strange dilemma. 'If I have not faith, I am lost; if I have faith, I can work miracles.' He was tempted to cry to the puddles between Elstow and Bedford, 'Be ye dry,' and to stake his eternal hopes on the event!

"Then he took up a notion that the day of grace for Bedford and the neighboring villages was past; that all who were to be saved in that part of England were already converted; and that he had begun to pray and strive some months too late.

"Then he was harassed by doubts whether the Turks were not in the right, and the Christians in the wrong. Then he was troubled by a maniacal impulse which prompted him to pray to the trees, to a broomstick, to the parish bull!" ‡

Civil war raging in England, he enlisted in the parliamentary army at the age of seventeen. The incident already quoted, in reference to his comrade who volunteered to take his place and was shot, occurred at the siege of Leicester in June, 1645. His military experience enriched his style with many embellishments and happy illustrations.

At nineteen he married his first wife. Little better than a gipsy, he had saved nothing of his earnings, and the bride was equally destitute. "We came together as poor as poor might be, not having so much household stuff as a dish or spoon betwixt us both; yet this she had for her part, *The Plain Man's Pathway to Heaven*, and *The Practice of Piety*, which her father had left when he died." Tenderly and faithfully did this good woman strive to win her young husband from his wicked ways, and well was her fidelity rewarded. At first his reformation was only external. From the extremity of remorse and fear, he passed to the extreme of self-righteousness. "I would think with myself, 'God cannot choose but be now pleased with me;' yea, to relate it in my own way, I thought 'no man in England could please God better than I.' Thus I continued about a twelvemonth or more." Humiliation and despair followed.

At twenty-five all the storms had cleared away, to return only briefly and at long intervals. He had found that peace which the world cannot give nor take away. The

---

* *Grace Abounding to the Chief of Sinners*, § 7. † *Ibid.*, § 187. ‡ *Macaulay.*

terrible fire through which he had passed, had purged off the dross, and the pure gold of his intellect and heart was now ready to be moulded into shapes of beauty that will shine forevermore. He was admitted as a member of the Baptist Church at Bedford. At twenty-seven, on the death of their pastor, he was earnestly solicited to preach for them, and with modest reluctance he consented. For five years, though not regularly ordained, he officiated in the pulpit with singular eloquence.

But when Charles II. came to the throne, in the spring of 1660, dissenters were prohibited from holding religious meetings. In November of that year, Bunyan was arrested, tried before Justice Wingate, and sentenced to perpetual banishment for holding unlawful assemblies and conventicles. The sentence was commuted to imprisonment in Bedford jail, where he remained twelve and a half years. At any moment he might have been liberated, if he would promise to abstain from preaching. His self-denial in choosing imprisonment in this wretched hole cost him intense anguish. The partings from his distressed family, who were occasionally permitted to visit him, and particularly from his blind daughter, who lay nearer his heart than all the world besides, were, he says, "like tearing the flesh from the bones." The jailer was kind, and allowed him to give religious instruction to the other prisoners.

Tinkering being ended for him, he learned to make long tagged thread-laces.* It appears that his wife and children usually wove them, and he used to fasten the tags on. These laces were sold to peddlers, and thus the family were supported. Towards the end of his imprisonment, its rigor was relaxed, and he was allowed to go out into the village; and once, it appears, he even went to London while a prisoner.

In prison he had few, if any, books, other than the Bible and Fox's Book of Martyrs. These he deeply studied. Pen, ink, and paper were allowed him, and he produced several religious works; among them, *Pilgrim's Progress.* He wrote it more as a recreation, than as a work of any importance. After it was finished, a long time elapsed before he made up his mind to publish it. He consulted friends.

> "Some said, 'John, print it,' others said, 'Not so.'
> Some said, 'It might be good;' others said, 'No.'"

About 1675 appeared the first edition, comprising Part I.; in 1678, a second edition, containing also the second part. In the next seven years it was reprinted eight times, and from that day to this, its popularity has been second to that of the Bible only.

In the last year of his imprisonment, he was ordained a minister in place of his old friend, Rev. Mr. Gifford. Released in 1672 through the kind intercession of Barlow, Bishop of Lincoln, he entered heartily upon the work of the ministry. A *barn* was purchased for £50 and fitted up as a chapel. Here (and elsewhere as itinerant preacher) he labored sixteen years, annually riding to London, where he addressed large congregations of non-conformists. His influence and authority became so great among the Baptists that he was popularly called *Bishop* Bunyan, and the fine scholars and rich gentry were compelled to recognize his power, though they despised his homely garb and manners, and hated what they termed his fanaticism.

In 1685 he appears to have been again in some danger, many prosecutions being then brought against the non-conformists. There is a tradition that he was forced to disguise himself as a wagoner, and that he preached in a smock-frock with a whip in his hand. About this time he published his *Holy War*, which Lord Macaulay pronounces superior to all other allegories, the *Pilgrim's Progress* excepted.

In 1687 a courtier came from London to remodel the corporation of Bedford, and, it was supposed, to offer some municipal dignity to Bunyan, if he could but gain the

* *Wire-snares*, says Taine.

"Baptist bishop" over to the support of King James; but the sturdy preacher refused even to speak with the royal emissary.

Bunyan wrote, in all, some sixty works. Many of these were controversial; against the Quakers, against the Catholics, against the liturgy of the English Church, against Arminians and Pelagians, and against believers in "Close-communion." Among the most important, after the *Pilgrim's Progress* and *the Holy War*, are his autobiography, entitled, *Grace Abounding to the Chief of Sinners; Life and Death of Dr. Badman; The Barren Fig-tree.*

In the summer of 1688, he made a journey from Reading to London, to reconcile an angry father to a son, whom the sire had threatened to disinherit. The attempt was successful, but it cost Bunyan his life. Riding through a heavy rain, he contracted a severe cold, which brought on a fever. In a few days he lay dead at his lodgings on Snow Hill. A plain grave-stone, bearing in faint lettering the simple words, "Here lies John Bunyan," was erected over his grave in the humble cemetery at Bunhill Fields.

There are many little defects in the *Pilgrim's Progress*, yet for two centuries it has been, and it seems likely to continue, the most popular of allegories. This is due to its vivid painting; its stirring action; its all-important theme; its quiet humor, whose lambent flames light many a dark page; its tenderness for the weak; its perfectly intelligible language, whole pages of which contain no word which any child of eight years may not understand; and, above all, its strong human interest, which makes every Christian feel that he is reading the story of his own inner life, while he recognizes the portrait of many a neighbor in those representative characters, which Bunyan delineates with a pen hardly less felicitous than Shakespeare's.

To this list of qualities we add another, its sweet *rhythm*. The subject of rhythm in prose is a field comparatively unexplored, but well deserving the attention of students of rhetoric and elocution. There are books which edify a chosen few, but whose discordant sentences are chips and sawdust to the masses. The *Pilgrim's Progress* is a prose poem. Like Christian himself, it has, running through it, an inner melody, which often breaks forth into actual song. Its sweetness enters the heart by the ear as well as by the eye. Only a few changes are necessary to make it a poem in *form*. For example, see how easily the following passage runs into dactylic hexameters :—

> "Só they went | úp to the | moúntains to (be-) | hóld the | gárdens and | órchards, the víneyards and | főuntains of | water, where | álso they | dránk and | wáshed themsélves, and did | fréely | eát of the | víneyards. Now (there) | wére on the | tóps of those mountains, | shépherds | feéding their | flócks ; and they | stoód by the | híghway-síde. The | pílgrims | thérefore went | tó them, and | léaning up- | ón their stáffs, as is | cómmon with | wéary | pílgrims, when (they) | stánd to | tálk with ány (by) the | wáy, they | ásk-ed | 'whóse de- | léctable | móuntains are thése, and | whose be the | shéep that | féed upon | them ?'"

Write down in chronological order the leading events in the life of Bunyan, including the publication of his principal books and treatises. Give some account of the *Pilgrim's Progress*, its origin, the circumstances under which it was composed, its circulation during its author's life, its popularity, its influence, and its place among the works of literary genius. (See Macaulay's Essay on Southey's Edition of *Pilgrim's Progress* and on *John Bunyan*; Southey's *Life of Bunyan*; Collier's *History of English Literature*; Angus's *Hand-Book of English Literature*; Craik's *English Literature*; Taine's *History of English Literature*; Chambers's *Cyclopedia of English Literature*; Cleveland's *Compendium*; Wickens's *Introduction to Pilgrim's Progress*; Allibone's *Dictionary of Authors*, under the title *Bunyan*, and the works there referred to.)

THE PILGRIM'S PROGRESS:

UNDER THE SIMILITUDE OF A DREAM.

PART I.

As I walked through the wilderness* of this world, I lighted on a certain place, where was a den; and laid me down in that place to sleep; and as I slept, I dreamed a dream. I dreamed, and behold, I saw a man clothed with rags, standing in a certain place, with his face from his own house, a book in his hand, and a great burthen upon his back. I looked and saw

* **Walked through the wilderness.** Note the alliteration. The careful reader will all along be struck with the highly scriptural language and imagery of this work. See Judges xi., 16.—**Lighted on.** Gen. xxviii., 11.—**Den.** In 1660, Bunyan was tried before Justice Wingate and convicted of holding unlawful assemblies and conventicles, and thereupon was committed to Bedford jail, where he was confined for twelve years. It was a vile place, fitly characterized as a *den.* Bunyan, however, found it not a bad place for meditation and the study of the Bible. During his imprisonment he said, "I never had in all my life so great an *inlet* into the Word of God as now." See Macaulay's two brilliant essays on Bunyan, one of them in the *Encyclopedia Britannica.* See Heb. xi., 38.—**Laid me down.** Ps. iii., 5; iv., 8; Gen. xxviii., 11, 12, etc. By consulting Cruden's *Concordance* a multitude of biblical expressions and associations will appear, of which a number will be indicated in these foot-notes.—**Dreamed a dream.** Gen. xxxvii., 5, 9.—**Rags.** Prov. xxiii., 21; Is. lxiv., 6.—**Face from.** Luke xiv., 33.—**Burthen.** Ps. xxxviii., 4.

I walked. These two words constitute a *simple* sentence; that is, a sentence containing but one subject and one predicate. It is a *declarative* sentence; that is, a sentence not interrogative, imperative, conditional, nor exclamatory.

I is the *subject; i. e.*, that of which something is said. Walked is the predicate; *i. e.*, that which is said of the subject. The connection of subject with predicate must exist in every sentence. It may be called *The Subject-and-Predicate Combination*, and may be expressed by a bracket [connecting the two, as shown below.

The *subject* is always a noun, a pronoun, or something standing for a noun. The *predicate* may be a verb, as in this case.

MODEL OF ANALYSIS.

SYNTACTICAL. (Logical, etc.)			SYNTACTICAL. (Parsing.)	HISTORICAL. (Compara. Philology, etc.)
Simple Declar. Sentence.	┌I	Subj.	Pers. pr., 1st, sing., masc., nom.	A. S. *ic;* Lat. *ego;* Gr. ἐγώ; Ger. *ich;* Fr. *je.* See pp. 283, 284.
	└**walked.**	Pred.	Weak v., intr., ind., past, 1st, sing.	A. S. *wealcan*, to roll; Ger. *walken*, to *full* (whence *walker* = a fuller), originally, to *go;* Ger. *wallen*, to move with undulations; Goth. *valka*, to walk.

This may be read according to the following

FORMULA:

I walked is a simple declarative sentence.
I walked is a *subject-and-predicate combination.*
I is the subject; *walked*, the predicate.
I is a pers. pron., first pers., sing. num., masc. gend., nom. case, subject of walked. Rule—The subject of a finite verb, etc.
Walked is a weak (*i. e., regular*[1]) verb, intrans., indic. mood, past tense, first pers., sing. num., agreeing with *I.* Rule—A verb must agree with its subject, etc.
I is akin to the Anglo-Sax. *ic;* Lat. *ego;* Gr. ἐγώ; Ger. *ich;* Fr. *je.* *Walked* is from the Anglo-Sax. *wealcan*, to roll; akin to Ger. *walken*, to full (whence the proper name *walker*, a fuller), originally = to *go;* Ger. *wallen*, to move in an undulatory manner; Goth. *valka*, to walk.

Analyze, according to the same model, *I lighted.*

[1] *Regular* verbs are called *weak*, because they require the aid of *-d* or *-ed* added to the present to form the imperfect; *i. e., past*, or *preterit. Irregular* verbs are called *strong*, because they require no aid from without to form the imperfect. There are less than two hundred of the latter, but about four thousand of the former. The suffix *-d* or *-ed* is probably abridged from an ancient auxiliary verb signifying *to do.* So that *love -d* is equivalent to *love -did*, or *did love; form -ed* is equivalent to *form -did*, or *did form.*

him open the book, and read therein; and as he read, he wept, and trembled;* and, not being able longer to contain, he broke out with a lamentable cry, saying, "What shall I do?"

In this plight, therefore, he went home, and refrained himself as long as he could, that his wife and children should not perceive his distress; but he could not be silent long, because that his trouble increased. Wherefore at length he brake his mind to his wife and children, and thus he began to talk to them: "O my dear wife," said he, "and ye the children of my bowels, I, your dear friend, am in myself undone, by reason of a burthen that lieth hard upon me: moreover, I am certainly informed, that this our city will be burned with fire from heaven; in which fearful overthrow, both myself, with thee my wife, and you my sweet babes, shall miserably come to ruin; except, the which yet I see not, some way of escape may be found whereby we may be delivered."

At this, his relations were sore amazed; not for that they believed that what he had said to them was true, but because they thought some frenzy-distemper had got into his head. Therefore, it drawing towards night, and they hoping that sleep might settle his brains, with all haste they got him to bed. But the night was as troublesome to him as the day. Wherefore, instead of sleeping, he spent it in sighs and tears. So when the morning was come, they would know how he did. He told them, "Worse and worse." He also set to talking to them again; but they began to be hardened. They also thought to drive away his distemper by harsh and surly carriage to him: sometimes they would deride, sometimes they would chide, and sometimes they would quite neglect him. Wherefore he began to retire himself to his chamber to pray for and pity them, and also to condole his own misery. He would also walk solitarily in the fields, sometimes reading and sometimes praying; and thus for some days he spent his time.

Now I saw upon a time, when he was walking in the fields, that he was, as he was wont, reading in his book and greatly distressed in his mind; and as he read he burst out, as he had done before, crying, "What shall I do to be saved?"

I saw also that he looked this way, and that way, as if he would run; yet he stood still; because, as I perceived, he could not tell which way to go. I looked then, and saw a man named Evangelist, coming to him, and [he] asked, "Wherefore dost thou cry?"

He answered, "Sir, I perceive by the book in my hand that I am condemned to die, and after that to come to judgment; and I find that I am not willing to do the first, nor able to do the second."

---

* **Trembled.** Acts xvi., 29, etc.; ii., 37.—**Contain,** *restrain himself.* Obs. in this sense. In this first paragraph the following words are not of Anglo-Saxon origin: *certain, place, face, trembled, able, contain, lamentable, cry.* This great preponderance of Anglo-Saxon words is very marked in Bunyan. For the relative proportion of Anglo-Saxon and of foreign words in each of the leading English authors, see Marsh's *Lectures on the English Language.*—**Burned.** 2 Pet. iii., 10.—**In this plight,** etc. This passage, as far as, "I saw also," is not in the earliest edition.—**Evangelist** (Gr. εὐαγγελιστής, one who brings good tidings, a messenger of good; εὖ, well, good, ἄγγελος, messenger.)—**Condemned to die.** Heb. ix., 27, and *passim.*

Trouble increased. Analyze according to the model on p. 289.

Then said Evangelist: "Why not willing to die, since this life is attended with so many evils?" The man answered, "Because I fear that this burthen that is upon my back will sink me lower than the grave; and I shall fall into Tophet.* And, sir, if I be not fit to go prison, I am not fit to go to judgment, and from thence to execution; and the thoughts of these things make me cry."

Then said Evangelist, "If this be thy condition, why standest thou still?" He answered, "Because I know not whither to go." Then he gave him a parchment roll, and there was written within, *Fly from the wrath to come.*

The man therefore read it, and looking upon Evangelist very carefully, said, "Whither must I fly?" Then said Evangelist, pointing with his finger over a very wide field, "Do you see yonder wicket gate?" The man said, "No." Then said the other, "Do you see yonder shining light?" He said, "I think I do." "Then," said Evangelist, "keep that light in your eye, and go up directly thereto. So shalt thou see the gate; at which, when thou knockest, it shall be told thee what thou shalt do."

So I saw in my dream, that the man began to run. Now, he had not run far from his own door, but his wife and children, perceiving it, began to cry after him to return; but the man put his fingers in his ears, and ran on, crying "Life! life! eternal life!" So he looked not behind him, but fled towards the middle of the plain.

The neighbors also came out to see him run; and as he ran, some mocked, others threatened, and some cried after him to return; and among those that did so, there were two that were resolved to fetch him back by force. The name of the one was Obstinate, and the name of the other, Pliable.

Now, by this time, the man was got a good distance from them; but, however, they were resolved to pursue him; which they did, and in a little time they overtook him. Then said the man, "Neighbors, wherefore are ye come?" They said, "To persuade you to go back with us:" but he said, "That can by no means be. You dwell," said he, "in the City of Destruc-

---

* **Tophet.** Is. xxx., 33. (Heb. *tuph*, to spit out; *tophet*, a place to be spit on, an abominable place. *Webster*. Others derive it from Heb. *toph*, a drum, "since drums were used to drown the cries of children offered to the idol Moloch." The valley of Hinnom, southeast of Jerusalem, was called Tophet, because good King Josiah, angered by the worship of Moloch and other idols there, defiled the place by casting into it carcasses and the refuse of the city. Fires were kept perpetually burning there.) *Hell.*

> "The pleasant valley of Hinnom, Tophet thence
> And black Gehenna called, the type of *hell.*"—*Par. Lost*, I., 404, 405.

Fly from the wrath. Matt. iii., 7.—**Wicket gate.** Matt. vii., 7, 13, 14. The gate is *prayer*. Macaulay (Essay on Bunyan in the *Encyclopedia Britannica*) points out some curious blunders of zealots who have remodelled the *Pilgrim's Progress*, to make it serve sectarian purposes. One champion of infant baptism represents the wicket gate as symbolical of that ordinance. Another will have it that the House Beautiful is the eucharist. Can the student point out the self-destructive character of such reasoning?—**Shining light.** Ps. cxix., 105; Prov. iv., 18.—**Looked not behind.** Gen. xix., 17.—**Came out.** Jer. xx., 10.

Obstinate, stubborn, contumacious, mulish, headstrong, heady. Point out the peculiar meaning of each of these, and illustrate all by appropriate sentences. Has Bunyan chosen the best word for the character? This exercise on synonymes should be written.

Pliable, pliant, flexible, subtle, limber. Distinguish the peculiar meaning of each of these, and illustrate it by a sentence. Has Bunyan selected the most appropriate word? **Make this a** written exercise.

Neighbors came. Analyze this according to the model on p. 289.

tion, the place also where I was born. I see it to be so; and dying there sooner or later, you will sink lower than the grave, into a place that burns with fire and brimstone. Be content, good neighbors, and go along with me."

"What," said Obstinate, "and leave our friends and our comforts behind us?"

"Yes," said Christian, for that was his name; "because that all that which you shall forsake, is not worthy to be compared* with a little of that that I am seeking to enjoy: and if you will go along with me, and hold it, you shall fare as I myself: for there, where I go, is enough and to spare. Come away, and prove my words."

Obstinate. What are these things you seek, since you leave all the world to find them?

Christian. I seek an inheritance incorruptible, undefiled, and that fadeth not away; and it is laid up in heaven, and safe there; to be bestowed, at the time appointed, on them that diligently seek it. Read it so, if you will, in my book.

Obstinate. Tush! away with your book. Will you go back with us or no?

Christian. No, not I: because I have laid my hand to the plough.

Obstinate. Come, then, neighbor Pliable, let us turn again, and go home without him. There is a company of these crazy-headed coxcombs, that when they take a fancy by the end, are wiser in their own eyes than seven men that can render a reason.

Pliable. Do not revile: if what the good Christian says, is true, the things he looks after are better than ours. My heart inclines to go with my neighbor.

---

* **Worthy to be compared**, etc. Rom. viii., 18.—**To spare.** Luke xv., 17.—**Fadeth not.** 1 Pet. i., 4.—**Laid up.** 2 Tim. iv., 8.—**Tush.** Make a phonetic analysis of this word. See pp. 60, 61, 62.—**Plough.** Luke ix., 62.—**Coxcombs** (cock's comb; A. S. *cocc;* Fr. *coq*, the male of the domestic fowl; A. S. *cemban*, Ger. *kämmen*, to comb; *camb*, a comb; *cock's-comb*, a piece of red cloth notched and shaped like the comb of a cock, and which licensed fools used to wear in their caps), fops, vain pretenders. "Coxcomb tells us [by its spelling] nothing now; but it did when spelt, as it used to be, *cockscomb*, the comb of a cock being a sort of ensign or token, which the fool was accustomed to wear." *Trench.*—**Seven men**, etc. Prov. xxvi., 16.

Good Christian says.

Any notion *added to* a noun, but not asserted of it, or to a word or words used as a noun, is said to be joined to it *adjectively*, if added for the purpose of more exact description. This union of the adjective, or adjective words, with the noun, is called *The Adjective Combination.* The half mark of a parenthesis ( ) may be used to indicate *the adjective combination;* thus:—

SYNTACTICAL. (Logical, etc.)			ETYMOLOGICAL, etc. (Parsing.)	HISTORICAL. (Compara. Philology, etc.)
Simple	**Good**)	A.[1]	Adj., posi., etc.	A. S. *god;* Ger. *gut*, etc.
Declarative	┌**Christian**)	S.	N., prop., masc., etc.	
Sentence.	└**says.**	P.	Strong (or weak ?) v., etc.	

Let the student complete the analysis according to the model on p. 289.
Analyze, after the same model, *My heart inclines.*

[1] *I. e.*, adjective combination.

Obstinate. What! more fools still? Be ruled by me, and go back. Who knows whither such a brain-sick fellow will lead you? Go back, go back and be wise.

Christian. Nay, but do thou come with thy neighbor Pliable. There are such things to be had which I spoke of, and many more glories besides. If you believe not me, read here in this book, and for the truth of what is expressed therein, behold, all is confirmed by the blood* of Him that made it!

Pliable. Well, neighbor Obstinate, I begin to come to the point. I intend to go along with this good man, and to cast in my lot with him. But, my good companion, do you know the way to this desired place?

Christian. I am directed by a man whose name is Evangelist, to speed me to a little gate that is before us; where we shall receive instructions about the way.

Pliable. Come, then, good neighbor, let us be going.

Then they went both together.

Obstinate. And I will go back to my place. I will be no companion of such misled, fantastical fellows.

Now I saw in my dream, that when Obstinate was going back, Christian and Pliable went talking over the plain; and thus they began their discourse.

Christian. Come, neighbor Pliable, how do you do? I am glad you are persuaded to go along with me. Had even Obstinate himself but felt what I have felt of the powers and terrors of what is yet unseen, he would not thus lightly have given us the back.

Pliable. Come, neighbor Christian, since there are none but us two here, tell me now, farther, what the things are, and how to be enjoyed, whither we are going?

Christian. I can better conceive of them with my mind, than speak of them with my tongue; but yet, since you are desirous to know, I will read of them in my book.

Pliable. And do you think that the words of your book are certainly true?

Christian. Yes, verily, for it was made by Him that cannot lie.

Pliable. Well said. What things are they?

Christian. There is an endless kingdom to be inhabited, and everlasting life to be given us, that we may inhabit that kingdom forever.

Pliable. Well said: and what else?

Christian. There are crowns of glory to be given us, and garments that will make us shine like the sun in the firmament of heaven.

Pliable. This is very pleasant: and what else?

Christian. There shall be no more crying, nor sorrow; for He that is owner of this place will wipe all tears from our eyes.

Pliable. And what company shall we have there?

Christian. There we shall be with seraphims and cherubims, creatures

---

* **Confirmed by the blood.** Heb. ix., 12-21.—**Cannot lie.** Titus i., 2.—**Crowns.** 2 Tim. iv., 8; Rev. ii., 10.—**Like the sun.** Matt. xiii., 43; Dan. xii., 3.—**All tears.** Rev. xxi., 4.—**Cherubims.** The proper plural of *cherub* is *cherubs;* or, as in the Hebrew, *cherubim;* that of *seraph* is *seraphs;* or, as in the Hebrew, *seraphim.* But the forms *cherubims* and *seraphims* are uniformly used in the Bible, and are often found in good authors. See Is. vi., 2; Ex. xxvi., 1.

Brain sick fellow will lead. Analyze as directed on p. 292.

that will dazzle your eyes to look on them. There also we shall meet with thousands and ten thousands that have gone before us to that place; none of them are hurtful, but loving and holy, every one walking in the sight of God, and standing in his presence with acceptance forever. In a word, there we shall see the elders * with their golden crowns; there we shall see the holy virgins with their golden harps; there we shall see men, that by the world were cut in pieces, burnt in flames, eaten of beasts, drowned in the seas, for the love that they bare to the lord of the place;—all well clothed with immortality as with a garment.

Pliable. The hearing of this is enough to ravish one's heart. But are these things to be enjoyed? How shall we get to be sharers thereof?

Christian. The Lord, the Governor of the country, hath recorded that in this book; the substance of which is, if we be truly willing to have it, he will bestow it upon us freely.

Pliable. Well, my good companion, glad am I to hear of these things. Come on, let us mend our pace.

Christian. I cannot go so fast as I would, by reason of this burthen that is on my back.

Now I saw in my dream, that just as they had ended their talk, they drew nigh to a very miry slough that was in the midst of the plain, and they, being heedless, did both fall suddenly into the bog. The name of the slough was Despond. Here therefore they wallowed for a time, being grievously bedaubed with dirt; and Christian, because of the burthen that was upon his back, began to sink in the mire.

---

* **Elders.** Rev. iv., 4.—**Harps.** Rev. xiv., 2, 4, 5.—**Cut in pieces,** etc. Heb. xi., 36, 37, 38.—**Clothed.** 2 Cor. v., 2, 3, 4; 1 Cor. xv., 53.—**Freely.** Is. lv., 1; Rev. xxii., 17; xxi., 6.—**Began to sink,** etc. Bunyan makes use of the same metaphor in relating his own experience: "I found myself in a miry bog, that shook if I did but stir."

The Lord, the Governor, hath recorded.

Here is another form of the *adjective combination.* (See p. 292.) It consists of a noun explained by a noun in apposition. The connection of the article *the* with its noun is also clearly an adjective combination. As the two words *hath recorded* together constitute the predicate, we may indicate the fact, as shown in the diagram. The following form may be used:

SYNTACTICAL.			ETYMOLOGICAL.	HISTORICAL.
Simple	The	A.	Adj., etc.	A. S. *the;* Goth. *tho*, etc.
	governor,	A.	Noun, etc.	
Declarative	the	A.	Adj., etc.	
	Lord	S.	Noun, etc.	
Sentence.	hath	P.	Auxil. verb, etc.	
	recorded.	P.	Weak verb, etc.	

Let the student complete the analysis according to the model on p. 289.

Then said Pliable, "Ah, neighbor Christian, where are you now?"

"Truly," said Christian, "I do not know."

At this Pliable began to be offended, and angrily said to his fellow, "Is this the happiness you have told me all this while of? If we have such ill speed at our first setting-out, what may we expect betwixt this and our journey's end? May I but get out again with my life, you shall possess the brave country alone for me." And with that he gave a desperate struggle or two, and got out of the mire on that side of the slough which was next his own house. So away he went, and Christian saw him no more.

Wherefore Christian was left to tumble in the Slough of Despond alone: but still he endeavored to struggle to that side of the slough that was farther from his own house, and next to the wicket-gate. The which he did, but could not get out, because of the burthen that was upon his back. But I beheld in my dream, that a man came to him, whose name was Help, and asked him what he did there.

"Sir," said Christian, "I was bid to go this way, by a man called Evangelist, who directed me also to yonder gate, that I might escape the wrath to come. And as I was going thither, I fell in here."

Help. But why did you not look for the steps?

Christian. Fear followed me so hard, that I fled the next way and fell in.

Then said Help, "Give me thy hand." So he gave him his hand, and he drew him out, and set him upon sound ground,* and bade him go on his way.

Then I stepped to him who plucked him out, and said, "Sir; wherefore, since over this place is the way from the city of Destruction to yonder gate, is it that this plat is not mended, that poor travellers might go thither with more security?" And he said unto me: "This miry slough is such a place as cannot be mended. It is the descent whither the scum and filth that attend conviction for sin, do continually run; and therefore it is called the Slough of Despond; for, still as the sinner is awakened about his lost condition, there arise in his soul many fears and doubts and discouraging apprehensions, which all of them get together, and settle in this place: and this is the reason of the badness of this ground. It is not the pleasure of the king that this place should remain so bad. His laborers also have, by the direction of his Majesty's surveyors, been for above these sixteen hundred years employed about this patch of ground, if perhaps it might have been mended. Yea, and to my knowledge," said he, "here have been swallowed up at least twenty thousand cart-loads, yea, millions of wholesome instructions, that have at all seasons been brought from all places of the king's dominions, (and they that can tell, say, they are the best materials to make good ground of the place,) if so be it might have been mended. But it is the Slough of Despond still; and so will be, when

---

* **Sound ground.** Ps. xl., 2.—**Remain so bad.** Is. xxxv., 3-10.

Badness, illness. Other synonymes? Differentiate, etc.

Christian was left. Analyze according to the model on p. 289. See the form on p. 294.

they have done what they can. True, there are, by the direction of the Lawgiver, certain good and substantial steps, placed even through the very midst of this slough: but at such time as this place doth much spew out of it filth, as it doth against change of weather, these steps are hardly seen; or, if they be, men, through the dizziness of their heads, step beside; and then they are bemired to some purpose, notwithstanding the steps be there. But the ground is good when they are once got in at the gate."

Now I saw in my dream, that by this time Pliable was got home to his house. So his neighbors came to visit him; and some of them called him wise man for coming back; and some called him fool for hazarding himself with Christian. Others again did mock his cowardliness, saying, "Surely, since you began to venture, I would not have been so base to have given out for a few difficulties." So Pliable sat sneaking among them. But at last he got more confidence, and then they all turned their tales and began to deride poor Christian behind his back. And thus much concerning Pliable.

Now, as Christian* was walking solitarily by himself, he espied one afar off, crossing over the field to meet him; and their hap was to meet, just as they were crossing the way to each other. The gentleman's name that met him was Mr. Worldly Wiseman. He dwelt in the town of Carnal Policy, a very great town, and also hard by from whence Christian came. This man, then, meeting with Christian, and having some knowledge of him,—for Christian's setting forth from the city of Destruction, was much noised abroad, not only in the town where he dwelt, but also it began to be the town talk in some other places,—Mr. Worldly Wiseman, therefore, having some guess of him, by beholding his laborious going, by observing his sighs and groans and the like, began thus to enter into some talk with Christian:

Worldly Wiseman. How now, good fellow, whither away after this burthened manner?

Christian. A burthened manner, indeed, as ever I think poor creature had! And whereas you ask me, "Whither away?" I tell you, sir, I am going to yonder wicket gate before me; for there, as I am informed, I shall be put in a way to be rid of my heavy burthen.

---

* **Now as Christian,** etc. This passage and what follows, as far as, "So, in process of time, Christian got up to the gate" (p. 302), were not in the earliest edition.

Christian's setting forth was noised.

Here we have another form of the *adjective combination*, the adjective word being a noun in the possessive (or genitive) case. The two words *setting forth* may, for this occasion, be considered as constituting a noun, and they may be written on the same line. So the two words in the predicate, *was noised*, may be united. The following diagram may be used:

Christian's	A.
setting forth	S.
was noised.	P.

Let the student complete the analysis according to the model on p. 289. For the etymological and historical analyses, the four words, *setting*, *forth*, *was*, *noised*, may be written in a new vertical column.

Worldly Wiseman. Hast thou a wife and children ?

Christian. Yes; but I am so laden with this burthen, that I cannot take pleasure in them as formerly: methinks I am as if I had none.*

Worldly Wiseman. Wilt thou hearken to me if I give thee counsel ?

Christian. If it be good, I will; for I stand in need of good counsel.

Worldly Wiseman. I would advise thee, then, that thou with all speed get thyself rid of thy burthen; for thou wilt never be settled in thy mind till then: nor canst thou enjoy the benefits of the blessings which God hath bestowed upon thee, till then.

Christian. That is that which I seek for, even to be rid of this heavy burthen; but get it off myself, I cannot; nor is there a man in my own country that can take it off my shoulders. Therefore am I going this way, as I told you, that I may be rid of my burthen.

Worldly Wiseman. Who bade thee go this way to be rid of thy burthen ?

Christian. A man that appeared to me to be a very great and honorable person. His name, as I remember, is Evangelist.

Worldly Wiseman. Beshrew him for his counsel. There is not a more dangerous and troublesome way in the world, than is that unto which he hath directed thee; and that thou shalt find, if thou wilt be ruled by his counsel. Thou hast met with something, as I perceive, already; I see the dirt of the Slough of Despond is upon thee. But that slough is the beginning of the sorrows that attend those that go on in that way. Hear me, I am older than thou. Thou art like to meet with, in the way which thou goest, wearisomeness, painfulness, hunger, perils, nakedness, sword, lions, dragons, darkness; and, in a word, death, and what not. These things are certainly true, having been confirmed by many testimonies. And why should a man so carelessly cast away himself, by giving heed to a stranger ?

Christian. Why, sir, this burthen on my back is more terrible to me, than are all these things which you have mentioned. Nay, methinks I care not what I meet with in my way, if so be I can also meet with deliverance from my burthen.

Worldly Wiseman. How camest thou by the burthen at first ?

Christian. By reading this book in my hand.

Worldly Wiseman. I thought so, and it has happened unto thee as to other weak men, who, meddling with things too high for them, do suddenly fall into thy distractions: which distractions do not only unman men, as thine

---

* **As if I had none.** 1 Cor. vii., 29.—**Beshrew him,** *curse him.* The prefix *be-* or *by-* (Goth. *bi-;* O. Sax. *bi-;* Ger. *be-*, *bei-;* Dutch *be-*) denotes nearness, or is intensive. Sometimes it seems to have lost its force. Sometimes it renders an intransitive verb transitive; as, *beseem*, *befall*, *bemoan;* or it changes the direction of the transitive relation; as, *behold*, *beset*, *betake;* or it spreads the action of the verb; as, *bedaub*, *bedeck*, *bespot*. *Shrew* is from Low Ger. *schrauen*, to bawl or brawl; D. *schreeuwen*, Ger. *schreien*, to cry, scream. *Shrewd* was formerly always used in an unfavorable sense, as *shrew* is yet. *Beshrew* was used in petty or playful cursing.—**Wearisomeness,** etc. 2 Cor. xi., 25, 26, 27. The passage in Paul's epistle possesses extraordinary pathos and beauty. In the intensity of their feelings there was a remarkable similarity between Paul and Bunyan.

Counsel, *advice*, *instruction*, *warning*. Discriminate, etc.

I would advise. Analyze as in the model on p. 289.

I perceive have done thee, but they run them upon desperate ventures, to obtain they know not what.

Christian. I know what I would obtain: it is ease from my heavy burthen.

Worldly Wiseman. But why wilt thou seek for ease this way, seeing so many dangers attend it? especially, since, hadst thou but patience to hear me, I could direct thee to the obtaining of what thou desirest, without the dangers that thou in this way wilt run thyself into. Yes, and the remedy is at hand. Besides, I will add, that instead of these dangers thou shalt meet with much safety, friendship, and content.

Christian. Pray, sir, open the secret to me.

Worldly Wiseman. Why, in yonder village, the village is named Morality,* there dwells a gentleman whose name is Legality, a very judicious man, and a man of very good name, that has skill to help men off with such burthens as thine is, from their shoulders. Yea, to my knowledge, he hath done a great deal of good this way; and besides, he hath skill to cure those that are somewhat crazed in their wits with their burthen. To him, as I said, thou mayest go, and be helped presently. His house is not quite a mile from this place; and if he should not be at home himself, he hath a pretty young man to his son, whose name is Civility, that can do it, to speak on, as well as the old gentleman himself. There, I say, thou mayest be eased of thy burthen: and if thou art not minded to go back to thy former habitation, as indeed I would not wish thee; thou mayest send for thy wife and children to thee to this village, where there are houses now standing empty, one of which thou mayest have at a reasonable rate. Provision is there also cheap and good; and that which will make thy life more happy is, to be sure, there thou shalt live by honest neighbors, in credit and good fashion.

Now was Christian somewhat at a stand; but presently he concluded, "If this be true which this gentleman hath said, my wisest course is to take his advice." And with that he thus farther spake, "Sir, which is my way to this honest man's house?"

Worldly Wiseman. Do you see yonder high hill?

Christian. Yes, very well.

Worldly Wiseman. By that hill you must go, and the first house you come at is his.

So Christian turned out of his way to go to Mr. Legality's house for help. But behold, when he was got now hard by the hill, it seemed so high, and also that side of it that was next the wayside, did hang so much over, that Christian was afraid to venture farther, lest the hill should fall on his head. Wherefore there he stood still, and knew not what to do. Also his burthen now seemed heavier to him than while he was in his way. There came also

---

* **Morality**, etc. The Puritans, Baptists, and others argued with great earnestness that *legality* was not enough—that outward *morality* and decorum, without a total change of heart, had no saving merit.

Happy, lucky, fortunate, felicitous, blessed, blissful, joyful, glad. Write out the appropriate meaning of each, and illustrate as before.

Legality's house stood. Analyze as shown in the model on p. 239, and as directed on p. 296. *His burthen seemed.* Analyze.

flashes of fire out of the hill,* that made Christian afraid that he should be burned. Here, therefore, he sweat and did quake for fear. And now he began to be sorry that he had taken Mr. Worldly Wiseman's counsel; and with that he saw Evangelist coming to meet him; at the sight also of whom he began to blush for shame. So Evangelist drew nearer and nearer, and coming up to him, he looked upon him with a severe and dreadful countenance and thus began to reason with Christian.

"What dost thou here, Christian?" said he. At which words Christian knew not what to answer. Wherefore at present he stood speechless before him. Then said Evangelist farther, "Art not thou the man that I found crying without the walls of the City of Destruction?"

Christian. Yes, dear sir, I am the man.

Evangelist. Did not I direct thee the way to the little wicket-gate?

Christian. Yes, dear sir.

Evangelist. How is it, then, that thou art so quickly turned aside? For thou art now out of the way.

Christian. I met with a gentleman so soon as I had got over the Slough of Despond, who persuaded me that I might, in the village before me, find a man that could take off my burthen.

Evangelist. What was he?

Christian. He looked like a gentleman, and talked much to me, and got me at last to yield. So I came hither; but when I beheld this hill, and how it hangs over the way, I suddenly made a stand, lest it should fall on my head.

Evangelist. What said that gentleman to you?

Christian. Why, he asked me whither I was going. And I told him.

Evangelist. And what said he then?

Christian. He asked me if I had a family. And I told him. "But," said I, "I am so loaded with the burthen that is on my back, that I cannot take pleasure in them as formerly."

Evangelist. And what said he then?

Christian. He bade me with speed get rid of my burthen; and I told him it was ease that I sought: "And," said I, "I am therefore going to yonder gate, to receive further direction how I might get to the place of deliverance." So he said that he would show me a better way, and short, not so attended with difficulties, as the way, sir, that you set me in. "Which way," said he, "will direct you to a gentleman's house that has skill to take off these burthens." So I believed him, and turned out of that way into this, if happily I might be soon eased of my burthen. But when I came to this place,

---

* **Flashes of fire out of the hill.** Ex. xix., 16-18; Heb. xii., 18-21. Bunyan says of himself: "I saw I had a heart that *would* sin, and that lay under a law that would condemn . . . . . Sin and corruption would as naturally bubble out of my heart as water would bubble out of a fountain. I thought now that every one had a better heart than I had. I could have changed heart with anybody. I thought none but the devil himself could equalize me for inward wickedness and pollution. I fell, therefore, at the sight of my own vileness, deeply in despair."

Severe, austere, stern, grave, morose. Write out the peculiar meanings, as before. Illustrate. Has Bunyan chosen the best word?

That gentleman said. Analyze as before.

and beheld things as they are, I stopped for fear, as I said, of danger. But I now know not what to do.[1]

Evangelist. Then stand still a little, that I may show thee the words of God.

So he stood trembling. Then said Evangelist, "See that you refuse not* him that speaketh; for, if they escaped not who refused him that spake on earth, much more shall not we escape, if we turn away from him that speaketh from heaven." He said moreover, "Now the just shall live by faith; but if any man draw back, my soul shall have no pleasure in him." He also did thus apply them: "Thou art the man that art running into this misery; thou hast begun to reject the counsel of the Most High and to draw back thy foot from the way of peace, even almost to the hazarding of thy perdition."

Then Christian fell down at his feet as dead, crying, "Wo is me, for I am undone!" At the sight of which, Evangelist caught him by the right hand, saying, "All manner of sin and blasphemies shall be forgiven unto men: be not faithless, but believing." Then did Christian again a little revive, and stood up trembling, as at first, before Evangelist.

Then Evangelist proceeded, saying, "Give more earnest heed to the things that I shall tell thee of. I will now show thee who it was that deluded thee, and who it was also to whom he sent thee. The man that met thee is one Worldly Wiseman; and rightly he is so called: partly because he savoreth only of the doctrine of this world; therefore he always goes to the town of Morality to church: and partly because he loveth that doctrine best; for it saveth him from the cross. And because he is of this carnal temper, therefore he seeketh to prevent my ways, though right. Now there are three things, in this man's counsel, that thou must utterly abhor: 1. His turning thee out of the way. 2. His laboring to render the cross odious to thee. 3. And his setting thy feet in that way that leadeth unto the administration of death.

"First, thou must abhor his turning thee out of the way; yea, and thine own consenting thereto: because this is to reject the counsel of God, for the sake of the counsel of a worldly-wise man. The Lord says, 'Strive to enter in at the strait gate,' the gate to which I send thee; 'for strait is the gate

---

* **Refuse not.** Heb. xii., 25.—**No pleasure.** Heb. x., 38.—**Worldly Wiseman.** 1 John iv., 5.—**Saveth him from the cross.** Gal. vi., 12.—**Strait gate.** Luke xiii., 24. "The straitness of this gate is not to be understood carnally, but mystically. You are not to understand it as if the entrance into heaven was some little pinching wicket. No, the straitness of this gate is quite another thing. This gate is wide enough for all them that are truly gracious and sincere lovers of Jesus Christ; but so strait as that none of the other can by any means enter in. . . . The gates of the temple were six cubits wide; yet they were so strait that none that were unclean in anything might enter in thereat." 2 Chr. xxiii., 19. Bunyan's *Strait Gate.*

Deluded, deceived, imposed upon, misled, beguiled. Name other synonymes. Has Bunyan selected the best? Write out, etc., as before.

Thou hast begun. Analyze as before.

---

[1] When Christians unto carnal men give ear,
Out of their way they go, and pay for 't dear;
For Master Worldly Wiseman can but show
A saint the way to bondage and to woe.

that leadeth unto life, and few there be * that find it.' From this little wicket-gate, and from the way thereto, hath this wicked man turned thee, to the bringing of thee almost to destruction. Hate, therefore, his turning thee out of the way, and abhor thyself for hearkening to him.

"Secondly. Thou must abhor his laboring to render the cross odious unto thee; for thou art to prefer it before the treasures in Egypt. Besides, the King of Glory hath told thee, that he that will save his life, shall lose it; and, he that comes after him, and hates not his father and mother, and wife and children, and brethren and sisters, yea, and his own life also, 'he cannot be my disciple.' I say, therefore, for a man to labor to persuade thee that that shall be thy death, without which, the Truth has said, thou canst not have eternal life,—this doctrine thou must abhor.

"Thirdly. Thou must hate his setting of thy feet in the way that leadeth to the ministration of death. And for this thou must consider to whom he sent thee, and also how unable that person was to deliver thee from thy burthen. He to whom thou wast sent for ease, being by name Legality, is the son of the bond woman which now is, and is in bondage with her children; and is, in a mystery, this Mount Sinai, which thou hast feared will fall on thy head. Now, if she with her children are [is] in bondage, how canst thou expect by them to be made free? This Legality, therefore, is not able to set thee free from thy burthen. No man was as yet ever rid of his burthen by him; no, nor ever is like to be. Ye cannot be justified by the works of the law; for by the deeds of the law no man living can be rid of his burthen. Therefore Mr. Worldly Wiseman is an alien, and Mr. Legality a cheat. As for his son Civility, notwithstanding his simpering looks, he is but a hypocrite, and cannot help thee. Believe me, there is nothing in all this noise that thou hast heard of these sottish men, but a design to beguile thee of thy salvation, by turning thee from the way in which I have set thee."

After this, Evangelist called aloud to the heavens for confirmation of what he had said. And with that there came words and fire out of the

---

* **Few there be.** Matt. vii., 13, 14.—**Treasures in Egypt.** Heb. xi., 26.—**Save his life, shall,** etc. Matt. x., 39; Mark viii., 35; John xii., 25.—**Hates not.** Luke xiv., 26.—**This Mount Sinai.** Gal. iv., 21-26. Travellers and geographers are still disputing as to the precise locality of this famous mountain. It seems clear that it was in Arabia Petræa, in a cluster of which Horeb was one of the most northerly.

The King of Glory hath told. Here is another instance of the *adjective combination*, the words *of glory* having an adjective force.

Simple	**The**
	of glory
Declarative	
	King
Sentence.	**hath told.**

Complete the analysis, parsing each word, giving derivations, etc., according to the model on page 289. The words *of glory* and *hath told* may, for the purposes of the etymological and historical analysis, be written in a second vertical column.

Analyze in the same way, *The man of the gate asked.*

mountain under which poor Christian stood, that made the hair of his flesh* stand up. The words were thus pronounced: "As many as are of the works of the law are under the curse. For it is written, cursed is every one that continueth not in all things which are written in the book of the law to do them."

Now Christian looked for nothing but death, and began to cry out lamentably: even cursing the time in which he met with Mr. Worldly Wiseman; still calling himself a thousand fools for hearkening to his counsel. He also was greatly ashamed to think that this gentleman's arguments, flowing only from the flesh, should have the prevalency with him as to cause him to forsake the right way. This done, he applied himself again to Evangelist in words and sense as follows:—

Christian. Sir, what think you? Is there hope? May I now go back, and go up to the wicket-gate? Shall I not be abandoned for this, and sent back from thence ashamed? I am sorry I have hearkened to this man's counsel: but may my sin be forgiven?

Evangelist. Thy sin is very great; for by it thou hast committed two evils: thou hast forsaken the way that is good, to tread in forbidden paths. Yet will the man at the gate receive thee, for he has good-will for men. Only take heed that thou turn not aside again; lest thou perish from the way, when his wrath is kindled but a little.

Then did Christian address himself to go back; and Evangelist, after he had kissed him, gave him one smile and bid him God speed.

So Christian went on with haste; neither spake he to any man by the way; nor, if any asked him, would he vouchsafe them an answer. He went like one that was all the while treading on forbidden ground, and could by no means think himself safe, till again he was got into the way which he left to follow Mr. Worldly Wiseman's counsel. So, in process of time, Christian got up to the gate. Now over the gate there was written, "Knock, and it shall be opened unto you." He knocked, therefore, more than once or twice, saying,—

"May I now enter here? Will he within
Open to sorry me, though I have been
An undeserving rebel? Then shall I
Not fail to sing his lasting praise on high."

At last there came a grave person to the gate, named Goodwill; who asked who was there, and whence he came, and what he would have.

Christian. Here is a poor burthened sinner. I came from the City of Destruction, but am going to Mount Zion, that I may be delivered from the wrath to come. I would therefore, sir, since I am informed that by this gate is the way thither, know if you are willing to let me in.

Goodwill. I am willing with all my heart.

And with that he opened the gate.

* **Hair of his flesh,** etc. See Job iv., 15.—**Cursed is every one,** etc. Gal. iii., 10.—**Wrath.** Ps. ii., 12.—**Knock.** Matt. vii., 7.—**Address,** prepare. This is a frequent signification of the word in our old writers. See p. 129.—**God speed,** 2 John 10.

This gentleman's arguments should have. Analyze as before.

So when Christian was stepping in, the other gave him a pull. Then said Christian, "What means that?" The other told him: "A little distance from this gate, there is erected a strong castle, of which Beelzebub is the captain. From thence both he, and they that are with him, shoot arrows at those that come up to the gate, if happily* they may die before they can enter in."

Then said Christian, "I rejoice and tremble." So when he was got in, the man of the gate asked him who directed him thither.

Christian. Evangelist bade me come hither and knock, as I did; and he said, that you, sir, would tell me what I must do.

Goodwill. An open door is before thee, and no man can shut it.

Christian. Now I begin to reap the benefits of my hazards.

Goodwill. But how is it that you come alone?

Christian. Because none of my neighbors saw their danger as I saw mine.

Goodwill. Did any of them know of your coming?

Christian. Yes, my wife and children saw me at the first, and called after me to turn again; also some of my neighbors stood crying and calling after me to return. But I put my fingers in my ears, and so came on my way.

Goodwill. But did none of them follow you, to persuade you to go back?

Christian. Yes, both Obstinate and Pliable: but when they saw that they could not prevail, Obstinate went railing back, but Pliable came with me a little way.

Goodwill. But why did he not come through?

Christian. We indeed came both together, until we came to the Slough of Despond, into the which we also suddenly fell; and then was my neighbor Pliable discouraged, and would not adventure further. Wherefore, getting out again on that side next to his own house, he told me I should possess the brave country alone for him: so he went his way, and I came mine; he after Obstinate, and I to this gate.

Goodwill. Alas, poor man! Is the celestial glory of so small esteem with him that he counteth it not worth running the hazard of a few difficulties to obtain it?

Christian. I have told you truly concerning Pliable; and if I should also say all the truth of myself, it will appear there is no betterment betwixt him and myself. 'Tis true, he went back to his own house; but I also turned aside to go in the way of death, being persuaded thereto by the carnal argument of one Mr. Worldly Wiseman.

Goodwill. Oh! did he light upon you? What, he would have had you sought for ease at the hands of Mr. Legality! They are both of them very cheats. But did you take his counsel?

---

* **Happily** (for *haply*), perhaps. Obs. in this sense.—**No man can shut it.** Rev. iii., 8.

Persuade, entice, prevail upon, exhort. Write out, etc., as before.

My neighbor Pliable was discouraged. Analyze according to the model, pp. 289, 294.

Christian. Yes, as far as I durst. I went to find out Mr. Legality, until I thought that the mountain that stands by his house would have fallen upon my head: wherefore, there I was forced to stop.

Goodwill. That mountain has been the death of many, and will be the death of many more. It is well you escaped being dashed in pieces by it.

Christian. Why, truly, I do not know what had become of me there, had not Evangelist happily met me again as I was musing in the midst of my dumps.* But it was God's mercy that he came to me again, for else I had never come hither. But now, I am come, such a one as I am; more fit indeed for death by that mountain, than thus to stand talking with my Lord. But O what a favor is this to me, that yet I am admitted entrance here!

Goodwill. We make no objections against any. Notwithstanding all that they have done before they came hither, they in no wise are cast out; and therefore, good Christian, come a little way with me, and I will teach thee about the way thou must go. Look before thee; dost thou see this narrow way? That is the way thou must go. It was cast up by the Patriarchs, Prophets, Christ, and his Apostles; and it is as straight as a rule can make it. This is the way thou must go.

Christian. But, good sir, are there no turnings nor windings by which a stranger may lose his way?

Goodwill. Yes; there are many ways butt down upon this; and they are crooked and wide: but thus thou mayest distinguish the right from the wrong—the right only being straight and narrow.

Then I saw in my dream, that Christian asked him further, if he could not help him off with the burthen that was upon his back: for as yet he had not got rid thereof; nor could he by any means get it off without help.

He told him; "As to thy burthen, be content to bear it, until thou comest to the place of deliverance, for there it will fall from thy back of itself."

Then Christian began to gird up his loins, and to address himself to his journey. So the other told him, that by that he was gone some distance from the gate, he would come at the house of the Interpreter; at whose door he should knock, and he would show him excellent things. Then Christian took his leave of his friend, and he again bid him God speed.

Then went Christian on, till he came at the house of the Interpreter,

---

* **Dumps** (Ger. *dumpf*, damp, gloomy; *dampf*, vapor; Ice. *dampi*, fog, steam; D. *dom*, dull, blunt, stupid; Ger. *dumm;* allied to Eng. *dumb*). *despondency*, *melancholy*.—**Cast out.** John vi., 37.—**Butt down** (Gael. *buta*, butt, mask; Fr. *bot*, end, extremity; Gael. *bot*, mound; W. *bot*, any round body; Fr. *bout*, end; A. S. *butan*, without, outside; Fr. *aboutir*, to come out, to end; Eng. *abut*, to terminate, to meet), *border upon*, *meet*.—"Beware of by-paths: take heed thou dost not run into those lanes which lead out of the way. There are crooked paths—paths in which men go astray—paths that lead to death and damnation. Some of them are dangerous because of practice; some, because of opinion. . . . . Though the way to heaven be but one, yet there are many crooked lanes and by-paths shoot down upon it, as I may say." Bunyan's *Heavenly Footman*. See Prov. iv., 14, 15, 18, 19, 26, 27.—**Narrow.** Matt. vii., 14. See Bunyan's explanation of "straitness" or narrowness, at the bottom of p. 300.

They are crooked. Analyze as before.

Interpreter, *explainer*, *expounder*, *expositor*, *translator*. Write out, etc., as before.

where he knocked over and over:* at last, one came to the door, and asked who was there.

Christian. Sir, here is a traveller, who was bid by an acquaintance of the good man of this house to call here for my profit: I would therefore speak with the master of the house.

So he called for the master of the house; who, after a little time, came to Christian, and asked him what he would have.

Christian. Sir, I am a man that am come from the City of Destruction, and am going to the Mount Zion: and I was told by the man that stands at the gate at the head of this way, that, if I called here, you would show me excellent things, such as would be a help to me in my journey.

Interpreter. Come in; I will show thee that which will be profitable to thee.

So he commanded his man to light the candle, and bade Christian follow him. So he had him into a private room, and bid his man open a door; the which when he had done, Christian saw the picture of a very grave person hang up against the wall; and this was the fashion of it: it had eyes lifted up to heaven, the best of books in his hand, the law of truth was written upon his lips, the world was behind his back; he stood as if he pleaded with men; and a crown of gold did hang over his head.

Then said Christian, "What meaneth this?"

Interpreter. The man whose picture this is, is one of a thousand: he can beget children, travail in birth with children, and nurse them himself when they are born. And whereas thou seest him with his eyes lift up to heaven,

---

* **Over and over,** *again and again.*—**For my profit.** It would be more grammatically correct to say, *for his profit;* but *his* would have been ambiguous.—**His man,** *his servant.* So *man* is often used in the old writers.—**Had him into,** *took him into.*—**Eyes lift up,** etc. "Similar to these are the evidences which Mr. Wesley required of his 'helpers' as proof of their ministry, *grace, gifts,* and *fruit.* 'As long,' he says, 'as these marks concur in any one, we believe he is called of God to preach. These we receive as sufficient proof that he is moved thereto by the Holy Ghost.'" *Wickens.* For the form of the participle *lift*, see Abbott's *Shakespearian Grammar*, 343.—**Children.** See 1 Cor. iv., 15; Gal. iv., 19.

Private, secret, hidden, concealed, retired, secluded. Name other synonymes. Write out, etc., as before.

I am a man. We saw on p. 289 that the predicate may be a verb alone. It may also be a verb with a noun, a verb with an adjective, or a verb with a prepositional phrase. Here it is a verb with a noun. In the example below, it is a verb with an adjective.

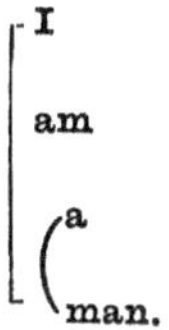

Complete the analysis, etc. In like manner analyze, etc., *This was the fashion.*

Which will be profitable. See analysis diagram of, *Though this be so*, p. 308.

Which

will be profitable.

Another *subject-and-predicate* combination. Complete the analysis as directed in the footnotes on pp. 289, 290.

the best of books in his hand, and the law of truth written on his lips; it is to show thee, that his work is to know and unfold dark things * to sinners; even as also thou seest him stand as if he pleaded with men. And whereas thou seest the world as cast behind him, and that a crown hangs over his head; that is to show thee, that, slighting and despising the things that are present, for the love that he hath to his Master's service, he is sure, in the world that comes next, to have glory for his reward. Now, said the Interpreter, I have showed thee this picture first, because the Man whose picture this is, is the only man whom the Lord of the place whither thou art going hath authorized to be thy guide in all difficult places thou mayest meet with in the way. Wherefore, take good heed to what I have showed thee, and bear well in thy mind what thou hast seen; lest in thy journey thou meet with some that pretend to lead thee right, but their way goes down to death.

Then he took him by the hand, and led him into a large parlor that was full of dust, because never swept: the which after he had reviewed a little while, the Interpreter called for a man to sweep. Now, when he began to sweep, the dust began abundantly to fly about, so that Christian had almost therewith been choked. Then said the Interpreter to a damsel that stood by, "Bring hither the water, and sprinkle the room:" the which when she had done, it was swept and cleansed with pleasure.

Then said Christian, "What means this?"

The Interpreter answered, "This parlor is the heart of a man that was never sanctified by the sweet grace of the Gospel. The dust is his original sin and inward corruptions that have defiled the whole man. He that began to sweep at first, is the Law; but she that brought water, and did sprinkle it, is the Gospel. Now, whereas thou sawest, that as soon as the first began to sweep, the dust did so fly about that the room by him could not be cleansed, but that thou wast almost choked therewith; this is to show thee that the Law, instead of cleansing the heart, by its working, from sin, doth revive, put strength into, and increase it in the soul, even as it doth discover and forbid it; for it doth not give power to subdue it. Again, as thou sawest the damsel sprinkle the room with water, upon which it was cleansed with pleasure; this is to show thee, that, when the Gospel comes, in the sweet and precious influences thereof, to the heart; then, I say, even as thou sawest the damsel lay the dust by sprinkling the floor with water, so is sin vanquished and subdued, and the soul made clean, through the faith of it, and consequently fit for the King of Glory to inhabit."

---

* **Dark things,** *mysteries.*—**The Interpreter.** Whom are we to understand by the Interpreter? John xvi., 13, 14; and 1 Cor. ii., 9, 10, 11, 12.—**Because the man.** Jesus Christ.—**Cleansing the heart,** etc. Rom. vii., 9. **Put strength into.** 1 Cor. xv., 56.—**Discover,** *reveal,* bring to light. See p. 216.—**Subdued.** Rom. v., 20.—**Made clean.** John xv., 2; Eph. v., 26; Acts xv., 9. The reader will observe the skill with which Bunyan blends narrative, dialogue, allegory, and doctrinal discussion; and the air of reality with which he nevertheless invests all.

Authorized, empowered, accredited. Other synonymes. Differentiate, etc.

This parlor is the heart. Analyze fully.

I saw, moreover, in my dream, that the Interpreter took him by the hand, and had him into a little room,* where sat two little children, each one in his chair. The name of the eldest was Passion, and the name of the other, Patience. Passion seemed to be much discontented, but Patience was very quiet. Then Christian asked, "What is the reason of the discontent of Passion?" The Interpreter answered, "The Governor of them would have him stay for his best things till the beginning of the next year; but he will have all now: but Patience is willing to wait."

Then I saw that one came to Passion, and brought him a bag of treasure, and poured it down at his feet; the which he took up, and rejoiced therein, and withal laughed Patience to scorn. But I beheld but a while, and he had lavished all away, and had nothing left him but rags.

Then said Christian to the Interpreter, "Expound this matter more fully to me."

Interpreter. These two lads are figures; Passion, of the men of this world, and Patience, of the men of that which is to come. For, as here thou seest, Passion will have all now, this year; that is to say, in this world: so are the men of this world; they must have all their good things now; they cannot stay till next year, that is, until the next world, for their portion of good. That proverb, *A bird in the hand is worth two in the bush*, is of more authority with them than are all the divine testimonies of the good of the world to come. But as thou sawest that he had quickly lavished all away, and had presently left him nothing but rags; so will it be with all such men at the end of this world.

Christian. Now I see that Patience has the best wisdom, and that upon many accounts. 1. Because he stays for the best things. 2. And also because he will have the glory of his, when the other has nothing but rags.

Interpreter. Nay, you may add another; to wit the glory of the next world will never wear out; but these are suddenly gone. Therefore Passion had not so much reason to laugh at Patience, because he had his good things first, as Patience will have to laugh at Passion, because he had his best things last: for, first must give place to last, because last must have its time to come: but last gives place to nothing; for there is not another to succeed. He, therefore, that hath his portion first, must needs have a time to spend it; but he that has his portion last, must have it lastingly. Therefore it is said of Dives, "In thy lifetime thou receivedst thy good things, and likewise Lazarus evil things: but now he is comforted, and thou art tormented."

Christian. Then I perceive it is not best to covet things that are now; but to wait for things to come.

---

* **Had him into a little room,** i. e., *took him into*, etc.—**He had his good things first.** Who? Note the imperfection of the English language. Let the student reconstruct the sentence beginning, "Therefore Passion," etc.—**Dives** (Lat. *dives*, rich; *divitia*, riches), the rich man in the parable.—**Lazarus.** Luke xvi., 25.

That proverb is of authority. Analyze. See pp. 289, 296, 305. The words *of authority* have evidently an *adjective* force, and are equivalent to *authoritative*.

Discontent, uneasiness. Other synonymes? Differentiate, etc.

Interpreter. You say truth; for the things that are seen are temporal; but the things that are not seen, eternal.* But though this be so, yet since things present and our fleshly appetite are such near neighbors one to another; and again, because things to come and carnal sense are such strangers one to another; therefore it is that the first of these so suddenly fall into amity, and that distance is so continually between the second.

Then I saw in my dream, that the Interpreter took Christian by the hand, and led him into a place where was a fire burning against a wall, and one standing by it always casting much water upon it, to quench it: yet did the fire burn higher and hotter.

Then said Christian, "What means this?"

The Interpreter answered; "This fire is the work of grace that is wrought in the heart: he that casts water upon it, to extinguish and put it out, is the devil. But in that thou seest the fire, notwithstanding, burn higher and hotter; thou shalt also see the reason of that."—So he had him about the backside of the wall, where he saw a man with a vessel of oil in his hand, of the which he did also continually cast (but secretly) into the fire.

Then said Christian, "What means this?"

The Interpreter answered: "This is Christ, who continually, with the oil of his grace, maintains the work already begun in the heart; by the means of which, notwithstanding what the devil can do, the souls of his people prove gracious still. And in that thou sawest that the man stood behind the wall to maintain the fire; this is to teach thee, that it is hard for the tempted to see how this work of grace is maintained in the soul."

I saw, also, that the Interpreter took him again by the hand and led him into a pleasant place, where was built a stately palace, beautiful to behold; at the sight of which Christian was greatly delighted. He saw also upon the top thereof certain persons walking, who were clothed all in gold.

Then said Christian, "May we go in thither?"

Then the Interpreter took him, and led him up towards the door of the palace; and behold, at the door stood a great company of men, as desirous to go in, but durst not. There also sat a man at a little distance from the

---

* **Not seen, eternal.** 2 Cor. iv., 18.—**Oil of his grace.** 2 Cor. xii., 9.—**How this work of grace is maintained.** Some of Bunyan's editors seize upon this passage to prove that he was not an Arminian. Thus, one writes, "No, it is plain that Mr. Bunyan was not an Arminian; he did not ascribe any of that glory to the work and power of the creature, which is solely due to the Lord, who is the Alpha and the Omega, the First and the Last, the Beginning, Carrier-on, and Finisher of his work in sinners' hearts," etc. *Kelley's* edition, p. 37.

Beautiful, handsome. Other synonymes? Differentiate, etc.

Though this be so. We have seen (p. 305) that a predicate may be a verb with a noun, a verb with an adjective, or a verb with a prepositional phrase. It may also be a verb with an *adverb.*

Though
┌**this** S.
└**be so.** P.

Complete this work as required in the preceding pages. As to the construction of *though*, it may be remarked that it was in its origin, as Horne Tooke shows, the imperative of the A. S. *thafigan*, to allow, grant, and it still retains a concessive force. *Though this be so = grant that this is so.* In the etymological analysis, it will suffice to call it a *concessive conjunction.* *So* being an adverb here, we have another form of the *subject-and-predicate* combination; the predicate being *be so.* Analyze, *The souls of his people prove gracious.*

door, at a table-side with a book, and his ink-horn* before him, to take the name of him that should enter therein: he saw also that in the door-way stood many men in armor to keep it, being resolved to do to the men that would enter what hurt and mischief they could. Now was Christian somewhat in amaze. At last, when every man started back for fear of the armed men, Christian saw a man of very stout countenance come up to the man that sat there to write, saying, "Set down my name, Sir." The which when he had done, he saw the man draw his sword and put a helmet upon his head and rush toward the door upon the armed men, who laid upon him with deadly force; but the man, not at all discouraged, fell to cutting and hacking most fiercely. So after he had received, and given many wounds to those that attempted to keep him out, he cut his way through them all, and pressed forward into the palace; at which there was a pleasant voice heard from those that were within, even of those that walked upon the top of the palace, saying,

"Come in, come in!
Eternal Glory thou shalt win."

So he went in, and was clothed with such garments as they. Then Christian smiled, and said, "I think, verily, I know the meaning of this."

"Now," said Christian, "let me go hence."—"Nay, stay," said the Interpreter, "till I have showed thee a little more; and after that thou shalt go on thy way."—So he took him by the hand again, and led him into a very dark room, where there sat a man in an iron cage.

Now the man, to look on, seemed very sad; he sat with his eyes looking down to the ground, his hands folded together, and he sighed as if he would break his heart. Then said Christian, "What means this?" At which the Interpreter bid him talk with the man.

Then said Christian to the man, "What art thou?" The man answered, "I am what I was not once."

Christian. What wast thou once?

Man. I was once a fair and flourishing professor, both in my own eyes and also in the eyes of others. I once was, as I thought, fair for the Celestial City, and had then even joy at the thoughts that I should get thither.

Christian. Well, but what art thou now?

Man. I am now a man of despair, and shut up in it, as in this iron cage. I cannot get out. Oh, now I cannot!

---

* **Ink-horn,** *inkstand.* These articles were formerly made of horn. *Ink*, fr. Lat. *encaustum*, a purple-red fluid with which the Roman emperors signed their edicts. This from Gr. ἔγκαυστον, burnt in, encaustic; ἐν, in. and καίω, future καύσω, to burn; ἐγκαίειν, to burn in, to paint in encaustic, *i. e.*, with colors mixed with wax; Lat. *encausto pingere*. *Horn* is from Lat. *cornu;* Gr. κέρας, horn. See Grimm's Law. pp. 23, 240.—**Bid him talk.** *Bid* and *bade* are both correct (A. S. *biddan*, to ask).—**Professor.** This word is often technically used by the old writers, as here, to denote a "professing Christian."—**A man of despair.** Bunyan is here drawing from the rich stores of his own experience. He had passed through all that he describes. Of one of these terrible seasons he says, "Down fell I, as a bird that is shot from the top of a tree, into great guilt and fearful despair. . . . Then did I, for whole days together, feel my very body as well as my mind, to shake and totter under the sense of this dreadful judgment of God, such a clogging and heat at my stomach by reason of this my terror, that I was sometimes as if my breast-bone would split asunder!" Bunyan's *Grace Abounding.*

Flourish, thrive, prosper, grow. Write out, etc., as before.

A pleasant voice was heard. Analyze.

Christian. But how camest thou into this condition?

Man. I left off to watch * and be sober; I laid the reins upon the neck of my lusts; I sinned against the light of the world and the goodness of God; I have grieved the Spirit, and he is gone; I tempted the Devil, and he is come to me; I have provoked God to anger, and he has left me; I have so hardened my heart that I cannot repent.

Then said Christian to the Interpreter, "But is there no hope for such a man as this?" "Ask him," said the Interpreter.

Then said Christian, "Is there no hope, but you must be kept in the iron cage of despair?"

Man. No, none at all.

Christian. Why? The Son of the Blessed is very pitiful.

Man. I have crucified him to myself afresh; I have despised his person; I have despised his righteousness; I have counted his blood an unholy thing; I have done despite to the Spirit of grace. Therefore I shut myself out of all the promises; and there now remains to me nothing but threatenings, dreadful threatenings, fearful threatenings of certain judgment and fiery indignation, which shall devour me as an adversary.

Christian. For what did you bring yourself into this condition?

Man. For the lusts, pleasures, and profits of this world; in the enjoyment of which I did then promise myself much delight: but now every one of those things also bite me, and gnaw me, like a burning worm.

Christian. But canst thou not repent and turn?

Man. God hath denied me repentance; his word gives me no encouragement to believe; yea, himself hath shut me up in this iron cage; nor can all the men in the world let me out. O eternity! eternity! how shall I grapple with the misery that I must meet with in eternity!

Then said the Interpreter to Christian, "Let this man's misery be remembered by thee, and be an everlasting caution to thee."

Christian. Well, this is fearful! God help me to watch and be sober, and to pray that I may shun the cause of this man's misery. Sir, is it not time for me to go on my way now?

Interpreter. Tarry till I shall show thee one thing more; and then thou shalt go on thy way.

So he took Christian by the hand again, and led him into a chamber, where there was one rising out of bed; and as he put on his raiment, he shook and trembled. Then said Christian, "Why doth this man thus tremble?" The Interpreter then bade him to tell Christian the reason of his so doing.

---

* **Left off to watch,** omitted to watch, ceased to watch.—**Laid the reins upon the neck of,** *gave loose rein to.*—**Pitiful,** full of pity.—**Crucified afresh.** Heb. vi., 6.—**Despised his person.** Luke xix., 14.—**Done despite.** Heb. x., 28, 29.—**Every one . . . . also bite.** *Bite* should be *bites*, the subject being singular. So *gnaw* should be *gnaws*. See Abbott's *Shakes. Grammar*, 412.—**Well, this is fearful.** Indeed it is. The despair of this man is painted in colors that are hardly surpassed in literature. How simple, yet how vivid are the pictures! "I preached," says Bunyan, "what I felt, what I smartingly did feel."

Dreadful, awful, fearful. Other synonymes? Distinguish among them, and illustrate each. Has Bunyan selected the best?

The Son of the Blessed is pitiful. Analyze.

So he began and said, "This night as I was in my sleep, I dreamed: and behold! the heavens grew exceeding black; also it thundered and lightened in most fearful wise, that it put me into an agony. So I looked up in my dream, and saw the clouds rack an unusual rate; upon which I heard a great sound of a trumpet,* and saw also a Man sit upon a cloud, attended with the thousands of heaven. They were all in flaming fire, also the heavens were in a burning flame. I heard then a voice saying, 'Arise, ye dead, and come to judgment!' and with that the rocks rent, the graves opened, and the dead that were therein came forth. Some of them were exceeding glad and looked upward; and some sought to hide themselves under the mountains. Then I saw the Man that sat upon the cloud open the book and bid the world draw near. Yet there was, by reason of a flame which issued out and came before him, a convenient distance betwixt him and them, as betwixt the judge and the prisoners at the bar. I heard it also proclaimed to them that attended on the Man that sat on the cloud, 'Gather together the tares, the chaff, and stubble, and cast them into the burning lake:' and with that the bottomless pit opened, just whereabout I stood: out of the mouth of which there came, in an abundant manner, smoke, and coals of fire, with hideous noises. It was also said to the same persons, 'Gather my wheat into the garner.' And with that I saw many catched up, and carried away into the clouds; but I was left behind. I also sought to hide myself, but I could not; for the man that sat upon the cloud still kept his eye upon me: my sins also came into my mind, and my conscience did accuse me on every side. Upon this, I awakened from my sleep."

Christian. But what was it that made you so afraid of this sight?

Man. Why, I thought the Day of Judgment was come, and that I was not ready for it. But this frighted me most, that the angels gathered up several, and left me behind: also, the pit of hell opened her mouth just

* **Trumpet.** 1 Cor. xv., 52; 1 Thess. iv., 16.—**Thousands.** Jude 14.—**Flaming fire.** 2 Thess. i., 8.—**Heard a voice.** John v., 28.—**The dead.** Rev. xx., 12, 13.—**Hide themselves.** Rev. vi., 16.—**Flame which issued.** Dan. vii., 9, 10.—**A convenient distance,** a *proper* distance.—**Chaff.** Matt. iii., 12; Mal. iv., 1.—**Bottomless.** Rev. xx., 1, 3.—**Wheat.** Luke iii., 17; Matt. xiii., 30.—**Catched.** This word is nearly obsolete. See Index.—**Clouds.** 1 Thess. iv., 17—**Accuse me.** Rom. ii., 14.—**Pit of hell.** Hell is represented in the Bible as a pit. See Rev. xx., 1. *Hell.* (A. S. *hell*, from A. S. *helan*, to cover, conceal; akin to A. S. *hol*, hole, cavern; and to Lat. *celare*, to conceal. Apply Grimm's law to show how *cel* in *celare*, may become *hel* in *hell.*)—**Opened her mouth.** It is clear that Bunyan is all along relating his own astonishing experience. The student will do well to read carefully Southey's charming and sympathetic biography of him.

Hide, *conceal*, *secrete*. Differentiate, etc.

The heavens were in a burning flame. *In a burning flame* is equivalent to *afire*, or *conflagrant*, and, with *were*, makes a *subject-and-predicate combination* with *heavens*.

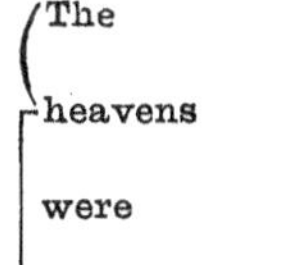

The
heavens
were
in a burning flame. *I. e.*, The heavens were *conflagrant.*

Complete this analysis.

Analyze *I was in my sleep*

where I stood. My conscience, too, afflicted me; and, as I thought, the Judge had always his eyes* upon me, showing indignation in his countenance.

Then said the Interpreter to Christian, "Hast thou considered all these things?"

Christian. Yes; and they put me in hope and fear.

Interpreter. Well, keep all things so in thy mind, that they may be as a goad in thy sides, to prick thee forward in the way thou must go.

Then Christian began to gird up his loins, and to address himself to his journey. Then said the Interpreter, "The Comforter be always with thee, good Christian, to guide thee in the way that leads to the city?"

So Christian went on his way, saying:

> "Here I have seen things rare and profitable:
> Things pleasant, dreadful things to make me stable
> In what I have begun to take in hand:
> Then let me think on them, and understand
> Wherefore they showed me were, and let me be
> Thankful, O good Interpreter, to thee."

Now I saw in my dream, that the highway up which Christian was to go, was fenced on either side with a wall, and that wall was called Salvation. Up this way, therefore, did burthened Christian run; but not without great difficulty, because of the load on his back.

He ran thus till he came at a place somewhat ascending, and upon that place stood a cross, and a little below, in the bottom, a sepulchre. So I saw in my dream, that just as Christian came up with the cross, his burthen loosed from his shoulders, and fell from off his back, and began to tumble, and so continued to do, till it came to the mouth of the sepulchre; when it fell in, and I saw it no more!

Then was Christian glad and lightsome, and said with a merry heart,

---

* **Had always his eyes,** etc. Doubtless the author here describes one of his own terrible visions. See Macaulay's Essay on *Bunyan.*—**Goad** (A. S. *gâd*, a pointed instrument used to urge on a beast to move faster), *a stimulus*, an instrument to drive cattle.—**Salvation.** Is. xxvi., 1. The path that is walled on either hand by eternal principles often leads away from riches and fame.—**Saw it no more.** After all, perhaps, the best evidence of the truth of the Christian religion is its power to change the heart, to set the whole inner man in harmony with all that is good, and to give satisfaction and peace. Here is an argument with which infidelity and atheism never grapple; a test which science does not even touch.

Indignation, anger, resentment, wrath, ire. Write out, etc.

I have seen things rare. Another syntactical combination is here found. The *object* of the action *completes* the predicate. It unites with the verb which governs it, to form the *Objective Combination.* It may be expressed by a brace { connecting the two. It is marked O.

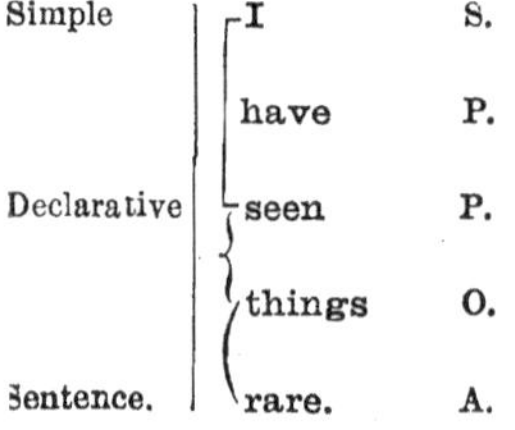

Let the student complete this work according to model, p. 289.

"He hath given me rest by his sorrow, * and life by his death." Then he stood still a while to look and wonder: for it was very surprising to him, that the sight of the cross should thus ease him from his burthen. He looked, therefore, and looked again, even till the springs that were in his head sent the waters down his cheeks.

Now, as he stood looking and weeping, behold three Shining Ones came to him and saluted him, with, "Peace be to thee." So the first said to him, "Thy sins be forgiven thee;" the second stripped him of his rags, and clothed him with change of raiment; the third also set a mark on his forehead, and gave him a roll with a seal upon it, which he bade him look on as he ran, and that he should give it in at the Celestial Gate. So they went their way. Then Christian gave three leaps for joy, and went on singing:—

"Thus far did I come, laden with my sin;
Nor could aught ease the grief that I was in,
Till I came hither. What a place is this!
Must here be the beginning cf my bliss?
Must here the burthen fall from off my back?
Must here the strings that bind it to me, crack?
Blest Cross! blest Sepulchre! blest rather be
The MAN that there was put to shame for me!"

I saw then in my dream, that he went on thus, even until he came at the bottom; where he saw, a little out of the way, three men fast asleep, with fetters upon their heels. The name of the one was Simple; another, Sloth, and the third, Presumption.

Christian, then, seeing them lie in this case, went to them, if peradventure he might awake them; and cried, "You are like them that sleep on the top of a mast, for the dead sea is under you, a gulf that has no bottom. Awake, therefore, and come away; be willing also, and I will help you off with your irons." He also told them, "If he that goeth about like a roaring lion comes by, you will certainly become a prey to his teeth." With that they looked upon him, and began to answer in this sort: Simple said, "I see no danger." Sloth said, "Yet a little more sleep;" and Presumption said, "Every tub must stand upon his own bottom." And so they lay down to sleep again, and Christian went on his way.

Yet was he troubled to think, that men in that danger should so little esteem the kindness of him that so freely offered to help them, both by the awakening of them, counselling of them, and proffering to help them off with their irons. And as he was troubled thereabout, he espied two men come tumbling over the wall, on the left hand of the narrow way; and they

* **Rest by his sorrow.** "I remember one day, as I was travelling in the country and musing on the wickedness and blasphemy of my heart, and considering the enmity there was in me to God, this Scripture came into my mind, 'He hath made peace by the blood of his cross;' by which I was made to see, both again and again, that day, that God and my soul were friends by his blood. This was a good day to me! I hope I shall never forget it." Bunyan's *Grace Abounding.*—**Sins be forgiven.** Matt. ix., 2.—**Rags.** Zech. iii., 4; Rev. iii., 5, 18.—**Forehead.** Rev. vii., 3.—**Roll** (Lat. *rota*, a wheel), a document written on parchment or other material which may be rolled up, *a scroll.*—**Top of a mast** (Prov. xxiii., 34), the height of insecurity.—**Lion.** 1 Pet. v., 8.—**Both.** Is this use of *both* correct? See p. 222.

Christian gave three leaps. Analyze as directed on pp. 289, 312.

made up apace to him. The name of the one was Formalist,* and the name of the other Hypocrisy. So, as I said, they drew up unto him, who thus entered with them into discourse.

Christian. Gentlemen, whence came you, and whither go you?

Formalist and *Hypocrisy.* We were born in the land of Vain-glory, and are going for praise to Mount Zion.

Christian. Why came you not in at the gate which standeth at the beginning of the way? Know you not that it is written, that "he that cometh not in by the door, but climbeth up some other way, the same is a thief and a robber?"

Formalist and Hypocrisy then said, that to go to the gate for entrance, was by all their countrymen counted too far about; and therefore, the usual way was to make a short cut of it, and to climb over the wall as they had done.

Christian. But will it not be counted a trespass against the Lord of the city, whither we are bound, thus to violate his revealed will?

They told him, that, as for that, he needed not to trouble his head thereabout; for what they did, they had custom for, and could produce, if need were, testimony that would witness it for more than a thousand years.

Christian. But will it stand a trial at law?

They told him, that custom, it being of so long standing as above a thousand years, would doubtless now be admitted as a thing legal by an impartial judge. "And besides," said they, "if we get into the way, what's matter which way we get in? If we are in, we are in. Thou art but in the way, who, as we perceive, came in at the gate; and we are also in the way, that came tumbling over the wall. Wherein now is thy condition better than ours?"

Christian. I walk by the rule of my master; you walk by the rude working of your fancies. You are counted thieves already by the Lord of the way: therefore I doubt you will not be found true men at the end of the way. You came in by yourselves, without his direction, and shall go out by yourselves, without his mercy.

To this they made him but little answer; only they bid him look to himself.

Then I saw, that they went on, every man in his way, without much conference one with another; save that these two men told Christian, that, as to laws and ordinances, they doubted not but they should as conscientiously do them as he. "Therefore," say they, "we see not wherein thou differest

---

* **Formalist.** "The formalist is a man that hath lost all but (or never had more than) the *shell* of religion. He is hot, indeed, for his form; and no marvel; for that is his all to contend for. But his form being without the power and spirit of godliness, it will leave him in his sins; nay, he standeth now in them in the sight of God, and is one of the 'many' that 'shall seek to enter in and shall not be able.'" Bunyan's *Strait Gate.*—**Robber.** John x., 1.—**Doubt you will not be found,** *fear* or *suspect* that you will not be found. So below, *I doubt* [suspect that] *you want.*—**Laws and ordinances.** Gal. ii., 16; Col. ii., 20.

Legal, lawful, legitimate, authorized, licit. Write out, etc.

They could produce testimony. Analyze as before.

from us, but by the coat that is on thy back, which was, as we trow, given thee by some of thy neighbors, to hide the shame of thy nakedness.

Christian. By laws and ordinances you will not be saved, since you came not in by the door. And as for this coat that is on my back, it was given me by the Lord of the place whither I go; and that, as you say, to cover my nakedness with. And I take it as a token of kindness to me; for I had nothing but rags before; and besides, thus I comfort myself as I go: "Surely," think I, "when I come to the gate of the city, the Lord thereof will know me for good, since I have his coat on my back; a coat that he gave me freely in the day that he stripped me of my rags." I have, moreover, a mark in my forehead, of which perhaps you have taken no notice, which one of my Lord's most intimate associates fixed there in the day that my burthen fell off my shoulders. I will tell you, moreover, that I had then given me a roll sealed, to comfort me by reading as I go on the way. I was also bid to give it in at the Celestial Gate, in token of my certain going in after it. All which things I doubt you want, and want them because you came not in at the gate.

To these things they gave him no answer; only they looked upon each other and laughed. Then I saw that they went on all, save that Christian kept before, who had no more talk but with himself, and that sometimes sighing, and sometimes comfortably; also he would be often reading in the roll that one of the Shining Ones gave him, by which he was refreshed.

I beheld then, that they all went on till they came to the foot of the hill Difficulty, at the bottom of which was a spring.* There were also in the same place two other ways besides that which came straight from the gate: one turned to the left hand, and the other to the right, at the bottom of the hill; but the narrow way lay right up the hill, and the name of the going up the side of the hill is called Difficulty. Christian now went to the spring, and drank thereof to refresh himself, and then began to go up the hill, saying:—

"The hill, though high, I covet to ascend;
The difficulty will not me offend,
For I perceive the way to life lies here:
Come, pluck up heart, let's neither faint nor fear.
Better, though difficult, the right way to go,
Than wrong, though easy, where the end is wo."

The other two also came to the foot of the Hill: but when they saw that the hill was steep and high; and that there were two other ways to go; and supposing also that these two ways might meet again with that up which Christian went, on the other side of the hill; therefore they were resolved

* **Spring.** Isaiah xlix., 10.—**The name of the going.** Going seems here to mean *road* or *path.*—**The way to life lies there.** "If thou wouldst be faithful to do that work that God hath appointed thee, then beware thou do not stop and stick when hard work comes before thee. It is with Christians as it is with other scholars; they sometimes meet with hard lessons: but these thou must also learn, or thou canst not do thy work." Bunyan on *Paul's Departure and Crown.*

The way to life lies. "*To life*" modifies "*way*"; an adjective combination. Analyze.

to go in those ways. Now the name of one of those ways was Danger, and the name of the other, Destruction. So the one took the way which is called Danger, which led him into a great wood; and the other took directly up the way to Destruction, which led him into a wide field full of dark mountains, where he stumbled and fell, and rose no more.

I looked then after Christian, to see him go up the hill; where I perceived he fell from running to going, and from going to clambering upon his hands and his knees, because of the steepness of the place. Now, about the midway to the top of the hill was a pleasant arbor, made by the Lord of the hill, for the refreshing of weary travellers. Thither, therefore, Christian got, where also he sat down to rest him. Then he pulled his roll out of his bosom, and read therein to his comfort. He also now began afresh to take a review of the coat or garment that was given him as he stood by the cross. Thus pleasing himself awhile, he at last fell into a slumber, and thence into a fast sleep;* which detained him in that place until it was almost night; and in his sleep, his roll fell out of his hand. Now, as he was sleeping, there came one to him, and awaked him, saying, "Go to the ant, thou sluggard: consider her ways, and be wise." And with that Christian suddenly started up and sped him on his way, and went apace till he came to the top of the hill.

---

* **Fast sleep** (Goth. *fasten;* A. S. *fäst*, firm, fixed), *firm* or *deep sleep*, profound sleep.—**Roll fell out.** This was the roll given to Christian by one of the "three Shining Ones." Another roll had been committed to him by Evangelist at the beginning of his pilgrimage, and in it was written, "Fly from the wrath to come."—**Be wise.** Prov. vi., 6, also xxx., 24, 25.—**Apace.** Lat. *passus*, step; *pandere*, to spread; Fr. *pas*, *footstep*, *pace*. The mixed character of the English language is well illustrated by the prefix *a*, of which we note the following different origins: 1. The A. S. prefix *a* or *ge*, once equivalent to Lat. *co* or *con*, signifying *with*, *together with*, but afterwards intensive in its force, and now common without special significancy, as in *awake*, *arise*. 2. The A. S. preposition *an* or *on*, meaning *in* or *on;* as, *abed*, in bed, *aground*, *asleep*. 3. The article *a* or *an*, A. S. *ane*, Lat. *unus*, one; as, *awhile*, *apiece*, *i. e.*, *one* piece. 4. The French preposition *à*, Lat. *ad*, to, in words derived from the French, as *adieu*, to God, *abandon*, *à ban donner*, to give to interdiction. 5. The Lat. *a* or *ab*, from, away; as, *avert*, turn away. 6. Lat. *e* or *ex* in some words that come through the French; as, *amend*, Fr. *amender*, Lat. *amendare*, to amend. 7. Greek ἀ negative, ἀν before a vowel, as *anarchy*, without government. 8. Greek ἀ copulative, as *acolyte*, a companion, from ἀκολουθεῖν. The full form of ἀ in this case is ἅμα, with, allied to no. 1, above.

Danger, *peril*, *hazard*. Other synonymes? Write out, etc.
Review, *survey*. Other synonymes? Differentiate, etc.

The way is called Danger. *Danger* may here be called a *factitive* object, from *facĕre*, to make. "There are some verbs which require, besides the simple passive object of the thing, another object of the effect." Thus, *They made him king.* Here *king* is the factitive object. The same object appears when the verb is in the passive voice; thus, *He is made* (appointed, constituted, chosen, called, etc.) *king*. The Latin verb *facĕre*, to make, being a type of verbs of this class, this object, thus completing the action of the verb, is called a *factitive object*. It may be marked *fac.* This then, is another example of the *objective combination.*

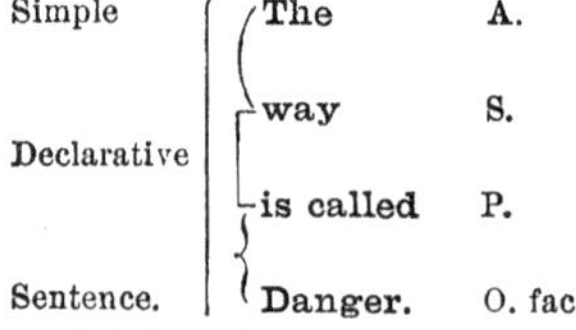

Let the student complete this according to the model on p. 289.

He began to take a review. Analyze. It will be observed that the words *to take a review* are the object of *began;* and *a review*, the object of take. Note the force of *re-* in *review.*

Now when he was got up to the top of the hill, there came two men running to meet him amain.* The name of the one was Timorous, and of the other, Mistrust. To whom Christian said, "Sirs, what is the matter you run the wrong way?" Timorous answered, that they were going to the City of Zion, and had got up that difficult place. "But," said he, "the farther we go, the more danger we meet with; wherefore we turned, and are going back again."

"Yes," said Mistrust, "for just before us lie a couple of lions in the way: whether sleeping or waking, we know not; and we could not think, if we came within reach, but they would presently pull us in pieces."

Then said Christian, "You make me afraid. But whither shall I flee, to be safe? If I go back to my own country, that is prepared for fire and brimstone, and I shall certainly perish there. If I can get to the celestial city, I am sure to be in safety there. I must venture. To go back is nothing but death; to go forward is fear of death, and life everlasting beyond it. I will yet go forward."

So Mistrust and Timorous ran down the hill, and Christian went on his way. But thinking again of what he had heard from the men, he felt in his bosom for his roll, that he might read therein and be comforted; but he felt, and found it not! Then was Christian in great distress, and knew not what to do; for he wanted that which used to relieve him, and that which should have been his pass into the celestial city. Here, therefore, he began to be much perplexed, and knew not what to do. At last he bethought himself that he had slept in the arbor that is on the side of the hill; and, falling down upon his knees, he asked God's forgiveness for that his foolish act, and then went back to look for his roll. But all the way he went back, who can sufficiently set forth the sorrow of Christian's heart? Sometimes he sighed, sometimes he wept, and oftentimes he chid himself for being so foolish as to fall asleep in that place, which was erected only for a little refreshment for his weariness. Thus therefore he went back, carefully looking on this side and on that all the way as he went, if happily he might find the roll that had been his comfort so many times in his journey. He went thus till he came again within sight of the arbor where he sat and slept: but that sight renewed his sorrows the more, by bringing

---

* **Amain,** with force, with energy. *Main* is A. S. *mägen, mägn;* Ice. *magn*, strength, vigor; fr. A. S. *magan*, to be able or strong; Ger. *mögen*. Hence *may, might*, and the obsolete *mought*. See *a* in *apace*, p. 316.—**What is the matter,** etc. *Matter* here means the *cause* of the trouble. What is the difficulty or trouble? Milton uses the word in the same way, thus, "And this is the *matter* why interpreters will not consent it to be a true story."

He began to be perplexed. The construction of the infinitive is that of a noun in the neuter gender. Here *to be perplexed* is the object of the transitive verb begins.

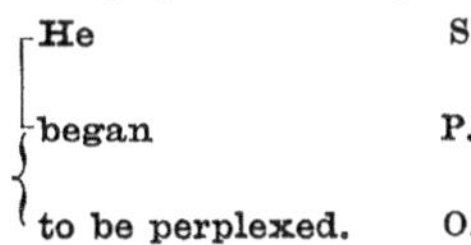

Let the student complete the analysis, etc., according to the directions previously given.

To go forward is fear of death. Analyze as before directed. *To go forward* is the subject.

again, even afresh, his evil of sleeping into his mind. Thus, therefore, he now went on bewailing his sinful sleep, saying, "O wretched man that I am! that I should sleep in the day time!* that I should sleep in the midst of difficulty! that I should so indulge the flesh, as to use that rest for ease to my flesh, which the Lord of the hill hath erected only for the relief of the spirits of the pilgrims! How many steps have I took in vain! Thus it happened to Israel; for their sin they were sent back again by way of the Red Sea; and I am made to tread these steps with sorrow, which I might have trod with delight, had it not been for this sinful sleep. How far might I have been on my way by this time! I am made to tread those steps thrice over, which I needed not to have trod but once: yea, now also I am like to be benighted, for the day is almost spent. O, that I had not slept!"

Now by this time he was come to the arbor again; where for a while he sat down and wept: but at last, as Providence would have it, looking sorrowfully down under the settle, there he espied his roll; the which he with trembling and haste catched up and put into his bosom. But who can tell, how joyful this man was, when he had gotten his roll again? For this roll was the assurance of his life and acceptance at the desired haven. Therefore he laid it up in his bosom, gave God thanks for directing his eye to the place where it lay, and with joy and tears betook himself again to his journey. But, oh how nimble now did he go up the rest of the hill! Yet, before he got up, the sun went down upon Christian; and this made him again recall the vanity of his sleeping to his remembrance; and thus he again began to condole with himself: "O thou sinful sleep! how for thy sake am I like to be benighted in my journey! I must walk without the sun, darkness must cover the path of my feet, and I must hear the noise of doleful creatures, because of my sinful sleep."—Now also he remembered the story that Mistrust and Timorous told him of, how they were frighted with the sight of the lions. Then said Christian to himself again, "These beasts range in the night for their prey; and if they should meet with me in the dark, how should I shift them? How should I escape being by them torn in pieces?" Thus he went on his way: but while he was thus bewailing his unhappy miscarriage, he lift up his eyes, and behold, there was a very stately palace before him, the name of which was Beautiful; and it stood just by the highway side.

So I saw in my dream, that he made haste and went forward, that, if possible, he might get lodging there. Now, before he had gone far, he entered into a very narrow passage, which was about a furlong off the por-

---

* **Sleep in the day time.** 1 Thess. v., 7, 8.—**Took.** See Abbott's *Shak. Gram.* 343. Milton uses this for the past participle in his epitaph on Shakespeare,—

"Each heart,
Hath from the leaves of thy unvalued book
Those Delphic lines with deep impression took."—

Settle (A. S. *sitel*, from *sittan*, to sit; Lat. *sedere*, to sit), a high-back bench. Apply Grimm's law.—**He lift up his eyes.** *Lift*, A. S. *lyft*, air. Hence *lift* is to raise into the *air*. See *on loft*, p. 26. *Lift* was sometimes used instead of *lifted*. Thus, "Lift up your heads, O ye gates; and be ye *lift* up, ye everlasting doors." *Psalms*, xxiv., 7.

This roll was the assurance of his life. Analyze fully.

ter's lodge, and, looking very narrowly before him as he went, he espied two lions in the way. "Now," thought he, "I see the danger that Mistrust and Timorous were driven back by." The lions were chained, but he saw not the chains. Then he was afraid, and thought also himself to go back after them, for he thought nothing but death was before him: but the porter at the lodge, whose name is *Watchful*,* perceiving that Christian made a halt, as if he would go back, cried unto him, saying, "Is thy strength so small! Fear not the lions; for they are chained, and are placed there for trial of faith, where it is, and for discovery of those that have none. Keep in the midst of the path, and no hurt shall come unto thee."

Then I saw that he went on trembling for fear of the lions; but taking good heed to the direction of the porter, he heard them roar, but they did him no harm. Then he clapped his hands, and went on till he came and stood before the gate where the porter was. Then said Christian to the porter, "Sir, what house is this? and may I lodge here to-night?" The porter answered, "This house was built by the Lord of the hill; and he built it for the relief and security of pilgrims." The porter also asked, whence he was, and whither he was going.

Christian. I am come from the City of Destruction, and am going to Mount Zion: but because the sun is now set, I desire, if I may, to lodge here to-night.

Porter. What is your name?

Christian. My name is now Christian; but my name at the first was Graceless. I came of the race of Japhet, whom God will persuade to dwell in the tents of Shem.

Porter. But how did it happen that you came so late? The sun is set.

Christian. I had been here sooner, but that, wretched man that I am, I slept in the arbor that stands on the hill side. Nay, I had, notwithstanding that, been here much sooner, but that in my sleep I lost my evidence, and came without it to the brow of the hill; and then feeling for it and finding it not, I was forced, with sorrow of heart, to go back to the place where I slept my sleep: where I found it, and now I am come.

Porter. Well, I will call out one of the virgins of this place, who will, if she likes your talk, bring you in to the rest of the family according to the rules of the house.

---

* **Porter at the lodge whose name is Watchful.** Mark xiii., 34. "The palace called Beautiful, into which Christian desires admission, is supposed to represent a visible church of Christ, of which Watchful, the Porter, is the pastor. The previous questioning of the Pilgrim by Watchful and others denotes the carefulness with which churches should examine those who apply for admission."—**Japhet.** Gen. ix., 27.

Whom God will persuade. The predicate is here completed by a pronoun.

God	S.
will persuade	P.
whom.	O.

The student will complete the work as before. Analyze *What moved you?*

So Watchful, the porter, rang a bell; at the sound of which, came out of the door of the house a grave and beautiful damsel, named Discretion; * and asked why she was called.

The porter answered, "This man is in a journey from the City of Destruction to Mount Zion; but being weary and benighted, he asked me if he might lodge here to-night: so I told him I would call for thee, who, after discourse had with him, mayest do as seemeth thee good, even according to the law of the house."

Then she asked him, whence he was, and whither he was going? and he told her. She asked him also, how he got into the way? and he told her. Then she asked him, what he had seen and met with in the way? and he told her. And at last she asked his name? So he said, "It is Christian; and I have so much the more desire to lodge here to-night, because, by what I perceive, this place was built by the Lord of the hill, for the relief and security of pilgrims." So she smiled; but the water stood in her eyes; and, after a little pause, she said, "I will call forth two or three more of my family."

So she ran to the door, and called out Prudence, Piety, and Charity; who, after a little more discourse with him, had him into the family; and many of them, meeting him at the threshold of the house, said, "Come in, thou blessed of the Lord; this house was built by the Lord of the hill, on purpose to entertain such pilgrims in." Then he bowed his head, and followed them into the house. So when he was come in, and set down, they gave him something to drink, and consented together, that, until supper was ready, some of them should have some particular discourse with Christian, for the best improvement of time; and they appointed Piety, and Prudence, and Charity, to discourse with him; and thus they began:—

Piety. Come, good Christian, since we have been so loving to you, to receive you into our house this night; let us, if perhaps we may better ourselves thereby, talk with you of all things that have happened to you in your pilgrimage.

Christian. With a very good will, and I am glad that you are so well disposed.

Piety. What moved you at first to betake yourself to a pilgrim's life?

Christian. I was driven out of my native country by a dreadful sound

---

* **Discretion.** Prov. ii., 11.—**But the water stood in her eyes.** An exquisite touch of nature, reminding us of *Cordelia* in *Lear*, Act IV., sc. 3.

> "You have seen
> Sunshine and rain at once; her smiles and tears
> Were like a better May. . . . . There she shook
> The holy water from her heavenly eyes."—

Had him into the family, brought him into the midst of the family.—**To entertain such pilgrims in.** "If thou wouldst be faithful to do that work that God hath allotted thee to do in this world for his name, labor to live in the savor and sense of thy freedom and liberty by Jesus Christ. This is of absolute use in this matter; yea, so absolute that it is impossible for any Christian to do his work christianly without some enjoyment of it." Bunyan's *Paul's Departure and Crown.*

Discretion, judgment, prudence, circumspection. Other synonymes? Write out, etc.

that was in my ears; to wit, that unavoidable destruction did attend me, if I abode in that place where I was.

Piety. But how did it happen that you came out of your country this way?

Christian. It was as God would have it: for when I was under the fears of destruction, I did not know whither to go; but by chance there came a man, even to me, as I was trembling and weeping, whose name is Evangelist; and he directed me to the wicket-gate,* which else I should never have found, and so set me into the way that hath led me directly to this house.

Piety. But did you not come by the house of the Interpreter?

Christian. Yes; and did see such things there, the remembrance of which will stick by me as long as I live: especially three things; to wit, how Christ, in despite of Satan, maintains his work of grace in the heart; how the man had sinned himself quite out of hope of God's mercy; and also the dream of him that thought in his sleep the Day of Judgment was come.

Piety. Why, did you hear him tell his dream?

Christian. Yes; and a dreadful one it was, I thought. It made my heart ache as he was telling of it; but yet I am glad I heard it.

Piety. Was this all you saw at the house of the Interpreter?

Christian. No: he took me, and had me where he showed me a stately palace, and how the people were clad in gold that were in it; and how there came a venturous man and cut his way through the armed men that stood at the door to keep him out; and how he was bid to "come in, and win eternal glory!" Methought those things did ravish my heart. I would have staid at that good man's house a twelvemonth, but that I knew I had farther to go.

Piety. And what saw you else in the way?

Christian. Saw! Why, I went but a little farther, and I saw one, as I thought in my mind, hang bleeding upon a tree; and the very sight of him made my burthen fall off my back; for I groaned under a very heavy

---

* **Wicket-gate.** Matt. vii., 13, 14. See pp. 291, 302.—**In despite of Satan.** Bunyan's conception of a personal devil was intensely vivid. At times Satan seemed to prevail. At other times he says, "Methought I saw as if the tempter did leer and steal away from me as being ashamed of what he had done."

He was telling of it. This is another instance of the objective combination. The predicate is completed by the words *of it.*

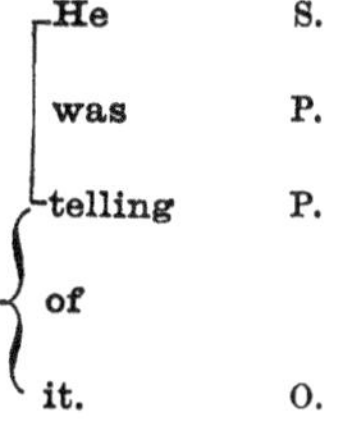

Let the student complete the analysis as before.

Those things did ravish my heart. Analyze.

burthen; but then it fell down from off me. 'Twas a strange thing to me, for I never saw such a thing before. Yea, and while I stood looking up, for then I could not forbear looking, three Shining Ones came to me. One of them testified that my sins were forgiven me; another stripped me of my rags and gave me this embroidered coat which you see; and the third set the mark which you see in my forehead, and gave me this sealed roll.

And with that he plucked it out of his bosom.

Piety. But you saw more than this, did you not?

Christian. The things that I have told you, were the best. Yet some other matters I saw; as, namely, I saw three men, Simple, Sloth, and Presumption, lie asleep a little out of the way as I came, with irons upon their heels: but do you think I could awake them? I also saw Formality and Hypocrisy come tumbling over the wall, to go, as they pretended, to Zion: but they were quickly lost; even as I myself did tell them, but they would not believe. But above all, I found it hard work to get up this hill, and as hard to come by the lions' mouths; and truly, if it had not been for the good man, the porter that stands at the gate, I do not know but that, after all, I might have gone back again. But now I thank God I am here, and I thank you for receiving of me.

Then Prudence thought good to ask him a few questions and desire his answers to them.

Prudence. Do you not think sometimes of the country from whence you came?

Christian. Yea, but with much shame and detestation. Truly, if I had been mindful of that country * from whence I came out, I might have had opportunity to have returned. But now I desire a better country, that is, a heavenly one.

Prudence. Do you not yet bear away with you some of the things that then you were conversant withal?

Christian. Yes; but greatly against my will: especially my inward and carnal cogitations, with which all my countrymen, as well as myself, were delighted. But now all those things are my grief; and might I but choose mine own things, I would choose never to think of those things more; but when I would be doing of that which is best, that which is worst is with me.

Prudence. Do you not find sometimes as if those things were vanquished, which at other times are your perplexity?

Christian. Yes; but that is but seldom. But they are to me golden hours, in which such things happen to me.

---

* **Mindful of that country,** *very attentive to that country,* or *fond* of it.—**Opportunity to have returned.** Heb. xi., 15, 16.—**Worst is with me.** Rom. vii., 15, 19. 22, 23.—**Then Prudence thought good,** etc. "Prudence must be joined to piety. Christian prudence should be visible in every step of the Christian; for, says Solomon, 'I, Wisdom, dwell with prudence.' Prov. viii., 12; and, 'the wisdom of the prudent is to understand his way,' Prov. xiv., 8." *Newton.*

Hypocrisy, dissembling, deception, pretense, cheat. Other synonymes? Write out, etc.

I desire a better country. Analyze.

Prudence. Can you remember by what means you find your annoyances at times, as if they were vanquished?

Christian. Yes; when I think what I saw at the Cross, that will do it; and when I look upon my embroidered coat, that will do it; and when I look into the roll that I carry in my bosom, that will do it; and when my thoughts wax warm about whither I am going, that will do it.

Prudence. And what is it that makes you desirous to go to Mount Zion?

Christian. Why, there I hope to see him alive that did hang dead on the Cross; and there I hope to be rid of all those things, that to this day are in me an annoyance to me: there, they say, there is no death;* and there I shall dwell with such company as I like best. For, to tell you truth, I love Him, because I was by him eased of my burthen; and I am weary of my inward sickness: I would fain be where I shall die no more, and with the company that shall continually cry, "Holy, holy, holy!"

Then said Charity to Christian, "Have you a family? are you a married man?"

Christian. I have a wife and four small children.

Charity. And why did you not bring them along with you?

Then Christian wept, and said, "Oh! how willingly would I have done it! but they were all of them utterly averse to my going on Pilgrimage!"

Charity. But you should have talked to them, and have endeavored to have shown them the danger of being behind.

Christian. So I did, and told them also what God had shown to me of the destruction of our city; but I seemed to them as one that mocked, and they believed me not.

Charity. And did you pray to God, that he would bless your counsel to them?

Christian. Yes, and that with much affection; for you must think that my wife and poor children were very dear unto me.

Charity. But did you tell them of your own sorrow, and fear of destruction? for I suppose that destruction was visible enough to you.

Christian. Yes, over and over and over. They might also see my fears in my countenance, in my tears, and also in my trembling under the apprehension of the judgment that did hang over our heads. But all was not sufficient to prevail with them to come with me.

Charity. But what could they say for themselves why they came not?

Christian. Why, my wife was afraid of losing this world; and my children were given to the foolish delights of youth. So, what by one thing and what by another, they left me to wander in this manner alone.

Charity. But did you not, with your vain life, damp all that you, by words, used by way of persuasion to bring them away with you?

* **No death.** Rev. xxi., 4.—**Then said Charity.** This dialogue between Christian and Charity is not found in the first edition. Is there, or is there not, in these questions and answers, an appropriateness, as corresponding to the different qualities of piety, prudence, and charity?—**Endeavored to have shown.** Point out the error.—**Mocked.** Gen. xix., 14.

You should have endeavored to show. Analyze.

Christian. Indeed I cannot commend my life; for I am conscious to myself of many failings therein. I know, also, that a man * by his conversation may soon overthrow what by argument or persuasion he doth labor to fasten upon others for their good. Yet this I can say, I was very wary of giving them occasion, by any unseemly action, to make them averse to going on pilgrimage. Yea, for this very thing, they would tell me I was too precise, and that I denied myself of things, for their sakes, in which they saw no evil. Nay, I think I may say, that, if what they saw in me did hinder them, it was my great tenderness in sinning against God, or of doing any wrong to my neighbor.

Charity. Indeed, Cain hated his brother, because his own works were evil, and his brother's righteous; and if thy wife and children have been offended with thee for this, they thereby show themselves to be implacable to good; and thou hast delivered thy soul from their blood.

Now I saw in my dream, that thus they sat talking together until supper was ready. So when they had made ready, they sat down to meat. Now the table was furnished with fat things, and with wine that was well refined; and all their talk at the table was about the Lord of the hill; as namely, about what he had done, and wherefore he did what he did, and why he had built that house. And by what they said, I perceived that he had been a great warrior, and had fought with and slain him that had the power of death; but not without great danger to himself; which made me love him the more.

For, as they said, "And as I believe," said Christian, "he did it with the loss of much blood; but that which put glory of grace into all he did, was, that he did it of pure love to his country."—And besides, there were some of them of the household that said, they had been and spoke with him since he died on the cross; and they have attested that they had it from his own lips, that he is such a lover of poor pilgrims that the like is not to be found from the east to the west.

---

* **By his conversation,** etc. "Dost thou love thy friends? dost thou love thy enemies? dost thou love thy family, or relations, or the church of God? Then cry for strength from heaven, and for wisdom to walk wisely before them." Bunyan's *Paul's Departure and Crown.*—**His brother's righteous.** 1 John iii., 12.—**From their blood.** Ezek. xxxiii., 5, 9.—**Well refined.** Isaiah xxv., 6.—**Power of death.** Heb. ii., 14.

Occasion, opportunity, cause. Other synonymes? Write out, etc.

They saw no evil. Here the predicate is enlarged by an adjective used as a noun. As before the objective combination is indicated by the brace.

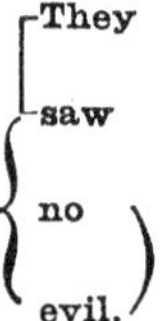

Let the student complete this analysis.

His own works were evil. Analyze.

They, moreover, gave an instance of what they affirmed; and that was, he had stript himself of that glory, that he might do this for the poor; and that they heard him say and affirm that he would not dwell in the mountain of Zion alone. They said, moreover, that he made many pilgrims princes,* though by nature they were beggars born, and their original had been the dunghill.

Thus they discoursed together till late at night; and after they had committed themselves to their Lord for protection, they betook themselves to rest. The Pilgrim they laid in a large upper chamber, whose windows opened towards the sun-rising. The name of the chamber was Peace; where he slept till break of day, and then he awoke and sang:—

Where am I now? Is this the love and care
Of Jesus for the men that Pilgrims are,
Thus to provide! that I shall be forgiven,
And dwell already the next door to heaven!

So in the morning, they all got up; and, after some more discourse, they told him that he should not depart till they had showed him the rarities of that place. And at first they had him into the study, where they showed him records of the greatest antiquity; in which, as I remember in my dream, they showed him first the pedigree of the Lord of the hill; that he was the Son of the Ancient of Days, and came by that eternal generation. Here also were more fully recorded the acts that he had done, and the names of many hundreds that he had taken into his service; and how he had placed them in such habitations that could neither by length of days nor decays of nature be dissolved.

Then they read to him some of the worthy acts that some of his servants had done; as how they had subdued kingdoms, wrought righteousness, obtained promises, stopped the mouths of lions, quenched the violence of fire, escaped the edge of the sword, out of weakness were made strong, waxed valiant in fight, and turned to flight the armies of the aliens.

Then they read again in another part of the records of the house, where

---

* **Pilgrims princes.** 1 Sam. ii., 8; Ps. cxiii., 7.—**Ancient of Days.** Dan. vii., 9, 13, 22. —**Worthy acts.** Hab. xi., 33, 34. We see in these pages the strong hold which military scenes had taken upon Bunyan's mind. Life with him was a battle. His second great allegory shows still more clearly the depth of the impressions made upon him by his experience as a soldier in the parliamentary army. It is entitled, "*The Holy War made by King Shaddai upon Diabolus, for the Regaining the Metropolis of the World, or the Losing and Retaking of Mansoul.*"

They showed him records. Here we have the predicate completed by a *double* object: *records* being the *direct*, and *him* the indirect or *dative* object (so called from the Lat, *dative*, the case that follows *dare*, to give: the case of the remoter object; the case which "denotes that *to* or *for* which anything is or is done").

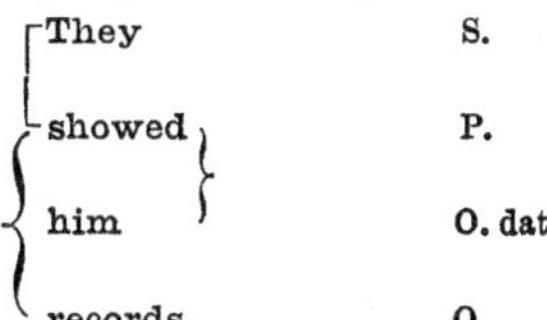

S.

P.

O. dat.

O

Let the student complete, as before.

it was shown how willing their Lord was to receive into his favor, any, even any, though they in time past had offered great affronts to his person and proceedings. Here also were several other histories of many other famous things, of all which Christian had a view; as of things both ancient and modern; together with prophecies and predictions of things that have their certain accomplishment, both to the dread and amazement of enemies, and the comfort and solace of pilgrims.

The next day they took him, and had him into the armory;* where they showed him all manner of furniture, which the Lord had provided for pilgrims, as sword, shield, helmet, breast-plate, all-prayer, and shoes that would not wear out: and there was here enough of this to harness out as many men, for the service of their Lord, as there be stars in the heaven for multitude.

They also showed him some of the engines with which some of his servants had done wonderful things. They showed him Moses's rod; the hammer and nail with which Jael slew Sisera; the pitchers, trumpets, and lamps too, with which Gideon put to flight the armies of Midian. Then they showed him the ox's goad, wherewith Shamgar slew six hundred men. They showed him also the jaw-bone with which Samson did such mighty feats. They showed him moreover the sling and stone with which David slew Goliath of Gath; and the sword also with which their Lord will kill the man of sin, in the day that He shall rise up to the prey. They showed him, besides, many excellent things, with which Christian was much delighted. This done, they went to their rest again.

Then I saw in my dream, that on the morrow he got up to go forwards, but they desired him to stay until the next day also; "And then," said they, "we will, if the day be clear, show you the Delectable Mountains;" which, they said, would yet farther add to his comfort, because they were nearer the desired haven than the place where at present he was. So he consented and staid.

When the morning was up, they had him to the top of the house, and bade him look south. So he did; and behold! at a great distance, he saw a most pleasant mountainous country, beautified with woods, vineyards, fruits of all sorts, flowers also, with springs and fountains, very delectable to behold. Then he asked the name of the country. They said it was Immanuel's Land: "And it is as common," said they, "as this hill is to and for all the Pilgrims. And when thou comest there, from thence thou mayest see to the gate of the Celestial City, as the shepherds that live there will make appear."

Now he bethought himself of setting forward, and they were willing he should. "But first," said they, "let us go again into the armory." So they did; and when he came there, they harnessed him from head to foot, with

* **Armory**, etc. See Eph. vi., 11-18.—**Moses's rod.** Ex. iv.—**Jael.** Judges iv., 21; v., 26.—**Gideon.** Judges vii.—**Shamgar.** Judges iii., 31.—**Samson.** Judges xv., 15.—**Goliath.** 1 Sam. xvii.—**Immanuel's** (Heb. *im*, with; *amu*, us; *el*, God; God with us). See Isaiah vii., 14; Matt. i., 23.—**Harnessed.** See *harness*, pp. 175, 251.

His servants had done wonderful things. Analyze.

what was of proof,* lest perhaps he should meet with assaults in the way. He being, therefore, thus accoutred, walked out with his friends to the gate, and there he asked the Porter, if he saw any Pilgrims pass by? Then the Porter answered, "Yes."

Christian. Pray, did you know him?

Porter. I asked his name, and he told me it was Faithful.

Christian. O, I know him! He is my townsman, my near neighbor: he comes from the place where I was born. How far do you think he may be before?

Porter. He is got by this time below the hill.

Christian. Well, good Porter, the Lord be with thee, and add to all thy blessings much increase for the kindness thou hast shown to me.

Then he began to go forward; but Discretion, Piety, Charity, and Prudence would accompany him down to the foot of the hill. So they went on together, reiterating their former discourses, till they came to go down the hill. Then said Christian, "As it was difficult coming up, so, so far as I can see, it is dangerous going down." "Yes," said Prudence, "so it is; for it is a hard matter for a man to go down into the Valley of Humiliation, as thou art now, and to catch no slip by the way." "Therefore," said they, "are we come out to accompany thee down the hill." So he began to go down, but very warily; yet he caught a slip or two.

Then I saw in my dream, that these good companions, when Christian was got down to the bottom of the hill, gave him a loaf of bread, a bottle of wine, and a cluster of raisins; and then he went his way.

> While Christian is among his godly friends,
> Their golden mouths make him sufficient mends
> For all his griefs; and when they let him go,
> He's clad with northern steel from top to toe.

But now in this Valley of Humiliation, poor Christian was hard put to it; for he had gone but a little way before he espied a foul fiend coming over the field to meet him: his name is Apollyon. Then did Christian begin to be afraid, and to cast in his mind whether to go back, or to stand his ground. But he considered again that he had no armor for his back, and therefore thought that to turn the back to him might give him greater advantages with ease to pierce him with his darts: therefore he resolved to venture, and stand his ground. "For," thought he, "had I no more in my eye than the saving of my life, it would be the best way to stand."

So he went on, and Apollyon met him. Now the monster was hideous to behold. He was clothed with scales like a fish, and they are his pride: he had wings like a dragon, feet like a bear, and out of his belly came fire and

---

* **Proof.** See p. 112.—**Faithful.** If the palace Beautiful represents "the visible church," how does it happen that Faithful is not admitted? Is this a blunder of Bunyan?—**While Christian is,** etc. These four lines are not in the first edition.—**Apollyon** (Gr 'Απολλύων, the destroyer; fr. ἀπόλλυμι, I destroy. See Rev. ix., 11).—**For his back.** "St. Paul, in his enumeration of the various parts of a Christian's panoply, makes no mention of armor for the back." Eph. vi., 11-17.—**To stand.** Eph. vi., 13.—**Scales are his pride.** Job xli., 15.

Faithful, trusty, trustworthy. Other synonymes? Write out, etc.
Gave him a loaf of bread. Analyze fully.

smoke, and his mouth was as the mouth of a lion. When he was come up to Christian, he beheld him with a disdainful countenance, and thus began to question him:—

Apollyon. Whence come you? and whither are you bound?

Christian. I am come from the City of Destruction, which is the place of all evil; and am going to the City of Zion.

Apollyon. By this I perceive thou art one of my subjects: for all that country is mine, and I am the prince and god of it. How is it, then, that thou hast run away from thy king? Were it not that I hope thou mayest do me more service, I would strike thee now at one blow to the ground.

Christian. I was born, indeed, in your dominions; but your service was hard, and your wages* such as a man could not live on; for the wages of sin is death. Therefore when I was come to years, I did as other considerate persons do; look out, if perhaps I might mend myself.

Apollyon. There is no prince that will thus lightly lose his subjects; neither will I, as yet, lose thee. But since thou complainest of thy service and wages, be content to go back. What our country will afford, I do here promise to give thee.

Christian. But I have let myself to another, even to the King of princes; and how can I, with fairness, go back with thee?

Apollyon. Thou hast done in this according to the proverb, Change a bad for a worse. But it is ordinary for those that have professed themselves his servants, after a while to give him the slip and return again to me. Do thou so too, and all shall be well.

Christian. I have given him my faith, and sworn my allegiance to him. How, then, can I go back from this, and not be hanged as a traitor?

Apollyon. Thou didst the same to me; and yet I am willing to pass by all, if now thou wilt yet turn and go back.

Christian. What I promised thee, was in my nonage; and besides, I count that the Prince under whose banner now I stand, is able to absolve me; yea, and to pardon also what I did as to my compliance with thee.

---

* **Wages such as a man could not live on.** A stroke of Bunyan's humor. Rom. vi., 23.—**Nonage** (Lat. *non*, not; *ætas*, age; fr. *ævitas*, fr. *ævum*, fr. αἰών, age, fr. ἀεί, always). *minority*, the time of life before a person becomes 'of age,' *i. e.*, provious to his becoming twenty-one years old. Bunyan evidently understood the principle of law that a contract made by a minor is not binding upon him, unless ratified after attaining majority. He would appear, also, by what goes before, to have some understanding of the law involved in self-expatriation.

Ordinary, common, usual, customary, vulgar. Other synonymes? Differentiate, etc.

Change a bad.

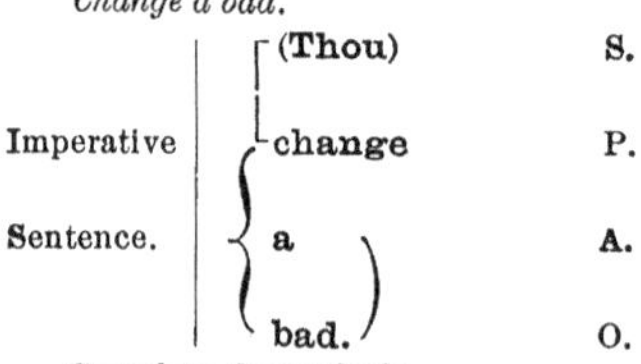

Complete the analysis.
I have given him my faith. Analyze.

And besides, O thou destroying* Apollyon, to speak truth, I like his service, his wages, his servants, his government, his company, and his country, better than thine; and therefore leave off to persuade me farther. I am his servant, and I will follow him.

Apollyon. Consider, again, when thou art in cool blood, what thou art like to meet with in the way that thou goest. Thou knowest that, for the most part, his servants come to an ill end, because they are transgressors against me and my ways. How many of them have been put to shameful deaths! And besides, thou countest his service better than mine; whereas, he never came yet from the place where he is, to deliver any that served him out of their hands. But as for me, how many times, as all the world very well knows, have I delivered, either by power or fraud, those that have faithfully served me, from him and his, though taken by them? And so I will deliver thee.

Christian. His forbearing at present to deliver them is on purpose to try their love, whether they will cleave to him to the end; and as for the ill end thou sayest they come to, that is most glorious in their account. But for present deliverance, they do not much expect it: for they stay for their glory; and then they shall have it, when their prince comes in his and the glory of his angels.

Apollyon. Thou hast already been unfaithful in thy service to him; and how dost thou think to receive wages of him?

Christian. Wherein, O Apollyon, have I been unfaithful to him?

Apollyon. Thou didst faint at first setting out, when thou was almost choked in the gulf of Despond. Thou didst attempt wrong ways to be rid of thy burthen, whereas thou shouldst have staid till thy prince had taken it off. Thou didst sinfully sleep, and lose thy choice things. Thou wast, also, almost persuaded to go back at the sight of the lions; and when thou talkest of thy journey, and of what thou hast heard and seen, thou art inwardly desirous of vain-glory in all that thou sayest or doest.

Christian. All that is true, and much more, which thou hast left out. But the prince whom I serve and honor, is merciful and ready to forgive. But, besides, these infirmities possessed me in thy country; for there I sucked them in, and I have groaned under them, been sorry for them, and I have obtained pardon of my prince.

Then Apollyon broke out into a grievous rage, saying, "I am an enemy to this prince; I hate his person, his laws, and people; I am come out on purpose to withstand thee."

Christian. Apollyon, beware what you do; for I am in the King's highway, the way of holiness; therefore take heed to yourself.

Then Apollyon straddled quite over the whole breadth of the way, and said, "I am void of fear in this matter. Prepare thyself to die; for I swear by my infernal den, that thou shalt go no farther! here will I spill thy soul!"

---

* **O thou destroying.** "*Thou*, in Shakespeare's time, was very much like "du" now among the Germans, the pronoun of (1) affection towards friends, (2) good-humored superiority to servants, and (3) contempt or anger to strangers. It had, however, already fallen somewhat into disuse, and being regarded as archaic, was naturally adopted (4) in the higher poetic style and in the language of solemn prayer." Abbott's *Shakespearian Grammar*, Sec. 231.—**The King's highway.** Isaiah xxxv., 8.

And with that he threw a flaming dart at his breast; but Christian held a shield in his hand, with which he caught it, and so prevented the danger of that.

Then did Christian draw; for he saw it was time to bestir him; and Apollyon as fast made at him, throwing darts as thick as hail. By the which, notwithstanding all that Christian could do to avoid it, Apollyon wounded him in his head,* his hand, and foot. This made Christian give a little back. Apollyon, therefore, followed his work amain; and Christian again took courage, and resisted as manfully as he could.

This sore combat lasted for above half a day, even till Christian was almost quite spent. For you must know, that Christian, by reason of his wounds, must needs grow weaker and weaker.

Then Apollyon, espying his opportunity, began to gather up close to Christian, and wrestling with him, gave him a dreadful fall; and with that Christian's sword flew out of his hand. Then said Apollyon, "I am sure of thee now!" And with that he had almost pressed him to death; so that Christian began to despair of life. But, as God would have it, while Apollyon was fetching his last blow, whereby to make a full end of this good man, Christian nimbly reached out his hand for his sword, and caught it, saying, "Rejoice not against me, O mine enemy! when I fall I shall arise:" and with that gave him a deadly thrust, which made him give back, as one that had received his mortal wound. Christian, perceiving that, made at him again; saying, "Nay, in all these things we are more than conquerors through Him that loved us." And with that Apollyon spread forth his dragon's wings, and sped him away, so that Christian saw him no more.

In this combat, no man can imagine, unless he had seen and heard, as I did, what yelling and hideous roaring Apollyon made all the time of the fight. He spake like a dragon. And on the other side, what sighs and groans burst from Christian's heart. I never saw him all the while give so much as one pleasant look, till he perceived he had wounded Apollyon with his two-edged sword. Then, indeed, he did smile, and look upward. But it was the dreadfullest sight that ever I saw.

So when the battle was over, Christian said, "I will here give thanks to Him that hath delivered me out of the mouth of the lion; to Him that did help me against Apollyon." And so he did, saying,

"Great Beelzebub, the captain of this fiend,
Designed my ruin. Therefore, to this end,
He sent him harnessed out; and he, with rage
That hellish was, did fiercely me engage:

---

* **In his head,** etc. Bunyan, in a marginal note, explains this as meaning, "*in his understanding, his faith, and his conversation.*"—**Needs.** This word is here an adverb. It is formed from the genitive (possessive) of *need.* So in Shakespeare; as,

"There must be needs a like proportion
Of lineaments, of manners, and of spirit."—*Merchant of Venice,* III., 4.

Needs is frequently so used in the Bible, and is not yet obsolete.—**Rejoice not.** Micah vii., 8.—**More than conquerors.** Rom. viii., 37.—**Sped him away.** James iv., 7.

Design, propose, purpose, plan, intend, mean, project. Other synonymes? Write out, etc.

Great Beelzebub, the captain of this fiend, designed my ruin. Analyze.

But blessed Michael helped me; and I
By dint of sword, did quickly make him fly.
Therefore to Him let me give lasting praise.
And thanks, and bless his holy name always."

Then there came to him a hand with some of the leaves of the tree of life; the which* Christian took and applied to the wounds that he had received in the battle, and was healed immediately. He also sat down in that place, to eat bread, and to drink of the bottle that was given him a little before. So, being refreshed, he addressed himself to his journey, with his sword drawn in his hand, "For," he said, "I know not but some other enemy may be at hand." But he met with no other affront from Apollyon quite through the Valley.

Now, at the end of this valley was another, called the Valley of the Shadow of Death; and Christian must needs go through it, because the way to the Celestial City lay through the midst of it. Now this Valley is a very solitary place. The prophet Jeremiah thus describes it: "A wilderness; a land of deserts, and of pits; a land of drought and of the shadow of death; a land that no man (but a Christian) passeth through; and where no man dwelt."

Now here Christian was worse put to it than in his fight with Apollyon; as by the sequel you shall see.

I saw then in my dream, that when Christian was got to the borders of the Shadow of Death, there met him two men, children of them that brought up an evil report of the good land, making haste to go back. To whom Christian spake as follows:—

Christian. Whither are you going?

Men. Back! back! and would have you to do so too, if either life or peace is prized by you.

Christian. Why, what is the matter?

Men. Matter! We were going that way as you are going, and went as far as we durst; and, indeed, we were almost past coming back. For, had we gone a little farther, we had not been here to bring the news to thee.

Christian. But what have you met with?

Men. Why, we were almost in the Valley of the Shadow of Death; but that by good hap we looked before us, and saw the danger, before we came to it.

Christian. But what have you seen?

Men. Seen! Why, the valley itself, which is as dark as pitch. We also saw there the hobgoblins, satyrs, and dragons of the pit. We heard also in

---

* **The which.** This use of *the* with *which* is common in Shakespeare, the Bible, and many of our old writers. Why should *the* be so used with *which*, and not with *who?* Because *who* is definite and stands for a noun, while *which* is properly an indefinite adjective. Similarly in French we find *lequel*, but not *lequi.*—**Was healed.** See Rev. xxii., 2. "As a leaf for medicine, when applied to a sore in the body, doth supple, mollify, and heal the wound; so the word of promise, when rightly applied to the soul, doth supple, mollify, and heal the wounded conscience." Bunyan's *Holy City.*—**Needs.** See p. 330 and Index.—**Jeremiah.** Jer. ii., 6. —**Shadow of death.** Ps. xxiii., 4; xliv., 19; cvii., 14. The valley of the shadow of death must not be interpreted to mean actual dying. It denotes a dark and dismal passage, from which one shrinks as from death. *Valley of death-shade* would be a better translation. Bunyan here describes his own terrible internal conflicts.—**Evil report.** Num. xiii., 32.

that Valley a continual howling and yelling, as of people under unutterable misery, who there sat bound in affliction and irons. Over that Valley hang the discouraging clouds of confusion.* Death also doth always spread his wings over it. In a word, it is every whit dreadful, being utterly without order.

Christian. I perceive not yet, by what you have said, but that this is my way to the desired haven.

Men. Be it thy way; we will not choose it for ours.

So they parted, and Christian went on his way, but still with his sword drawn in his hand, for fear lest he should be assaulted.

I saw then in my dream, so far as this Valley reached, there was on the right hand a very deep ditch. That ditch is it, into which the blind have led the blind in all ages, and have both there miserably perished. Again, behold, on the left hand, there was a very dangerous quag, into which if a good man falls, he finds no bottom for his foot to stand on. Into that quag king David once did fall, and had, no doubt, therein been smothered, had not He that is able plucked him out.

The path-way was here also exceeding narrow, and therefore good Christian was the more put to it; for when he sought, in the dark, to shun the ditch on the one hand, he was ready to tip over into the mire on the other: also, when he sought to escape the mire, without great carefulness he would be ready to fall into the ditch. Thus he went on, and I heard him here sigh bitterly. For, besides the danger mentioned above, the path-way was here so dark, that ofttimes, when he lift up his foot, to set forward, he knew not where, or upon what, he should set it next.

About the midst of this valley, I perceived the mouth of hell to be; and it stood also hard by the way-side. Now, thought Christian, what shall I do? And ever and anon the flame and smoke would come out in such abundance, with sparks and hideous noises, things that cared not for Christian's sword, as did Apollyon before, that he was forced to put up his sword and betake himself to another weapon called all-prayer. So he cried in my hearing, "O Lord, I beseech thee, deliver my soul." Thus he went on a great while; yet still the flames would be reaching towards him. Also he heard doleful voices, and rushings to and fro, so that sometimes he thought he should be torn to pieces, or trodden down like mire in the streets. This frightful sight was seen, and these dreadful noises were heard by him, for several miles together. And coming to a place where he thought he heard a company of fiends coming forward to meet him, he stopped and began to muse what he had best to do. Sometimes he had half a thought to go back; and then, again, he thought he might be half-way through the

* **Clouds of confusion,** etc. Job iii., 5; x., 22.—**Whit.** See *wight*, p. 24.—**David.** Ps. lxix., 14.—**When he lift.** The *-ed*, as in *lifted*, is omitted in many cases by the old English writers. Such omission is for the sake of euphony. "If the root of a verb ends in *-d* or *-t* doubled or preceded by another consonant, the *-de* or *-te* of the past tense, and *-d* or *-t* of the past participle, are omitted." Morris's *Specimens of Early English*, xxxv.—**All-prayer.** Eph. vi., 18.—**Deliver my soul.** Ps. cxvi., 4.

Smothered, *suffocated*, *stifled*. Other synonymes? Write out and illustrate each.

I perceived the mouth of hell. Analyze.

Valley. He remembered, also, how he had already vanquished many a danger, and that the danger of going back might be much more than for to go forward. So he resolved to go on; yet the fiends seemed to come nearer and nearer. But when they were come even almost at him, he cried out with a most vehement voice, "I will walk in the strength* of the Lord God." So they gave back, and came no farther.

One thing I would not let slip. I took notice, that now poor Christian was so confounded that he did not know his own voice! and thus I perceived it. Just when he was come over against the mouth of the burning pit, one of the wicked ones got behind him, and stept up softly to him, and, whispering, suggested many grievous blasphemies to him, which he verily thought had proceeded from his own mind. This put Christian more to it than anything that he met with before, even to think that he should now blaspheme him that he loved so much before. Yet, if he could have helped it, he would not have done it; but he had not the discretion either to stop his ears, or to know from whence those blasphemies came.

When Christian had traveled in this disconsolate condition some considerable time, he thought he heard the voice of a man, as going before him, saying, "Though I walk through the Valley of the Shadow of Death, I will fear no ill, for thou art with me."

Then was he glad, and that for these reasons:—

First; because he gathered from thence, that some who feared God were in this valley as well as himself.

Secondly; that he perceived that God was with them, though in that dark and dismal state:—"And why not," thought he, "with me? Though by reason of the impediment that attends this place, I cannot perceive it."

Thirdly; for that he hoped, could he overtake them, to have company by and by.

So he went on, and called to him that was before; but he knew not what to answer; for that he also thought himself to be alone. And by and by the day broke. Then said Christian, "He hath turned the shadow of death into the morning."

Now, morning being come, he looked back, not out of desire to return, but to see by the light of the day what hazards he had gone through in

---

* **In the strength.** Ps. lxxi., 16.—**Verily thought,** etc. Here Bunyan is relating his own experience. He says, "Whole floods of blasphemies were poured upon my spirit to my great confusion and astonishment, and did so overweigh my heart, both with their number, continuance, and fiery force, that I felt as if God had, in very wrath to my soul, given me up to them, to be carried away with them as with a mighty whirlwind." See Southey's *Life of Bunyan.* —**Though I walk.** Ps. xxiii.—**Cannot perceive it.** Job ix., 11; xxiii., 8.—**Turned the shadow.** Amos v., 8.

Vanquish, conquer, subdue, overcome, surmount. Other synonymes? Write out, etc.

Analyze *He hath turned the shadow of death.*

N. B. In all these exercises in analysis the pupil should, (1) state the kind of sentence; (2) connect by the proper signs the words that are syntactically combined; (3) [1] place the proper capital letters opposite the separate words; (4) parse each; (5) give derivations, etc.

[1] This may be omitted, when the student has become perfectly familiar with the method and signs.

the dark. So he saw more perfectly the ditch that was on the one hand, and the quag that was on the other; also how narrow the way was which led betwixt them both. Also he saw the hobgoblins,* and satyrs, and dragons of the pit, but all afar off. For, after break of day, they came not nigh, yet they were discovered to him, according to that which is written. "He discovereth deep things out of darkness, and bringeth out to light the shadow of death."

Now was Christian much affected with his deliverance from all the dangers of his solitary way. Which dangers, though he feared them more before, yet he saw them more clearly now, because the light of the day made them conspicuous to him; and about this time the sun was rising. And this was another mercy to Christian. For you must note, that though the first part of the Valley of the Shadow of Death was dangerous; yet this second part, which he was yet to go, was, if possible, far more dangerous. For, from the place where he now stood, even to the end of the Valley, the way was all along set so full of snares, traps, gins, and nets here, and full of pits, pit-falls, deep holes, and shelvings down there; that, had it now been dark, as it was when he came the first part of the way, had he had a thousand souls, they had in reason been cast away. But, as I said, just now the sun was rising. Then said he, "His candle shineth on my head, and by his light I go through darkness."

In this light, therefore, he came to the end of the Valley. Now I saw in my dream, that at the end of this valley lay blood, bones, ashes, and mangled bodies of men, even of Pilgrims that had gone this way formerly. And while I was musing what should be the reason, I espied a little before me a cave, where two giants, Pope and Pagan, dwelt in old time; by whose power and tyranny, the men, whose bones, blood, ashes, etc., lay there, were cruelly put to death. But by this place Christian went without danger; whereat I somewhat wondered. But I have learnt since, that Pagan has been dead many a day; and as for the other, though he be yet alive, he is, by reason of age, and also of the many shrewd brushes that he met with in his younger days, grown so crazy and stiff in his joints that he can now do little more than sit in his cave's mouth, grinning at Pilgrims as they go by, and biting his nails because he cannot come at them.

So I saw, that Christian went on his way; yet at the sight of the old man that sat at the mouth of the cave, he could not tell what to think; especially because he spake to him, though he could not go after him; saying, "You will never mend, till more of you be burnt." But he held his peace, and set a good face on it, and so went by and catched no hurt. Then sang Christian—

---

* **Hobgoblins.** *Hob*, the goblin. *Hob* is *Rob*, *Robin*, *Bob*; just as *Hodge* is *Roger*; *goblin* is the Fr. *gobelin*, Ger. *kobold*. *Keightley*. *Hobgoblin* or *Puck* was the name formerly given to *Robin Goodfellow*; for which, see New American Cyclopedia; also Robin Hood, Robin Goodfellow in *Vocabulary of Noted Names of Fiction* in Appendix to Webster's *Dictionary*.—**Discovereth deep things.** Job xii., 22.—**Candle shineth.** Job xxix., 3.

Valley, vale, dale, glen. Other synonymes? Distinguish, etc.

The first part of the Valley of the Shadow of Death was dangerous. Analyze.

O world of wonders!—I can say no less,—
That I should be preserved in that distress
That I have met with here! O, blessed be
That hand that from it hath delivered me!
Dangers in darkness, devils, hell, and sin,
Did compass me, while I this vale was in.
Yea, snares, and pits, and traps, and nets did lie
My path about, that worthless, silly I
Might have been catched, entangled, and cast down:
But since I live, let Jesus wear the crown.

Now, as Christian went on his way, he came to a little ascent, which was cast up on purpose that pilgrims might see before them. Up there, therefore, Christian went; and, looking forward, he saw Faithful before him upon his journey. Then said Christian aloud, "Ho, ho! So, ho! Stay, and I will be your companion." At that, Faithful looked behind him; to whom Christian called again, "Stay, stay, till I come up to you." But Faithful answered, "No, I am upon my life, and the avenger of blood is behind me." *

At this, Christian was somewhat moved; and putting to all his strength, he quickly got up with Faithful, and did also overrun him. So the last was first. Then did Christian vaingloriously smile, because he had gotten the start of his brother. But, not taking good heed to his feet, he suddenly stumbled and fell, and could not rise again until Faithful came to help him.

Then I saw in my dream they went very lovingly on together, and had sweet discourse of all things that had happened to them in their pilgrimage; and thus Christian began.

Christian. My honored and well-beloved brother Faithful, I am glad that I have overtaken you; and that God has so tempered our spirits, that we can walk as companions in this so pleasant a path.

Faithful. I had thought, dear friend, to have had your company quite from our town, but you did get the start of me. Wherefore I was forced to come thus much of the way alone.

Christian. How long did you stay in the City of Destruction, before you set out after me on your pilgrimage?

Faithful. Till I could stay no longer: for there was a great talk, presently after you were gone out, that our city would, in a short time, with fire from heaven, be burnt down to the ground.

Christian. What! did your neighbors talk so?

Faithful. Yes, it was for a while in everybody's mouth.

Christian. What! and did no more of them but you come out to escape the danger?

Faithful. Though there was, as I said, a great talk thereabout, yet I do not think they did firmly believe it. For, in the heat of the discourse, I heard some of them deridingly speak of you and of your desperate journey;

* **The avenger of blood is behind me.** Deut. xix., 6; xxxii., 43. Speaking of such conduct as that of Faithful in this paragraph, Bunyan remarks, "Thus wise are men when they run for corruptible things, and thus thou shouldst do; and thou hast more cause to do so than they, forasmuch as they run but for things that last not, but thou for an incorruptible glory." Bunyan's *Heavenly Footman.*

Discourse, conversation, discussion, speech, conference, talk. Other synonymes? Write out, etc.

for they so called this your pilgrimage. But I did believe,* and do still, that the end of our city will be with fire and brimstone from above; and therefore I have made my escape.

Christian. Did you hear no talk of neighbor Pliable ?

Faithful. Yes, Christian: I heard that he followed you till he came to the Slough of Despond; where, as some said, he fell in; but he would not be known to have so done. But I am sure he was soundly bedaubed with that kind of dirt.

Christian. And what said the neighbors to him ?

Faithful. He hath, since his going back, been had greatly in derision, and that among all sorts of people; some do mock and despise him, and scarce will any set him on work. He is now seven times worse than if he had never gone out of the city.

Christian. But why should they be so set against him, since they also despise the way that he forsook ?

Faithful. O! they say, "Hang him; he is a turncoat! he was not true to his profession." I think God has stirred up even his enemies to hiss at him, and make him a proverb, because he hath forsaken the way.

Christian. Had you no talk with him before you came out ?

Faithful. I met him once in the streets; but he leered away on the other side, as one ashamed of what he had done. So I spake not to him.

Christian. Well, at my first setting out I had hopes of that man: but now I fear he will perish in the overthrow of the city. For it has happened to him according to the true proverb, "The dog is turned to his vomit again; and the sow that was washed, to her wallowing in the mire."

Faithful. They are my fears of him too; but who can hinder that which will be ?

Christian. Well, neighbor Faithful, let us leave him, and talk of things that more immediately concern ourselves. Tell me now, what you have met

* **But I did believe,** etc. "Let me tell thee, soul, whoever thou art, that if thou didst but verily believe that thou must die and come to judgment, it would make thee turn over a new leaf. But this is the misery; the devil doth labor by all means to keep out of the heart, as much as in him lies, the thoughts of passing from this life into another world; for he knows, if he can but keep them from the serious thoughts of death, he shall the more easily keep them in their sins, and so, from closing with Christ." Bunyan's *Sighs from Hell.*—**Enemies to hiss.** Jer. xxix., 18.—**Dog.** 2 Pet. ii., 22.—**Is turned.** "With some few intransitive verbs, mostly of motion, both *be* and *have* are still used. 'He *is* gone, he *has* gone.' The *is* expresses the present state; the *has*, the activity necessary to cause that state. The *is* is evidently quite as justifiable as *has* (perhaps more so), but it has been found more convenient to make a division of labor, and assign distinct tasks to *is* and *has*. Consequently *is* has been almost superseded by *has* in all but the passive forms of transitive verbs." Abbott's *Shakes. Gram.*, 295.

To make him a proverb.

. . . . to

A form of the *objective* combination. *Proverb* is clearly a "factitive" object. See p. 316. Complete the analysis. Analyze, *He is a turncoat.*

with in the way as you came. For I know you have met with some things, or else it may be writ for a wonder.

Faithful. I escaped the slough that I perceived you fell into, and got up to the gate without that danger. Only I met with one whose name was Wanton, that had like to have done me a mischief.

Christian. It was well you escaped her net. Joseph* was hard put to it by her, and he escaped her as you did; but it had like to have cost him his life. But what did she do to you?

Faithful. You cannot think, but that you know something, what a flattering tongue she had. She lay at me hard to turn aside with her, promising me all manner of content.

Christian. Nay, she did not promise you the content of a good conscience.

Faithful. You know what I mean, all carnal and fleshly content.

Christian. Thank God you have escaped her. "The abhorred of the Lord shall fall into her ditch."

Faithful. Nay, I know not whether I did wholly escape her, or no.

Christian. Why, I trow, you did not consent to her desire?

Faithful. No, not to defile myself; for I remembered an old writing that I had seen, which said, "Her steps take hold of hell." So I shut mine eyes, because I would not be bewitched with her looks. Then she railed on me, and I went my way.

Christian. Did you meet with no other assault as you came?

Faithful. When I came to the foot of the hill called Difficulty, I met with a very aged man, who asked me what I was, and whither bound. I told him that I was a Pilgrim, going to the Celestial City. Then said the old man, "Thou lookest like an honest fellow: wilt thou be content to dwell with me for the wages that I shall give thee?" Then I asked him his name, and where he dwelt. He said his name was Adam the First, and that he dwelt in the town of Deceit. I asked him then, what was his work, and what the wages that he would give. He told me that his work was many delights; and his wages, that I should be his heir at last. I further asked him what house he kept, and what other servants he had. So he told me that his house was maintained with all the dainties in the world; and that his servants were those of his own begetting. Then I asked how many children he had. He said that he had but three daughters, The Lust of the Flesh, The Lust of the Eyes, and The Pride of Life; and that I should marry one of them, if I would. Then I asked, how long time he

---

* **Joseph.** Gen. xxxix., 11-13.—**The abhorred.** Prov. xxii., 14.—**Trow,** *think.* See *trowed*, Index.—**Her steps take hold of hell.** Prov. v., 5.—**Mine eyes.** Job xxxi., 1.—**Old man.** Eph. iv., 22.—**Thou lookest,** etc. For this use of *Thou*, see p. 329.—**Adam the First.** 1 Cor. xv., 45. "Adam the First represents man's original, carnal, and corrupt nature, described by the apostle as 'the old man which is corrupt according to the deceitful lusts.'"—**Lust of the flesh,** etc. 1 John ii., 16.

Deceit, art, cunning, deception, duplicity, double-dealing, fraud, guile. Other synonymes? Write out, etc.

His name was Adam the First. Analyze.

would have me live with him. And he told me, as long as he lived himself.

Christian. Well; and what conclusion came the old man and you to at last?

Faithful. Why, at first I found myself somewhat inclinable to go with the man, for I thought he spake very fair.* But looking in his forehead, as I talked with him, I saw there written, "Put off the old man with his deeds."

Christian. And how then?

Faithful. Then it came burning hot into my mind, whatever he said, and however he flattered, when he got me home to his house, he would sell me for a slave. So I bade him forbear to talk, for I would not come near the door of his house. Then he reviled me, and told me that he would send such a one after me that should make my way bitter to my soul. So I turned to go away from him. But just as I turned myself to go thence, I felt him take hold of my flesh, and give me such a deadly twitch back, that I thought he had pulled part of me after himself. This made me cry, "O wretched man!" So I went on my way up the hill. Now when I had got above half-way up, I looked behind me, and saw one coming after me swift as the wind. So he overtook me just about the place where the settle stands.

Christian. Just there did I sit down to rest me; but being overcome with sleep, I there lost this roll out of my bosom.

Faithful. But, good brother, hear me out. So soon as the man overtook me, he was but a word and a blow: for down he knocked me, and laid me for dead. But when I was a little come to myself again, I asked him wherefore he served me so? He said, because of my secret inclining to Adam the First. And with that he struck me another deadly blow on the breast: he beat me down backward. So I lay at his foot as dead, as before. When I came to myself again, I cried him mercy. But he said, "I know not how to show mercy;" and with that knocked me down again. He had doubtless made an end of me, but that one came by and bade him forbear.

Christian. Who was that that bade him forbear?

Faithful. I did not know him at first. But as he went by, I perceived the holes in his hands and in his side. Then I concluded that he was our Lord. So I went up the hill.

Christian. That man that overtook you was Moses. He spareth none; neither knoweth he how to show mercy to those that transgress his law.

Faithful. I knew it very well; it was not the first time that he has met

---

* **Spake very fair.** *Fair* is here an adverb. In early English, adverbs were often formed from adjectives by adding *e*, the ending of the dative case, to the positive degree; as *bright*, adj., *brighte*, adv. In time the *e* was dropped, but the adverbial use was retained. By a false analogy, many adjectives which could never form adverbs in *e*, were used as adverbs. See Abbott's *Shakespearian Grammar*, 1.—**Put off the old,** etc. Eph. iv., 22.—**O wretched.** Rom. vii., 24.—**Cried him mercy.** *Mercy* is derived by some from Lat. *misericordia*, heartfelt pity. Others make it from Lat. *merces*, a reward; and they assert that *I cry you mercy* meant I cry to you for *ransom*. See Worcester's Dictionary.

with me. It was he that came to me when I dwelt securely at home, and that told me he would burn my house over my head if I stayed there.

Christian. But did you not see the house that stood there, on the top of the hill on the side of which Moses met you ?

Faithful. Yes, and the lions too, before I came at it. But for the lions, I think they were asleep; for it was about noon; and because I had so much of the day before me, I passed by the Porter and came down the hill.

Christian. He told me, indeed, that he saw you go by. But I wish you had called at the house; for they would have shown you so many rarities that you would scarce have forgot them to the day of your death. But pray tell me, did you meet nobody in the Valley of Humility ?

Faithful. Yes, I met with one Discontent, who would willingly have persuaded me to go back again with him. His reason was, for that the Valley was altogether without honor. He told me, moreover, that there to go, was to disoblige all my friends, as Pride, Arrogancy, Self-Conceit, Worldly-Glory, with others, who, he knew, as he said, would be very much offended, if I made such a fool of myself as to wade through this valley.

Christian. Well, and how did you answer him ?

Faithful. I told him, that although all these that he named might claim a kindred of me, and that rightly, for indeed they were my relations according to the flesh, yet, since I became a pilgrim, they have disowned me, as I also have rejected them: and therefore they were to me now no more than if they had never been of my lineage. I told him moreover, that as to this valley, he had quite misrepresented the thing; for, "Before honor* is humility," and "A haughty spirit, before a fall." Therefore, said I, I had rather go through this valley to the honor that was so accounted by the wisest, than choose that which he esteemed most worthy of our affections.

Christian. Met you with nothing else in that valley ?

Faithful. Yes, I met with Shame; but of all the men that I met with

---

* **Before honor,** etc. Prov. xv., 33.—**Haughty spirit,** etc. Prov. xvi., 18.—**Had rather.** *Had* is A. S. *häfed, häfd,* i. e., *hav-ed. Rather* is the comparative of *rathe,* early, quick, soon. *Had rather = would sooner.* The expression is idiomatic. See *had lever,* p. 33; also, *had as lief,* in Craik's *English of Shakespeare,* Rolfe's edition, Boston, 1868, pp. 156, 157, 158. See Ps. lxxxiv., 10, "I had rather be a door-keeper in the house of the Lord," etc.

I dwelt securely. Here we have the fourth and last of the *syntactical combinations;* to wit, the *adverbial* (marked *Adv.*). It should be understood, however, as a matter of strict science, that the objective combination, which consists of two factors; viz., a verb or adjective involving the idea of action, and an object to which such activity is directed; really *includes* the adverbial. The treating of the adverbial combination as a separate one, is only for convenience and in conformity to usage. This combination may be expressed by a brace with a loop or circle in the centre, or by a brace with a straight side, and an angle in the middle; thus, { In this way its character, as a form of the objective combination, will be made visible. It will be found that the brace with a loop or circle in the middle is the easier to make, and it is therefore preferable.

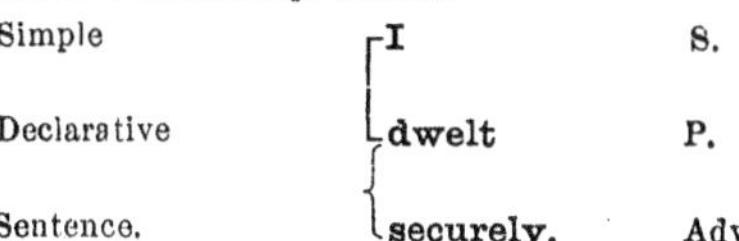

S.
P.
Adv.

Let the student complete this analysis as before. Analyze *Christian modestly smiled.*

in my pilgrimage, he, I think, bears the wrong name. The other would be said nay, after a little argumentation, and somewhat else. But this bold-faced Shame would never have done.

Christian. Why, what did he say to you?

Faithful. What! why he objected against Religion itself. He said it was a pitiful, low, sneaking business for a man to mind Religion. He said, that a tender conscience was an unmanly thing; and that for a man to watch over his words and ways, so as to tie up himself from that hectoring liberty that the brave spirits of the times accustom themselves unto, would make him the ridicule of the time. He objected also, that few of the mighty,* rich, or wise, were ever of my opinion; nor any of them neither, before they were persuaded to be fools, and to be of a voluntary fondness to venture the loss of all, for nobody else knows what. He moreover objected the base and low estate and condition of those that were chiefly the pilgrims of the times in which they lived; also their ignorance and want of understanding in all natural science. Yea, he did hold me to it at that rate also, about a great many more things than I here relate; as, that it was a shame to sit whining and mourning under a sermon, and a shame to come sighing and groaning home; that it was a shame to ask my neighbor forgiveness for petty faults, or to make restitution where I have taken from any. He said also, that religion made a man grow strange to the great, because of a few vices, which he called by finer names, and made him own and respect the base, because of the same religious fraternity. "And is not this," said he, "a shame?"

Christian. And what did you say to him?

Faithful. Say! I could not tell what to say at first. Yea, he put me to it, that my blood came up in my face; even this Shame fetched it up, and had almost beat me quite off. But, at last, I began to consider, that which is highly esteemed among men, is held in abomination with God. And I thought again, "This Shame tells me what men are; but it tells me nothing what God, or the word of God is." And I thought moreover, that at the day of doom we shall not be doomed to death or life, according to the hectoring spirits of the world, but according to the wisdom and law of The Highest. "Therefore," thought I, "what God says is best, though all the men in the world are against it. Seeing, then, that God prefers his religion; seeing, God prefers a tender conscience; seeing, they that make themselves fools for the kingdom of heaven are wisest; and that the poor man that loveth Christ, is richer than the richest man in the world, that hates him; Shame, depart! thou art an enemy to my salvation. Shall I entertain thee against

* **Few of the mighty,** etc. 1 Cor. i., 26; iii., 18.—**Fondness,** foolishness. See *fond*, p. 28.

"Fondness it were for any, being free,
To covet fetters, though they golden be." *Spenser.*

—**Loss of all,** etc. Philip. iii., 7, 8, 9.—**Abomination.** Luke xvi., 15.—**Are wisest.** "He that cometh unto God by Christ is no little-spirited fellow." Bunyan's *Christ a Complete Saviour.*

Ridicule, laugh at, banter, deride, mock, rally, burlesque, satirize, lampoon. Other synonymes? Write out, etc.

my sovereign Lord? how then shall I look him in the face at his coming?* Should I now be ashamed of his ways and servants, how can I expect the blessing! But indeed, this Shame was a bold villain; I could scarce shake him out of my company. Yea, he would be haunting of me, and continually whispering me in the ear, with some one or other of the infirmities that attend religion. But at last I told him, it was but in vain to attempt further in this business; for those things that he disdained, in those did I see most glory: and so at last I got past this importunate one. And when I had shaken him off, then I began to sing:—

The trials that those men do meet withal,
That are obedient to the heavenly call,
Are manifold, and suited to the flesh,
And come, and come, and come again afresh;
That now, or some time else, we by them may
Be taken, overcome, and cast away.
O, let the Pilgrims, let the Pilgrims then,
Be vigilant, and quit themselves like men!

Christian. I am glad, brother, that thou didst withstand this villain so bravely. For, of all, as thou sayest, I think he has the wrong name; for he is so bold as to follow us in the streets, and to attempt to put us to shame before all men; that is, to make us ashamed of that which is good. But if he was not himself audacious, he would never attempt to do as he does. But let us still resist him; for, notwithstanding all his bravadoes, he promoteth the fool, and none else. "The wise shall inherit glory," said Solomon, "but shame shall be the promotion of fools."

Faithful. I think we must cry to Him for help against Shame, that would have us to be valiant for truth upon earth.

Christian. You say true. But did you meet nobody else in that valley?

Faithful. No, not I; for I had sunshine all the rest of the way through that, and also through the Valley of the Shadow of Death.

Christian. It was well for you. I am sure it fared far otherwise with me. I had for a long season, as soon almost as I entered into the valley, a dread-

* **At his coming.** Mark viii., 38.—**Meet withal.** *Withal* in the Old Eng. writers is (1) sometimes equivalent to *in addition to all this;* as, "I must have liberty withal." Shakespeare's *As You Like It;* (2) sometimes it is an emphatic form of *with;* but (3) it is usually equivalent to *with*, and is used for the sake of the metre at the end of a line or sentence.—**Promotion of fools.** Prov. iii., 35.

I look him in the face. Another form of the adverbial combination, '*in the face*' denoting *manner*.

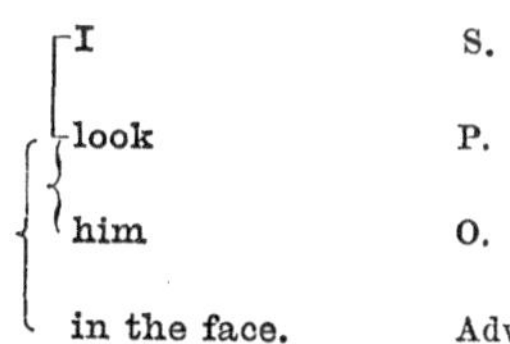

I	S.
look	P.
him	O.
in the face.	Adv.

Complete the analysis.

Analyze *I could shake him out of my company.*

ful combat with that foul fiend Apollyon: yea, I thought verily he would have killed me, especially when he got me down, and crushed me under him, as if he would have crushed me to pieces. For, as he threw me, my sword flew out of my hand. Nay, he told me he was sure of me; but I cried to God, and he heard me, and delivered me* out of all my troubles. Then I entered into the Valley of the Shadow of Death, and had no light for almost half the way through it. I thought I should have been killed there, over and over; but at last day broke, and the sun rose, and I went through that which was behind, with far more ease and quiet.

Moreover I saw in my dream, that, as they went on, Faithful, as he chanced to look on one side, saw a man whose name was Talkative, walking at a distance beside them: for in this place there was room enough for them all to walk. He was a tall man, and something more comely at a distance, than at hand. To this man Faithful addressed himself in this manner.

Faithful. Friend, whither away? Are you going to the heavenly country?

Talkative. I am going to the same place.

Faithful. That is well; then I hope we may have your good company?

Talkative. With a very good will, will I be your companion.

Faithful. Come on then, and let us go together, and let us spend our time in discoursing of things that are profitable.

Talkative. To talk of things that are good, to me is very acceptable, with you or with any other; and I am glad that I have met with those that incline to so good a work. For, to speak the truth, there are but few that care thus to spend their time, as they are in their travels; but choose much rather to be speaking of things of no profit. And this hath been a trouble to me.

Faithful. That is indeed a thing to be lamented. For, what thing so worthy the use of the tongue and mouth of men on earth, as are the things of the God of Heaven?

Talkative. I like you wonderful well; for your sayings are full of conviction; and I will add, What thing so pleasant and what so profitable, as to talk of the things of God?—What things so pleasant, that is, if a man hath any delight in things that are wonderful? For instance: if a man doth delight to talk of the history, or the mystery of things; or if a man doth love to talk of miracles, wonders, or signs, where shall he find things recorded so delightful, and so sweetly penned, as in the Holy Scripture?

Faithful. That is true: but to be profited by such things in our talk, should be our chief design.

Talkative. That is it that I said; for to talk of such things is most profitable. For, by so doing, a man may get knowledge of many things; as of the

---

* **Delivered me,** etc. Ps. cvii., 6, 13, 19.—**Something more comely at a distance,** etc. We can imagine a smile on Bunyan's grave face, as he writes this. Probably it is the portrait of some person well-known in Bedford.—**Wonderful well.** Another instance of the adverbial use of an adjective form. See *spake very fair*, p. 338.

Talkative, loquacious, garrulous. Other synonymes? Write out, etc.

vanity of earthly things, and the benefit of things above. Thus in general; but, more particularly, by this a man may learn the necessity of the new birth; the insufficiency of our works; the need of Christ's righteousness, etc. Besides, by this a man may learn what it is to repent, to believe, to pray, to suffer, or the like. By this, also, a man may learn what are the great promises and consolations of the Gospel, to his own comfort. Further; by this a man may learn to refute false opinions, to vindicate the truth, and also to instruct the ignorant.

Faithful. All this is true; and glad am I to hear these things from you.

Talkative. Alas! the want of this is the cause that so few understand the need of faith, and the necessity of works of grace in their soul, in order to eternal life; but ignorantly live in the works of the law, by which a man can by no means obtain the kingdom of heaven.

Faithful. But, by your leave, heavenly knowledge of these is the gift of God; no man attaineth to them by human industry, or only by the talk of them.

Talkative. All this I know very well. For a man can receive nothing except it be given him from heaven; all is of grace, not of works. I could give you an hundred scriptures for the confirmation of this.

Faithful. Well then, what is that one thing that we shall at this time found our discourse upon ?

Talkative. What you will. I will talk of things heavenly, or things earthly; things moral, or things evangelical; things sacred, or things profane; things past, or things to come; things foreign, or things at home; things more essential, or things circumstantial; provided that all be done to our profit.*

Now did Faithful begin to wonder; and stepping to Christian, for he walked all this while by himself, he said to him, but softly, "What a brave companion have we got! Surely this man will make a very excellent pilgrim."

At this Christian modestly smiled, and said, "This man, with whom you are so taken, will beguile, with this tongue of his, twenty of them that know him not."

Faithful. Do you know him then ?

Christian. Know him! Yea, better than he knows himself.

Faithful. Pray, what is he ?

Christian. His name is Talkative; he dwelleth in our town. I wonder you should be a stranger to him, only I consider our town is large.

Faithful. Whose son is he ? and whereabout does he dwell ?

Christian. He is the son of one Say-well; he dwelt in Prating-row; and he is known of all that are acquainted with him, by the name of Talkative, in Prating-row; and, notwithstanding his fine tongue, he is but a sorry fellow.

---

* **To our profit.** "O brave Talkative !" Bunyan's *marginal note* on this passage.

Modestly, diffidently. Other synonymes ? Write out, etc.

He dwelleth in our town. Analyze.

Faithful. Well, he seems to be a very pretty man.

Christian. That is, to them that have not a thorough acquaintance with him, for he is best abroad; near home he is ugly enough. Your saying that he is pretty man, brings to my mind what I have observed in the work of the painter whose pictures show best at a distance, but very near more unpleasing.

Faithful. But I am ready to think you do but jest, because you smiled.

Christian. God forbid that I should jest, though I smiled, in this matter; or that I should accuse any falsely! I will give you further discovery of him. This man is for any company, and for any talk. As he talketh now with you, so he will talk when he is on the ale-bench; and the more drink he hath in his crown, the more of these things he hath in his mouth. Religion hath no place in his heart, or house, or conversation; all he hath lieth in his tongue; and his religion is to make a noise therewith.

Faithful. Say you so? Then I am in this man greatly deceived.

Christian. Deceived! you may be sure of it: Remember the proverb, "They say, and do not:" * But "The kingdom of God is not in word, but in power." He talketh of prayer, of repentance, of faith, and of the new birth; but he knows but only to talk of them. I have been in his family, and have observed him both at home and abroad; and I know what I say of him is the truth. His house is empty of religion, as the white of an egg is of savor. There is there neither prayer, nor sign of repentance for sin; yea, the brute, in his kind, serves God far better than he. He is the very stain, reproach, and shame of religion, to all that know him; it can hardly have a good word in all the end of the town where he dwells, through him. Thus say the common people that know him, "A saint abroad, and a devil at home." His poor family finds it so; he is such a churl, such a railer at, so unreasonable with his servants, that they neither know how to do for, or to speak to him, men that have any dealings with him. It is better to deal with a Turk than with him; for fairer dealing they shall have at their hands. This Talkative, if it be possible, will go beyond them; defraud, beguile, and overreach them. Besides he brings up his sons to follow his steps; and if he finds in any of them a foolish timorousness, for so he calls the first appearance of a tender conscience, he calls them fools and blockheads, and by no means will employ them in much, or speak to their commendation before others. For my part, I am of opinion that he has, by his wicked life, caused many to stumble and fall; and will be, if God prevents not, the ruin of many more.

Faithful. Well, my brother, I am bound to believe you; not only because

---

* **Say and do not.** Matt. xxiii., 3.—**But in power.** 1 Cor. iv., 20.—**Shame of religion.** Rom. ii., 24. "A professor, and practice such villanies as these! Such an one is not worthy to bear that name any longer. Go, professors, go; leave off profession, unless you will lead your lives according to your profession. Better never profess than make profession a stalking-horse to sin, deceit, to the devil and hell." Bunyan's *Life and Death of Dr. Badman.*—**White of an egg.** See Job vi., 6.—**With a Turk.** The English had a special horror of the Turks. Why?

Empty, vacant, void, devoid, unfurnished, unoccupied. Other synonymes? Write out, etc.

This Talkative will go beyond them. Analyze.

you say you know him, but also because, like a Christian, you make your reports of men. For I cannot think that you speak these things of ill-will, but because it is even so as you say.

Christian. Had I known him no more than you, I might perhaps have thought of him as at the first you did. Yea, had he received this report at their hands only, that are enemies to religion, I should have thought it had been a slander, a lot that often falls from bad men's mouths upon good men's names and professions. But all these things, yea, and a great many more as bad, of my own knowledge, I can prove him guilty of. Besides, good men are ashamed of him; they can neither call him brother nor friend; the very naming of him among them makes them blush, if they know him.

Faithful. Well, I see that saying and doing are two things; and hereafter I shall better observe this distinction.

Christian. They are two things, indeed, and are as diverse as are the soul and the body. For, as the body without the soul is but a dead carcass; so saying, if it be alone, is but a dead carcass also. The soul of religion is the practical part. "Pure religion and undefiled, before God and the Father, is this: to visit the fatherless and widows in their affliction, and to keep himself unspotted * from the world." This, Talkative is not aware of; he thinks that hearing and saying will make a good Christian; and thus he deceiveth his own soul. Hearing is but as the sowing of the seed; talking is not sufficient to prove that fruit is indeed in the heart and life; and let us assure ourselves, that at the day of Doom, men shall be judged according to their fruit. It will not be said then, "Did you believe?" but, "Were you doers, or talkers only?" And accordingly shall they be judged. The end of the world is compared to a harvest; and you know men at harvest regard nothing but fruit. Not that anything can be accepted, that is not of faith; but I speak this to show you how insignificant the profession of Talkative will be at that day.

Faithful. This brings to my mind that of Moses, by which he described the beast that is clean. He is such an one that parteth the hoof and cheweth the cud; not that parteth the hoof only, or that cheweth the cud only. The hare cheweth the cud; but yet is unclean, because he parteth not the hoof. And this truly resembleth Talkative; he cheweth the cud; he seeketh knowledge, he cheweth upon the Word: but he divideth not the hoof; he parteth not with the way of sinners; but as the hare, he retaineth the foot of a dog or bear, and therefore he is unclean.

Christian. You have spoken, for aught I know, the true Gospel sense of those texts. And I will add another thing; Paul calleth some men, yea, and those great talkers too, "sounding brass," and "tinkling cymbals." That is, as he expounds them in another place, "things without life, giving

* **Unspotted.** James i., 27.—**According to their fruit.** Matt. vii., 16-20.—**Cheweth the cud.** Lev. xi., 3-8.—**The true Gospel sense.** Bunyan loved to study the hidden meaning of the Old Testament "types, shadows, and metaphors;" of "pins and loops, calves and sheep, heifers and rams, birds and herbs," etc.

. . . . "Happy is he
That finds the light and grace that in them be." Bunyan's *Apology*.

—**Cymbals.** 1 Cor. xiii., 1.

sound;" *—things without life, that is without the true faith and grace of the Gospel; and consequently, things that shall never be placed in the kingdom of Heaven among those that are the children of life; though their sound, by their talk, be as it were the tongue or voice of an angel.

Faithful. Well, I was not fond of his company at first: but I am sick of it now. What shall we do to be rid of him?

Christian. Take my advice, and do as I bid you, and you shall find that he will soon be sick of your company too; except God shall touch his heart and turn it.

Faithful. What would you have me to do?

Christian. Why, go to him, and enter into some serious discourse about the power of Religion; and ask him plainly, when he has approved of it, for that he will, whether this thing be set up in his heart, house, or conversation!

Then Faithful stepped forward again, and said to Talkative, "Come, what cheer? how is it now?"

Talkative. Thank you, well. I thought we should have had a great deal of talk by this time.

Faithful. Well, if you will, we will fall to it now; and since you left it with me to state the question, let it be this, "How doth the saving grace of God discover itself, when it is in the heart of man?"

Talkative. I perceive then that our talk must be about the power of things. Well, it is a very good question, and I shall be willing to answer you. And take my answer in brief thus: First, where the grace of God is in the heart, it causeth there a great outcry against sin. Secondly,—

Faithful. Nay, hold, let us consider of one at once. I think you should rather say, it shows itself by inclining the soul to abhor its sin.

Talkative. Why, what difference is there between crying out against and abhorring of sin?

Faithful. Oh! a great deal. A man may cry out against sin, of policy; but he cannot abhor it but by virtue of a godly antipathy against it. I have heard many cry out against sin in the pulpit, who yet can abide it well enough in the heart, house, and conversation. Joseph's mistress cried out with a loud voice, as if she had been very holy; but she would willingly, notwithstanding that, have committed uncleanness with him. Some cry out against sin, even as a mother cries out against her child in her lap, when she calleth it "slut" and "naughty girl," and then falls to hugging and kissing it.

Talkative. You lie at the catch, I perceive.

---

* **Giving sound.** 1 Cor. xiv., 7.—**What cheer?** *Cheer* is Gr. χαρά, joy; It. *cera*, cheer; Span. *cara*, countenance; Fr. *chère*, entertainment. *What cheer?* is a common salutation; like, *What's the good word?*—**Uncleanness.** Gen. xxxix.—**Lie at the catch.** *Catch* is fr. Lat. *captare*, *captivare*, *capĕre*, to catch, seize. To *lie at the catch* is to be watching the opportunity to seize. Addison has "to *lie on the catch*." Fuller says, "The common and the canon law . . . . *lie at catch*, and wait advantages one against another."

Holy, pious, devout, religious, sacred, hallowed, divine. Other synonymes? Write out, etc.

Joseph's mistress cried out with a loud voice. Analyze.

Faithful. No, not I. I am only for setting things right. But what is the second thing, whereby you would prove a discovery of a work of grace in the heart?

Talkative. Great knowledge of gospel mysteries.

Faithful. This sign should have been first; but first, or last, it is also false. For knowledge, great knowledge, may be obtained in the mysteries of the gospel, and yet no work of grace in the soul. Yea, if a man have all knowledge,* he may yet be nothing; and so, consequently, be no child of God. When Christ said, "Do you *know* all these things?" and the disciples had answered, "Yes;" he added, "Blessed are ye, if ye *do* them." He doth not lay the blessings in the knowing of them, but in the doing of them. For there is a knowledge that is not attended with doing. "He that knoweth his master's will, and doeth it not." A man may know like an angel, and be no Christian: therefore your sign of it is not true. Indeed, to *know* is a thing that pleaseth talkers and boasters; but to *do* is that which pleaseth God. Not that the heart can be good without knowledge: for, without that, the heart is naught. There are, therefore, two sorts of knowledge: knowledge that resteth in the bare speculation of things; and knowledge that is accompanied with the grace of Faith and Love; which puts a man upon doing even the will of God from the heart. The first of these will serve the talker; but, without the other, the true Christian is not content. "Give me understanding, and I shall keep thy law; yea, I shall observe it with my whole heart."

Talkative. You lie at the catch again. This is not for edification.

Faithful. Well, if you please, propound another sign how this work of grace discovereth itself where it is.

Talkative. Not I; for I see we shall not agree.

Faithful. Well, if you will not, will you give me leave to do it?

Talkative. You may use your liberty.

Faithful. A work of grace in the soul discovereth itself either to him

* **All knowledge.** 1 Cor. xiii., 2.—**Give me understanding.** Ps. cxix., 34.—**Edification** (Lat. *ædes*, a building; *facĕre*, to make), a building-up in Christian graces. It is interesting to observe the change which this word has undergone in meaning. Once it referred to architecture. Thus Spenser speaks of "a holy chapel *edified*."

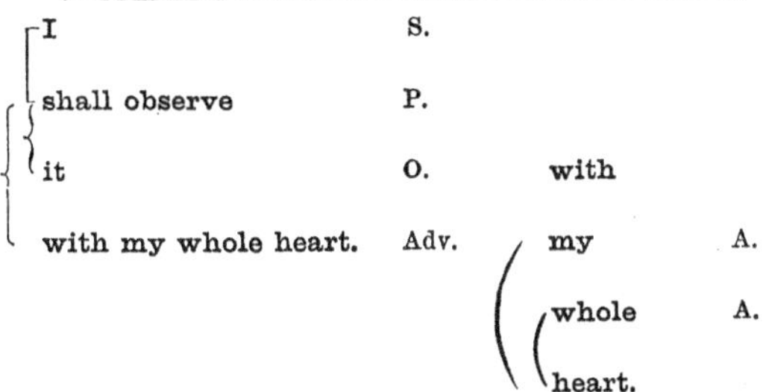

Here we have the four syntactical combinations. Complete the analysis.

A man may know like an angel. Analyze.

that hath it, or to standers by. To him that hath it, thus: it gives him conviction of sin, especially the defilement of his nature, and the sin of unbelief;* for the sake of which he is sure to be damned, if he findeth not mercy at God's hand, by faith of Jesus Christ. This sight and sense of things worketh in him sorrow and shame for sin. He findeth, moreover, revealed in him the Saviour of the world, and the absolute necessity of closing with him for life; at the which he findeth hungerings and thirstings after him; to which hungerings, etc., the promise is made. Now, according to the strength or weakness of his faith in his Saviour, so is his joy and peace, so is his love to holiness, so are his desires to know Him more and also to serve him in this world. But though, I say, it discovereth itself thus unto him, yet it is but seldom that he is able to conclude that this is a work of grace; because his corruptions now and his abused reason make his mind to misjudge in this matter. Therefore, in him that hath this work, there is required a very sound judgment before he can with steadiness conclude that this is a work of grace. To others it is thus discovered: 1. By an experimental confession of his faith in Christ. 2. By a life answerable to that confession, to wit, a life of holiness; heart holiness, family holiness, if he hath a family, and by conversation holiness in the world. Which in the general teacheth him inwardly to abhor his sin, and himself for that, in secret; to suppress it in his family, and to promote holiness in the world; not by talk only, as a hypocrite or talkative person may do, but by a practical subjection in faith and love to the power of the word. And now, sir, as to this brief description of the work of Grace, and also the discovery of it, if you have aught to object, object; if not, then give me leave to propound to you a second question.

Talkative. Nay, my part is not now to object, but to hear. Let me therefore have your second question.

Faithful. It is this: Do you experience this first part of the description of it? and doth your life and conversation testify the same? or standeth your religion in *word* or *tongue*, and not in *deed* and *truth?* Pray, if you incline to answer me in this, say no more than you know the God above will say *amen* to: and also nothing but what your conscience can justify you in. "For not he that commendeth himself, is approved; but whom the Lord commendeth." Besides to say, "I am thus and thus," when my conversation and all my neighbors tell me I lie, is great wickedness.

Then Talkative at first began to blush; but recovering himself, thus he replied.

Talkative. You come now to experience, to conscience, and God; and to appeal to him for justification of what is spoken. This kind of discourse I

* **Sin of unbelief.** John xvi., 8, 9; Ps. xxxviii., 18.—**Sorrow and shame.** Jer. xxxi., 19.—**Hungerings.** Matt. v., 6.—**Conversation holiness.** *Conversation* is here used in the now obsolete sense of *general course of conduct.* *Conversation holiness* is holiness in one's intercourse with the world. See 1 Pet. ii., 12.—**Experimental confession.** Philip. iii., 17. *Experimental* is used by the old theologians to indicate that which is taught by practical *experience* or derived from it.—**Lord commendeth.** 2 Cor. x., 18.—**Tell me I lie.** Job xxiv., 25.

It discovereth itself thus unto him. Analyze.

did not expect: nor am I disposed to give an answer to such questions, because I count not myself bound thereto, unless you take upon you to be a *catechiser;* and though you should so do, yet I may refuse to make you my *judge.* But I pray, will you tell me why you ask me such questions?

Faithful. Because I saw you forward to talk, and because I knew not that you had aught else but notion. Besides, to tell you all the truth, I have heard of you, that you are a man whose religion lies in *talk*, and that your conversation gives this your profession the lie. They say, you are a spot* among Christians; and that religion fareth the worse for your ungodly conversation; that some already have stumbled at your wicked ways, and that more are in danger of being destroyed thereby. Your religion and an ale-house, and covetousness, and uncleanness, and swearing, and lying, and vain-company-keeping, etc., will stand together. The proverb is true of you, which is said of a whore; to wit, that "she is a shame to all women." So are you a shame to all professors.

Talkative. Since you are ready to take up report, and to judge so rashly as you do, I cannot but conclude you are some peevish or melancholy man not fit to be discoursed with; and so, adieu.

Then came up Christian, and said to his brother, "I told you how it would happen. Your words and his lusts could not agree. He had rather leave your company than reform his life; but he is gone, as I said. Let him go, the loss is no man's but his own; for, he continuing, as I suppose he will do, as he is, he would have been but a blot in our company. Besides, the apostle says, 'From such withdraw thyself.'"

Faithful. But I am glad we had this little discourse with him; it may happen that he will think of it again. However, I have dealt plainly with him, and so am clear of his blood, if he perisheth.

Christian. You did well to talk so plainly to him as you did; there is but little of this faithful dealing with men now-a-days, and that makes religion to stink so in the nostrils of many, as it doth. For they are these talkative fools, whose religion is only in word, and are debauched and vain in their conversation; that, being so much admitted into the fellowship of the godly, do puzzle the world, blemish Christianity, and grieve the sincere. I wish that all men would deal with such, as you have done. Then should they either be made more conformable to religion, or the company of saints would be too hot for them.

Then did Faithful say,

> How Talkative at first lifts up his plumes!
> How bravely doth he speak! how he presumes

* **A spot.** Jude 12.—**Religion lies in talk.** "Let me a little expostulate the matter with you, O ye professors, whose religion lieth only in your tongues: I mean you who are little or nothing known from the rest of the rabble of the world, only you can talk better than they. Hear me a word or two. 'If I speak with the tongues of men and angels, and have not charity'—that is, love to God and Christ and saints and holiness—'I am nothing,' no child of God, and so have nothing to do with heaven. A prating tongue will not unlock the gates of heaven, nor blind the eyes of thy Judge. Look to it." Bunyan's *Discourse on the Strait Gate.*—**Withdraw thyself.** 1 Tim. vi., 5.

Catechiser, questioner, inquirer, interrogator, asker. Write out, etc.

To drive down all before him! But so soon
As Faithful talks of heart-work; like the moon
That's past the full, into the wane he goes:
And so will all but he that heart-work knows.

Thus they went on, talking of what they had seen by the way; and so made that way easy, which would otherwise no doubt have been tedious to them. For they went through a wilderness.

Now when they were got almost quite out of this wilderness,* Faithful chanced to cast his eye back, and espied one coming after them, and he knew him. "Oh!" said Faithful to his brother, "who comes yonder?" Then Christian looked, and said, "It is my good friend Evangelist." "Aye, and my good friend too," said Faithful, "for it was he that set me the way to the Gate." Now Evangelist came up unto them, and thus saluted them: "Peace be with you, dearly beloved; and peace be your helper."

Christian. Welcome, welcome, my good Evangelist! The sight of thy countenance brings to my remembrance thy ancient kindness and unwearied labors for my eternal good.

"And a thousand times welcome," said good Faithful. "Thy company, O sweet Evangelist, how desirable is it to us poor pilgrims!" Then said Evangelist, "How hath it fared with you, my friends, since the time of our last parting? what have you met with; and how have you behaved yourselves?" Then Christian and Faithful told him of all things that had happened to them in the way; and how, and with what difficulty, they had arrived to that place. "Right glad am I," said Evangelist; "not that you have met with trials, but that you have been victors, and for that you have, notwithstanding many weaknesses, continued in the way to this very day—I say, right glad am I of this thing, and that for mine own sake and yours. I have sowed, and you have reaped; and the day is coming when both he that sowed and they that reap shall rejoice together: that is, if you hold out; for in due time you shall reap, if you faint not. The crown is before you, and it is an incorruptible one: So run, that you may obtain it. Some there be that set out for this crown, and, after they have gone far for it, another comes in and takes it from them. Hold fast, therefore, that you have; let no man take your crown; you are not yet out of the gunshot of the devil. You have not resisted unto blood, striving against sin. Let the kingdom be always before you, and believe steadfastly concerning things that are invisible. Let nothing that is on this side the other world get within you: and, above all, look well to your own hearts and to the lusts thereof; for they are deceitful above all things, and desperately wicked. Set your faces like a flint. You have all power in heaven and earth on your side."

---

* **Now when they had got**, etc. This passage, relating the interview between Evangelist and the two pilgrims, as far as the words, "Then I saw in my dream," is not found in the first edition.—**I have sowed**, etc. John iv., 36, 37; Gal. vi., 9; 1 Cor. ix., 24-27; Rev. iii., 11.

Gunshot, stone's-throw, ear-shot. Other synonymes? Has Bunyan selected the best word?

You have continued in the way to this very day. Analyze.

Then Christian thanked him for his exhortation; but told him withal that they would have him speak farther to them for their help the rest of the way; and the rather, for that they well knew that he was a prophet, and could tell them of things that might happen unto them, and how they might resist and overcome them. To which request, Faithful also consented. So Evangelist began as followeth:—

"My sons, you have heard in the words of the truth of the Gospel, 'that you must, through many tribulations, enter into the kingdom of heaven;' and again, 'that in every city,* bonds and afflictions abide you:' and therefore you cannot expect that you should go long on your pilgrimage without them, in some sort or other. You have found something of the truth of these testimonies upon you already; and more will immediately follow. For now, as you see, you are almost out of this wilderness; and therefore you will soon come into a town that you will by and by see before you; and in that town you will be hard beset with enemies, who will strain hard but they will kill you. And be you sure that one or both of you must seal the testimony which you hold, with blood. But be you faithful unto death, and the king will give you a crown of life. He that shall die there, although his death will be unnatural, and his pain, perhaps, great; he will yet have the better of his fellow: not only because he will be arrived at the Celestial City soonest, but because he will escape many miseries that the other will meet with in the rest of his journey. But when you are come to the town, and shall find fulfilled what I have here related, then remember your friend, and quit yourselves like men, and commit the keeping of your souls to your God in well-doing, as unto a faithful Creator."

Then I saw in my dream, that when they were got out of the wilderness, they presently saw a town before them; and the name of the town is

---

* **In every city**, etc. Acts xx., 23.—**Crown of life.** Rev. ii., 10.—**Fellow.** See Index.—**Will be arrived.** See *is turned*, p. 336.—**Quit yourselves like men.** *Quit* is the same as *acquit, conduct, behave.* Thus in Milton,

Samson hath quit himself
Like Samson.—

Then I saw in my dream. This interview with Evangelist, was not in the earliest edition. Was Bunyan wise in inserting it? Why?—**When they were got out of the wilderness,** *i. e.*, Christian and his new companion, Faithful.

Expect, await, wait for, look for. Other synonymes? Write out, etc.

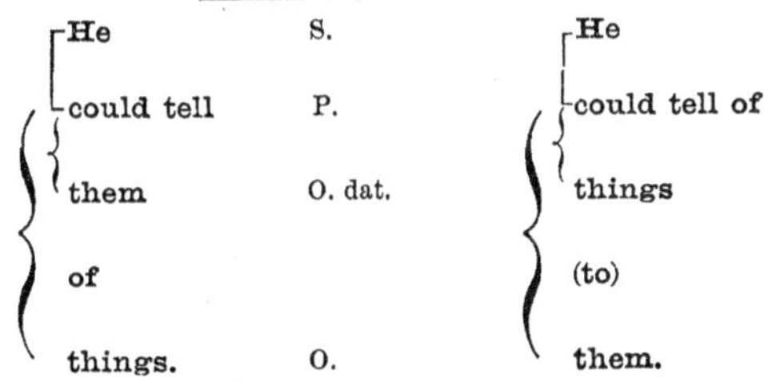

Them is a *dative* object; *things*, a passive.

The king will give you a crown of life. Analyze.

Vanity; and at the town there is a fair kept, called Vanity Fair. It is kept all the year long. It beareth the name of Vanity Fair, because the town where it is kept is lighter than Vanity! * and also, because all that is there sold, or that cometh thither, is Vanity. As is the saying of the wise, "All that cometh is vanity." This fair is no new-erected business, but a thing of ancient standing. I will show you the original of it. Almost five thousand years agone, there were pilgrims walking to the Celestial City, as these two honest persons are; and Beelzebub, Apollyon, and Legion, with their companions, perceiving by the path that the pilgrims made, that their way to the city lay through this town of Vanity, they contrived here to set up a fair; a fair wherein should be sold all sorts of vanity; and that it should last all the year long. Therefore at this fair, are all such merchandises sold, as houses, lands, trades, places, honors, preferments, titles, countries, kingdoms, lusts, pleasures, and delights of all sorts, as whores, bawds, wives, husbands, children, and masters, servants, lives, blood, bodies, souls, silver, gold, pearls, precious stones, and what not! And, moreover, at this fair there are at all times to be seen, jugglings, cheats, games, plays, fools, apes, knaves, and rogues, and that of every kind. Here are to be seen too, and that for nothing, thefts, murders, adulteries, false-swearers, and that of a blood-red color. And as in other fairs of less moment, there are several rows and streets under their proper names, where such and such wares are vended; so here likewise, you have the proper places, rows, streets, (viz., countries and kingdoms,) where the wares of this fair are soonest to be found. Here is the Britain-Row, the French-Row, the Italian-Row, the Spanish-Row, the German-Row; where several sorts of vanities are to be sold. But, as in other fairs, some one commodity is as the chief of all the fair, so the ware of Rome and her merchandise is greatly promoted in this fair. Only, our English nation, with some others, have taken a dislike thereat.

Now, as I said, the way to the Celestial City lies just through the town where this lusty Fair is kept; and he that will go to the city, and yet not go through this town, must needs go out of the world. The Prince of princes himself, when here, went through this town to his own country, and

* **Lighter than vanity.** Ps. lxii., 9; Eccles. xii., 8.—**Agone,** *ago.* Obs.—**Legion.** Mark v., 9.—**Blood-red color,** *flagrant,* deeply-dyed in iniquity.—**This town of Vanity.** "The City of Destruction in its gala dress."—**Is greatly promoted.** Subject of *is?* In Shakespeare, "The inflection in *s* is of frequent occurrence when two or more singular nouns precede the verb." Abbott's *Shakes. Gram.*, 336.—**Our English nation.** When did the English Church separate from the Romish? See Henry the Eighth in Froude's History.—**Go out of the world.** 1 Cor. v., 10.

Vanity Fair

is

kept

all the year.

The predicate is here supplemented by a phrase denoting *time.* Complete the analysis.

Her merchandise is greatly promoted in this fair. Analyze.

that upon a fair-day too. Yea, and, as I think, it was Beelzebub, the Chief lord of this fair, that invited him to buy of his vanities; yea, would have made him lord of the fair, would he but have done him reverence as he went through the town. Yea, because he was such a person of honor, Beelzebub had him from street to street and showed him all the kingdoms* of the world in a little time, that he might, if possible, allure that Blessed One to cheapen and buy some of his vanities. But he had no mind to the merchandise, and therefore left the town without laying out so much as one farthing upon these vanities. This fair, therefore, is an ancient thing, of long standing, and a very great fair.

Now these pilgrims, as I said, must needs go through the fair. Well, so they did. But behold, even as they entered into the fair, all the people in the fair were moved and the town itself, as it were, in a hubbub about them; and that for several reasons. For,

First. The pilgrims were clothed with such kind of raiment as was diverse from the raiment of any that traded in that fair. The people, therefore, of the fair made great gazing upon them. Some said, they were fools; some, they were bedlams; and some, they were outlandish men.

Secondly. And as they wondered at their apparel, so they did likewise at their speech; for few could understand what they said. They naturally spoke the language of Canaan; but they that kept the fair were the men of this world; so that, from one end of the fair to the other, they seemed barbarians to each other.

Thirdly. But that which did not a little amuse the merchandisers, was that these pilgrims set very light by all their wares. They cared not so much as to *look* upon them; and if they called upon them to buy, they would put their fingers in their ears, and cry, "Turn away mine eyes from beholding vanity;" and look upwards, signifying that their trade and traffic were in heaven.

Fourthly. One chanced mockingly, beholding the carriages of the men, to say unto them, "What will ye buy?" But they, looking gravely upon him, said, "We buy the truth." At that, there was an occasion taken to despise the men the more; some mocking, some taunting, some speaking reproachfully, and some calling upon others to smite them.

At last, things came to a hubbub, and great stir in the fair; insomuch that all order was confounded. Now was word presently brought to the

---

* **Showed him all the kingdoms,** etc. See Matt. iv., 1-11. "Satan is here a mighty artist and can show us all earthly things in a multiplying glass. . . . Much of this world and its glory is permitted of God to be disposed of by the devil, and he is called both the prince and the god thereof." Bunyan's *Paul's Departure and Crown.*—**Hubbub.** A. S. *hwôpan*, to cry out. Hence *whoobub*, now obsolete, and *whoop*. One would suppose this word to be onomatopoetic. See Wedgwood's *Dictionary of English Etymology.*—**Such kind of raiment.** Matt. xxii., 11; Rev. iii., 5, etc.—**Language of Canaan.** 1 Cor. ii., 7, 8.—**Beholding vanity.** Ps. cxix., 37.—**Beholding the carriages,** beholding the *conduct* or *behavior.*—**Buy the truth.** Prov. xxiii., 23. "Buy the truth and sell it not." The meaning of this injunction is, "Gain the truth by labor, study, and expense, and never dispossess thyself of it."

Language, speech, tongue, dialect, idiom. Write out, etc. See Smith's *Synonymes Discriminated.*

Hubbub, noise, din, hurly-burly. Other synonymes? Write out, etc.

Analyze, *We buy the Truth.*

great one of the fair; who quickly came down and deputed some of his most trusty friends to take those men into an examination, about whom the fair was almost overturned. So the men were brought to examination; and they that sat upon them,* asked them, whence they came, whither they went, and what they did there in such an unusual garb? The men told them, that they were pilgrims and strangers in the world; and that they were going to their own country, which was heavenly Jerusalem; and that they had given no occasion to the men of the town, nor yet to the merchandisers, thus to abuse them and to stop them in their journey; except it was for that, when one asked them what they would buy, they said, they would *buy the truth.*

But they that were appointed to examine them, did not believe them to be any other than bedlams and mad, or else such as came to put all things into a confusion in the fair. Therefore they took them and beat them, and besmeared them with dirt; and then put them into the cage, that they might be made a spectacle to all the men in the fair.

There, therefore, they lay for some time, and were made the object of any man's sport, or malice, or revenge; the great one of the fair laughing still at all that befell them. But the men being patient, and not rendering railing for railing, but contrarywise blessing; and giving good words for bad, and kindness for injuries done; some men in the fair, that were more observing and less prejudiced than the rest, began to check and blame the baser sort for their continual abuses done by them to the men. They, therefore, in angry manner let fly at them again, counting them as bad as the men in the cage; and telling them, that they seemed confederates, and should be made partakers of their misfortunes. The others replied, that for aught they could see, the men were quiet and sober, and intended nobody any harm; and that there were many that traded in their fair, that were more worthy to be put into the cage, yea, and pillory too, than were the men that they had abused.

Thus, after diverse words had passed on both sides, the men behaving themselves all the while very wisely and soberly before them, they fell to some blows among themselves, and did harm one to another. Then were these two poor men brought before their examiners again, and there charged

---

* **Sat upon them.** A technical phrase meaning "held a session, inquest, or investigation in regard to them." We still say, "The jury sat upon the body."—**Heavenly Jerusalem.** Heb. xi., 13, 14, 15, 16.—**Bedlams and mad.** *Bedlam* is said to be from *Bethlehem*, the name of a religious house in London, afterwards converted into a hospital for lunatics. Hence *bedlams* are *lunatics*.—**Into the cage,** into the jail with its grated windows. So in *Lovelace's* lines,

> "Stone walls do not a prison make,
> Nor iron bars a *cage*.
> Minds innocent and quiet take
> That for a hermitage."

Pillory. "A frame of wood erected on posts, with movable boards and holes, through which the head and hands of a criminal were formerly put, to punish him." *Webster.* The pillory was commonly erected in the most public square or open place in a city or town.—**Had passed on both sides.** "O, it is hard work to pocket up the reproaches of all the foolish people, as if we had found great spoil, and to suffer all their revilings, lies, and slanders, without cursing them as Elisha did the children." Bunyan on *Paul's Departure and Crown.*

The men intended nobody any harm. Analyze.

of being guilty of the late hubbub that had been in the fair. So they beat them pitifully; and hanged irons upon them, and led them in chains up and down the fair, for an example and terror to others, lest any should speak in their behalf or join themselves unto them.

But Christian and Faithful behaved themselves yet more wisely, and received the ignominy and shame that was cast upon them, with so much meekness and patience that it won to their side, though but few in comparison with the rest, several of the men in the fair. This put the other party yet into greater rage; insomuch, that they concluded the death of these two men. Wherefore they threatened, that neither cage nor irons should serve their turns, but that they should die for the abuse they had done, and for deluding the men of the fair.

Then were they remanded to the cage again, until farther order should be taken with them. So they put them in, and made their feet fast in the stocks.

Here, therefore, they called again to mind what they had heard from their faithful friend Evangelist;* and were the more confirmed in their ways and sufferings by what he told them would happen to them. They also now comforted each other, that whose lot it was to suffer, even he should have the best on it: therefore each man secretly wished that he might have that preferment: but committing themselves to the all-wise disposal of Him that ruleth all things, with much content they abode in the condition in which they were, until they should be otherwise disposed of.

Then, a convenient time being appointed, they brought them forth to their trial, in order to their condemnation. When the time was come, they were brought before their enemies, and arraigned. The judge's name was lord *Hategood:* their indictment was one and the same in substance, though somewhat varying in form; the contents whereof were these:—

"That they were enemies to, and disturbers of, their trade; that they had made commotions and divisions in the town, and had won a party to their own most dangerous opinions, in contempt of the law of their prince."

Then Faithful began to answer, "That he had only set himself against that which had set itself against Him that is higher than the highest. And," said he, "as for disturbance, I make none, being myself a man of peace: the parties that were won to us, were won by beholding our truth and innocence; and they are only turned from the worse to the better. And as to the king you talk of, since he is *Beelzebub*, the enemy of our Lord, I defy him and all his angels."

* **Evangelist.** This reference to Evangelist is not in the first edition.—**Should have the best on it.** *On* is often thus used for *of* in Shakespeare. Thus in *Macbeth* in some editions, "Banquo's buried: he cannot come out *on's* grave." So in *Coriolanus*, 'one *on's* ears," "worth six *on* him," and in the *Tempest* "my profit *on't*." The explanation seems to be that *of* is shortened in rapid conversation to *o'*; and then, before a vowel sound, *o'* was changed to *on*, just as *a* before a vowel sound becomes *an*. See Abbott's *Shakes. Gram.* 182. But this usage is now confined to the vulgar.—**Brought them forth to their trial.** This description of the trial is a pretty good take-off. Bunyan himself had been through it; and the proceedings related are not more scandalous than some over which Judge Jeffries presided. See Life of Richard Baxter, and see p. 358.—**Beelzebub.** Scholars tell us that this name should be spelled *Beelzebul;* and that it may mean *lord of the dwellings*, or *lord of the dunghill*, or *lord of idols*, or *god of flies!*

They had made commotions in the town. Analyze.

Then proclamation was made, "That they that had aught to say for their lord the king against the prisoner at the bar, should forthwith appear, and give in their evidence." So there came in three witnesses; to wit, *Envy*, *Superstition*, and *Pickthank*.* They were then asked, If they knew the prisoner at the bar; and what they had to say for their lord the king against him?

Then stood forth *Envy*, and said to this effect: "My lord, I have known this man a long time, and will attest upon my oath before this honorable bench, that he is—"

Judge. Hold—give him his oath.

So, they sware him. Then he said, "My lord, this man, notwithstanding his plausible name, is one of the vilest men in our country. He neither regardeth prince nor people, law nor customs; but doth all that he can to possess all men with certain of his disloyal notions, which he in the general calls *principles of faith and holiness*. And in particular, I heard him once myself affirm that Christianity and the customs of our town of Vanity were diametrically opposite and could not be reconciled. By which saying, my lord, he doth, at once, not only condemn all our laudable doings but us in the doing of them."

Judge. Hast thou any more to say?

Envy. My lord, I could say much more, only I would not be tedious to the court. Yet, if need be, when the other gentlemen have given in their evidence, rather than any thing shall be wanting that will despatch him, I will enlarge my testimony against him.

So he was bidden to stand by.

Then they called Superstition, and bade him look upon the prisoner. They also asked, what he could say for their lord the king against him. Then they sware him. So he began.

Superstition. My lord, I have no great acquaintance with this man, nor do I desire to have further knowledge of him. However, this I know, that he is a very pestilent fellow, from some discourse that the other day I had with him in this town; for then, talking with him, I heard him say that our religion was naught, and such by which a man could by no means please God. Which saying of his, my lord,—your lordship very well knows what necessarily thence will follow, to wit, that we still do worship in vain, are yet in our sins, and finally shall be damned. And this is that which I have to say.

Then was Pickthank sworn, and bidden to say what he knew in behalf of their lord the king, against the prisoner at the bar.

Pickthank. My lord, and you gentlemen all, this fellow I have known of a long time, and have heard him speak things that ought not to be spoke.

---

* **Pickthank.** "An officious fellow who does what he is not desired to do, for the sake of gaining favor; a whispering parasite." *Webster.* (Correct, by transposition of words, this definition from Webster's *Dictionary*.)—**To possess all men with,** etc., *to put all men in possession of*. This use of *possess* is found in Shakespeare; as, "Record a gift . . . . of all he dies possessed unto his son." *Merchant of Venice.* So Dryden, "Of fortune's favor long possessed." Addison says, "It is of unspeakable advantage to possess our minds with an habitual good intention." So we say a person is "well *read*."—**Spoke,** *spoken*. See Abbott, 343.

Superstition, fanaticism. Other synonymes? Write out, etc.

I will enlarge my testimony against him. Analyze.

For he hath railed on our noble prince Beelzebub, and hath spoke contemptibly of his honorable friends, whose names are, the lord *Old Man*, the lord *Carnal Delight*, the lord *Luxurious*, the lord *Desire of Vain-Glory*, my old lord *Lechery*, sir *Having-Greedy*, with all the rest of our nobility; and he hath said, moreover, that if all men were of his mind, if possible, there is not one of these noblemen should have any longer a being in this town. Besides, he hath not been afraid to rail on you, my lord, who are now appointed to be his judge; calling you an ungodly villain; with many other such like vilifying terms, with which he hath bespattered most of the gentry of our town.

When this Pickthank had told his tale, the judge directed his speech to the prisoner at the bar, saying, "Thou renegade,* heretic, and traitor, hast thou heard what these honest gentlemen have witnessed against thee?"

Faithful. May I speak a few words in my own defence?

Judge. Sirrah, sirrah, thou deservest to live no longer, but to be slain immediately upon the place. Yet, that all men may see our gentleness towards thee, let us hear what thou hast to say.

Faithful. 1. I say then, in answer to what Mr. Envy hath spoken, I never said aught but this, That what rule, or laws, or custom, or people, were flat against the Word of God, are diametrically opposite to Christianity. If I have said amiss in this, convince me of my error, and I am ready here before you to make my recantation.

2. As to the second, to wit, Mr. Superstition, and his charge against me, I said only this, That in the worship of God, there is required a divine faith; but there can be no divine faith without a divine revelation of the will of God. Therefore, whatever is thrust into the worship of God, that is not agreeable to divine revelation, can be done but by a human faith, which faith will not be profitable to eternal life.

3. As to what Mr. Pickthank hath said, I said, (avoiding terms, as that I am said to rail, and the like,) That the prince of this town, with all the rabblement his attendants, by this gentleman named, are more fit for being in hell than in this town and country. And so the Lord have mercy upon me!

Then the judge called to the jury, who all this while stood to hear and observe, "Gentlemen of the jury, you see this man, about whom so great an uproar hath been made in this town. You have also heard what these worthy gentlemen have witnessed against him. Also you have heard his reply and confession. It lieth now in your breasts to hang him or save his life; but yet I think meet to instruct you in our law. There was an act made in the days of Pharaoh the Great, servant to our prince, that, lest those of a contrary religion should multiply and grow too strong for him, their males should be thrown into the river. There was also an act made in

* **Renegade** (Lat. *re-*, again; *negare*, to deny; Fr. *renégat; renier*, to deny), one faithless to principle; an *apostate*. Some editions have *runagate*, which is a corruption of *renegade*, very much as the illiterate British sailors mistook the classic name of the French ship *Bellerophon* for *Bully-ruffian!*—**Into the river.** Ex. i., 22.

The judge called to the jury. Analyze.

days of Nebuchadnezzar the Great, another of his servants, that whoever would not fall down and worship his golden image, would be thrown into a fiery furnace.* There was also an act made in the days of Darius, that whoso for some time called upon any God but him, should be cast into the lion's den. Now the substance of these laws this rebel has broken, not only in thought, which is not to be borne, but also in word and deed: which must therefore needs be intolerable. For that of Pharaoh, his law was made upon a supposition to prevent mischief, no crime being yet apparent. But here is a crime apparent. For the second and third, you see he disputeth against our religion; and for the treason he hath confessed, he deserveth to die the death."

Then went the jury out; whose names were Mr. Blindman, Mr. No-good, Mr. Malice, Mr. Love-lust, Mr. Live-loose, Mr. Heady, Mr. High-mind, Mr. Enmity, Mr. Liar, Mr. Cruelty, Mr. Hate-light, and Mr. Implacable; who every one gave in his private verdict against him among themselves, and afterwards unanimously concluded to bring him in guilty before the judge. And first among themselves, Mr. Blindman the foreman said, "I see clearly, that this man is a heretic."—Then said Mr. No-good, "Away with such a fellow from the earth."—"Ay," said Mr. Malice, "for I hate the very looks of him."—Then said Mr. Love-lust, "I could never endure him." "Nor I," said Mr. Live-loose, "for he would always be condemning my way."—"Hang him, hang him," said Mr. Heady.—"A sorry scrub," said Mr. High-mind.—"My heart riseth against him," said Mr. Enmity.—"He is a rogue," said Mr. Liar.—"Hanging is too good for him," said Mr. Cruelty.—"Let us despatch him out of the way," said Mr. Hate-light. Then said Mr. Implacable, "Might I have all the world given me, I could not be reconciled to him; therefore let us forthwith bring him in guilty of death." And so they did: therefore he was presently condemned to be had from the place where he was, to the

* **Furnace.** Dan. iii.—**Den.** Dan. vi., 7.—**To die the death.** Judge Hategood's character is not a whit more infamous than those of some live judges in Bunyan's day. On the trial of Baxter in 1684, Judge Jeffreys called the prisoner an "old blockhead," an "unthankful villain," a "conceited, stubborn, fanatical dog." "Ah! Richard, Richard!" said he, "thou art an old fellow and an old boy! Thou hast written as many books as would load a cart, every one of which is as full of sedition as an egg is full of meat. . . . I know thou hast a mighty party, but by the grace of Almighty God, I will crush you all. Come, what do you say for yourself, you old knave! Come, speak up. I am not afraid of you, for all the snivelling calves you have got about you" (alluding to some of Baxter's friends who were weeping).—**Mr. Heady,** etc. Bunyan evidently has in mind the enumeration made by St. Paul in 2 Timothy, iii., 4, and context: perhaps also Romans i., 31. **Heady** is *headstrong, precipitate, wilful.* The reader will notice how closely each juror's utterance accords with the peculiar character as indicated by the name.

Malice, rancor, spite, malignity, malignancy, bitterness, maliciousness. Other synonymes? Write out, etc.

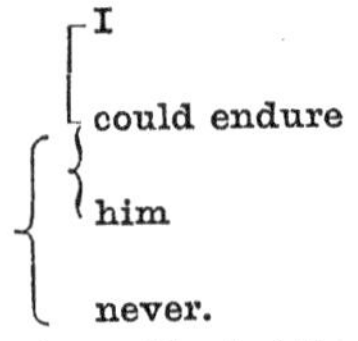

Never is an adjunct of time. Complete the analysis.

place from which he came, and there to be put to the most cruel death that could be invented.

They therefore brought him out, to do with him according to their law. At first they scourged him,* then they buffeted him, then they lanced his flesh with knives; after that, they stoned him with stones, then pricked him with their swords; and, last of all, they burnt him to ashes at the stake. Thus came Faithful to his end.

Now I saw, that there stood behind the multitude a chariot and a couple of horses waiting for Faithful; who, so soon as the adversaries had despatched him, was taken up into it, and straightway was carried up through the clouds with sound of trumpet, the nearest way to the Celestial Gate.

But as for Christian, he had some respite, and was remanded back to prison. So he there remained for a space. But He that overrules all things, having the power of their rage in his own hand, so brought it about, that Christian for that time escaped them and went his way. And as he went, he sung, saying:—

> "Well, Faithful, thou hast faithfully professed
> Unto thy Lord; with whom thou shalt be blest,
> When faithless ones, with all their vain delights,
> Are crying out under their hellish plights.
> Sing, Faithful, sing; and let thy name survive:
> For though they kill thee, thou art yet alive."

Now I saw in my dream, that Christian went not forth alone; for there was one whose name was Hopeful, being so made by the beholding of Christian and Faithful in their words and behaviour, in their sufferings at the Fair, who joined himself unto him, and, entering into a brotherly covenant, told him he would be his companion. Thus one died to bear testimony to the truth; and another rises out of his ashes, to be a companion with Christian in his pilgrimage. This Hopeful also told Christian, that there were many more of the men in the Fair, that would take their time, and follow after.

So I saw, that quickly after they were got out of the Fair, they overtook one that was going before them, whose name was By-ends. So they said to him, "What countryman, sir? and how far go you this way?" He told them, "That he came from the town of Fair-speech; and he was going to the Celestial City;" but told them not his name.

"From Fair-speech!" said Christian: "Is there any good that lives there?"

"Yes," said By-ends; "I hope."

---

* **Scourged him,** etc. As a specimen of the rough treatment accorded to heretics in Bunyan's day, we might cite the case of William Prynne, who was twice pilloried, had both ears cut off, both cheeks branded, and then was sentenced to perpetual imprisonment; or that of Dr. Leighton, who, for a treatise in favor of Presbyterian church government, was repeatedly pilloried, publicly flogged, had his nostrils slit, his ears cropped, and his cheeks branded. Bunyan's father, too, might have seen two Arians burnt at the stake, in 1614, one at Smithfield, and the other at Burton-on-Trent.—**Thou art yet alive.** "Was not this man, think you, a giant? Had he not also hold of the shield of faith? And did he not behave himself valiantly? Was not his mind elevated a thousand degrees beyond sense, carnal reason, fleshly love, self-concerns, and the desires of embracing temporal things? . . . His mind was captivated with delights invisible. He coveted to show his love to his Lord, by laying down his life for his sake. . . . He was a man of a thousand." Bunyan's *House of the Forest of Lebanon.*

Christian. Pray, sir, what may I call you?

By-ends. I am stranger to you, and you to me. If you be going this way, I shall be glad of your company; if not, I must be content.

Christian. This town of Fair-speech I have heard of; and, as I remember, they say it is a wealthy place.

By-ends. Yes, I will assure you that it is; and I have very many rich kindred there.

Christian. Pray who are your kindred there, if a man may be so bold?

By-ends. Almost the whole town:* and in particular, my lord Turn-about; my lord Time-server; my lord Fair-speech, from whose ancestors that town first took its name; also Mr. Smooth-man; Mr. Facing-both-ways; Mr. Any-thing; and the parson of our parish, Mr. Two-tongues, was my mother's own brother by father's side. And, to tell you the truth, I am become a gentleman of good quality; yet my great-grandfather was but a waterman, looking one way and rowing another, and I got most of my estate by the same occupation.

Christian. Are you a married man?

By-ends. Yes: and my wife is a very virtuous woman, the daughter of a virtuous woman. She was my lady Feigning's daughter; therefore she came of a very honorable family, and is arrived to such a pitch of breeding, that she knows how to carry it to all, even to prince and peasant. It is true, we somewhat differ in religion from those of the stricter sort; yet but in two small points; first, we never strive against wind and tide: secondly, we are always most zealous when Religion goes in silver slippers; we love much to walk with him in the street, if the sun shines and the people applaud him.

Then Christian stepped a little aside to his fellow Hopeful; saying, "It runs in my mind that this is one By-ends, of Fair-speech. And if it be he, we have as very a knave in our company as dwelleth in all these parts." Then said Hopeful, "Ask him. Methinks he should not be ashamed of his name."

So Christian came up with him again, and said: "Sir, you talk as if you knew something more than all the world doth; and, if I take not my mark amiss, I deem I have a guess of you. Is not your name Mr. By-ends, of Fair-speech?"

By-ends. This is not my name, but indeed it is a nick-name that is given me by some that cannot abide me; and I must be content to bear it as a reproach, as other good men have borne theirs before me.

Christian. But did you never give an occasion to men to call you by this name?

By-ends. Never, never! The worst that ever I did to give them an occa-

---

* **Almost the whole town,** etc. This account of the kindred of By-ends is not in the first edition. Has Bunyan been judicious in adding it?—**Waterman,** etc. Another of Bunyan's grave jokes.—**Arrived to,** arrived *at*. *To* is obsolete after *arrive*, in the sense of *reach*. *Arrive* is Lat. *ad*, to; *ripa*, bank; and means originally *to come* to a *bank* or *shore*. Fr. *arriver*.

We never strive against wind and tide. Analyze.

sion to give me this name was, that I had always the luck to jump in my judgment with the present way of the times, whatever it was; and my chance was to get thereby. But if things are thus cast upon me, let me count them a blessing; but let not the malicious load me therefore with reproach.

Christian. I thought, indeed, that you were the man that I heard of; and, to tell you what I think, I fear this name belongs to you more properly than you are willing we should think it doth.

By-ends. Well, if you will thus imagine, I cannot help it. You will find me a fair company-keeper, if you will still admit me your associate.

Christian. If you will go with us, you must go against wind and tide: the which, I perceive, is against your opinion. You must also own Religion in his rags as well as when he is in his silver slippers; and stand by him, too, when bound in irons, as well as when he walketh the streets with applause.

By-ends. You must not impose, nor lord it over my faith. Leave me to my liberty, and let me go with you.

Christian. Not a step farther, unless you will do, in what I propound, as we.

Then said By-ends, "I shall never desert my old principles, since they are harmless and profitable. If I may not go with you, I must do as I did before you overtook me, even go by myself until some overtake me that will be glad of my company."

Then I saw in my dream,* that Christian and Hopeful forsook him, and kept their distance before him. But one of them, looking back, saw three men following Mr. By-ends; and, behold! as they came up with him, he made them a very low congé; and they also gave him a compliment. The men's names were, Mr. Hold-the-world, Mr. Money-love, and Mr. Save-all; men that Mr. By-ends had formerly been acquainted with. For, in their minority they were school-fellows and taught by one Mr. Gripeman, a schoolmaster in Love-gain; which is a market-town in the county of Coveting, in the North. This schoolmaster taught them the art of getting, either by violence, cozenage, flattery, lying, or by putting on a guise of religion; and these four gentlemen had attained much of the art of their master, so that they could each of them have kept such a school themselves.

Well, when they had, as I said, thus saluted each other, Mr. Money-love said to Mr. By-ends, "Who are they upon the road before us?" for Christian and Hopeful were yet within view.

By-ends. They are a couple of far countrymen, that, after their mode, are going on pilgrimage.

---

* **Then I saw in my dream,** etc. The conversation of Mr. By-ends with his three friends is not found in the first edition. The added part extends from, *Then I saw in my dream*, to, *Then Christian and Hopeful outwent them again.*—**Congé** (Lat. *con-*, together; *meare*, to go; *commeatus*, going back and forth, a parting ceremony, leave of absence, furlough; Fr. *congé*, leave, permission), *the act of taking leave, parting ceremony; bow*, or *courtesy*.

Imagine, *conceive*, *apprehend*, *suppose*, *fancy*, *think*, *apprehend*, *deem*. Other synonymes? Write out, etc.

Money-love. Alas! why did they not stay, that we might have had their good company? For they, and we, and you, sir, I hope, are going on pilgrimage.

By-ends. We are so, indeed; but the men before us are so rigid, and love so much their own notions, and do also so lightly esteem the opinions of others, that, let a man be never so godly, yet if he jumps* not with them in all things, they thrust him quite out of their company.

Save-all. That is bad; but we read of some that are "righteous overmuch;" and such men's rigidness prevails with them to judge and condemn all but themselves. But I pray, what, and how many, were the things wherein you differed?

By-ends. Why, they, after their headstrong manner, conclude that it is their duty to rush on their journey all weathers; and I am for waiting for wind and tide. They are for hazarding all for God at a clap; and I am for taking all advantages to secure my life and estate. They are for holding their notions, though all other men be against them; but I am for Religion, in what and so far as the times and my safety will bear it. They are for Religion, when in rags and contempt; but I am for him when he walks in his silver slippers, in the sunshine, and with applause.

Hold-the-world. Ay, and hold you there still, good Mr. By-ends; for, for my part, I can count him but a fool, that, having the liberty to keep what he has, shall be so unwise as to lose it. Let us be wise as serpents. It is best to make hay when the sun shines: you see how the bee lieth still all the winter, and bestirs her only when she can have profit with pleasure. God sends sometimes rain, and sometimes sunshine. If they be such fools to go through the first, yet let us be content to take fair weather along with us. For my part, I like that religion best that will stand with the security of God's blessing unto us: for who can imagine, that is ruled by his reason, since God hath bestowed upon us the good things of this life, but that he would have us keep them for his sake? Abraham and Solomon grew rich in religion. And Job says that a good man "shall lay up gold as dust." But he must not be such as the men before us, if they be as you have described them.

Save-all. I think that we are all agreed in this matter, and therefore there needs no more words about it.

Money-love. No, there needs no more words about this matter, indeed; for he that believes neither Scripture nor reason, and you see we have both on our side, neither knows his own liberty nor seeks his own safety.

By-ends. My brethren, we are, as you see, going all on pilgrimage;

---

* **Jumps,** agrees, tallies. So in Shakespeare, "It jumps with my humor."—**Righteous overmuch.** Eccles. vii., 16.—**At a clap,** at a stroke, on a sudden, all at once. Shakespeare says,

"What, fifty of my followers at a clap!"

A. S. *clappan;* Ger. *klopfen*, to strike.—**God's blessing unto us.** "They that look upon their outward enjoyments to be tokens of God's special grace unto them, are deceived. . . . . This is a trap in which the devil hath caught many thousands of poor souls." Bunyan's *Sighs from Hell.*—**Lay up gold as dust.** Job xxii., 24.

Profit, benefit, advantage, gain, emolument, lucre, avail, service. Write out, etc.

and, for our better diversion from things that are bad, give me leave to propound unto you this question.

Suppose a man, a minister or a tradesman, etc., should have an advantage lie before him, to get the good blessings of this life; yet so as that he can by no means come by them, except, in appearance at least, he becomes extraordinary zealous* in some points of religion, that he meddled not with before. May he not use this means to attain his end, and yet be a right honest man?

Money-love. I see the bottom of your question; and, with these gentlemen's good leave, I will endeavor to shape you an answer. And first, to speak to your question as it concerns a minister himself. Suppose a minister, a worthy man, possessed but of a very small benefice, and has in his eye a greater, more fat and plump by far; he has also now an opportunity of getting it, yet so as by being more studious, by preaching more frequently and zealously, and, because the temper of the people requires it, by altering some of his principles. For my part, I see no reason but a man may do this, provided he has a call; ay, and a great deal more besides; and yet be an honest man. For why?

1. His desire of a greater benefice is lawful, (this cannot be contradicted,) since it is set before him by Providence. So then he may get it if he can, making no question for conscience' sake.

2. Besides, his desire after that benefice makes him more studious, a more zealous preacher, etc.; and so makes him a better man; yea, makes him better improve his parts; which is according to the mind of God.

3. Now, as for his complying with the temper of his people, by deserting, to serve them, some of his principles,—this argueth, (1,) that he is of a self-denying temper; (2,) of a sweet and winning deportment; (3,) and so more fit for the ministerial function.

4. I conclude, then, that a minister that changes a small for a great should not, for so doing, be judged as covetous; but rather, since he is improved in his parts and industry hereby, be counted as one that pursues his call and the opportunity put into his hands to do good.

And now to the second part of the question, which concerns the tradesman you mention. Suppose such a one to have but a poor employ in the world, but, by becoming religious, he may mend his market; perhaps get a rich wife, or more and far better customers to his shop. For my part I see no reason but this may be lawfully done. For why?

1. To become religious is a virtue, by what means soever a man becomes so.

2. Nor is it unlawful to get a rich wife, or more custom to my shop.

3. Besides, the man that gets these by becoming religious, gets that which is good of them that are good, by becoming good himself. So then

---

* **Extraordinary zealous.** *Extraordinary* is here an adverb. See Abbott's *Shakes. Gram.* § 1.—**A rich wife.** "Professors perhaps there may be, who make profession a stalking-horse to beguile their neighbors out of their estates, as Mr. Badman himself did, when he beguiled her that is now with sorrow his wife." Bunyan's *Life and Death of Mr. Badman.*

A minister changes a small for a great. Analyze.

here is a good wife, and good customers, and good gain; and all these by becoming religious, which is good. Therefore, to become religious to get all these, is a good and profitable design.

This answer, thus made by Mr. Money-love to Mr. By-ends' question was highly applauded by them all. Wherefore they concluded, upon the whole, that it was most wholesome and advantageous. And because, as they thought, no man was able to contradict it; and because Christian and Hopeful were yet within call, they jointly agreed to assault them with the question, as soon as they overtook them; and the rather because they had opposed Mr. By-ends before. So they called after them; and they stopt and stood still till they came up to them; but they concluded, as they went, that not Mr. By-ends, but old Mr. Hold-the-world should propound the question to them; because, as they supposed, their answer to him would be without the remainder of that heat that was kindled between Mr. By-ends and them at their parting a little before.

So they came up to each other; and after a short salutation Mr. Hold-the-world propounded the question to Christian and his fellow, and bade them to answer it if they could.

Then said Christian; "Even a babe in religion may answer ten thousand such questions. For, if it be unlawful to follow Christ for loaves, as it is, John vi., 26, how much more abominable is it to make of him and religion a stalking-horse to get and enjoy the world? Nor do we find any other than heathens, hypocrites, devils, and witches, that are of this opinion.

"1. Heathens: for when Hamor and Shechem had a mind to the daughter and cattle of Jacob; and saw that there was no way for them to come at them, but by becoming circumcised, they said to their companions, 'If every male of us be circumcised, as they are circumcised; shall not their cattle, and their substance, and every beast of theirs be ours?' Their daughters and their cattle were that which they sought to obtain; and their religion the stalking-horse they made use of to come to them. Read the whole story, Gen. xxxiv., 20–23.

"2. The hypocritical Pharisees were also of this religion; long prayers were their pretence; but to get widows' houses was their intent; and greater damnation was from God their judgment. Luke xx., 46, 47.

"3. Judas* the devil was also of this religion; he was religious for the bag, that he might be possessed of what was therein: but he was lost, cast away, and the very son of perdition.

"4. Simon the witch was of this religion too; for he would have had the Holy Ghost, that he might have got money therewith; and his sentence from Peter's mouth was according. Acts viii., 9–24.

---

* **Judas.** Matt. xxvi., 14, 15; xxvii, 3, 5. See John vi., 70; xii., 6.—**Witch,** same as wizard, in the old writers. "Our examination of the various notices of magic in the Bible gives this general result: They do not, so far as we can understand, once state positively that any but illusive results were produced by magical rites. They, therefore, afford no evidence that man can gain supernatural power to use at his will." Smith's *Dictionary of the Bible*, Art. *Magic.*

Propounded, proposed, suggested. Other synonymes? Has Bunyan used the best? Write out, etc.

"5. Neither will it go out of my mind, but that that man that takes up religion for the world, will throw away religion for the world. For, so surely as Judas resigned the world in becoming religious, so surely did he also sell religion and his Master for the same. To answer the question therefore affirmatively, as I perceive you have done; and to accept of, as authentic, such an answer, is both heathenish, hypocritical, and devilish; and your reward will be according to your works."

Then they stood staring one upon another; but had not wherewith to answer Christian. Hopeful also approved of the soundness of Christian's answer. So there was a great silence among them. Mr. By-ends and his company also staggered and kept behind, that Christian and Hopeful might outgo them. Then said Christian to his fellow: "If these men cannot stand before the sentence of men, what will they do with the sentence of God? and if they are mute when dealt with by vessels of clay, what will they do when they shall be rebuked by the flames of a devouring fire?"

Then Christian and Hopeful outwent them again; and went till they came to a delicate plain called Ease, where they went with much content. But that plain was but narrow; so they were quickly got over it. Now, at the farther side of that plain was a little hill called Lucre, and in that hill a silver mine, which some of them that had formerly gone that way, because of the rarity of it, had turned aside to see; but, going too near the brink of the pit, the ground, being deceitful under them, broke, and they were slain. Some also had been maimed there, and could not, to their dying day, be their own men again.

Then I saw in my dream, that a little off the road, over against the silver mine, stood Demas,* gentleman-like, to call passengers to come and see; who said to Christian and his fellow, "Ho! turn aside hither; I will show you a thing."

Christian. What thing is so deserving as to turn us out of the way?

Demas. Here is a silver mine, and some digging in it for treasure. If you will come, with a little pains you may richly provide for yourselves.

Hopeful. Let us go see.

Christian. "Not I," said Christian: "I have heard of this place before now, and how many have there been slain. And besides, that treasure is a snare to those that seek it; for it hindereth them in their pilgrimage."

* **Demas.** Paul had a companion by the name of Demas, who deserted the apostle through love of this world. See Philem. 24; Col. iv., 14; 2 Tim. iv., 10. The name is probably contracted from Demetrius or Demarchus.—**Let us go see.** See note on *Desire to go see*, p. 367.

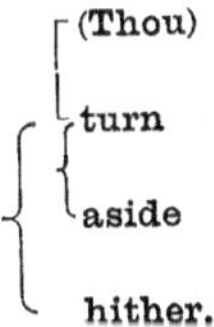

Hither is an adjunct of *place;* so is *aside.* Complete the analysis. Analyze, *In this meadow they lay.*

Then Christian called to Demas, saying, "Is not the place dangerous? hath it not hindered many in their pilgrimage?"

Demas. "Not very dangerous, except to those that are careless." But withal, he blushed as he spake.

Then said Christian to Hopeful, "Let us not stir a step, but still keep on our way."

Hopeful. I will warrant you, when By-ends comes up, if he hath the same invitation as we, he will turn in thither to see.

Christian. No doubt thereof, for his principles lead him that way; and a hundred to one but he dies there.

Then Demas called again, saying, "But will you not come over and see?"

Then Christian roundly answered, saying: "Demas, thou art an enemy to the right ways of the Lord of this way; and hast been already condemned for thine own turning aside, by one of his Majesty's justices; and why seekest thou to bring us into the like condemnation? Besides, if we at all turn aside, our Lord the King will certainly hear thereof, and will there put us to shame, where we would stand with boldness before him."

Demas cried again that he also was one of their fraternity; and that if they would tarry a little, he also himself would walk with them.

Then said Christian, "What is thy name? Is it not the same by which we have called thee?"

Demas. Yes, my name is Demas. I am the son of Abraham.

Christian. I know you. Gehazi was your great-grandfather, and Judas your father; and you have trod in their steps. It is but a devilish prank that thou usest. Thy father was hanged for a traitor; and thou deservest no better reward. Assure thyself, that when we come to the King we will tell him of this thy behavior.

Thus they went their way.

By this time By-ends and his companions were come again within sight; and they at the first beck went over to Demas. Now, whether they fell into the pit by looking over the brink thereof, or whether they went down to dig, or whether they were smothered in the bottom by the damps that commonly arise; of these things I am not certain: but this I observed, that they never were seen again in the way.

Then sang Christian:—

"By-ends and silver Demas both agree;
One calls, the other runs, that he may be
A sharer in his lucre. So these do
Take up in this world, and no farther go."

Now I saw, that, just on the other side of this plain, the pilgrims came

---

* **Gehazi.** 2 Kings iv.; v., 20–27. Gehazi, the servant of Elisha, fraudulently obtained money and garments from Naaman, was miraculously smitten with incurable leprosy, and was dismissed from the prophet's service. He is mentioned again in 2 Kings, viii., 4–6.

Reward, recompense, compensation, remuneration, pay, requital. Other synonymes? Write out, etc.

Thy father was hanged for a traitor. Analyze.

to a place where stood an old monument, hard by the highway side; at the sight of which they were both concerned, because of the strangeness of the form thereof; for it seemed to them as if it had been a woman transformed into the shape of a pillar. Here, therefore, they stood looking and looking upon it, but could not for a time tell what they should make thereof. At last, Hopeful espied, written upon the head thereof, a writing in an unusual hand. But he, being no scholar, called to Christian, for he was learned, to see if he could pick out the meaning. So he came, and, after a little laying of the letters together, he found the same to be this, "Remember Lot's Wife." * So he read it to his fellow; after which, they both concluded that that was the pillar of salt into which Lot's wife was turned, for looking back with a covetous heart, when she was going from Sodom for safety. Which sudden and amazing sight gave them occasion of the following discourse.

Christian. Ah, my brother! this is a seasonable sight. It came opportunely to us after the invitation which Demas gave us to come over to view the hill Lucre: and had we gone over, as he desired us, and as thou wast inclined to do, my brother, we had, for aught I know, been made, like this woman, a spectacle for those that shall come after, to behold.

Hopeful. I am sorry that I was so foolish, and am made to wonder that I am not now as Lot's wife. For wherein was the difference between her sin and mine? She only looked back, and I had a desire to go see. Let Grace be adored, and let me be ashamed that ever such a thing should be in mine heart!

Christian. Let us take notice of what we see here, for our help for time to come. This woman escaped one judgment; for she fell not by the destruction of Sodom: yet she was destroyed by another. As we see, she is turned into a pillar of salt.

Hopeful. True; and she may be to us both caution and example; caution, that we should shun her sin; or a sign of what judgment will overtake such as shall not be prevented by this caution. So Korah, Dathan, and Abiram, with the two hundred and fifty men that perished in their sin, did also become a sign or example to beware. But above all, I muse at one thing; to wit, how Demas and his fellows can stand so confidently yonder to look for that treasure, which this woman but for looking behind her after, for we read not that she stepped one foot out of the way, was turned into a pillar of salt; especially since the judgment which overtook her did make her an example, within sight of where they are. For they cannot choose but see her, did they but lift up their eyes.

---

* **Lot's wife.** Gen. xix., 26.—**Korah,** etc. Num. xxvi., 9, 10; xvi., 31, 32, 33. This passage about the "old monument," from "Now I saw," p. 366, to "I saw then that they went," p. 368, is not found in the earliest edition.—**Desire to go see.** In early English the infinitive ended in *-en.* When this *-en* fell into disuse, *to* was inserted as a sort of substitute; but it was never much used before *go* and *come.* See *Shakespearian Grammar*, 349.

Remember, recollect. Discriminate. See Smith's *Synonymes Discriminated.* Write out, etc.

His fellows can stand confidently. Analyze.

Christian. It is a thing to be wondered at, and it argueth that their hearts are grown desperate in the case; and I cannot tell who* to compare them to so fitly as to them that pick pockets in the presence of the judge, or that will cut purses under the gallows. It is said of the men of Sodom, "that they were sinners exceedingly," because they were sinners "before the Lord," that is, in his eye-sight, and notwithstanding the kindness he had showèd them: for the land of Sodom was now like the garden of Eden heretofore. This, therefore, provoked him the more to jealousy, and made their plagues as hot as the fire of the Lord out of heaven could make it. And it is most rationally to be concluded that such, even such as these are, that shall sin in the sight, yea, and that too in despite of such examples, that are set continually before them to caution them to the contrary, must be partakers of the severest judgment.

Hopeful. Doubtless thou hast said the truth: but what a mercy is it, that neither thou, but especially I, am not made myself this example! This ministereth occasion to us to thank God, to fear before him, and always to remember Lot's wife.

I saw then that they went on their way to a pleasant river; which David the king called the river of God; but John, the river of the water of life. Now their way lay just upon the bank of this river. Here, therefore, Christian and his companion walked with great delight: they drank also of the water of the river, which was pleasant and enlivening to their weary spirits. Besides, on the banks of this river, on either side, were green trees of all manner of fruit; and the leaves they did eat to prevent surfeits and other diseases that are incident to those that heat their blood by travels. On either side of the river was also a meadow, curiously beautiful with lilies; and it was green all the year long. In this meadow they lay down and slept: for here they might lie down safely. When they awoke, they gathered again of the fruit of the trees, and drank again of the water of the river, and then lay down again to sleep. Thus they did several days and nights. Then they sang,—

"Behold ye, how these crystal streams do glide,
To comfort pilgrims, by the highway side.
The meadows green, besides their fragrant smell,
Yield dainties for them: and he that can tell
What pleasant fruit, yea, leaves, these trees do yield
Will soon sell all, that he may buy this field."

* **Who,** *whom.* So, often in Shakespeare, the inflection of *who* is omitted. See *for who*, p. 165.—**Sodom.** Gen. xiii., 13.—**Eden.** Gen. xiii., 10.—**Neither thou, but especially I, am,** etc. Such a coupling of pronouns with the verb is awkward, though common in colloquial use. The verb *to be* should agree with the first, when its subjects are pronouns of different persons and of the singular number connected by *or* or *nor*. Reconstruct the sentence thus, "What a mercy is it that thou art not made this example, and, especially, that I am not!" Avoid such colloquialisms.—**River of God.** Ps. lxv., 9.—**River of the water of life.** Rev. xxii., 1. "This water of life is nothing else but the manifold grace of God in Christ; for both the words *water* and *life* are but metaphorical sayings, under which is held forth some better and more excellent thing. . . . From this water of life come all those heavenly and spiritual quickenings and revivings that do fetch again and cheer up the sinking soul."—Bunyan's *Holy City.* —**Green trees.** Ezek. xlvii., 12; Rev. xxii., 2.—**Lay down and slept.** Ps. xxiii., 2.—**Lie down safely.** Is. xiv., 30.

His companion walked with great delight. Analyze.

So when they were disposed to go on, for they were not as yet at their journey's end, they did eat and drink, and departed.

Now I beheld in my dream,* that they had not journeyed far, but the river and the way for a time parted; at which they were not a little sorry, yet they durst not go out of the way. Now, the way from the river was rough, and their feet tender by reason of their travels: so the souls of the pilgrims were much discouraged because of the way. Wherefore, still as they went on they wished for a better way. Now, a little before them, there was on the left hand of the road a meadow, and a stile to go over into it; and that meadow is called By-path Meadow. Then said Christian to his fellow, "If this meadow lieth along by our way-side, let us go over into it." Then he went to the stile to see; and behold, a path lay along by the way on the other side of the fence. "It is according to my wish," said Christian: "here is the easiest going; come, good Hopeful, and let us go over."

Hopeful. But how if this path should lead us out of the way?

Christian. That is not likely. Look, doth it not go along by the way-side?

So Hopeful, being persuaded by his fellow, went after him over the stile. When they were gone over, and were got into the path, they found it very easy for their feet; and withal, they, looking before them, espied a man walking as they did, and his name was Vain Confidence. So they called after him, and asked him whither that way led? He said, "To the celestial gate." "Look," said Christian, "did not I tell you so? By this you may see we are right." So they followed; and he went before them. But, behold, the night came on, and it grew very dark; so that they that were behind lost the sight of him that went before.

He therefore that went before, Vain Confidence by name, not seeing the way before him, fell into a deep pit, which was on purpose there made by the prince of those grounds, to catch vain-glorious fools withal; and was dashed in pieces with his fall.

Now Christian and his fellow heard him fall. So they called to know the matter; but there was none to answer; only they heard a groaning. Then said Hopeful, "Where are we now?" Then was his fellow silent, as mistrusting that he had led him out of the way. And now it began to rain and thunder and lighten in a most dreadful manner; and the waters rose amain.

Then Hopeful groaned in himself, saying, "Oh, that I had kept on my way!"

Christian. Who would have thought that this path should have led us out of the way?

---

* **I beheld in my dream,** etc.

> "Wouldst thou be in a dream, and yet not sleep?
> Or wouldst thou in a moment laugh and weep?
> Wouldst read thyself, and read thou knowest not what,
> And yet know whether thou art blest or not,
> By reading the same lines? O, then, come hither,
> And lay my book, thy head, and heart together."—Bunyan's *Apology*.

—**Discouraged.** Num. xxi., 4.

Discouraged, disheartened, dispirited, dejected. Write out, etc. Has Bunyan chosen the best?

Hopeful. I was afraid of it at the very first; and therefore gave you that gentle caution. I would have spoke plainer, but that you are older than I.

Christian. Good brother, be not offended; I am sorry I have brought thee out of the way, and that I have put thee into such imminent danger. Pray, my brother, forgive me; I did not do it of an evil intent.

Hopeful. Be comforted, my brother, for I forgive thee; and believe too, that this shall be for our good.

Christian. I am glad I have met with a merciful brother. But we must not stand thus; let us try and go back again.

Hopeful. But, good brother, let me go before.

Christian. No; if you please, let me go first, that, if there be any danger, I may be first therein, because by my means we are both gone out of the way.

Hopeful. No, you shall not go first; for your mind, being troubled, may lead you out of the way again.

Then, for their encouragement, they heard the voice of one saying, "Let thine heart be towards the highway;* even the way that thou wentest: turn again."

But by this time the waters were greatly risen; by reason of which the way of going back was very dangerous. Then I thought that it is easier going out of the way when we are in, than going in when we are out. Yet they adventured to go back; but it was so dark, and the flood so high, that in their going back they had like to have been drowned nine or ten times.

Neither could they, with all the skill they had, get again to the stile that night. Wherefore, at last lighting under a little shelter, they sat down there till the day-break: but being weary, they fell asleep. Now there was not far from the place where they lay a castle, called Doubting Castle, the owner whereof was Giant Despair; and it was in his grounds they now were sleeping. Wherefore he, getting up in the morning early, and walking up and down in his fields, caught Christian and Hopeful asleep in his grounds.

* **The highway.** Jer. xxxi., 21.—**The going back was very dangerous.** "Indeed I have found it as difficult to come to God by prayer, after backsliding from him, as to do any other thing. O the shame that did now attend me! especially when I thought I am now going to pray to Him for mercy that I had so lightly esteemed but a while before." Bunyan's *Grace Abounding.*—**They had like.** This use of *like* is colloquial. It is explained in Webster's *Dictionary* as equivalent to *come near to, escaped with difficulty; like* being regarded as an intransitive verb.

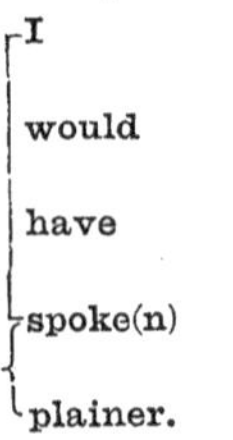

Plainer is an adjunct of *manner*. Complete the Analysis.

Analyze *The waters were risen greatly*. *Greatly* is an adjunct of *degree*.

Then with a grim and surly voice, he bade them awake, and asked them whence they were, and what they did in his grounds. They told him they were pilgrims, and that they had lost their way. Then said the giant, "You have this night trespassed on me by trampling and lying on my ground; and therefore you must go along with me." So they were forced to go, because he was stronger than they. They also had but little to say, for they knew themselves in a fault.

The giant therefore drove them before him and put them into his castle, into a very dark dungeon, nasty and stinking to the spirits of these two men. Here then they lay from Wednesday morning till Saturday night, without one bit of bread, or drop of drink, or light, or any to ask how they did. They were therefore here in evil case, and were far from friends* and acquaintance. Now, in this place, Christian had double sorrow, because it was through his unadvised counsel that they were brought into this distress.

Now, Giant Despair had a wife, and her name was Diffidence. So when he was gone to bed, he told his wife what he had done; to wit, that he had taken a couple of prisoners, and cast them into his dungeon for trespassing on his grounds. Then he asked her, also, what he had best to do further to them? So she asked him what they were, whence they came, and whither they were bound? and he told her. Then she counselled him, that when he arose in the morning he should beat them without mercy. So when he arose, he getteth him a grievous crab-tree cudgel, and goes down into the dungeon to them, and there first falls to rating of them as if they were dogs, although they gave him never a word of distaste. Then he falls upon them, and beats them fearfully, in such sort that they were not able to help themselves, or turn them upon the floor. This done, he withdraws, and leaves them there to condole their misery and to mourn under their distress. So all that day they spent their time in nothing but sighs and bitter lamentations. The next night she talked with her husband about them further; and understanding that they were yet alive, did advise him to counsel them to make away with themselves. So when morning was come, he goes to them in a surly manner, as before, and perceiving them to be very sore with the stripes that he hath given them the day before, he told them, that since they were never like to come out of that place, their only way would be forthwith to make an end of themselves, either with knife, halter, or poison. "For why," said he, "should you choose life, seeing it is attended with so much bitterness?" But they desired him to let them go. With which he looked ugly upon them, and, rushing to

* **Far from friends.** Ps. lxxxviii., 18.—**Giant Despair had a wife.** This whole account of Giant Despair's wife to, "Well, on Saturday, about midnight," p. 374, is not found in the earliest edition.—**Beats them fearfully.** In the edition of 1682 this passage is illustrated by a most grotesque cut, showing Giant Despair's castle, the two pilgrims behind a grated window, and a hideous giant with a big club. Under the picture are the words,—

"The Pilgrims now, to gratifie the Flesh,
Will seek its ease: but, Oh! how they afresh
Do thereby plunge themselves new griefs into!
Who seek to please the Flesh, themselves undo."

Diffidence, modesty, bashfulness, timidity. Write out, etc.

them, had doubtless made an end of them himself, but that he fell into one of his fits; for he sometimes, in sunshiny weather, fell into fits, and lost for a time the use of his hand. Wherefore he withdrew and left them as before, to consider what to do. Then did the prisoners consult between themselves, whether it was best to take his counsel or no. And thus they began to discourse:

"Brother," said Christian, "what shall we do? The life that we now live is miserable! For my part, I know not whether it is best to live thus, or to die out of hand. My soul chooseth strangling,* and death rather than life, and the grave is more easy for me than this dungeon! Shall we be ruled by the giant?"

Hopeful. Indeed our present condition is dreadful; and death would be far more welcome to me, than thus forever to abide. But let us consider, the Lord of the country to which we are going, hath said, "Thou shalt do no murder;" no, not to another man's person. Much more then are we forbidden to take his counsel to kill ourselves. Besides, he that kills another, can but commit murder upon his body; but for one to kill himself is to kill body and soul at once. And moreover, my brother, thou talkest of ease in the grave; but hast thou forgotten the hell; whither, for certain, the murderers go? For, "No murderer hath eternal life," etc. And let us consider again, that all the law is not in the hand of the Giant Despair: others, so far as I can understand, have been taken by him, as well as we; and yet have escaped out of his hands. Who knows but that God, who made the world, may cause that Giant Despair may die, or that, at some time or other, he may forget to lock us in; or that he may, in a short time, have another of his fits before us, and may lose the use of his limbs? And if ever that should come to pass again, for my part I am resolved to pluck up the heart of a man, and to try my utmost to get from under his hand. I was a fool that I did not try to do it before; but, however, my brother, let us be patient and endure awhile. The time may come that may give us a happy release. But let us not be our own murderers.

With these words, Hopeful at present did moderate the mind of his brother; so they continued together in the dark that day in their sad and doleful condition.

Well, towards evening the giant goes down into the dungeon again, to see if his prisoners had taken his counsel. But when he came there, he found them alive; and, truly, alive was all; for now, what for want of bread and water, and by reason of the wounds they received when he beat them, they could do little but breathe. But, I say, he found them alive; at which he fell into a grievous rage, and told them, that, seeing that they had dis-

* **Strangling.** Job vii., 15.—**Have another of his fits.** The "sunshiny weather, in which the giant had "fits," represents seasons of hope in the midst of gloom. Thus Bunyan says of his own experience in the midst of depressing doubts, "I had some supports in this temptation; but they were but hints, touches, and short visits, though very sweet when present. Only they lasted not, but, like to Peter's sheet, of a sudden were caught up from me to heaven again."—**Hopeful did moderate,** etc. The student will do well to note carefully Bunyan's skill in drawing characters.

Strangling, choking. Other synonymes? Discriminate, etc.

obeyed his counsel, it should be worse with them than if they had never been born.

At this they trembled greatly; and I think that Christian fell into a swoon. But, coming a little to himself again, they renewed their discourse about the giant's counsel, and whether yet they had best take it or no. Now Christian again seemed to be for doing it; but Hopeful made his second reply as followeth:—

Hopeful. My brother, rememberest thou not how valiant thou hast been heretofore? Apollyon could not crush thee; nor could all that thou didst hear, or see, or feel, in the Valley of the Shadow of Death. What hardships, terror, and amazement hast thou already gone through! and art thou now nothing but fear? Thou seest that I am in the dungeon with thee; a far weaker man by nature than thou art; also this giant has wounded me as well as thee, and has also cut off the bread and water from my mouth; and, with thee, I mourn without the light. But let us exercise a little more patience: remember how thou playedst the man at Vanity Fair, and wast neither afraid of the chain nor cage, nor yet of bloody death. Wherefore let us, at least to avoid the shame that becomes not a Christian to be found in, bear up with patience as well as we can.

Now night being come again, and the giant and his wife being in bed, she asked him concerning the prisoners, and if they had taken his counsel. To which he replied, "They are sturdy rogues: they choose rather to bear all hardships, than to make away with themselves." Then said she, "Take them into the castle-yard to-morrow, and show them the bones and skulls of those that thou hast already despatched; and make them believe, ere a week comes to an end thou wilt also tear them in pieces as thou hast done their fellows before them."

So when the morning was come, the giant goes to them again, and takes them into the castle-yard, and shows them as his wife had bidden him. "These," said he, "were pilgrims, as you are, once; and they trespassed in my grounds, as you have done; and when I thought fit, I tore them in pieces; and so within ten days I will do you.* Go, get you down to your den again." And with that he beat them all the way thither.

They lay therefore all day on Saturday in lamentable case, as before. Now when night was come, and Mrs. Diffidence and her husband, the giant were gone to bed, they began to renew their discourse of their prisoners; and withal, the old giant wondered that he could neither by his blows nor counsel bring them to an end. And with that his wife replied: "I fear," said she, "that they live in hopes that some will come to relieve them, or that they have picklocks about them, by the means of which they hope to

---

* **And so within ten days I will do you.** "Then hath the tempter come upon me with such discouragements as these: 'You are very hot after mercy, but I will cool you; this frame shall not last always; many have been as hot as you for a spirt, but I have quenched their zeal.' And with this, such and such who were fallen off would be set before mine eyes. Then I would be afraid that I should do so too!" Bunyan's *Grace Abounding*.

Crush, break, overwhelm, destroy, annihilate. Write out, etc.
They lay all day on Saturday in lamentable case. Analyze.

escape." "And sayest thou so, my dear?" said the giant, "I will therefore search them in the morning."

Well, on Saturday, about midnight, they began to pray; and continued in prayer till almost break of day.*

Now, a little before it was day, good Christian, as one half amazed, brake out in this passionate speech: "What a fool," quoth he, "am I, thus to lie in a stinking dungeon, when I may as well walk at liberty! I have a key in my bosom, called Promise, that will, I am persuaded, open any lock in Doubting Castle." Then said Hopeful, "That is good news, good brother; pluck it out of thy bosom, and try."

Then Christian pulled it out of his bosom, and began to try at the dungeon door; whose bolt, as he turned the key, gave back, and the door flew open with ease; and Christian and Hopeful both came out. Then he went to the outward door that leads into the castle-yard, and with this key opened that door also. After, he went to the iron-gate, for that must be opened too; but that lock went very hard: yet the key did open it. Then they thrust open the door to make their escape with speed; but that gate, as it opened, made such a creaking that it waked Giant Despair; who, hastily rising to pursue his prisoners, felt his limbs to fail; for his fits took him again, so that he could by no means go after them. Then they went on, and came to the king's highway, and so were safe, because they were out of the giant's jurisdiction.

Now, when they were gone over the stile, they began to contrive with themselves, what they should do at the stile, to prevent those that should come after from falling into the hand of Giant Despair. So they consented to erect there a pillar, and to engrave upon the stile thereof this sentence: "Over this stile is the way to Doubting Castle; which is kept by Giant Despair; who despiseth the King of the Celestial Country, and seeks to destroy his Holy Pilgrims." Many, therefore, that followed after, read what was written, and escaped the danger. This done, they sang as follows:—

" Out of the way we went, and then we found
What 'twas to tread upon forbidden ground.
And let them that come after have a care,
Lest they, for trespassing, his prisoners are,
Whose castle's Doubting, and whose name's Despair."

---

* **Continued in prayer till almost break of day.** "Prayer wrestleth with the devil, and will overthrow him; prayer wrestleth with God, and will overcome him; prayer wrestleth with all temptations, and makes them fly. Great things have been done by prayer, even by the prayer of those that have contracted guilt, and by their sins lost the smiles and sense of the favor of God. Therefore, when this needy, this evil time has overtaken thee, *pray!* Ply it hard!" Bunyan's *Saint's Privilege.*

I will therefore search them.

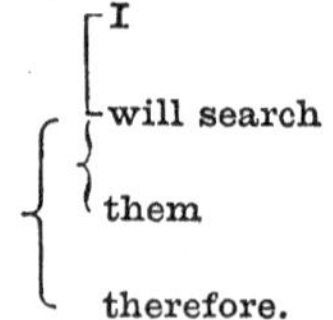

Therefore is an adjunct of *cause.*

They went then till they came to the Delectable Mountains; which mountains belong to the Lord of that hill of which we have spoken before. So they went up to the mountains,* to behold the gardens and orchards, the vineyards and fountains of water; where also they drank and washed themselves, and did freely eat of the vineyards. Now there were on the tops of those mountains shepherds feeding their flocks; and they stood by the highway side. The pilgrims therefore went to them, and leaning upon their staffs, as is common with weary pilgrims, when they stand to talk with any by the way, they asked, "Whose delectable mountains are these? and whose be the sheep that feed upon them?"

Shepherds. These mountains are Emanuel's Land: and they are within sight of his city; and the sheep also are his, and He laid down his life for them.

Christian. Is this the way to the Celestial City?

Shepherds. You are just in the way.

Christian. How far is it thither?

Shepherds. Too far for any but those that shall get thither indeed.

Christian. Is the way safe or dangerous?

Shepherds. Safe for those for whom it is to be safe; "But transgressors shall fall therein."

Christian. Is there in this place any relief for pilgrims, that are weary and faint in the way?

Shepherds. The Lord of these mountains hath given us a charge "not to be forgetful to entertain strangers." Therefore the good of the place is before you.

I also saw in my dream, that when the shepherds perceived they were wayfaring men, they also put questions to them, to which they made answer as in other places; as, "Whence came you?" and, "How got you into the way?" and, "By what means have you so persevered therein? for, but few of them that begin to come hither, do show their faces at these mountains." But when the shepherds heard their answers; being pleased therewith, they looked very lovingly upon them, and said, "Welcome to the Delectable Mountains!"

The shepherds, I say, whose names were *Knowledge*, *Experience*, *Watchful*, and *Sincere*, took them by the hand, and had them to their tents, and made them partake of that which was ready at present. They said, moreover, "We would that you should stay here awhile, to be acquainted with us; and yet more to solace yourselves with the good of the Delectable Mountains." Then they told them, that they were content to stay; so they went to their rest that night, because it was very late.

Then I saw in my dream, that in the morning the shepherds called up

---

* **So they went up to the mountains,** etc. See this passage quoted in the sketch of Bunyan's Life, p. 288. In this delightful transition from the gloom and terror of Doubting Castle to the soft splendor and joy of the Delectable Mountains, Bunyan has unwittingly displayed consummate art. "It is as ordinary as for the light to shine, for God to make black and dismal dispensations to usher in bright and pleasing; yea, and the more frightful that is which goes before, the more comfortable is that which follows after." Bunyan's *Antichrist and its Ruin.*—**Shall fall therein.** Hos. xiv., 9.—**Entertain strangers.** Heb. xiii., 2.

The shepherds took them by the hand. Analyze.

Christian and Hopeful to walk with them upon the mountain.* So they went forth with them and walked awhile, having a pleasant prospect on every side. Then said the shepherds one to another, "Shall we show these pilgrims some wonders?" So, when they had concluded to do it, they had them first to the top of a hill, called *Error;* which was very steep on the farthest side; and bade them look down to the bottom. So Christian and Hopeful looked down, and saw, at the bottom several men dashed all to pieces by a fall that they had from the top. Then said Christian, "What meaneth this?" The shepherds answered, "Have you not heard of them that were made to err, by hearkening to Hymeneus and Philetus; as concerning the faith of the resurrection of the body?" They answered, "Yes." Then said the shepherds, "Those that you see dashed in pieces at the bottom of this mountain, are they: and they have continued to this day unburied, as you see, for an example for others to take heed how they clamber too high, or how they come too near to the brink of this mountain.'

Then I saw, that they had them to the top of another mountain; and the name of this is Caution; and bade them look afar off. Which when they did, they perceived, as they thought, several men, walking up and down among the tombs that were there: and they perceived that the men were blind; because they stumbled sometimes upon the tombs, and because they could not get out from among them. Then said Christian, "What means this?"

The shepherds then answered: "Did you not see a little below these mountains a stile that led into a meadow, on the left-hand of this way?" They answered, "Yes." Then said the shepherds, "From the stile there goes a path that leads directly to Doubting Castle, which is kept by Giant Despair; and these men (pointing to them among the tombs) came once on pilgrimage, as you do now, even till they came to that same stile. And because the right way was rough in that place, they chose to go out of it into that meadow; and there were taken by Giant Despair, and cast into Doubting Castle; where, after they had been a while kept in a dungeon, he at last did put out their eyes, and led them among those tombs, where he has left them to wander to this very day, that the saying of the wise man might be fulfilled, "He that wandereth out of the way of understanding shall remain in the congregation of the dead." Then Christian and Hopeful looked upon one another with tears gushing out, but yet said nothing to the shepherds.

Then I saw in my dream, that the shepherds had them to another place

---

* **To walk with them upon the mountain.** In the old editions, thirteen of which were published prior to 1693, there were fourteen rude wood-cuts, and under each were four lines of rhyme. Under the one representing the shepherds entertaining the pilgrims on the Delectable Mountains were the following:—

" Mountains Delectable they now ascend,
Where shepherds be, which to them do commend
Alluring things, and things that cautions are.
Pilgrims are steady kept by faith and fear."

Hymeneus, etc. 2 Tim. ii., 17, 18.—**Saying of the wise man.** Prov. xxi., 16.

Analyze, *They have continued unburied, for an example.* The last three words introduce a *purpose* or *end* (what is termed the *final cause*).

Analyze, *They come too near.* *Too* denotes *degree.*

in a bottom, where was a door in the side of a hill: and they opened the door, and bade them look in. They looked in therefore, and saw that; within, it was very dark and smoky; they also thought that they heard there a rumbling noise, as of fire; and a cry of some tormented; and that they smelt the scent of brimstone. Then said Christian, "What means this?" The shepherds told him, "This is a by-way to hell; a way that hypocrites go in at; namely, such as sell their birth-right, with Esau; such as sell their master, with Judas; such as blaspheme the gospel, with Alexander; and that lie and dissemble, with Ananias and Sapphira his wife."

Then said Hopeful to the shepherds, "I perceive that these had on them, even every one, a show of pilgrimage, as we have now. Had they not?"

Shepherds. Yes; and held it a long time too.

Hopeful. How far might they go on pilgrimage in their days; since they, notwithstanding, were thus miserably cast away?

Shepherds. Some farther, and some not so far as these mountains.

Then said the pilgrims one to another, "We have need to cry to the strong for strength."

Shepherds. Ay, and you will have need to use it, when you have it, too.

By this time the pilgrims had a desire to go forwards, and the shepherds a desire they should. So they walked together towards the end of the mountains. Then said the shepherds one to another, "Let us here show the pilgrims the gates to the Celestial City, if they have skill to look through our perspective glass." * The pilgrims then lovingly accepted the motion. So they had them to the top of a high hill called Clear, and gave them the glass to look through.

Then they tried to look; but the remembrance of the last things that the Shepherds had showed them made their hands shake; by means of which impediment they could not look steadily through the glass. Yet they thought they saw something like the gate, and also some of the glory of the place. Then they went away, and sang,—

* **Perspective glass.** Just about the time that Bunyan was writing this, or a little earlier, Milton was composing the famous lines in which he calls the telescope of Galileo an "*optic glass.*"

. . . . . "The moon, whose orb
Through optic glass the Tuscan artist views,
At evening, from the top of Fesolé."—*Par. Lost*, I., 288.

Perceive, discern, distinguish, see, recognize, comprehend, observe, understand. Write out, etc.

They went and sang. Here are two sentences in one, a compound sentence. The two are co-ordinate, or mutually independent, though connected. The sentence is a *Co-ordinate Compound Sentence* (Co. Com. Sent.)

Two or more subjects or predicates are essential to the compound sentence, whereas the simple sentence has but one of each.

Co-ordinate	**They**	
	went	
Compound	**and**	**Connective.**
	(they)	
Sentence.	**sang.**	

Complete the analysis.

"Thus by the Shepherds, secrets are revealed,
Which from all other men are kept concealed.
Come to the Shepherds then, if you would see
Things deep, things hid, and that mysterious be."

When they were about to depart, one of the shepherds gave them a note of the way. Another of them bade them beware of the Flatterer. The third bade them take heed that they stepped not upon the enchanted ground. And the fourth bade them God-speed! So I awoke from my dream.

And I slept, and dreamed again, and saw the same two pilgrims going down the mountains along the highway towards the City. Now, a little below these mountains, on the left hand, lieth the country of Conceit; from which country there comes into the way in which the pilgrims walked, a little crooked lane. Here, therefore, they met with a very brisk lad, that came out of that country; and his name was Ignorance. So Christian asked him from what parts he came, and whither he was going?

Ignorance. Sir, I was born in the country that lieth off there on the left hand, and am going to the Celestial City.

Christian. But how do you think to get in the gate? for you may find some difficulty there.

Ignorance. As other people do.

Christian. But what have you to show at that gate, that the gate should be opened to you?

Ignorance. I know my Lord's will, and have been a good liver. I pay every man his own. I pray, fast, pay tithes, and give alms, and have left my country for whither I am going.

Christian. But thou camest not in at the Wicket-gate that is at the head of this way. Thou camest in hither through that same crooked lane; and therefore, I fear, however thou mayest think of thyself, when the reckoning-day shall come, thou shalt have laid to thy charge that thou art "a thief and a robber," instead of getting admittance into the city.

Ignorance. Gentlemen, ye be utter strangers to me. I know you not. Be content to follow the religion of your country, and I will follow the religion of mine.* I hope all will be well. And as for the gate that you talk of, all the world knows that this is a great way off our country. I cannot think that any men in all our parts do so much as know the way to it; nor need they matter whether they did or no, since we have, as ye see, a fine pleasant green lane, that comes down from our country, the next way into it.

When Christian saw that the man was wise in his own conceit, he said to Hopeful whisperingly, "There is more hope of a fool than of him;"

---

* **I will follow the religion of mine.** "There is the wilfully ignorant professor, or him [he] who is afraid to know more through fear of the cross. When he is at any time overtaken by arguments or awakenings of conscience, he uses to heal all by 'I was not brought up in this faith'; as if it were unlawful for Christians to know more than hath been taught them at first. There are many scriptures that lie against this man, as the mouths of great guns." Bunyan's *Strait Gate*.—**More hope of a fool.** Prov. xxvi., 12.

Reveal, divulge, unveil, make known, publish, disclose, discover. Other synonymes? Write out, etc.

Analyze *I slept and dreamed.*

and said moreover, "When he that is a fool walketh by the way, his wisdom faileth him, and he saith to every one that he is a fool.* What, shall we talk further with him, or outgo him at present; and so leave him to think of what he had heard already, and then stop again for him afterwards, and see if, by degrees, we can do any good of him?"

Then said Hopeful:—

"Let Ignorance a little while now muse
On what is said; and let him not refuse
Good counsel to embrace, lest he remain
Still ignorant of what's the chiefest gain.
God saith, those that no understanding have,
Although he made them, them he will not save."

He farther added, "It is not good, I think, to say to him all at once; let us pass him by, if you will, and talk to him anon, even as he is able to bear it."

So they both went on, and Ignorance—he came after. Now, when they had passed him a little way, they entered into a very dark lane, where they met a man whom seven devils had bound with seven strong cords, and were carrying of him back to the door that they saw on the side of the hill. Now good Christian began to tremble, and so did Hopeful, his companion; yet, as the devils led away the man, Christian looked to see if he knew him; and he thought it might be one Turnaway, that dwelt in the town of Apostasy. But he did not perfectly see his face; for he did hang his head like a thief that is found. But being gone past, Hopeful looked after him, and espied on his back a paper, with this inscription, "Wanton Professor and Damnable Apostate."

Then said Christian to his fellow: "Now I call to remembrance that which was told me of a thing that happened to a good man hereabout. The name of the man was Little-faith; but a good man, and he dwelt in the town of Sincere. The thing was this: at the entering in at this passage, there comes down from Broadway Gate a lane called Dead Man's Lane; so called because of the murders that are commonly done there. And this Little-faith, going on pilgrimage as we do now, chanced to sit down there, and slept. Now there happened at that time to come down the lane from Broadway Gate, three sturdy rogues, and their names were Faint-heart, Mistrust, and Guilt, three brothers; and they, espying Little-faith, where he was, came galloping up with speed. Now the good man was just awakened from his sleep, and was getting up to go on his journey. So they came up all to him, and with threatening language bade him stand. At this Little-faith looked as white as a clout, and had neither power to fight nor fly. Then said Faint-heart, 'Deliver thy purse;' but he making no haste to do it, for he was loth to lose his money, Mistrust ran up to him, thrusting his hand

* **He is a fool.** Eccles. x., 3.—**Seven devils.** Matt. xii., 45.—**Cords.** Prov. v., 22—**Wanton professor and damnable apostate.** "If Judas the traitor, or Francis Spira the backslider, were but now alive in this world, to whisper these men in the ear a little, and tell them what it hath cost *their* souls for backsliding, surely it would stick by them and make them afraid of running back again, so long as they had one day to live in this world." Bunyan's *Strait Gate.*

into his pocket, and pulled out thence a bag of silver. Then he cried out, 'Thieves! Thieves!' With that Guilt, with a great club that was in his hand, struck Little-faith on the head, and with that blow felled him flat to the ground; where he lay bleeding as one that would bleed to death. All this while, the thieves stood by. But at last, they hearing that some were upon the road, and fearing lest it should be one *Great-grace*, that dwells in the city of Good-Confidence, they betook themselves to their heels and left this good man to shift for himself. Now, after a while, Little-faith came to himself, and, getting up, made a shift to scrabble on his way. This was the story."

Hopeful. But did they take from him all that ever he had?

Christian. No: the place where his jewels were, they never ransacked: so those he kept still. But, as I was told, the good man was much afflicted for his loss; for the thieves got most of his spending-money. That which they got not, as I said, were jewels; also, he had a little odd money left, but scarce enough * to bring him to his journey's end. Nay, if I was not misinformed, he was forced to beg as he went, to keep himself alive; for his jewels he might not sell. But beg and do what he could, he went, as we say, with many a hungry belly the most part of the rest of the way.

Hopeful. But is it not a wonder they got not from him his certificate, by which he was to receive his admittance at the Celestial Gate?

Christian. It is a wonder. But they got not that; though they missed it not through any good cunning of his. For he, being dismayed with their coming upon him, had neither power nor skill to hide anything. So it was more by good Providence than by his endeavor, that they missed that good thing.

Hopeful. But it must needs be a comfort to him, that they got not his jewels from him.

Christian. It might have been great comfort to him, had he used it as he should. But they that told me the story, said that he had made but little use of it all the rest of the way; and that because of the dismay that he had in the taking away his money. Indeed he forgot it a great part of the rest of his journey; and besides, when at any time it came into his mind, and he began to be comforted therewith, then would fresh thoughts of his loss come again upon him, and those thoughts would swallow up all.

Hopeful. Alas, poor man! this could not but be a great grief to him!

Christian. Grief! ay, a grief indeed! Would it not have been so to any of us, had we been used as he? to be robbed and wounded too, and that in a strange place, as he was? It is a wonder he did not die with grief, poor heart! I was told that he scattered almost all the rest of the way with

---

* **Scarce enough,** etc. 1 Pet. iv., 18.—**A hungry belly the most part of the rest of the way.** "Little-faith is a type of those feeble and sickly, yet sincere professors, who, giving way to spiritual sloth and remissness in Christian duties, become weary and faint." *Wickens.* "If they had but the grace to add to their faith, virtue, etc., they might have more peace, live better lives, and not have their heads so often *in a bag.*" Bunyan's *Strait Gate.*—**Must needs.** See *needs* in Index.

He had neither power nor skill. Analyze.

nothing but doleful and bitter complaints; telling also to all that overtook him, or that he overtook in the way as he went, where he was robbed and how; who they were that did it, and what he lost; how he was wounded; and that he hardly escaped with his life.

Hopeful. But it is a wonder that his necessity did not put him upon selling or pawning some of his jewels, that he might have wherewithal to relieve himself in his journey.

Christian. Thou talkest like one upon whose head is the shell* to this very day. For what should he pawn them ? or to whom should he sell them ? In all that country where he was robbed, his jewels were not accounted of; nor did he want that relief which could from thence be administered to him. Besides, had his jewels been missing at the gate of the Celestial City, he had, and that he knew well enough, been excluded from an inheritance there; and that would have been worse to him than the appearance and villany of ten thousand thieves.

Hopeful. Why art thou so tart, my brother ? Esau sold his birth-right, and that for a mess of pottage, and that birth-right was his greatest jewel; and if he, why might not Little-faith do so too ?

Christian. Esau did sell his birth-right indeed, and so do many besides; and by so doing, exclude themselves from the chief blessings, as also that caitiff did. But you must put a difference betwixt Esau and Little-faith, and also betwixt their estates. Esau's birth-right was typical; but Little-faith's jewels were not so. Esau's belly was his god; but Little-faith's belly was not so. Esau's want lay in his fleshly appetite; Little-faith's did not so. Besides, Esau could see no farther than to the fulfilling of his lusts. "For I am at the point to die," said he; "and what good will this birth-right do me ?" But Little-faith, though it was his lot to have but a little faith, was by his little faith kept from such extravagances and made to see and prize his jewels more than to sell them, as Esau did his birth-right. You read not anywhere that Esau had faith, no, not so much as a little. Therefore no marvel, if, where the flesh only bears sway, as it will in that man where no faith is to resist, he sells his birth-right and his soul and all, and that to the devil of hell; for it is with such as it is with the ass, who in her occasions cannot be turned away. When their minds are set upon their lusts, they will have them, whatever they cost. But Little-faith was of another temper; his mind was on things divine; his livelihood was upon things that were spiritual, and from above. Therefore, to what end should he that is of such a temper, sell his jewels, had there been any that would have bought them, to fill his mind with empty things ? Will a man give a penny to fill his

---

* **Head is the shell.** See next page.—**Esau.** "Esau was a thorough *Bedawy*, a 'son of the desert,' who delighted to roam free as the wind of heaven, and who was impatient of the restraints of civilized or settled life." Esau was reckless; Jacob was selfish, grasping. Jacob takes a mean advantage of his brother's distress to rob him of that which was as dear as life itself to an eastern patriarch. See Smith's *Bible Dictionary*.—**Pottage.** Heb. xii., 16.—**What good will this,** etc. Gen. xxv., 32.—**Who in her occasions.** This use of *who* to represent animals is not uncommon in the old writers.—**Cannot be turned.** Jer. ii., 24.

Villany, knavery, rascality, scoundrelism, depravity, atrocity, roguery. Write out, etc.

belly with hay ? or can you persuade the turtle-dove to live upon carrion like the crow ? Though faithless ones can, for carnal lusts, pawn or mortgage, or sell what they have, and themselves outright to boot;* yet they that have faith, saving faith, though but a little of it, cannot do so. Here, therefore, my brother, is thy mistake.

Hopeful. I acknowledge it; but yet your severe reflection had almost made me angry.

Christian. What! I did but compare thee to some of the birds that are of the brisker sort, who will run to and fro in untrodden paths, with the shell upon their heads. But pass by that and consider the matter under debate, and all shall be well betwixt thee and me.

Hopeful. But, Christian, these three fellows, I am persuaded in my heart, are but a company of cowards. Would they have run else, think you, as they did, at the noise of one that was coming on the road ? Why did not Little-faith pluck up a greater heart ? He might, methinks, have stood one brush with them, and have yielded when there had been no remedy.

Christian. That they are cowards, many have said; but few have found it so in the time of trial. As for a great heart, Little-faith had none; and I perceive by thee, my brother, hadst thou been the man concerned, thou art but for a brush and then to yield. And verily, since this is the height of thy stomach, now they are at a distance from us, should they appear to thee, as they did to him, they might put thee to second thoughts.

But consider again, they are but journeymen thieves; they serve under the king of the bottomless pit; who, if needs be, will come in to their aid himself, and his voice is "as the roaring of a lion." I myself have been engaged as this Little-faith was, and I found it a terrible thing. These three villains set upon me; and I beginning like a Christian to resist, they gave but a call, and in came their master. I would, as the saying is, have given my life for a penny; but that, as God would have it, I was clothed with armor of proof. Ay, and yet, though I was so harnessed, I found it hard work to quit myself like a man. No man can tell what in that combat attends us, but he that hath been in battle himself.

Hopeful. Well, but they ran, you see, when they did but suppose that one Great-grace was in the way.

Christian. True, they have often fled, both they and their master, when Great-grace hath but appeared: and no marvel; for he is the King's champion. But, I trow, you will put some difference between Little-faith and the King's champion. All the King's subjects are not his champions; nor can

* **To boot.** See *boot*, Index.—**The height of thy stomach.** Stomach is used for courage by the old writers. Thus in Shakespeare's *Henry V.*,

> "Rather proclaim it, Westmoreland, through my host,
> That he which hath no *stomach* to this fight
> Let him depart."

—**Armor of proof.** See *proof*, p. 112.

Acknowledge, confess, own, avow, admit, concede, allow. Write out, etc.

They serve under the king of the bottomless pit. Analyze.

they, when tried, do such feats of war as he. Is it meet to think that a little child should handle Goliah * as David did ? or, that there should be the strength of an ox in a wren ? Some are strong, some are weak; some have great faith, some have little; this man was one of the weak, and therefore he went to the wall.

Hopeful. I would it had been Great-grace, for their sakes!

Christian. If it had been he, he might have had his hands full. For I must tell you, that though Great-grace is excellent good at his weapons, and has, and can, so long as he keeps them at the sword's point, do well enough with them; yet if they get within him, even Faint-heart, Mistrust, or the other, it will go hard, but they will throw up his heels. And when a man is down, you know, what can he do ?

Whoso looks well upon Great-grace's face, shall see those scars and cuts there that shall easily give demonstration of what I say. Yea, once I heard that he should say, and that when he was in the heat of combat, "We despaired even of life." How did these sturdy rogues, and their fellows, make David groan, mourn, and roar ? Yea, Heman and Hezekiah too, though champions in their days, yet were forced to bestir them, when by these assaulted; and yet, notwithstanding, they had their coats soundly brushed by them. Peter, upon a time, would go try what he could do; but though some do say of him, that he is the prince of the Apostles, they handled him so that they made him at last afraid of a sorry girl.

Besides, their king is at their whistle; and is never out of hearing; and if at any time they be put to the worst, he, if possible, comes in to help them. And of him it is said, "The sword of him that layeth at him cannot hold; the spear, the dart, nor the habergeon: he esteemeth iron as straw, and brass as rotten wood. The arrows cannot make him fly, sling-stones are turned, with him, into stubble; darts are counted as stubble; he laugheth at the shaking of a spear." What can a man do in this case ? It is true, if a man could at every turn have Job's horse, and had skill and courage to ride him, he might do notable things: "For his neck is clothed with thunder: he will not be afraid of the grasshopper; the glory of his nostrils is terrible; he paweth in the valley, rejoiceth in his strength, and goeth out to meet the armed men. He mocketh at fear, and is not affrighted, neither turneth back from the sword. The quiver rattleth against him, the glittering spear and the shield. He swalloweth the ground with fierceness and rage, neither believeth he that it is the sound of the trumpet. He saith among the trumpets, ha, ha! and he smelleth the battle afar off, the thundering of the captains and the shoutings."

But for such footmen as thee and I are, let us never desire to meet with

---

* **Handle Goliah.** The reader will be struck with the colloquialisms in this dialogue. Many of them are yet in use "in the rural districts;" as, "went to the wall," "had his hands full," "throw up his heels," "coats soundly brushed," "at their whistle." How much of Bunyan's popularity is due to his every-day style?—**Heman.** Southey's edition has *Mordecai* instead of *Heman*. The latter is mentioned in 1 Chron. xv., 17 ; xxv., 5, and elsewhere.—**Afraid of a sorry girl.** Matt. xxvi., 69, etc.—**Shaking of a spear.** Job xli., 29.—**Job's horse.** Job xxxix., 19-25.—**Thee and I are.** *Thee* for *thou*.

an enemy; nor vaunt as if we could do better, when we hear of others that they have been foiled; nor be tickled at the thoughts of our manhood; for such commonly come by the worst when tried. Witness Peter, of whom I made mention before; he would swagger, ay he would, as his vain mind prompted him to say, do better, and stand more for his Master than all men. But who so foiled and run down by these villains, as he?

When, therefore, we hear that such robberies are done on the King's highway, two things become us to do. First, to go out harnessed, and to be sure to take a shield with us: for it was for the want of that, that he that laid so lustily at Leviathan could not make him yield; and, indeed, if that be wanting, he fears us not at all. Therefore, he that hath skill hath said, "Above all, take the shield of faith, wherewith ye shall be able to quench all the fiery darts of the wicked."

It is good also that we desire of the King a convoy, yea, that He will go with us himself. This made David rejoice when in the valley of the shadow of death; and Moses was rather for dying where he stood, than to go one step without his God. O my brother, if He will but go along with us, what need we be afraid of ten thousands that shall set themselves against us? But without Him, the proud helpers fall under the slain.

I, for my part, have been in the fray before now; and though through the goodness of Him that is best, I am, as you see, alive; yet cannot I boast of my manhood. Glad shall I be, if I meet with no more such brunts; though I fear we are not gone beyond all danger. However, since the lion and the bear have not as yet devoured me, I hope God will also deliver us from the next uncircumcised Philistine.

Then sang Christian:

> "Poor Little-faith! hast been among the thieves?
> Wast robb'd? remember this whoso believes;
> And get more faith. Then shall you victors be
> Over ten thousand; else, scarce over three."

So they went on, and Ignorance followed. They went then till they came at a place where they saw a way put itself into their way, and seemed withal to lie as straight as the way which they should go; and there they knew not which of the two to take, for both seemed straight before them. Therefore here they stood still to consider. And as they were thinking about the way; behold, a man black of flesh, but covered with a very light robe, came to them, and asked them, why they stood there? They answered, "They were going to the Celestial City, but knew not which of these ways to take." "Follow me," said the man; "it is thither that I am going." So they followed him in the way that but now came into the road; which

---

* **All the fiery darts.** Eph. vi., 16.—**Valley of the shadow.** Ps. xxiii., 4.—**Moses.** Ex. xxxiii., 15.—**Ten thousands.** Ps. iii., 6: xxvii., 3.—**Fall under the slain.** Is. x., 4.

I
fear
we are not yet gone beyond all danger.

Here the sentence, *we are not yet gone beyond all danger*, is the direct *object* of *fear*. It is accordingly connected with *fear* by a curved brace. See p. 312. Complete the analysis.

by degrees turned, and turned them so from the city that they desired to go to, that in a little time their faces were turned away from it: yet they followed him. But, by and by, before they were aware, he led them both within the compass of a net, in which they were both so entangled, that they knew not what to do: and with that, the white robe fell off the black man's back. Then they saw where they were. Wherefore there they lay crying some time, for they could not get themselves out.

Then said Christian to his fellow, "Now do I see myself in an error. Did not the shepherds bid us beware of the flatterers? As is the saying of the wise man, so we have found it this day: 'A man that flattereth his neighbor, spreadeth a net* for his feet.'"

Hopeful. They also gave us a note of directions about the way, for our more certain finding thereof; but therein we have also forgotten to read, and have not kept ourselves from the paths of the destroyer. Here David was wiser than we; for, said he, "Concerning the works of men, by the words of thy lips I have kept me from the paths of the destroyer."

Thus they lay bewailing themselves in the net. At last they espied a shining one coming towards them with a whip of small cord in his hand. When he was come to the place where they were, he asked them whence they came, and what they did there? They told him, that they were poor pilgrims going to Zion, but were led out of their way by a black man clothed in white; "Who bade us," said they, "follow him, for he was going thither too." Then said he with the whip, "It is the Flatterer, a false apostle, that hath transformed himself into an angel of light."

So he rent the net, and let the men out. Then said he to them, "Follow me, that I may set you in your way again." So he led them back to the way which they had left to follow the Flatterer. Then he asked them, saying, "Where did you lie the last night?" They said, "With the shepherds upon the Delectable Mountains." He asked them then, if they had

---

* **Spreadeth a net.** Prov. xxix., 5.—**Paths of the destroyer.** Ps. xvii., 4.—**Transformed himself.** 2 Cor. xi., 14. "Luther was wont to caution against the white devil as much as the black one." *Mason.*

Bewail, bemoan, lament, deplore, mourn. Write out, etc.

They lay bewailing. This kind of sentence, involving a *participial*, is called *intermediate* between simple and compound. *They lay bewailing* is nearly, but not quite, the same as, *They lay and bewailed.* The gerund *bewailing*, expresses, like other gerunds, *concomitant action.*

They
lay
bewailing.

Complete the analysis.

Analyze, *He asked them, saying.*

They	S.
told	P.
him	O. dat.
that they were poor pilgrims.	O. pass. or trans.

The clause, *that they were poor pilgrims*, is a direct object of told. Complete the analysis. The sentence is complex. See Fowler's *English Grammar*, p. 638.

not a note of directions for the way? They answered, "Yes." "But did you," said he, "when you were at a stand, pluck out and read your note?" They answered, "No." He asked them, "Why?" They said they forgot. He asked, moreover, if the shepherds did not bid them beware of the Flatterer? They answered, "Yes. But we did not imagine," said they, "that this fine-spoken man had been he."

Then I saw in my dream, that he commanded them to lie down.* Which when they did, he chastised them sore, to teach them the good way wherein they should walk: and as he chastised them he said, "As many as I love, I rebuke and chasten; be zealous, therefore, and repent." This done, he bade them go their way, and take good heed to the other directions of the shepherds. So they thanked him for all his kindness, and went softly along the right way, singing,—

"Come hither, you that walk along the way;
See how the pilgrims fare, that go astray:
They catched are in an entangled net,
'Cause they good counsel lightly did forget.
'Tis true, they rescued were; but yet you see
They're scourged to boot. Let this your caution be."

Now, after a while they perceived, afar off, one coming softly and alone all along the highway to meet them. Then said Christian to his fellow, "Yonder is a man with his back toward Zion; and he is coming to meet us."

Hopeful. I see him; let us take heed to ourselves now, lest he should prove a flatterer also.

So he drew nearer and nearer, and at last came up to them. His name was Atheist; and he asked them whither they were going?

Christian. We are going to Mount Zion.

Then Atheist fell into a very great laughter.

Christian. What is the meaning of your laughter?

Atheist. I laugh to see what ignorant persons you are to take upon you so tedious a journey, and yet are like to have nothing but your travel for your pains.

Christian. Why, man? Do you think we shall not be received?

Atheist. Received! There is no such place as you dream of, in all this world.

Christian. But there is in the world to come.

Atheist. When I was at home in mine own country, I heard as you now affirm; and from that hearing, went out to see, and have been seeking this city these twenty years, but find no more of it than I did the first day I set out.

---

* **Lie down.** Deut. xxv., 2.—**As many as**, etc. Rev. iii., 19.—**Scourged to boot.** See *boot* in Index.—**Seeking this city.** Eccles. x., 15.

Ignorant, untaught, illiterate, unlearned, unlettered, uninstructed, unenlightened, uninformed, unknowing. Write out, etc.

He
asked
whither they were going.

The clause, *whither they were going*, is a direct object. Another complex sentence. Complete the analysis.

Christian. We have both heard and believe that there is such a place to be found.

Atheist. Had not I, when at home, believed, I had not come thus far to seek; but finding none—and yet I should, had there been such a place to be found, for I have gone to seek it farther than you—I am going back again, and will seek to refresh myself with the things that I then cast away for hopes of that which, I now see, is not.

Then said Christian to Hopeful, his companion, "Is it true which this man has said?"

Hopeful. Take heed; he is one of the flatterers. Remember what it has cost us once already for our hearkening to such kind of fellows. What! No Mount Zion! Did we not see, from the Delectable Mountains, the gate of the city? Also, are we not now "to walk by faith?" * Let us go on, lest the man with the whip overtake us again. You should have taught me that lesson, which I will round you in the ears withal, "Cease, my son, to hear the instruction that causeth to err from the words of knowledge:" I say, my brother, cease to hear him, and let us believe to the saving of the soul.

Christian. My brother, I did not put the question to thee, for that I doubted of the truth of your belief myself; but to prove thee, and to fetch from thee a fruit of the honesty of thy heart. As for this man, I know that he is blinded by the god of this world. Let thou and I go on, knowing that we have belief of the truth, and no lie is of the truth.

Hopeful. Now do I rejoice in the hope of the glory of God.

So they turned away from the man; and he, laughing at them, went his way.

I saw then in my dream, that they went until they came into a certain country whose air naturally tended to make one drowsy, if he came a stranger into it. And here Hopeful began to be very dull and heavy to sleep. Wherefore he said unto Christian, "I do now begin to grow so drowsy that I can scarcely hold open my eyes. Let us lie down here and take one nap."

---

* **Walk by faith.** 2 Cor. v., 7.—**Round** (A. S. *runian*, to whisper; *run*, a magic letter; O. Eng. *roun*, to whisper; *runic*, of the *Runes*, the mysterious letters of the ancient Norsemen), *whisper*.—**Causeth to err.** Prov. xix., 27.—**Saving of the soul.** Heb. x., 39.—**Let thou and I.** This is clearly ungrammatical.—**Lie.** 1 John i., 6; ii., 21.

Finding none, I am going back. Another *intermediate* sentence containing an "*adverbial quasi-clause.*" The nominative absolute and its modifiers often express *time*, *cause*, *condition*, *concession*, or *accompanying circumstance*. Here, *finding none* is the *cause*. See Fowler's *English Grammar*, p. 638.

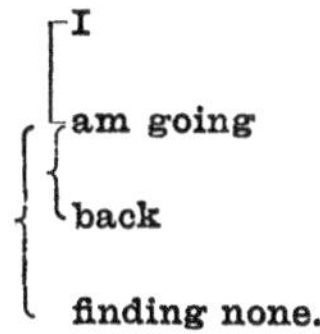

Complete the analysis.

He, laughing, went his way. Analyze.

Christian. By no means, lest, sleeping, we never awake more.

Hopeful. Why, my brother? Sleep is sweet to the laboring man. We may be refreshed, if we take a nap.

Christian. Do you not remember that one of the shepherds bade us beware of the Enchanted Ground? He meant by that, that we should beware of sleeping. Wherefore, "Let us not sleep as others do, but let us watch and be sober." *

Hopeful. I acknowledge myself in a fault; and, had I been here alone, I had by sleeping run the danger of death. I see it is true that the wise man saith, "Two are better than one." Hitherto hath thy company been my mercy; and thou shalt have good reward for thy labor.

Christian. Now, then, to prevent drowsiness in this place, let us fall into good discourse.

Hopeful. With all my heart.

Christian. Where shall we begin?

Hopeful. Where God began with us: but do you begin if you please.

Christian. I will sing you, first, a song:

"When saints do sleepy grow, let them come hither
And hear how these two pilgrims talk together:
Yea, let them learn of them in any wise
Thus to keep ope their drowsy slumb'ring eyes.
Saints' fellowship, if it be managed well,
Keeps them awake, and that in spite of hell."

Then Christian began, and said, "I will ask you a question. How came you to think at first of so doing as you do now?"

Hopeful. Do you mean, how came I at first to look after the good of my soul?

Christian. Yes: that is my meaning.

Hopeful. I continued a great while in the delight of those things which were seen and sold at our Fair; things which I now believe would, had I continued in them still, have drowned me in perdition and destruction.

Christian. What things were they?

Hopeful. All the treasures and riches of the world. Also I delighted much in rioting, revelling, drinking, swearing, lying, uncleanness, sabbath-breaking, and what not, that tended to destroy the soul. But I found at last, by hearing and considering of things that are divine, which indeed I heard of you, as also of beloved Faithful, that was put to death for his faith and good-living in Vanity-Fair, that the end of these things is death; and that, for these things' sake, "The wrath of God cometh upon the children of disobedience."

---

* **Watch and be sober.** 1 Thess. v., 6. **Two are better.** Eccles. iv., 9.—**The end of these things.** Rom. vi., 21, 22, 23.—**Wrath of God.** Eph. v., 6.

I	S.
see	P.
it is true.	O.

Complete the analysis.

Christian. And did you presently fall under the power of this conviction ?

Hopeful. No: I was not willing presently to know the evils of sin, nor the damnation that follows upon the commission of it; but endeavored, when my mind at first began to be shaken with the Word, to shut mine eyes against the light thereof.

Christian. But what was the cause of your carrying of it* thus to the first workings of God's Spirit upon you ?

Hopeful. The causes were, 1. I was ignorant that this was the work of God upon me. I never thought that by awakenings from sin, God at first begins the conversion of a sinner. 2. Sin was yet very sweet to my flesh, and I was loth to leave it. 3. I could not tell how to part with my own companions; their presence and actions were so desirable unto me. 4. The hours in which convictions were upon me, were such troublesome and heart-affrighting hours, that I could not bear, no, not so much as the remembrance of them upon my heart.

Christian. Then, as it seems, sometimes you got rid of your trouble ?

Hopeful. Yes, verily, but it would come into my mind again, and then I would be as bad, nay, worse than I was before.

Christian. Why, what was it that brought your sins to mind again ?

Hopeful. Many things; as, 1. If I did but meet a good man in the streets; or, 2. If I have heard any read in the Bible; or, 3. If mine head did begin to ache; or, 4. If I were told that some of my neighbors were sick; or, 5. If I heard the bell toll for some that were dead; or, 6. If I thought of dying myself; or, 7. If I heard that sudden death happened to others. 8. But especially when I thought of myself, that I must quickly come to judgment.

Christian. And could you at any time, with ease, get off the guilt of sin, when by any of these ways it came upon you ?

Hopeful. No, not I; for then they got faster hold of my conscience; and then, if I did but think of going back to sin, though my mind was turned against it, it would be double torment to me.

Christian. And how did you then ?

Hopeful. I thought I must endeavor to mend my life; for else, thought I, I am sure to be damned.

Christian. And did you endeavor to mend ?

Hopeful. Yes; and fled from, not only my sins, but sinful company too; and betook me to religious duties; as praying, reading, weeping for sin, speaking truth to my neighbors, etc. These things did I, with many others, too much here to relate.

Christian. And did you think yourself well then ?

---

* **Carrying of it,** *behavior.*—**If I did but meet.** "I trembled at the sight of the saints of God, especially those that greatly loved me; for they did, both in their words, their carriage, and all their expressions of tenderness and fear to sin against their precious Saviour, condemn, and also add continual affliction to my soul." Bunyan's *Grace Abounding.*

Companion, associate, comrade, mate, compeer, coadjutor. Write out, etc.

Hopeful. Yes, for a while; but at the last my trouble came tumbling upon me again, and that over the neck of all my reformation.

Christian. How came that about, since you was now reformed?

Hopeful. There were several things brought it upon me, especially such sayings as these: "All our righteousnesses are as filthy rags;"* "By the works of the law, no man shall be justified;" "When ye have done all these things say, 'We are unprofitable;'" with many more such like. From whence I began to reason with myself thus:—If all my righteousnesses are as filthy rags; if by the deeds of the law no man can be justified; and if, when we have done all, we are unprofitable; then it is but folly to think of heaven by the law. I farther thought thus: If a man runs a hundred pounds into the shop-keeper's debt, and after that shall pay for all that he shall fetch; yet if this old debt stands still in the book uncrossed, the shop-keeper may sue him for it, and cast him into prison till he shall pay the debt.

Christian. Well; and how did you apply this to yourself?

Hopeful. Why, I thought thus with myself: I have by my sins run a great way into God's book, and that my now reforming will not pay off that score; therefore I should think, still under all my present amendments, "But how shall I be freed from that damnation that I brought myself in danger of by my former transgressions?"

Christian. A very good application. But pray go on.

Hopeful. Another thing that hath troubled me ever since my late amendments is, that if I look narrowly into the best of what I do now, I still see sin, new sin, mixing itself with the best of what I do: so that now I am forced to conclude, that, notwithstanding my former fond conceits of myself and duties, I have committed sins enough in one day, to send me to hell, though my former life had been faultless.

Christian. And what did you then?

Hopeful. Do! I could not tell what to do, till I broke my mind to Faithful; for he and I were acquainted: and he told me, that, unless I could obtain the righteousness of a man that never had sinned, neither mine own, nor all the righteousnesses of the world could save me.

Christian. And did you think he spake true?

Hopeful. Had he told me so when I was pleased and satisfied with mine own amendments, I had called him fool for his pains; but now, since I see mine own infirmity, and the sin which cleaves to my best performance, I have been forced to be of his opinion.

Christian. But did you think, when at first he suggested it to you, that

---

* **Rags.** Is. lxiv., 6.—**Justified.** Gal. ii., 16.—**Unprofitable.** Luke xvii., 10.

Suggest, hint, intimate, insinuate. Write out, etc.

Another thing that hath troubled me is. Analyze thus:

Another	A.
that hath troubled me	A.
thing	S.
is, etc.	P.

The clause, *that hath troubled me*, evidently modifies *thing* adjectively. A complex sentence.

there was such a man to be found, of whom it might justly be said, that he never committed sin?

Hopeful. I must confess the words at first sounded strangely; but after a little more talk and company with him, I had full conviction about it.

Christian. And did you ask him what man this was, and how you must be justified by him?

Hopeful. Yes; and he told me it was the Lord Jesus, that dwelleth on the right hand of the Most High: * "And thus," said he, "you must be justified by him, even by trusting to what he hath done by himself in the days of his flesh, and suffered when he did hang on the tree." I asked him further, how that man's righteousness could be of that efficacy as to justify another before God? And he told me, He was the mighty God: and did what he did, and died the death also, not for himself, but for me; to whom his doings, and the worthiness of them should be imputed, if I believed on him.

Christian. And what did you do then?

Hopeful. I made my objection against my believing, for that I thought he was not willing to save me.

Christian. And what said Faithful to you then?

Hopeful. He bade me go to him and see. Then I said, it was presumption. He said, "No;" for I was invited to come. Then he gave me a book of Jesus's inditing, to encourage me the more freely to come; and he said, concerning that book, that every jot and tittle thereof stood firmer than heaven and earth. Then I asked him, what I must do when I came. And he told me, I must entreat upon my knees, with all my heart and soul, the Father to reveal him to me. Then I asked him further, "How I must make my supplication to him?" And he said, "Go and thou shalt find him upon a mercy-seat, where he sits all the year long, to give pardon and forgiveness to them that come." I told him that I knew not what to say when I came. And he bade me say to this effect: "God be merciful to me a sinner; and make me know and believe in Christ;

---

* **Right hand of God.** Heb. x., 12.—**Justified.** Rom. iv., 25;—**Flesh.** Col. i., 22. —**Tree.** 1 Pet. ii., 24.—**Not for himself, but for me.** "Here is his willingness asserted, as well as his power suggested. These words, therefore, are sufficient ground to encourage any coming sinner that Christ is willing to receive him; and since he hath power also to do what he will, there is no ground at all left to the coming sinner any more to doubt; but to come in full hope of acceptance, and to be received unto grace and mercy." Bunyan's *Come and Welcome.* —**Go to him.** Matt. xi., 28.—**Firmer.** Matt. xxiv., 35; v., 18.—**Knees.** Ps. xcv., 6; Dan. vi., 10.—**Heart.** Jer. xxix., 13.—**Mercy-seat.** Ex. xxv., 22; Lev. xvi., 2; Num. vii., 89; Heb. ix., 5.

He bade me go. Here is another proposition *intermediate* between the simple and the compound. See Fowler's *English Grammar*, p. 638. The sense is nearly, *He bade me that I should go.* The incompleteness of the combination (of subject and predicate) may be expressed by an incomplete bracket, [

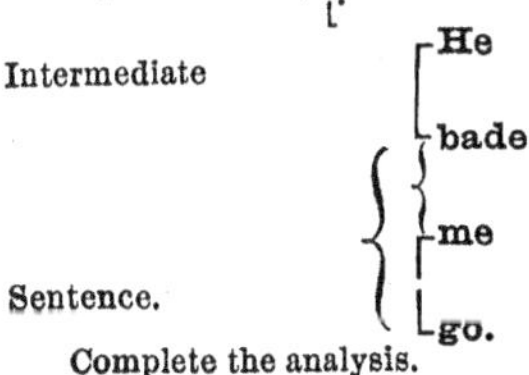

Complete the analysis.

for I see, that if this righteousness had not been, or I have not faith in that righteousness, I am utterly cast away. Lord, I have heard that thou art a merciful God, and hast ordained that thy Son Jesus Christ should be the Saviour of the world; and, moreover, that thou art willing to bestow him upon such a poor sinner as I am; and I am a sinner indeed! Lord, take therefore this opportunity and magnify thy grace in the salvation of my soul, through thy Son Jesus Christ. Amen."

Christian. And did you do as you were bidden?

Hopeful. Yes: over and over and over.

Christian. And did the Father reveal the Son to you?

Hopeful. Not at first, nor second, nor third, nor fourth, nor fifth; no, nor at the sixth time neither.

Christian. What did you do then?

Hopeful. What! why, I could not tell what to do.

Christian. Had you no thoughts of leaving off praying?

Hopeful. Yes; and a hundred times twice told.

Christian. And what was the reason you did not?

Hopeful. I believed that that was true, which hath been told me, to wit, that without the righteousness of this Christ, all the world could not save me: and therefore thought I with myself, "If I leave off, I die; and can but die at the throne of Grace." And withal, this came into my mind, "If he tarry, wait for him; because he will surely come, and will not tarry."* So I continued praying until the Father showed me his Son.

Christian. And how was he revealed unto you?

Hopeful. I did not see him with my bodily eyes, but with the eyes of mine understanding; and thus it was. One day I was very sad, I think sadder than at any one time of my life; and this sadness was through a fresh sight of the greatness and vileness of my sins. And as I was then looking for nothing but hell, and the everlasting damnation of my soul; suddenly, as I thought, I saw the Lord Jesus look down from heaven upon me, and saying, "Believe on the Lord Jesus Christ, and thou shalt be saved." But I replied, "Lord, I am a great, a very great sinner." And he answered, "My grace is sufficient for thee." Then I said, "But, Lord, what is believing?" And then I saw from that saying, "He that cometh to me shall never hunger, and he that believeth on me shall never thirst," that believing and coming was all one; and that he that came, that is, ran out in his heart and affections after salvation by Christ; he indeed believed in Christ. Then the water stood in mine eyes, and I asked further, "But,

* **Will not tarry.** Heb. x., 37.—**Eyes of understanding.** Eph. i., 18.—**Believe . . . . saved.** Acts xvi., 31.—**Grace is sufficient.** 2 Cor. xii., 9.—**He that cometh.** John vi., 35.

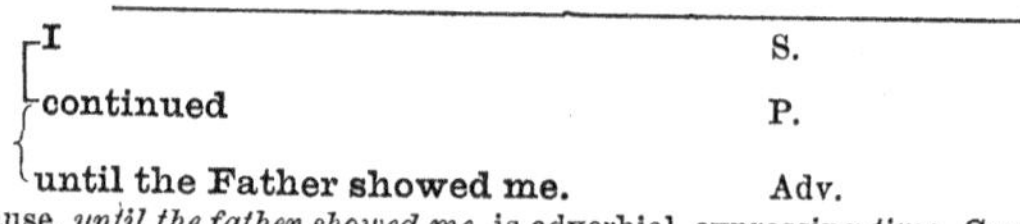

The clause, *until the father showed me*, is adverbial, expressing *time*. Complete the analysis. Analyze *It made me see.*

Lord, may such a great sinner as I am be indeed accepted of thee, and be saved by thee?" And I heard him say, "And him that cometh to me, I will in no wise cast out."* Then I said, "But how, Lord, must I consider of thee in my coming to thee, that my faith must be placed aright upon thee?" Then he said, "Christ came into the world to save sinners. He is the end of the law for righteousness to every one that believes. He died for our sins, and rose again for our justification. He loved us, and washed us from our sins in his own blood. He is a Mediator betwixt God and us. He ever liveth to make intercession for us." From all which I gathered, that I must look for righteousness in his person, and for satisfaction for my sins by his blood; that what he did in obedience to his Father's Law, and in submitting to the penalty thereof, was not for himself, but for him that will accept it for his salvation, and be thankful. And now was my heart full of joy, mine eyes full of tears, and mine affections running over with love to the name, people, and ways of Jesus Christ.

Christian. This was a revelation of Christ to your soul indeed! But tell me particularly, what effect this had upon your spirits?

Hopeful. It made me see that all the world, notwithstanding all the righteousness thereof, is in a state of condemnation. It made me see that God the Father, though he be just, can justly justify the coming sinner. It made me greatly ashamed of the vileness of my former life, and confounded me with the sense of mine own ignorance; for there never came a thought into my heart before now, that showed me so the beauty of Jesus Christ. It made me love a holy life, and long to do something for the honor and glory of the name of the Lord Jesus; yea, I thought that, if I had now a thousand gallons of blood in my body, I could spill it all for the sake of the Lord Jesus!

I saw in my dream, that Hopeful looked back and saw Ignorance, whom they left behind, coming after. "Look," said he to Christian, "how far yonder youngster loitereth behind!"

Christian. Ay, ay, I see him; he careth not for our company.

Hopeful. But I trow it would not have hurt him, had he kept pace with us hitherto.

Christian. That is true; but I will warrant you he thinketh otherwise.

Hopeful. That I think he doth; but however, let us tarry for him. So they did.

Then Christian said to him, "Come away, man; why do you stay so behind?"

Ignorance. I take my pleasure in walking alone; even more a great deal than in company, unless I like it better.

---

* **Cast out.** John vi., 37.—**Save sinners.** 1 Tim. i., 15.—**End of the law.** Rom. 10., 4.—**Our justification.** Rom. iv., 25. "Do not conclude thy cause is lost because thou dost not hear from court. Cry, if thou wilt, 'O when wilt thou come unto me?' but never let such a wicked thought pass through thy heart, saying, 'Why should I wait upon the Lord any longer?'" Bunyan's *Advocateship of Jesus Christ.*—**I trow.** See Index.

Warrant, guarantee. Other synonymes? Write out, etc.

I will warrant you he thinketh otherwise. Analyze.

Then said Christian to Hopeful, but softly, "Did I not tell you he cared not for our company? But however," said he, "come up, and let us talk away the time in this solitary place." Then directing his speech to Ignorance, he said, "Come, how do you do? How stands it between God and your soul now?"

Ignorance. I hope, well; for I am always full of good motions that come into my mind, to comfort me as I walk.

Christian. What good motions? Pray tell us.

Ignorance. Why, I think of God and Heaven.

Christian. So do the devils* and damned souls.

Ignorance. But I think of them, and desire them.

Christian. So do many, that are never like to come there. "The soul of the sluggard desires, and hath nothing."

Ignorance. But I think of them, and leave all for them.

Christian. That I doubt; for to leave all is a very hard matter; yea, a harder matter than many are aware of. But why, or by what, art thou persuaded that thou hast left all for God and Heaven?

Ignorance. My heart tells me so.

Christian. The wise man says, "He that trusteth in his own heart is a fool."

Ignorance. This is spoken of an evil heart: but mine is a good one.

Christian. But how dost thou prove that?

Ignorance. It comforts me in hopes of heaven.

Christian. That may be through its deceitfulness; for a man's heart may minister comfort to him in the hopes of that thing for which he has yet not ground to hope.

Ignorance. But my heart and my life agree together; and therefore my hope is well grounded.

Christian. Who told thee that thy heart and life agree together?

Ignorance. My heart tells me so.

Christian. Ask my fellow if I be a thief? Thy heart tells thee so! Except the word of God beareth witness in this matter, other testimony is of no value.

Ignorance. But is it not a good heart that has good thoughts? And is not that a good life that is according to God's commandments?

Christian. Yes; that is a good heart that hath good thoughts; and that is a good life that is according to God's commandments. But it is one thing indeed to have these, and another thing only to think so.

---

* **So do devils.** Jas. ii., 19.—**Sluggard.** Prov. xiii., 4.—**Is a fool.** Prov. xxviii., 26.—**Other testimony.** Is. viii., 20; John v. 31, 32.

Witness, testimony, evidence, proof, deposition. Other synonymes? Write out, etc.

My	A.
heart and life	S.
agree.	P.

Here the subject is *compound.* Complete the analysis.

Ignorance. Pray, what count you good thoughts and a life according to God's commandments?

Christian. There are good thoughts of divers kinds: some, respecting ourselves; some, God; some, Christ; and some, other things.

Ignorance. What be good thoughts respecting ourselves?

Christian. Such as agree with the word of God.

Ignorance. When do our thoughts of ourselves agree with the word of God?

Christian. When we pass the same judgment upon ourselves which the Word passes. To explain myself: The Word of God saith of persons in a natural condition, "There is none righteous;* there is none that doeth good." It saith also, that "every imagination of the heart of man is only evil, and that continually." And again, "The imagination of man's heart is evil, from his youth." Now, then, when we think thus of ourselves, having sense thereof; then are our thoughts good ones, because according to the Word of God.

Ignorance. I will never believe that my heart is thus bad.

Christian. Therefore thou never hadst one good thought concerning thyself in thy life. But let me go on. As the Word passeth a judgment upon our heart, so it passeth judgment upon our ways; and when the thoughts of our hearts and ways agree with the judgment which the Word giveth of both, then are both good, because agreeing thereto.

Ignorance. Make out your meaning.

Christian. Why, the Word of God saith, that man's ways are crooked ways, not good, but perverse. It saith, "They are naturally out of the good way; that they have not known it." Now, when a man thus thinketh of his ways, I say—when he doth sensibly and with heart humiliation thus think—then hath he good thoughts of his own ways, because his thoughts now agree with the judgment of the Word of God.

Ignorance. What are good thoughts concerning God?

Christian. Even, as I have said concerning ourselves, when our thoughts of God do agree with what the Word saith of him. And that is, when we think of his being and attributes, as the Word hath taught; of which I cannot now discourse at large. But to speak of Him in reference to us: then we have right thoughts of God, when we think that He knows us better

* **None righteous.** Rom. iii., 10, 12.—**Every imagination.** Gen. vi., 5.—**From his youth.** Gen. viii., 21.—**Crooked ways.** Ps. cxxv., 5; Prov. ii., 15.—**Naturally out of the good way.** Rom. iii., 12-18.

Righteous, godly, upright, holy, sacred. Write out, etc.

Good
of divers kinds
thoughts
are
there

Complete the analysis. *There* is an expletive, but may be regarded as having a slight adverbial force.

than we know ourselves, and can see sin in us when and where we can see none in ourselves; when we think He knows our inmost thoughts; and that our heart, with all its depths, is always open unto his eyes: also, when we think that all our righteousness stinks in his nostrils; and that, therefore, he cannot abide to see us stand before him in any confidence, even of all our best performances.

Ignorance. Do you think that I am such a fool as to think God can see no farther than I ? or that I would come to God in the best of my performances ?

Christian. Why, how dost thou think in this matter ?

Ignorance. Why, to be short, I think I must believe in Christ for justification.

Christian. How! Think thou must believe in Christ, when thou seest not thy need of Him! * Thou neither seest thy original nor actual infirmities, but hast such an opinion of thyself, and of what thou doest, as plainly renders thee to be one that did never see a necessity of Christ's personal righteousness to justify thee before God. How then dost thou say, "I believe in Christ" ?

Ignorance. I believe well enough, for all that.

Christian. How dost thou believe ?

Ignorance. I believe that Christ died for sinners; and that I shall be justified before God, from the curse, through his gracious acceptance of my obedience to his law. Or thus: Christ makes my duties, that are religious, acceptable to his Father by virtue of merits; and so shall I be justified.

Christian. Let me give an answer to this confession of thy faith.—1. Thou believest with a fantastical faith; for this faith is nowhere described in the Word.—2. Thou believest with a false faith, because it taketh justification from the personal righteousness of Christ, and applies it to thy own.—3. This faith maketh not Christ a justifier of thy person, but of thy actions; and of thy person, for thy actions' sake, which is false.—4. Therefore this faith is deceitful; even such as will leave thee under wrath in the day of God Almighty: for, true justifying faith puts the soul, as sensible of its lost condition by the law, upon flying for refuge unto Christ's righteousness; which righteousness of his is not an act of grace by which he maketh, for justification, thy obedience accepted with God, but his personal obedience to the law, in doing and suffering for us what that required at our hands; this righteousness, I say, true faith accepteth; under the skirt of which, the soul being shrouded, and by it presented as spotless before God, it is accepted, and acquitted from condemnation.

Ignorance. What! would you have us trust to what Christ in his own

---

* **Seest not thy need,** etc. A man must have brains before he can have religion.

You
do think
that I am such a fool?

Complete the analysis.

person hath done without us! This conceit would loosen the reins of our lust, and tolerate us to live as we list; for, what matter how we live, if we may be justified, by Christ's personal righteousness, from all, when we believe it?

Christian. Ignorance is thy name; and as thy name is, so art thou. Even this thy answer demonstrateth what I say. Ignorant thou art of what justifying righteousness is, and as ignorant how to secure thy soul, through the faith of it, from the heavy wrath of God. Yea, thou also art ignorant of the true effects of saving faith in this righteousness of Christ; which is to bow and win over the heart to God in Christ, to love his name, his word, ways, and people, and not as thou ignorantly imaginest.

Hopeful. Ask him if ever he had Christ revealed to him from Heaven?

Ignorance. What! you are a man for revelation! I do believe that what both you and all the rest of you say about that matter, is but the fruit of distracted brains.

Hopeful. Why, man! Christ is so hid in God from the natural apprehensions of the flesh, that he cannot by any man be savingly known, unless God the Father reveals Him to them.

Ignorance. That is your faith, but not mine. Yet mine, I doubt not, is as good as yours, though I have not in my head so many whimseys as you.*

Christian. Give me leave to put in a word. You ought not to speak so slightly of this matter. For this I will boldly affirm, even as my good companion hath done, that no man can know Jesus Christ but by the revelation of the Father. Yea, and faith too, by which the soul layeth hold upon Christ, if it be right, must be wrought by the exceeding greatness of his mighty power. The working of which faith, I perceive, poor Ignorance, thou art ignorant of. Be awakened, then; see thine own wretchedness, and fly to the Lord Jesus; and by his righteousness, which is the righteousness of God, for he himself is God, thou shalt be delivered from condemnation.

Ignorance. You go so fast, I cannot keep pace with you. Do you go on before; I must stay awhile behind.

Then they said,—

"Well, Ignorance, wilt thou yet foolish be,
To slight good counsel, ten times given thee?
And if thou yet refuse it, thou shalt know,
Ere long, the evil of thy doing so.
Remember, man, in time; stoop, do not fear:
Good counsel, taken well, secures; then hear.
But if thou yet shalt slight it, thou wilt be
The loser, Ignorance, I'll warrant thee."

Then Christian addressed himself thus to his fellow:—

Christian. Well, come, my good Hopeful; I perceive that thou and I must walk by ourselves again.

---

* **I have not in my head so many whimseys as you.** "There is no man more at ease in his mind, with such ease as it is, than the man that hath not closed with the Lord Jesus, but is shut up in unbelief. O! but this is the man that stands convict before God, and that is bound over to the great *assize!*" Bunyan on *Justification.*—**Whimsey** (Ice. *hvim*, a quick movement; W. *chwim*, a brisk motion; Sp. *quimera*, a wild fancy), *a whim, caprice, freak.*—**No man can know,** etc. Matt. xi., 27.—**Mighty power.** Eph. i., 19.

So I saw in my dream, that they went on apace before, and Ignorance—he came hobbling after. Then said Christian to his companion, "I am much grieved for this poor man. It will certainly go hard with him at the last."

Hopeful. Alas! there are abundance in our town in this condition; whole families, yea, whole streets; and that of pilgrims too: and if there be so many in our parts, how many, think you, must there be in the place where he was born?

Christian. Indeed the Word saith, "He hath blinded their eyes, lest they should see," etc. But now we are by ourselves, what do you think of such men? Have they at no time, think you, convictions of sin; so, consequently, fears that their state is dangerous?

Hopeful. Nay, do you answer that question yourself, for you are the elder man.

Christian. Then I say, sometimes, as I think, they may; but they, being naturally ignorant, understand not that such convictions tend to their good; and, therefore, they do desperately seek to stifle them, and presumptuously continue to flatter themselves in the way of their own hearts.

Hopeful. I do believe, as you say, that fear tends much to men's good, and to make them right at their beginning to go on pilgrimage.

Christian. Without all doubt it doth, if it be right; for says the Word, "The fear of the Lord is the beginning of wisdom."*

Hopeful. How will you describe right fear?

Christian. True or right fear is discovered by three things: 1. By its rise: it is caused by saving convictions for sin. 2. It driveth the soul to lay fast hold of Christ for salvation. 3. It begetteth and continueth in the soul a great reverence of God, his word and ways; keeping it tender, and making it afraid to turn from them, to the right hand or to the left, to anything that may dishonor God, break its peace, grieve the Spirit, or cause the enemy to speak reproachfully.

Hopeful. Well said. I believe you have said the truth. Are we now almost got past the Enchanted Ground?

---

* **Beginning of wisdom.** Job xxviii., 28; Ps. cxi., 10; Prov. i., 7; ix., 10.

Fear tends to make them right. *To make them right* adverbially modifies tends. Here is another *intermediate* proposition. See Fowler's *Grammar*, p. 638.

Fear
tends
to make them right.

To may here be considered a sign of the adverbial combination; *them* is a transitive or passive object; *right* is a factitive. Complete the analysis.

It
doth
without all doubt, **if**
it
be right.

Here we have a compound sentence. Complete the analysis.

Christian. Why, art thou weary of this discourse ?

Hopeful. No, verily; but that I would know where we are.

Christian. We have not now above two miles farther to go thereon. But let us return to our matter. Now, the ignorant know not that such convictions as tend to put them in fear are for their good; and therefore they seek to stifle them.

Hopeful. How do they seek to stifle them ?

Christian. 1. They think that those fears are wrought by the devil; though indeed they are wrought of God; and thinking so, they resist them, as things that directly tend to their overthrow. 2. They also think that these fears tend to the spoiling of their faith; when, alas for them, poor men that they are! they have none at all: and, therefore, they harden their hearts against them. 3. They presume they ought not to fear: and, therefore, in despite of them, wax presumptuously confident. 4. They see that those fears tend to take away from them their pitiful old self-holiness; and, therefore, they resist them with all their might.

Hopeful. I know something of this myself. Before I knew myself, it was so with me.

Christian. Well, we will leave at this time our neighbor Ignorance by himself, and fall upon another profitable question.

Hopeful. With all my heart, but you shall still begin.

Christian. Well, then, did you know, about ten years ago, one *Temporary* in your parts, who was a forward man in religion then ?

Hopeful. Know him! yes; he dwelt in *Graceless*, a town about two miles off *Honesty*, and he dwelt next door to one *Turnback*.

Christian. Right, he dwelt under the same roof with him. Well, that man was much awakened once. I believe that then he had some sight of his sins, and of the wages that were due thereto.

Hopeful. I am of your mind; for my house not being above three miles from him, he would ofttimes come to me, and that with many tears. Truly, I pitied the man, and was not altogether without hope of him: but one may see, "It is not every one that cries, Lord, Lord."

Christian. He told me once that he was resolved to go on pilgrimage as we go now; but all on a sudden he grew acquainted with one *Save-self*, and then he became a stranger to me.

Hopeful. Now, since we are talking about him, let us a little inquire into the reason of the sudden backsliding of him and such others.

Christian. It may be very profitable; but do you begin.

Hopeful. Well, then, there are, in my judgment, four reasons for it.

Believe, think, suppose, deem, imagine. **Other synonymes? Write out, etc.**

They
do seek
to stifle them
how?

Complete the analysis.

1. Though the consciences of such men are awakened, yet their minds are not changed; therefore, when the power of guilt weareth away, that which provoketh them to be religious ceaseth. Wherefore they naturally turn to their own course again, even as we see the dog* that is sick of what he hath eaten, so long as his sickness prevails, he vomits and casts up all; not that he doth this of a free mind, if we may say a dog has a mind, but because it troubleth his stomach. But now, when his sickness is over, and so his stomach eased, his desires being not at all alienated from his vomit, he turns him about and licks up all; and so it is true which is written, "The dog is turned to his own vomit again." Thus, I say, being hot for heaven, by virtue only of the sense and fear of the torments of hell; as their sense of hell and fear of damnation chills and cools, so their desires for heaven and salvation cool also; so, then, it comes to pass that, when their guilt and fear are gone, their desires for heaven and happiness die, and they return to their course again.

2. Another reason is, they have slavish fears, that do overmaster them. I speak now of the fears that they have of men, for "The fear of men bringeth a snare." So then, though they seem to be hot for heaven so long as the flames of hell are about their ears, yet, when that terror is a little over, they betake themselves to second thoughts; namely, that 'tis good to be wise, and not run, for they know not what, the hazard of losing all; or, at least, of bringing themselves into unavoidable and unnecessary troubles. And so they fall in with the world again.

3. The shame that attends religion lies also as a block in their way. They are proud and haughty, and religion in their eye is low and contemptible. Therefore, when they have lost their sense of hell and the wrath to come, they return again to their former course.

4. Guilt, and to meditate terror, are grievous to them. They like not to

---

* **The dog.** 2 Pet. ii., 22.—**Bringeth a snare.** Prov. xxix., 25.

Sickness, illness, indisposition, malady, disease, distemper, disorder, ailment. Write out, etc.

The shame that attends religion lies. This is a *compound* (or, more specifically, *complex*) sentence, having more than one subject and predicate. The sentence, *that attends religion*, has the force of an *adjective* modifying *shame*. We term it an *adjective subordinate sentence*. Some grammarians would term the whole proposition a *subordinative complex sentence*. The main proposition may be written for analysis thus: —

The

that attends religion,

shame,

lies.

The subordinate sentence may be analyzed separately, and written thus:—

Adjective Subordinate Sentence.	**That** **attends** **religion.**

Let the student complete the work of analysis in each case.

see their misery before they come into it; though perhaps the sight of it at first, if they loved that sight, might make them fly whither the righteous run and are safe. But because they do, as I hinted before, even shun the thoughts of guilt and terror; therefore, when once they are rid of their awakenings about the terrors and wrath of God, they harden their hearts gladly, and choose such ways as will harden them more and more.

Christian. You are pretty near the business, for the bottom of all is for want of a change in their mind and will. And, therefore, they are but like the felon that standeth before the Judge. He quakes and trembles, and seems to repent most heartily: but the bottom of all is the fear of the halter, not that he hath any detestation of the offence: as is evident, because, let but this man have his liberty, and he will be a thief and so a rogue still; whereas, if his mind was changed, he would be otherwise.

Hopeful. Now I have showed you the reason of their going back, do you show me the manner thereof.

Christian. So I will willingly.

1. They draw off their thoughts, all that they may, from the remembrance of God, death, and judgment to come.

2. Then they cast off by degrees private duties, as closet-prayer, curbing their lusts, watching, sorrow for sin, and the like.

3. Then they shun the company of lively and warm Christians.

4. After that, they grow cold to public duty, as hearing, reading, godly conference, and the like.

5. They then begin to pick holes, as we say, in the coats of some of the godly, and that devilishly, that they may have a seeming color to throw religion, for the sake of some infirmities they have spied in them, behind their backs.

6. Then they begin to adhere to and associate themselves with carnal, loose, and wanton men.

7. Then they give way to carnal and wanton discourses in secret; and glad are they, if they can see such things in any that are counted honest, that they may the more boldly do it through their example.

8. After this they begin to play with little sins openly.

9. And then, being hardened, they show themselves as they are. Thus being launched again into the gulf of misery, unless a miracle of grace prevent it, they everlastingly perish in their own deceivings.

Now I saw in my dream, that by this time the pilgrims were got over the Enchanted Ground; and, entering into the country of Beulah,* whose air was very sweet and pleasant, the way lying directly through it, they solaced themselves there for a season. Yea, here they heard continually the singing of birds, and saw every day the flowers appear in the earth, and heard the voice of the turtle in the land. In this country the sun shineth night and

* **Beulah.** Isaiah lxii., 4, 5. *Beulah* means *married.*—**Voice of the turtle.** Song of Solomon ii., 11, 12.

Pleasant, agreeable, pleasing, gratifying. Write out, etc.

Being hardened, they show themselves as they are. Analyze.

day. Wherefore it was beyond the Valley of the Shadow of Death;* and also out of the reach of Giant Despair: neither could they from this place so much as see Doubting Castle. Here they were within sight of the city they were going to; also here met them some of the inhabitants thereof; for in this land the shining ones commonly walked, because it was open to the borders of heaven. In this land also, the contract between the Bride and the Bridegroom was renewed. Yea, here, as the bridegrom rejoiceth over the bride; so did their God rejoice over them. Here they had no want of corn and wine; for in this place they met with abundance of what they had sought for in all their pilgrimage. Here they heard voices from out of the city, loud voices, saying, "Say ye to the daughter of Zion, Behold, thy Salvation cometh! Behold, his reward is with him!" Here all the inhabitants of the country called them, "the holy people, the redeemed of the Lord, sought out," etc.

Now, as they walked in this land, they had more rejoicing than in parts more remote from the kingdom to which they were bound; and drawing nearer to the city yet, they had a more perfect view thereof. It was built of pearls and precious stones; also the streets thereof were paved with gold; so that by reason of the natural glory of the city, and the reflection of the sun-beams upon it, Christian with desire fell sick. Hopeful also had a fit or two of the same disease; wherefore here they lay by it awhile, crying out, because of their pangs, "If you see my Beloved, tell him that I am sick of love."

---

* **Valley of the Shadow of Death.** See Ps. xxiii. "Valley of death-shade" is said to be a more literal translation. It does not mean death itself, as many erroneously suppose.—**Giant Despair** and **Doubting Castle.** See pp. 370, 371, etc.—**Shining ones.** Luke xxiv., 4.—**Bridegroom rejoiceth.** Isai. lxii., 5.—**Corn and wine,** etc. Isai. lxii., 8, 9.—**Sought out.** Isai. lxii., 12.—**Sick of love,** sick *because* of love. Sol. Song ii., 5; v., 8.

Contract, *agreement*, *compact*, *covenant*, *stipulation*. Other synonymes? Write out, etc.

Tell him that I am sick. *That I am sick* is equivalent to *my sickness*. It is, therefore, a *substantive* subordinate proposition constituting the complementary object.

(Thou)
tell
him
that I am sick.

that
I
am sick.

Complete the analysis. Analyze by itself the subordinate clause.
N.B. A subordinate clause may also be the *subject* of a sentence; as, *That I am sick is true.*

I
am
sick
of
love.

Sick of love is *love-sick*. *Love* may be called the *genitive* object (*i. e.*, the object that *produces* the sickness). See Fowler's *English Grammar*, pp. 632, 637, etc. Thus adjectives take *objects* of different kinds. Complete the analysis.

But being a little strengthened, and better able to bear their sickness, they walked on their way, and came yet nearer and nearer where were orchards, vineyards, and gardens, and their gates opened into the highway. Now as they came up to these places, behold, the gardener stood in the way; to whom the pilgrims said, "Whose goodly vineyards and gardens are these?" He answered, "They are the King's, and are planted here for his own delight, and also for the solace of pilgrims."* So the gardener had them into the vineyards, and bade them refresh themselves with dainties. He also showed them there the King's walks and arbors, where he delighted to be: and here they tarried and slept.

Now I beheld, in my dream, that they talked more in their sleep at this time than ever they did in all their journey. And being in a muse thereabout, the gardener said even to me, "Wherefore musest thou at the matter? It is the nature of the fruit of the grapes of these vineyards to go down so sweetly as to cause the lips of them that are asleep to speak."

So I saw, that when they awoke, they addressed themselves to go up to the city. But, as I said, the reflection of the sun upon the city, for the city was pure gold, was so extremely glorious that they could not as yet with open face behold it, but through an instrument made for that purpose. So I saw that, as they went on, there met them two men in raiment that shone like gold; also their faces shone as the light.

These men asked the pilgrims whence they came; and they told them. They also asked them where they had lodged; what difficulties and dangers, what comforts and pleasures, they had met with in the way. And they told them. Then said the men that met them, "You have but two difficulties more to meet with; and then you are in the city."

Christian then and his companion asked the men to go along with them. So they told them that they would. "But," said they, "you must obtain it by your own faith." So I saw, in my dream, that they went on together till they came in sight of the gate.

Now I farther saw that betwixt them and the gate was a river; but there was no bridge to go over, and the river was very deep. At the sight, therefore, of this river, the pilgrims were much stunned. But the men that went with them said, "You must go through, or you cannot come at the gate."

The pilgrims then began to inquire, if there was no other way to the gate. To which they answered, "Yes; but there hath not any, save two, to wit, Enoch and Elijah, been permitted to tread that path since the foundation of the world; nor shall until the last trumpet shall sound." The pil-

---

* **Solace of pilgrims.** Deut. xxiii., 24.—**Go down so sweetly.** Sol. Songs vii., 9.—**Addressed themselves.** Prepared themselves. *Addressed* is commonly used in this sense in Shakespeare, as in *Julius Cæsar*, Act III., Sc. 1.—**Pure gold.** Rev. xxi., 18.—**An instrument.** 2 Cor. iii., 18; 1 Cor. xiii., 12.—**Enoch and Elijah.** Gen. v., 22, 23, 24. For Enoch's translation to heaven, see Heb. xi., 5. For an account of Elijah's, see 2 Kings ii., 10–12.—**You must go through,** etc. "The day of death, when I am to pack up all to be gone from hence, is a time of need. Now the greatest trial is come, excepting that of the day of judgment. Now a man is to be stripped of all but that which cannot be shaken. Now a man grows near the borders of eternity; now he begins to see into the skirts of the next world. Now death is death, and the grave the grave indeed." Bunyan's *Saint's Privilege.*—**Trumpet shall sound.** 1 Cor. xv., 52; 1 Thess. iv., 16.

grims then, especially Christian, began to despond in their minds, and looked this way and that; but no way could be found by them by which they might escape the river. Then they asked the men, if the waters were all of a depth? They said, "No;" yet they could not help them in that case. "For," said they, "you shall find it deeper or shallower, as you believe in the king of the place."

Then they addressed themselves to the water, and, entering, Christian began to sink; and, crying out to his good friend Hopeful, he said, "I sink in deep waters; the billows go over my head; all the waves go over me.* Selah."

Then said the other, "Be of good cheer, my brother; I feel the bottom, and it is good." Then said Christian, "Ah! my friend; the sorrows of death have compassed me about; I shall not see the land that flows with milk and honey." And with that, a great darkness and horror fell upon Christian, so that he could not see before him. Also he in a great measure lost his senses, so that he could neither remember nor orderly talk of any of those sweet refreshments that he had met with in the way of his pilgrimage; but all the words that he spake still tended to discover that he had horror of mind, and heart-fears that he should die in that river and never obtain entrance in at the gate. Here, also, they that stood by perceived he was much in the troublesome thoughts of the sins that he had committed, both since and before he began to be a pilgrim. It was also observed that he was troubled with apparitions of hobgoblins and evil spirits: for, ever

---

* **All the waves go over me.** See Ps. xlii., 7.—**Selah.** "A word of doubtful meaning, occurring very frequently in the Psalms; by some supposed to signify silence or a pause in the musical performance of the song; by others, to indicate special attention to the subject." *Webster.* "The Septuagint translators and some commentators look upon it as a mere musical mark; whilst others, from the probable derivation of the word, consider it as synonymous with *Hallelujah*, and used therefore at the end of passages which the writer would point out as worthy of the most attentive observation." *Eden.*—**Compassed me.** Ps. xviii., 5.

Sins he had committed since he began to be a pilgrim. The clause beginning with *since*, is a subordinate adverbial clause denoting *time*. In like manner adverbial clauses may denote *place*, *reason*, *cause*, *manner*, *degree*, etc. See Fowler's *English Grammar*, pp. 635, 638, etc.

He

had committed

since he began to be a pilgrim.

Complete this analysis.

Since

he

began

to be a pilgrim.

Complete the analysis.

It was also observed that he was troubled, etc. Here the subordinate sentence, *that he was troubled*, is in apposition to *it*, and has the force of a substantive. The syntactical combinations might be expressed thus :—

That he was troubled,

it

was also observed.

and anon, he would intimate so much by words. Hopeful, therefore, here had much ado to keep his brother's head above water: yea, sometimes he would be quite gone down; and then, ere a while, he would rise up again half dead. Hopeful did also endeavor to comfort him, saying, "Brother, I see the gate, and men standing by to receive us:" but Christian would answer, "It is you, it is you they wait for. You have been hopeful * ever since I knew you." "And so have you," said he to Christian. "Ah, brother!" said he, "surely if I was right, he would now rise to help me; but for my sins he hath brought me into the snare and left me." Then said Hopeful, "My brother, you have quite forgot the text, where it is said of the wicked, 'There are no bands in their death; but their strength is firm; they are not troubled as other men, neither are they plagued like other men.' These troubles and distresses that you go through in these waters, are no sign that God hath forsaken you; but are sent to try you, whether you will call to mind that which heretofore you have received of his goodness, and live upon him in your distresses."

Then I saw in my dream, that Christian was in a muse awhile. To whom also Hopeful added these words, "Be of good cheer; Jesus Christ maketh thee whole." And with that, Christian brake out with a loud voice, "Oh! I see him again; and he tells me, 'When thou passest through the waters, I will be with thee; and through the rivers, they shall not overflow thee.'" Then they both took courage; and the enemy was after that as still as a stone, until they were gone over. Christian, therefore, presently found ground to stand upon; and so it followed, that the rest of the river was but shallow. Thus they got over.

Now, upon the bank of the river, on the other side, they saw the two shining men again, who there waited for them. Wherefore, being come out of the river, they saluted them, saying, "We are ministering spirits sent forth to minister to those that shall be heirs of salvation." Thus they went along toward the gate.

Now you must note, that the city stood upon a mighty hill; but the pilgrims went up that hill with ease, because they had these two men to lead them up by the arms: they had likewise left their mortal garments behind them in the river; for, though they went in with them, they came out without them. They, therefore, went up here with much agility and speed, though the foundation upon which the city was framed was higher than the

---

* **You have been hopeful.** Like Shakespeare, Bunyan does not stick at a *pun*, even in the most serious circumstances.—**No bands.** Ps. lxxiii., 4, 5. No pangs that cramp and bind; no terrors that constrain.—**Distress.** "Sick-bed temptations are oftentimes the most violent, because then the devil is to play his last game with us; he is never to assault us more. But out of all these the Lord will deliver his people. He shall save Israel out of all his troubles, out of sick-bed troubles as well as others." Bunyan's *Saved by Grace*.—**Maketh thee whole.** Acts ix., 34.—**Overflow thee.** Isai. xliii., 2.—**As still as a stone.** So in Chaucer, "In creepeth age alway *as still as stone*."—**Ministering spirits.** Heb. i., 14.

Distress, *affliction*, *trouble*, *perplexity*, *grief*, *suffering*, *pain*, *misery*, *calamity*, *misfortune*, *adversity*, *agony*. Other synonymes? Write out, etc.

Analyze, *When thou passest through the waters, I will be with thee.*

clouds. They therefore went up through the region of the air, sweetly talking as they went, being comforted because they safely got over the river and had such glorious companions to attend them.

The talk that they had with the Shining Ones, was about the glory of the place; who told them, that the beauty and glory of it was* inexpressible. "There," said they, "is Mount Zion, the heavenly Jerusalem, the innumerable company of angels, and the spirits of just men made perfect. You are going now," said they, "to the paradise of God, wherein you shall see the tree of life and eat of the never-fading fruits thereof: and when you come there, you shall have white robes given you; and your walk and talk shall be every day with the King, even all the days of eternity. There you shall not see again such things as you saw when you were in the lower region upon the earth; to wit, sorrow, sickness, affliction, and death. For the former things are passed away. You are now going to Abraham, Isaac, and Jacob, and to the prophets; men that 'God hath taken away from the evil to come,' and that are now 'resting upon their beds, each one walking in his uprightness.'" The men asked, "What must we do in the holy place?" To whom it was answered, "You must there receive the comforts of all your toil, and have joy for all your sorrow; you must reap what you have sown, even the fruit of all your prayers and tears, and sufferings for the King by the way. In that place you must wear crowns of gold, and enjoy the perpetual sight and vision of the Holy One; for there you shall see Him as he is. There, also, you shall serve him continually with praise, with shouting and thanksgiving, whom you desired to serve in the world, though with much difficulty because of the infirmity of your flesh. There your eyes shall be delighted with seeing and your ears with hearing the pleasant voice of the Mighty One. There you shall enjoy your friends again, that are gone thither before you: and there you shall with joy receive even every one that follows into the holy places after you. There also you shall be clothed with glory and majesty, and put into an equipage fit to ride out with the King of Glory. When he shall come with sounding trumpet in the clouds, as upon the wings of the wind, you shall come with him; and when he shall sit upon the throne of judgment, you shall sit by him; yea, and when he shall pass sentence upon all the workers of iniquity, let them be angels or men, you also shall have a voice in that judgment, because they were his and your enemies. Also

* **Beauty and glory was.** *Beauty* and *glory* form a single subject; hence "*was.*"—**Innumerable.** Heb. xii., 22, 23.—**Tree of life.** Rev. ii., 7; xxii., 2; Gen. ii., 9; iii., 22.—**White robes.** Rev. iii., 4; vii., 13.—**Passed away.** Rev. xxi., 4; Isai. xxxv., 10.—**Evil to come.** Isai. lvii., 1.—**In his uprightness.** Isai. lvii., 2—**See him as he is.** 1 John iii., 2.—**Sit by him.** Rev. iii., 21; Matt. xix., 28.—**Be they angels or men.** 1 Cor. vi., 2, 3.

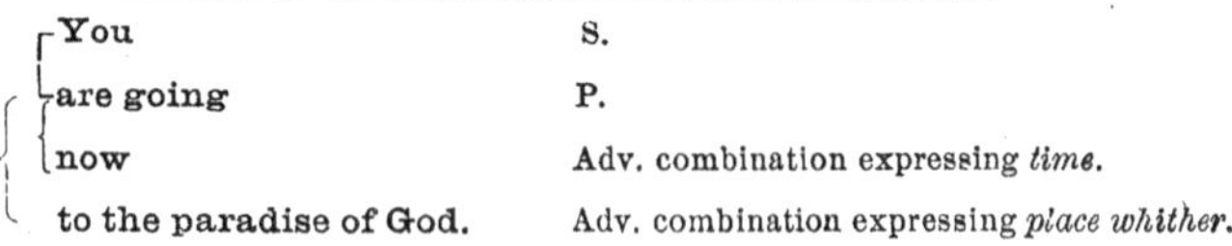

when he shall again return to the City, you shall go too with sound of trumpet, and be ever with him."

Now, while they were thus drawing towards the gate, behold, a company of the heavenly host came out to meet them! To whom it was said by the other two shining ones, "These are the men that have loved our Lord when they were in the world, and that have left all for His holy name; and He hath sent us to fetch them; and we have brought them thus far on their desired journey, that they may go in, and look their Redeemer in the face with joy." Then the heavenly host gave a great shout, saying: "Blessed are they that are called to the marriage supper* of the Lamb." There came out also at this time to meet them several of the King's trumpeters, clothed in white and shining raiment; who, with melodious noises and loud, made even the heavens to echo with the sound. These trumpeters saluted Christian and his fellow with ten thousand welcomes from the world; and this they did with shouting and sound of trumpet.

This done, they compassed them round about on every side. Some went before, some behind, and some on the right hand, some on the left, as it were to guard them through the upper regions; continually sounding, as they went, with melodious noises in notes on high; so that the very sight was to them that could behold it, as if heaven itself was come down to meet

---

* **Marriage supper.** Rev. xix., 9.—**There came out also at this time to meet them.** This passage about the trumpeters, as far as, "Thus they came up to the gate," p. 408, is not in the earliest edition.

You shall go and be ever with him. We have seen (p. 377) that two co-ordinate or independent propositions united as here, constitute a *co-ordinative compound sentence* (or *proposition*). There are several kinds of these. (1) The *copulative*, where the conjunction is *and*, or some nearly equivalent conjunction or connecting words; as, *also*, *as well as*, *not only . . . but also*. (2) The *adversative*, where the contrast is such that the co-ordinate clause restricts or denies the thought of the preceding clause. Here the conjunction is *but*, or *yet*, or some kindred word; as, *He is rich, but honest.* (3) The *disjunctive*, where the two clauses unite to form one whole, but one excludes the other. Here the conjunction is *or*, *nor*, *otherwise than*, *as . . . as*. Thus, *You must either work or starve.* (4) The *causal*, where the latter clause denotes a cause, reason, effect, or inference, and the conjunction is *because*, *therefore*, *on that account*, or the like. Thus, *He studies because he fears a whipping.*

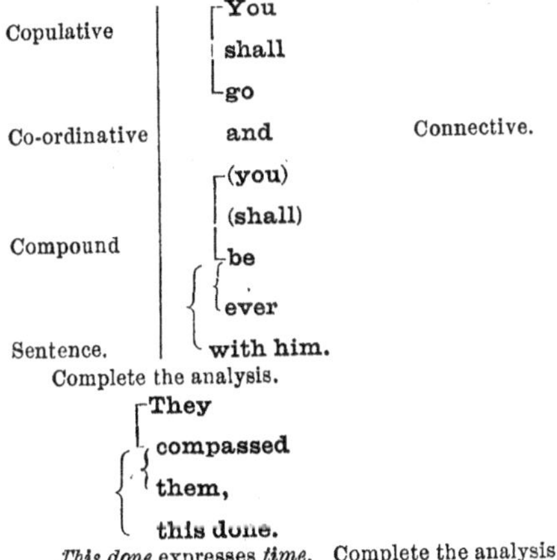

Complete the analysis.

This done expresses *time*. Complete the analysis.

them. Thus, therefore, they walked on together; and, as they walked, ever and anon these trumpeters, even with joyful sound, would, by mixing their music with looks and gestures, still signify to Christian and his brother how welcome they were into their company, and with what gladness they came to meet them. And now were these two men, as it were, in heaven before they came at it; being swallowed up with the sight of angels and with hearing their melodious notes. Here also they had the city itself in view, and thought they heard all the bells therein to ring, to welcome them thereto. But, above all, the warm and joyful thoughts that they had about their own dwelling there with such company, and that for ever and ever! Oh! by what tongue or pen can their glorious joy be expressed!—Thus they came up to the gate.

Now, when they were come up to the gate, there was written over it in letters of gold, "Blessed are they that do his commandments, that they may have right to the tree of life, and may enter in through the gates * into the city."

Then I saw in my dream, that the two shining men bade them call at the gate. The which when they did, some from above looked over the gate, to wit, Enoch, Moses, and Elijah, etc.; to whom it was said, "These pilgrims are come from the City of Destruction, for the love that they bear to the King of this place:" and then the pilgrims gave in unto them each man his certificate, which they had received in the beginning. Those, therefore, were carried in to the King; who, when he had read them, said, "Where are the men?" To whom it was answered, "They are standing without the gate." The King then commanded to open the gate, "That the righteous nation," said he, "that keepeth truth, may enter in."

Now I saw in my dream, that these two men went in at the gate; and lo! as they entered they were transfigured; and they had raiment put on that shone like gold. There were also that met them with harps and crowns, and gave them to them; the harps to praise withal, and the crowns in token of honor. Then I heard, in my dream, that all the bells in the city rang again for joy; and that it was said unto them, "Enter ye into the joy of your Lord." I also heard the men themselves, that they sang with a loud voice, saying, "Blessing, and honor, and glory and power, be unto Him that sitteth upon the throne, and to the Lamb, for ever and ever!"

Now, just as the gates were opened to let in the men, I looked in after them; and behold, the city shone like the sun: the streets also were paved

* **Through the gates.** Rev. xxii., 14.—**May enter in.** Isai. xxvi., 2.—**The joy of your Lord.** Matt. xxv., 21, 23.—**For ever and ever.** Rev. v., 13.

Company, society, troop, association, assemblage, circle. Other synonymes? Write out, etc.

They
were transfigured
as they entered.

Complete the analysis. See p. 407.

with gold, and in them walked many men with crowns on their heads, palms in their hands, and golden harps to sing praises withal.

There were also of them that had wings; and they answered one another without intermission, saying, "Holy, holy, holy,* is the Lord." And after that, they shut up the gates. Which when I had seen, I wished myself among them.

Now, while I was gazing upon all these things, I turned my head to look back, and saw Ignorance coming up to the river-side. But he soon got over, and that without half the difficulty which the other two men met with. For it happened that there was then at that place one Vain-hope, a ferry-man, that with his boat helped him over. So he, as the others I saw, did ascend the hill to come up to the gate: only he came alone; neither did any man meet him with the least encouragement. When he was come up to the gate, he looked up to the writing that was above, and then began to knock, supposing that entrance should have been quickly administered to him. But he was asked by the men that looked over the top of the gate, "Whence came you? and what would you have?" He answered, "I have eaten and drunk in the presence of the King; and he has taught in our streets." Then they asked him for his certificate, that they might go in and show it to the King. So he fumbled in his bosom for one, and found none. Then they said, "Have you none?" But the man answered never a word. So they told the King; but he would not come down to see him, but commanded the two shining ones that conducted Christian and Hopeful to the city, to go out and take Ignorance, and "Bind him hand and foot, and have him away." Then they took him up, and carried him through the air to the door that I saw on the side of the hill, and put him in there. Then I saw

---

* **Holy, holy, holy.** Isai. vi., 3.—**I wished myself among them.** "Here, assuredly, the story ought to have ended, leaving the reader to shut the book, with the closing gates of heaven in his eye, and the author's pious wish in his heart. But the stern justice of John Bunyan to every part of his subject compelled him to add, what, indeed, is a very seasonable warning to those who go on pilgrimage, that though the right-minded Christian cannot fail at last, the presumptuous sinner cannot escape." *Montgomery.*—**Taught in our streets.** See Luke xiii., 26.—**Bind him,** etc. Matt. xxii., 13.

Answer, reply, rejoin, respond. Other synonymes? Write out, etc.

Analyze, *So they told the King, but he would not come.*

They
took up
him
then,
and
(they)
carried
him
through the air
to the door that I saw on the side of the hill,

that there was* a way to hell, even from the gates of heaven, as well as from the City of Destruction.

So I awoke; and behold, it was a dream.

---

* **There was.** *There is* would have been better.

```
and                      ...... to the door
(they)                                  (that
put                                       I
him                                       saw
in there.                                 on the side
                                              of the hill.
```

Complete the analysis.

The student should exercise his ingenuity in devising convenient groupings of the words in the sentence to be analyzed. For convenience, a word may occasionally (like "*that*" in the foregoing example) be allowed to stand out of its usual order, and the fact may be indicated by placing the sign on the right, as above. See pp. 411, 412, etc.

Write a brief abstract (what is technically termed the "argument") of the story of *Pilgrim's Progress*. Write an essay on the genius of Bunyan; on the peculiar merits of his *Pilgrim's Progress;* on the simple character of his language; on the peculiar training he had for his work; on his opportunities for mental improvement; on the great events that took place in England during his life, and his part in them; on *intensity of feeling* as an element in *genius;* on alliteration; on the rhythmic movement of Bunyan's language; on allegories; on the literary works that have been produced in prison. Is Bunyan wholly consistent in the conduct of his allegory? Does Faithful pass through the river? Does he join a church organization? Might any of the characters have been omitted without impairing the allegory as a work of art? Can you think of others that should have been inserted? Is it strange that, while on his pilgrimage, he has no communication with his own family? Write an essay covering the ground of any one or more of these questions. Write an essay on each of the prominent characters in *Pilgrim's Progress*, pointing out merits and defects in Bunyan's conception or development of them respectively.

ANALYSIS.

A complete analysis of a passage would contain,—

1. A *syntactical* analysis, showing syntactical combinations and relations.

2. An *etymological* or *grammatical* analysis, distinguishing the parts of speech with their modifications, and the particulars usually included in the term *parsing*.

3. An *historic* word-analysis, pointing out the origin, original form, and history of each word and of each significant part of the written word.

4. A *phonetic* analysis, showing the elementary sounds and their natural or proper significancy, etc.

5. An *orthographic* analysis, showing the origin, form, power, combinations, etc., of the letters in each word.

6. An *elocutionary* analysis, showing the ideas and sentiments as influencing vocal delivery.

7. A *rhetorical* analysis, naming, describing, and criticising the rhetorical forms, figures, and constituent parts of discourse viewed in a rhetorical light.

8. A *poetical* analysis, naming, describing, and criticising the poetical language, forms, and devices.

9. A *logical* analysis, naming and describing the logical forms, and criticising the conduct of the thought.

In this volume we give the first six of the above, reserving the others for succeeding volumes. The following sentences and marks develop and illustrate a convenient

MODE OF SENTENCE ANALYSIS.

1. *I walked.* (See p. 289.)

┌**I**
└**walked.**

The *subject and predicate* combination in its simplest form.

2. *Good Christian says.* (See p. 292.)

(**Good**
┌**Christian**
└**says.**

The *adjective combination* in its simplest form.

3. *The Lord, the governor, hath recorded.* (See p. 294.)

```
  ( The
( ( governor,
( ( the
┌ Lord
│ hath
└ recorded.
```

A second form of the *adjective combination;* consisting of a noun explained by a noun in apposition.

4. *Christian's setting forth was noised.* (See p. 296.)

```
( Christian's
┌ setting-forth
│ was
└ noised.
```

A third form of the *adjective combination;* the adjective word being a noun in the possessive.

5. *The King of Glory hath told.* (See p. 301.)

```
(   The
( ( of glory
┌ King
│ hath
└ told.
```

A fourth form of the *adjective combination;* the adjective words being a preposition and its case.

6. *I am a man.* (See p. 305.)

```
┌ I
│ am
│ ( a
└ ( man.
```

A second form of the *subject and predicate* combination; the predicate consisting of a copulative verb and a noun. (See p. 289, and No. 19, *post.*)

7. *Which will be profitable.* (See p. 305. See, also, *That proverb is of authority*, p. 307, and No. 19, *post.*)

```
┌ Which
│ will
│ be
└ profitable.
```

A third form of the *subject and predicate* combination; consisting of the subject with a copulative verb and an adjective.

8. *Though this be so.* (See p. 308.)

Though (Omit the consideration of the conjunction for the present. But see note at bottom of p. 308.)

this
be
so.

A fourth and less common form of the *subject and predicate* combination; the predicate consisting of a copulative verb and an adverb. *So* has here nearly the force of *such.*

9. *The heavens were in a burning flame.* (See p. 311.)

The
heavens
were
in
a
burning
flame.

A fifth form of the *subject and predicate* combination; the predicate consisting of a copulative verb and a substantive with a preposition. (The word *burning* is not an essential part of the prepositional phrase.) *In a burning flame* has nearly the force of *afire* or *conflagrant.*

10. *I have seen things rare.* (See p. 312. See *Whom God will persuade,* p. 319; and *They saw no evil,* p. 324. See also the 15th and 34th examples.)

I
have
seen
things
rare.

A new syntactical combination, the *objective,* is here seen in its simplest form. It expresses the complementary object (*i. e.*, an object *completing* the predicate). The complementary object *things* is in this sentence the object of the transitive verb *seen,* and may be called "passive object."

11. *The way is called Danger.* (See p. 316.)

The
way
is
called
Danger.

A second form of the *objective* combination; consisting of the union of the predicate with the "*factitive*" (or produced) object. *Care must be taken not to confound the word* OBJECT *with* OBJECTIVE CASE. *Danger*, the "factitive" object, is in the nominative. It completes the predicate, and is therefore a *complementary* object.

12. *He began to be perplexed.* (See p. 317.)

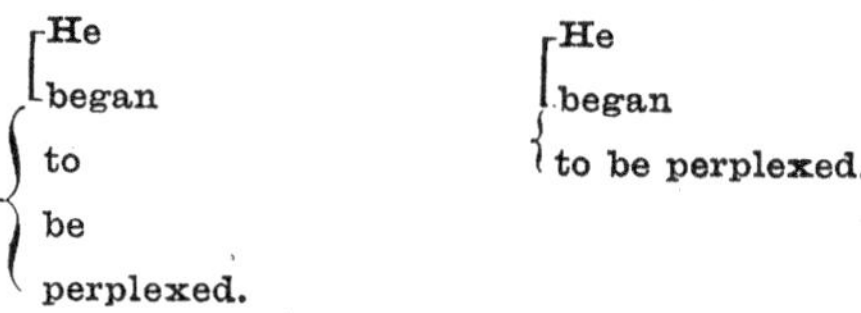

A third form of the *objective* combination; the object consisting of an infinitive mood. Some grammarians would treat this as identical with the first form, which includes "passive" objects. It completes the predicate, and so is called a *complementary* object.

13. *He was telling of it.* (See pp. 321, 351. See *Fowler's Grammar*, § 535.)

He
was
telling
of
it.

A fourth form of the *objective* combination, nearly identical with the first, the object consisting of an objective case governed by a preposition. This, too, is a *complementary* object. (See p. 312.)

14. *They saw no evil.* (See p. 324.)

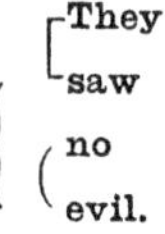

A fifth form of the *objective* combination; the object consisting of an adjective used as a noun. This form may be regarded as substantially one with the first. (See the 10th example.) The object completes the predicate.

15. *They showed him records.* (See pp. 325, 351.)

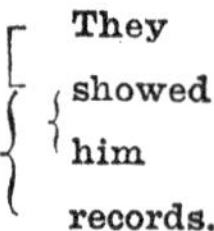

A sixth form of the *objective* combination; there being two objects, both *complementary.* In strictness *him* might be called the "indirect" or "dative" object; and *records*, the "direct," "passive," or "transitive." (See the 10th example.)

16. *He could tell them of things.* (See pp. 351, 385. See also, *He was telling of it*, p. 321.)

He
could
tell
them
of
things.

A seventh form of the *objective* combination; closely akin to the foregoing, there being two *complementary* objects, one a "dative," and the other depending on a preposition.

17. *Thou change a bad.* (See p. 328.)

Thou
change
a
bad.

(See No. 14, above.)

18. . . . . *To make him a proverb.* (See pp. 336, 316.)

. . . . to
make
him
a
proverb.

An eighth form of the *objective* combination, there being two objects, one a "passive" and the other a "factitive." Both are *complementary.*

19. *He remained true to his profession.* (See p. 305. See also *Fowler's Grammar*, p. 637; and, especially, § 513, p. 593.)

He
remained
true to his profession.

It is difficult to distinguish this form from that of the *subject and predicate* combination. (See the 6th example, above.) Some grammarians, however, would treat the phrase, *true to his profession*, as a *supplementary* adverbial phrase. In the latter view, a straight brace, as shown in No. 20, should be used; thus,

remained
true to, etc.

But perhaps the best disposal of such cases is to regard the verbs *to re-*

main, *to seem*, *to become*, *to feel*, and many others, as *copulative* verbs, like the substantive verb *am*. With such verbs, "The whole predicate is made up of the predicate element in the verb, taken with the adjective. Each verb, as compared with the substantive verb, may be regarded as a strengthened copula." (See *Fowler's Grammar*, p. 593.)

20. *I dwelt securely.* (See p. 339. See, too, pp. 370, 399.)

I
dwelt
securely.

Here we have a fourth syntactical combination, called *the adverbial*. The predicate is enlarged or restricted by a *supplementary* word or words. Here the supplementary expression is an adverb of *manner*. The combination may be most easily expressed with pencil or crayon by an ordinary curved brace with a circle at the point in the middle. For convenience, however, we here use a straight brace; thus

21. *I look him in the face.* (See pp. 341, 347.)

I
look
him
in the face.

This, like the preceding, is an *adverbial* combination; the predicate being supplemented by a phrase denoting *manner* or *direction*.

22. *Vanity Fair is kept all the year.* (See pp. 352, 358, 392, 407, 408.)

Vanity Fair
is kept
all the year.

A third *adverbial* combination; the predicate being supplemented by a phrase denoting *time*.

23. *I could never endure him.* (See p. 358.)

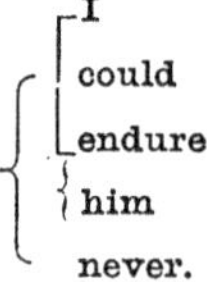

This, like the preceding, denotes *time*.

24. (*Thou*) *turn aside hither.* (See pp. 365, 406.)

(Thou)
turn
aside
hither.

A fourth *adverbial* combination; *aside* and *hither* both presenting the supplementary idea of *place.*

25. *I will therefore search them.* (See p. 374.)

I
will
search
them
therefore.

A fifth *adverbial* combination, presenting the idea of *cause* or *reason.* Here we have the *logical ground.* (See No. 26.)

26. *They have continued unburied, for an example.* (See p. 376.)

They
have
continued
for an example.

The words *for an example* express the *final cause* or the *purpose.*

27. *I am a very great sinner.* (See bottom of pp. 352, 376.)

I
am
a
sinner
great
very.

I
am
a
very
great
sinner.

A sixth *adverbial* combination, presenting the idea of *degree.* Such propositions are sometimes called propositions of *intensity. Very* is the representative word in this sentence.

28. *They went and sang.* (See pp. 377, 394.)

They
went
and
(they)
sang.

Here we have a *co-ordinative compound sentence* in its simplest form.

29. *They lay bewailing.* (See p. 385.)

They
lay
bewailing.

This is a proposition *intermediate* between the simple and the compound.

A participle used adverbially is called a *gerund.* The gerund modifies the predicate by another separate accompanying action or state. The combination is not quite equivalent to, *They lay and they bewailed.*

30. *Finding none, I am going back.* (See p. 387.)

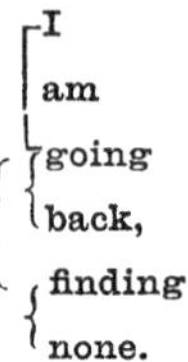

Another *intermediate* proposition. Here the participle expresses *cause.* The sentence is not quite equivalent to, *I find none and am going back.*

31. *He bade me say.* (See p. 391.)

He
bade
me
say.

Another form of the proposition *intermediate* between simple and compound. The incompleteness of the *subject and predicate* combination may be visibly expressed, if that be desired, by the incomplete bracket [. The sentence is nearly equivalent to, *He bade me that I should say.*

32. *Fear tends to make them right.* (See p. 398.)

Fear
tends
to make them right.

Another form of the *adverbial* proposition *intermediate.* It might be crudely expressed thus, *Fear tends so that it shall make them right. To make them right* denotes *direction,* or *result.*

33. *The shame that attends religion, lies.* (See pp. 400, 390, 404.)

The,
that attends religion,
shame
lies.

This is a subordinative compound, or, more specifically, *complex* proposition. All dependent clauses have the force of substantives, adjectives, or adverbs. *That attends religion* has here an *adjective* force.

34. *Tell him that I am sick.* (See p. 402.)

(Thou)
tell
him
that I am sick.

Here we have a dependent clause that has the power of a *substantive.* It is a "passive" or "transitive" or "direct" object; *him* being a "dative." (See bottom of pp. 384, 385, 386, 388, 396.)

35. (*Sins*) *he had committed since he began to be a pilgrim.* (See pp. 404, 317, 352, 358, 392.)

He
had committed
since he began to be a pilgrim.

A subordinative complex proposition, with adverbial clause denoting *time.*

36. *You shall go and be ever with him.* (See pp. 407, 377, 394.)

You
shall go,
and
(you)
shall be
ever
with him.

Another instance of the copulative co-ordinative compound sentence. (See No. 28, *ante.*)

37. *So they told the King, but he would not come.* (See p. 409.)

They
told
the King,
but
he
would come
not.

An adversative co-ordinative compound sentence.

38. *Then they took him up, and carried him through the air to the door that I saw on the side of the hill, and put him in there.* (See pp. 409, 410.)

They
took up
him
then,
and
(they)
carried
him
through the air
to the door that I saw on the side of the hill,
and
(they)
put
him
in there.

A copulative co-ordinative complex sentence.

The clause, *that I saw on the side of the hill*, may be resolved separately as follows:—

(door)
that
I
saw
on the **side**
of the hill.

For convenience *that* is placed *before* the predicate. Being out of the usual order, the fact may be indicated by placing the brace on the right.

APPLICATION OF THE FOREGOING PRINCIPLES.

1. Write first at the top any conjunction that unites the sentence to the preceding; then the modifiers of the subject, one under the other in a column. Preserve, so far as practicable, the natural order of the words, phrases, and clauses.
2. Next underneath write the subject.
3. Under the subject write the predicate.
4. Under the predicate write its modifiers.
5. On the left of this column name the kind of sentence, using abbreviations if necessary.
6. Connect the words and clauses by the proper marks to indicate syn-

tactical combinations. The order of the modifiers of the subject may make it unnecessary to connect them visibly with it.

7. Having thus disposed of the *syntactical combinations*, write opposite each word that stands alone the *etymological analysis* (*parsing*), using abbreviations; and, still further on the right, the *historical analysis* (showing the derivation of the word and of its significant elements, giving the kindred words, etc.).

8. Next, take the words in the successive *groups*, if any; write them in similar order one under the other, and proceed as before.

9. If thought desirable, the office performed by each word or group of words may be written next to it on the right.

A partial analysis on this plan is shown by the following

MODEL.

There came out also at this time to meet them, several of the King's trumpeters, clothed in white and shining raiment, who, with melodious voices, made even the heavens to echo with their sound.—Bunyan.

SYNTACTICAL.			ETYMOLOGICAL.	HISTORICAL.
Sub-ordi-native com-plex declar-ative sen-tence.	also,		Adverbial cop. conj.	A. S. *ealswa*, *alswa*, fr. *eal*, all, *swa*, so; Goth. *alls*, all; *sva*, so; O. Eng. *al so*. Synonymes, *likewise*, *too*.
	of the King's trumpeters,			
	clothed in white and shining raiment,			
	several	Subj.	Pronom. adj., always plu., not compared, subj. nom. to *came*.	Lat. *separare*, to separate; Lat. *se*, apart; *parare*, to prepare; Fr. *sevrer*, to separate, to wean; *several*.
	came	Pred.	Str. v., intrans., ind., im., 3d, pl.	A. S. *cuman*; Goth. *qviman*; Ger. *kommen*, to come; Sans. *gam*, to go.
	out		Adv. of place; not compared.	Goth. *ut*; A. S. *ût*; Ger. *aus*, out; D. *uit*.
	at this time			
	to meet them			
	there,		Adv.; here merely euphonic.	A. S. *thar*, *thaer*, *ther*, there; akin to Goth. *thata*; Eng. *this*. *Th* has demonstrative force akin to Gr. το, etc. See pp. 19, 25, 60.

The prepositional phrase *of the King's trumpeters* may be analyzed as follows:—

Adjective prepositional phrase.	**(Several)**			
	of	Sign of adj. combination.	Prep. showing rel. bet. *several* and *trumpeters.*	A. S. *of;* O. Fris. *af*, of; Goth., Sw., Dan., *af.* Akin to Ger. and Lat. *ab*, Gr. ἀπό, from.
	the		Def. art. belonging to *king.*	Gr. τό; A. S. *the* or *se;* akin to Sans. *tat*, that; Goth. *tho*, *sa*, *thata;* Ger. *der*, *die*, *das;* Ice. *sa*, *se*, that; Low Ger. *de*, *dat.* See *there*, p. 421.
	king's		N., c., m., 3, s., pos. belonging to *trumpeters.*	A. S. *cyng*, *cynig*, *cyning;* O. Sax. *cuning*, king; fr. A. S. *cunnan*, to know, be able. The King, then, was the *wisest, ablest man!* 'S is a relic of A. S. gen. in *-es*, *-is*, or *-ys*, and was introduced in the 16th century. See Index, under "possessive case."
	trumpeters		N., c., m., 3, pl., ob.	Fr. *trompe*, trumpet; akin perhaps to Lat. *tuba*, trumpet, or to Ice. *trumba*, a drum. Perhaps onomat. *-Et* is orig. diminutive. See p. 229. *-Er* denotes the active agent, fr. A. S. *-r*, *-or*, *-er*, Lat. *-or*, Goth. *-r*. *S* is for *-es*, the plu. ending of the Semi-Saxon.

The foregoing sufficiently indicates the method of etymological and historical analysis. The syntactical combinations in the remainder of the sentence may be expressed as follows:—

Particip. clause. | (**(Several)**
clothed in white and shining raiment.)

This might be written in connection with the word *came*, as a proposition intermediate between the simple and the compound sentence. See *Fowler's Grammar*, p. 638. In the latter case, a broken bracket may be used to denote the incompleteness of the predication. Thus:—

Several
came (and)

several (were)
clothed in white and shining raiment.

The expression *clothed in white and shining raiment* may be written thus:—

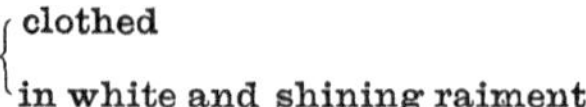

clothed
in white and shining raiment.

The phrase *in white and shining raiment* may be expanded thus:—

Prepositional phrase of manner.	**in**	Sign of adverb. comb.
	white	
	(raiment)	
	and	Connective.
	shining	
	raiment.	

The phrase *at this time* is similarly expanded.

The clause *came to meet them* may be regarded as a proposition intermediate between the simple and the compound, being equivalent to *came that they might meet them*, and the imperfect predication might be expressed thus:—

(Several) to
meet
them.

It may, however, be sufficient to regard the phrase *to meet them* as an adverbial expression of purpose; and with *came*, it may be written thus:—

came
to meet them.

The phrase *to meet them* is readily resolved into,—

Prepositional phrase of purpose.	**to**	sign of adverbial comb.
	meet	
	them.	obj.

The clause, *who, with melodious voices, made even the heavens to echo with their sound*, may be resolved into the following:—

(Several)

Adjective subordinate sentence.	**who**
	made,
	with melodious voices,
	even the heavens to echo with their sound.

The words *with melodious voices* are a prepositional phrase adverbially expressing means. They may be written thus:—

(made)	
with	sign of adv. combination.
melodious	
voices.	

The word *even*, in the clause *made even the heavens*, is an adverb of *degree*, and may be combined thus:—

made
even

Made the heavens to echo is another intermediate proposition between the simple and the compound, being equivalent to *made the heavens that they did echo*. The incompleteness of the predication may be expressed as before by a broken bracket, thus:—

Quasi subject and predicate combination.	**the**
	heavens
	to
	echo
	with their sound.

The words *with their sound* are a prepositional phrase of means. Their combination with *echo* has just been shown. For further analysis they may be written thus:—

with — sign of adverbial combination.

(**their**
(**sound.**

NOTE. The mark [[ ] which we have used to indicate the combination of subject and predicate, may be shortened to a straight line; that for the adverbial combination may be simplified into a plane angle [<]. For example, the four syntactical combinations may be marked as in the following sentence:—

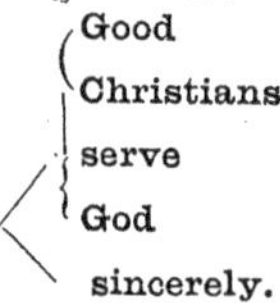

If it be thought desirable to retain in the column the original order of the words, a deviation from the order which we have adopted in the rules on page 420 may be indicated by placing on the right hand the marks that indicate syntactical combinations. See, for illustration, the word *that* on pp. 410, 420.

INDEX.

The figures refer to pages.

www.ingramcontent.com/pod-product-compliance
Lightning Source LLC
LaVergne TN
LVHW021131110826
845150LV00005B/992

* 9 7 8 1 4 2 5 5 5 0 5 1 6 *